D0023437

ENCYCLOPEDIA OF CONTEMPORARY AMERICAN SOCIAL ISSUES

ENCYCLOPEDIA OF CONTEMPORARY AMERICAN SOCIAL ISSUES

VOLUME 3
FAMILY AND SOCIETY

Michael Shally-Jensen, Editor

 ABC-CLIO

Santa Barbara, California • Denver, Colorado • Oxford, England

Copyright 2011 by ABC-CLIO, LLC

All rights reserved. No part of this publication may be reproduced, stored in a retrieval system, or transmitted, in any form or by any means, electronic, mechanical, photocopying, recording, or otherwise, except for the inclusion of brief quotations in a review, without prior permission in writing from the publisher.

Library of Congress Cataloging-in-Publication Data

Encyclopedia of contemporary American social issues / Michael Shally-Jensen, editor.
    v. ; cm.
  Includes bibliographical references and index.
  Contents: Vol. 1: business and economy — Vol. 2: criminal justice — Vol. 3: family and society — Vol. 4: environment, science, and technology.
    ISBN 978-0-313-39204-7 (set : alk. paper) — ISBN 978-0-313-39205-4 (set ebook)
  1. United States—Social conditions—Encyclopedias. 2. United States—Economic conditions—Encyclopedias. 3. United States—Politics and government—Encyclopedias.
I. Shally-Jensen, Michael.
  HN59.2.E343 2011
  306.0973—dc22   2010041517

ISBN: 978-0-313-39204-7
EISBN: 978-0-313-39205-4

15 14 13 12 11   1 2 3 4 5

This book is also available on the WorldWideWeb as an eBook.
Visit www.abc-clio.com for details.

ABC-CLIO, LLC
130 Cremona Drive, P.O. Box 1911
Santa Barbara, California 93116-1911

This book is printed on acid-free paper ∞

Manufactured in the United States of America

Contents

VOLUME 2: CRIMINAL JUSTICE

VOLUME 3: FAMILY AND SOCIETY

VOLUME 4: ENVIRONMENT, SCIENCE, AND TECHNOLOGY

Preface

The growing prominence of news, information, and commentary of all kinds, and in every medium, has unfortunately not always been matched by a deepening or a widening of consumers' understanding of the issues at hand. In this era of tweets and peeks (information and video clips), of blogging and befogging (electronic opining), people of all stripes are under increased pressure to make snap judgments about matters about which they may know little. The fact that so many of the issues of the day—corporate misdoings, criminal violence, the condition of the schools, environmental disasters—touch the lives of so many Americans suggests that awareness of them at *any* level is a good thing. At some point, however, one needs to move beyond the news feeds and sound bites and begin to appreciate current issues for the complex matters that they are. This is precisely what the *Encyclopedia of Contemporary American Social Issues* is designed to do.

As with other works of its kind, the present encyclopedia is intended to serve as a bridge between the knowledge of experts and the knowledge of those new to the subjects it covers. We present here, then, scholarly research on a broad array of social issues in a format that is accessible and interesting, yet informative. The contributors have taken care with both the quality of their prose and the accuracy of their facts, the aim being to produce entries that are clear, accurate, and thorough. Contributors and editors alike have paid attention to the language of the entries to ensure that they are written in an intelligible style without losing sight of the terms and conventions employed by scholars writing within their disciplines. Thus, readers will find here thoughtful introductions to some of the most pressing issues currently confronting American society.

Scope

The *Encyclopedia of Contemporary American Social Issues* is divided into four volumes: (1) Business and Economy; (2) Criminal Justice; (3) Family and Society; and (4) Environment, Science, and Technology. Within each volume, the entries are arranged in alphabetical order. There are just over 200 entries in the encyclopedia, the essays ranging in length from about 1,500 words to more than 8,000. Each essay discusses a contemporary issue and ends with suggestions for further reading.

The first problem in compiling an encyclopedia of this type, of course, is determining what constitutes a social issue. It would seem a common enough term about whose meaning there is general consensus. Still, the matter bears a quick review. The *American Heritage Dictionary* defines an issue as:

a. a point or matter of discussion, debate, or dispute;

b. a matter of public concern;

c. a misgiving, objection, or complaint;

d. the essential point, crux.

In other words, not only a matter of public debate or discussion but also a point of concern or matter about which there are misgivings or objections. Included in the mix, moreover, is the idea of a neat summary or something boiled down to its essentials.

In the present encyclopedia, readers will find entries reflecting these varied senses of the term *issue*. There are entries, for example, such as "Health Care," "Oil Drilling," and "Gun Control" whose subjects one often hears debated in public forums. On the other hand, there are entries such as "Globalization," "Sprawl," and "Social Justice" whose subjects are rather harder to identify as clear-cut matters for public debate and seem more like general areas of concern. Of course, more than the general public, it is scholars who routinely examine the ins and outs of various subjects; and for scholars there is little doubt that globalization and the like are key issues requiring careful description and analysis. Fortunately for readers of this encyclopedia, included here are the considered opinions of some 170 scholars and professionals from a variety of different fields, all of whom were asked to lay out "the essential points" for lay readers.

No encyclopedia can encompass the complete spectrum of issues within the contemporary United States. The question of what to include and what to omit is one that has vexed us from the start. The best strategy, we found, was to keep constantly in mind the readers who turn to a work like the *Encyclopedia of Contemporary American Social Issues,* whether in a school or college library or in a public library reference center. We recognize that reference works like this serve a range of purposes for the reader, from gleaning facts to preparing a research paper or introducing oneself to a subject in order to appreciate where it fits within the world at large. In the end, as editors who have been around school curricula and have worked in library reference publishing for many years, we followed our own counsel in deciding upon the contents of this work. We do so knowing that we cannot satisfy all readers; we hope, however, that we have satisfied the majority of those in need of the kind of information presented here.

Although the emphasis is on *contemporary* social issues, the entries generally situate their topics in historical context and present arguments from a variety of perspectives. Readers are thus able to gain an understanding of how a particular issue has developed and the efforts that have been made in the past—including in the most recent times—to address it. Thus, perennial issues such as taxes, education, and immigration are examined in their latest permutations, and newer developments such as cloning, identity theft, and media violence are discussed in terms of both their antecedents and the conversations currently surrounding them. If there is any trend to be noted with respect to contemporary American social issues, it might only be that with each step forward comes the likelihood of further steps yet to be negotiated. We get from point A to point B only by making good use of our democratic heritage and anticipating the prospect of multiple voices or multiple intermediary steps. The *Encyclopedia of Contemporary American Social Issues* reflects that fact and advances the idea that it is useful to know where and how a question first arose before attempting to answer it or move it forward in the public agenda.

There is an established tradition in sociology that focuses on "social problems" and the many means by which these problems can be and have been researched and analyzed. Always something of an eclectic enterprise, and drawing on the collective wisdom of social scientists working in a variety of different fields (including criminology, demography, anthropology, policy studies, and political economy), in recent years the social problems tradition has widened its range still further to include questions about the environment, corporations, the media, gender politics, and even science and technology. It is this expanded version of the sociological traditional that the present encyclopedia takes as its animating vision. Encompassed herein are all of the above fields and more. We welcome the expansion and see it as linked to the broader meaning of the term *social issues*.

The four volumes assembled here—Business and Economy; Criminal Justice; Family and Society; and Environment, Science, and Technology—have benefited from work done earlier by others, work hereby democratically brought forward and expanded in scope. Specifically, we have drawn upon a series of books published previously by Greenwood Press and entitled *Battleground*. Key entries from that series have been updated, revised, rewritten, and in some cases replaced through the efforts of either the original authors or experienced editors knowledgeable in the applicable fields. In addition, some two dozen entries appear here for the first time, the aim being to ensure that issues emerging in the last few years receive the attention they deserve. Among this latter group of entries are "Bank Bailouts," "Cybercrime," "Consumer Credit and Household Debt," and "Airport and Aviation Security."

Acknowledgments

It is to the contributors, then, that I, personally, owe the greatest debt of gratitude. Without their patience and understanding, their expertise and professionalism, this work would not have been possible. An associate editor, Debra Schwartz, and development editor Anne Thompson provided invaluable service in the preparation of entries for publication, and the assistance of Scott Fincher in this regard is happily acknowledged as well. Acquisitions editor Sandy Towers, with whom I first worked in conceiving the project, proved a valuable friend and professional asset throughout the process. Also present from the beginning was Holly Heinzer, whom I thank for her support. Many thanks, too, to the production staffs at both ABC-CLIO and Apex CoVantage for their invaluable assistance in helping to refine the text and set up the volumes for publication. I am grateful to Jeff Dixon for handling the graphics.

—*Michael Shally-Jensen*

A

ABORTION

Jonelle Husain

Abortion refers to the premature end or termination of a pregnancy after implantation of the fertilized ovum in the uterus and before fetal viability or the point in fetal development at which a fetus can survive outside a woman's womb without life support. The term refers to the expulsion of the fetus, fetal membranes, and the placenta from the uterus and includes spontaneous miscarriages and medical procedures performed by a licensed physician intended to end pregnancy at any gestational age.

Abortion Procedures

An early abortion procedure, performed during the first trimester, or the first 12 weeks of pregnancy, is one of the safest types of medical procedures when performed by a trained health care professional in a hygienic environment. The risk of abortion complications is minimal, with less than 1 percent of all patients experiencing a serious complication. In the United States, the risk of death resulting from abortion is less than 0.6 per 100,000 procedures. The risks associated with abortion are less than those associated with childbirth.

There are two major types of procedures used to terminate a pregnancy. These procedures include both medical abortions and surgical abortions. The type of procedure that will be used is selected by the physician and the patient after determining the stage of pregnancy. Early-term abortions, or those occurring in the first trimester of pregnancy, may be either medical or surgical. Surgical abortions are used in later-stage abortions, or those occurring in the second or third trimester.

Early First-Trimester Abortions

Early first-trimester abortions are defined as those performed within the first eight weeks of pregnancy. Two procedures may be used: medical (nonsurgical) or surgical abortions. Medical abortions involve the administration of oral medications that cause expulsion of the fetus from the uterus (miscarriage). Medical abortions include the use of RU-486, commonly referred to as the abortion pill, as well as other combinations of drugs, depending on the stage of pregnancy. Typically, a combination of methotrexate and misoprostol are used to end pregnancies of up to seven weeks in duration. RU-486, a combination of mifepristone and misoprostol, is used to terminate pregnancies between seven and nine weeks in duration. Women opting for a medical abortion are typically administered methotrexate orally or by injection in a physician's office. Misoprostal tablets are administered orally or vaginally during a second office visit that occurs five to seven days later. The procedure is then followed up with a visit to the physician to confirm complete expulsion of the fetus and the absence of any complications. Many women find that medical abortions are more private and more natural than surgical abortions.

A surgical abortion involves the use of suction aspiration to remove the fetus from the uterus. Surgical abortion is generally used to end pregnancies between 6 and 14 weeks duration. Vacuum aspiration uses suction to expel the contents of the uterus through the cervix. Vacuum aspiration is performed in a doctor's office or clinic setting and typically takes less than 15 minutes. Patients receive an injection into the cervix to numb the cervical area. The physician inserts dilators to open the cervix, where a sterile cannula is inserted. The cannula, attached to tubing that is attached to a vacuum or manual pump, gently empties the contents of the uterus. The procedure is highly effective and is used most often in first-trimester abortions.

Second-Trimester Abortions

Second-trimester abortions refer to abortions performed between the 13th and 20th weeks of pregnancy. In some cases, second-trimester abortions may be performed as late as the 24th week of pregnancy. Second-trimester abortions carry a greater risk of complications due to the later stage of fetal development and are performed under local or general anesthesia. The cervix is dilated and a curette or forceps are inserted through the vagina, and the fetus is separated into pieces and extracted. Second-trimester abortions are typically performed in cases where a woman has not had access to early medical care and has only recently had a pregnancy confirmed, or in cases where a recent diagnosis of genetic or fetal developmental problems has been made.

The available abortion procedures provide many options to women. Pregnancy terminations performed between the 6th and 12th weeks of pregnancy are safe and include both medical and surgical procedures. Medical abortions, accomplished with a combination of drugs that induce a miscarriage, provide women with the option of ending a pregnancy in the privacy of her home in a relatively natural way. Surgical abortion, by using vacuum aspiration, gently removes the fetus from the uterus and includes minimal risks. These risks are usually limited to cramping and bleeding that last from a few hours to several days after the procedure. Most women who abort during the first trimester are able to return to their normal routines the following day. Antibiotics are generally prescribed following a first-trimester abortion to decrease any risk of infection, and a follow up visit several weeks later makes first-trimester abortions safer than childbirth.

Abortion as a Social Issue

As a contemporary social issue, elective abortion raises important questions about the rights of pregnant women, the meaning of motherhood, and the rights of fetuses. Since the late 1960s, abortion has been a key issue in the contemporary U.S. culture wars. The term *culture wars* refers to ongoing political debates over contemporary social issues, including not only abortion but also homosexuality, the death penalty, and euthanasia. Culture wars arise from conflicting sets of values between conservatives and progressives. The culture war debates, particularly those surrounding the issue of abortion, remain contentious among the American public. The debates have resulted in disparate and strongly held opinions and have resulted in the emergence of activist groups taking a variety of positions on abortion. Activists include those who support a woman's right to abortion (epitomized in groups such as the National Abortion Rights Action League—NARAL Pro-Choice America) and those who oppose abortion on religious or moral grounds (such as right-to-life organizations).

Researchers suggest that the continuing debates over abortion have called into question traditional beliefs about the relations between men and women, raised vexing issues about the control of women's bodies and women's roles, and brought about changes in the division of labor in the family and in the broader occupational arena. Elective abortion has called into question long-standing beliefs about the moral nature of sexuality. Further, elective abortion has challenged the notion of sexual relations as privileged activities that are symbolic of commitments, responsibilities, and obligations between men and women. Elective abortion also brings to the fore the more personal issue of the meaning of pregnancy.

Historically, the debate over abortion has been one of competing definitions of motherhood. Pro-life activists argue that family, and particularly motherhood, is the cornerstone of society. Pro-choice activists argue that reproductive choice is central to women controlling their own lives. More contemporary debates focus on the ethical and moral nature of personhood and the rights of the fetus. In the last 30 years, these debates have become politicized, resulting in the passage of increasingly restrictive laws governing abortion, abortion doctors, and abortion clinics.

Early Abortion Laws

Laws governing abortion up until the early 19th century were modeled after English Common Law, which criminalized abortion after "quickening," or the point in fetal gestational development where a woman could feel fetal movement. Prior to quickening, the fetus was believed to be little more than a mass of undifferentiated cells. Concurrent with the formal organization of the American Medical Association in the mid-1800s, increasingly restrictive abortion laws were enacted. In general, these laws were designed to decrease competition between physicians and midwives, as well as other lay practitioners of medicine, including pharmacists. A few short years later, the New York Society for the Suppression of Vice successfully lobbied for passage of the Comstock Laws, a series of laws prohibiting pornography and banning contraceptives and information about abortion. With the formal organization of physicians and the enactment of the Comstock Laws, pregnancy and childbirth shifted from the realm of privacy and control by women to one that was increasingly public and under the supervision of the male medical establishment. Specifically, all abortions were prohibited except therapeutic abortions that were necessary in order to save the life of the pregnant woman. These laws remained unchallenged until the early 1920s, when Margaret Sanger and her husband were charged with illegally distributing information about birth control. An appeal of Sanger's conviction followed, and contraception was legalized, but only for the prevention or cure of disease. It was not until the early 1930s that federal laws were enacted that prohibited government inference in the physician-patient relationship as it related to doctors prescribing contraception for their women patients. Unplanned pregnancies continued to occur, and women who had access to medical care and a sympathetic physician were often able to obtain a therapeutic abortion. These therapeutic abortions were often performed under less-than-sanitary conditions because of the stigma attached to both the physicians performing them and to the women who sought to abort.

By the 1950s, a growing abortion reform movement had gained ground. The movement sought to expand the circumstances under which therapeutic abortions were available; it sought to include circumstances in which childbirth endangered a woman's mental or physical health, where there was a high likelihood of fetal abnormality, or when pregnancy was the result of rape or incest. The abortion reform movement also sought to end the threat of "back-alley" abortions performed by questionable practitioners or performed under unsanitary conditions that posed significant health risks to women and often resulted in death.

By the 1960s, although the abortion reform movement was gaining strength, non-therapeutic abortion remained illegal, and therapeutic abortion was largely a privilege of the white middle to upper classes. A growing covert underground abortion rights collective emerged in the Midwest. Known as the Jane Project, the movement included members of the National Organization for Women, student activists, housewives, and mothers who believed access to safe, affordable abortion was every woman's right. The

Jane Project was an anonymous abortion service operated by volunteers who provided counseling services and acted in an intermediary capacity to link women seeking abortions with physicians who were willing to perform the procedure. Members of the collective, outraged over the exorbitant prices charged by many physicians, learned to perform the abortion procedure themselves. Former members of the Jane Project report providing more than 12,000 safe and affordable abortions for women in the years before abortion was legalized.

Activists involved in the early movement to reform abortion laws experienced their first victory in 1967, when the Colorado legislature enacted less restrictive regulations governing abortion. By 1970, four additional states had revised their criminal penalties for abortions performed in the early stages of pregnancy by licensed physicians, as long as the procedures followed legal procedures and conformed to health regulations. These early challenges to restrictive abortion laws set into motion changes that would pave the way to the legal right to abortion.

The Legal Right to Abortion

Two important legal cases reviewed by the U.S. Supreme Court in the 1970s established the legal right to abortion. In the first and more important case, *Roe v. Wade* (1973), the court overturned a Texas law that prohibited abortions in all circumstances except when the pregnant woman's life was endangered. In a second companion case, *Doe v. Bolton* (1973), the high court ruled that denying a woman the right to decide whether to carry a pregnancy to term violated privacy rights guaranteed under the U.S. Constitution's Bill of Rights. These decisions, rendered by a 7–2 vote by the Supreme Court justices in 1973, struck down state statutes outlawing abortion and laid the groundwork for one of the most controversial public issues in modern history.

The Supreme Court decisions sparked a dramatic reaction by the American public. Supporters viewed the Court's decision as a victory for women's rights, equality, and empowerment, while opponents viewed the decision as a frontal attack on religious and moral values. Both supporters and opponents mobilized, forming local and national coalitions that politicized the issue and propelled abortion to the forefront of the political arena. Opponents of abortion identified themselves as "antiabortion" activists, while those who supported a woman's right to choose whether to carry a pregnancy to term adopted the term "pro-choice" activists. These two groups rallied to sway the opinions of a public that was initially disinterested in the issue.

The Early Years Post *Roe*

Following the *Roe* decision, antiabortion activists worked to limit the effects of the Supreme Court decision. Specifically, they sought to prevent federal and state monies from being used for abortion. In 1977, the Hyde Amendment was passed by Congress, and limits were enacted that restricted the use of federal funds for abortion. In the ensuing years, the amendment underwent several revisions that limited Medicaid coverage for abortion to cases of rape, incest, and life endangerment. The Hyde Amendment significantly impacted low-income women and women of color. It stigmatized abortion care by limiting federal and state health care program provisions for basic reproductive health care.

As antiabortion and pro-choice advocates mobilized, their battles increasingly played out in front of abortion clinics throughout the country, with both groups eager to promote their platforms about the legal right to abortion. Abortion clinics around the country became the sites of impassioned protests and angry confrontations between activists on both sides of the issue. Confrontations included both antiabortionists who pled with women to reconsider their decision to abort, and pro-choice activists working as escorts for those who sought abortions, shielding the women from the other activists who were attempting to intervene in their decision. Many clinics became a battleground for media coverage and 30-second sound bites that further polarized activists on both sides of the issue. Moreover, media coverage victimized women who had privately made a decision to abort by publicly thrusting them into the middle of an increasingly public battle.

By the mid-1980s, following courtroom and congressional defeats to overturn the *Roe v. Wade* decision and a growing public that was supportive of the legal right to abortion, antiabortion activists broadened their strategies and tactics to focus on shutting down abortion clinics. Moreover, antiabortionist groups began identifying themselves as "pro-life" activists to publicly demonstrate their emphasis on the sanctity of all human life and to reflect their concern for both the pregnant woman and the fetus. The change in labels was also an attempt to neutralize the negative media attention resulting from a number of radical and militant antiabortion groups that emerged in the 1980s, many of which advocated the use of intimidation and violence to end the availability of abortion and to close down clinics. For these more radical groups, the use of violence against a fetus was seen as justification for violence that included the bombing and destruction of abortion clinics and included, in some cases, the injury or murder of physicians and staff working at the clinics.

The polarization of activists on both sides of the issue and the increased incidence of violence at abortion clinics resulted in the passage of the Freedom of Access to Clinic Entrance Act (FACEA). FACEA prohibited any person from threatening, assaulting, or vandalizing abortion clinic property, clinic staff, or clinic patients, as well as prohibited blockading abortion clinic entrances to prevent entry by any person providing or receiving reproductive health services. The law also provided both criminal and civil penalties for those breaking the law. Increasingly, activists on both sides of the issue shifted their focus from women seeking to abort and abortion clinics to the interior of courtrooms, where challenges to the legal right to abortion continue to be heard. Meanwhile, increasingly restrictive laws governing abortion and abortion clinics were passed.

The Later Years Post *Roe*

With the legal right to abortion established and the battle lines between pro-life and pro-choice activists firmly drawn, key legislative actions impacting the legal right to abortion characterized the changing landscape of the abortion debate. In the 1989 *Webster v. Reproductive Health Services* case, the Supreme Court affirmed a Missouri law that imposed restrictions on the use of state funds, facilities, and employees in performing, assisting with, or counseling about abortion. The decision for the first time granted specific powers to states to regulate abortion and has been interpreted by many as the beginning of a series of decisions that might potentially undermine the rights granted in the *Roe* decision.

Following the *Webster* case, the U.S. Supreme Court reviewed and ruled in *Planned Parenthood of Southeastern Pennsylvania v. Casey* (1992), a case that challenged five separate regulations of the Pennsylvania Abortion Control Act as being unconstitutional under *Roe v. Wade*. Specifically, the Pennsylvania act required doctors to provide women seeking abortion with a list of possible health complications and risks of abortion prior to the procedure, required married women to inform their husbands of an abortion beforehand, required parental or guardian consent for minors having an abortion, imposed a 24-hour waiting period before a woman could have an elective abortion, and mandated specific reporting requirements for clinics where abortions were performed. The court upheld four of the five provisions, striking down the spousal consent rule, which was found to give excessive power to husbands over their wives and possibly exacerbate spousal abuse. Moreover, the Court allowed for waivers for extenuating circumstances in the parental notification requirement. *Casey* was the first direct challenge to *Roe,* and the court modified the trimester framework that *Roe* had created. It also restructured the legal standard by which restrictive abortion laws were evaluated. *Casey* gave states the right to regulate abortion during the entire period before fetal viability, and they could do so for reasons other than to protect the health of the mother. The increased legal rights provided to states to impose restrictions on laws governing abortion resulted in a tightening of the requirements for clinics providing abortions and adversely affected many women who sought abortions, particularly low-income women and women who lived in rural areas. As a result of the increased power granted to states to regulate abortion, women were required to attend a pre-abortion counseling session before the procedure, in which they received information on the possible risks and complications from abortion, and they were required to wait at least 24 hours after the counseling session to undergo the procedure. For poor women or for women who lived in states where there were no abortion clinics available, the costs associated with the procedure rose dramatically because of the associated travel and time off from work.

Since *Casey,* the Supreme Court has heard only one case related to abortion. In *Stenberg v. Carhart* (2000), the constitutionality of a Nebraska law prohibiting so-called partial birth abortions was heard by the high court. The Nebraska law prohibited this form of abortion—known as intact dilation and extraction (IDX) within the medical community—under any circumstances. Physicians who violated the law were charged with a felony, fined, sentenced to jail time, and automatically had their license to practice medicine revoked. The IDX procedure is generally performed in cases where significant fetal abnormalities have been diagnosed and represents less than one-half of one percent of all abortions performed. The pregnancy is terminated by partially extracting the fetus from the uterus, collapsing its skull, and removing its brain. In the *Stenberg* case, the court ruled that the law was unconstitutional because it did not include a provision for an exception in cases where the pregnant woman's health was at risk. However, in 2007, the decision was reversed in *Gonzales v. Carhart*, the ban reinstated. The court held that the IDX prohibition did not unduly affect a woman's ability to obtain an abortion.

The Shift in Recent Debates

The differences between activist groups involved in the abortion debates have tradition-ally crystallized publicly as differences in the meaning of abortion. Pro-life activists define abortion as murder and a violation against the sanctity of human life. Pro-choice activists argue that control of reproduction is paramount to women's empowerment and autonomy. More recently the issues have focused on questions about the beginning of life and the rights associated with personhood. Technological advancements in the field of gynecology and obstetrics are occurring rapidly and influencing how we understand reproduction and pregnancy. Advances in the use of ultrasound technology, the rise in fetal diagnostic testing to identify genetic abnormalities, and the development of intra-uterine fetal surgical techniques to correct abnormalities in the fetus prior to birth all contribute to defining the fetus as a wholly separate being or person from the woman who is pregnant.

These new constructions of the fetus as a separate person, coupled with visual tech-nologies that allow for very early detection of pregnancy and images of the developing fetus, give rise to debates about what constitutes personhood and the rights, if any, the state of personhood confers upon the entity defined as a person. The issue of viability, defined as the developmental stage at which a fetus can survive without medical inter-vention, is complicated in many respects by these technological advances. Those who identify themselves as pro-life argue that all life begins at the moment of conception and point to technology to affirm their position. Many pro-life activists argue that the fetus is a preborn person with full rights of personhood—full rights that justify all actions to preserve, protect, and defend the person and his or her rights before and after the birth process. Those who identify themselves as pro-choice argue that personhood can only be conferred on born persons and that a developing fetus is neither a born person nor a fully developed being. These contemporary debates concerning personhood and rights con-tinue to divide the public and are particularly germane to the issue of fetal surgery. Fetal surgery is cost-prohibitive, success rates are very low, and some argue that the scarcity of medical resources should be directed toward a greater number of patients or toward the provision of services that have greater success rates.

At the state level, the battle has recently been fought in terms of pre-abortion counseling, including the issue of whether to require ultrasounds and whether pregnant women should be shown the ultrasound images. Twenty states now require that an ultrasound be done prior to an abortion and that the pregnant woman be given an opportunity to view the image. One state, Oklahoma, requires both that an ultrasound be done and that the woman view the image, although the law is currently in litigation (National Right to Life Committee 2010).

The Impact of Restrictive Abortion Legislation

Abortion is one of the most common and safest medical procedures that women age 15 to 44 can undergo in the United States. According to the U.S. Census Bureau's *2010 Statistical Abstract*, which combines figures reported by the Centers for Disease Control and the individual states, approximately 1.2 million abortions were performed in the United States in 2005. Among women aged 15 to 44, the abortion rate declined from 27 out of 1,000 in 1990 to 19.4 out of 1,000 in 2005. The number of abortions and the rate of abortions have declined over the years, partly as a result of improved methods of birth control and partly as a result of decreased access to abortion services.

The number of physicians who provide abortion services has declined by approximately 39 percent, from 2,900 in 1982 to less than 1,800 in 2000. Although some of the decline is the result of a shift from hospital-based providers to specialized clinics offering abortion procedures, this shift is further exacerbated by the number of clinics that have closed in recent years due to increased regulatory requirements that make remaining open more difficult. Moreover, the decline in providers of abortion services means that some women will experience a more difficult time in locating and affording services. Today, only 13 percent of the counties in the United States provide abortion services to women; that is, abortion services are unavailable in 87 percent of U.S. counties. Moreover, the Hyde Amendment preventing federal funds from being used to pay for abortion services was reaffirmed in March 2010 by President Barack Obama as part of an overall health care reform legislative package.

The Food and Drug Administration's (FDA) approval of Plan B, an emergency contraceptive best known as "the morning after pill" and mifepristone (RU-486) for early medication-induced abortions may be shifting the location of abortion procedures away from abortion clinics to other locations such as family planning clinics and physicians' offices. However, neither of these recent FDA approvals eliminates the need for reproductive health care that includes abortion care. While the issue of abortion may spawn disparate opinions about the meaning of motherhood, family values, the changing dynamics of male-female relations, and sexual morality, as well as raise issues about personhood and rights, unintended pregnancies disproportionately impact women and their children. This is especially true of poor women and women of color whose access to reproductive health care may be limited or nonexistent. Historically, women from the middle and upper classes have had access to abortion—be that access legal, illegal, therapeutic or nontherapeutic—while women from less privileged backgrounds have often been forced to rely on back-alley abortionists whose lack of training and provision of services cost women their health and, often, their lives.

See also **Birth Control; Teen Pregnancy**

Further Reading

Ehrenreich, Nancy, ed., *The Reproductive Rights Reader: Law, Medicine, and the Construction of Motherhood.* New York: Routledge, 2008.

Ginsberg, Faye, D., *Contested Lives: The Abortion Debate in an American Community,* rev. ed. Berkeley: University of California Press, 1998.

Herring, Mark Youngblood, *The Pro-Life/Choice Debate.* Westport, CT: Greenwood Press, 2003.

Luker, Kristen, *Abortion and the Politics of Motherhood.* Berkeley: University of California Press, 1984.

Maxwell, Carol J. C., *Pro-Life Activists in America: Meaning, Motivation, and Direct Action.* Cambridge, England: Cambridge University Press, 2002.

McBride, Dorothy E., *Abortion in the United States: A Reference Handbook.* Santa Barbara, CA: ABC-CLIO, 2008.

National Right to Life Committee, "Woman's Right to Know: States that Offer Ultrasound Option" (September 1, 2010). http://www.nrlc.org/WRTK/UltrasoundLaws/StateUltrasound Laws.pdf

Page, Cristina, *How the Pro-Choice Movement Saved America: Freedom, Politics, and the War on Sex.* New York: Basic Books, 2006.

Riddle, John M., *Eve's Herbs: A History of Contraception and Abortion in the West.* Cambridge, MA: Harvard University Press, 1997.

Rose, Melody, *Safe, Legal, and Available? Abortion Politics in the United States.* Washington, DC: CQ Press, 2007.

Shrage, Laurie, *Abortion and Social Responsibility: Depolarizing the Debate.* New York: Oxford University Press, 2003.

Solinger, Ricki, *Pregnancy and Power: A Short History of Reproductive Politics in America.* New York: New York University Press, 2005.

ADDICTION AND FAMILY

Angela Sparrow

Addiction has become an increasingly large problem in the United States over the past few decades. Jails have become overcrowded with those who are caught selling and using addictive substances. It has become the social norm for celebrities to be in and out of addiction rehabilitation centers every other week, and activities such as gambling and overeating have been labeled, along with substances such as alcohol and cocaine, as potentially addictive.

Once a narrowly defined term, *addiction,* or *dependence,* has been expanded to describe behaviors or activities that one wouldn't normally think of as being addictive. Among the more recent uses of the term are food addicts, sex addicts, and Internet addicts. With this expanding definition has come a heightened desire to uncover the causes behind addiction, whether it is to a traditional addictive drug or to a certain behavior. While the use of certain substances and certain activities often become addictions, not everyone who engages in these activities or consumes these substances becomes addicted to them, further complicating the issue. As a result, addiction counselors believe that there are certain reasons why one person becomes addicted more easily than another. Personality and biological factors are among some of the proposed reasons. Research into the topic has produced many debates over the subject of dependency and addiction, including conflicts over the cause and treatment of addiction and whether the term should apply to behavioral issues as well as to mood-altering substances.

Addiction has begun to play a large role in family life in the United States. Conceptions of harmonious family life suggest that serious problems such as addiction exist only in other people's families. As a consequence of this view, many families fail to recognize, deal with, and recover from a problem in their midst. The development, maintenance, and treatment of substance abuse are intimately connected with families. Families that have an addicted individual undergo a large assortment of effects, ranging from children lacking a parent due to addiction, to parents struggling to help their child to overcome an addiction, to divorce of marital partners when the lack of communication inherent with addiction leads to a breakdown of the marriage. Regardless of the stance one takes on the origin of addiction, it is important to remember that all addictions can be managed, and overcoming addiction is often achieved with the help of loved ones. Thus, family plays a central role in the recovery process.

Background

Addiction is a recurring compulsion or need by an individual to engage in some particular activity or to consume some specific substance. The activity or substance becomes the sole focus in an addicted individual's life. He or she begins to lose interest in other activities, loses focus on goals that were once important, and will begin to abandon normal behavior in order to gain access to the addictive activity. As the need for the activity or substance grows, the individual will do anything for the substance. In extreme cases, the addict even breaks laws in order to continue engaging in the activity or substance. Family is often the target of the illegal activity and may pay stiff penalties in personal and financial security as an addiction (particularly to illicit drugs) escalates.

When the term *addiction* was first coined, it clearly referred to the use of a tolerance-inducing drug. This definition recognizes that humans can become quickly addicted to various drugs. The modern understanding of chemical transmission in the brain, and how substances can lead to addiction, began in the mid-1800s in France. From this initial research by Claude Bernard, scientists began to discover how the body responds to drugs.

Addictions develop because the substance or activity produces a pleasure response in the individual, who then wants to receive more of the pleasure. For example, if an individual ingests a substance such as crack cocaine, he or she will feel a euphoric high feeling. As the drug enters the brain, it triggers the body's natural pleasure sensor to release endorphins, which results in a pleasurable sensation. The individual wants to continue to feel this euphoric high, but, as the addiction builds, the individual's tolerance to the substance grows. Over time, greater dosages of the drug must be used to produce an identical effect.

Over the years, however, as a medical model of behavior gained prominence, addiction began to be defined as a disease. This is in reference to the physiological changes that occur when one becomes addicted to a substance. The influence of both the medical and the psychological communities has been crucial in the area of addiction research. Two types of addiction—physical dependence and psychological dependence—have been identified through their combined efforts.

Physical Addiction

Physical addiction is determined by the appearance of withdrawal symptoms when the substance is suddenly discontinued. Withdrawal refers to the symptoms that appear when a drug that is regularly used for a long time is suddenly discontinued or decreased in dosage. The symptoms of withdrawal are often the opposite of the drug's direct effect. Sudden withdrawal from addictive drugs can be harmful or even fatal, so the drug should not be discontinued without a doctor's supervision and approval. Part of the rehabilitation process is to wean the addict off of the drugs in a safer and less traumatic manner.

Alcohol, nicotine, and antidepressants are examples of substances that, when abused, can produce physical addiction. The speed at which an individual develops an addiction depends on the substance, the frequency of use, the intensity of the pleasure that the drug induces, the means of ingestion, and the individual person.

Psychological Addiction

Psychological addiction is the dependency of the mind and leads to psychological withdrawal symptoms such as cravings, insomnia, depression, and irritability. Psychological addiction is believed to be strongly associated with the brain's reward system. It is possible to be both psychologically and physically dependent at the same time. Some doctors make little distinction between the two types of addiction, because they both result in substance abuse. The cause and characteristics of the two types of addiction are quite different, as are the types of treatment. Psychological dependence does not have to be limited only to substances; activities and behavioral patterns can be considered addictions within this type of dependency. The popularity of Internet usage, video games, pornography, and social networking services such as Facebook and Twitter have all been characterized in this manner.

Medical Debates

Not all doctors agree on what constitutes addiction. Traditionally, addiction has been defined as only possible when a substance is ingested that temporarily alters the natural chemical behavior of the brain to produce the euphoric high associated with these drugs. However, over time, people have begun to feel that there should be an alteration of the definition of addiction to include psychological dependency on such things as gambling, food, sex, pornography, computers, work, exercise, cutting, shopping, and so forth. These activities do not alter the natural chemical behavior of the brain when they are performed; thus, they do not fit into the traditional views of addiction, despite their impacts on social interactions and family life.

Those who support the contemporary view of addiction show that symptoms mimicking withdrawal occur when the individual stops the addictive behavior, even if it is not a physiologically acting substance. Those who support the traditional view purport that these withdrawal-like symptoms are not strictly reflective of an addiction, but rather of a behavioral disorder. Proponents of the traditional view say that the overuse of the term may cause the wrong treatment to be used, thus failing the person with the behavioral problem.

The contemporary view of dependency and addiction acknowledges the possibility that individuals who are addicted to a certain activity feel a sense of euphoria, much like the euphoria received from addictive substances. For example, when a person who is addicted to shopping is satisfying his or her craving by engaging in the behavior, chemicals that produce a feel-good effect, called endorphins, are produced and released within the brain, enforcing the person's positive associations with the behavior. Additionally, there could be negative, real-life consequences to participation in the activity, including isolation from family and friends, increased debt, and so forth.

Debate over the Causes of Addiction

The causes of addiction have been debated for years within the scientific community. One school of thought believes that addiction is a disease that cannot be controlled by the individual. This theory states that addiction is an inherited disease, and an individual with the inherited trait of the disease is permanently ill with the addiction located at a genetic level. Even those with long periods of overcoming the addiction will always contain the disease. This viewpoint states that if one's parent was addicted to something, whether a substance or an activity, he or she is predisposed to also develop the addiction. Even if the person avoids the substance or activity, he or she still technically has an addiction to it. The idea that "alcoholism runs in families" has a long tradition in the substance abuse field. Studies that compare alcoholism rates of natural and adopted children indicate that the adopted children of alcoholics have significantly lower rates of alcoholism than do their biologically related progeny. Additionally, a family history of alcoholism has been linked to a younger initial age of alcohol consumption.

Another school of thought argues that addiction is a dual problem caused by both a physical and a mental dependency on chemicals along with a preexisting mental disorder. This theory says that addiction is not caused by one factor alone but instead by many factors combined. Addiction is caused not just by the fact that a person's family member had the disease of addiction, but because the person's family member had the disease of addiction in addition to being emotionally unstable and prone to finding quick ways to happiness. Clearly, when a parent is "absent" due to his or her use of mood-altering substances, the socialization of the children is affected.

The social learning model suggests that the pattern of addiction is learned by watching or modeling the behavior of others. In families where addictive behaviors and substance abuse occur, children see role models of how to participate in addictive activities. This occurs even when parents attempt to hide their addictive behaviors. The fact that persons tend to share addictions over time through the process of assortative mating provides support for the idea that two persons with similar tendencies toward addictive behaviors will likely become partnered. There is scientific research to support all concepts of the causes of addiction. No one theory has emerged as having greater veracity in explaining and predicting dependency.

Effects within the Family

Addiction is the number one disease in the United States, with one in three families having at least one addicted member. With the problem of addiction so widespread, the effects on the family have become an important subject. Addiction affects the family in many ways. An addicted individual puts stress on the rest of the family. There is often a stigma of shame associated with addiction; this shame burdens the family and makes it harder for the family to seek help for the individual because of the fear of ridicule from the outside world. There is a substantial fear of discovery, and many families may hide the addiction for years without seeking the medical attention needed to help the addicted person. A significant loss of self-esteem in the addicted individual is noticed and may cause the addiction to get worse and the addicted individual to further deteriorate.

Many families that have an individual who has the disease of addiction are overcome by denial. They try to deny that there is a problem to everyone they know, including themselves. This act of denial will often lead to exaggerated feelings and may result in explosive behavior to which the family can become emotionally exhausted. One of the most concerning aspects of addiction in the family is that most illicit drug users are fairly young, of childbearing age (18 to 35 years), and thus are exposing children to addictive substances, behaviors, and outcomes.

Addiction may sometimes produce physical effects. Domestic violence—whether physical, emotional, or sexual—is increased in families that have an addicted member, particularly someone with alcoholism. Domestic violence can occur in well-educated families as well as families with less professional backgrounds. It is predicted that members of families where abuse due to addiction takes place are more likely to require medical care. Additionally, children of substance abusers who experienced physical or sexual abuse are more likely to experience psychiatric symptoms and marital instability than those persons in whose family there was not addictive behavior.

Typically, families experiencing substance abuse witness the allocation of the addict's role to others in the family. Often this "absent parent" cedes his or her responsibilities to a child. The child then must assume duties that are inappropriate to his or her age, even having to raise himself or herself because the parents were unavailable to nurture the child. As one can imagine, this leads to strained relationships, even as the child reaches adulthood. Resentment for a lost childhood is not uncommon.

Families with an individual who is an addict often withdraw from their community, are distrustful of others, and have severe financial difficulties. The fear of exposure and subsequent stigma may force the withdrawal. If the addict is engaging in illegal activities, it is possible that he or she will be caught and sentenced to jail. Indeed, 80 percent of women inmates are mothers, and the vast majority have children under the age of 18. If the individual has no one to care for the children during the incarceration, the children might be left alone, placed in foster care, or put into state-run child care facilities.

Another issue that families with an addict must face is the fact that children could be born to an addict and be drug dependent themselves. In these cases, the infants must go through detoxification and often have a low birth weight or other lingering physical and behavioral manifestations of the addiction. If the mothers remain addicted, they may have tremendous difficulty meeting the care needs of their child. One of the factors most associated with an increase in infants addicted to substances is the wide availability and low cost of crack cocaine.

Family and Recovery

The family often plays a large role in the recovery process for the family member who is an addict. Because denial is the primary barrier to effective treatment for addiction, the addict must admit that there is a problem. It is usually the family members who help the addict admit the addiction and realize that it is something that must be overcome. Wives routinely encourage husbands to seek treatment for alcoholism, for example. Today, most recovery programs involve the family members in counseling and behavior modification, suggesting that fewer relapses occur when family support networks are readily available.

In order for an addict to successfully overcome an addiction, he or she must have the support of his or her family. It is very important to find a treatment center or a recovery program that is a good fit for the person. Programs are available that can be easily adjusted to better suit the person undergoing the treatment. Online programs as well as weekly meetings with other recovering addicts are useful methods. There are also live-in treatment centers that take a drastic approach to help the person recover, though they may be avoided due to the stigma of their hospital-like approach.

Conclusion

Addiction is only one of many subjects relating to the importance of one's family in the world today. The debate over what specifically constitutes an addiction, its precise causes, and which disease metaphor is the most appropriate will likely continue for some time. The focus of these debates should transition into how to prevent addiction and to diminish the damaging effects that it has on the family. We live in a society where it is the social norm to associate addiction with a negative stigma. Ideally, we would live in a society where those with an addiction were embraced so that the recovery process could happen immediately with no shame or blame given to the family of the addict. When we reach this point, family members will be better able to relate to one another and will be more emotionally stable.

See also **Child Abuse; Domestic Violence—Behaviors and Causes; Drugs; Gambling; Juvenile Delinquency; Video Games; Internet (vol. 4)**

Further Reading

Ali, Syed F., and Michael J. Kuhar, eds., *Drug Addiction: Research Frontiers and Treatment Advances.* Boston: Blackwell, 2008.

Cheever, Susan, *Desire: Where Sex Meets Addiction.* New York: Simon & Schuster, 2008.

Clark, Neils, *Game Addiction: The Experience and the Effects.* Jefferson, NC: McFarland, 2009.

Harwood, Henrick J., and Tracy G. Myers, eds., *New Treatments for Addiction: Behavioral, Ethical, Legal, and Social Questions.* Washington, DC: National Academies Press, 2004.

Heyman, Gene M., *Addiction: A Disorder of Choice.* Cambridge, MA: Harvard University Press, 2009.

Lowinson, Joyce H., et al., eds., *Substance Abuse: A Comprehensive Textbook.* Philadelphia: Lippincott Williams & Wilkins, 2005.

Miller, William R., and Kathleen M. Carroll, *Rethinking Substance Abuse: What the Science Shows, and What We Should Do about It.* New York: Guilford Press, 2006.

Nutt, David, et al., eds., *Drugs and the Future: Brain Science, Addiction, and Society.* Burlington, MA: Academic Press, 2006.

ADOPTION—INTERNATIONAL AND TRANSRACIAL

HAYLEY COFER AND TARALYN WATSON

International adoption, also known as transnational adoption or intercountry adoption, is the process of a prospective adoptive parent seeking and obtaining a child for legal adoption from a country other than that of the parent's citizenship. For residents of the United States, children are available for adoption from over 50 countries. However, U.S. residents are ineligible to adopt from Canada, Australia, and Western Europe.

Transracial, or interracial, adoption is a form of adoption in which a family of one race legally adopts a child of a different race. Such adoptions have grown dramatically since black children started to be included regularly on adoption agency lists in the 1950s and 1960s. Also during that time, Asian children began entering the United States in adoption arrangements.

International Adoption

Residents of the United States adopt more children through intercountry adoption than do the residents of any other nation. The practice has garnered more attention in recent years as Hollywood celebrities flaunt their adoption-created families. Parents in the United States are turning increasingly to international adoptions as a way to create their families. Since 1971, close to 400,000 children have been adopted from foreign countries. Recent numbers indicate approximately 12,500 international adoptions by U.S. parents in 2009 (www.travel.state.gov). Comparably, in 1994, there were approximately 8,000 international adoptions.

The dramatic rise in international adoption can be attributed to war, poverty, and the lack of social welfare in the children's home countries. Factors in the United States that contribute to the increase in international adoptions are a disinclination toward foster care adoptions, perceived difficulties with domestic adoptions, and preference toward adopting infants in lieu of older children. As fewer healthy white infants became available in the United States, parents seeking children with these characteristics began to look elsewhere. Additionally, prospective parents in the United States have a greater amount of expendable income compared with couples from other developed countries. These financial resources are necessary, because an average international adoption processed through a private agency can easily cost between $7,500 and $30,000, depending on the child's country of origin and adoption service used (www.statistics.adoption.com).

In the United States, the vast majority of children who are in need of adoptive parents are older children. Statistics on the ages of children adopted in the United States gathered by the Adoption and Foster Care Analysis and Reporting System show that less than a quarter of the children in need of adoption are two years old or younger, whereas close to 40 percent of the adoptions that take place involve children from that age bracket. For families seeking an infant, international adoption is increasingly the answer. Most international adoptions are of infants and toddlers, with the majority of these children adopted from China, Guatemala, Russia, and South Korea. The number of children adopted from each of these countries varies from year to year, but these countries have been generally supportive of international adoptions. Increased infertility rates have also played a role in the rise in international adoptions. Infertility rates have been on the rise as more and more couples in the United States choose to postpone having children until later in life. For some of these couples, their goal of having a family can only be realized with an adoption.

With the large number of internationally adopted children entering the United States each year come many challenges concerning cultural socialization, developmental delays as a result of poor health, and potential behavioral issues. The language barrier alone causes many of the educational and social problems faced by children adopted from other countries. Additionally, these children sometimes face medical issues. According to the *International Adoption Guidebook,* children who are adopted from other countries are at risk for numerous medical conditions; the five most prevalent are hepatitis, HIV, fetal alcohol spectrum disorder, reactive attachment disorder, and sensory integration disorder. This creates special challenges for these families once they have navigated the bureaucracy to add the child to their family.

Popular International Adoption Countries

South Korean Adoptions

The Korean War (1950–1953) began the largest wave of international adoptions. In 1955, Harry Holt, an Oregon farmer and his wife Bertha, were so touched by the situation of the orphans from the Korean War that they adopted eight children from South Korea. This story sparked widespread media interest around the country, and many other Americans became eager to adopt South Korean children. In response, the Holts created Holt International Children's Services, which, by 2007, had placed around 60,000 Korean orphans into U.S. homes.

Foreign adoptions became so prevalent after the war that a special agency was created under the Ministry of Social Affairs in South Korea. In the 1950s, the majority of children adopted overseas were the mixed-race children of Korean women and U.S. servicemen. These children were referred to as the "dust of the streets" and were often treated cruelly in Korea. Eventually, the practice of adoption became so widespread in South Korea that not only mixed-race children were sent for adoption, but children of poverty-stricken families were put up for adoption as well. South Korea became the largest supplier of children to the United States and other developed countries. Since the end of the Korean War, over 200,000 Korean children have been sent overseas for adoption, 150,000 of them to the United States. To this day, Koreans comprise the largest group of adoptees in both the United States and Western Europe. Because unmarried Korean women often face a severe social stigma for nonmarital births, they are likely to put up their children for adoption because this makes the women eligible for substantial financial support.

Vietnamese Adoptions

In the 1970s, the Vietnam War was responsible for another wave of international adoptions by U.S. families. In 1975, Operation Baby Lift brought 2,000 Vietnamese and mixed-race children to the United States for adoption during the final days of the war. Critics questioned whether this hasty evacuation was in the best interest of the children. The most contentious point was whether these children were technically orphans who qualified for adoption. This operation was plagued with lost and inaccurate records, casting a negative light on international adoption. In several well-publicized instances, birth parents or other relatives later arrived in the United States requesting custody of children who had already been adopted by U.S. families. This effort was also criticized as another example of U.S. cultural imperialism.

Guatemalan Adoptions

Guatemala has in the recent past been a popular country for adopting U.S. couples; however, the number of Guatemalan adoptions has been dramatically curtailed, in part because of plans initiated by the former president of Guatemala, Oscar Berger. He announced that, as of 2008, all intercountry adoptions would be suspended. Thus, according to the U.S. State Department, whereas between 2004 and 2008 adoptions from Guatemala ranged from between 3,200 and 4,700 per year, by 2009, the figure had dropped to 756.

One of the primary reasons that so many children were available for so long in Guatemala relates to high levels of poverty, where birth parents may not be able to adequately care for all of their children and perceive adoption as a way to better their child's life. There also has been a long-standing concern that many Guatemalan children offered for adoption were actually stolen from their birth parents, who did not wish to tender them for adoption. As a result, Guatemalan children recently entering the United States via adoption have been subject to DNA testing to ensure that they are, in fact, eligible for adoption and that they were not kidnapped from their birth parents.

Chinese Adoptions

China routinely has a high number of children adopted by U.S. parents. This is due in part to China's one-child policy. In 1979, the Chinese government determined that Chinese couples residing in urban areas could have only one child without facing a penalty. If these couples had more than one child, they could receive jail time, pay heavy fines, and be ostracized from the community (www.china.adoption.com).

Additionally, China is a country where baby boys are revered and baby girls are seen as burdens on society. Inheritance and ties to the ancestral family are passed along the male line, so parents have a preference that their one child be a son. This is an important element in Chinese society. As a consequence of the preference for male heirs, there are many more baby girls than baby boys available for adoption. Historically, female fetuses were more likely to be aborted, and some female infants were killed by their parents. Rather than becoming the victims of infanticide, many times baby girls in China are abandoned in temples and hospitals or in subways or railway stations. When found, these children are taken to orphanages, where they can become eligible for adoption.

Former Soviet States and Adoption

In the early years of the 21st century, the former Soviet States, including Russia and Ukraine, were competing with China for the place from which the most children were being adopted by Americans. More recently, however, the numbers of children being adopted from Russia have declined, and, in April 2010, the government announced a halt to U.S. adoptions. The cessation came as the result of a case in which a Tennessee adoptive mother "returned" a seven-year-old boy whom she had adopted in 2009, claiming that the child was violent and posed a threat to the safety of herself and her family. The Russian government later announced that adoptions would continue, leaving many U.S. couples who had made plans to adopt from Russia both pleased and anxious about the prospects for completing the process.

Benefits of International Adoption

Parents face many challenges when attempting to adopt internationally. But the benefits may outweigh the difficulties in many cases. Among the most attractive reasons for international adoption is that the children are legally available for adoption before being advertised or listed with agencies. This means that there is very little chance that birth parents will change their mind and take back the child at the last minute, as has happened with some open adoptions in the United States.

Although the bureaucratic aspects of international adoption make it unlikely that one can adopt directly at a child's birth, as can happen in open adoptions in the United States, nearly one-half of the children who are adopted internationally are under the age of one when they meet their new parents, and almost all are under the age of four. This factor is very appealing to U.S. parents who would have many options for domestic adoptions if they preferred older children but few when they prefer the youngest children.

There is a tremendous variety in the children available for adoption. They are from different countries, of different ages and genders, and they have many different needs that adoptive parents might be able to fulfill. This variety means that parents can generally find the child with whom they will have the best fit. Multicultural families lead to greater tolerance and acceptance, supporting the politics of community and unity. Famous adoptive parents Angelina Jolie and Brad Pitt have such a multicultural family. Parents who have adopted children from poor countries often cite the opportunity they have to provide for the underprivileged child as a motivating factor in their decision.

While many domestic adoption agencies have limitations on who is eligible to adopt, some foreign agencies have less stringent guidelines, perhaps permitting older parents or singles to adopt when other avenues for domestic adoption are closed to them.

Concerns of International Adoption

Because everyone dreams of a healthy, happy child, potential adoptive parents need to recognize that they may not know about medical problems. Generally, parents receive information about the child's health, but they rarely know about the birth parents' health and backgrounds. The concerns extend to whether any prenatal care was available or attained by the birth mother. Children who were cared for in orphanages may have some additional special needs related to mental health and adjustment as a result of the institutional environment, though these are often resolved relatively quickly upon arrival in their new home.

International adoption remains costly, but, again, this varies by country. Agencies usually provide a list of expenses up front so that prospective parents can plan accordingly. The costs, however, do limit those persons eligible to adopt in this manner. This has led to the suggestion that international adoption agencies sell children to the highest bidders who can pay for fees, travel, and sometimes extended stays in foreign locales. Extortion has even been reported with some agencies. These scams claim a child is available, send details about the child, and get a commitment from prospective parents who send money to the agency, only to be told later that the fees have increased and more money is needed or the child is no longer available.

Adopting internationally can be a time-consuming and tedious process. The U.S. Citizenship and Immigration Service (USCIS) is a federal agency within the Department of Justice that is responsible for overseeing citizenship issues for foreign-born persons who wish to enter the United States, including children. The USCIS must provide permission for the adoptive child to lawfully enter the United States prior to the adoption being finalized in the child's country of origin. The average time frame for an international adoption is 12 to 18 months, but much of this depends on the country of origin and whether the U.S. paperwork is prepared properly.

The State of International Adoption Today

International adoption continues to be a subject that is fraught with questions and remains controversial. These questions are important as the number of international adoptions continues to rise. It remains to be seen whether international adoptions are in the best interest of the child. Even though conditions may not be perfect in their home country, would it not be of benefit to be raised in the culture to which one is born? Will the child suffer discrimination or have difficulty identifying with their U.S.-born parents? With all of the millions of dollars spent on legal processing, could it be better spent to improve conditions in these countries so that adoptions are no longer necessary?

Although these questions and others remain unanswered, they are very important to consider, because hundreds of thousands of children and their adoptive families would like to know the answers. In the earliest years of international adoption, the concerns expressed by adoptive parents and the general public were primarily about transitioning to the new family and adjustment, with an occasional question about transmitting cultural heritage; today, the concerns are expanded.

The concerns have shifted to include legal, criminal, and ethical issues affecting both birth and adoptive parents and the children. The options for parents who would like to adopt internationally are many, but they are always in flux. For example, as countries' laws regarding immigration or their political regimes change, they are more or less likely to permit children to be adopted to foreign families. Not only do policies, laws, and procedural requirements change in other countries, they change in the United States as well. The Hague Treaty on International Adoptions, when ratified by all Hague Convention nations, is designed to help ensure ethical adoption practices so that all parties will benefit and have their rights maintained. One of the primary goals was to prevent the abduction, trafficking, or sale of children through intercountry adoption. Additional provisions were designed to protect both the birth and adoptive parents' rights. The Intercountry Adoption Act of 2000 was passed in the United States to implement the provisions of the Hague Convention Treaty, ratified by the United States in April 2008. These provisions are forcing some changes in the ways that international adoptions occur. Specifically, agencies must have a national accreditation with consistent standards of practice, and there must be a mechanism for filing complaints.

As the procedure for international adoptions changes in response to the Hague Convention, this is a confusing time for those wishing to adopt internationally. As the nations adhering to the convention change, so do those nations' policies. There are also some shifts in which of the countries are being explored by prospective U.S. parents. In 2009, according to the U.S. Department of State, 2,277 Ethiopian children were adopted by U.S. citizens, a nearly eightfold increase from 2004. Changing patterns of adoption will be interesting to monitor.

Transracial Adoption

The most common form of transracial adoption in the United States is the adoption of a black child by white parents. Several reasons influence a couple's choice to adopt transracially, such as limited numbers of white children awaiting adoption, some people feeling a connection to a different race, others just wanting to adopt a child regardless of his or her race. Most advocates of transracial adoption feel that a loving family of any race is essential for a child, and yet there are opponents who believe firmly that children should be placed solely with families of their own race.

Transracial adoptions gained popularity in the 1950s and peaked through the 1960s and 1970s. With fewer healthy white infants available for adoption, adoption agencies began to consider placing a child of color into the home of a white family. The main reasons for the increase in transracial adoptions were long adoption waiting periods and a decreased number of white babies available due to advances in birth control, abortion, and societal acceptance of single mothers. The civil rights movement, too, with its emphasis on the breaking down of racial barriers, has been credited as a factor contributing to the increase in transracial adoptions.

The National Health Interview Survey found that 8 percent of adoptions were transracial in 1987. In 1998, the estimate of transracial or transcultural adoptions was 15 percent of the 36,000 foster children who were adopted. Of the 1.6 million children who were adopted in the United States in 2004, 17 percent were interracial adoptions and 13 percent were foreign born, according to the U.S. Census Bureau. Data compiled under the U.S. Health and Human Service's Adoption and Foster Care Analysis and Reporting System suggest that, in 2008, of the 123,000 children awaiting adoption from foster care, more than 60 percent were nonwhite.

The Debate

The numbers of transracial adoptions have increased, sparking controversy between those who do not believe that a white family can raise an African American child and those who believe that children are entitled to a loving home, no matter what racial barriers exist. The largest adversary of transracial adoptions historically and currently is the National Association of Black Social Workers (NABSW). Native Americans also oppose transracial adoptions, claiming that the practice is cultural genocide.

Arguments against Transracial Adoption

One of the main arguments against transracial adoption is that white parents will not be able to give a black child a cultural identity and survival skills in a racially diverse society. NABSW says that child socialization begins at birth, but the needs of black children differ from those of white children. Black children need to learn coping mechanisms to function in a society where racism is prevalent. Black families are capable of teaching these mechanisms in everyday life without having to seek out special projects or activities. They live their lives in a white-dominated society, and their children learn by daily interactions. Even when white adoptive families actively seek out interactions and activities with black families, they put an emphasis on the differences within their family.

Cultural support can be especially difficult to give if there is limited understanding of the cultural differences of family members. White couples are ill equipped in their understanding of African American culture to adequately prepare a child for life in an ethnic group other than that of the adoptive parents. Despite their best intentions, whites cannot fully understand life from a minority perspective, because they only experience it vicariously. The unique experiences of African Americans since their arrival on

U.S. soil mean that parenting strategies and coping mechanisms have been developed to help deflect hostility from the dominant members of society. Additionally, racial barriers exist in many different aspects of social life.

Over time, there has been a decline in the availability of white children to adopt. NABSW feels that white families adopt a black child so they do not have to wait for long periods of time to become parents. Adoption agencies cater to white middle-class prospective adoptive parents, and, because white children are not as available, the agencies try to persuade these families to adopt black children.

NABSW supports adoption agencies finding black families to adopt black children. It suggests that agencies should change adoption requirements so that black families wanting to adopt are not quickly eliminated from the process. NABSW also would like to see adoption agencies work harder to find extended family members who want to adopt and keep the child within the family. Financial help also should be available for these families, so adopted children have the opportunity to grow, develop, and socialize within the black community. In fact, NABSW has argued that the so-called genocide that results from the adoption of black children by white families could never promote the interests and well-being of black children.

In 1971, William T. Merritt, then president of NABSW, stated that black children who are in foster care or are adopted should only be in the home of a black family. His position paper the following year reiterated his perspective, and, as a consequence of the advocacy of NABSW, national adoption guidelines were changed to favor or promote race matching. In 1973, transracial placements decreased by 39 percent. In 1985, Merritt claimed that black children raised in white homes could not learn skills to function as a black person in society. He adamantly spoke out against transracial adoptions. Morris Jeff Jr., another past president of NABSW, called transracial adoption "the ultimate insult to black heritage."

Children who are adopted can sometimes face certain problems regardless of the adoptive parents' ethnicity. These problems, however, can become more intense when also dealing with racial barriers. Children placed for adoption have usually come from homes where abuse was common. They may be of an age to remember their biological parents and have unresolved conflicts because they were, in their minds, unwanted by their biological families. They often have to learn new ways of family life. In addition to adjustment issues, children who are adopted often have mental, physical, or emotional handicaps. Because adoption itself may require the child to make adjustments, the presence of racial identity questions enhances the difficulty of transitions.

Adoption comes with a certain stigma, and children who are adopted may face identity issues. Even though they accept their adoptive parents and families and appreciate being a part of the family, adopted children often have an intense desire to know their biological parents. Research shows that both adoptive parents and adult adoptees experience feelings of being stigmatized by others who question the strength of their ties with their adoptive families. This stigma can be heightened when the adoptee's ethnicity is different from that of the adoptive family.

Along with the cultural barriers and stigma of adoption, many opposed to transracial adoption say that there are enough black families interested in adoption to eliminate the placement of black children with white families. The National Urban League identified at least 3 million black families in 2000 who were interested in adoption. Adoption agencies have been faulted for contributing to the low numbers of available black adoptive families compared with white adoptive families. Critics say that many agencies do not have enough black social workers who are competent to make assessments of black families. Black families seeking to adopt may not receive equal treatment with their white counterparts, a situation that could be improved through the employment of more black social workers in adoption agencies.

Arguments for Transracial Adoption

Legislation has stepped in to terminate discrimination in the adoption process and eliminate race as the sole factor when determining the placement of a child for adoption. The Multi Ethnic Placement Act in 1994 was created to prohibit agencies or entities that receive money from the federal government from using race, color, or national origin as the critical criteria in the adoptive or foster parent or child decisions. While the Multi Ethnic Placement Act made improvements to the process of transracial adoptions, it still allowed for agencies to take into consideration whether prospective parents could adequately care for a child from a different race. The passage of the Adoption and Safe Families Act (1996) eliminated the use of any form of discriminatory tactics that would not allow prospective parents to transracially adopt. Any states that broke the laws would face reductions in their quarterly federal funds.

Those favoring transracial adoptions say that the statistics alone should be reason enough to disregard race as the determining factor in placement. In 2008, it was estimated that 123,000 children were awaiting adoption from foster care, and one-third of those were black children. In addition, the average black child waits more than four years before a permanent placement is obtained. Some of these inequities may be relieved if more transracial placements occurred.

The argument that suggests that harm will come to transracial adoptees because of the obviousness of the adoption and the constant reminder of being adopted may be interpreted positively. A child who is of a different race will learn sooner that he or she is adopted, and being forced to recognize this will make the adoption easier to talk about, thus making for a more open relationship with the parents. It has been suggested that there are direct benefits to the child in learning early about the adoption. They include a greater openness about the adoption, a positive self-identification with the adoptive status as well as racial identity, and recognition that there is no shared biology between the parents and child. Additionally, there is a positive affirmation for the child that he or she was chosen and wanted. Given that adoptive families are often open about the adoption and encourage their other-race children to become involved with the children's heritage, black children adopted by white parents are more likely to refer to themselves as black than are black children adopted within race. As a consequence of having to learn about more than one culture, studies suggest that these children have a greater tolerance for others different from themselves and are more accepting of cultural differences.

Because the adopted child knows that he or she was wanted by the family, there is also recognition that race is not a factor in how much the child will be loved. This visible reminder that the child was chosen to be a part of the family can help to increase the child's self-esteem. The visible differences can also help to remind the child that he or she does not share biology with the parents, but psychologically this can help the child realize that differences with the parents are expected and are not frowned upon. Any genetic expectations would be decreased as well so the child might feel less pressure to develop the same interests or talents as the parent.

Other concerns regarding the psychological health of transracially adopted persons have also been disputed. Many studies have refuted the claim that white parents are ill equipped to raise socially adapted African American children with high levels of self-esteem. Although this is a classic claim used by those opposed to transracial adoption, research data suggest that there are no significant differences in adjustment between transracially adopted children and those adopted within race. The most important factor influencing how the child adjusts to society is the age of the child at the time of adoption. Likewise, studies have not found a correlation between a child's adjustment and racial identity. It seems that the older a child is when adopted, the more problems there are with adjustment issues. However, this seemed to be the outcome whether the child was adopted by same-race or other-race parents.

The Simon-Altstein Longitudinal Study of adoption was a classic study that examined several aspects of transracial adoption. The study began in 1972, had three phases, and involved 204 families with nonwhite adopted children. The first phase of interviews asked the children about their racial identity by using the Kenneth Clark doll test. This phase concluded that the children in the study—both nonwhite and white—had no racial biases to either a black or white color doll. All knew their racial identities. Parents indicated that they used several means to introduce the racial culture of the adopted nonwhite children in the family.

The second phase of the study, conducted in 1983, measured self-esteem. The results of black, nonwhite, white adopted children, and white biological children were separated and compared. All groups had statistically equal levels of self-esteem. The transracially adopted children were asked about their relationships with their parents and white siblings. Most said that their relationship with their parents was better now in young adulthood than it had been when they were adolescents. Interestingly, this finding was the same for biological children and parents. Racial differences had no impact in most of the relationships between the transracially adopted children and their siblings who were the biological children of their shared parents. Transracially adopted children and biological children were almost equal in choosing a parent or sibling as the ones to whom they would go if they needed help, at 46.8 percent and 45 percent, respectively.

The third phase of this study, conducted in 1991, asked again to whom they would go if they needed help. The results showed that the adopted children would still turn to their parents or siblings for help. The study's overall findings provided strong evidence that white parents are capable of raising children of another race to have high self-esteem, positive identities, and close family ties.

Looking Ahead

There are several issues that families must consider before committing to transracial adoption. The most important thing to consider is the potential parents' own racial views. Another thing to consider is that the family will be in the minority after transracially adopting. Of concern may be how the parent and other members of the family will deal with opinions expressed by those outside of the family. Prospective parents could think about adopting siblings so that each child will have a familiar face to help with the transition.

Colorblind is a term frequently used by those who promote transracial adoptions. This refers to the ideal that everyone is seen equally and is not discriminated against due to race. The term is pertinent in adoption discussions, because it is illegal for adoption agencies to discriminate because of someone's skin color. In matching parents and children for adoption, the United States will probably never be a society that is totally colorblind. Colorblindness helps to promote fairness with regard to race, a difficult but necessary task. On the other hand, critics of the concept of colorblind contend that it erases a person's heritage and culture. Being colorblind does not erase the questions that arise about visual differences within families and communities. Ignoring differences can cause hurt and resentment. Because race and culture are so closely linked, to be colorblind to someone's race is to ignore his or her culture. Experts contend that children have a right to learn about their culture so that they can pass it down to the next generation.

Transracial adoption is not only a black and white issue; children are also adopted from foreign countries, although there is very little research to date on the adjustment experiences of these parents and children. Places like China and Ukraine are popular when families decide to adopt, because the high birth rates and poor economic conditions in these locales mean that there are often children readily available. There is not as much debate about the adoption of these children as there is over black children being adopted by white families, because adoption is seen as helping these children. The idea of saving a child is an idea that supporters of transracial adoption believe can happen right here in the United States by decreasing the numbers of children of all races awaiting placement with a permanent family.

See also **Foster Care; Gay Parent Adoption; Teen Pregnancy**

Further Reading

Adoption Media, http://www.adoption.com

Adoption.com. "Cost of Adopting," 2007. http://statistics.adoption.com/information/statistics-on-cost-of-adopting.html

Berquist, Kathleen Ja Sook, *International Korean Adoption: A Fifty-year History of Policy and Practice.* Binghamton, NY: Haworth Press, 2007.

Child Welfare Information Gateway, http://www.childwelfare.gov

Dorow, Sara K., *Transnational Adoption: A Cultural Economy of Race, Gender, and Kinship.* New York: New York University Press, 2006.

Fogg-Davis, Hawley, *The Ethics of Transracial Adoption.* Ithaca, NY: Cornell University Press, 2002.

Gailey, Christine Ward, *Blue-Ribbon Babies and Labors of Love: Race, Class, and Gender in U.S. Adoption Practice.* Austin: University of Texas Press, 2010.

Marre, Diana, and Laura Briggs, eds., *International Adoption: Global Inequalities and the Circulation of Children.* New York: New York University Press, 2009.

National Association of Black Social Workers, "Position Statement on Trans-Racial Adoption." September 1972. http://darkwing.uroegon.edu/~adoption/archive/NabswTRA.htm

National Council for Adoption, http://www.adoptioncouncil.org

Patton, Sandra, *BirthMarks: Transracial Adoption in Contemporary America.* New York: New York University Press, 2000.

Quiroz, Pamela Ann, *Adoption in a Color-Blind Society.* Lanham, MD: Rowman & Littlefield, 2007.

Simon, Rita J., and Rhonda M. Roorda, *In Their Own Voices Transracial Adoptees Tell Their Stories.* New York: Columbia University Press, 2000.

Simon, Rita J., and Rhonda M. Roorda, *In Their Parents' Voices: Reflections on Raising Transracial Adoptees.* New York: Columbia University Press, 2007.

Trenka, Jane Jeong, *Outsiders Within: Writing on Transracial Adoption.* Cambridge, MA: South End Press, 2006.

United States Department of Health and Human Services, http://www.hhs.gov

U.S. Department of State, Bureau of Consular Affairs. http://www.travel.state.gov

Volkman, Toby Alice, ed., *Cultures of Transnational Adoption.* Durham, NC: Duke University Press, 2005.

Yancy, George A., and Richard Lewis Jr., *Interracial Families: Current Concepts and Controversies.* New York: Routledge, 2009.

AFRICAN AMERICAN FATHERS AND ABSENTEEISM

Aaron D. Franks

African American fathers have come under much scrutiny in recent years. Most notable is the attention given to nonresidential fathers (those who do not live in the same home as their child), or what are sometimes referred to as absentee fathers. From the rise in African American juvenile crime to the increase in single-parented homes headed by black women, the African American man as a father has been consistently blamed for such occurrences. Statistics affirm that the majority of black children are without the presence of a father. About 70 percent of all African American births occur to unmarried women, and over 80 percent of African American children will spend some years of their childhood without a father in the home (Nelson, Clampet-Lundquist, and Edin 2002). With statistics such as these, the black father's role in the family has been closely examined. Although the validity of a number of arguments that blame black male fathering for many social ills seems legitimate, a number of speculations are false. As with most human endeavors, there are those who perform well and those who do not excel at the task of fatherhood. The role of black fathers is one of the strongest and most important traditions in the black community.

Background

Historical Influence

There is no question that, in their earliest years in the New World, enslaved African Americans were concerned about their fathers. Their loyalty to their fathers (and mothers) served as a target in the efforts of their white slaveholders to break their family bonds. In her book *Ain't I a Woman: Black Women and Feminism,* bell hooks asserts that scholars have examined and emphasized the impact that slavery has had on the consciousness of the black male. These scholars argued that black men, more so than black women, were the primary victims of the institution of slavery. She documents the case that "chauvinist historians and sociologists" have provided the American public with a perspective on slavery in which the most malicious and dehumanizing impact of slavery on the lives of black people was that black men were stripped of their masculinity. Historians and psychologists have argued that the overall interruption, but particularly the disbanding, of pre-emancipation black family structure has had an undeniable effect on family life. The fact that the African American father is a viable and resourceful entity in the home remains undeniable.

Media Influence

The traditional as well as unorthodox depictions of the strong African American father of the late 1970s and early 1980s in such programs as *Goodtimes* (James Evans) and *The Jeffersons* (George Jefferson), provided a glimpse into the more socially predominant view of the black father as strong, stern, and often frustrated due to his status as a black man in the United States. Although many of these stereotypes would have been true and relevant to the times, they also created a stigma of anger and questionable judgment on behalf of the notable black fathers who were portrayed. Viewers may recall the countless slurs George Jefferson would aim at his white counterparts as a means of expressing his distrust or dislike of them. Parallel to this was the consistent dejection, anger, and disappointment portrayed through James Evans, a barely-making-ends-meet father of three living in a public housing facility in Chicago. While these portraits and personalities were scripted, they were reflections of a society marked by inequity, social dysfunction, and frustration. However daunting these portrayals may have been, there was an alternate side to the coin. There was strength, resilience, and determination to provide for and keep the family afloat and together through the harshest of times.

This view would, however, shift as times have progressed into a more socially equitable age. As a result, along came *The Cosby Show*. This was the portrayal of the contemporary black father at his best. Here was a family headed by both parents, whose professions were doctor and lawyer. Above all, viewers saw a father who was not angry or frustrated; he was affluent and funny. This portrayal remains utopian and was, neither then nor now, as socially accepted as the aforementioned perspectives. Undeniably, the postemancipation African American father had to be of a stronger and stricter variety, but this was of necessity by his circumstances and not the result of natural inclination. To imply, as some have done, that such experiences as the Cosbys' did not exist throughout the course of African American history would be false.

Present Concerns

As society has progressed into a more technologically advanced social, economic, and academic age, the multiple uncertainties and social ills surrounding the family unit have come into focus. Likewise, attempts to fix what does not work in today's families have become more common. The black family and its supposed dysfunctions have been a prominent area of inquiry and concern, probably because of the continued higher numbers of such families in poverty. The absence of the black father in the home has been tagged as cause for a myriad of increasing social problems and irritations, including rises in black male juvenile crime, an increased number of black male juveniles with criminal records, an increase in the number of homes parented by single black mothers, increased numbers of illegitimate children, and the increased dependency of black women–headed households on the state. All of these can be attributed to the black fathers' recent absence from the home. In order to determine the effects of father absence, it is just as vital to denote the causes or sequential happenings that have led to the absence.

Possible Causes of Paternal Delinquency

In *The Woes of the Inner-City African-American Father,* renowned social inequality specialist William J. Wilson argues that there are structural and cultural explanations for the lack of black fathers in inner-city African American homes. He contends that structural economic forces such as deindustrialization and globalization have decreased the number of high-paying manufacturing jobs in the United States, which were replaced by lower-paying types of employment. Wilson argues that low pay and limited education have made it increasingly difficult for black men to marry. Also, the lack of employment and educational opportunities creates a cultural environment that allows black men to personally assimilate racist sentiments and negative attitudes about themselves. As a result, these African American men view fatherhood and marriage as burdens that they are unwilling to assume. Wilson also suggests that there needs to be a policy that addresses black men's self-esteem and creates readily available, higher-paying employment opportunities (Wilson 2002).

There is also the issue of divorce or separation that influences absence. Approximately two in three divorces are initiated not by the husbands but by the wives, and the children remain living with their mothers in 93 percent of these cases. Encouraged by the government, family courts have consistently taken the stance that if the mother does not want the child to see the father any more, then that must be what is best for the child. Consequently, following divorce or separation, 60 percent of fathers have no further meaningful relationship with their children. These fathers may be walking away and exhibiting negligence, but they are also being pushed out of their children's lives.

Black Family Awareness

There is a question of accountability and responsibility that black men must answer regarding the present state of many African American families, but as a culture and society there has to be a reciprocal solution. In a 2005 Chicago *Sun-Times* poll, of 11 response categories to the question, "What is the most important thing you do for your children?" the largest response (25 percent of the total responses) was to the category "provide." When asked what the idea of a good father meant, the category of nine possible answers that received the most responses was "being able to provide and protect." When asked about the worst aspect of having and raising children, 26 percent of the fathers responded that it was not being able to provide for them. The issue of basic needs provision was chosen most often in all conditions.

With so many African American fathers desiring to support their children but finding it difficult to do so, there has to be a strategy to combat the absence of black fathers and the systemic ills that accompany it. As an advocate for strengthening African American families, famous black actor and comedian Bill Cosby has been involved on many occasions in recent years in discussions about the role of black fathers. He has gone on speaking tours, appeared on television news programs, and penned books on the subject. With Harvard Medical School psychiatry professor Alvin Poussaint, Cosby coauthored the book *Come On, People: On the Path from Victims to Victors,* in which he argues that children in single-parent homes often do not receive the guidance they need or deserve. He suggests that, in a generational, fatherless situation, regardless of whether the father was married to the child's mother, where the male is not present, the child perceives the situation as abandonment. While his harsh criticism of some black families has not always been well received, he has done a very good job of bringing the issue to the public's attention.

Regarding family and personal relationships, today's African American men are no less sensitive than their forefathers. According to black psychologist Marvin Krohn, black men come to the psychiatrist's office in large numbers, in pain and genuinely seeking help. Krohn goes on to assert that African American fathers have little or nothing to say about the statistics, myths, and other sociological indictments so often made about them. Rather, many of them come in speaking of depression, unease, aggravation, fear, shame, esteem issues, and anger that are most often associated with the close, ongoing relations (child's mother) in their lives. This suggests that black men are as frustrated over their absence in their children's lives as is the rest of society.

Black Father Absenteeism

Formal Statistics

Father absenteeism has been explored by examining the physical and financial presence of the father in the home. Eighty percent of all African American children will spend part of their childhood living apart from their fathers. Seventy percent of African American children are born to unmarried mothers, and 40 percent of all children regardless of race live in homes without fathers. Further studies of African American fathers do indeed suggest that many young African American fathers are relatively uninvolved in the lives of their children.

The National Longitudinal Survey of Labor Market Experience of Youth indicated that, of African American children with mothers ages 20 to 25, about 40 percent primarily lived with both parents, compared to about 90 percent of non–African American children. Of the nonresident fathers, 20 percent had never visited in the past year or had seen their child only once (Lerman and Sorensen 2003). In a sample of 100 fathers and a comparison group of nonfathers, all but one of whom was African American, 18 months after the child's birth, only about 25 percent of the nonresident fathers reported seeing their children daily. A follow-up study of 110 boys mostly born to African American teen mothers in the Baltimore Parenthood Study revealed that over half of these young men have never lived with their father, and most of the nonresident fathers had irregular contact with their children. Only 20 percent of young fathers were living with their children five years after the child's birth, and an additional 20 percent visited regularly.

As it relates to economic support, there is even less information on child support payments by African American fathers. National studies tend to show that about 50 to 75 percent of fathers paid the full amount of court-ordered support in the preceding year. A study based on the Current Population Survey found that minority group fathers of children born to never-married mothers are less likely, overall, to pay child support.

INTERVENTION STRATEGIES

Although black father absenteeism is a significant problem, a number of individuals and community organizations are attempting to limit or even eradicate this phenomenon. Programs like the Academy of Black Fathers in Boston, Massachusetts, and the Father Focus program located in Baltimore, Maryland, are counseling programs that support, encourage, and help fathers develop and maintain close relationships with their children and families. These organizations also provide a society of men who can talk about the experiences of fatherhood.

There are also many government agencies that aid black fathers. One such office is the National Partnership for Community Leadership. Its mission is to improve the management and administration of nonprofit, tax-exempt organizations and strengthen community leadership through family and neighborhood empowerment.

The most recognizable and easily accessible institution with programs aimed at helping fathers is the YMCA (Young Men's Christian Association). A prominent YMCA fatherhood program based in Cleveland, Ohio, recently met with a number of public health officials to discuss programs that would help to prevent absenteeism and fatherlessness in the black community. The conference participants developed a three-level preventative solution to this problem. The first level educated black fathers about the positive side of fatherhood. The next level covered the needs of at-risk men who were consistently underemployed or involved in the criminal justice system. The third level counseled about the importance of relationships.

Henry E. Edward, author of *Black Families in Crisis: The Middle Class*, constructed a forum of solutions to alleviate the current strife in the black family as a societal unit. The initial solutions presented were to reach out to black fathers and to offer them support. Religion and spirituality were highlighted as a source of strength that could be used to aid in morality and accountability for these men. Because of a false sense of masculinity and manliness, black fathers may not want to acknowledge the need for religion. Indeed, rates of church attendance are significantly higher for black women compared to black men. He also discussed at length the effects that mass media have had in the desecration of the black male image and the African American father. Boycotts of radio stations, talk-show hosts, newspapers, and businesses that slander black fathers were proposed to draw attention to the issues. Ultimately, African American men and women were urged to oppose further cuts in jobs and social service programs, to support those programs and policies that allow black fathers to earn the money necessary to provide for their families, and to encourage full-time dads to join a black men's group, such as those structured in the inner cities. These programs help black men support other black men to be better fathers.

In short, previous research has generated a rather negative image of young African American fathers. Additionally, the portrayals of these men in the media highlight their struggles and absence as normative. They may even be shown as sexual predators, seeking personal gratification and likely to abandon the child and the child's mother when a better opportunity comes along. This image has found its way into the nation's consciousness about race and family, perhaps to the extent of influencing public policy on public assistance and associated issues. One of the most important limitations of much research on fatherhood is that nonresident fathers are highly underrepresented in household surveys, and therefore their perspectives are underrepresented in the literature. Data on young, urban, nonresident African American fathers are particularly thin, and the limited research that has focused on them continues to employ generally small, unrepresentative samples.

African American fathers often are seen as deadbeats due to their lack of economic support in the home, but it would be a bit fairer to say that they are dead broke as well. Seventy percent of the child support debts owed in 2003 were accumulated by men earning $10,000 a year or less. Over 2.5 million nonresident or absentee fathers of poor children are poor themselves, thus making it extremely difficult for them to fulfill the father role as it is currently conceived in U.S. society (Furstenberg and Weiss 2000).

Informal Statistics

Statistics that account for father support of children have largely been derived from formal child support payments; however, the unaccounted-for informal child support, which may constitute a significant percentage of the mother's resources, has been overlooked in many cases. Some researchers have suggested that the nonresident status of the fathers may not forecast their lack of involvement, as was previously believed. Some studies have indeed suggested that the contribution of both financial and nonfinancial support by nonresident African American fathers has exceeded expectations. Many African American men are practically involved in their children's lives and make nonfinancial contributions to their children. Diapers, milk, toys, and baby clothes are only a few of the noncash provisions.

Many have asked why these fathers who provide some basic items do not simply pay child support. There are a number of reasons why they do not. Many of the items a father brings to his children are physical support of his efforts to provide for them, despite his dismal economic conditions. In return, the bits and pieces have greater significance, visibility, and permanence than cash payments. Such cash payments often vanish almost instantaneously as bills are paid, they are misused by the custodial parent, or, in the case of children receiving public assistance, they are used to reimburse the government for necessities it has provided the children.

It is quite likely that black fathers have been assaulted, and their contributions in a number of categories have been unjustifiably denigrated. Research supports many assertions about the positive contributions of African American fathers. African American fathers in two-parent families spend more time with their children than do Hispanic or white fathers. African American fathers and black fathers in the Caribbean are more likely than white fathers to treat boys and girls similarly when they are babies. They also interact just as frequently with their young daughters as they do with their young sons.

On the other hand, in the United States, black families have higher divorce, separation, and never-living-together rates than white families. However, a top predictor that a black couple will stay together is the black man's enjoyment of, and interest in, being a father and sharing in the day-to-day care of his children (Fatherhood Institute 2005).

Rates of nonresident fathers being involved with very young children are surprisingly high among nonresident African American fathers, but father involvement drops off considerably as the children age. Correspondingly, as the time since the father has lived with his child increases, father involvement decreases. Most nonresident African American fathers speak movingly of the meaning of their children in their lives, even if they rarely see them. African American fathers sometimes say that when they cannot contribute financially, they feel too guilty to have ongoing contact with their children. Many times a pregnancy and the ensuing birth provide African American fathers who have been participating in frequent illegal activity a strong motive to leave their hazardous street lives. Because of this, African American fathers often claim that their children have literally saved them (Fatherhood Institute 2005).

However, low-income African American fathers are more likely than both black and white higher-income fathers to place an equal value on the breadwinning, provider role and on the relational functions of fatherhood. Both structural and behavioral factors, such as unemployment, drug use, criminal activity, and conflicts with their child's mother hinder black fathers from fulfilling the duties they say are necessary to be an adequate or good father.

Conclusion

There is a question of accountability and responsibility that black men have to answer regarding the present state of many African American families. At the same time, social and cultural supports could be enacted that would assist black men in more fully meeting their obligations. Given the constraints of living in poverty, many African American fathers are torn between their desires to effectively parent and their need to ensure their own survival. The general public, influenced by the stereotypical portrayals of black men in the media, may not recognize the roles that black men do play in the lives of their children.

Having an involved father has noticeable benefits to children. Fathers are important because they help to teach children values and lessons in solving the problems they may face, and they do so in a way that differs from what mothers contribute. Fathers also serve as role models in their children's lives that affect how well they relate to peers and adults outside the home and in society. When speaking of the benefits of being an involved father, focus is placed on the benefits that children receive from such a relationship. Being an involved father means being actively involved in nearly every aspect of a child's life, from direct contact, play, and accountability for child care to making oneself available to the child. Black men's social situations influence how well they may or may not meet these demands.

While the common stance regarding African American fathers today is that their absence results in significant financial and social harm to their offspring, it may not be universally true. Researchers studying the issue of paternal involvement for a substantial amount of time have found concise evidence supporting the importance of paternal participation. Recently, some researchers have found that African American fathers can contribute to the health and well-being of their children, even if they do not live in the same household. The results of investigations of the influences of nonresident father involvement on children indicate that positive father involvement relates to better child outcome.

Researchers note that it is the quality rather than quantity of time that youth spend with their fathers that is important for their well-being. Research has also shown that children whose fathers are involved in rearing them score higher on cognitive tests (they appear smarter) than those with relatively uninvolved fathers. These improved cognitive abilities are associated with higher educational achievement. In fact, fathers who are involved in their children's schools and academic achievement, regardless of their own educational level, increase the chances that their child will graduate from high school and perhaps go to a vocational school or a college. A father's involvement in his children's school activities protects at-risk children from failing or dropping out.

Research shows that fathers who are more involved with their children tend to raise children who experience more success in their careers. Career success can lead to greater income and greater financial stability. Involved fathering is related to lower rates of teen violence, delinquency, and other problems with the legal system. Furthermore, paternal involvement is associated with positive child characteristics such as understanding, self-esteem, self-control, psychological well-being, social competence, and life skills. Children who grow up in homes with involved fathers are more likely to take an active and positive role in raising their own children. For example, fathers who remember a safe, loving relationship with both parents were more involved in the lives of their children and were more supportive of their wives.

Finally, being an involved father brings benefits to the dads themselves. When fathers build strong relationships with their children and others in the family, they receive support and caring in return. Research has shown that healthy family relationships provide the strongest and most important support network a person can have, whether that person is a child or an adult. Being involved in their family members' lives helps fathers to enjoy a secure attachment relationship with their children, cope well with stressful situations and everyday problems, feel as if they can depend on others, feel more comfortable in their occupations, and feel that they can do their parenting job better.

The benefits listed above are only a small portion of what accrues for fathers and children in a healthy relationship. There may be others that the research has yet to uncover. Nevertheless, all of these benefits for both fathers and children in the African American community will require hard work, patience, support, and diligence. It seems a more prudent and wise use of resources to determine how African American men can be assisted to be present in their children's lives rather than to denigrate them for their absence.

See also **Deadbeat Parents; African American Criminal Injustice (vol. 2); Social Justice (vol. 2)**

Further Reading

Clayton, Obie, et al., eds., *Black Fathers in Contemporary American Society: Strengths, Weaknesses, and Strategies for Change.* New York: Russell Sage Foundation, 2005.

Coles, Roberta L., and Charles Green, eds., *The Myth of the Missing Black Father.* New York: Columbia University Press, 2010.

Connor, Michael E., and Joseph L. White, eds., *Black Fathers: An Invisible Presence in America.* Mahwah, NJ: Lawrence Erlbaum, 2006.

Cosby, Bill, and Alvin F. Poussaint Jr., *Come On, People: On the Path from Victims to Victors.* New York: Thomas Nelson, 2007.

Fatherhood Institute, "Finding Black Fathers in Families" (2005). http://www.fatherhoodinstitute. org/index.php?id=7&cID=82

Furstenberg, Frank E., and Christopher C. Weiss, "Intergenerational Transmission of Fathering Roles in At Risk Families." *Marriage and Family Review* 29 (2000): 181–202.

Hamer, Jennifer, *What It Means to Be Daddy: Fatherhood for Black Men Living Away from Their Children.* New York: Columbia University Press, 2001.

hooks, bell, *Ain't I a Woman: Black Women and Feminism.* Boston: South End Press, 1981.

Lerman, Robert, and Elaine Sorensen, "Child Support: Interactions between Private and Public Transfers." In *Means-Tested Transfer Programs in the U.S.,* ed. Robert Moffitt. Chicago: University of Chicago Press, 2003.

Nelson, T. J., Clampet-Lundquist, S., and K. Edin, "Sustaining Fragile Fatherhood: Father Involvement among Low-income, Noncustodial African American Fathers in Philadelphia." In *A Handbook of Father Involvement,* ed. Catherine S. Tamis-LeMonda and Natasha Cabrera. Mahwah, NJ: Lawrence Erlbaum, 2002.

Smith, Carolyn A., Marvin D. Krohn, R. Chu, and O. Best, "African American Fathers: Myths and Realities about Their Involvement with Their Firstborn Children." *Journal of Family Issues* 26, no. 7 (2005): 975–1001.

Wilson, William J., *The Woes of the Inner-City African-American Father.* New York: Cambridge University Press, 2002.

ATTENTION DEFICIT HYPERACTIVITY DISORDER (ADHD)

Nicole D. Garrett

Parents often agonize over a child's behavior, wondering if their child is just unruly or if there might be a medical cause to problems experienced in school and other rigid settings. Increasingly, parents are finding a diagnosis—attention deficit hyperactivity disorder (ADHD)—to account for some of the behavior issues that make parenting a particularly challenging activity. According to the medical community, ADHD is a neurological disorder primarily characterized by inattentiveness, hyperactivity, and impulsivity. ADHD is generally detected in childhood, but increasing numbers of individuals are being diagnosed in adulthood. The vast majority of identified ADHD sufferers are male. A heated debate centers on the nature of the disorder, including whether a medical label is appropriate and how it should be treated.

ADHD has received increased attention in the professional and popular literature in recent years. Most sources agree that ADHD diagnoses are on the rise in the United States. Comparing two similar data sources illustrates this increase. According to a 1987 study, the weighted national estimate of children receiving treatment for ADHD was approximately a half million. A follow-up to this research in 1997 reported a weighted national estimate of children receiving ADHD treatment of more than 2 million. These figures can be loosely compared to the most recent data available from the Centers for Disease Control and Prevention on the number of children in the United States ever diagnosed with ADHD. According to this source, this distinction applied to 4.5 million youth in 2006 (the most recent estimate). From this illustration emerges a general idea of the rate of change surrounding ADHD diagnoses in the United States.

Three Contested Perspectives

A crucial element of the ADHD debate involves its definition. Many physicians and psychologists believe that ADHD is a medical issue with neurological implications and genetic causes. Others—those who favor a more holistic approach to life or who may not have parented—feel that ADHD is a creation of overzealous practitioners and pharmaceutical companies. Still others see the phenomenon as social in origin, arising from changing values and ideals regarding childhood. Thus, three main perspectives exist in the ADHD controversy. The first is the medical perspective that views ADHD as a physiological disease. The second perspective describes ADHD as subject to the medicalization process that transforms many behavioral issues into medical problems. The third perspective portrays ADHD as a social issue arising from changing interpretations of behavior rather than children's physical disabilities.

ADHD as a Disease

The underlying assumption of a medical model of a disorder is that some recognized standard of behavior, one that is displayed by the majority of the populace, is absent in an individual. The absence of the expected behavior is attributed to an illness or disease, which, once properly diagnosed, can be treated to help bring about more desired behavior.

Many psychologists, psychiatrists, physicians, and other clinicians, as well as parents, teachers, and members of the general public, believe this model is appropriate for

ADHD. The idea that inattentiveness and hyperactivity in children indicate a disorder originated near the turn of the 20th century. The condition, then termed *hyperkinetic reaction of childhood*, was officially recognized by the American Psychiatric Association in the second edition of its *Diagnostic and Statistical Manual of Mental Disorders* (DSM-II) in 1968. For the DSM-III, the label was revised to *attention deficit disorder* (ADD). The terminology changed again for the revision of the third addition, the DSM-III-R, when the disorder was given the more inclusive title of *attention deficit hyperactivity disorder* or ADHD.

The current DSM-IV lists inattentiveness, hyperactivity, and impulsivity as the three primary characteristics of ADHD. The manual also indicates that an ADHD diagnosis is not appropriate unless symptoms have been present for at least six months, these symptoms occur to a degree that is developmentally deviant, and these symptoms were developed by the time the individual was seven years old.

The medical community has been searching for a verifiable physiological cause of ADHD for some time. Although no exact biological origin has been determined, researchers and clinicians have focused their efforts on the brain for answers to the root of the disorder. Among the proposed possibilities are chemical imbalances and brain deficiencies that may arise from low birth weight or premature birth. Some notable investigation has also been done on the frontal lobe, the area of the brain responsible for behavioral and emotional regulation. As this area matures, individuals gain the ability to plan before acting and, when necessary, to ignore the desire to act. Scientists have observed a difference in the size and shape of the frontal lobe in ADHD individuals compared to non-ADHD individuals. These variations may indicate a diminished capacity for self-control in people with the disorder. Yet this research has also proven inconclusive, even leading some who accept the medical view of ADHD to admit that no irrefutable biological cause has been discovered to explain it—a point that critics and skeptics are quick to emphasize.

In addition to the argument for neurological markers of ADHD, researchers have also proposed a genetic factor for the disorder. As science learns and understands more about human DNA, the quest to locate particular genetic sources for illnesses has expanded beyond physiological disease to behavioral disorders like ADHD. No one has yet pinpointed an ADHD gene, but many believe it will be discovered eventually. Other proponents of the medical understanding of ADHD see it as more complicated than that, feeling that a single ADHD gene is not likely to be identified. Those who hold this point of view assert that science is beginning to realize that mental disorders originate from complex interactions of genes, chemicals, and other neurological components, meaning that the isolation of a specific ADHD gene is not likely.

Strong arguments asserting that ADHD is a disease come from individuals, or from the relatives of individuals, who have ADHD. According to many of these advocates, ADHD causes much pain for those it touches, especially when not diagnosed and medical treatment can bring relief. ADHD literature contains a large number of personal stories by individuals dealing with the disorder. Many of these report that they were considered stupid, lazy, and unmotivated as children. They also describe deep feelings of guilt and isolation because they were unable to meet academic and social expectations. For these individuals who found relief and understanding after being diagnosed with ADHD, the validity of the medical model is unquestionable. The stories of ADHD sufferers can often be found alongside reports from family members who describe distress over not knowing how to relate to or help their loved one with ADHD. These personal accounts available in the literature give human voices to an issue that is dismissed by some critics as a myth and others as invention.

The Medicalization of ADHD

Another perspective on ADHD is that it, like a number of other social issues, has been subjected to the process of medicalization. Prominent medicalization researchers and others cite as key elements of the medicalizing of ADHD the changing views of children in the United States, the unprecedented power of the medical profession, and the clout of pharmaceutical companies offering so-called miracle drugs to fix behavioral problems.

Prior to the Industrial Revolution, children were seen as miniature adults rather than members of a special life stage prior to adulthood. Children were considered responsible and were expected to become productive members of society at early ages, for most this meant joining the labor force or helping on the family farm. At this time, the realms of child care and management rested squarely within the family.

But with urbanization came a decreased need for child labor and a greater emphasis on education. Eventually, society came to see children's proper place as in the classroom, and compulsory education arose. As youth were being thrust into schools, their parents were coming to view them as innocent creatures with little social power, dependent on the protection and care of adults. Over time, as people began to place more stock in the word of professionals and specialists over the teachings of folkways and tradition, parents more often sought out these specialized groups for ideas about how to properly rear children. This view of youth as innocent and dependent coupled with a loss of authority in the family is described by some as a prime contributor to the medicalization of untoward child behavior. Furthermore, because children are not considered mature enough to be culpable, their unacceptable actions cannot be labeled crimes, leaving only illness labels to explain their deviant conduct.

Before medicine gained respect as a scientific field, bad children were thought to be under the devil's influence, morally lacking, or subject to poor parenting. Religion and the family had the main responsibility for shaping society's views on appropriate and inappropriate behavior. However, once physicians began to make medical breakthroughs, including the advent of vaccinations, the profession began to build expert power. Over the last century or so, the medical field has acquired great authority and now has almost absolute control over how U.S. society defines disease, illness, and treatment. Thus, when physicians approach behavioral difficulties, such as those displayed with ADHD, as medical issues requiring medical treatment, most people accept this definition without question.

The makers of pharmaceuticals have also been gaining influence in society. Some now see these companies as a driving force behind the medicalization of a host of issues, including ADHD. Many people believe that if a drug exists that treats symptoms, then it proves disease is present. Such is often the case with ADHD. Psychostimulants, such as Ritalin and Adderall, have been shown to be very effective at helping children calm down and pay attention. Because of this success, despite the positive effects found for alternative treatments such as parent training programs, medications are considered the most useful method of curbing ADHD difficulties. Critics contend, however, that the efficacy of psychostimulants for adjusting the behavior of children diagnosed with ADHD is not valid evidence of a biological deficit, because these drugs produce similar results in children who do not have ADHD as well.

Following the view of some proponents, one primary reason aspects of human behavior are being increasingly tied to genetic explanations is because this is financially beneficial for drug manufacturers who are supposedly able to offer the only solutions to medical defects. Supporting this argument is the fact that, in the 1960s, pharmaceutical companies began to aggressively market psychostimulants for children with ADHD by using print advertisements in medical journals, direct mailing, and skilled representatives who promoted their products to doctors. These tactics proved effective, and more doctors and clinicians looked to psychostimulant medications as solutions for problematic behavior in children. Today, millions of people in the United States take these medications, causing some to fear that drugging children has become a new form of social control or that doctors are handing out prescriptions haphazardly to anyone claiming to have trouble concentrating or sitting still.

ADHD as Social Construction

In addition to the perspectives of ADHD as disease and the medicalization of ADHD is the view of ADHD as social construction. According to social psychology, humans are driven by the desire to make sense of the world around them. Individuals observe one another's behavior, interact in situations, and perform acts, all to which they constantly try to attach definitions to help them understand the world and their place in it. This process is social and varies based on situational, historical, and other factors, which means that society's understandings can change over time. Several authors believe this has occurred with the interpretation of youthful conduct.

Ideas about desirable and undesirable child behavior vary within and between cultures. Thus, no universal definitions of good and bad conduct exist. Some claim that, in the United States, children's actions have not changed so much as society's interpretations of them. U.S. society used to be more understanding of variations in children's behavior and allowed them outlets for excess energy, such as time for recess and physical education built into the school day. Recently, however, following the No Child Left Behind Act of 2001 and the thrust to improve standardized test scores, most schools have done away with these sanctioned play times.

In a scholastic atmosphere now calling for more productivity from even the youngest students, inattentiveness and hyperactivity are considered more of a problem than they were formerly. Some critics of this social development, such as Armstrong (2002), are troubled by the demands that they believe society places on children to be more like machines than human beings. Following this and some others' views, society, with pressure from experts, no longer sees disruptive students as exuberant or eccentric but rather as sick and in need of medication to put them back on the path to success, almost as if these children are broken and in need of repair.

The emergence of the field of developmental psychology also may have engendered a change in the social definitions of childhood conduct (Timimi 2005). Developmental psychology offers standardized ideals for child development. Milestones are prescribed based on age, and deviation from these standards is considered cause for alarm and is often approached from a medical standpoint. This discipline promotes developmental markers not only for areas such as physical growth, language use, and motor skills but for maturity, ability to attend to stimuli, and social interaction.

Some argue that, due to the prescriptions of developmental psychology, parents, teachers, and physicians are now more likely to view behaviors that are not deemed age appropriate or acceptable as highly problematic. What may have once been considered simply a difficult personality is often pathologized today. Authors who hold this view seem to apply a version of the Thomas Theorem to the issue, the basic idea of which is that anything perceived as real is real in its consequences. Following this, it appears to some that people, accurately or not, view ADHD as a real disorder and thus look for symptoms confirming it, causing real consequences for children who are given the resulting pathological label.

A final illustration of society's changing definitions surrounding this issue deals with the locus of blame for children's misbehavior. Some researchers today support the view that poor home environments can impact children such that they display symptoms of ADHD. According to these authors, chaos, disharmony, hostility, and dysfunction at home can cause children to have trouble focusing in class or to act out irrationally. Supporters of this view, however, are in the minority. Furthermore, prior to the medical diagnosis, behavioral difficulties characterizing ADHD were frequently thought to result from poor parenting, especially by mothers. Today, however, the prevailing professional opinion is that mothering behaviors are a consequence, not a cause, of children's behaviors. Thus, less desirable actions and reactions on the part of parents are now seen as a consequence of stress that builds up from dealing with a troubled child rather than a poorly behaved child being seen as a symptom of poor parenting. The emphasis on biology over parenting has taken responsibility away from parents and placed it on intangible sources deep within the child's brain.

Children with ADHD and Their Parents

While the debate rages on about the proper conceptualization of ADHD behaviors, parents and children are caught in the middle. Much research has found that actions consistent with ADHD in a child have negative implications for that child's relationship with his or her parents. In general, households with children who have ADHD are characterized by higher parental stress and distress and more parent-child conflict than households without children who have ADHD. Studies of parents' self-reports find that mothers and fathers of these children have trouble relating to their offspring, often lack a sense of closeness with the child, and view themselves as less skilled and competent as parents. Commonly, these parents experience feelings of hopelessness and desperation to find help. In efforts to address the challenges they face, some parents display negative reactions to their children, including being excessively controlling, viewing the youths less positively, and resorting to more authoritarian discipline styles.

In addition to these joint concerns, studies have found issues unique to mothers and to fathers regarding their children with ADHD. For example, research has found a correlation between depression in mothers and parenting children with ADHD. Following a social tradition of disproportionate responsibility for rearing children, many mothers internalize the notion that they are to blame when their sons or daughters misbehave. This history of mother blaming has been somewhat relieved by the rise of the medical model for ADHD, which takes the liability away from mothers and places it on the child's internal defects that are outside their control. Despite this, a number of mothers today are still deeply troubled when their children behave negatively, both out of concern for the quality of life of the child and for others' potentially hurtful perceptions about their parenting.

Many fathers of children with ADHD experience their role differently from mothers. For example, one study found that fathers were much less willing than mothers to accept the medical view of their children's difficulties. Additionally, this research noted that many fathers were not active in the diagnostic and treatment process of their children's disorder, but they did not stand in the way of it either. Often they were sidelined during this progression, some by choice and others in an effort to avoid conflict in the marital relationship.

One notable finding by researchers, such as psychiatrist Ilina Singh, is that a number of fathers feel guilt in connection to their sons' ADHD. The medical model for this behavioral disorder proposes a genetic linkage that passes ADHD from father to son. Due to this, some fathers blame themselves for causing their sons' problems. One consequence of acknowledging their possible responsibility is that men think back to their own child-hoods, in which they behaved similarly to their sons, and question whether they should have been given the same diagnosis.

Finally, discord can arise between a husband and wife as they struggle to deal with their child with ADHD for a number of reasons. One example is a disagreement over the true nature of their offspring's problems. Also, trouble can emerge simply from the general stress of the environment. Partners who are feeling upset about issues with their child may take out their emotions on one another. Another source of conflict might be a husband's opinion that his wife is at least somewhat responsible for their child's unruly behavior because she is too indulgent, a sentiment some fathers report they have.

A DEBATE WITHIN THE DEBATE

Millions of children in the United States are currently taking Ritalin, Adderall, or some other psychostimulant used to treat attention deficit hyperactivity disorder (ADHD). Although other treatment methods exist, medication is by far the treatment most often used. This rise in psychostimulant prescriptions, which has corresponded with the rapid increase in ADHD diagnoses, has sparked an intense debate within the overall ADHD controversy.

Although the conceptualization of a disorder called ADHD was decades in the future, a scientist in 1937 was the first to test the results of stimulants on children with behavioral problems. He was surprised to discover the seemingly illogical effect these drugs had of subduing unruly children. The most-prescribed ADHD drug, Ritalin, was created in the 1950s and was approved by the federal Food and Drug Administration for use in children in 1961. Since then, innumerable studies have been conducted to test the effects of psychostimulants on ADHD children. The majority of this research has reported these drugs as successful at calming children, helping them concentrate, and improving their short-term memory. Supporters of psychostimulant use see this as evidence of the medications' appropriateness and usefulness. They also report the extended effects of helping children learn and socialize better with peers, both of which improve self-esteem. Additionally, they claim that medications improve outcomes of other therapies when they are used in combination.

Critics of psychostimulant use point to the negative effects these drugs can have, some of which are rare. These include lethargy, compulsiveness, slight growth inhibition, appetite loss, dry mouth, seizures, and tics. They also note that the drugs' benefits are short-term. Once patients stop taking them, their ADHD difficulties return. This means that children, once placed on medication, have little hope of ever getting off of it and functioning effectively. Skeptics also point out that psychostimulants have been found to have similar calming and attention-focusing effects on people not considered to have ADHD. They believe this disproves the belief that a disease is present if medications can successfully treat it.

Critics of the medical model and of the medicalization of ADHD sometimes condemn parents for their willingness to accept such a label for their children. Some of these critics believe that parents today take the easy way out, choosing to take their children to a doctor for medication rather than altering their parenting styles to address difficult behavior. Contrary to this perception, however, many parents report experiencing great worry over the decision to seek treatment for their children. Many would likely report that these actions were a last resort. A great number of ADHD diagnoses are initiated at school. Parents are often called to school repeatedly to address a child's unruly behavior, and eventually a teacher or administrator suggests an ADHD evaluation. If a parent is reluctant, this suggestion may continue to be made until he or she gives in. Regardless of whether they feel the ADHD label is appropriate, if a practitioner tells a parent that a son or daughter has ADHD, that parent has additional pressure to take steps to address it. Many parents, who may see themselves as grossly unqualified to determine the nature of their children's problems, eventually defer to the opinion of the experts (teachers, doctors, psychologists) and accept the ADHD diagnosis and treatment. Despite critics' claims, these parents would surely report that this decision is anything but easy.

Conclusion

ADHD is an issue touching more and more lives in the United States each day. Extensive research has been done on this topic, ranging from medical investigation to social interpretation, yet it remains an area ripe for exploration and debate. Science continues to seek definitive proof that a deficiency or imbalance in the brain, transmittable by DNA, causes recognizable unwanted behaviors that can be labeled and treated as a disease. At the same time, those opposed to this view continue to study and question the social factors surrounding this issue and disprove any biological basis. Neither side has had absolute success, so the controversy continues.

Regardless of where one stands in the debate, it is hard to deny that an increasing number of parents and children are being faced with the ADHD label. Those parents who hear competing information from various sources in the controversy often feel torn over the right thing to do and experience negative feelings, regardless of their decision. Perhaps one day an irrefutable medical discovery will be made to mark ADHD as a disease. Perhaps social opinion on children's behavior will shift, and more rambunctious or unruly behavior will not be considered as problematic as it is today. Either of these events could result in an end to the debate surrounding ADHD. However, at this point, there is no indication that either type of solution will occur any time soon. Thus, ADHD diagnoses are sure to continue, with proponents' blessings and critics' curses.

See also **Inclusive Schooling; Mental Health**

Further Reading

Armstrong, Thomas, "ADD: Does It Really Exist?" In *Taking Sides: Clashing Views on Controversial Issues in Abnormal Psychology,* 3d ed., ed. Richard P. Halgin. Dubuque, IA: McGraw-Hill/Duskin, 2002.

Barkley, Russell A., *Attention-Deficit Hyperactivity Disorder: A Handbook for Diagnosis and Treatment,* 3d ed. New York: Guilford Press, 2006.

Conrad, Peter, and Joseph W. Schneider, *Deviance and Medicalization: From Badness to Sickness.* Philadelphia: Temple University Press, 1992.

Hallowell, Edward M., "What I've Learned from ADD." In *Taking Sides: Clashing Views on Controversial Issues in Abnormal Psychology,* 3d ed., ed. Richard P. Halgin. Dubuque, IA: McGraw-Hill/Duskin, 2002.

McBurnett, Keith, and Linda Pfifner, eds., *Attention Deficit Hyperactivity Disorder: Concepts, Controversies, New Directions.* New York: Informa Healthcare, 2008.

Singh, Ilina, "Boys Will Be Boys: Fathers' Perspectives on ADHD Symptoms, Diagnosis, and Drug Treatment," *Harvard Review of Psychiatry* 11 (2003): 308–316.

Timimi, Sami, *Naughty Boys: Anti-Social Behavior, ADHD and the Role of Culture.* New York: Palgrave Macmillan, 2005.

Wegandt, Lisa L., *An ADHD Primer,* 2d ed. Mahwah, NJ: Lawrence Erlbaum, 2007.

B

BILINGUAL EDUCATION

Lee Gunderson

Miriam Amanda Ferguson, known as Ma Ferguson, the first woman governor of Texas some 75 years ago, became involved in a debate about which languages should be used in teaching Texas schoolchildren. "If English was good enough for Jesus Christ, it's good enough for me," she said. This statement characterizes the seemingly irrational view many Americans have of English. Just like motherhood, justice, freedom, democracy, and apple pie, it seems that English has become a central symbol of American culture.

Many view English, especially reading and writing, as the prerequisite that allows both native-born and immigrant students' participation in schools, socialization into society, ability to learn, and academic and professional success. Many believe that the learning of English is a basic requirement of citizenship for immigrants; that it is their democratic responsibility. Many secondary teachers argue that English should be a prerequisite for entrance into their classes and are convinced that English should be a prerequisite for immigration. Issues relating to the use of languages other than English in the United States have become both contentious and politically charged. English has become so central that some states have passed English-only laws, and the group called U.S. English has organized to lobby for an amendment to the U.S. Constitution that would establish English as the official language. In 1998, 63 percent of the voters in California supported an anti-bilingual proposition called Proposition 227. Arizona has also passed a similar law. In the midterm election of 2006, voters of Arizona voted 849,772 (66 percent) to 295,632 (26 percent) in favor of Proposition 103 to make English the official language and to make businesses enforce the measure. A year later, Idaho and Kansas passed similar laws, and Oklahoma seemed set to pass an English-only law in November 2010. (See http://englishfirst.org/ for an interesting view of English.)

The passage of the law in California in 1998 neither made the advocates of English-only happy nor did it eliminate bilingual education. The bilingual lobby is now simply defying the state law. A front-page story in the *San Francisco Chronicle* headlined "Educators Working around Prop. 227" reports that, "in many Bay Area school districts, bilingual education lives." When kids got back to school, "they found bilingual education waiting for them." The bilingual education director in Contra Costa County defiantly said, "If a child is very limited in English proficiency, we will offer [native] language instruction. It's essentially the same as what we offered last year" (Amselle and Moore 1998, 2).

The mere mention of bilingual instruction disturbs many Americans. Those who speak English as a second language are seen as the culprits of lower reading scores in many jurisdictions. Unfortunately, students who speak languages other than English at home are less likely to succeed in schools. Spanish-speaking students are less likely to complete high school than English speakers and are also less likely to go on to university. Immigrants enrolled in secondary school English-only programs do not do well academically, and they drop out at alarming rates. Such students could be helped in their studies by some kind of support in their first languages. The political climate is such, however, that the use of languages other than English or bilingual instructional programs causes general societal and governmental angst. History, however, reveals that the United States is a country of diversity that has welcomed people who speak many different languages. How then, has it transpired that English-only is considered by so many as the only way; the American way?

Not All of the Founding Fathers Were English Speakers

The earliest European colonists to America were English speakers. However, by 1776, there were thousands of German settlers in what became the states of Pennsylvania, Maryland, Virginia, New York, and Ohio. The Continental Congress produced German versions of many of its proclamations. Heinz Kloss, in *The American Bilingual Tradition* (1998), notes that "the most important German publication of the Continental Congress was the German edition of the Articles of Confederation, which had the title: 'Artikel des Bundes under der immerwährenden Eintracht zwischen den Staaten'" (28). And the recognition of the German language was also a recognition of "a strong and enthusiastic participation of most of the German minority in the armed rebellion" (28).

According to Kloss, the Third Congress was asked in 1794 by individuals from Virginia to print copies of federal laws in German. This issue did not come up for a vote until 1795, when it lost, 41 to 42. Kloss notes these events gave rise to the "Muhlenberg legend." The legend is that the Congress wanted to make German rather than English the official language of Congress, and Muhlenberg, the speaker of the House, "thwarted" the action

(30). Kloss concludes that this is not true. It is true, however, that the first Constitutional Convention in the commonwealth of Pennsylvania on July 26, 1776, published records in German. Therefore, the use of German in state business is as old as the state itself.

Bilingual Instruction: An American Tradition

The state of Ohio first authorized German-English instruction in 1839. Laws authorized French and English programs in Louisiana in 1847 and Spanish and English in the territory of New Mexico in 1850. By the end of the 1800s, nearly a dozen states had established bilingual programs in languages such as Norwegian, Italian, Cherokee, Czechoslovakian, and Polish. Reports revealed that about 600,000 students were receiving some or all of their education in German. During the years before the First World War there were thousands of students enrolled in bilingual classes. Subjects such as mathematics and history were taught in students' first languages. However, it appears that the First World War signaled a hardening of attitudes toward instruction in languages other than English. This negative view appears to have solidified during the Second World War and did not change substantially until the 1960s. It is important to note that immigrant students did not do so well in their studies by being immersed in English-only programs. During the later 1800s and early 1900s, immigrant students did considerably worse than their English-speaking classmates.

Immigrant groups did much worse than the native-born, and some immigrant groups did much worse. The poorest were Italians. According to a 1911 federal immigration commission report, in Boston, Chicago, and New York, 80 percent of native white children in the seventh grade stayed in school another year, but 58 percent of Southern Italian children, 62 percent of Polish children, and 74 percent of Russian Jewish children did so. Of those who made it to the eighth grade, 58 percent of the native whites went on to high school, but only 23 percent of the Southern Italians did so. In New York, 54 percent of native-born eighth-graders made it to ninth grade, but only 34 percent of foreign-born eighth-graders did so (Olneck and Lazerson 1974.

By the mid-1940s, bilingual education had become unpopular in general, and it seems that an anti-German response was likely responsible.

The Exciting 1950s and 1960s

The space age was launched on October 4, 1957, by the Soviet Union. The successful launch of *Sputnik I* was followed by the launch of *Sputnik II* on November 3. A great feeling of failure became part of the American psyche, and a general angst focused Americans' attention on how the Soviet Union had been first. The schools became the target for critics who believed they were not producing the scientists required to keep the United States first in technology and science. In 1963, H. G. Rickover wrote *American Education: A National Failure.* As a result of his efforts, a focus turned to training students to become scientists. However, in the early 1960s, hundreds of thousands of

Spanish-speaking Cubans arriving in Florida resulted in a resurgence of and a refocus on bilingual education in an environment of the drive for civil rights.

Bilingual Education Redux

Systematic bilingual programs in the United States appeared in Dade County in Florida after the influx of thousands of Spanish-speaking Cubans. These bilingual programs were designed to be transitional; that is, the first language was used to support students until their English skills developed and they could learn in English. The majority of students' early education in this model was conducted in their first language, with a daily period reserved for English instruction. Students began to transition to English after they had attained a degree of English proficiency. These programs came to be known as transitional bilingual education, or TBE. It is interesting to note that, in 1968, Governor Ronald Reagan signed into law California Senate Bill 53 that allowed the use of other instructional languages in California public schools. Like other Republicans in the 1960s, he was a proponent of bilingual instruction.

Congress passed the Bilingual Education Act (known as Title VII) in 1968. The act specified that individuals who "come from environments where a language other than English has had a significant impact on their level of English language proficiency; and who, by reason thereof, have sufficient difficulty speaking, reading, writing, or understanding the English language" should be provided bilingual programs. All programs had to provide students "full access to the learning environment, the curriculum, special services and assessment in a meaningful way." Congress did not provide funding for Title VII. However, subsequently it provided support, and 27,000 students were served by Title VII–funded programs. The bill encouraged instruction in a language other than English, primarily Spanish.

Bilingual Programs and the Supreme Court

The U.S. Supreme Court in 1974 concluded that all students had the right to access educational programs in schools and that an individual's first language (L1) was a key to such access. The decision is referred to as *Lau v. Nichols*. In essence, the Court stated that school districts must have measures in place that make instruction comprehensible to English learners. The decision included a number of comments, as well, one of which was the following:

> Basic English skills are at the very core of what public schools teach. Imposition of a requirement that, before a child can effectively participate in the educational program, he must already have acquired those basic skills is to make a mockery of public education.

Title II of the Educational Amendments Act of 1974 mandated that language barriers were to be eliminated by instructional programs. School districts were required to have bilingual programs. The new teachers were told that any group having 20 or more speakers was to be provided bilingual programs. In another ruling, *Castañeda v. Pickard* (1981), the Supreme Court laid out guidelines for schools with respect to how to meet the needs of English language learners.

By the mid-1980s, however, it seemed that a more pessimistic view of bilingual education had taken hold across the United States. A form of ethnic politics came to dominate instructional decision making, and by the end of the decade there were calls in several states to make laws limiting or banning bilingual education. In 1992, an Arizona state court upheld a parent's claim that her child, an English language learner, was not being provided with sufficient English-language instruction to allow the child to succeed in school. The U.S. Supreme Court, however, taking up the matter years later (in *Horne v. Flores,* 2009), overturned the state court's decision and offered the opinion that the state could determine its own requirements as to English language learning instruction. Two decades of openness toward bilingual education on the part of the Court seemed to be in jeopardy.

Bilingual Education: The Research Base

Researchers became interested in exploring bilingual education beginning in the late 1960s and found evidence that a student's initial reading instruction, for instance, should be in their native language. The belief was that students should learn to read in their L1s first as the "native-language literacy axiom." Some early researchers, particularly those who looked at French-immersion programs in Canada, concluded that students do not necessarily learn to read best in their L1s. This is an argument that continues. Generally, however, the students in these early studies were from families in which both English and French were highly valued and the dominant language was English.

There are two kinds of language proficiencies to be learned: basic interpersonal communicative skill (BICS), the language of ordinary conversation or the manifestation of language proficiency in everyday communicative contexts, and cognitive academic language proficiency (CALP), the language of instruction and academic text. These labels might lead to a misinterpretation of the complexities they seek to describe and imply a deficit model of language. CALP has been likened to "test-wiseness" and is sometimes referred to by an additional acronym: SIN, or "skill in instructional nonsense," a term coined by C. Edelsky in *With Literacy and Justice for All: Rethinking the Social in Language and Education.* The two labels have generally, however, come to represent two categories of proficiency; one associated with face-to-face conversation (BICS) and the other with learning in the context-reduced cognitively demanding oral and written environment of the classroom (CALP). Older students use knowledge of academic material and concepts gained studying L1 to help them in L2, and the acquisition of L2 occurs faster. A number of researchers found that BICS requires about two to three years to develop and that CALP takes about five to seven years.

Cummins and Swain (1986) proposed a common underlying proficiency (CUP) model based on the notion that "literacy-related aspects of a bilingual's proficiency in L1 and L2 are seen as common or interdependent across languages" (82). Literacy experience in either language promotes the underlying interdependent proficiency base. This view suggests that "common cross-lingual proficiencies underlie the obviously different surface manifestations of each language" (82). There is evidence to support CUP; however, there is only modest evidence of transfer of language skills. Common underlying proficiency has also been referred to as the interdependence principle, and some research provides powerful long-term evidence that common underlying proficiency or interdependence does exist.

The 1990s brought a focused research effort to investigate bilingual education but resulted in little definitive evidence that transitional bilingual education is a superior strategy for improving language achievement. Bilingual immersion programs were designed to introduce minority students to English during the early years by integrating second-language instruction with content-area instruction. Immersion students showed an early significant advantage at grade four that disappeared by grade seven. One major difficulty in evaluating bilingual studies is that there are so many variations in programs across studies. A second major difficulty is that many studies are neither well designed nor well evaluated. A third difficulty is that authors often take for granted that what other authors claim is true of their findings is, in fact, true.

Dual-immersion programs were an alternative to TBE programs that gained popularity in the 1990s. Two-way immersion programs are defined as the integration of language-majority and language-minority students in the same classrooms, where: (1) language-minority and language-majority students are integrated for at least half of the day at all grade levels; (2) content and literacy instruction are provided in both languages to all students; and (3) language-minority and language-majority students are balanced. The support for dual-immersion programs, like other bilingual programs, is limited.

The director of the National Institute of Child Health and Human Development established the National Reading Panel in 1997 as a result of a congressional request (National Institute of Child Health and Human Development 2006). The issue of second-language learning was not included in the panel because it was to be addressed by a different research review. An additional National Literacy Panel was established to conduct a literature review on the literacy of language-minority children and youth. In August 2005, the U.S. Department of Education declined to publish the report of the National Literacy Panel, reportedly "because of concerns about its technical adequacy and the degree to which it could help inform policy and practice."

Research has found that secondary students in English-only schools disappeared from academic classes at about a 60 percent rate, and there were significant differences in disappearance rate among ethnolinguistic groups. The relatively high socioeconomic status students who were Mandarin speakers achieved at higher rates and had lower disappearance rates than did the low socioeconomic status students who were Spanish and Vietnamese speakers. Other research shows that structured English immersion resulted in higher success for English language learners.

There is a constant debate between advocates of English-only and advocates of bilingual programs. The claims that one instructional approach is superior to any other appear to be founded on limited or questionable evidence. At best, inferences about best approaches appear to have limited empirical support. It is impossible to conduct scientific research in a typical school, because there are too many confounding variables to control. Unfortunately, hundreds of thousands of English language learners are failing to learn in school and are dropping out. In the United States, Spanish-speaking students are less likely to complete high school than English speakers and are also less likely to go on to university. The 2005 National Assessment of Adult Literacy report states that, "Perhaps most sobering was that adult literacy dropped or was flat across every level of education, from people with graduate degrees to those who dropped out of high school" (National Institute for Literacy 2006). It also states that those who have higher literacy levels made about $50,000 a year, which is $28,000 more than those who had only minimal literacy skills. It is estimated that the loss of potential wages and taxes in the United States alone over the lifespan of the total number of dropouts in a year is approximately $260 trillion. For countries like the United States that are striving to have a technically trained work force and to remain technically superior, dropouts are a serious difficulty. It is a significant problem that seems to be ignored in favor of arguments about the language of instruction. It remains to be seen what the Obama administration will do in the area of bilingual education, but Secretary of Education Arne Duncan has stated that educating bilingual students is a matter of civil rights and has requested $800 million for English language learner programs in 2011.

Conclusion

The struggle to learn English and to learn academic content is extremely difficult. English language learners deal with the trials and tribulations of growing into adulthood while trying to master English and multiple sets of expectations from their schoolmates, their friends, their teachers, and their parents. Many hundreds of thousands drop out. Proponents and opponents of bilingual education argue their viewpoints vehemently, often referring to research or to political views to support their beliefs. Most bilingual research is focused on younger students, and what happens in secondary and postsecondary situations has had little attention. Much like Ma Ferguson, modern-day critics often make statements that are not always logical. Bob Dole, for instance, argued that "We must stop the practice of multilingual educations as a means of instilling ethnic pride, or as a therapy for low self-esteem, or out of guilt over a culture built on the traditions of the west." The former speaker of the House, Newt Gingrich, concluded: "Bilingualism keeps people actively tied to their old language and habits and maximizes the cost of transition to becoming American," and "Without English as a common language, there is no such civilization." He also has stated, "When we allow children to stay trapped in bilingual programs where they do not learn English, we are destroying their economic future."

The scandalous situation is that English language learners are not learning the academic skills to allow them to enter into our technological society, and they are dropping out at high rates—some groups more than others. Meanwhile, educators, researchers, politicians, and others seem intent on proving that their views of English-only or bilingual instruction are right rather than on searching for the best programs to assure that all students, including English language learners, learn the vital skills they need to participate in this technologically based society. Is learning English in a bilingual program so evil? It seems time to wake up to history. Diversity has worked well for the United States in the past; one wonders, why not today?

See also Immigration Reform; Immigrant Workers (vol. 1); Social Justice (vol. 2)

Further Reading

Amselle, J., and S. Moore, "North of the Border—Mexico Lobbies for Specific U.S. Educational Policies" (includes related article on California's Proposition 227). *National Review* (October 12, 1998): 22–24.

Cummins, Jim, and Merill Swain, *Bilingualism in Education: Aspects of Theory, Research, and Practice.* New York: Longman, 1986.

Edelsky, Carole, *With Literacy and Justice for All: Rethinking the Social in Language and Education.* New York: Falmer Press, 1991.

Gandara, Patricia, and Megan Hopkins, *Forbidden Language: English Learners and Restrictive Language Policies.* New York: Teachers College Press, 2010.

Garcia, Eugene E., *Teaching and Learning in Two Languages: Bilingualism and Schooling in the United States.* New York: Teachers College Press, 2005.

Gunderson, Lee, *English-Only Instruction and Immigrant Students in Secondary Schools: A Critical Examination.* Mahwah, NJ: Lawrence Erlbaum, 2007.

Kloss, Heinz, *The American Bilingual Tradition.* McHenry, IL: Center for Applied Linguistics, 1998 (orig. 1977, Newbury House).

National Center for Education Statistics, *Language Minorities and Their Educational and Labor Market Indicators—Recent Trends.* Washington, DC: U.S. Department of Education, Institute of Education Sciences, 2004.

National Institute for Literacy, "Adults with Basic and Below Basic Literacy Levels: Findings from NAAL and Implications for Practice" (2006). http://www.nifl.gov/webcasts/NAALfindings/webcast081506.html

National Institute of Child Health and Human Development, "Report of the National Reading Panel" (2006). http://www.nichd.nih.gov/publications/nrp/intro.cfm

Olneck, M. R., and M. Lazerson, "The School Achievement of Immigrant Children: 1900–1930." *History of Education Quarterly* (Winter 1974): 453–482.

Salomone, Rosemary C., *True Americans: Language, Identity, and the Education of Immigrant Children*. Cambridge, MA: Harvard University Press, 2010.

Samway, Katharine Davies, and Denise McKeon, *Myths and Realities: Best Practices for English Language Learners*, 2d ed. Portsmouth, NH: Heinemann, 2007.

BIRTH CONTROL

Jonelle Husain

Birth control is the control of fertility, or the prevention of pregnancy, through one of several methods. Another common name for birth control is contraception, because that is precisely what the various birth control methods do; they prevent the viable sperm and egg from uniting to form a fertilized embryo. Though discussing birth control is no longer likely to lead to an arrest, as it did in the days of birth control pioneer Margaret Sanger, public debates remain. Some debates address which methods of birth control are the most effective at attaining one's reproductive goals, while others address whether insurance benefits should include the cost of birth control, the likely long- and short-term effects of their use, how to increase the use of birth control among sexually active young people, and questions over why there are still so many more methods that focus on women's fertility compared with those that focus on men's fertility.

Introduction

Controlling fertility affects the well-being of women, men, children, families, and society by providing methods and strategies to prevent unplanned pregnancies. Planned fertility positively impacts the health of children, maternal longevity, and the empowerment of women. Access to birth control provides women and men with choices regarding family size, timing between pregnancies, and spacing of children. Additionally, controlling fertility reduces the prevalence of chronic illness and maternal death from pregnancy-related conditions.

Globally, approximately 210 million women become pregnant each year. Of these pregnancies, nearly 40 percent are unplanned. In the United States, 49 percent of pregnancies are estimated to be unplanned. Research shows that unintended pregnancies can have devastating impacts on not only women but also children and families. An unintended pregnancy places a woman at risk for depression, physical abuse, and the normal risks associated with pregnancy, including maternal death. Pregnancies that are spaced closely together present risks to children, including low birth weight, increased likelihood of death in the first year, and decreased access to resources necessary for healthy development. Unintended pregnancies can have devastating impacts on the well-being of the family unit. An unplanned pregnancy often pushes families with limited economic resources into a cycle of poverty that further limits their opportunities for success.

Although control of fertility spans approximately 30 years of men's and women's reproductive life, preferences for birth control methods and strategies vary among individuals and across the life course and are influenced by multiple social factors. These factors may include socioeconomic status, religious or moral beliefs, purpose for using birth control (permanent pregnancy prevention, delay of pregnancy, or spacing between births), availability of birth control products, access to medical care, willingness to use birth control consistently, concern over side effects, and variability in the failure rates of different types of birth control products. Although the primary purpose of birth control is to control fertility, increases in the prevalence of sexually transmitted infections (STIs) and the human immunodeficiency virus (HIV), which causes acquired immunodeficiency syndrome (AIDS), have created pressures to develop new pregnancy prevention options that combine contraception and STI prevention. The availability of contraceptive options allows women and men the opportunity to maximize the benefits of birth control while minimizing the risks of contraceptive use according to their needs.

The availability of birth control has raised important questions about reproductive control and the relationships between men and women. Traditionalists argue that pregnancy and child rearing are the natural or biologically determined roles of women, given their capacity to become pregnant and give birth. Opponents of this view argue that reproduction and motherhood are one of many choices available to women. Providing options to women and men that allow them to control their fertility has shifted pregnancy and motherhood from a position of duty to one of choice. This shift is a consequence of changes to the work force, increased opportunities for women, and changes in the economic structure of contemporary families. These changes, along with ongoing developments in fertility control research, provide women and men today with many innovative choices concerning birth control. These choices allow women and men to tailor birth control to their individual needs and life circumstances.

Today, birth control debates focus on the advantages and disadvantages of different birth control methods. The most common debates focus on the merits of temporary versus permanent methods of pregnancy prevention. Other debates examine the benefits of natural versus barrier methods of controlling reproduction. Still other debates examine the advantages and disadvantages of male and female contraception. With the growing pandemic of AIDS in sub-Saharan Africa and Asia and the increasing prevalence of sexually transmitted diseases that threatens world health, contemporary debates about birth control focus on the feasibility and practicality of combining STI prevention and contraception.

Brief History of Contraception

Although women have sought to control their fertility since ancient times, safe and effective contraception was not developed until the 20th century. The large influx of immigrants in the 1900s and the emergence of feminist groups working for women's rights helped bring to the forefront large-scale birth control movements in the United States and abroad. Ancient forms of birth control included potions, charms, chants, and herbal recipes. Ancient recipes often featured leaves, hawthorn bark, ivy, willow, and poplar, believed to contain sterilizing agents. During the Middle Ages, potions containing lead, arsenic, or strychnine caused death to many women seeking to control their fertility. Additionally, crude barrier methods were used in which the genitals were covered with cedar gum or alum was applied to the uterus. Later, pessary mixtures of elephant dung, lime (mineral), and pomegranate seeds were inserted into a woman's vagina to prevent pregnancy. Other barrier methods believed to prevent pregnancy included sicklewort leaves, wool tampons soaked in wine, and crudely fashioned vaginal sponges.

Later birth control developments were based on more accurate information concerning conception. Condoms were developed in the early 1700s by the physician to King Charles II. By the early 1800s, a contraceptive sponge and a contraceptive syringe were available. By the mid-1800s, a number of more modern barrier methods to control conception were available to women. However, it was illegal to advertise these options, and most were available only through physicians and only in cases that were clinically indicated. Thus, early modern conception was limited to health reasons.

Modern contraceptive devices such as the condom, diaphragm, cervical cap, and intrauterine device (IUD) were developed in the 20th century and represented a marked advance in medical technology. Effectiveness was largely dependent on user compliance. Although these methods represented a significant improvement over more archaic methods, contraceptive safety remained an issue. Other modern methods included the insertion of various substances (some toxic) into the vagina, resulting in inflammation or irritation of the vaginal walls, while other devices often caused discomfort.

The birth control pill, developed in the 1950s by biologist Charles Pincus, represented a major advance in fertility control. Pincus is credited with the discovery of the effects of combining estrogen and progesterone in an oral contraceptive that would prevent pregnancy. The development and mass marketing of the birth control pill provided women with a way to control not only their fertility but also their lives.

Overview of Traditional Contraceptive Methods

Traditional contraception includes both temporary and permanent methods of controlling fertility. Temporary contraception provides temporary or time-limited protection from becoming pregnant. Permanent contraception refers to surgical procedures that result in a lasting or permanent inability to become pregnant. The choice of contraception takes into consideration several biological and social factors, including age, lifestyle (frequency of sexual activity, monogamy or multiple partners), religious or moral beliefs, legal issues, family planning objectives, as well as medical history and concerns. These factors vary among individuals and across the life span.

Traditional Contraceptive Methods

Traditional contraceptive methods provide varying degrees of protection from becoming pregnant and protection from STIs. While some of these methods provide non-contraceptive benefits, they require consistent and appropriate use and are associated with varying degrees of risks. Traditional contraception includes both hormonal and non-hormonal methods of preventing pregnancy and sexually transmitted diseases. These methods provide protection as long as they are used correctly but their effects are temporary and reversible once discontinued. Traditional contraceptive methods include sexual abstinence, coitus interruptus, rhythm method, barrier methods, spermicides, male or female condoms, IUDs, and oral contraceptive pills.

Sexual abstinence refers to the voluntary practice of refraining from all forms of sexual activity that could result in pregnancy or the transmission of sexually transmitted diseases. Abstinence is commonly referred to as the only form of birth control that is 100 percent effective in preventing pregnancy and STIs; however, failed abstinence results in unprotected sex which increases the risks of unintended pregnancy and transmission of STIs.

Coitus interruptus is the oldest method of contraception and requires the man to withdraw his penis from the vagina just prior to ejaculation. Often referred to as a so-called natural method of birth control, coitus interruptus is highly unreliable because a small amount of seminal fluid, containing sperm, is secreted from the penis prior to ejaculation and can result in conception. This method offers no protection from sexually transmitted diseases.

The *rhythm method* of birth control developed in response to research on the timing of ovulation. Research findings indicate that women ovulate approximately 14 days before the onset of their menstrual cycle. The rhythm method assumes that a woman is the most fertile during ovulation. To determine an individual cycle of ovulation, this method requires a woman to count backward 14 days from the first day of her menstrual period. During this time period, a woman should abstain from sexual activity or use another form of birth control (such as condoms) to avoid pregnancy. The rhythm method is another natural form of birth control that is highly risky. Few women ovulate at the exact same time from month to month, making accurate calculations of ovulation difficult. Additionally, sperm can live inside a woman for up to seven days, further complicating the calculations of safe periods for sex. Finally, the rhythm method does not provide protection from sexually transmitted diseases.

Barrier methods of contraception prevent sperm from reaching the fallopian tubes and fertilizing an egg. Barrier methods include both male and female condoms, diaphragms, cervical caps, and vaginal sponges. With the exception of the male condom, these methods are exclusively used by women. Barrier contraception is most often used with a spermicide to increase effectiveness. Spermicides contain nonoxynol-9, a chemical that immobilizes sperm to prevent them from joining and fertilizing an egg. Barrier methods of contraception and spermicides provide moderate protection from pregnancy and sexually transmitted diseases although failure rates (incidence of pregnancy resulting from use) vary from 20 to 30 percent.

Condoms, a popular and non-prescription form of barrier contraception available to both men and women, provides moderate protection from pregnancy and STIs. The male condom is a latex, polyurethane, or natural skin sheath that covers the erect penis and traps semen before it enters the vagina. The female condom is a soft, loosely fitting polyurethane tube-like sheath that lines the vagina during sex. Female condoms have a closed end with rings at each end. The ring at the closed end is inserted deep into the vagina over the cervix to secure the tube in place. Female condoms protect against pregnancy by trapping sperm in the sheath and preventing entry into the vagina. Used correctly, condoms are between 80 and 85 percent effective in preventing pregnancy and the transmission of STIs. Risks that decrease the effectiveness of condoms include incorrect usage, slippage during sexual activity, and breakage. Natural skin condoms used by some males do not protect against the transmission of HIV and other STIs.

The female diaphragm is a shallow, dome-shaped, flexible rubber disk that fits inside the vagina to cover the cervix. The diaphragm prevents sperm from entering the uterus. Diaphragms are used with spermicide to immobilize or kill sperm and to prevent fertilization of the female egg. Diaphragms may be left inside the vagina for up to 24 hours but a spermicide should be used with each intercourse encounter. To be fully effective, the diaphragm should be left in place for six hours after intercourse before removal. Approximately 80 to 95 percent effective in preventing pregnancy and the transmission of gonorrhea and Chlamydia, the diaphragm does not protect against the transmission of herpes or HIV.

Cervical caps are small, soft rubber, thimble-shaped caps that are fitted inside the woman's cervix. Cervical caps prevent pregnancy by blocking the entrance of the uterus. Approximately 80 to 95 percent effective when used alone, effectiveness is increased when used with spermicides. Unlike the diaphragm, the cervical cap may be left in place for up to 48 hours. Similar to the diaphragm, the cervical cap provides protection against gonorrhea and chlamydia but does not provide protection against herpes or HIV.

Vaginal sponges, removed from the market in 1995 due to concerns about possible contaminants, are round, donut-shaped polyurethane devices containing spermicides and a loop that hangs down in the vagina allowing for easy removal. Sponges prevent pregnancy by blocking the uterus and preventing fertilization of the egg. Vaginal sponges are approximately 70 to 80 percent effective in preventing pregnancy but provide no protection against STIs. Risks include toxic shock syndrome if left inside the vagina for more than 24 hours.

Barrier methods of birth control provide moderate protection from pregnancy and STIs but are not fail-safe. Effectiveness is dependent on consistency and proper use. Advantages include lower cost, availability without a prescription, and ease of use (with the exception of the diaphragm). Disadvantages include lowered effectiveness as compared to other forms of birth control and little or no protection against certain STIs.

Non-Barrier Contraceptive Methods

Two other traditional contraceptive methods are the IUD and oral contraceptive pills. Both of these methods are characterized by increased effectiveness if used properly. The IUD is a T-shaped device inserted into a woman's vagina by a health professional. Inserted into the wall of the uterus, the IUD prevents pregnancy by changing the motility (movement) of the sperm and egg and by altering the lining of the uterus to prevent egg implantation. The effectiveness of IUDs in preventing pregnancy is approximately 98 percent, however, IUDs do not provide protection from STIs. Oral contraceptive pills are taken daily for 21 days each month. Oral contraceptives prevent pregnancy by preventing ovulation, the monthly release of an egg. This form of contraception does not interfere with the monthly menstrual cycle. Many birth control pills combine progesterone and estrogen, however, newer oral contraceptives contain progesterone only. Taken regularly, oral contraceptives are approximately 98 percent effective in preventing pregnancy but do not provide STI protection.

New Contraceptive Technologies

In spite of the availability of a broad range of contraceptive methods, the effectiveness of traditional contraceptive methods is largely dependent on user consistency and proper use. Even with consistent and proper use, each method is associated with varying degrees of risk. Risks include the likelihood of pregnancy, side effects, and possible STI transmission. New developments in contraceptive technology focus on improvement of side effects and the development of contraceptives that do not require users to adhere to a daily regiment. These new technologies are designed to make use simpler and more suitable to users' lives. Additionally, many of the new technologies seek to combine fertility control with protection from STIs.

The *vaginal contraceptive ring* is inserted into a woman's vagina for a period of three weeks and removed for one week. During the three week period, the ring releases small doses of progestin and estrogen, providing month-long contraception. The release of progestin and estrogen prevents the ovaries from releasing an egg and increases cervical mucus that helps to prevent sperm from entering the uterus. Fully effective after seven days, supplementary contraceptive methods should be used during the first week after insertion. Benefits include a high effectiveness rate, ease of use, shorter and lighter menstrual periods, and protection from ovarian cysts and from ovarian and uterine cancer. Disadvantages include spotting between menstrual periods for the first several months and no protection against STIs.

Hormonal implants provide highly effective, long-term, but reversible, protection from pregnancy. Particularly suitable for users who find it difficult to consistently take daily contraceptives, hormonal implants deliver progesterone by using a rod system inserted underneath the skin. Closely related to implants are hormonal injections that are administered monthly. Both hormonal implants and injections are highly effective in preventing pregnancy but may cause breakthrough bleeding. Neither provides protection from STIs at this stage of development.

Contraceptive patches deliver a combination of progestin and estrogen through an adhesive patch located on the upper arm, buttocks, lower abdomen or upper torso. Applied weekly for three weeks, followed by one week without, the contraceptive patch is highly effective in preventing pregnancy but does not protect against the transmission of STIs. The use of the patch is associated with withdrawal bleeding during the week that it is not worn. Compliance is reported to be higher than with oral contraceptive pills.

ABORTION

Abortion, defined as the intentional termination of a pregnancy, was legally established in 1973 with the Supreme Court decision in *Roe v. Wade* (*Roe v. Wade* 410 U.S. 113). The decision spawned disparate and strongly held opinions among the American public and the emergence of activist groups taking a variety of positions on abortion. The availability of elective abortion has called into question traditional beliefs about the relations between men and women, has raised vexing issues about the control of women's bodies, and has intensified contentious debates about women's roles and brought about changes in the division of labor, both in the family and in the broader occupational arena. Elective abortion has called into question long-standing beliefs about the moral nature of sexuality. Further, elective abortion has challenged the notion of sexual relations as privileged activities that are symbolic of commitments, responsibilities, and obligations between men and women. Elective abortion also brings to the fore the more personal issue of the meaning of pregnancy.

Historically, the debate over abortion has been one of competing definitions of motherhood. Pro-life activists argue that family, and particularly motherhood, is the cornerstone of society. Pro-choice activists argue that reproductive choice is central to women controlling their lives. More contemporary debates focus on the ethical and moral nature of personhood and the rights of the fetus. In the last 30 years, these debates have become politicized, resulting in the passage of increasingly restrictive laws governing abortion, abortion doctors, and abortion clinics. Currently, South Dakota is the only state that has passed laws making abortions illegal except in cases in which the woman's life is endangered. Other states are considering passage of similarly restrictive legislation.

The consequences of unintended pregnancy are well documented and contribute to the need for the continued development of contraceptive options that will meet the needs and goals of diverse populations whose reproductive needs change throughout their life course. By definition abortion is not a type of contraception but is an option when contraceptive efforts did not prevent pregnancy.

Levonorgestrel intrauterine systems provide long-term birth control without sterilization by delivering small amounts of the progestin levonorgestrel directly to the lining of the uterus to prevent pregnancy. Delivered through a small T-shaped intrauterine plastic device implanted by a health professional, the levonorgestrel system provides protection from pregnancy for up to five years. It does not currently offer protection from STIs.

New contraceptive technologies are designed to provide longer-term protection from pregnancy and to remove compliance obstacles that decrease effectiveness and increase the likelihood of unintended pregnancies. The availability of contraceptive options provides users with choices that assess not only fertility purposes but also variations in sexual activity. However, until new contraceptive technologies that combine pregnancy and STI prevention are readily available, proper use of male and female condoms provides the most effective strategy for prevention of sexually transmitted diseases and HIV.

Permanent Contraception

Permanent contraception refers to sterilization techniques that permanently prevent pregnancy. Frequently referred to as sterilization, permanent contraception prevents males from impregnating females and prevents females from becoming pregnant.

Tubal ligation refers to surgery to tie a woman's fallopian tubes, preventing the movement of eggs from the ovaries to the uterus. The procedure is considered permanent and involves the cauterization of the fallopian tubes. However, some women who later choose to become pregnant have successfully had the procedure reversed. The reversal of tubal ligation procedures are successful in 50 to 80 percent of cases.

Hysterectomy refers to the complete removal of a woman's uterus or the uterus and cervix, depending on the type of procedure performed, and results in permanent sterility. Hysterectomies may be performed through an incision in the abdominal wall, vaginally, or by using laparoscopic incisions on the abdomen.

Vasectomy refers to a surgical procedure for males in which the vas deferens are tied off and cut apart to prevent sperm from moving out of the testes. The procedure results in permanent sterility although the procedure may be reversed under certain conditions.

Permanent contraception is generally recommended only in cases in which there is no desire for children, family size is complete, or in cases where medical concerns necessitate permanent prevention of pregnancy.

Emergency Contraception

Emergency contraception, commonly referred to as postcoital contraception or the so-called morning-after pill, encompasses a number of therapies designed to prevent pregnancy following unprotected sexual intercourse. Emergency contraception is also indicated when a condom slips or breaks, a diaphragm dislodges, two or more oral contraceptives are missed or the monthly regimen of birth control pills are begun two or more days late, a hormonal injection is two weeks overdue, or a woman has been raped. Emergency contraception prevents pregnancy by preventing the release of an egg from the ovary, by preventing fertilization, or by preventing attachment of an egg to the uterine wall. Most effective when used within 72 hours of unprotected sex, emergency contraception does not affect a fertilized egg already attached to the uterine wall. Emergency contraception does not induce an abortion or disrupt an existing pregnancy; it prevents a pregnancy from occurring following unprotected sexual intercourse.

Conclusion

Ideally, birth control should be a shared responsibility between a woman and her partner. In the U.S., approximately 1.6 million pregnancies each year are unplanned. Unplanned pregnancies position women, men, and families in a precarious situation that has social, economic, personal and health consequences. An unintended pregnancy leaves a woman and her partner facing pregnancy termination, adoption, or raising an unplanned child—often times under less-than-ideal conditions. Contraceptive technologies and research developments in the transmission of sexually transmitted diseases represent increased opportunities for not only controlling fertility but also improving safe sex practices.

See also **Abortion; Teen Pregnancy**

Further Reading

Caron, Simone M., *Who Chooses? American Reproductive History since 1830.* Gainsville, FL: University Press of Florida, 2008.

Connell, Elizabeth B., *The Contraception Sourcebook.* New York: McGraw-Hill, 2002.

Gebbie, Alisa E., and Katharine O'Connell White, *Fast Facts: Contraception.* Albuquerque, NM: Health Press, 2009.

Glasier, Anna, and Alisa Gebbie, eds., *Handbook of Family Planning and Reproductive Healthcare.* New York: Churchill Livingstone/Elsevier, 2008.

Lord, Alexandra M., *Condom Nation: The U.S. Government's Sex Education Campaign from World War I to the Internet.* Baltimore: Johns Hopkins University Press, 2010.

May, Elaine Tyler, *America and the Pill: A History of Promise, Peril, and Liberation.* New York: Basic Books, 2010.

Weschler, Toni, *Taking Charge of Your Fertility.* New York: Harper Collins, 2006.

C

CHARTER SCHOOLS

Gary Miron

Charter schools have become one of the most sweeping school reforms in the United States in recent decades. Charter schools seek to reform public education through a blend of elements found in public schools (universal access and public funding) and elements often associated with private schools (choice, autonomy, and flexibility).

While the definition of charter schools varies somewhat by state, essentially they are nonsectarian public schools of choice that are free from many regulations that apply to traditional public schools. The charter agreement establishing a charter school is a performance contract that details, among other things, the school's mission, program, goals, and means of measuring success. Charters are usually granted for three to five years by an authorizer or sponsor (typically state or local school boards). In some states, public universities or other public entities may also grant charters.

Authorizers hold charter schools accountable for meeting their goals and objectives related to their mission and academic targets. Schools that do not meet their goals and objectives or do not abide by the terms of the contract can have their charter revoked or—when it comes time for renewal—not renewed. Because these are schools of choice and receive funding based on the number of students they enroll, charter schools also are accountable to parents and families who choose to enroll their child in them or choose to leave for another school.

The charter school movement has grown rapidly from two charter schools in Minnesota in 1992 to some 4,000 schools in 41 states and the District of Columbia as of 2010.

Despite this impressive growth, charter schools enroll only a few percent of the public school students in the United States. Some estimates suggest that charter schools enroll close to 1 million students in 2010. Although the impact of charter schools appears minimal at the national level, a few states and several cities have seen the proportion of charter school students rise to capture a quarter of all public school students.

Beyond the United States, charter school reforms can be found in Canada and Puerto Rico. The charter school concept is also very similar to reforms initiated in other countries at approximately the same time. The United Kingdom saw the creation of grant-maintained schools, and in New Zealand and Sweden independent schools were initiated. These various reforms are part of a larger set of national and international trends that have sought to restructure public education. Attempts to restructure schools in the 1980s focused largely on decentralization, site-based management, small-scale choice reforms, and the use of market mechanisms. Proponents argued that restructuring public education would make it more efficient and responsive. One of the main reasons for the rapid and widespread growth of the charter movement in the 1990s was that it provided a vehicle to pursue many or most of the goals related to school restructuring. Another reason for the growth of charter schools is that this reform has been championed by a wide range of supporters, from those who saw these schools as a stepping stone to vouchers to those who saw charter schools as a compromise that would avoid vouchers.

How and Why Charter Schools Work

The simplest and most direct way to explain the theory and ideas behind the charter school concept is to discuss it in terms of three key principles, which roughly correspond to three phases within an overall model of change. The three principles or phases are (1) structural change; (2) "opportunity space" or intermediate goals; and (3) outcomes or final goals. Each of these is discussed below.

Structural Change

At the start of any charter school initiative is the effort to bring about policy changes. These are changes in state law that alter the legal, political, and economic environment in which charter schools operate. They are *structural changes* because they seek to fundamentally alter the conditions under which schools operate. The structural changes provide an opportunity space in which charter schools may experiment. Thus, the charter concept is different from other education reforms in that it does not prescribe specific interventions; rather, it changes the conditions under which schools develop and implement educational interventions.

One of the most important ways in which the charter concept seeks to change schools' external environments is through *choice*. Charter schools are schools of choice in that, with some exceptions, students from any district or locale may attend any charter school. Advocates of school choice argue that choice will lead to sorting by preferences, which will reduce the amount of time schools spend resolving conflicts among school stake-holders, leaving them more time and energy to devote to developing and implementing educational programs. Advocates of school choice also argue that the very act of choice will dispose students, parents, and teachers to work harder to support the schools they have chosen.

Another theoretical argument for charter schools is that *deregulated and autonomous* schools will develop innovations in curriculum, instruction, and governance that will lead to improvements in outcomes. Traditional public schools could also improve by adopting the innovative practices that charter schools are expected to develop.

At the heart of the charter concept lies a bargain. Charter schools will receive en-hanced autonomy over curriculum, instruction, and operations. In exchange, they must agree to be held more accountable for results than other public schools. This new ac-countability holds charter schools accountable for outcomes—many of them articulated in the charter contract—and then employs deregulation to allow them to choose their own means for arriving at those goals. If charter schools do not live up to their stated goals, they can have their charter revoked by their sponsor, or they may not be able to renew the charter when it expires. Another form of accountability charter schools face is market accountability. Because these are schools of choice, and because money follows the students, charter schools that fail to attract and retain students will, in theory, go out of business.

Opportunity Space and Intermediate Goals

The autonomy granted to charter schools provides them with an opportunity space to create and operate schools in new ways. One important opportunity that charter schools have is to create their own governing boards. Charter school governing boards func-tion much as local district school boards. Unlike district school boards, however, charter school boards are appointed rather than elected. Depending on the state, the board members are selected by the sponsor of the school that granted the charter, or they are selected according to specific bylaws approved by the sponsor. This process helps ensure that the charter school can obtain a governing board that is focused and responsive to the specific needs of the school.

Charter school laws limit—to some extent—the opportunity space in which the schools operate by defining a number of intermediate goals. One such intermediate goal found in many states is the enhancement of *opportunities for parental and community in-volvement.* Parents who choose schools can be expected to be more engaged than those who do not. Beyond that, proponents of the charter concept contend that such involve-ment is a valuable resource that will ultimately lead to higher student achievement and other positive outcomes.

Another intermediate goal in most charter school laws is enhanced *professional au-tonomy and opportunities for professional development for teachers.* Charter schools are schools of choice for teachers as well as for parents and students. The charter school concept suggests that allowing teachers to choose schools with educational missions and approaches that closely match their own beliefs and interests will create school communities that can spend less time managing value conflicts among school stakeholders and more time implementing effective educational interventions. School choice can also promote a shared professional culture and higher levels of professional autonomy, which the literature suggests lead ultimately to improved levels of student achievement.

While it is true that many important regulations are not waived for charter schools, a few of the key freedoms charter schools are granted deal with teachers; for example, teachers are at-will employees, and most states do not require all charter school teachers to be certified. These provisions allow charter schools more flexibility in recruiting and structuring their teaching force to suit the specific needs of the school.

A third intermediate goal for charter schools is to develop *innovations in curriculum and instruction*. Put another way, proponents argue that charter schools can function as public education's research and development sector. As such, the benefits of charter schools will extend to noncharter students as traditional public schools adopt and emulate these innovations.

Finally, some charter school advocates hope the schools will be laboratories for experiments in the use of *privatized services*. According to these advocates, schools will run more efficiently by contracting out part or all the services they provide. Charter schools, as it turns out, have provided a quick and easy route for privatization, because many states allow private schools to convert to public charter schools, and most states allow charter schools to contract all or part of their services to private education management organizations (EMOs). Some states have no charter schools operated by EMOs, but others—such as Michigan—have more than three-quarters of their schools operated by EMOs. In total, it is estimated that between 20 and 25 percent of all charter schools in the United States are operated by EMOs.

The research base to support many of these theoretical arguments is largely borrowed from market research and remains unproven within the education sector. Nevertheless, proponents continue to argue that increased school choice and privatization will bring a much-needed dose of entrepreneurial spirit and a competitive ethos to public education. While the research base is still somewhat limited, in recent years more and more sound evaluation and research has replaced the rhetorical or theoretical pieces that earlier dominated the literature on charter schools.

Outcomes

Accountability is the price that charter schools pay for their autonomy—specifically, accountability for results rather than accountability for inputs and processes. This, however, begs two additional questions. The first is: accountability for which outputs and outcomes? That is, which outcomes shall serve as the primary indicators of charter school quality? The second question is: accountability to whom? In other words, who will decide whether charter schools are making sufficient progress toward their goals?

The most commonly noted final outcomes for charter schools are student achievement and customer satisfaction, which are principles drawn from, respectively, the field of education and the field of business. There is some controversy over how policymakers and citizens should balance the values of student achievement and customer satisfaction. While many charter advocates argue that both are important, some libertarians and market conservatives view customer satisfaction as the paramount aim of public programs and agencies. Advocates of this position hold that a policy decision or outcome is good only if its customers think it is good and continue to "vote with their feet" for the service. Proponents of this position also maintain that it is the customers—parents and guardians—and not public officials who are best suited to know what is good for children. Interestingly, while most studies or evaluations of charter schools find that parents and students are generally satisfied with their charter school, the growing body of evidence indicates that, on the whole, charter schools are not performing better on standardized tests than are traditional public schools. Although there are a few successful states, the overall results are mixed at best.

The Future of Charter Schools

Charter schools are here to stay. Few will question that. However, two unanswered questions are of particular interest to the future of charter schools: What will be the likely rate of growth of charter schools? Will charter schools remain a distinct and separate school form, or will they be dragged back into the fold and come to resemble and operate like traditional public schools? Answers to these questions will depend greatly on how charter schools respond to a variety of potential threats that are both external and internal to the movement.

External threats to charter schools include state deficits and re-regulation. School systems are under increasing pressure owing to large budget deficits at local, state, and national levels. In times like these, governments need to focus on core education services and are less likely to start or expand reforms such as charter schools. Although some may argue that charter schools can be more efficient, to date there is insufficient evidence to support these claims. Another potential threat to charter schools is re-regulation. Requirements that charter schools administer the same standardized tests and have the same performance standards as traditional public schools mean that they cannot risk developing and using new curricular materials. New mandates regarding outcomes pressure charter schools to conform and restrict the autonomy they were intended to enjoy.

Charter schools also face a number of internal threats from within the movement. These include the following:

- Growing school and class sizes that are now approaching the sizes found in traditional public schools.

- Unchecked expansion of private EMOs. Claims that EMOs can make charter schools more effective have not been substantiated by research.
- While charter schools were originally intended to be autonomous and locally run, increasingly they are being started by EMOs rather than community groups and steered from distant corporate headquarters.
- Lack of innovation and limited diversity of school options. True school choice requires a diversity of options from which to choose, but charter schools are becoming increasingly similar to traditional public schools.
- Lack of support and standards for authorizers. Many authorizers have no funds allocated for oversight activities. Also, many authorizers are unprepared and sometimes unwilling to be sponsors of charter schools.
- Attrition of teachers and administrators is extremely high in charter schools. A number of studies suggest that annual attrition of teachers ranges from 15 to 30 percent. The loss of teachers leads to greater instability in the schools and represents a loss of investment. Some of this attrition may be functional, as charter school administrators exercise their autonomy in determining which teachers to hire and fire.
- Rapid growth of reforms. As with any sound reform process, it is important to test charter school reforms on a small scale in order to make adjustments before implementing them on a large scale. Some states have implemented and expanded their charter school reforms very rapidly, resulting in a backlash of resistance as shortcomings in oversight and other neglected aspects of the reform become apparent.

Evaluating Schools or Evaluated Schools?

Charter schools—by their very design—were intended to be evaluating schools. The charter school concept is based on providing greater autonomy for charter schools in exchange for greater accountability. This implies that charter schools would be actively involved in evaluating their outcomes and reporting these outcomes to state agencies, the authorizer or sponsor, parents, and the public at large. Another reason that suggests that charter schools would be evaluating schools is that they embody site-based management, so there are no bureaucracies to deal with. Also, the smaller size of these schools and self-selection by teachers and staff should lead to higher levels of interpersonal trust and better collaborative relationships and professional culture. Reasons such as these suggest that charter schools would be more likely to use and incorporate evaluation into regular operations at the school.

Nevertheless, charter schools face a number of obstacles in using evaluation or fulfilling their obligations for accountability. These include vague, incomplete, and often unmeasurable goals and objectives included in the charter contracts and the overwhelming start-up issues that charter schools face. Given the enormous start-up challenges related to facilities, staffing, and recruiting students, it is no surprise that charter schools place evaluation low on the list of priorities. Further obstacles include the often new and inexperienced school leaders and the high turnover of teachers and administrators. Another critical obstacle is the weak signals that the schools might receive from oversight agencies.

While there are tremendous differences between and within states, it generally can be said that evaluation conducted by individual charter schools is weak and limited in scope. Because of demands for accountability and because they are not sufficiently proactive in demonstrating success, charter schools have largely become *evaluated* rather than *evaluating* schools.

Autonomy for Accountability

As noted earlier, the academic performance of charter schools is mixed at best. Defenders of charter schools rationalize or justify this less-than-expected performance by pointing out that many traditional public schools are also failing, and thus it is unfair to hold charter schools to high standards when other schools are not.

Nationally, between 6 and 7 percent of all charter schools have closed, which is surprising given their relatively weak performance. One reason for the lack of closures is insufficient evidence about school performance from which authorizers can make renewal, nonrenewal, or revocation decisions. Political and ideological factors can also explain—in part—why many authorizers are closing so few poor-performing charters.

Closing poor-performing charter schools will strengthen charter school reforms in two ways. First, removing these schools from the aggregate results for charter schools will increase their overall results. Second, closing such schools sends a strong message to other charter schools that the autonomy-for-accountability agreement is real.

While many traditional schools do perform far below established standards, this should not be used as a justification for excusing charter schools from the standards agreed upon in their contracts. The idea behind charter schools was not to replicate the existing system, which many argue suffers from a lack of accountability. Rather, they were envisioned as a means of pressuring traditional public schools to improve both by example and through competition. If charter schools are to serve as a lever for change, they must be better than traditional public schools, and they must be held accountable for their performance.

See also **Government Role in Schooling; No Child Left Behind; School Choice**

Further Reading

Buckley, Jack, and Mark Schneider, *Charter Schools: Hope or Hype?* Princeton, NJ: Princeton University Press, 2007.

Bulkley, K., and P. Wohlstetter, eds., *Taking Account of Charter Schools: What's Happened and What's Next.* New York: Teachers College Press, 2004.

Carnoy, Martin, Rebecca Jacobsen, Lawrence Mishel, and Richard Rothstein, *The Charter School Dust-Up: Examining the Evidence on Enrollment and Achievement*. Washington, DC: Economic Policy Institute; New York: Teachers College Press, 2005.

Fuller, B., ed., *Inside Charter Schools: The Paradox of Radical Decentralization*. Cambridge, MA: Harvard University Press, 2000.

Merseth, Katherine K., with Kristy Cooper, *Inside Urban Charter Schools: Promising Practices and Strategies in Five High-Performing Schools*. Cambridge, MA: Harvard Education Press, 2009.

Miron, G., and C. Nelson, *What's Public about Charter Schools? Lessons Learned about Choice and Accountability*. Thousand Oaks, CA: Corwin Press, 2002.

Noll, James William, ed., *Taking Sides: Clashing Views on Educational Issues*, 15th ed. Boston: McGraw Hill Higher Education, 2010.

Powers, Jeanne M., *Charter Schools: From Reform Imagery to Reform Reality*. New York: Palgrave Macmillan, 2009.

CHILD ABUSE

Amanda Singletary

Child abuse is generally defined in two ways. One is the nonaccidental injury to a child that requires medical attention. These are acts of commission. The second part of the definition is neglect, acts of omission where parents and other adults fail to meet the basic needs of the child. Nearly all experts concur that neglect is far more likely than other forms of abuse. The U.S. Department of Health and Human Services estimated that, in 2007, there were 794,000 victims of child abuse and neglect, approximately 1,500 of whom died as a result of the abuse. Sixty-two percent of the total victims experienced neglect, 18 percent were physically abused, sexual abuse harmed 10 percent, 7 percent were psychologically mistreated, and medical neglect accounted for 2 percent.

As with any abuse situation, the child abuse may be physical, psychological, emotional, sexual, or some combination. Clearly, these are broad categorizations for what constitutes the complex phenomenon of abuse, and this has made the whole domain of child abuse controversial. The societal expectation that parents are nearly exclusively in charge of the care and rearing of their children has meant that interventions into the private family setting have been likely only when abuse is very serious and can be documented.

The controversies surrounding child abuse are grounded in the question, Does the child stay in the home or get removed from the home? Society has made it known that abuse of a child is horrific. The problem is in how to stop the abuse with a solution that will best benefit the child. Specifically, the concern is over whether a child should be completely removed from the home or whether attempts should be made to maintain the family unit. When considering the solutions to child abuse, among the primary controversies are questions about exactly what constitutes abuse, particularly with regard to physical discipline, and how other forms of domestic violence complicate the scene.

Causes of Child Abuse

The causes of child abuse are many, and not all are found in all cases. Child abuse is mainly perpetrated by an adult who wields physical and emotional control over a child. Many factors can relate to someone's risk to abuse children. Some of the factors at work in child abuse are cultural, social, and personal. In very early studies of child abuse, the assumptions were that abusers must be mentally ill. While that is an easy supposition, the evidence suggests that only around 10 percent of abusers have psychoses or severe personality disorders. Reliance on mental illness as an explanation has hindered a more complete understanding of child abuse. This has led recent researchers, such as Richard Gelles, to broaden the discussion to include other factors that might make one prone to abuse a child.

Personal psychological factors in parents can play a significant role in the risk of abuse. However, these factors usually relate to the stressors that parents might experience. Stress can arise from many sources, not the least of which is the task of parenting itself. It is a permanent status that at times can seem overwhelming, particularly for persons with inadequate support networks. Some children with special needs require additional care that heightens caregiving stress. Not all babies are equally easy-going, and those that seem more prone to crying can lead parents to question their skills. Stress is increased when one is a single parent, has lower income or is unemployed, is ill, or experiences conflict with a romantic partner. Furthermore, environmental stressors such as the family ideal, work, finances, and even health issues can cause a large amount of stress.

The use of alcohol or drugs reduces inhibitions and heightens the abusers' awareness of personal insecurities. Both alcohol and drugs can, through aggravating stress and impairing judgment, cause an abuser to verbally or physically attack a child for some perceived wrong. If an individual is a victim of prior abuse, he or she is more likely to become an abuser, too, although the individual is not destined to be abusive. Estimates are that 30 percent of abused children will grow up to be abusers, in contrast to 3 percent of persons who were not abused. Low self-esteem and feelings of inadequacy have also been linked to a greater tendency to abuse when compared with persons with higher levels of self-esteem. After prolonged exposure to negative opinions, an individual may become violent as a way of venting the built-up pressure and anxiety caused by low self-esteem.

Abuse is also used as a method to gain control over a child. A person who has a poor self-concept, low self-esteem, or has been a victim of prior abuse has a stronger need for control and power, because it is the ability to gain power and control that validates the abuser. This cyclical pattern is difficult to break. Often parents have very little preparation for the tasks of parenting, have unrealistic expectations about what it entails, and have little understanding of how children can be expected to behave at various stages of development. The images of babies in most parenting magazines show a smiling, cooing, cherubic face; they don't show the child crying with a runny nose, messy diaper, or other distasteful daily occurrences of child rearing. Abuse may occur as an attempt to gain conformity from unruly children. For whatever reason, studies suggest that abusive parents tend to be much more demanding than nonabusive parents.

Society's focus on the ideal family creates stress when an individual realizes that he or she is not living up to society's standard of the modern family, be it by not making enough income, not living in the right neighborhood, or needing a two-income household in order to get by. Also, pressure from a boss at work may cause tension that adds to the build-up of stress. These stressors may create a volatile home life where abuse is the outlet for a massive release of pent-up stresses. And, unfortunately, children are likely to be the targets for the abusive release.

This inclusion of economic status in the likelihood of abuse is important. A number of studies suggest that child abuse is more likely in families from low socioeconomic backgrounds, although they differ on the reasons for why this is so. One explanation posits that it only appears that the rates are higher in poor families because they seek treatment in settings, such as public hospitals, in which the suspicion of abuse is likely

CHILD ABUSE ADVOCACY GROUPS

Child abuse prevention and advocacy Web sites have proliferated in recent years. Some are the Web sites of well-established nonprofit organizations, and others are solely cyberspace creations. Nearly all encourage visitors to the site to donate money to help the cause of education and advocacy. Because child abuse is an issue that commands attention and garners sympathy, particularly from those who identify with the child, it is a cause that persons are likely to donate toward. The so-called innocence of childhood is a strong cultural image, and it is easy to sell abuse as violating that innocence. This model of innocence is used as a contrast for data on abuse.

Some particularly useful Web sites and organizations devoted to child welfare include www.childhelp.org and www.cwla.org. Childhelp is a large nonprofit organization that uses celebrity ambassadors, product partnerships, and media outlets to spread the word about child abuse. Its hotline 1-800-4-A-Child is a well-publicized reporting mechanism. The Child Welfare League of America is the oldest and largest child abuse information and prevention organization in the country. In contrast to these long-standing organizations (Childhelp was founded in 1959; the Child Welfare League in 1920), www.childabuse.com is purely an online venture and promotes prevention through education and awareness.

to be reported. Wealthy families may seek care from a private physician who may be more reluctant to label a suspicious injury as abuse. So wealthier families may be better able to hide abuse. Another explanation for the link between poverty and abuse is the stress that accompanies poverty. Additionally, low-income parents have less education, inadequate support systems, higher rates of substance abuse, and are more likely to be young. Compounded, these risk factors make being a lower-class child a potentially harmful position. Low-income parents tend to be single parents. The risk of neglect among low-income children is an astounding 44 times higher than among middle- and upper-income children.

Contrary to the stereotype of women's constant nurturing, evidence indicates that, in cases of child abuse, women are as likely as men to be the perpetrators. The majority of low-income families are mother-only families. Some of these women are no doubt forced into the mothering role by a lack of well-paying or fulfilling employment, as well as by unplanned pregnancies. Unwanted children are an added mental and economic burden, making them prone to abuse.

Consequences of Child Abuse

Because the causes of abuse are many, it follows that the consequences of abuse are just as numerous. Although statistics cannot tell the whole story of the consequences of child abuse, they can give insight into the frequency and severity of the problem. However, statistics about child abuse must be viewed with caution. Given the unacceptability of harming a child, parents are often inaccurate in their reporting of such behaviors, fearing legal reprisal and social condemnation. A lot of the statistics, then, come from the reports of teachers, physicians, social workers, and others who must make assumptions about the origin of injuries.

There are nearly 3 million reports of child abuse made each year, suggesting that awareness of the issue is resulting in some action. However, estimates are that the actual rates of child abuse are at least three times what are reported. According to Childhelp, one of the largest and oldest nonprofit organizations dedicated to the issue of child abuse, children between birth and age three are the most likely group to experience abuse. They are victimized at a rate of 16.4 per 1,000 children, compared with a rate of 12.3 per 1,000 children for all children under age 18. This means that, for every 1,000 infants and toddlers, more than 16 of them will be abused. Around four children die every day from abuse or neglect, and 79 percent of these juvenile homicide victims are children younger than four years old.

Consequences also encompass the likely future outcomes for the victims of abuse. According to data compiled by the U.S. Department of Health and Human Services, there can be many long-term consequences for children who are abused. Among them is a 25 percent greater likelihood of teen pregnancy, abused teens being three times less likely than nonabused teens to practice safe sex, increasing their risks of contracting sexually transmitted diseases and AIDS. Abused children are nearly 30 percent more likely to abuse their own children.

Victimization through child abuse is also correlated with more contact with the criminal justice system. Children who experience child abuse and neglect are 59 percent more likely to be arrested as juveniles, 28 percent more likely to be arrested as adults, and 30 percent more likely to commit violent crime than are nonabused persons. Data indicate that, among the prison population, 36.7 percent of women inmates were abused as children, and 14.4 percent of men inmates were.

Psychological and psychiatric outcomes also are linked with child abuse. Eighty percent of young adults who had been abused met the diagnostic criteria for at least one psychiatric disorder at the age of 21. Common disorders among this group included depression, anxiety, eating disorders, and post-traumatic stress disorder. Sexual abuse compounds these issues. Children who are victims of sexual abuse are 2.5 times more likely to abuse alcohol and 3.8 times more likely to become addicted to drugs than their nonabused peers. In fact, nearly two-thirds of those persons in drug abuse treatment programs report having been abused as children.

Controversies

Controversies have surfaced when determining healthy solutions for child abuse victims. The key controversies concerning child abuse are the definition of abuse, the presence of other risk behaviors and factors, and whether the child should remain in or be removed from the home. Solutions to child abuse are difficult to create, because each child abuse case is different and the solution that works for one child may harm another child even more. When handling child abuse cases, caseworkers must do their absolute best not to add to the child's trauma. It is this desire to minimize an abused child's trauma that makes finding solutions to these controversies difficult.

Defining Abuse

The definitions of child abuse have changed significantly over time. No longer do parents have rights of life and death over children, as was common in the days of the Roman Empire, when children not blessed by their fathers were left to die through neglect. Nor can parents in the United States turn their children into commodities by selling them to the highest bidder. Today the question of abuse is focused on the point where a parent crosses the fine line between acceptable use of force and unacceptable abuse, and with what frequency. At what point should a neighbor, teacher, physician, or social worker intervene? Extreme cases, such as burning, imprisoning, or beating are easy to define as child abuse. However, there is much gray area in what is acceptable behavior of a parent toward a child.

Definitions that focus only on physically hurting the child might be too broadly interpreted. The result is that any physical act, such as tightly holding a toddler during a tantrum, becomes defined as abuse by some. The legal standard recognizes that it is not always easy to distinguish between physical discipline and abuse. The former condition is the result of what is considered reasonable by the cultural context. While 90 percent of parents of three- and four-year-olds have used spankings on their child and nearly that many consider it acceptable to do so, does that mean 90 percent of parents are abusive? This question is not easily answered but is important because the definition of abuse that is applied by social workers, courts, and so on can determine whether children are permitted to remain with the parent or whether they are taken in by the state. In fact, the American Bar Association has no universally recognized definition of child abuse to use in court settings.

As difficult as defining physical abuse is in practice, defining neglect is even more difficult. While abandonment or gross failure to provide for the basic needs of a child are clear, statutes that define parental negligence in broad ways may mean that different parenting models than the community norm, or failure to instill morals, or even permitting truancy are seen as negligent. In the early days of the home school movement, some parents were considered neglectful for not sending their children for standard classroom instruction.

Defining Abusers and Settings

For many years there have been concerns over who is most likely to abuse a child. Stereotypes hold that the particularly likely culprit is a stepfather. While it seems easy to place the blame on a male, nonbiological family member because of the expectation that men are more violent than women and the supposition that biological ties are stronger than social ties, this is inaccurate. Biological parents are more likely than other persons to abuse a child, and it is the mother who is most likely to do so. This pattern is particularly true for African American families, which have a greater proportion of single-parent homes. Does this then mean that single black mothers are profiled as child abusers?

Police who are called to homes to investigate domestic disturbance calls are taught to pay attention to any children who are present for signs of abuse. Statistics indicate that when women are abused in a domestic setting, their children have a higher likelihood of being abused as well. This might be abuse from the woman's abuser or, paradoxically, abuse from the woman herself. It is often extremely difficult to determine who in a household is abusing whom.

Interventions

Since the 1950s, many private and public agencies have dedicated themselves to helping children. One of the primary tasks of the agencies involves educating the public about the issues surrounding child abuse and proposing specific solutions. It has only been recently that laws have been developed to aid children, such as the Child Abuse

Prevention and Treatment Act of 1974. The goal of this act was to encourage states to develop their own laws and strategies to protect children from maltreatment and neglect. While every state handles child abuse cases in a slightly different way and relies on slightly different administrative structures, they have been fairly successful in their assault on child abuse and neglect.

One of the most traumatic aspects of child abuse and neglect is the decision to remove the child from the home, even on a temporary basis. This is granted under the states' rights to protect the interest of the child, but the question that is raised is what to then do with the child. Options are limited. For infants and young children, the foster care system is their destination, at least on a temporary basis while abuse claims are investigated. For adolescents and severely disabled children, the care is frequently provided in a group home, where a small number of similar children are tended by a staff of child care workers. These decisions to remove children from the care of their biological parents are controversial for several reasons.

First, the expanding definitions of child abuse mean that children can be removed with far less proof than was needed in the past. Additionally, the numbers of cases that social workers and child advocates are saddled with mean that it takes some time for the data regarding each case to be gathered, leaving the child in foster care for longer periods of time than most state regulations initially intended. Second, parents may be encouraged not to contest the child's removal in order to avoid damaging allegations of abuse. After an assessment, the child may be sent back home, sometimes with court supervision and follow-up services, but sometimes without.

When individuals hear about a case of child abuse, they automatically want the child removed from the home. It is true that removing the child from the home is the most effective way to stop the abuse. But is tearing a child away from the only home he or she has known really helping the child? Young children are particularly prone to be victims of violence, but there is a common cultural idea that very young children need their parents (particularly their mothers) more than at any other age. Indeed, federal laws governing foster care encourage states to work vigorously to reunite children with their parents. Unfortunately, the frequent court reviews of the cases often just mean moving the child to a new foster placement.

In extreme cases of child abuse where the child's life is at risk, removal is the only option. However, temporary removal or family counseling might be more productive in the end if the abuser is taught alternative ways of managing anger and stress instead of using abusive measures. These types of interventions require a great deal of time, effort, and energy on the part of the abuser and the state counseling agencies and are often something that cash-strapped states are unable to provide.

Critics of the foster care system suggest that the system is broken and badly needs repair. Children are moved from one foster family to another on a frequent basis. Due to an overwhelming need for foster care providers, many foster families receive little train-ing for their role and may be caring for too many children. One of the great concerns is what happens to children who age out of the foster care system. At age 18, they are no longer under state care but may be poorly prepared to live as independent adults.

In some cases, parents must give up their rights to a child when the abuse has been determined to be too severe to attempt reuniting the family. However, it is extremely difficult for this to happen, because there is a high legal burden of proof for the court to terminate parental rights. Sometimes, the threat of criminal charges will push parents to voluntarily terminate their rights. When a child cannot be returned to the biologi-cal family and parental rights are terminated, adoption becomes available to the child. Adoption is another area of controversy. Society generally views adoption by a blood rel-ative as the most beneficial for the child. However, abuse is a learned behavior. If a child's parent is the abuser, the assumption is that the parent's parent was probably abusive as well. In such a case, being adopted by a blood relative may be placing the child back in a potentially abusive situation. The underlying problem of these controversies remains, and until abuse can be prevented, no amount of intervention will be adequate.

See also **Corporal Punishment; Deadbeat Parents; Domestic Violence—Behaviors and Causes; Foster Care; Sex-Offender Registries (vol. 2)**

Further Reading

Child Welfare Information Gateway, http://www.childwelfare.gov

Child Welfare League of America, http://www.cwla.org

Childhelp USA Foundation, http://www.childhelpusa.org

Crosson-Tower, Cynthia, *Understanding Child Abuse and Neglect.* Boston: Allyn and Bacon, 2007.

Crouse, Janice Shaw, *Children at Risk: The Precarious State of Children's Well-Being in the United States.* New Brunswick, NJ: Transaction Publishers, 2010.

Dodge, Kenneth A., and Doriane Lambelet Coleman, *Preventing Child Maltreatment: Community Approaches.* New York: Guilford Press, 2009.

Finklehor, David, *Childhood Victimization: Violence, Crime, and Abuse in the Lives of Young People.* New York: Oxford University Press, 2008.

Flowers, R. Barri, *Domestic Crimes, Family Violence and Child Abuse: A Study of Contemporary American Society.* Jefferson, NC: McFarland, 2000.

Gelles, Richard J., *Intimate Violence in Families.* Thousand Oaks, CA: Sage, 1997.

Kurst-Swanger, Karel, and Jacqueline L. Petcosky, *Violence in the Home: Multidisciplinary Perspec-tives.* New York: Oxford University Press, 2003.

Monteleone, James A., *A Parent's and Teacher's Handbook on Identifying and Preventing Child Abuse.* St. Louis: G. W. Medical Publishing, 1998.

National Association to Protect Children, http://www.protect.org

National Children's Advocacy Center, http://www.nationalcac.org

Prevent Child Abuse America, http://www.preventchildabuse.org

CHILD CARE

Lori McNeil

Controversies concerning child care in the United States, which center on who should take responsibility, have moved in and out of the spotlight for more than 150 years. Social and moral issues concerning appropriate child care are motivated primarily by the dilemma of public versus private responsibility for the well-being of children.

Background

Although many people may believe that the issue of child care is relatively new, this issue has been part of the national landscape for quite some time. In fact, the first recorded formal day care began in 1854 in New York City (Rose 1999). At that time, these centers were called day nurseries, and they were modeled after the formal French day care centers called *crèches*. The primary purpose of the day nurseries was centered on issues of child neglect as opposed to a child care service. In the beginning, day nurseries were not federally funded ventures and instead tended to be funded by settlement houses and local service agencies.

During the Great Depression of the 1930s, however, child care use and offerings were greatly expanded as part of the Works Progress Administration (WPA) (Rose 1999). The major purpose for the inclusion of child care under WPA was to create jobs—in this case, jobs as child care workers. An even bigger expansion of child care occurred in 1943 under the Lanham Act. This expansion was necessary because of the incredible increase of women in the workforce during World War II. Because childcare offerings were not readily available during this era, the federal government funded more than 3,000 day care centers for approximately 60,000 children as part of this legislation. This expansion of child care extended to private business as well. During World War II, for example, the Kaiser Shipbuilding Corporation in Oregon was the first company to offer employer-sponsored child care. This offering consisted of two day care centers that operated 24 hours a day. When the war ended, so did the need for women in the workforce; thus, child care services greatly decreased at that time.

The 1950s saw continued allegiance to a more traditional mother's role—that is, one that is primarily focused on raising children. The 1950s ideology was questioned beginning in the 1960s, however, when a more liberal view of women's roles prevailed. At that time, more women were entering the workforce and that, in turn, influenced the amount of child care that was necessary. Since the 1960s, child care offerings and use have increased dramatically. This is so even in light of the demise of the first Comprehensive Child Development Bill in 1971. This bill would have authorized more than $2 billion specifically for child care services. President Nixon vetoed the bill, stating that, "for the Federal Government to plunge headlong financially into supporting child care development would commit the vast moral authority of the National Government to the side of communal approaches to child rearing" (Robertson 2003, 7). Despite Nixon's veto in 1971, both federal and state governments have been major contributors to child care definitions, regulations, finance, and structure.

What Is Child Care?

Typically, child care is defined as care provided for children by those who are not the children's parents or guardians. Most often, the caregiving work for children is financially compensated. The federal government has attached an age requirement for its definition of child care that spans from birth through 12 years of age. The age category specifies eligibility of child care subsidy and tax credits regulated at the federal level.

Child care structure occurs in several arrangements: relative care, day care center care, family day care, and in-home care. Relative care is care provided by a family member outside the immediate family, most often by the grandmother of the child. Even though the grandparent or other family relative may be a blood relative to the child, financial compensation may still be part of the arrangement. In the past, relative care had been the most utilized style of child care arrangement. Today, day care centers are the most common type of child care used.

A day care center arrangement is care provided by a nonrelative that occurs in a public setting much like a school setting. In fact, day care centers are often part of school systems but also can be part of a workplace setting as well as a freestanding facility. The increased popularity of day care center care is due in part to the education environment it commonly offers. Traditionally, day care centers deliver child care services to a large number of children of wide-ranging ages. Because day care centers normally operate as a business venture—that is, occurring in a public setting and with a trained and fully compensated staff—day care centers tend to be described as the most reliable style of child care arrangement.

Family day care offerings are commonly located in the child care provider's home. Normally, a family day care provider serves as few as one child but usually not more than six children because of licensing regulations. Family day care tends to be used by families with younger children, because the setting is considered more homelike than the more institutionalized setting of day care centers. Thus, the transition for very young children from home to day care, it is reasoned, will be somewhat less stressful, as the care setting tends to be similar to a child's own home.

In-home child care is the least used style of child care arrangement, mainly because it is the most expensive form. In-home child care is care by a nonrelative that occurs in the child's home. This style of arrangement is also commonly known as care performed by a nanny or au pair. The child care provider provides care to a single child or family of siblings. Babysitting is not included in formal child care arrangements, because babysitting services are more likely those that are retained while a parent is involved in errands or other functions not associated with the workplace.

Another way to describe child care is based on licensing status. Child care is regulated by individual states. Although some subsidies originate from the federal government, each state sets standards for child care delivery, usually in the form of child care licensure. The states use regulation standards through the licensing of child care providers. The issue at hand is that much child care exists in an underground fashion—that is, unlicensed. Estimations of unlicensed child care in the United States range from 50 percent to as high as 80 percent (Clarke-Stewart and Allhusen 2005). Because unlicensed child care is virtually impossible to detect and thus regulate, issues such as child safety and the quality of care children receive are major concerns. Beyond the issue of licensing, a crucial component of child care involves the responsibility of caregiving.

Oppositional Terrains

The private responsibility debate suggests that children are best cared for within the family, preferably when the mother provides the hands-on daily care of her child(ren) (Robertson 2003). The assumption is that the rearing of children is a private matter, and caregiving is a natural purview of women generally and of mothers specifically. This ideology stems from the concept of the "cult of true womanhood." Here, women's highest calling is rooted in caregiving. That is, to be a woman means caregiving and that, in turn, means mothering.

THE COLUMBINE HIGH SCHOOL SHOOTINGS: A CASE FOR STAY-AT-HOME PARENTAL CHILD CARE

Unsupervised children indulged by affluent parents may be a recipe for disaster, and disaster is exactly what transpired at Columbine High School in April 1999. Opponents of day care suggest that it was precisely this combination that was the root cause for the Columbine atrocity. The shooters, Dylan Klebold and Eric Harris, came from homes where both parents worked outside the home, with the boys enjoying considerable autonomy and freedom. Although warning signs existed about the upcoming shootings, such as the videotapes explaining the plans, fascination with violent video games, and reports from school authorities about the boys' aggressive and threatening behavior, these signs appeared to go unnoticed by their parents. Harris's voice on a video saying, "thank God my parents never searched my room," offers support to these allegations of inattentive parenting. Moreover, Klebold describes a great deal of anger surrounding day care experiences, such as being teased and mocked. These experiences continued and were magnified during high school, and, interestingly, he pens an essay in his creative writing class about a day care center in hell that was operated by Satan (Robertson 2003). Examples such as these contribute to the private responsibility debate whose proponents contend that often the investment in a dual-career family occurs at the expense of children because little time exists to properly attend to the monitoring and well-being of children.

Arguments supporting the private responsibility debate often center on the issue of children's developmental health. This focus claims that children are likely harmed developmentally in day care settings. For example, children may have higher levels of aggressive behavior such as bullying or classroom disruptions when they have spent more time in daycare (Robertson 2003). This perspective originates from infant attachment theory posited by John Bowlby in 1951 in his highly influential work, *Maternal Care and Mental Health*. His work suggested that these harmful behaviors are found in children who have not had adequate opportunities to bond with their mothers, because the children are in day care settings instead of at home with their mothers.

The public responsibility debate centers on the notion that children are the collective responsibility of communities, states, and of the entire nation. Collective responsibility extends to the social, political, educational, and economical realm. Thus, this perspective suggests that child rearing is akin to education. Whereas education is funded and regulated at both the state and national level, so also should child care. This ideology gained momentum and notoriety with Hillary Clinton's book, *It Takes a Village* (1996).

Clinton (1996) argued that to create a strong and thriving nation, communities must be fully committed to children in every sense. Moreover, families need support and resources to grow strong children who are contributing members of society. Applied to the issue of child care, the contention is that child care must be made available and financed so that children are not left unsupervised and are not subjected to substandard child care venues. Thus, as part of our societal offerings and commitment to children, child care needs to be widely available, of high quality, and affordable.

Child Care and Media Influence

Although both the public and the private responsibility debate have merit, these dichotomous perspectives have been reduced to a clash between working and stay-at-home mothers. This controversial and very public debate, however, encompasses the much more complex issue of defining women's proper role in society.

Perhaps one of the best examples of this clash is one that played out in the media in the 1990s. The case of Jennifer Ireland garnered national attention and the media spotlight after she gave birth to her daughter when she was a 16-year-old high school student (Frost-Knappman and Cullen-Dupont 1997). The father of the child, Steven Smith, was also a high school student. After graduating from high school, Ireland was a recipient of a college scholarship at the University of Michigan. In 1993, Ireland attended the university and at that time enrolled her daughter in the university-affiliated day care center. In 1994, Smith sued Ireland for custody of the child, claiming that she was an unfit mother. Part of the claim centered on the assertion that Ireland was more interested in her academic career than in her daughter, because she chose to put her child in day care while she attended to her studies.

Initially, Smith won the case. Smith, who also was attending college, resided with his parents, explaining that his mother would provide care for his daughter while he worked and attended classes. The judge, Raymond Cachen, agreeing with Smith, concluded that a child, "raised and supervised by blood relations" as opposed to being "supervised a great part of the day by strangers" would be the better arrangement for the youngster (Frost-Knappman and Cullen-Dupont 1997). A public uproar ensued over the decision. Allegations of a backlash against women, specifically career women, were declared. A year later, the decision was overturned on appeal. The *Ireland v. Smith* case brought the day care debate into the media spotlight, as well as into public discourse.

A precursor to the Ireland case, the McMartin Preschool scandal likely wielded considerable influence in the original Ireland decision, as well as to public opinion surrounding the issue of child care. This case was first filed in 1983 with allegations of sexual abuse of a child while the child attended the McMartin Preschool day care center (Douglas and Michaels 2004). The case grew from abuse of a single child to more than 125 children, with accusations extending from torture and satanism to secret tunnels existing beneath the day care facility. The children's silence surrounding the abuse was allegedly coerced through the viewing of atrocities such as cutting the ears off live rabbits, smashing baby turtles, and beating a horse to death. Children reported abuse over an approximate 10-year span and/or including many members of the McMartin family in their allegations. After a lengthy trial, the allegations were found to be unsubstantiated, and the case was dropped by 1990 after an unsuccessful retrial. The impact of the unsupported allegations of nightmarish and perverse atrocities against young children lingered in the media and likely in many parents' minds as well. Since the McMartin case, cadres of other similar day care abuse cases have been played out in the media and consequently on a national platform. Some of the claims were certainly founded, but many others were reported to be pure fabrication. The media influence of the McMartin and Ireland cases, in part, explains the hypervisibility of child care. To have a full understanding of child care issues, however, an overview of the challenges families face in the provision of care for their children is necessary.

Child Care Challenges

Formalized child care has often been described as a patchwork system of caring for children. This description of child care is used because there is no formal or comprehensive style of caring for children outside of the immediate family. Parents, especially mothers, often feel immense frustration, because few options and conversely many gaps exist in securing child care. For example, licensed child care rarely exists after 6:00 P.M. This can be an insurmountable problem for women whose work hours do not fit the typical 9-to-5 workday.

The securing of infant care can also add to the challenge of child care. Normally, infant care is quite time intensive for providers, and they must subsequently reduce their child care load to care for an infant. Because of this situation, providers are less likely to engage in infant child care, because they can earn higher incomes caring for toddlers and preschoolers. The very issue of child care cost continues to add to the challenges of child care. The cost of caring for children is staggering. For a single child in 2003, full-time child care costs averaged $4,000 to $6,000 per year and were significantly higher for infant care (Clarke-Stewart and Allhusen 2005).

The issues of child care gaps presented here, as well as child care cost generally, create the market for unlicensed child care that currently exists. Although many parents may feel they have no other options than to use unlicensed child care, it is important to note that unlicensed child care is not eligible for child care subsidies or tax credits. A parent, for example, may use a licensed day care center for one child and unlicensed care for her infant because either licensed care is not available or is too expensive. Because day care centers typically do not offer services beyond 6:00 P.M., the same mother may also need to employ yet another person to pick up the child care slack should her workday extend beyond 6:00 P.M. As parents patch together many different types of child care to successfully meet their child care needs, the patchwork system will likely be less stable and can be prone to last-minute cancellations and changes. In the previous example, only one of the three arrangements needs to fail, causing the mother to scramble to locate another last-minute arrangement. The alternative is that the working mother misses work, which also may translate to less money—money that is likely critical to the maintenance of the family.

The patchwork system of child care provision is a less-than-compelling one, but proponents of stay-at-home parental child care suggest that the problem in terms of changing the system is rooted in how the federal government organizes tax subsidies. At issue is the increasing of options to families as opposed to increasing the offerings of formal

THE DEVALUING OF PUBLIC CHILD CARE

It is surprising that child care provider pay is among the lowest of all professions, given the fact that child care cost is often described as exorbitant. In fact, it is commonplace for child care providers to earn wages far below poverty rates. Gas station attendants, zoo employees whose primary job is feeding animals, and bank employees responsible for counting money command higher wages than do child care providers. These startling examples provide motivation for child care providers to seek other employment out of financial desperation. Provider turnover rates are estimated to be 30 percent (Clarke-Stewart and Allhusen 2005). This rate is among the highest of all professions and more than four times that of teachers. Many child care experts caution, however, that what we call turnover, children experience as loss. Thus, turnover represents the loss of someone who is important in the lives of children, to whom children may have developed an important emotional attachment.

child care. This perspective focuses on working parents' discomfort with formalized child care and how, despite their uneasiness, they feel forced to participate in a dual-career formulation. Instead, they seek financially viable opportunities as an avenue to providing daily care for their children (Robertson 2003).

The challenge becomes an economic one for families who prefer stay-at-home parental child care. To begin addressing this concern, it is proposed that corporations should be encouraged to provide family-friendly policies such as flextime, part-time, and job-sharing options, as well as priority scheduling and telecommuting opportunities for parents. These offerings would provide families with choices to be able to construct workdays that promote direct caregiving to their children.

Moreover, the government can continue to increase options by raising the personal exemption allowance. This would reduce the tax burden on families, thereby allowing for one parent to remain at home to care for children. A more direct measure would include the expansion of the dependent care tax credit to extend beyond families who use formal child care to parents who provide stay-at-home parental child care. Currently, subsidy exists only for families who use formal child care and this, it is argued, occurs at the expense of stay-at-home parents. Thus, the organization of tax subsidy literally compels families to pay others to care for their children.

Conclusion

Whether, it takes a village or a stay-at-home mom and exactly what serves the best interests of children are still unknown. How children may be hindered developmentally or helped educationally is a controversy with a long history. The debate over public versus private responsibility to children will likely continue to be portrayed in the media and pondered within the home. As families continue to grapple with this issue, it is likely that communities, states, and the federal government will as well. Nonetheless, the struggle over women's appropriate role in contemporary society remains an active site of contention for all Americans.

See also **Early Childhood Education; Poverty and Public Assistance; Working Mothers**

Further Reading

Bowlby, John, *Maternal Care and Mental Health*. Geneva: World Health Organization, 1951.

Clarke-Stewart, Alison, and Virginia D. Allhusen, *What We Know about Childcare*. Cambridge, MA: Harvard University Press, 2005.

Clinton, Hillary, *It Takes a Village*. New York: Simon & Schuster, 1996.

Douglas, Susan, and Meredith Michaels, *The Mommy Myth: The Idealization of Motherhood and How It Has Undermined All Women*. New York: Free Press, 2004.

Family Research Council, http://www.frc.org

Fox, Isabel, and Norman Lobsenz, *Begin There: The Benefits of a Stay-at-Home Parent*. Hauppage, NJ: Barrons Educational Series, 1996.

Frost-Knappman, Elizabeth, and Kathryn Cullen-Dupont, *Women's Rights on Trial: 101 Historic Trials from Anne Hutchinson to Virginia Military Cadets.* Detriot: Gale, 1997.

Jackson, Mick, *Indictment: The McMartin Case.* HBO Home Video, 1995, 132 min.

Robertson, Brian, *Day Care Deception: What the Child Care Establishment Isn't Telling Us.* New York: Encounter Books, 2003.

Rose, E., *A Mother's Job: A History of Day Care 1890–1960.* New York: Oxford University Press, 1999.

Waldfogel, Jane, *What Children Need.* Cambridge, MA: Harvard University Press, 2008.

Zigler, Edward, Katherine Marsland, and Heather Lord, *The Tragedy of Child Care in America.* New Haven, CT: Yale University Press, 2009.

CLERGY SEX-ABUSE SCANDAL

Paul Boudreau

Beginning in the mid-1980s, a series of court cases began to reveal the extent of sexual abuse committed by clergy in various religious contexts. Although the popular press has tended to associate the clergy abuse scandals as a "Catholic" issue, in fact, the problem is widespread in many religious contexts, including non-Christian religions as well. Although the focus here is on the crisis in the American Catholic Church, in 1990, a survey conducted by the Center for Ethics and Social Policy at the Graduate Theological Union in Berkeley, California, discovered that 10 percent of clergy from across many Protestant Christian denominations that were surveyed said that they had been sexually active with an adult parishioner ("Clergy and Sexuality" 1990). It is believed that sexual abuse among rabbis approximates that found in the Protestant clergy. According to one study, 73 percent of women rabbis report instances of sexual harassment (Shaefer 2003). Sadly, an attempt at damage control has kept things quiet. Fear of lawsuits and bad publicity have dictated an atmosphere of hushed voices and outrage against those who dare to break ranks by speaking out.

In the 1990s, information started to become public about sexual abuse of children in Hare Krishna–movement schools of the 1970s and 1980s.

As universal as the problem of religious leaders and personnel sexually abusing the faithful is in the United States, the problem became most widely known (perhaps unfairly) when it was connected to the Roman Catholic Church. In fact, about 4 percent of the Catholic clergy that served between 1950 and 2002 sexually molested minors. Statistically, that is about average for the U.S. population in general.

The Catholic Church Faces a Crisis

On October 18, 1984, a grand jury in Louisiana returned a 34-count criminal indictment against Gilbert Gauthe, a Catholic priest of the diocese of Lafayette. The charges included 11 counts of aggravated crimes against nature, 11 counts of committing sexually immoral acts with minors, 11 counts of taking pornographic photographs of juveniles, and a single count of aggravated rape, sodomizing a child under the age of 12. In an arrangement with prosecutors, Gauthe pled guilty to multiple counts of contributing to the delinquency of a minor and possession of child pornography and was sentenced to 20 years in prison. The family of one of the victims sued the diocese of Lafayette and was awarded $1.25 million. It was the first time in history that details of a Catholic priest's sexual abuse of children was brought to the public's attention, and it marked the beginning of what became the most horrifying and damaging scandal ever to hit the Catholic Church in the United States.

The year following Gauthe's conviction, his attorney, Raymond Mouton, along with Dominican Fr. Thomas Doyle, a canon lawyer on the staff of the Vatican's representative to the United States, and Fr. Michael Peterson, president of St. Luke's Institute, a resident treatment facility for troubled clergy, prepared a 100-page report titled *The Problem of Sexual Molestation by Roman Catholic Clergy: Meeting the Problem in a Comprehensive and Responsible Manner.* The report was presented to the Committee on Research and Pastoral Practices of the National Conference of Catholic Bishops/U.S. Catholic Conference (NCCB/USCC). The committee was headed by the archbishop of Boston, Cardinal Bernard Law. Every diocesan bishop in the United States received a copy of the report.

After studying the document, the NCCB/USCC committee concluded that the issues raised by the report and the report's recommendations had been adequately addressed by the bishops' conference, and no further action on the report was taken. The task of responding to allegations of sexual abuse by clergy was therefore left up to the individual dioceses.

The Bishops' Response

For the next 15 years, the NCCB/USCC (in 2001, the conference was renamed the United States Conference of Catholic Bishops, or USCCB) continued to study the problem. In 1993, the conference formed the Ad Hoc Committee on Sexual Abuse to make recommendations to the dioceses. These recommendations included:

- *Dealing effectively with priests who sexually abuse minors and others.* The committee sought to assist with diocesan policies, evaluate treatment centers, provide education through topical articles by competent authors, and act as a clearinghouse in related matters.
- *Assisting victims and survivors.* The committee provided articles focused on victims and survivors of clergy sexual abuse, along with a special section in the report on diocesan policies, and met with representatives of various national organizations and with individual victims/survivors. It also developed a 42-page article entitled "Responding to Victims-Survivors."

- *Addressing morale of bishops and priests.* The committee provided focal points to deal with criticism and presented regular reports to bishops to help deal effectively with allegations of clergy sexual misconduct. It also urged the Committees for Bishops' Life and Ministry and Priestly Life and Ministry, the National Federation of Priests' Councils, and the National Organization for Continuing Education of Roman Catholic Clergy to address this concern.
- *Screening candidates for ministry.* Working with the Committee on Priestly Formation and the National Catholic Educational Association, the committee surveyed seminaries on psychological screening and formation of candidates for ordination, focusing on issues of sexuality. Twenty-nine of 36 diocesan seminaries and 24 out of 42 college seminaries responded. They reported varying levels of psychological screening and formation of candidates. The committee proposed specific goals for consideration by the conference.
- *Assisting bishops in assessing possible reassignment.* The issue of reassigning offending clergy to nonparish ministry remained unresolved due to canon laws protecting the rights of clergy. (USCCB 2002).

In 1997, a jury awarded 11 plaintiffs $119.6 million in a record judgment against the diocese of Dallas, Texas. Later that same year, the diocese settled another sexual abuse lawsuit, agreeing to pay five victims $5 million. The following year, the diocese agreed to pay $23.4 million to eight former altar boys and the family of a ninth, who say they were sexually victimized by a priest, Rudolph Kos, who was subsequently removed from the priesthood by the Vatican and is serving a life sentence in prison. Still, the Catholic clergy sexual abuse scandal in the United States remained a sleeping giant.

The Scandal Breaks

On January 6, 2002, the *Boston Globe* launched a series of articles on the case of John Geoghan, a priest of the archdiocese of Boston who had been accused of molesting 130 children, convicted of fondling a 10-year-old boy, and sent to prison. (While in prison, Geoghan was murdered by another inmate.) The *Globe* investigation revealed a widespread pattern of sexual abuse by priests that was covered up by archdiocesan officials. The ensuing public uproar resulted in the resignation of Boston's archbishop, Cardinal Bernard Law, the following December.

It became evident that, despite years of programs, reports, and directives from the USCCB, the archdiocese had done little to respond to complaints of clergy sexual abuse. On the contrary, archdiocesan documents made public and testimony by victims and their families showed an unwillingness by archdiocesan officials to address the issue of clergy sexual abuse of minors. The report further revealed a pattern of intimidation of victims and their families and of protection of offending priests. The Pulitzer Prize–winning series sparked a national crisis of epic proportions.

In April 2002, Pope John Paul II requested a meeting of all U.S. cardinals and USCCB officers with Vatican officials in Rome to discuss the situation. In his address to the meeting, the Pope said:

> The abuse which has caused this crisis is by every standard wrong and rightly considered a crime by society; it is also an appalling sin in the eyes of God. To the victims and their families, wherever they may be, I express my profound sense of solidarity and concern. (Kennedy 2002)

The meeting concluded with a directive from the Vatican that the U.S. bishops prepare a set of national standards and policies for dealing with the sexual abuse of minors by clergy and other church personnel in the United States.

The Dallas Meeting

The following June, *The Charter for the Protection of Children and Young People* was adopted by the USCCB at its general meeting in Dallas, Texas, by a vote of 239–13. The Office of Child and Youth Protection is organized to implement the charter, and a National Review Board (NRB) was formed to monitor the function of the office. At its next general meeting in November, the USCCB adopted the text of the *Essential Norms for Diocesan / Eparchial Policies Dealing with Allegations of Sexual Abuse of Minors by Priests or Deacons.* At its promulgation the following March, the *Essential Norms* became particular law, binding on all dioceses in the United States.

At the same time, the John Jay College of Criminal Justice of the City University of New York was commissioned to embark on a descriptive study of the nature and scope of the problem of sexual abuse of minors by clergy within the Catholic Church in the United States. All diocesan bishops were directed to cooperate fully with the study.

The Scope of the Problem

In February 2004, the NRB released *A Report on the Crisis in the Catholic Church in the United States.* The NRB report was combined with the findings of the John Jay College report entitled *The Nature and Scope of the Problem of Sexual Abuse of Minors by Catholic Priests and Deacons in the United States.* The John Jay study found that, between 1950 and 2002, 10,667 individuals made allegations of sexual abuse against 4,392 priests, roughly 4 percent of the 109,694 priests serving during those 52 years. During that time, approximately 3,300 allegations were not investigated because the accused clergymen were dead, and another 1,000 or so claims proved to be unsubstantiated.

The report estimates that the total cost to the church for payment to victims, for their treatment and the treatment of priests, and legal expenses for defending lawsuits exceeded $533 million. The study also found that more abuse occurred in the 1970s than any other decade, peaking in 1980, and that approximately one-third of all cases were reported in 2002–2003, and two-thirds have been reported since 1993. Prior to 1993, only one-third of cases were known to the church officials.

The ages of the victims vary widely: 27.3 percent were between ages 15 and 17; 50.9 percent were between the ages of 11 and 14; 16 percent were between ages 8 and 10; and 5.8 percent were under age 7. Of the victims, 81 percent were boys and 19 percent were girls. It was found that 149 priests caused 27 percent of allegations. More than half of the accused priests had 1 victim, and 3.5 percent of the priests were accused by more than 10 victims. The following are some highlights of the National Review Board report.

- There were inadequate screening procedures by dioceses and seminaries to weed out candidates unfit for the priesthood.
- There was inadequate seminary formation in the area of celibacy and sexuality.
- There is need of further study concerning the sexual orientation of priests, since 81 percent of the abuse was same-sex in nature.
- There is need of further study concerning celibacy, since the instances of sexual abuse reveal a malformation of human sexuality.
- There are special issues of spiritual life for bishops and priests, since both the acts of abuse by priests and the failure of bishops to put an end to it were "grievously sinful."

Additionally, the report found that, for many bishops, their responses to allegations of abuse "were characterized by moral laxity, excessive leniency, insensitivity, secrecy and neglect." Among issues it cited regarding the bishops were:

- A failure to understand the nature and scope of the abuse and the harm it caused.
- A failure to respond adequately to victims, both pastorally and legally.
- Making unwarranted presumptions in favor of the priest when assessing allegations.
- A culture of clericalism that sought to protect the accused priest.
- Aspects of church law that made it difficult to assess criminal penalties, even when it was clear the priest had violated the law.
- A culture of leniency that failed to recognize the horror of the abuse and the need to condemn it.
- An emphasis on secrecy and avoidance of scandal at all costs.
- Failure to report actions that were civil crimes to civil authorities.
- Overreliance on corrective therapy, depending on psychologists and psychiatrists to "cure" offenders and make them fit to return to ministry.
- Overreliance on attorneys, treating allegations as primarily legal problems rather than problems of pastoral and moral concern.

The report acknowledged that some bishops were aware of the serious nature of the problem early on and spent years trying to convince authorities to change church law so abusers could be taken out of ministry and dealt with more effectively. The study also said that bishops were often ill-served by the therapists and lawyers they depended on for guidance.

The report drew particular attention to the bishops who protected abusers and was very critical of those bishops who failed to act on behalf of victims. Such bishops, the report states, were guilty of neglect and insensitivity toward victims. They not only allowed the abuse to continue, they also spread the abuse and multiplied the number of victims by reassigning molesters to new and unsuspecting parishes.

Developing Safe Environments

With the publication of *The Charter for the Protection of Children and Young People*, 194 of 195 dioceses and archdioceses in the United States enacted Safe Environment programs designed to prevent further sexual abuse of children. All clergy, religious and lay church workers, school teachers, and volunteers must submit to fingerprinting and background checks by the FBI and the Department of Justice. Safe Environment classes and workshops are mandatory for all clergy and lay diocesan, parish, and school personnel. All diocesan and parish personnel must undergo instruction in mandated reporting, the legal responsibility of reporting to police any suspicion of sexual abuse of children. Pastoral settings must provide for adequate supervision of adults with children. No adult, clergy or lay, can be left alone or out of sight of another responsible adult while meeting with children. Children must be taught the dangers of sexual abuse by adults and how to recognize inappropriate behavior by adults. All adults, and especially parents, need to learn how to listen to their children and recognize the signs that a child is being sexually abused.

Developments after 2002

In 2003, the archdiocese of Boston paid $85 million to 552 people who claimed sexual abuse by Roman Catholic priests. In 2004, the diocese of Orange in California settled 90 abuse claims for $100 million. In November 2004, the USCCB established a data collection procedure, whereby dioceses make annual reports regarding allegations of sexual abuse of minors by priests and deacons and the costs associated with the abuse. The Center for Applied Research in the Apostolate (CARA) at Georgetown University was given responsibility for compiling and reporting the data.

According to the CARA reports, there were 898 new allegations of sexual abuse of minors by clergy in 2004, 695 new allegations in 2005, and 635 new allegations against 394 priests or deacons in 2006, in 193 of the 195 dioceses in the United States (Office of Child and Youth Protection et al. 2008). (Two dioceses refused to participate in the survey.) About 70 percent of the reported incidents of sexual abuse occurred between 1960 and 1984. About 70 percent of the accused offenders were either deceased, had already been removed from ministry, or had left the priesthood.

About 60 percent of the priests or deacons named in 2006 had already been accused in previous cases. About 55 percent of the allegations were reported by the victim, according to CARA, and about 80 percent of the victims were boys.

In 2006, dioceses in the United States paid out more than $220 million in settlements to victims. In addition, another $180 million was spent for therapy, support, and legal fees. That compares to a $466.9 million total in 2005. Dioceses also spent over $25 million implementing the prevention and protection programs initiated by the charter.

On July 16, 2007, a judge approved a $660 million settlement between the Roman Catholic archdiocese of Los Angeles and more than 500 alleged victims of clergy abuse. The deal came after more than five years of negotiations and is by far the largest payout by any diocese since the clergy abuse scandal began. The archdiocese also paid $60 million the previous year to settle 45 cases that were not covered by sexual abuse insurance. Before that, the archdiocese, its insurers, and various Roman Catholic orders had paid more than $114 million to settle 86 claims.

In the following years, seven Catholic dioceses declared bankruptcy due to the enormous financial burdens of the settlements. They are Portland, Oregon; Tucson, Arizona; Spokane, Washington; Davenport, Iowa; San Diego, California; Fairbanks, Alaska; and Wilmington, Delaware.

By 2009, there was evidence that cases of abuse had declined sharply and that most of those that did arise were from decades before. Church leaders observed that, while the scandal was an extremely serious matter, it was, in practical terms, caused by a small fraction—perhaps no more than 1 percent—of the total number of 400,000 Catholic priests worldwide. Some Church leaders, such as Archbishop Silvano Maria Tomasi of Geneva, Switzerland, argued, moreover, that the abuse did not stem from the condition of pedophilia as it affected the various clerical offenders but rather was rooted in homosexuality, an argument that angered many gay rights groups for its implication that homosexuality is inherently deviant and/or harmful.

In Ireland, in November 2009, a report was released that revealed the existence of many abuses and various systemic problems in that country, and this was followed in early 2010 by a wave of similar revelations involving other European countries. The scandal once again was in the international headlines, and Church officials, including Pope Benedict XVI, made the matter a top priority. An additional round of new cases in the United States also caught the public's eye. Commentators noted that the gap between lay people's expectations (prosecution of abusers) and the Church's tendency to protect its own (clerical offenders) was finally beginning to close.

Is This Largely a "Catholic Problem"?

The crisis has given rise to considerable controversies and questions. For example, many asked whether priests are more likely to be pedophiles than nonclergy. The term *pedophile* has been used to describe priests accused of sexually abusing children. The American Psychiatric Association defines a pedophile as a person who has intense sexually arousing fantasies, sexual urges, or behaviors involving sexual activity with a prepubescent child or children. A prepubescent child is generally considered to be under age 13. But because prepubescence can be hard to determine, courts generally have set the age below which an accuser may be considered the victim of a pedophile at 11 years. Statistics show that 20 percent of clergy abusers can be accurately described as pedophiles; most have been accused of abusing victims who are younger adolescents.

Why Do Priests Sexually Abuse Minors?

In 1972, and again in 1977, studies by the NCCB/USCC found that more than half of all Catholic priests in the United States were underdeveloped emotionally, and that 8 percent were psychosexually maladjusted. It has been suggested by some researchers that this is due in part to the past practice of recruiting boys into training for the priesthood at an age when they have not yet begun their psychosexual development. At these pre-developing and developing ages, boys perceive the discipline of celibacy simply in terms of avoiding all thoughts, words, and deeds of a sexual nature.

Lacking the opportunities for social and emotional development in these areas, boys can grow into adulthood without the psychological tools needed to function normally in society. Their development can be frozen or fixated at a very early age, so that while they may be chronologically adults, they might still be children emotionally. Therefore, since they lack the ability to control sexual urges when they normally arise, those urges may be directed toward individuals who correspond to the levels of their development. In other words, they may direct their sexual urges toward children and adolescents.

Why Are the Victims Mostly Boys?

It has been suggested by some, most notably Vatican officials, that the problem is largely due to homosexuals in the priesthood. While that may be true, two factors must be considered. The first is that pedophiles, adults who are sexually attracted to prepubescent children, are not necessarily gender specific in their orientation. In other words, pedophiles are not attracted to boys or girls, but rather to children who are not yet sexually differentiated.

Second, in the Catholic culture of the 1950s, 1960s, and 1970s, priests generally had unrestricted access to young boys and adolescent boys. Girls were not permitted to be altar servers, and, in most cases, boys and girls were segregated in Catholic school classrooms and in many parish activities. Catholic parents generally perceived the attentions of priests toward their sons as a good thing. On the other hand, priests who sought the company of girls were regarded with suspicion. Additionally, priests were expected to encourage vocations to the priesthood, and their close association with boys in the parish was considered normal. This allowed much greater freedom for predator priests to target boys.

Why Wasn't the Abuse Reported by Church Officials?

Since the Council of Trent some 400 years ago, the discipline of priestly celibacy had been rigorously enforced. Additionally, bishops were bound by church law to maintain strict secrecy when it came to violations of celibacy. All records of misbehavior by clergy were kept in confidential files, and officials were obliged not to reveal anything that might cause scandal. Any sexual misbehavior by priests was considered a violation of celibacy.

When credible allegations of sexual abuse did arise, offending priests were ordered to cease the behavior. In many instances, the offending priest was transferred to another parish where the sexual abuse continued. When it was determined that a priest had an ongoing problem, he was often sent to a treatment facility where he underwent therapy to resolve the problem. After a period of time, it was determined that the offending priest was no longer a threat to children, and he was returned to parish ministry. At the time, church law would have made it extremely difficult for a bishop to remove a priest from active ministry.

Why Did Bishops Allow the Abuse to Continue?

In some cases, bishops were simply negligent. It has been suggested by some researchers that many bishops lacked the expertise to properly evaluate the suitability of their priests to work safely with children. These bishops relied on the advice and counsel of experts, which, in many cases, was unreliable.

Additionally, it has been suggested that the culture of bishops effectively distanced them from any awareness of the damage sexual abuse was causing children. Insulated from family life and the mainstream of society, they lacked the awareness and sensitivity to adequately understand the problem. They perceived their first responsibility to be the protection of their own, and the welfare of the children became a secondary consideration. Therefore, they failed in their responsibility to care for their people.

Why Didn't Parents Force the Issue?

In the Catholic culture of the 1950s, 1960s, and 1970s, when most of the abuse occurred, respect and reverence for clergy was placed very high on the social scale. It was inconceivable to parents that priests would do such things to their children. The parents, when informed of the abuse, often reacted with denial. Plus, the credibility of children was often questioned. The word of the priest held sway over the stories reported by the children. Compounding the problem, the children lacked the experience and vocabulary to adequately describe what was happening to them. When a child is sexually victimized by a superior adult, the child believes the adult is right, and it is the child who has misbehaved. During testimony that came out in the investigations, many adults who were sexually abused as children reported that they had tried to inform parents but were rebuffed.

Why Did It Take So Long for the Victims to Come Forward?

When a child is sexually abused, he or she must deal with the horror in the only ways available. Without adult allies, children will often repress the memory of abuse in the same way a person will not remember a terrible car accident. The memory of childhood sexual abuse may remain submerged for years until something like a newspaper article or television report will awaken the memory. Adults who have lived for decades with sexual and relational difficulties may suddenly become aware of the events that led to their dysfunction. When that happens, they may still lack the courage to come forward. The experience of shame is a very powerful motivator. It is only with a great deal of effort that individuals can break through the barrier of guilt and report their experiences.

Are Children Safe in Church?

With the implementation of Safe Environment programs in the dioceses, the Catholic Church may now be the safest place for a child to be. Statistics indicate that most sexual abuse of children occurs in the home by family members, trusted family friends, and neighbors. If anything, the sexual abuse scandal has provided society with a new awareness of the threat of sexual predators. The United States will no longer be deaf or blind to the plight of its children.

Church Scandals: Who Is Punished for Church Scandals?

Few would debate that guilty clergy and religious leaders should face legal penalties for their behavior in the same manner that any other citizen should. Furthermore, punitive financial damages (often into the millions of dollars) are a common form of legal recourse in the United States in legal actions against large institutions. However, in the case of a church, are there circumstances that make this a complex issue of justice? There have been church members, both clergy and laity, who have openly wondered whether large-scale financial suits are the most effective, or even fair and just, manner to deal with the issues. In fact, it has been argued that many entirely innocent people are punished by punitive financial awards against a church institution that must then sell property (often quickly), lay off staff, and/or lower salaries, because of the abuses of a minority of church staff and officials. Often the most vulnerable properties, offices, and personnel, are those dealing with minority or marginal communities within the church—and it is arguable that this is much more common in the cases of church institutions losing a large financial court case than a major industrial or commercial company facing a major financial payment. Who, in fact, is paying the price for these settlements of abuse scandals?

See also **Child Abuse; Sex-Offender Registries (vol. 2); Sexual Assault and Sexual Harassment (vol. 2)**

Further Reading

Bausch, William J., *Brave New Church: From Turmoil to Trust.* New London, CT: Twenty-Third Publications, 2001.

Berry, Jason, *Lead Us Not into Temptation: Catholic Priests and the Sexual Abuse of Children.* New York: Doubleday, 1992.

Boston Globe Investigative Staff, *Betrayal: The Crisis in the Catholic Church.* Boston: Little Brown, 2002.

"Clergy and Sexuality," *Christian Century* (March 7, 1990).

Cozzens, Donald B., *The Changing Face of the Priesthood: A Reflection on the Priest's Crisis of Soul.* Collegeville, MN: Liturgical Press, 2000.

Doyle, Thomas P., A. W. Richard Sipe, and Patrick Wall, *Sex, Priests, and Secret Codes: The Catholic Church's 2,000-Year Paper Trail of Sexual Abuse.* Santa Monica, CA: Bonus Books, 2006.

Frawley-O'Dea, Mary Gail, *Perversion of Power: Sexual Abuse in the Catholic Church.* Nashville: Vanderbilt University Press, 2007.

Greeley, Andrew M., *Priests: A Calling in Crisis.* Chicago: University of Chicago Press, 2004.

Jenkins, Phillip, *Pedophiles and Priests: Anatomy of a Contemporary Crisis.* New York: Oxford University Press, 1996.

John Jay College of Criminal Justice, *The Nature and Scope of the Problem of Sexual Abuse of Minors by Catholic Priests and Deacons in the United States.* United States Conference of Catholic Bishops, 2002. http://www.usccb.org/nrb/johnjaystudy/

Kennedy, Frances, "Pope Finally Proclaims That Child Abuse Is Not Just a Sin. It Is a Crime." *Independent* (April 24, 2002).

Lytton, Timothy D., "Clergy Sexual Abuse Litigation: The Policymaking Role of Tort Law." *Connecticut Law Review* 39, no. 3 (February 2007): 809–895.

McMackin, Robert A., et al., eds., *Understanding the Impact of Clergy Sexual Abuse: Betrayal and Recovery.* New York: Routledge, 2009.

Office of Child and Youth Protection, *Charter for the Protection of Children and Young People.* United States Conference of Catholic Bishops, 2005. http://www.usccb.org/ocyp/charter.shtml

Office of Child and Youth Protection, National Review Board, and United States Conference of Catholic Bishops, *Report on the Implementation of the Charter for the Protection of Children and Young People.* March 2008. http://fl1.findlaw.com/news.findlaw.com/hdocs/docs/abuse/usccbabuserpt308.pdf

Plante, Thomas G., ed., *Sin against the Innocent: Sexual Abuse by Priests and the Role of the Catholic Church.* Westport, CT: Praeger, 2004.

Shaefer, Arthur Gross, "Rabbi Sexual Misconduct Crying Out for a Communal Response." *Reconstructionist Rabbinical College Journal* (November 24, 2003).

United States Conference of Catholic Bishops, *Essential Norms for Diocesan/Eparchial Policies Dealing with Allegations of Sexual Abuse of Minors by Priests or Deacons.* 2002. http://www.usccb.org/bishops/norms.shtml

CORPORAL PUNISHMENT

Susan Cody-Rydzewski

One of the most divisive debates in contemporary family sociology and child psychology centers on corporal punishment, known to most persons as spanking. Corporal punishment is the most widespread and well-documented form of family violence. In recent years, scholars as well theologians have debated the question of whether corporal punishment is an appropriate form of child discipline. This debate is particularly interesting in that it is relatively new and it taps into an area of firmly entrenched beliefs and values held by most Americans: that family is a private institution and that government should be minimally involved in guiding or mandating parenting practices. Furthermore, for most of U.S. history, it was assumed that good parents used physical discipline and that an absence of physical punishment would be detrimental to the normal development of children. Indeed, the Society for the Prevention of Cruelty to Animals was established prior to any such organization formed on behalf of children's welfare. Both social as well as religious ideologies strongly legitimated the use of physical punishment in the home. The debate over corporal punishment is so volatile that the few scholars who dare study it empirically seldom have intellectual comrades. This is one area of social life in which even the most progressive-minded individuals find themselves in dissension with academia and perhaps personally conflicted. Indeed, one of the most prominent and widely recognized scholars in this area confronted quite a bit of resistance from publishers when attempting to market his book.

The scholarly study of corporal punishment is relatively new, with the vast majority of empirical studies conducted since the late 1950s. However, a few references to corporal punishment or harsh parenting appeared as early as the 1920s. Interestingly, in the 1960s, a popular magazine reported that there were more child deaths due to parental infliction than due to diseases. Despite this claim, many parental advice books make no mention of corporal punishment whatsoever, suggesting that the decision of whether to use it is a private one and must be decided by individuals. Culturally as well, the phenomenon is often either ignored or presumed normal and inevitable. Not surprisingly, most of these early works found that the vast majority of parents queried admitted to the use of physical punishment. Furthermore, in the early to mid-1900s, the majority of child psychologists approved of or ignored corporal punishment. To be sure, the trend among early scholars and child experts was to either actively endorse or tolerate the use of corporal punishment by parents against children, at least on occasion. One notable exception to this was Benjamin Spock, who was perhaps the most well known pediatrician and parenting expert of the 20th century. In his popular book, *Baby and Child Care,* he argued against the use of corporal punishment unless absolutely necessary. Spock later changed his position, arguing against the use of corporal punishment under all circumstances. Critics of Spock suggest that he led the trend toward more permissive parenting.

Today, experts are divided on the issue, although awareness of the potentially harmful consequences of corporal punishment is higher today than ever before. Consequently, disapproval of corporal punishment seems to have grown somewhat among scholars and those who offer parenting advice, although, even as late as the early 1990s, relatively high levels of support have been found among general practitioners and pediatricians.

Attitudes toward Corporal Punishment

The vast majority of U.S. parents support the use of corporal punishment. This is peculiar in light of the purported overwhelming concern that Americans have about violence in society generally and certainly in relation to children and adolescents. In fact, parents who choose not to spank their children are in violation of a strong social norm and often encounter conflict with others. They may feel the need to justify their decision not to spank, whereas no justification for spanking is required.

Overall, corporal punishment is still commonly being used against U.S. children. A number of Americans actually favor corporal punishment over other methods of child discipline. Most studies of the incidence of corporal punishment reveal that more than 90 percent of children and adolescents have experienced some form of physical punishment. What may be surprising, however, is that the use of corporal punishment is fairly common across the life course of a child, often beginning during infancy and continuing well into adolescence and even into young adulthood. Approximately three-quarters of U.S. parents believe that spanking or slapping a 12-year-old child is necessary sometimes. Furthermore, studies of college students reveal that a significant proportion of them report having been slapped or hit by a parent in the recent past. One study found that one in four 17-year-olds is still being hit by a parent (Straus 2001). The only significant decline is in the use of the most severe kinds of child discipline.

It should be noted, however, that attitudes and actions can be incongruent with regard to corporal punishment. Many Americans who do not verbally endorse corporal punishment do, in fact, spank or slap their children. On the other hand, some of those who endorse it may not use it. Interestingly, attitudes do not predict behavior for parents of toddlers. Almost all U.S. parents of four-year-olds spank regardless of their approval or disapproval of corporal punishment. On the other hand, when looking at older children, attitudes are predictive of behavior. Parents of 16-year-olds who score high on approval of corporal punishment are more likely to use it. Personal experience with corporal punishment seems to be a strong predictor of attitudes as well as actions. Individuals who were spanked or slapped by a parent are more likely than others to indicate that they favor spanking. Furthermore, those who say that they were hit by a parent are more likely to hit their own children, regardless of the children's age. Interestingly, in one study of parents who were hit but later chose not to hit or spank their own children, the influential variables seemed to be the educational level of the parents and their age at parenthood. The parents who decided to go against their upbringing—those who chose *not* to hit—were more highly educated and became parents at later ages.

All states give parents the right to use physical punishment against their children, regardless of the children's age. It may be surprising to learn that even spanking or hitting with an object such as a belt remains legal in the United States. More than 95 percent of parents of three-year-olds reported that they had been hit by their parents. Approximately 60 percent of parents admit to hitting their 10- to 12-year-old children. The lasting effect or mental imprint of having been physically punished is evident in the finding that 40 percent of adults over the age of 60 can recall being hit by their parents.

Little difference has been found between single-parent and two-parent families when it comes to the use of corporal punishment. It does appear that boys are hit more often than girls, although rates are not vastly discrepant. Adolescent boys are hit by both mothers and fathers, while adolescent girls are more often hit by mothers. There is evidence to show that mothers, in general, use corporal punishment more often than fathers, but this is generally assumed to be a consequence of the different amounts of time parents spend with children, with mothers spending considerably more time with children than fathers. Since it is known that men are more physically aggressive and more violent in all other areas of social life, it is assumed that if men spent as much time with children as women did, the use of corporal punishment by fathers would exceed that of mothers.

Religiosity, Region, and Corporal Punishment

Support for corporal punishment in the United States historically has always been high and is often linked to religious or regional factors. Violence against children and babies is well documented and dates back to the biblical period. Historically, most forms of child punishment would today be considered severe child abuse. Parents were instructed to chastise and control errant children through such methods as swaddling, whipping, burning, drowning, castration, and abandonment. Puritans held a strict belief in original sin, and parents were instructed to, in a very literal sense, beat the devil out of their children. Early U.S. schools used corporal punishment so frequently that the birch rod became a symbol of education. The not-too-distant past contains reports of special education teachers twisting and grabbing students' arms, hitting or banging their heads onto desks, and smearing hot sauce into their faces and mouths.

In the 1970s, it was found that Baptists were more likely to have experienced physical punishment at home than were persons from other denominations. In general, corporal punishment is more strongly supported by conservative or fundamentalist Protestants than by others. This association is explained by the emphasis on biblical literalism, biblical inerrancy, and original sin found among these religious traditions. In addition, Christians from more conservative traditions often embrace a view of the family that is hierarchical—with children, as well as wives, subsumed under the headship of men. Fundamentalist Protestants and conservative Catholics are also more likely than others to support the use of corporal punishment in schools. Not surprisingly, it also has been found that conservative Protestants are, for the most part, not persuaded by social science research to modify their familial practices. On the contrary, conservatives may identify social science scholarship, as well as intellectual pursuits more generally, as antithetical to Christian beliefs and threatening to family life. Popular theologian and author James Dobson, for example, has explicitly rejected the use of scientific inquiry to explore the appropriateness of various parenting practices. Dobson has also suggested that children suffer from an inherent predisposition toward selfishness and rebellion.

ALTERNATIVES TO CORPORAL PUNISHMENT

Past studies have considered the effects of using various methods of discipline on child outcomes. For instance, the use of reasoning alone has proven to be just as effective in correcting disobedience as the use of reasoning combined with corporal punishment. Time-out is a type of punishment in which a child is removed from a volatile situation for a short period of time. The rationale underlying time-out is that removing someone from a reinforcing situation deters and discourages him or her from repeating the offense. Time-out is based on a contingency model of human behavior that suggests that some combination of removal of or provision of valued or devalued resources will shape behaviors. Parents and teachers may increase good behaviors and decrease bad behaviors by either giving the child something he or she values, such as praise, toys, or tokens, or by removing something important or by removing the child from a pleasurable or enjoyable experience.

It has been shown that mothers who use time-out without physical correction are just as effective in controlling their children as mothers who use time-out with physical enforcement. Long-term studies reveal that behavior problems improve if and when parents desist in the use of corporal punishment. Today, many parenting experts and family scholars recommend some combination of providing clear guidelines, role modeling, rewarding good behavior, and demonstrating love and affection to children as the most effective ways to elicit good behavior. Screaming, criticizing, and limiting recognition of bad behavior are all discouraged, because they exacerbate behavior problems in children. In general, children whose parents give them prescriptive or affirmative instructions (telling children what to do rather than what not to do), praise them often, model appropriate behavior, and use calming reinforcements, such as time-out, are more well adjusted and better behaved than children whose parents rely on escalating methods such as yelling and spanking. Over time, children's noncompliance may result in the parents intensifying these methods, which increases the risk of physical or verbal abuse against the child.

Attitudes toward corporal punishment vary regionally as well. In general, persons living in the Southeast are more likely to approve of corporal punishment, both at home and in schools. This is not surprising in light of other findings that reveal that Southerners hold more conservative attitudes in many areas, including gender roles, sexuality, race, and religion. In particular, the association between region and approval of corporal punishment has been linked to the predominance of religious conservatism and biblical literalism found in the southern region of the United States. In fact, a small number of states concentrated in what is commonly referred to as the Bible Belt—including Alabama, Mississippi, Tennessee, Georgia, and South Carolina—account for the majority of school spankings nationally. Interestingly, recent studies demonstrate that the most noteworthy aspect of regional variation in corporal punishment attitudes does not center on the South's approval of corporal punishment, but rather the rejection of corporal punishment found in the Northeast. In general, the Northeastern region has the least amount of legitimate, or culturally sanctioned, violence.

Southern support for corporal punishment has also been linked to lower levels of education, lower household incomes, and racial composition. It should be noted, however, that research in this area has resulted in a myriad of findings, some of which are complex and contradictory. For example, African American parents have been shown to express approval for corporal punishment at higher levels than whites, although some studies find that white parents are more likely than African American parents to use corporal punishment. In addition, some studies find little or no correlation between the use of corporal punishment and socioeconomic status, presumably because support for corporal punishment in the United States has been, and continues to be, extremely high due to a variety of social, cultural, and religious reasons.

In conclusion, it has been found that mothers spank more than fathers and younger parents more than older parents. Individuals who were spanked as children are more likely than others to spank their own children. Also, spouses involved in violent marriages are more likely to hit their children than spouses in nonabusive relationships. The relationship between social class and use of corporal punishment has been researched extensively, and this research has produced mixed findings. Perhaps an accurate summary statement is that, while some studies find greater approval and more use of corporal punishment among lower-income households, corporal punishment is so widely accepted and approved in U.S. culture that it is commonly found among and across all social classes.

Effects of Corporal Punishment

The effects of corporal punishment are well documented and sobering. Studies reveal that individuals who were physically punished by parents or caregivers are more likely to be physically aggressive with others, including one's spouse; to severely attack one's siblings; to imagine or engage in masochistic sexual practices; to physically abuse one's children; to have depressive symptoms and suicidal thoughts; to become delinquent as a juvenile; and to have lower lifetime earnings. The more often one was subjected to corporal punishment during adolescence, the lower the chances of being in the top 20 percent of all wage earners. It is worth reiterating that, contrary to conventional wisdom, a number of studies demonstrate that spanking children actually places them at greater risk for adjustment and behavior problems.

It has also been found that states in which teachers are permitted to hit children have a higher rate of student violence as well as a higher homicide rate. Nations that approve of the use of corporal punishment by teachers have higher infant murder rates than do other nations. This association is explained by using a so-called cultural spillover theory. That is, nations that strongly support corporal punishment in schools tend to have wide levels of support for the practice and consequently high rates of its usage at all ages and across varying circumstances and situations. Therefore, the likelihood that someone—a parent, teacher, day care worker, or clergyperson—will use corporal punishment, even against an infant, is higher in such societies. Furthermore, the likelihood of corporal punishment resulting in death is obviously much higher for infants than for other age groups.

See also **Child Abuse**

Further Reading

Bitensky, Susan H., *Corporal Punishment of Children: A Human Rights Violation.* Ardsley, NY: Transnational Publishers, 2006.

Crary, Elizabeth, *Without Spanking or Spoiling: A Practical Approach to Toddler and Preschool Guidance.* Seattle: Parenting Press, 1993.

Donnelly, Michael, and Murray A. Stras, eds., *Corporal Punishment of Children in Theoretical Perspective.* New Haven, CT: Yale University Press, 2005.

Hyman, Irwin A., *Reading, Writing, and the Hickory Stick: The Appalling Story of Physical and Psychological Abuse in American Schools.* Lexington, MA: Lexington Books, 1990.

Spock, Benjamin, *Baby and Child Care.* New York: Simon & Schuster, 1996.

Straus, Murray A., *Beating the Devil out of Them: Corporal Punishment in American Families and Its Effects on Children.* New Brunswick, NJ: Transaction Publishers, 2001.

Wyckoff, Jerry L., and Barbara C. Unell, *Discipline without Shouting or Spanking: Practical Solutions to the Most Common Preschool Behavior Problems.* Minnetonka, MN: Meadowbrook Press, 2002.

CREATIONISM, INTELLIGENT DESIGN, AND EVOLUTION

Glenn Branch

Evolution is clearly the most controversial topic in the public school science curriculum in the United States. Among scientists worldwide, there is no significant controversy about the basic scientific issues: the Earth is ancient (about 4.5 billion years old); living things have descended, with modification, from common ancestors; and natural selection, by adapting living things to their environments, is a major driving force in the history of life. As the National Academy of Sciences (2008) observes, "The scientific consensus around evolution is overwhelming." Recognizing the centrality of evolution to biology, the National Association of Biology Teachers and the National Science Teachers Association have taken a firm stand on the pedagogical necessity of teaching evolution. Teaching evolution is a matter of social controversy, however, because of the prevalence of creationism—the rejection of a scientific explanation of the history of life in favor of a supernatural account—among the public. Not all antievolutionists are creationists, and not all creationists are fundamentalist Christians—there are creationists who identify themselves with Jewish, Islamic, Hindu, New Age, and Native American religious traditions. But the juggernaut of antievolutionist activity in the United States is propelled above all by Christian fundamentalism.

The Creationist Crusade

Creationists are not unanimous in their attitudes toward the antiquity of the Earth, common ancestry, and the efficacy of natural selection. Those who reject all three are called young-Earth or recent creationists; young-Earth creationism is currently the dominant form of creationism in the United States. Those who reject only the latter two are usually called old-Earth creationists; different forms of old-Earth creationism, corresponding to different interpretations of the book of Genesis to accommodate the antiquity of the Earth, include Day/Age and Gap creationism. There is not a standard term for creationists who reject only the efficacy of natural selection, perhaps reflecting their relative unimportance in the debate. The latest incarnation of creationism—intelligent design—is strategically vague in its attitudes toward the age of the Earth and common ancestry, in the hope of maintaining a big tent under which creationists of all varieties are welcome to shelter; its representatives run the gamut from antiselectionist creationists to young-Earth creationists, while the bulk of its public support seems to be provided by young-Earth creationists.

In its traditional forms, creationism is typically based on biblical inerrantism—the belief that the Bible, as God's word, is necessarily accurate and authoritative in matters of science and history as well as in matters of morals and doctrine. Inerrantism allows for the nonliteral interpretation of metaphorical or figurative language, and thus young-Earth and old-Earth creationists are able to agree on the principle of inerrantism while disagreeing on its application. Mindful of the legal failures of attempts to include creationism in the public school classroom, proponents of intelligent design sedulously disavow any commitment to the Bible, but such a commitment tends to surface nevertheless—for example, in their frequent invocation of the Gospel of John's opening verse, "In the beginning was the Word…"Whether avowing inerrantism or not, creationists typically express a passionate concern for the supposed moral consequences

CREATIONISM, INTELLIGENT DESIGN, AND EVOLUTION WEB SITES

Following is a sampling of organizations (and their Web sites) that are active in controversies over creationism, evolution, and their places in public science education. Where applicable, a relevant subsection of the Web sites is identified.

Creationist Web Sites

Young-Earth Creationist Organizations

- Answers in Genesis: http://www.answersingenesis.org
- Creation Research Society: http://www.creationresearch.org
- Institute for Creation Research: http://www.icr.org

Old-Earth Creationist Organization

- Reasons to Believe: http://www.reasons.org

Intelligent Design Organizations

- The Discovery Institute's Center for Science and Culture: http://www.discovery.org/csc
- Intelligent Design Network: http://www.intelligentdesignnetwork.org

Evolution Web Sites

Scientific Organizations

- American Association for the Advancement of Science: http://www.aaas.org/news/press_room/evolution
- The National Academies: http://www.nationalacademies.org/evolution/

Science Education Organizations

- National Association of Biology Teachers: http://www.nabt.org/
- National Science Teachers Association: http://www.nsta.org/publications/evolution.aspx

Anticreationist Organizations

- National Center for Science Education: http://www.ncseweb.org
- TalkOrigins Foundation: http://www.talkorigins.org

of the acceptance of evolution; the "tree of evil"—with evolution at its root and various evils, real and imagined, as its branches—is a common image in creationist literature. Creationism is primarily a moral crusade.

It is a crusade that is waged against any public exposition of evolution—in recent years, national parks, science museums, public television stations, and municipal zoos have faced challenges to their presentations of evolution—but the primary battleground is the public school system. Attempts to remove, balance, or compromise the teaching of evolution occur at every level of governance: from the individual classroom (where teachers may be creationists, or may mistakenly think it fair to present creationism along with evolution, or may decide to omit evolution to avoid controversy), to the local school district, to the state government's executive or legislative branch or even—rarely, and then usually as a mere token of support—to the federal government. Such attempts are a recurring feature of U.S. science education from the 1920s onward, in a basically sinusoidal trajectory. Whenever there is a significant improvement in the extent or quality of evolution education, a creationist backlash quickly ensues, only to meet with resistance and ultimately defeat in the courts.

From *Scopes* to *Edwards*

The first phase of the antievolutionist movement in the United States, beginning after the close of World War I, involved attempts to constrain or ban the teaching of evolution in response to its appearance in high school textbooks around the turn of the century. Due in part to the rise of organized fundamentalism, antievolution legislation was widely proposed (in 20 states between 1921 and 1929) and sometimes enacted (in Arkansas, Florida, Mississippi, Oklahoma, and Tennessee). It was Tennessee's Butler Act, which forbade teachers in the public schools "to teach any theory that denies the story of the Divine Creation of man as taught in the Bible, and to teach instead that man has descended from a lower order of animals," under which John Thomas Scopes was prosecuted in 1925. Although Scopes's conviction was overturned on appeal, on a technicality, the trial exerted a chilling influence on science education. Under the pressure of legislation, administrative decree, and public opinion, evolution swiftly disappeared from textbooks and curricula across the country.

It was not until after the launching of *Sputnik* in 1957 that evolution returned to the public school science classroom. Fearing a loss of scientific superiority to the Soviet Union, the federal government funded a massive effort to improve science education, which included a strong emphasis on evolution. Particularly important were the biology textbooks produced by the Biological Science Curriculum Study (BSCS), established in 1959 by a grant from the National Science Foundation to the education committee of the American Institute of Biological Sciences. The popular BSCS textbooks, written with the aid of biologists such as Hermann J. Muller (who complained of the inadequate treatment of evolution in biology textbooks in a famous address entitled "One Hundred Years without Darwin Are Enough"), treated evolution as a central theme, and commercial publishers began to follow suit. Meanwhile, the Tennessee legislature repealed the Butler Act in 1967, anticipating the Supreme Court's decision in *Epperson v. Arkansas* (1968) that laws prohibiting the teaching of evolution in the public schools violate the Establishment Clause of the First Amendment.

After it was no longer possible to ban the teaching of evolution, creationists increasingly began to argue that creationism was a viable scientific alternative that deserved to be taught alongside evolution. Poised to take the lead was young-Earth creationism,

> This textbook contains material on evolution. Evolution is a theory, not a fact, regarding the origin of living things. This material should be approached with an open mind, studied carefully, and critically considered.
>
> ***Approved by***
> ***Cobb County Board of Education***
> ***Thursday, March 28, 2002***

Figure 1. The Cobb County, Georgia, evolution warning sticker (2002–2005)

in the form of the creation science movement, which contended that there is scientific evidence that the Earth (and the universe) are relatively young (on the order of 10,000 years), that the Earth was inundated by a global flood responsible for a mass extinction and for major geological features such as the Grand Canyon, and that evolution is impossible except within undefined but narrow limits (since living things were created to reproduce "after their own kind"). Organizations such as the Creation Research Society (CRS) and the Institute for Creation Research (ICR) were founded in 1963 and 1972, respectively, ostensibly to promote scientific research supporting creationism. Creation science remained absent from the scientific literature but was increasingly prominent in controversies over science education.

During the second phase of the antievolution movement, science teachers, school administrators, and textbook publishers found themselves pressured to provide equal time to creation science. Creationists started to prepare their own textbooks, such as the CRS's *Biology: A Search for Order in Complexity* (1970) and the ICR's *Scientific Creationism* (1974), for use in the public schools. The movement received a boost in 1980 from Republican presidential nominee Ronald Reagan, who endorsed teaching creationism whenever evolution was taught. And legislation calling for equal time for creationism was introduced in no fewer than 27 states, successfully in both Arkansas and Louisiana in 1981. But both laws were ruled unconstitutional, the Arkansas law by a federal district court (*McLean v. Arkansas* 1982) and the Louisiana law ultimately by the Supreme Court (*Edwards v. Aguillard* 1987), on the grounds that teaching creationism in the public schools violates the Establishment Clause.

Intelligent Design

In the wake of the decision in *Edwards,* which held that the Louisiana law impermissibly endorsed religion "by advancing the religious belief that a supernatural being

A MESSAGE FROM THE ALABAMA STATE
BOARD OF EDUCATION

This textbook discusses evolution, a controversial theory some scientists present as a scientific explanation for the origin of living things, such as plants, animals and humans.

No one was present when life first appeared on earth. Therefore, any statement about life's origins should be considered as theory, not fact.

The word "evolution" may refer to many types of change. Evolution describes changes that occur within a species. (White moths, for example, may "evolve" into gray moths.) This process is microevolution, which can be observed and described as fact. Evolution may also refer to the change of one living thing to another, such as reptiles into birds. This process, called macroevolution, has never been observed and should be considered a theory. Evolution also refers to the unproven belief that random, undirected forces produced a world of living things.

There are many unanswered questions about the origin of life which are not mentioned in your textbook, including:

- Why did major groups of animals suddenly appear in fossil record (known as the "Cambrian Explosion")?

- Why have no new major groups of living things appeared in the fossil record for a long time?

- Why do major groups of plants and animals have no transitional forms in the fossil record?

- How did you and all living things come to possess such a complete and complex set of "Instructions" for building a living body?

Figure 2. The Alabama evolution warning sticker (1996–2001)

created humankind," a group of creationists sought to devise a form of creationism able to survive constitutional scrutiny. A scant two years after *Edwards,* intelligent design was introduced to a wide audience in *Of Pandas and People* (1989; second edition 1993), produced by a fundamentalist organization called the Foundation for Thought and Ethics (FTE) and intended for use as a supplementary biology textbook. Like its creation science predecessors, *Of Pandas and People* contended that evolution was a theory in crisis, on the common creationist assumption that (supposed) evidence against evolution is perforce evidence for creationism. Unlike them, however, it attempted to maintain a studied neutrality on the identity and nature of the designer, as well as on issues, such as the age of the Earth, on which creationists differ.

During the 1990s, the intelligent design movement coalesced, with its de facto headquarters shifting from FTE to the Center for the Renewal of Science and Culture (later renamed the Center for Science and Culture), founded in 1996 as a division of the Discovery Institute, a think tank based in Seattle. At the same time, as states began to introduce state science standards, which provide guidelines for local school districts to follow in their individual science curricula, the treatment of evolution was improving, penetrating even to districts and schools where creationism was taught—the Supreme Court's decision in *Edwards* notwithstanding—or where evolution was downplayed or omitted altogether. (The importance of state science standards was cemented by the federal No Child Left Behind Act, enacted in 2002, which requires states to develop and periodically revise standards.) The stage was set for the third phase of the antievolution movement, which is going on today.

Like the creation science movement before it, the intelligent design movement claimed to favor a top-down approach, in which the scientific establishment would be convinced first, with educational reform following in due course. But like creation science before it, intelligent design was in fact aimed at the public schools. Supporters of intelligent design have attempted to have *Of Pandas and People* approved for use in Alabama and Idaho; proposed laws to require or allow the teaching of intelligent design in at least eight states; and attempted to rewrite state science standards in at least four states, including Kansas, where, in 2005, the state board of education rewrote the standards to disparage the scientific status of evolution. As with a similar episode in 1999, the antievolution faction on the board lost its majority in the next election, and the rewritten standards were abandoned in 2007. Such activity at the state level was mirrored at the local level, where attempts to require or allow the teaching of intelligent design caused uproar sporadically across the country.

In the small Pennsylvania town of Dover, the result was the first legal challenge to the constitutionality of teaching intelligent design in the public schools, *Kitzmiller v. Dover.* After a summer of wrangling over evolution in biology textbooks, the Dover school board adopted a policy in October 2004 providing that "[s]tudents will be made aware of gaps/problems in Darwin's Theory and of other theories of evolution including, but not limited to, intelligent design." The board subsequently required a disclaimer to be read aloud in the classroom, according to which evolution is a "Theory…not a fact," "Gaps in the Theory exist for which there is no evidence," and intelligent design as presented in *Of Pandas and People* is a credible scientific alternative to evolution. Eleven local parents filed suit in federal district court, arguing that the policy violated the Establishment Clause. The court agreed, writing that it was "abundantly clear that the Board's ID Policy violates the Establishment Clause," adding, "In making this determination, we have addressed the seminal question of whether ID is science. We have concluded that it is not, and moreover that ID cannot uncouple itself from its creationist, and thus religious, antecedents."

The Fallback Strategy

Like *McLean, Kitzmiller* was tried in a federal district court, and the decision is directly precedential only in the district. (The Dover school board chose not to appeal the decision, in part because the supporters of the policy on the school board were defeated at the polls.) Thus, there is no decisive ruling at the highest judicial level that explicitly addresses the constitutionality of teaching intelligent design in the public schools so far, and it is possible that a future case will ultimately produce a decision by the Supreme Court. Even before the *Kitzmiller* verdict, however, the Center for Science and Culture was already retreating from its previous goal of requiring the teaching of intelligent design in favor of what it called "teaching the controversy"—in effect, a fallback strategy of attacking evolution without mentioning any creationist alternative. To its creationist supporters, such a strategy offers the promise of accomplishing the goal of encouraging students to acquire or retain a belief in creationism while not running afoul of the Establishment Clause. Unless there is a significant change in church/state jurisprudence, forms of the fallback strategy are likely to become increasingly prominent in the antievolution movement.

A perennially popular form of the fallback strategy involves oral and written disclaimers. Between 1974 and 1984, for example, the state of Texas required textbooks to carry a disclaimer that any material on evolution included in the book is to be regarded as "theoretical rather than factually verifiable"; in 1984, the state attorney general declared that the disclaimer was unconstitutional. The state of Alabama began to require evolution disclaimers in textbooks in 1996; the original disclaimer (since revised twice) described evolution as "a controversial theory some scientists present as a scientific explanation for the origin of living things, such as plants, animals and humans." Disclaimers have been challenged in court twice. In *Freiler v. Tangipahoa* (1997), a policy requiring teachers to read a disclaimer that conveyed the message that evolution is a religious viewpoint at odds with accepting the Bible was ruled to be unconstitutional. In *Selman v. Cobb County* (2005), a textbook disclaimer describing evolution as "a theory, not a fact" was ruled to be unconstitutional, but the decision was vacated on appeal and remanded to the trial court, where a settlement was reached.

Attacking the content of textbooks is also a perennially popular form of the fallback strategy, especially in so-called adoption states, where textbooks are selected by a state agency for use throughout the state, and the publishers consequently have a strong incentive to accommodate the demands of the agency. In Texas, Educational Research

Associates (ERA), founded by the husband-and-wife team of Mel and Norma Gabler, lobbied the state board of education against evolution in textbooks, succeeding in having the BSCS textbooks removed from the list of state-approved textbooks in 1969. Owing both to changes in the Texan political landscape and opposition from groups concerned with civil liberties and science education, ERA's influence waned in the 1980s. But the tradition is alive and well: while evaluating biology textbooks for adoption in 2003, the Texas board of education was inundated with testimony from creationists complaining of mistaken and fraudulent information in the textbooks. All 11 textbooks under consideration were adopted nevertheless.

Calling for critical analysis of evolution—and, significantly, *only* of evolution, or of evolution and a handful of issues that are similarly controversial, such as global warming or stem-cell research—is the latest form of the fallback strategy. Its most conspicuous venture so far was in Ohio, where, in 2002, after a dispute over whether to include intelligent design in the state science standards was apparently resolved, the state board of education voted to include in the standards a requirement that students be able to "describe how scientists continue to investigate and critically analyze aspects of evolutionary theory." The requirement served as a pretext for the adoption in 2004 of a corresponding model lesson plan that, relying on a number of creationist publications, appeared to be intended to instill scientifically unwarranted doubts about evolution. Following the decision in *Kitzmiller* and the revelation that the board ignored criticisms of the lesson plan from experts at the Ohio Department of Education, the board reversed itself in 2006, voting to rescind the lesson plan and to remove the "critical analysis" requirement from the standards.

Conclusion

The United States is not the only country with controversies about evolution in the public schools: In recent years, such controversies have been reported in Brazil, Canada, Germany, Italy, Malaysia, the Netherlands, Poland, Russia, Serbia, Turkey, and the United Kingdom. But the United States is clearly exceptional in the amount and influence of creationist activity—and of creationist belief. Comparing the levels of acceptance of evolution in the United States with those in 32 European countries and Japan, a recent report noted, "Only Turkish adults were less likely to accept the concept of evolution than American adults" (Miller, Scott, and Okamoto 2006) and plausibly attributed resistance to evolution among the U.S. public to three factors: the acceptance of fundamentalist religious beliefs, the politicization of science, and the widespread ignorance of biology. Longitudinally, the report adds, "After 20 years of public debate, the percentage of U.S. adults accepting the idea of evolution has declined from 45% to 40% and the percentage of adults overtly rejecting evolution declined from 48% to 39%. The percentage of adults who were not sure about evolution increased from 7% in 1985 to 21% in 2005."

These attitudes appear to be reflected in the public's attitude toward the teaching of evolution in the public schools. According to a pair of national polls (CBS News, November 2004; *Newsweek,* December 2004), a majority—60–65 percent—favors teaching creationism along with evolution, while a large minority—37–40 percent—favors teaching creationism instead of evolution. The situation is perhaps not quite so dire as these data suggest, however; in a poll that offered respondents a wider array of choices, only 13 percent favored teaching creationism as a "scientific theory" along with evolution, and 16 percent favored teaching creationism instead of evolution (DYG Inc., on behalf of the People for the American Way Foundation, November 1999). Still, it seems clear that, among the public, there is a reservoir of creationist sentiment, which frequently splashes toward the classroom. In a recent informal survey among members of the National Science Teachers Association (March 2005), 30 percent of respondents indicated that they experienced pressure to omit or downplay evolution and related topics from their science curriculum, while 31 percent indicated that they felt pressure to include nonscientific alternatives to evolution in their science classroom.

In addition to whatever creationist sympathies there are in the public at large, reinforced by the efforts of a creationist counterestablishment, there are also systemic factors that combine to sustain creationism and inhibit evolution education. Perhaps the most important among these is the decentralized nature of the public school system in the United States. There are over 15,000 local school districts, each with a degree of autonomy over curriculum and instruction, typically governed by a school board comprised of elected members of the community usually without any special training in either science or education. Each district thus offers a chance for creationist activists—who may, of course, be elected to school boards themselves—to pressure the school board to remove, balance, or compromise the teaching of evolution. Also important is the comparative lack of attention to preparing educators to understand evolution and to teach it effectively. Especially in communities with a tradition of ignorance of, skepticism about, and hostility toward evolution, it is not surprising that teachers who are neither knowledgeable about evolution nor prepared to teach it effectively often quietly decide to avoid any possible controversy.

There are signs of hope for supporters of the teaching of evolution, however, in addition to the consistency with which courts have ruled against the constitutionality of efforts to remove, balance, or compromise the teaching of evolution. Rallied by the spate of intelligent design activity, the scientific community is increasing its public engagement and advocacy, including outreach efforts to science educators in the public schools. Academic work in the burgeoning field of science and religion is producing a renewed interest in exploring ways to reconcile faith with science, while over 10,000 members of the Christian clergy have endorsed a statement affirming the compatibility of evolution with their faith. And the increasing economic importance of the applied biological sciences, of which evolution is a central principle, is likely to be increasingly cited in defense of the teaching of evolution. Still, controversies over the teaching of evolution are clearly going to continue for the foreseeable future.

See also **Prayer in Public Schools; Religious Symbols on Government Property**

Further Reading

Alters, B. J., and S. M. Alters, *Defending Evolution: A Guide to the Evolution/Creation Controversy,* Sudbury, MA: Jones and Bartlett, 2001.

Bowler, Peter J., *Monkey Trials and Gorilla Sermons: Evolution and Christianity from Darwin to Intelligent Design.* Cambridge, MA: Harvard University Press, 2007.

Giberson, Karl, *Saving Darwin: How to Be a Christian and Believe in Evolution.* New York: HarperOne, 2008.

Larson, Edward J., *Trial and Error: The American Controversy over Creation and Evolution,* 3d ed. New York: Oxford University Press, 2003.

Miller, J. D., E. C. Scott, and S. Okamoto, "Public Acceptance of Evolution." *Science* 313 (2006): 765–766.

Miller, Kenneth R., *Only a Theory: Evolution and the Battle for America's Soul.* New York: Viking Press, 2008.

Moore, Randy, and Mark D. Decker, *More than Darwin: An Encyclopedia of the People and Places of the Evolution-Creationism Controversy.* Westport, CT: Greenwood Press, 2008.

National Academy of Sciences and Institute of Medicine, *Science, Evolution, and Creationism.* Washington DC: National Academies Press, 2008.

Numbers, Ronald J., *The Creationists: From Scientific Creationism to Intelligent Design,* rev. ed. Cambridge, MA: Harvard University Press, 2006.

Petto, Andrew J., and Laurie R. Godfrey, *Scientists Confront Intelligent Design and Creationism.* New York: W. W. Norton, 2007.

Scott, Eugenie C., *Evolution vs. Creationism: An Introduction,* 2d ed. Berkeley: University of California Press, 2009.

Singham, Mano, *God vs. Darwin: The War between Evolution and Creationism in the Classroom.* Lanham, MD: Rowman & Littlefield Education, 2009.

D

DEADBEAT PARENTS

A question that has appeared in recent years, largely as a result of the increases in divorce and nonmarital child bearing, is the question of whether child support enforcement leads to an increase in deadbeat parents. Over the last few decades, the United States has witnessed an increase in the number of parents, mainly fathers, who are not taking responsibility for their children. Many of these parents have come to public attention through the child support system. The child support system is fundamentally an economic phenomenon run by the various states with federal oversight and guidelines. Historically, its focus was on either recovering welfare money for the government or on preventing the government from having to expend money on single mothers and their children. However, in recent years, the focus has expanded to include ensuring the health and well-being of the nation's children. Along with this expanded focus has come an increase in the strict enforcement of child support obligations. Consequently, some parents who fail to comply with their child support obligations, for whatever reason, are at risk for fines and imprisonment and are labeled deadbeat parents. In fact, the Deadbeat Parents Punishment Act makes it a federal offense for a noncustodial parent to willfully fail to pay past-due support obligations for a child residing in another state.

Referring to these parents as deadbeats has spawned great debate regarding how child support is conducted in the United States. On one side of the debate are child advocates who suggest that we need to be more aggressive with child support policies in an effort to reduce childhood poverty. On the other side are fathers' rights activists who argue that the current child support system is unjust in that it favors women in most actions that pertain to the child, leaving fathers out.

Child Support

Child support is the transfer of resources to a child living apart from a parent. The most common type of transfer is direct financial payment to the custodial parent on behalf of the child. However, child support can be indirect in the form of medical insurance and care, dental care, child care, or educational support.

The transfer of resources occurs at both the private and public level. Private child support is paid by the noncustodial parent to the custodial parent. The majority of custodial parents have some type of agreement or court award to receive financial and nonfinancial support from the noncustodial parent for their children. In most cases, these are legal agreements established by a court or other governmental entity, such as the local child support agency. Although the majority of custodial parents have legal agreements for child support, about 40 percent of custodial parents do not have such agreements or have informal agreements with the noncustodial parent. According to the U.S. Census Bureau, the three most-often cited reasons for the lack of child support agreements are: (1) custodial parents did not feel the need to go court or to get legal agreements; (2) the other parent provided what he or she could for support; and (3) the other parent could not afford to pay child support.

On the other hand, public child support is paid for by the state on behalf of a child living in poverty in the form of public assistance, such as Temporary Assistance to Needy Families (TANF); food stamps; Medicaid; or Women, Infants, and Children. Roughly, about one-third of all custodial parents receive some form of child support–related assistance from the state. Historically, child support was a means for the state to receive reimbursement from noncustodial fathers for public child support expenditures. In the case of public child support, it is the government and not the custodial parent who is the direct beneficiary of the noncustodial parent's financial payment. In fact, some scholars and fathers' rights activists suggest that it is the reimbursement of public child support that has stimulated interest in stricter child support enforcement.

The Transformation of Child Support in the United States

Child support in its present form has not always existed. Initially child support was considered a civil matter. Since the arrival of settlers in America, child support has existed in some form, with parental responsibility at the heart of collections of aid. Child support has its foundations in the Elizabethan Poor Laws of 1601, sometimes referred to as the English Poor Laws. The English Poor Laws were a system of relief to the poor that was financed and administered at the local level (parishes). The poor were divided into three groups: able-bodied adults, children, and the elderly or non–able-bodied. The overseers of the poor relief system were to put the able-bodied to work, to give apprenticeships to poor children, and to provide "competent sums of money" to relieve the non–able-bodied. It is this system of assistance to the needy that British settlers brought with them to America.

Child Support in Colonial America

Colonial child support had a slow start. In colonial America, when a couple married, the wife's identity merged with that of her husband. Women did not have the right to hold property, so the husband controlled and managed all property. In return, the husband was obligated to provide for his wife and children. Fathers had a *nonenforceable* duty to support their children. Under the Poor Laws, child support was considered a civil matter. Although desertion was rare, when a man did desert his family, the local community would provide for the mother and child to prevent destitution. In return, local communities would attempt to recover from the father monies spent in support of the mother and child. The money collected from the father was put back into the poor relief system's reserves. However, near the end of the 18th century, as the population increased, there was an accompanying increase in the numbers of individuals needing assistance, which eventually caused a breakdown of the colonial poor relief system.

Child Support Enforcement and the Making of the Deadbeat Dad

The revolutionary changes brought about by the industrialization and urbanization of the 19th century encouraged courts to strengthen the child support system. During this period, divorce and child custody laws were transformed. For instance, child custody laws that had previously favored the fathers in divorce began to favor the mother, increasingly granting custody of the child to mothers. Therefore, when divorce and desertion rates increased, many mothers and their children became dependent on the state for subsistence. In response to this rise in the utilization of and dependency on public resources, states began to make child support a criminal matter by establishing a legally *enforceable* child support duty. State legislators passed desertion and nonsupport statutes that criminalized and punished fathers for their refusal to support their child, especially if the mother and child were recipients of public child support. Fathers who failed to comply with child support were either fined or imprisoned.

Despite states' efforts to improve child support enforcement and to reduce public child support expenditures, a sizable number of fathers and husbands fled the state to avoid their child support obligations, leaving a host of mothers and children destitute and dependent on public child support services. In the mid-20th century, the Uniform Reciprocal Enforcement of Support Act implemented federal guidelines that made fathers who moved from state to state to avoid child support still responsible for their children through both civil and criminal enforcement. Yet these guidelines caused confusion between states regarding the jurisdiction of child support; hence, some fathers could have multiple child support orders. Throughout the remainder of the 20th century, state and federal child support enforcement programs continued to address interstate inconsistencies that provided irresponsible parents with a means of avoiding their child support obligations.

The Personal Responsibility and Work Opportunity Reconciliation Act (PRWORA) of 1996, known to most Americans as welfare reform, emphasized parental responsibility for the financial support of their children as well as implemented more aggressive enforcement techniques and additional provisions that unified state collection efforts. For instance, to reduce delay in establishing wage withholding for parents who are delinquent in their child support payments, PRWORA requires employers to report all new hires to child support enforcement authorities. As a result, the National Directory of New Hires, a centralized electronic system, was developed to match all employees with parents who owe child support and are listed in the federal case registry. In fiscal year 1998, the National Directory of New Hires located 1.2 million parents who were delinquent in their child support payments; in fiscal year 1999, the directory identified an additional 2.8 million delinquent parents.

The most recent child support enforcement effort focused on curtailing deadbeat parents is the creation of the Deadbeat Parents Punishment Act (DPPA), which makes it a federal offense for a noncustodial parent to willfully fail to pay a past-due child support obligation, with respect to a child residing in another state. Under the DPPA, if the obligation remains unpaid for longer than one year or is greater than $5,000, then a misdemeanor charge may be considered. Behaviors that constitute a felony offense are: (1) traveling in interstate or foreign commerce with the intent to evade a

POLITICS AND CHILD SUPPORT

The issue of child support is just one of many topics related to the changing family. Scholars and politicians continually debate whether the traditional family is in decline. On one side of the debate are those who think the family is in decline. Proponents of this perspective hail the traditional family—that is, a breadwinner husband, a stay-at-home wife and mother, and children—as the best environment for children. Along with this perspective come terms such as *family values* or *families first* that are used to affirm and clarify the merits of the two-parent home. Thus, the federal government spends millions of dollars on marriage promotion programs that are mainly aimed at the poor. Some argue that if marriage promotion works, we will witness more stable families and a reduction in government spending on public child support–related services.

On the other side of the debate are those who argue that the family is not in decline but is changing in response to societal shifts. This perspective also contends that it is unlikely that American families will ever return to the traditional family. Therefore, terms such as *family values* and *families first* should be used in relation to all family types. If we accept all families, then more aggressive efforts will be made to support single-parent households and to assist in moving families out of the poverty trap.

support obligation if the obligation has remained unpaid for longer than one year or is greater than $5,000 or (2) willfully failing to pay a support obligation regarding a child residing in another state if the obligation has remained unpaid for longer than two years or is greater than $10,000. Maximum penalties for a misdemeanor are six months incarceration and a $5,000 fine. Maximum penalties for a felony offense are two years and a $250,000 fine.

The past few centuries have seen a noteworthy transformation in the child support system in the United States. Yet there is scholarly and political debate about whether the current system works and, if so, for whom.

Child Advocates

Child advocates argue that the child support system has improved but suggest that more changes are needed to improve the health and well-being of children and to lift families out of poverty. For instance, the number of custodial parents receiving full private child support payments has increased over the last 10 years, from 36.9 percent to 45.3 percent. In contrast, among custodial parents who live below the poverty line, only 35 percent received all the private child support that was due.

In terms of public child support–related services, advocates argue that these services rarely prevent poverty and, in fact, are a poverty trap. Public child support services provide meager, below-poverty-level benefits, reduce benefits when mothers earn more, and take away medical benefits when a mother leaves welfare. A strategy such as this promotes dependency and perpetuates the cycle of poverty.

However, child advocates note that closely related to the poverty trap is the child support enforcement trap. Specifically, advocates are concerned that custodial parents receiving public child support such as TANF are required to assign their right to private child support to the governmental welfare entity before cash assistance can be received. Moreover, custodial parents must pursue child support from the noncustodial parent, which is then diverted to the welfare assistance program instead of the custodial parent. Child support payments that are used to reimburse government public assistance costs deprive many poor children of much of the child support paid on their behalf. Even after the family leaves welfare and is struggling to avoid return, in some circumstances child support collections will go to repay government arrears before going to the family. What's more, child advocates note, if the amount of private child support paid equals or exceeds the public child support assistance, the family is moved off of TANF, the cash assistance part of the program.

Finally, the federal government through the Social Security Administration provides up to $4.1 billion in financial incentives to states that create child support and arrearage orders. Again, child advocates argue that this type of child support enforcement system is a trap that perpetuates the cycle of poverty and is more beneficial for the state and federal government than for children and families.

Fathers' Rights Activists

Overall, fathers' rights activists find that the current child support system is a gender-biased system that discriminates against men. However, these activists' dissatisfaction with the child support system begins prior to the child support order, with the divorce proceedings. Many divorced men argue that awarding sole maternal custody denies a father equal rights. Yet many fathers admit that they do not want the responsibility of caring for their children on a daily basis but do want to continue the parenting role and visit with their children regularly.

A second issue that concerns fathers' rights activists is that mothers are awarded unjust child support payments; that is, more money than is needed to care for the child. Furthermore, fathers seem to resent that they have no control in the manner in which support payments are spent. Even more, fathers who pay child support become angry when visitation with their children is limited, again blaming a gender-biased system for these problems.

Activists also take issue with the term *deadbeat dad*. They contend that the concept of deadbeat dad carries the connotation of an affluent man who fails to meet his parental responsibility to provide for his children. Some activists suggest that the majority of dads who are labeled as deadbeats do not fit this image. In fact, they argue, many fathers just are not financially able to provide for their children, yet the court awards child support payments that he is unable to afford. For instance, activists assert that men characterized as deadbeats are either (1) remarried and the second family is worse off financially than the original family because the father is supporting his biological children and stepchildren; (2) living in poverty, homeless, or incarcerated; (3) fathers who are providing indirect support to the child and custodial parent such as repairing items around the custodial parent's house; (4) fathers who cannot find their children because the mother has moved, but the mother has filed a case with the local child support enforcement entity; (5) fathers with high arrearages in relation to their current economic circumstance; or (6) fathers who are truly child support resistors—that is, deadbeat dads.

Finally, some activists claim that child support enforcement benefits all entities related to the divorce industry. They point out that the divorce and child support industry creates jobs for many. For example, family court judges earn $90,000 to $160,000 per year, and each judge requires a staff, not to mention child support staff, social workers, private collections agencies, and attorneys. In addition, they note the availability of federal funding for the administration of child support enforcement programs under the Social Security Act. Federal funding incentives have led a number of for-profit and privately held corporations to offer services to state and local child support agencies ranging from consultation to payment processing. Thus, fathers' rights activists argue that the current child support system actually tears families apart while benefiting government and child support–related businesses.

See also **Child Abuse; Divorce; Poverty and Public Assistance**

Further Reading

Crowley, Jocelyn, *The Politics of Child Support in America*. New York: Cambridge University Press, 2003.

Duerr, Jill, and Bruce Fuller, eds., *Good Parents or Good Workers? How Policy Shapes Families' Daily Lives*. New York: Palgrave Macmillan, 2005.

Mandel, Deena, *Deadbeat Dads: Subjectivity and Social Construction*. Toronto: University of Toronto Press, 2002.

DESEGREGATION

Erica Frankenberg and Chinh Q. Le

For many, the 50th anniversary of *Brown v. Board of Education* in 2004 provided an opportunity to celebrate the decision as a victory for racial justice and to presume that large-scale racial inequality was an artifact of the past, of little concern to us today. Yet it is clear that segregated or near-segregated schools continue to exist and that school resegregation has been on the rise since the 1980s.

Public school segregation has increased over the past two decades not because we have learned that desegregation failed or because Americans have turned against it. In fact, there is now more information about the benefits of integration than ever before, and public support for integrated education remains high, particularly among those who have personal experience with desegregated schools. Rather, resegregation has been primarily a result of the changing legal and political landscape, which in recent years has severely limited what school districts must—or may—do to promote racial integration in their schools.

Why Desegregation?

Why should we care about segregation? Public school segregation can have a powerfully negative impact on students, an impact that prompted the Supreme Court to declare segregated schools unconstitutional in 1954. One of the common misconceptions about desegregation is that it is simply about seating black students next to white students in a classroom. If skin color were not systematically and inextricably linked to other forms of inequality, perhaps segregation would have less educational or legal significance. But when we talk about schools that are segregated by race, we are also usually talking about schools that are segregated along other dimensions as well, including poverty and English language learner status.

Racial segregation is highly correlated with the concentration of student poverty, and the differences by race and ethnicity in students' exposure to poverty are striking. Nationally, about half of all black and Latino students attend schools in which three-quarters or more students are poor, while only 5 percent of white students attend such schools. No fewer than 80 percent of students in schools of extreme poverty are black or Latino. As a result, minority students in these segregated schools are isolated not only from white students but from schools with students from middle-class families, and exposure to students with middle-class backgrounds is a predictor of academic success. Further, Latino English language learner students are even more isolated from whites than their native-speaking Latino peers and, as a result, have little exposure to native English speakers who could aid their acquisition of English.

Racially isolated minority schools are also often vastly unequal to schools with higher percentages of white students in terms of other tangible resources, such as qualified, experienced teachers and college preparatory curriculum, as well as intangible resources, such as lower teacher turnover and more college-bound peers—all of which are associated with higher educational outcomes. Social science research, then, confirms that the central premise of *Brown* remains true: Racially minority segregated schools offer students an inferior education, which is likely to harm their future life opportunities, such as graduation from high school and college. While a handful of successfully segregated minority schools certainly exist across the nation, these schools represent the exception to the general trend and are typically places with stable, committed leadership and faculty that are difficult to replicate on a large scale.

Desegregation has offered an opportunity to study how interracial schools can affect the education of students. Research generally concludes that integrated schools have important benefits for students who attend these schools and for the society in which these students will one day be citizens and workers. While early studies of the effects of desegregation focused on its impact on minority students, more recent research has revealed that white students, too, benefit from racial integration. Of course, these benefits depend on how desegregation is structured and implemented within diverse schools.

Over 50 years ago, Harvard University psychologist Gordon Allport suggested that one of the essential conditions to reducing prejudice was that people needed to be in contact with one another. Research in racially integrated schools confirms that, by allowing for students of different races and ethnicities to be in contact with one another, students can develop improved cross-racial understanding and experience a reduction of racial prejudice and bias.

Additionally, black and Latino students in desegregated schools have higher achievement than their peers in segregated schools, while the achievement of white students in racially diverse but majority white schools remains unaffected. Some evidence also suggests that diverse classrooms can improve the critical thinking skills of all students.

Benefits from such environments extend beyond the time spent in schools to improved life opportunities. Students in integrated schools are more likely to graduate from high school and go on to college than their segregated peers, meaning that integrated schools result in a more highly skilled workforce. These students are also connected to social networks that give them information about and access to competitive colleges and higher-status jobs. Perhaps because of this access or the fact that students who attend integrated schools tend to be more likely to attain graduate degrees, labor market studies show that African Americans who attend integrated schools have higher salaries than their peers from segregated schools. Finally, students who attend racially diverse schools are more likely to be civically engaged after graduation and to feel comfortable working in diverse settings.

There are important benefits for communities with racially diverse schools. For example, students who graduate from integrated schools will have experience and will be adept working with people of other racial and ethnic backgrounds, an important skill for the demands of the workforce in the global economy. Research also indicates that communities with extensive school desegregation have experienced declines in residential integration. Further, desegregation that encompasses most of a region can stem white flight. Communities with integrated schools tend to experience higher levels of parental involvement in and support for the schools.

It is no wonder, then, that over the years, many school districts have come to realize the value of racial and ethnic diversity and its important influence on educating future citizens. A number of these school districts, as a result, have voluntarily enacted policies and student assignment methods designed to promote racial integration in their schools. In other words, more and more school districts are trying to create diverse learning environments not out of legal obligation but on their own accord as an essential part of their core educational mission. They do so in recognition of the critical role schools play in fostering racial and ethnic harmony in an increasingly heterogeneous society and of the significance of an integrated school experience in shaping students' worldviews. Yet even these efforts may be imperiled.

The Development of School Desegregation Law

Most scholars and laypersons alike consider *Brown v. Board of Education* the most famous U.S. Supreme Court ruling in U.S. history. That landmark 1954 decision was the culmination of decades of civil rights litigation and strategizing to overturn the deeply entrenched doctrine from *Plessy v. Ferguson* (1896) of "separate but equal," which had applied to 17 Southern states where segregated schools were required. *Brown* held for the first time that racially segregated public schools violate the equal protection guarantees of the Fourteenth Amendment of the U.S. Constitution.

Although an enormous moral victory for civil rights advocates—indeed for the entire nation—*Brown* itself did not require the immediate elimination of segregation in the nation's public schools. In fact, one year later, in a follow-up decision popularly known as *Brown II,* the Supreme Court allowed racially segregated school systems to move forward in dismantling their segregative practices "with all deliberate speed"—an infamous phrase that, for many years, meant without any speed or urgency at all. Further, *Brown II* placed the duty to supervise school desegregation squarely on local federal district courts and then provided these courts little guidance.

Thus, despite the efforts of countless black communities across the nation demanding immediate relief in the wake of the *Brown* decision—often at the risk of grave danger and violence, and mostly in the segregated South, where resistance was greatest—a full decade passed with virtually no progress in desegregating schools. By 1963, when President John F. Kennedy asked Congress to pass legislation prohibiting racial discrimination in all programs receiving federal aid (including schools), well over 98 percent of Southern black students were still attending segregated schools.

A social and cultural revolution was sweeping the country during the civil rights era, however, and, by the mid-1960s and early 1970s, school desegregation too began to take hold. Congress enacted Kennedy's proposed legislation as the Civil Rights Act of 1964, which empowered the Department of Justice to initiate desegregation lawsuits independent of private plaintiffs. The act also authorized the Department of Health, Education, and Welfare to deny federal funds to segregating school districts. With these new governmental tools and allies, civil rights attorneys used the power of America's courts and television sets against recalcitrant school districts that refused to comply with the law.

During these critical years, the Supreme Court, also frustrated by the lack of progress in school desegregation, issued a number of important decisions that lent valuable support and legitimacy to the cause. For instance, in *Green v. County School Board of New Kent County* (1968), the Court expressly defined what desegregation required: the elimination of all traces of a school system's prior segregation in every facet of school operations—from student, faculty, and staff assignment to extracurricular activities, facilities, and transportation.

Three years later, the Supreme Court ruled unanimously in *Swann v. Charlotte-Mecklenburg Board of Education* (1971) that lower courts supervising the desegregation of individual school districts could order the use of transportation, or busing, to achieve desegregated student assignments. In so doing, it rejected the argument that formerly dual school systems had discharged their desegregation duties by assigning students to segregated schools that happened to correspond with segregated neighborhoods.

Shortly thereafter, the Supreme Court decided *Keyes v. School District No. 1* (1973), a case originating in Denver, Colorado, that extended school desegregation obligations to systems outside the South that had employed discriminatory policies. The *Keyes* case was also the first to order desegregation for Latino students. Federal district courts took guidance from these and other Supreme Court decisions as they ordered desegregation plans unique to the communities for which they were responsible. In response to these decisions, the federal judiciary began more actively issuing detailed desegregation orders and then monitoring the school districts' progress, or lack thereof, on a regular basis. Segregation was on the run.

Judicial Retrenchment

By the mid-1970s, significant changes in the Supreme Court's composition rendered its reputation as a champion of civil rights relatively short-lived. In perhaps the most significant case from this latter era, *Milliken v. Bradley* (1974), the Court dealt a serious blow to school desegregation by concluding that lower courts could not order interdistrict desegregation remedies that encompass urban as well as suburban school districts without first showing that the suburban district or the state was liable for the segregation across district boundaries. The practical impact of the decision was the establishment of a bright line between city and suburban school systems beyond which the courts could not traverse in designing their desegregation plans. Whites who for decades had tried to flee school desegregation finally had a place to go where they could avoid it.

Just one year prior to *Milliken*, the Supreme Court had decided a case, *San Antonio Independent School District v. Rodriguez* (1973), that seriously undermined a parallel strategy of the educational equity movement. The Court refused to strike down a public school financing scheme that resulted in significantly lower expenditures for poor and minority children who lived in school districts with lower tax property bases in comparison to their more affluent, white neighbors who lived in the neighboring district. In so doing, the Court foreclosed an important argument that civil rights lawyers had tried to advance in both school funding and segregation cases: that public education was a fundamental right under the Constitution, which must be available on an equal basis. With this legal avenue shut down by *Rodriguez,* and with interdistrict remedies effectively eliminated by *Milliken,* the Supreme Court's brief, forward charge on school desegregation law had officially come to a screeching halt.

Soon the executive branch of government, which had been fairly aggressive in litigation and enforcement of school desegregation cases, followed the increasingly more conservative federal courts. In the 1980s, the Reagan administration adopted a new philosophy that focused on school choice—rather than on the firm insistence of compliance with court orders requiring mandatory student assignments—to accomplish school desegregation. As a result, scores of school districts abandoned busing as a remedy and began more actively employing strategies and tools such as magnet schools and "controlled-choice plans" as the primary means of advancing desegregation. In general, the government's focus during this era turned away from educational equity and toward other issues—namely, an emphasis on standards-based accountability to improve student achievement.

The 1990s ushered in another phase of judicial retreat from school desegregation. Between 1991 and 1995, the Supreme Court handed down three important decisions: *Oklahoma City Board of Education v. Dowell* (1991), *Freeman v. Pitts* (1992), and *Missouri v. Jenkins* (1995). Taken together, these cases essentially invited school districts to initiate proceedings to bring their desegregation obligations to an end. They permitted federal district courts overseeing desegregation plans to declare a school system "unitary" if they determined that the system had done all that was feasible to eliminate the effects of past racial discrimination. In contrast to earlier decisions, now, according to the Supreme Court, a good faith effort to desegregate along with reasonable compliance with prior desegregation orders for a decent period of time were considered sufficient for a school district to achieve unitary status and thus have its desegregation orders permanently dissolved—even if severe racial isolation or other racial disparities remained. Advocates of school desegregation view these changes as a significant dilution of the desegregation obligations the Supreme Court had placed on school districts in the previous decades.

In the years since that trilogy of cases was decided, a large number of school systems have been declared unitary. In some instances, the school district itself sought to end federal court supervision, arguing it had met its constitutional obligations. In others, parents opposed to desegregation led the attack to relieve the school district of any continuing legal duties to desegregate, leaving the district in the awkward position of having to defend the kinds of policies that it had, ironically, resisted implementing in prior decades. Recently, in fact, a handful of federal courts have declared districts unitary even when the school district itself argued that its desegregation policies were still necessary to remedy past discrimination.

Once a school district has been declared unitary, it is no longer under a legal duty to continue any of the desegregation efforts that it had undertaken in the decades when it was under court order. The school district remains, of course, under a broad constitutional obligation—as do all districts—to avoid taking actions that intentionally create racially segregated and unequal schools. However, courts presume that the school district's actions are innocent and legal, even if they produce racially disparate results, unless there is evidence of *intentional* discrimination. The past history of segregation and desegregation is completely wiped away in the eyes of the law. These fully discretionary, "innocent and legal" policies in many instances have contributed to a disturbing phenomenon of racial resegregation in public schools, which are more racially separate now than at any point in the past two decades.

Trends in Desegregation and Resegregation

As a result of the courts' guidance, there were dramatic gains in desegregation for black students in the South, a region with the most black students and the most integrated region of the country by the late 1960s due to court-ordered desegregation and federal enforcement of desegregation plans. Desegregation of black students remained stable for several decades; by 1988, 43.5 percent of Southern black students were in majority white schools. During the 1990s, however, the proportion of black students in majority white schools in the region steadily declined as desegregation plans were dismantled. In 2003, only 29 percent of Southern black students were in majority white schools, lower than any year since 1968.

When there was a concerted effort to desegregate black and white students in the South during the mid- to late-1960s, there was major progress, demonstrating that desegregation can and has succeeded. We are experiencing a period of steady decline in desegregation since the late 1980s, and much of the success that led to several decades of desegregated schooling for millions of students in the South is being undone. Nevertheless, black and white students in the South attend schools that are considerably more integrated than before the time of *Brown*.

The judicial changes discussed above have had a major impact on the desegregation of schools at a time of racial transformation of the nation's public school enrollment. Since the end of the civil rights era, the racial composition of our nation's public school students has changed dramatically. The United States was once overwhelmingly white, but that is no longer the case. Minority students now comprise more than 40 percent of all U.S. public school students, nearly twice their share of students during the 1960s.

Not only are there more minority students than ever before, but the minority population is also more diverse than it was during the civil rights era, when most nonwhite students were black. Black and Latino students now comprise more than a third of all students in public schools. The most rapidly growing racial/ethnic group is Latinos, whose numbers almost quadrupled from 1968 to 2000 to 7.7 million students. Asian enrollment, like that of Latinos, is also increasing. Meanwhile, by 2003, whites comprised only 58 percent of the public school enrollment. There were 7 million fewer white public school students at the beginning of the 21st century than there were at the end of the 1960s. As a result of this growing diversity, nearly 9 million students in 2003 attended schools with at least three racial groups of students.

U.S. public schools are more than two decades into a period of rapid resegregation. The desegregation of black students has now declined to levels not seen in three decades. Latinos, by contrast, have never experienced a time of increased integration and today are the most segregated minority group in U.S. schools.

Remarkably, almost 2.4 million students attend schools that are 99–100 percent minority, including almost one in six of black students and one in nine Latino students. Nearly 40 percent of both black and Latino students attend intensely segregated schools (90–100 percent of students are nonwhite); yet less than 1 percent of white students attend such schools. Nearly three-fourths of black and Latino students attend predominantly minority schools.

Whites are the most racially isolated group of students in the United States. In a perfectly integrated system of schools, the racial composition of every school would mirror that of the overall U.S. enrollment. The typical white public school student, however, attends a school that is nearly 80 percent white, which is much higher than the white percentage of the overall public school enrollment (58 percent). This means that white students, on average, attend schools in which only one in five students are of another race, which, conversely, reduces the opportunities for students of other races to be in schools with white students. Schools with high percentages of white students are also likely to have overwhelmingly white faculties, meaning that such schools have few people of color.

Black and Latino students are also extremely isolated from students of other races, and they are particularly isolated from whites. Blacks and Latinos attend schools where two-thirds of students are also black and Latino, and over half of the students in their schools are students of their same race. Despite earlier progress in desegregation, the percentage of white students who attend schools with black students, another measure of school desegregation, has been declining since 1988. Asians are the most desegregated of all students; three-fourths of students in their schools are from other racial and ethnic groups, and only a small percentage of Asian students are in segregated minority schools.

The resegregation of blacks and Latinos is a trend seen in almost every large school district since the mid-1980s. One reason is that the public school districts in many of the nation's largest cities, which educate one-tenth of all public school students in the 26 largest districts, contain few white students—without which even the best designed desegregation plans cannot create substantial desegregation. While the largest urban districts (enrollment greater than 60,000) enroll over one-fifth of all black and Latino students, less than 1 in 40 white students attend these central city schools.

Minority students in suburban districts generally attend schools with more white students than their counterparts in central city districts, although there is substantial variation within the largest suburban districts. In over half of the suburban districts with more than 60,000 students, the typical black and Latino student attends schools that, on average, have a white majority. However, black and Latino students in these districts are more segregated from whites than was the case in the mid-1980s. In some large suburban districts, there has been drastic racial change in a short time span, and these districts are now predominantly minority like the urban districts discussed above. Countywide districts, or districts that encompass both city and suburban areas, have often been able to create stable desegregation. In rural districts, there is generally less segregation since there are fewer schools for students to enroll in, although, in some rural areas, private schools disproportionately enroll white students, while public schools remain overwhelmingly minority.

Current Status of the Law

In recent years, a number of school districts that have been released from their formal, constitutional desegregation obligations—as well as some that had never had any legal duty to desegregate in the first place—have adopted voluntary measures to promote integration in their schools. These voluntary school integration measures, in other words, are designed not by courts to be imposed on school districts, with the goal of curing historical, illegal segregation, but rather by the districts themselves, often with the support of and input from parents, students, and others in the community. They are future-oriented and are intended to assist the school districts realize *Brown*'s promise and vision of equal opportunity and high-quality integrated public education for all.

Odd as it may seem, however, it may turn out that a unitary school district's voluntary consideration of race for the laudable goal of stemming resegregation and promoting integration is illegal. Despite the success and popularity of well-designed voluntary school integration plans, opponents of desegregation in a handful of communities have sued their school systems for adopting them, alleging that such efforts violate the same constitutional equal protection guarantees that outlawed segregated schools 50 years ago in *Brown*. Indeed, in June 2007, the U.S. Supreme Court issued a much-anticipated and sharply divided ruling in two cases challenging voluntary integration plans in Seattle and Louisville. The court struck down aspects of the student assignment plans because they were not sufficiently tailored to achieve those goals. But a majority of justices left the window open for school districts to take race-conscious measures to promote diversity.

Even though it dramatically changed the landscape of school integration, this Supreme Court decision did not provide a clear set of rules and principles for school districts, creating some confusion about what can be done to promote integration. How communities and school districts will react to the ruling, and whether they choose to forge ahead with new ways to fulfill *Brown*'s promise of equal, integrated public education, remain open questions.

See also **Charter Schools; Government Role in Schooling; School Choice; Social Justice (vol. 2)**

Further Reading

Boger, John Charles, and Gary Orfield, eds., *School Resegregation: Must the South Turn Back?* Chapel Hill: University of North Carolina Press, 2004.

Clotfelter, Charles T., *After Brown: The Rise and Retreat of School Desegregation.* Princeton, NJ: Princeton University Press, 2006.

Dunn, Joshua M., and Martin R. West, eds., *From Schoolhouse to Courthouse: The Judiciary's Role in American Education.* Washington, DC: Brookings Institution Press, 2009.

Frankenberg, Erica, and Gary Orfield, eds., *Lessons in Integration: Realizing the Promise of Racial Diversity in America's Schools.* Charlottesville: University of Virginia Press, 2007.

Kluger, Richard, *Simple Justice: The History of* Brown v. Board of Education *and Black America's Struggle for Equality,* rev. ed. New York: Knopf, 2004.

NAACP Legal Defense Fund. Statement from the NAACP Legal Defense Fund on the Supreme Court's Rulings in Seattle and Louisville School Cases. June 28, 2007. http://www.naacp/df.org/content.aspx?article=1181

Orfield, Gary, and Chungmei Lee, *Racial Transformation and the Changing Nature of Segregation.* Cambridge, MA: Civil Rights Project at Harvard University, 2006.

Smrekar, Claire E., and Ellen B. Goldring, eds., *From the Courtroom to the Classroom: The Shifting Landscape of School Desegregation.* Cambridge, MA: Harvard Education Press, 2009.

Wells, Amy Stuart, Jennifer Jellison Holme, Anita Tijerina Revilla, and Awo Korantemaa Atanda, *Both Sides Now: The Story of School Desegregation's Graduates.* Berkeley: University of California Press, 2009.

DIVORCE

Kimberly P. Brackett and Donald Woolley

Divorce can, with some justification, be viewed as either a problem, a symptom, or a solution. Which of these is or should be the prevailing view depends on who is looking at the subject. Different stakeholders are concerned with the quality of family life and the effects that divorce might have on individuals and the culture as a whole. Among the groups with a vested interest in divorce are politicians, religious groups, counselors, educators, and families themselves.

Persons viewing divorce as a problem tend to focus on statistics indicating a high likelihood of divorces for first marriages and direct much of their concern toward the effects of postdivorce circumstances on children. These stakeholders have been very successful at getting their message to a wide audience. Among those viewing divorce as a problem are clinical psychologist Judith Wallerstein, James Dobson of Focus on the Family, and the Institute for American Values.

Persons who indicate that divorce is a symptom, express the sentiment that modern society is too quick to seek easy solutions to problems and suggest that couples' expectations of marriage are too idealistic. Additionally, those who see divorce as a symptom of a larger problem argue that the moral standards and values of society as a whole are in decline. They also tend to focus on individualism, secularization, and instant gratification as responsible for the increases in divorce. Advocates for this approach include the Institute for American Values, Maggie Gallagher, and Barbara Dafoe Whitehead.

Persons who emphasize the solution elements of divorce often point to decreases in violence and anger between the former partners as the biggest benefit to divorce. Likewise they would suggest that divorce is a solution for persons who entered a marriage unwisely or who were unprepared to assume the responsibilities of a lifetime commitment. Divorce is seen as a solution when the environment at home is one of constant tension and anger. Persons coming from this perspective tend to emphasize constructing a meaningful life after the divorce for both the couple and any children and include Constance Ahrons, the American Academy of Matrimonial Lawyers, and Mavis Hetherington.

Brief History of Divorce

It seems that persons of all recent societies place value on a marriagelike or lasting union between a man and woman. As a result, most societies historically and presently have frowned upon the ending of such unions and have generally put barriers in the way of dissolving the relationships, although surviving documents indicate that divorces occurred at least as far in the past as ancient Mesopotamia. While the process is formal and legal in the United States and other westernized societies, at other historic periods and places the mechanism has been quite different. Ancient Greeks were unlikely to place a high premium on marriages for other than the legitimating of heirs, and divorce was available provided the reasons a person was requesting a divorce were approved by a governmental official. In the later years of the Roman Empire, a couple could simply agree to divorce and it would be done. In other societies, the husband was the only party who could petition for and receive a divorce.

For the most part, the widespread acceptance of Christianity in the Middle Ages served to decrease the availability of divorce and to enact stringent limitations on the rare instances when it would be permitted. This pattern reflects the fact that marriage at the time was a religious sacrament and under the control of the Church rather than the civil authority. Annulment was the more available path to marital dissolution. In an annulment granted by the Church, the marriage was declared null, as if it had never occurred. This stance regarding divorce remains a hallmark of Roman Catholicism. Even today, devout Catholics and clergy chastise Catholic lawyers who facilitate divorce proceedings. Annulment is also a legal term that is used when a condition existed prior to the marriage that would have prevented the marriage from being legally permitted or recognized. Thus, in the eyes of the law, the marriage never existed.

Divorce has always been available in some capacity in the United States, although the ease with which one could attain divorce and the likelihood of social rejection for doing so has varied over time. The United States has a more liberal history of divorce than does Great Britain and other Western European countries, despite the reliance on English Common Law as the basis for U.S. civil authority. The first recorded divorce in what is now the United States was granted in the Plymouth Colony in 1639 to a woman whose husband had committed bigamy (was married to two women simultaneously). Divorces were rare, however, in the colonial period. This is likely due to the influence of religious beliefs, but also to the economic necessity of partners working together to survive the sometimes harsh conditions of colonial life. A wife was sometimes referred to as a "helpmeet" in colonial literature, reinforcing the role that she assumed in the success of the farm or family business.

While the United States was more liberal than many European countries regarding divorce, grounds for divorce had to be established before a divorce would be permitted. Traditional grounds for divorce included adultery, cruelty, nonsupport, desertion, and incarceration. It was not until 1970 that any state statutes permitted divorce simply because the partners were incompatible. The bold move by California of instituting the first no-fault divorce laws paved the way for partners to divorce for other than traditional grounds. By 1985, when South Dakota became the last state to permit no-fault divorce, all states had some provisions for these divorces, although a few states (such as New York) required a mandatory waiting period before such a divorce could occur. No-fault divorce meant that neither partner had committed a crime against the other; thus, the traditional grounds for divorce had not been met. Under no-fault divorce, couples agreed that they could no longer be married and would like to have their legal marital contract dissolved.

Divorce Statistics

Divorce is measured by using several different statistics. One of the most widely used is the crude divorce rate. This tells the number of divorces in a given year per 1,000 population. This rate was 4.2 for the year 1998. This statistic makes divorce look fairly uncommon and is not very useful because it includes all persons in society, whether married or not. Another measure of divorce, which academics feel is more accurate, is known as the refined divorce rate. It considers the number of divorces in a given year divided by the number of married women in the population. By focusing on married couples (women), it includes only those persons who are eligible to divorce. In the United States for the year 2004, the refined divorce rate was 17.7. This statistic allows for more comparisons between countries and periods to determine meaningful differences in divorce.

A statistic often quoted in the discussions of divorce is that 50 percent of marriages will end in divorce. This statistic is rather misleading, if not wholly inaccurate, because it is very difficult to predict what will happen over the duration of a marriage. In an average year in the United States, there are about 2.4 million marriages and 1.2 million divorces. It is from these data that the 50 percent figure is derived. However, experts who take into account the factors that lead to divorce for given social groups and historical eras put the likelihood of marriages beginning today and subsequently ending in divorce at around 40 percent.

For women who are college educated and have family incomes over $30,000, the likelihood of divorce decreases to around 25 percent. Race and ethnicity play a part in the likelihood of getting a divorce as well. After 10 years of marriage, 32 percent of non-Hispanic white women's first marriages end in divorce, compared with 34 percent of Hispanic women's first marriages, approximately 50 percent of black women's first marriages, and 20 percent of Asian women's first marriages. Current dissolution rates for first marriages indicate that approximately 20 percent of first marriages end within five years.

For the past 100 years, there has been a generally upward trend in divorce in the United States. A slight decrease in divorce occurred during the early years of the 1930s. The economic troubles of the Great Depression likely influenced the divorce rate, but economic recessions since that time have not showed the same pattern regarding divorce. While divorce declined in the 1930s, it spiked dramatically in the second half of the 1940s. This change has been attributed to the effects of World War II. It seems reasonable that some partners found others during the time they were apart, women discovered independence through their work in the war effort, or persons were changed by the separation so that they were no longer compatible. Another probable explanation for the spike was that marriages contracted hastily before or during the war were no longer appealing to the partners when the war was over.

Despite the changes brought about in the era immediately following World War II, the time of most rapid increase in divorce was from the early 1960s to 1980, when the divorce rate more than doubled. Factors that have been proposed to account for the increase in divorce include the second wave of feminism (also known as the modern women's movement), an increase in women attending college and perceiving options outside of married life, increases in the accessibility and effectiveness of birth control, increases in opportunities for cohabitation (living together without being married), and the introduction of no-fault divorce statutes. During the last 20 years, the divorce rate has declined from its all-time high but continues to be high when compared with the rates of divorce in other countries. Among the factors related to the recent decrease in divorce is that persons are waiting until later to marry for the first time. Early marriages, particularly among those younger than age 20, have a much higher chance of ending in divorce.

Divorce as Problem

While divorce rates in the United States have been stable or declining for 20 years, Americans express an overwhelming anxiety about the state of marriage. The rate of divorce peaked around 1980, but persons from all across the political spectrum propose that divorce is a serious problem in the United States today. Persons who see divorce as a problem come from the perspective that current divorce rates are unnaturally high and that society should work to reduce them. There is a long history stemming from religious prohibitions and middle-class morality suggesting that divorce is a problem.

Divorce is defined as a problem because of the trauma of the breakup as well as the aftereffects for both the partners who divorce and any children that are involved. Divorce is a problem for couples through both psychological and financial costs. Divorce is seen by many, including the divorcing partners, as a failure of the couple. They experience guilt, loss of self-esteem, and anger. Divorced people are more likely to commit suicide than are married people.

Additionally, divorce has financial consequences for couples. Many times they sell their jointly held assets to divide the results equally. Because men provide, on average, more than 60 percent of household income, women may face a difficult decline in standard of living following divorce. Research suggests that more than 25 percent of divorced women experience at least some time in poverty during the five years following a divorce. Financial concerns are perhaps heightened for women, because they are more likely to receive custody of and be caring for children than are their former husbands. This situation leads to an increase in the numbers of single-parent families in society.

DIVORCE AND CHILDREN

In any given year, about 1 million children discover that their parents are divorcing. Approximately 60 percent of all divorces in the United States involve children. Prior to the 1970s, social scientists believed, as did the general public, that, to have an adult life without added emotional and behavioral problems, a person had to grow up living with his or her biological parents. Early studies seemed to substantiate this, showing that children were scarred by divorce and left with emotional insecurities that continued when they became adults.

Later research has not shown this blanket concept to be true. Research shows that, of the 1 million children of divorce created each year, about 750,000 to 800,000 will suffer no long-term effects as they transition into adulthood. These children are able to function in the same way as those children reared by two parents. Indeed, many of these children may end up better off than they would have if their parents had remained together.

The concept of staying together for the children was born out of the popular belief of the need for two parents in the household. It was thought that a child had to grow up under the direct influence of both parents in order to mature socially and emotionally. Additionally, staying together for the sake of the children was generally considered to be noble and selfless. Parents were expected to sacrifice their personal happiness as a way of protecting their children from the stress of being part of a divorce.

During much of the 20th century in the United States, divorce was stigmatized. It was discouraged by many religions and often viewed as deviant by the public. Because of this atmosphere, the existence of children in a marriage was often used as an excuse to not get a divorce. While on the decline as an idea, staying together for the children was common prior to the 1970s, when divorce became more publicly acceptable.

However, for proper development, a child needs to grow up in a warm and loving environment that may not exist in a household racked by conflict. In these cases, the emotional well-being of children may be better if their parents divorce, at minimum reducing much of the daily discord and possibly even allowing the parents to find happier relationships elsewhere. Staying together for the children may do more harm than good in these situations.

Society's concern with the effects of divorce on children has been a recent phenomenon but a politically useful tack. The presence of children does little to prevent parents from divorcing; it only seems to delay it. Each year, more than 1 million children are involved in the divorce of their parents. For those advocates who see a two-parent home as essential for rearing well-adjusted children, divorce creates additional problems by creating single-parent families.

Divorce decreases the economic and social resources available to children. In terms of economics, children reared by one parent are far more likely to live in poverty than those reared in a two-parent home. There is less disposable income available to splurge on leisure activities or academic endeavors. Among the potential social consequences of divorce are problems in school, marrying at a young age or never marrying, and abusing alcohol or drugs. Children may experience depression and have less chance to be equally bonded with both parents. Usually it is the father who misses out on the experiences of the child's life. Some older studies of the consequences of divorce for children pointed to divorce as a factor in children's delinquency, truancy, and difficulty with peer relations. Judith Wallerstein (2000) has been particularly vocal about the long-term consequences of divorce for children, including the increased chance that their marriages are more likely to end in divorce than those of children whose parents did not divorce.

Those most likely to view divorce as a problem in society are groups that desire to strengthen marriage as an institution. Marriage is viewed by many as the only acceptable way to live an adult life and the only situation in which to rear children. It is in the context of a nuclear family that children learn the skills that will enable them to be successful and productive members of society. One of the primary concerns of those who oppose divorce is that the option of divorce weakens the institution of marriage. In other words, as more couples divorce, the decision to get a divorce is more acceptable.

Religious organizations such as Focus on the Family have been critical of divorce for not only the negative consequences for adults, children, and society, but for issues of morality as well. Given Christian ideals that marriage is a sacrament before God lasting a lifetime, the only reasonable ending for a marriage is the death of one of the partners. There are, therefore, moral or religious consequences for the violation of holy law by divorcing. One of the most intriguing questions researchers are currently exploring with regard to divorce is how persons who hold some of the most conservative views on divorce have divorce rates higher than the national average. Born-again Christians and Baptists had divorce rates of 27 and 29 percent, respectively, in a study by the religion-motivated Barna Research Group. The conservative religious right opposes divorce, but the Southern Bible belt states have the highest rates. The Catholic Church has been a harsh critic of divorce and lobbied hard to keep divorce options out of countries around the world.

Divorce as Symptom

Divorce is a symptom of the pressure that Americans put on the marital relationship to be all things to the partners. The romantic notion of marriage—that one perfect person will make all of your dreams come true—may be partly responsible for the high rates of divorce. Asking one person to be your everything is putting a lot of faith in and pressure on that individual. While partners are expected to marry for life, they are given very little preparation, other than what they have witnessed in the marriages of their parents and other adults, about how to make a marriage work. Divorce is a symptom of the inadequate preparation for marriage that exists in U.S. society. To combat this, clergy and counselors have developed programs for persons contemplating marriage in attempts to strengthen marriages. One popular program is known by the acronym PREPARE.

Pamela Paul (2002) has suggested that, because cultural notions of marriage have changed very little over time while society has changed a great deal, Americans are particularly likely to find that marriage is not meeting their needs. She suggests that several trends in society today are largely responsible for why marriages are likely to end in divorce: (1) people are living twice as long as they did 100 years ago; (2) the most intensive active parenting takes only about 20 years, so the couple likely has 40 or more years without children in the home; (3) persons are likely to have multiple careers over their lifetimes, so change becomes normative; (4) persons who marry today have grown up in a time in which the stigma of divorce has decreased, and they may have personally experienced divorce as a young person; and (5) the increased likelihood that both spouses are employed frees women to explore nonfamilial roles and to experience economic independence from their husbands. Given these changing circumstances of social life, Paul suggests that it may be unrealistic for spouses chosen while people are in their 20s to be appropriate partners at other life stages.

The Family Research Council has argued that divorce occurs because people are misguided about the purpose of marriage. Marriage is the institution in which children are to be reared, and that is the primary function of marriage. It is not for the fulfillment of the couple but rather for the fulfillment of procreation that marriage is intended to provide.

The phrase "divorce culture" reflects the notion that, in today's world, divorce might be seen as a rather common, even expected, occurrence. The cavalier attitude Americans display toward divorce, argue the critics, makes the harmful effects of divorce seem small. Thus, divorce might be chosen even when a couple has not seriously tried to resolve any difficulties. This choice locates the desire of the individual above the good of the family group. This is particularly criticized when children are involved. Divorce, then, is a sign of selfishness and individuality. Others would argue that it is the no-fault divorce provisions that make divorce quick and easy and thus permit Americans to have a selfish attitude toward marriage. If no-fault divorces were not an option and couples had to go through the court system to end their marriages, they would work harder to keep them together and resolve the difficulties.

Organizations such as the Institute for American Values and the National Marriage Project routinely suggest that the increases in divorce and continuing high divorce rates are the result of a loosening of the moral code in the United States and an increase in individuality. The freedoms that Americans have to conduct personal relationships today have consequences for the individuals and the whole society. One area of concern is the prevalence of media images that depict divorce positively and marriage negatively. Additionally, a more secular society, one that is less apt to follow all aspects of religious teachings, has been blamed for an increase in divorce. Likewise, they suggest that removing the stigma from divorce has meant there is less social pressure to stay in a marriage.

One of the behaviors related to an increase in divorce and a questioning of morality is cohabitation. Cohabitation, living with a partner in a marriagelike relationship without being married, has increased dramatically in the last 30 years. There are now around 5.5 million households of heterosexual cohabitors in the United States. In some communities, as many as 60 percent of couples marrying in a given year are currently cohabiting at the time they apply for the marriage license. Research suggests that, despite the common rationale for cohabitation—that the couple is testing the relationship for compatibility—persons who cohabit before marriage are more likely to divorce than those who do not live together first.

Divorce as Solution

For partners who do not grow together in terms of interests and expectations, married life can be stifling. Divorce permits couples in unhappy unions to end their relationships and start anew. While ending a marriage is a difficult, even traumatic, life transition, it does permit persons to make meaningful life changes and experience a renewal in their lives. This notion of being renewed after severing ties from an unsatisfactory relationship is particularly likely to be mentioned by women after a divorce. In some communities, a woman's female friends might even throw her a liberation party to celebrate her newly single status.

Despite the potential for some women to experience financial difficulties after divorce, when dealing with their children, divorced women are often calmer and more effective parents than when they were in the conflicted marriage. Women also tend to have decreased tension and fewer bouts of depression when they are single. Clearly for women (and children) who were victims of abuse during a marriage, divorce is a solution to the daily threat to their safety.

Children who experience high levels of conflict or even violence in their families enjoy an increase in well-being after a divorce has occurred. Most children from divorced families, even those without a violent past, live good lives after overcoming some initial difficulties. Staying together for the sake of the children, while a politically provocative idea, does not seem to have the desired outcomes. In fact, Constance Ahrons (1994) has indicated that a good divorce is much better for kids than a bad marriage, because they see a healthier way to interact that validates the feelings of the partners and permits them to strive for greater happiness in their lives. Divorce may even lead to better parenting, because the time with the children is coordinated and special. Partners no longer have to disagree about the problems of the marriage but can work on the most effective way to parent the children that they share. Positive outcomes are particularly likely when parents and children attend special classes on how to build their skills in dealing with family issues.

Persons who view divorce as a solution tend to point to studies that argue that, not only can children be reared successfully in arrangements other than a traditional two-parent family, but adults can also find fulfillment in situations other than marriage. Those taking this view would not suggest that divorce or its consequences are easy; it is a highly stressful transition. However, it does permit adults a second chance at happiness and permits children to escape from a dysfunctional home life. In fact, Stephanie Coontz (1992) argues that we have made the traditional two-parent family look so good in our nostalgic yearning for the past that even the most functional of families would have difficulty living up to the expectations.

Perhaps it is the unrealistic expectations of married life that push some people to marry in the first place. While there are no overt penalties for singlehood nor current laws in the United States that indicate that one must be married by a certain age, there may be social pressure to demonstrate adult status by marrying. For these persons, marriage may not meet with their expectations, they may have married the wrong person, or they may have married too early. Research consistently shows that persons who are teenagers when they marry have far higher rates of divorce than do persons who wait until they are slightly older to marry. For these persons divorce may be a solution to a decision made when they were not yet mature. Likewise, persons who marry due to a premarital conception have higher rates of divorce than those whose children are conceived after the wedding.

Divorce may be characterized as a problem, symptom, or solution. At the present time, popular conceptions of divorce give more support to the notion of divorce as a problem to be solved. It is a problem of both long-term and short-term consequences. It is a problem of individuals as well as society. It is also a symptom of how much we might value personal relationships. We value them so highly that we want them to be all things to all persons, and we feel betrayed when they are not. Perhaps it is a symptom of the freedoms that U.S. society permits its citizens. Divorce is also a solution for those situations and times in which no other options seem to work or when staying in the marriage might have devastating emotional or physical consequences for the participants.

See also **Child Care; Deadbeat Parents**

Further Reading

Ahrons, Constance, *The Good Divorce: Keeping Your Family Together When Your Marriage Comes Apart.* New York: Harper Collins, 1994.

Ahrons, Constanct, *We're Still Family: What Grown Children Have to Say about Their Parents' Divorce.* New York: Harper Paperbacks, 2005.

Celello, Kristin, *Making Marriage Work: A History of Marriage and Divorce in the United States.* Chapel Hill: University of North Carolina Press, 2009.

Coontz, Stephanie, *The Way We Never Were: American Families and the Nostalgia Trap.* New York: HarperCollins, 1992.

Demo, David, and Mark A. Fine, *Beyond the Average Divorce.* Thousand Oaks, CA: Sage, 2009.

Emery, Robert E., *Marriage, Divorce and Children's Adjustment,* 2d ed. Thousand Oaks, CA: Sage, 1999.

Hetherington, E. Mavis, and John Kelly, *For Better or For Worse: Divorce Reconsidered.* New York: W. W. Norton, 2002.

Karney, Benjamin J., *Families under Stress: An Assessment of Data, Theory, and Research on Marriage and Divorce in the Military.* Santa Monica, CA: Rand Corporation, 2007.

Metz, Tamara, *Untying the Knot: Marriage, the State, and the Case for Divorce.* Princeton, NJ: Princeton University Press, 2010.

Paul, Pamela, *The Starter Marriage and the Future of Matrimony.* New York: Villard, 2002.

Swallow, Wendy, *Breaking Apart: A Memoir of Divorce.* New York: Hyperion, 2001.

Wallerstein, Judith, Julia Lewis, and Sandra Blakeslee, *The Unexpected Legacy of Divorce.* New York: Hyperion, 2000.

DOMESTIC PARTNERSHIPS

MARION C. WILLETTS

Over the last 25 years, numerous legal options have emerged for same-sex and opposite-sex couples wishing to legitimize their intimate unions in ways other than through heterosexual legal marriage. Four of these options are civil unions, same-sex marriages, reciprocal beneficiaries, and licensed domestic partnerships.

Legal Options

Civil Unions

Four states (Vermont in 2000, Connecticut in 2005, New Jersey in 2007, and New Hampshire in 2008) have implemented *civil union* legislation. In all four states, only same-sex couples are eligible to enter into a civil union; with the exception of sexual orientation, they must also meet the eligibility requirements for legal marriage. At the state level, civil unions are the functional equivalent of legal marriage in that they provide to couples all of the benefits and protections of marriage afforded to spouses. Due to the federal Defense of Marriage Act signed into law by President Bill Clinton in 1996, which defines marriage as consisting of the legal union of one man and one woman, these couples do not enjoy any of the benefits or protections at the federal level afforded to legally married couples. Furthermore, while nonresidents are eligible to form civil unions in these four states, only in New Jersey do they receive any legal acknowledgment, benefits, or protections associated with their unions (Vermont and Connecticut do not grant legal acknowledgment to civil unions contracted elsewhere; nor does any state without civil union legislation).

Legally dissolving a civil union involves the same process as dissolving a marriage: one partner must file for divorce. In Vermont, for example, at least one partner must

DEFENSE OF MARRIAGE ACT (1996)

Passed by the U.S. Congress in 1996, the Defense of Marriage Act (DOMA) defined marriage as existing only between a man and a woman, specifically when in reference to federal laws affecting taxes, pensions, Social Security, and other federal benefits. DOMA also gave the states the individual freedom to refuse to recognize gay marriages performed in other states. This meant that, regardless of where the marriage had been performed, there was a strong likelihood that it would not be recognized at all anywhere in the United States. Because marriages are certified at the state rather than the federal level, this act gave states permission to ignore the common practice of reciprocity with regard to homosexual couples. For heterosexual couples, reciprocity (the recognition that a marriage is legal in other states regardless of the state in which it was performed) still applied. However, this federal legislation did not dampen the spirits of the same-sex marriage proponents. If anything, it likely fueled the fire to a new level of frenzy.

The passing of DOMA likely resulted in the drafting and implementation of a Federal Marriage Amendment (FMA), which first saw activation in Colorado in 2002 and again in 2003. The FMA was an attempt to squash objections that DOMA had overstepped its constitutional authority by allowing states to disregard legal agreements (contracts) that other states had considered valid and binding. Supporters of an FMA felt that this constitutional amendment would clarify any gray areas regarding marriage, defining it solely as a man-woman union, as well as including a clause that stated that no state constitution or other body of law was to be construed as being forced to allow and recognize same-sex marriages. By the early 21st century, nearly four-fifths of all states had already passed laws or amended their own constitutions to ban same-sex marriages from within their borders. The action that had the largest impact on the opposition of same-sex marriage was taken by President George W. Bush in 2004, as he announced his support for a constitutional amendment prohibiting gay marriage. As with the creation and enactment of DOMA, Bush's support of a constitutional ban on gay marriage likely did nothing but temporarily boost his image and fuel the fire for gay rights equality in the marriage arena.

reside in the state for a minimum of six months prior to filing for dissolution, and that partner must reside in Vermont for at least one year prior to the hearing date for final dissolution of the civil union. If a couple that entered into a civil union either relocates to or are residents of another state and they wish to legally dissolve their union, the lack of acknowledgement of civil unions in other states means that a legal divorce is difficult, if not impossible, to obtain. Indeed, two couples who entered into civil unions in Vermont currently are struggling to dissolve their unions in other states (one in Connecticut, initially heard before the court in 2002, and one in Texas, initially heard before the court in 2003). In both cases, decisions about whether the unions may be legally dissolved in these states are yet to be rendered.

Same-Sex Marriage

Another legal option made available to couples living in five states (Connecticut, Iowa, Massachusetts, New Hampshire, and Vermont) and the District of Columbia is *same-sex marriage*. The federal Defense of Marriage Act dictates that states are not required to legally recognize the same-sex marriages contracted in any other state, although most of the states that allow them also recognize them from other states. New Jersey legally translates these marriages, in addition to the legal same-sex marriages contracted in other countries (same-sex marriage was legalized in the Netherlands in 2001, Belgium in 2003, Canada and Spain in 2005, and South Africa in 2006), into civil unions if the couples relocate there and provides to these couples all of the state-level benefits and protections of legal marriage. Similar to civil unions, same-sex marriage in the states in which it exists grants to couples all of the benefits and protections afforded to legally married couples at the state level, but these couples do not enjoy any of the benefits or protections afforded to legally married couples at the federal level as a result of the Defense of Marriage Act.

Reciprocal Beneficiaries

A third legal option, available only in the state of Hawaii, is *reciprocal beneficiaries*. According to Hawaii's Reciprocal Beneficiaries Law, implemented in 1997, same-sex couples, as well as unmarried relatives and friends of heterosexual and homosexual individuals legally barred from marrying each other, are eligible to register with the Hawaii Department of Health as reciprocal beneficiaries. Hawaii's policy is unique because it extends eligibility to those not in an intimate union. The law grants some of the benefits of marriage to reciprocal beneficiaries, including property rights, protection under the state's domestic violence laws, the ability to visit a beneficiary in the hospital and to make medical decisions for him or her, to sue for the wrongful death of a beneficiary, and to inherit property without a will. Because individuals in reciprocal beneficiaries are legally single, dissolving the relationship legally simply involves informing the Hawaii Department of Health of its termination.

Licensed Domestic Partnerships

A fourth legal option is *licensed domestic partnerships*. These partnerships were first instituted in Berkeley, California, in 1984 and were originally intended to grant public acknowledgment to the unions of same-sex couples. Local government officials at that time determined that unmarried opposite-sex couples also needed legal acknowledgment of their unions, particularly with regard to protecting the so-called weaker party in the relationship upon the dissolution of it; thus, eligibility for participation in licensed domestic partnerships was extended to them as well. Since then, a few other states (Nevada, Oregon, and Washington) have implemented domestic partnership ordinances, as have over a dozen counties and more than 50 cities. An analysis of the domestic

SUPPORTERS AND OPPONENTS OF SAME-SEX MARRIAGE

Supporters

Advocacy groups in support of same-sex marriage have utilized the ever-changing social environment to their advantage, ultimately giving support to their position that a just society translates as one that accepts the practice of same-sex marriage as one of simple fairness, full and complete citizenship, and equal rights. While many involved in the battle over same-sex marriage approach it from a religious standpoint, those that are religiously affiliated but do not attack the issue on a negative level, such as the Unitarian Universalist Association, have called for fully legalized same-sex marriage. In 2005, the United Church of Christ (with some 1.3 million estimated adult members) became the first Christian denomination endorsing the right of homosexual marriage, concluding that "in the Gospel we find ground for a definition of marriage and family relationships based on affirmation of the full humanity of each partner, lived out in mutual care and respect for one another" (www.ucc.org). Some churches have not come to grips with a full decision regarding the topic. The Episcopal Church (with 3 million adult members) has not sanctioned full marriage rights, specifically in terms of actually enacting legal documentation. However, in 2003, the leaders of the Episcopal denomination in the United States approved a resolution at their annual convention that states that under the pretenses of "local faith communities operating within the bounds of our common life as they explore and experience the celebration of and blessing of same-sex unions" (Sheridan and Thrall 2003). In a roundabout way, the Episcopal Church has thrown in a pro-vote without necessarily donning a rainbow banner in the middle of the sanctuary.

Stepping back onto the secular side of the pro-argument, the biggest players on this team are advocacy groups. Examples of these groups include the American Civil Liberties Union, the Human Rights Campaign, the National Gay and Lesbian Task Force, as well as numerous others. Their ability to create change through lobbying, campaigning, fundraising, and numerous other tactics depends on a number of factors, specifically environmental conditions and policies favored strongly by the public. However, public policy is not strong enough to stand on its own as a deciding factor. It must be approached from the right angle at the right point in time for the advocacy groups to pull through as effective promoters of change. To obtain substantial legislative change, these groups must start at the ground level and work their way up, persuading everyone in their path to their reasoning of the argument in order to cut a path of agreeable successes from the starting line to the finish. One thing that must be kept in mind when considering the groups advocating same-sex marriage is that they are much smaller in number, poorer in financial resources, and more deeply polarized in political ideology than their opposition counterparts.

Opponents

Like their counterparts who support same-sex marriage, interest groups opposing same-sex marriage have their work cut out for them. With the ever-changing social environment and the turbulent political waters surrounding the issue, the battle has certainly been a heated one and will likely continue as such. Examples of interest groups in opposition of same-sex marriage include the Family Research Council, Focus on the Family (brought to the headlines of politics by its founder James Dobson), the Christian Coalition (with figures such as Pat Robertson at the helm), and many others. These groups have substantial advantages over the proponents of same-sex marriage in a number of areas. The first is that these groups need only keep things in their favor or keep the status quo. This specifically applies to legislation that these groups do not have to advance. Rather, they must simply block the pro–same-sex marriage groups from advancing their own legislative measures. Their second and perhaps largest advantage is that a large majority of these groups are religiously affiliated; thus, they are interconnected with a number of networks of individuals with various resources readily available for opposition mobilization, ready for attack at any sign of progressive successes. While blocking policy change is a deep advantage for the opposition, as a group, they have not been pleased with their successes in this area. These same groups are also responsible for enacting laws and legislation at various levels that will ultimately define marriage in all finality as being defined as the union of a man and a woman.

An example of one of these groups' arguments was found posted in an essay on the Family Research Council's Web site that specifically states that they oppose same-sex marriage "not because homosexuality is a greater sin than any other. It's not because we want to deprive homosexuals of their fundamental human rights. It's not because we are afraid to be near homosexuals, and it's not because we hate homosexuals. On the contrary, I desire the very best for them. And desiring the best for someone, and acting to bring that about, is the essence of love" (Sprigg 2004). One aspect of same-sex marriage that the opposition has recently chosen to utilize is the prominence, presence, and well-being of the children involved in these proceedings.

partnership records provided by most locales (some do not release this information due to confidentiality concerns) indicates that most licensed couples are in same-sex unions. Several other states grant partial benefits to couples in domestic partnerships.

Domestic partnership ordinances typically define partners as two financially interdependent adults who live together and share an intimate bond but are not related by blood or law. Couples wishing to license their cohabiting unions complete an affidavit attesting that they are not already biologically or legally related to each other or legally married to someone else, that they agree to be mutually responsible for each other's welfare, and that they will notify the local government records office if there is a change in the status of the relationship, either by dissolution or by legal marriage. Along with a fee, the affidavit is then submitted to the local records office or, in some locales, may be notarized to register the partnership. To dissolve a licensed partnership, one partner must inform the office where the partnership was registered. Within six months after this notification, an individual in most locales may then register another domestic partnership.

As noted, the first state to implement a domestic partnership ordinance was California in 1999; in that state, both same-sex and opposite-sex couples are eligible to become licensed partners, although the age-eligibility requirements differ. Specifically, both partners in a same-sex couple must be at least 18 years of age to become licensed partners. One partner in an opposite-sex couple, however, must be at least 62 years of age and meet eligibility requirements for old-age benefits under the Social Security Act. These differing eligibility requirements were implemented to encourage legal marriage among opposite-sex couples, while also recognizing that remarrying after the death of a spouse imposes financial costs in terms of reductions in Social Security benefits to those remarrying as opposed to remaining single. Upon implementation of the legislation, licensed domestic partners in California received a number of tangible benefits that the legally married enjoyed; since 2005, essentially all state-level rights and responsibilities of marriage have been extended to licensed partners.

In the state of Maine, both opposite- and same-sex couples are eligible to register as licensed domestic partners, with the same age eligibility requirements (both partners must be at least 18 years of age). To become licensed, both partners must be residents of Maine for at least one year. Licensed partners in Maine also enjoy limited benefits, including protection under the state's domestic violence laws, the right to inherit property from a partner without a will, making funeral and burial arrangements for a partner, entitlement to be named the partner's guardian in the event he or she becomes incapacitated, and to make decisions regarding organ or tissue donation for a deceased partner.

At least three of the dozen counties and 5 of the 50-plus cities that have implemented domestic partnership ordinances restrict eligibility to same-sex couples. Furthermore, in at least 13 locales, both partners must be either residents of the city or county or couples must include at least one partner who is an employee of the city or county. Thus, couples throughout the United States may become licensed domestic partners in many locales, although they do not reside there. Their home city or county will not acknowledge their licensed status, however, and they will receive no benefits or protections as a function of being licensed partners. Most locales, however, do not offer any tangible benefits or protections to licensed partners anyway, regardless of where the couple resides. The benefits granted by the handful of counties and cities that do provide them include health insurance coverage for a partner, visitation rights in hospitals and correctional facilities, and bereavement leave.

Current Controversies

Those most concerned with the implementation of policies legitimizing various coupling options are divided along ideological lines to form two competing camps. The pro-marriage camp consists of those promoting legal marriage as the sole form of public acknowledgement of intimate unions. Individuals and organizations in this camp may be divided further into two classes: one that promotes heterosexual marriage and desires the exclusion of legal recognition of all other types of unions based on religious beliefs (referred to here as the religiously-oriented) and one that fears the institution of marriage, along with its beneficial aspects to men, women, children, and society, are threatened by legally acknowledging other forms of relationships (referred to here as the family decline–oriented). Specifically, those motivated by religious arguments assert that only heterosexual relationships within the context of legal marriage are natural or ordained by God and that recognition of same-sex unions and nonmarital forms of heterosexual unions undermines the inherent value of legal marriage and violates the will of God. They view marriage as much more than simply a civil contract; rather, it is a holy sacrament. Those motivated by concerns over family decline assert that there are tangible and emotional benefits to marriage that accrue only to individuals residing within the context of legal marriage and that all of society benefits from the well-being these individuals enjoy. Those in this class are concerned that legal acknowledgement of other forms of coupling undermines marriage as the so-called gold standard and that couples will be less likely to aspire to marriage as a result, leading to a host of social ills.

The other side involved in this debate, referred to here as the pro-inclusivity camp, advocates for legal recognition of both marital and nonmarital relationships. They assert that legal marriage for many couples is either unavailable or undesirable as an option to legitimizing a union. They argue that other forms of legitimization must be made available to these couples as a civil rights issue. Advocates of inclusivity argue that the well-being of men, women, children, and society would be advanced by the implementation of policies promoting their choices and protecting their interests, whereas denying them either the opportunity to legitimize their unions or forcing them into an all-or-nothing situation, where they must either marry and receive benefits and protections or not marry and receive no benefits or protections, harms the individuals in these families as well as the well-being of society.

The success of both the pro-marriage and the pro-inclusivity camps in promoting their views is mixed. As noted, an increasing number of locales are implementing legislation that grants acknowledgement to various forms of coupling. At the same time, however, an increasing number of states have implemented their own Defense of Marriage Acts or amended their state constitutions to define marriage as consisting of the legal union of one man and one woman. Currently, only 10 states do not have a version of this act or a substantively similar constitutional amendment.

Clearly, the most controversial issue surrounding the implementation of policies legitimizing various methods of coupling concerns public acknowledgment of same-sex unions. States in particular have struggled with determining what type of acknowledgment to provide, if any, and what terminology should be employed to grant this acknowledgment (e.g., civil unions, licensed partnerships). As noted, only four states have made legal marriage available to resident same-sex couples. Other states have attempted to strike a compromise in this debate by implementing similar legislation but referring to it as something other than legal marriage. The result of the compromise is that parties on both sides of the debate are left dissatisfied. Pro-marriage advocates are alarmed that the unions of same-sex couples are receiving any acknowledgement all; for many same-sex couples and their advocates, however, anything short of legal marriage is simply not enough, as marriage enjoys a cultural aura and subsequent social support that is bolstered by history and religion and that does not exist in any other form of coupling.

It is important to note that even homosexual individuals and organizations promoting their civil rights and well-being are divided on the issue of whether marriage should be extended legally to same-sex couples. Some argue for equal legal treatment between same-sex and opposite-sex couples, whereas others argue that legal marriage has never been an institution in which spouses, especially wives, enjoy equality and the benefits and protections of marriage that have been traditionally enjoyed by husbands. It appears, however, that most organizations serving as advocates for homosexual individuals and their intimate unions are fighting for access to legal marriage.

Although they receive much less public attention, heterosexual licensed domestic partnerships are also a source of controversy. Those promoting heterosexual legal marriage on the basis of family decline concerns argue that opposite-sex couples are engaging in a rational-choice approach to coupling, looking to attain the benefits of marriage while attempting to avoid its costs and obligations. For example, they assert that cohabiting couples, licensed and otherwise, wish to enjoy the financial benefits of marriage by sharing household expenses, while also maintaining financial independence from their partners. Similarly, they are looking to attain the companionship found in marriage while also desirous of more emotional independence from their partners than spouses have from each other. Those in the family decline camp assert that by licensing heterosexual cohabitation, and thereby encouraging couples to cohabit rather than marry, legal marriage is losing its social status as the ultimate method of coupling in society and is being redefined as simply one of several equally valid and valued coupling options. The repercussions, they argue, are significant: adults reduce their sense of commitment and are less likely to fulfill their obligations to others, leading to less security for both adults and children.

Advocates of licensed domestic partnerships, however, assert that emotional commitment and the sense of obligation to partners and children do not differ among licensed partners or the legally married. Instead, marriage is associated with liabilities that may be avoided in licensed partnerships without undermining the quality of or obligations in intimate unions. For example, in legal marriage, spouses are responsible for each other's debts, whereas in licensed domestic partnerships, because the partners are legally single, the financial well-being of one partner is protected from the financial problems of the other partner. Because the partners reside together, the economic well-being of both partners and any children residing with them is protected. Similarly, marriage for some is associated with the oppression of women. Some women in licensed domestic partnerships believe that they are able to avoid what they see as the patriarchal nature of marriage by becoming licensed partners instead. As a result, they assert that they have attained equitable relationships that would not be possible in legal marriage.

In summary, civil unions, same-sex marriage, reciprocal beneficiaries, and licensed domestic partnerships provide some, but not all, of the legal benefits and protections of heterosexual marriage. As a result, these options are not, to date, the legal equivalent of marriage. Furthermore, these couples do not enjoy the social or cultural support promoting the maintenance of their unions that legally married couples enjoy. If indeed individuals in families engaging in nonheterosexual or nonmarital forms of coupling experience lower levels of well-being (and to date, research has not been conducted exploring this issue), the reasons should not be surprising.

See also **Gay Parent Adoption**

Further Reading

Cantor, Donald J., Elizabeth Cantor, James C. Black, and Campbell D. Barrett, *Same-Sex Marriage: The Legal and Psychological Evolution in America.* Middletown, CT: Wesleyan University Press, 2006.

Human Rights Campaign, "HRC: Civil Unions." http://www.hrc.org/Template.cfm?Section= Civilunions1&Template=/TaggedPage/TaggedPageDisplay.cfm&TPLID=23&ContentID= 21804

Human Rights Campaign, "HRC: Domestic Partners." http://www.hrc.org/Template.cfm?Section= Domesticpartners1&Template=/TaggedPage/TaggedPageDisplay.cfm&TPLID=23&Content ID=103

Human Rights Campaign, "Massachusetts Marriage/Relationship Recognition Law." http://www. hrc.org/Template.cfm?Section=Center&CONTENTID=27640&TEMPLATE=/Content Management/ContentDisplay.cfm

Pinello, D. R., *America's Struggle for Same-sex Marriage.* New York: Cambridge University Press, 2006.

Popenoe, D., *State of Our Unions: The Social Health of Marriage in America, 1999.* New Brunswick NJ: National Marriage Project, 1999.

Rimmerman, Craig A., and Clyde Wilcox, *The Politics of Same-Sex Marriage.* Chicago: University of Chicago Press, 2007.

Sheridan, Sharon, and James Thrall, "Deputies Approve Compromise Resolution on Same-Sex Unions." *Episcopal News Service* (August 8, 2003). http://www.episcopalchurch.org/3577_18576_ ENG_HTM.htm

Sprigg, Peter, "Homosexualty: The Threat to the Family and the Attack on Marriage." March 29, 2004. http://www.frc.org/get.cfm?i=PD04F01

Willetts, M. C., "An Exploratory Investigation of Heterosexual Licensed Domestic Partners." *Journal of Marriage and Family* 65 (2003): 939–952.

Willliams, H. K., and R. E. Bowen, "Marriage, Same-sex Unions, and Domestic Partnerships." *Georgetown Journal of Gender and Law* 1 (2000): 337–359.

DOMESTIC VIOLENCE—BEHAVIORS AND CAUSES

Rachel Birmingham

Domestic violence, also known as intimate partner violence, is a significant concern in society today. It is estimated that 9 million couples, or one in six marriages, experience some form of intimate partner violence, with 21 percent of all violent crimes committed against women perpetrated by a romantic partner (Strong, DeVault, and Cohen 2010). Although violence against women in intimate relationships has existed for centuries, it has only become widely acknowledged as problematic since the latter half of the 20th century. Many credit this increased awareness to social and political movements such the second wave of feminism, also known as the modern women's movement, that have argued for equality and basic rights regardless of gender. Also, in association with an increase in activity in the academic, medical, social, and political communities, legislation has been enacted for the purposes of domestic violence protection, prevention, and education.

Policies such as the 1994 Violence against Women Act help to empower women through the funding of prevention and intervention programs. Despite the fact that social change has been credited with spurring protective legislation and social awareness concerning intimate partner violence, many claim that there has been a limited social understanding of the experiences of women in violent relationships, and there remains a victim-blaming bias in how we have responded to domestic violence as a society.

As an aside, it is thoroughly acknowledged that women are not the only victims of domestic violence, because this is a social problem that victimizes men as well. However, research shows that the vast majority of reported domestic abuse victims in U.S. society are women. Additionally, the injuries suffered by women tend to be more severe than those suffered by men. Therefore, we will focus on domestic violence as it affects women primarily.

Abuse Behaviors

Behaviors associated with intimate partner violence are usually categorized into the following groups: physical abuse, emotional abuse, sexual abuse, and financial abuse. Although all are harmful, when there are limited resources in a community, leaders must choose where to direct these resources to do the most good. The most visible category is physical abuse, which has received the most attention from research and advocacy groups. This does not, however, imply that it is the most harmful or important abuse behavior. The following definitions of abusive behaviors have been taken from the National Center for Injury Prevention and Control (2008) and will be described here in greater detail.

Physical Abuse

Physical abuse is defined as the intentional use of physical force with the potential for causing death, disability, injury, or harm. Physical violence includes, but is not limited to, scratching, pushing, shoving, throwing, grabbing, biting, choking, shaking, slapping, punching, burning, use of a weapon, and use of restraints or one's body, size, or strength against another person. Consequences associated with physical abuse are severe and far reaching, resulting in death in extreme cases. This is what most persons stereotypically picture when they hear the phrase "battered wife."

Emotional Abuse

Psychological or emotional abuse involves trauma to the victim caused by acts, threats of acts, or coercive tactics. This can include, but is not limited to, humiliating the victim, controlling what the victim can and cannot do, withholding information, deliberately doing something to make the victim feel diminished or embarrassed, isolating the victim from friends and family, threatening or terrorizing, and denying access to basic resources. Scholars have reported that as many as 80 to 90 percent of women will experience psychological maltreatment at some point in an intimate relationship (Neufeld, McNamara, and Ertl 1999). The consequences of such abuse have been found to have devastating impacts on survivors as well. In fact, due to the devastating consequences of emotional abuse, many survivors report that they would rather be physically hit than emotionally abused by an intimate partner.

Sexual Abuse

The National Center for Injury Prevention and Control, a subgroup of the Centers for Disease Control and Prevention, defines and divides sexual abuse into three categories: (1) the use of physical force to compel a person to engage in a sexual act against his or her will, regardless of whether the act is completed; (2) an attempted or completed sex act involving a person who is unable to understand the nature or condition of the act, to decline participation, or to communicate unwillingness to engage in the sexual act (e.g., because of illness, disability, the influence of alcohol or other drugs, or because of intimidation or pressure); and (3) abusive sexual contact. Studies show that between 10 and 14 percent of wives have been forced into sexual activity by their partners (Strong, DeVault, and Cohen 2010). It is often difficult for women who are sexually abused by an intimate partner to seek help, because it is often the case that sexual activity within relationships, whether voluntary or coerced, is not recognized as abusive. Although sexual abuse within intimate relationships has achieved more recognition through increased research and media attention, it is still often very difficult for a victim to seek help or to receive the validation needed to overcome such traumatic experiences.

Financial Abuse

Financial abuse is usually characterized by an abuser withholding funds, stealing assets, stealing property, or compromising a partner's financial liberties. It can be difficult for the victim to seek relationship alternatives in situations where financial abuse is present, because the victim is often totally dependent on the abuser to provide for basic needs. This is especially true when children are involved. With this lack of resources available to the victim, there is also an increased risk of homelessness for the women and children impacted by violent relationships—an issue that will be discussed in further detail later.

Common Couple Violence Versus Intimate Terrorism

Among the issues that have made it difficult to get the needed attention for domestic violence is the wide range of behaviors that fall under the umbrella of abuse. For many years, there was a stereotypical image of a battered woman who was the victim of abusive beatings. However, recent thinking about domestic abuse has expanded to include a variety of unwanted violent acts. Intimate partner violence takes many forms and involves many behaviors that are detrimental to the victim. In addition, some theoretical and methodological considerations in relation to intimate partner violence must be examined. Based on the work of Michael Johnson (1995), several theoretical distinctions have been made regarding domestic abuse. These categories originally arose during a comparison of samples of domestic violence victims gathered from the general population and those from shelters. They also differ in areas related to power dynamics and behavioral characteristics as well as on overall outcomes for victims. Johnson terms these distinctions *common couple violence* and *intimate terrorism.*

Common Couple Violence

Common couple violence is considered the most common type of violence that occurs in relationships and is a less dangerous form of intimate partner violence. In situations where violence is present, conflict usually arises from a mutual disagreement between the partners and is equally perpetrated among partners, although women are more likely to be injured during violent episodes. It is important to recognize that both partners can be violent in this scenario. This form of violence rarely escalates over time and is more likely to be identified through surveys of the general population.

Intimate Terrorism

Intimate terrorism, also referred to as patriarchal terrorism, is severe and can be lethal. In situations where intimate terrorism is present, the abuser usually demonstrates power and control in order to dominate the partner. Conflict in these relationships is usually one-sided and intense. In these relationships, conflict usually escalates over time and increases in both frequency and intensity. Intimate terrorism is frequently characterized by a physical or emotional domination of the victim and often involves social isolation, financial dependence, and emotional degradation and is characterized by feelings of fear and hopelessness. Johnson reported that victims of intimate terrorism are more likely to be identified through research that focuses on specific samples, such as women in shelter settings.

While Johnson's work has been credited with uncovering a broad range of domestic violence types, there is some concern with defining domestic violence in this way. For example, the term *common couple violence* suggests that all partners participate and it must therefore be normal to do so. If this type of violence is assumed to be a normal part of relationships, that changes how society is willing to respond. There is a concern that a partner's requests for help may not be taken seriously if she were violent against her spouse. This could set up a situation in which only victims of intimate terrorism may be seen as worthy of assistance by shelters and other agencies. A victim of common couple violence, then, may be blamed for putting herself in a situation in which she and the partner resorted to violence.

Why Doesn't She Just Leave?

A common question that arises in relation to domestic violence is *why doesn't she just leave?* Surely women do not enjoy being treated this way, so why don't abused women get out? Many feel that if a victim of domestic violence *really* wanted to leave the relationship, she would just move on. However, as will be discussed further, the circumstances that often surround domestic violence, especially in situations where intimate terrorism is present, tend to be complex, and choosing to leave can be much more difficult, if not more lethal, than most people may realize. The suggestion that she should just leave blames any future abuse on her decision to stay; thus, the victim blaming becomes acute.

Barriers to Seeking Help

Due to various social barriers, many abused women do not perceive their decision to remain in a violent relationship as a choice at all, because few, if any, reasonable alternatives may be available. Common barriers that exist for victimized women include social isolation, financial dependence, fear of repercussions, pressure to keep the family together, and a lack of appropriate community response. Advocates for the victims of domestic abuse debate which of these exerts the most pressure on women to stay in abusive situations.

Social Isolation

As noted in the discussion of Johnson's concept of intimate terrorism, social isolation is a common factor found in most cases of domestic abuse. It is quite common in situations of intimate terrorism, because isolating one from the external support system enables the abuser to maintain power and control through forcing dependency of the victim on the abuser. This can include instances in which the victim is moved, often repeatedly, from place to place to ensure a lack of social contacts such as friends and family and external support such as community resources. In our individualistic society, this isolation is especially problematic because of cultural norms regarding the right to privacy of the family. The practice of purposeful isolation usually involves limiting access to friends, family, and coworkers or forbidding outside employment altogether. Increasing isolation of the victim greatly decreases the perceived and actual availability of support in situations of abuse. Therefore, escape from abusive relationships becomes all the more difficult. In fact, isolation increases the likelihood that a woman will live with an abusive partner from 12 to 25 percent (Bosch and Schumm 2004).

Financial Dependence

Studies show that domestic violence is more likely to occur in situations where couples are less educated and live in poor economic conditions. Poverty, which is directly correlated with lower levels of education, is also a strong predictor of domestic violence. In fact, among all couples, a top cause of conflict is related to economic stress and strain. In addition, a woman living in poverty is more likely to be financially dependent on her abuser, especially if she is unable to work. Therefore, for many women, the reality is that if she chooses to leave her abuser, the alternative is an inability to provide for her children and herself and possibly experiencing homelessness.

Fear of Repercussion

Many women remain in violent relationships because they are afraid to leave; the abuser has threatened severe violence, or he has threatened to kill the woman or her children. This fear may be quite valid, because most of the severe acts of violence tend to be perpetrated against women who have left or attempted to leave a violent relationship. Furthermore, a woman is more likely to be murdered during the first six months following her exit from an abusive relationship than at any other time in her life, and at least 67 percent of women homicide victims had a history of physical abuse by an intimate partner (National Center for Victims of Crime 2009).

Many women who exit abusive relationships are stalked by their abuser. Stalking is an issue of significant concern because it often results in psychological problems, including anxiety, insomnia, fear, depression, loss of work time, and the need for legal protective orders. Furthermore, the risk of homicide for stalked women is substantial; 76 percent of women who are murdered were stalked by their killer during the year prior to their death (National Center for Victims of Crime 2009).

Pressure to Keep the Family Together

Societal norms and values concerning the family often create pressure for women to keep their families together. Therefore, if a woman—especially a married woman—is in an abusive relationship, she may find it difficult to separate her family. Many women believe that if their children are not being directly physically assaulted, they are being protected from the abuse. This is seldom the case, because most children are much more aware of domestic violence than their parents realize. Furthermore, many women have been raised to believe that the outcomes of raising children in a single-parent home would be a far worse alternative to the abuse. Also, many abused women receive messages from friends, family members, or members their religious community that steps must be taken to ensure the family is kept together, regardless of the presence of abuse. This not only places women and children at risk but also places responsibility for the family health on the abused women.

Lack of Appropriate Community Response

Another barrier that domestic violence victims face is a lack of appropriate community response. Often, the seriousness of abuse situations is underestimated, or blame is placed on the victim. Survivors of abuse often report that they experienced being mocked, blamed, or completely ignored by law enforcement. It is also common for abuse victims to not report the abuse because they feel hopeless about the situation—as if it would not make a difference or things would only worsen. Thus, abused women may be abandoned by the system and left in a more dangerous situation with a perpetrator who has been agitated by her attempts to seek help.

In addition, a common concern experienced by abused mothers is that they will lose their children if they attempts to sever ties with the abuser. This concern is valid, because there are many documented cases of women losing custody of the children to an abuser, especially when domestic violence is present. A common misconception in society is that mothers are favored for custody within the court system. However, abused women increasingly are losing custody of their children on the basis of an inappropriate judicial response to domestic violence. For example, Parental Alienation Syndrome is a scientifically invalid condition in which a woman is accused of making up accusations of violence and abuse with the expressed purpose of alienating her children from the abuser. Although the syndrome has been debunked and deemed as so-called junk science, it still remains one of the most widely used arguments in the U.S. legal system to award primary child custody to abuse perpetrators.

Learned Helplessness?

A commonly taught principal on college campuses today regarding domestic violence victims is that of learned helplessness. The theory, originally derived from Martin Seligman's experiments with dogs, has been applied to abused women and was commonly accepted as an explanation regarding why a woman might not leave an abusive situation. In developing her concept of battered woman syndrome, psychologist Lenore Walker (2000) drew heavily on this idea. The argument is that a victim who has been repeatedly worn down both physically and emotionally by an abuser will reach a psychological state where she perceives that she is neither able nor worthy enough to escape her situation. Consequently, she loses her will to leave the relationship. Therefore, learned helplessness focuses a great deal on the psychological condition of victims, who commonly report having feelings of low self-esteem, depression, self-blame, passivity, and guilt, as well as experiences of repeated victimization, including those during childhood and adulthood.

In contrast, many argue that learned helplessness fails to take into account the fact that women often remain in relationships for rational reasons, such as those discussed previously, and not for psychopathological reasons. In addition, many criticize the approach that learned helplessness takes to domestic violence victimization in that it places the primary reasoning behind and responsibility for abusive relationships on women. This constitutes another form of blaming the victim. Those who are skeptical of the learned helplessness argument suggest that domestic violence should be viewed in terms of the context of the situation and the resources, or lack thereof, available to the victim, including the social response to domestic violence, as opposed to the characteristics of the victim.

What Resources Are Available?

In many communities, domestic violence organizations exist in some capacity. Common services provided by these groups are adult victim counseling, child counseling, legal assistance, voucher plans (for necessities such as food, clothing, and furniture), shelter services and protection if deemed necessary, transitional housing for women and children, safety planning, and coordination of or participation in community activism on behalf of domestic violence victims.

Many online educational resources exist pertaining to domestic violence as well. Some focus exclusively on the victim by providing information on abuse signs and symptoms, safety planning and tips, building healthy relationships, and prevention by providing information on local community resources. Such resources can be found through the Department of Health and Human Services, the Centers for Disease Control and Prevention, Womenshealth.gov, or MEDLINEplus.

Other services include those sponsored by the National Coalition against Domestic Violence. The cell phone program accepts donations of old cell phones to provide means of emergency communication for domestic abuse victims in need of immediate help. In addition, the National Domestic Violence Hotline (1-800-799-SAFE) exists for anyone who may need help or advice pertaining to domestic abuse. Anyone who suspects that they, or someone they know, may be in an unhealthy or abusive relationship is advised to seek the guidance of one of the above listed organizations. Taking a step that is as simple as making a phone call can save a life.

Finally, national movements such as Take Back the Night exist to provide individuals and communities with the opportunity to be empowered through providing a voice to victims to be heard and to live lives that are free from violence and abuse.

Conclusion

A common critique pertaining to research on and response to domestic violence is that most approaches to this social problem are oriented from a victim-blaming perspective. Even in this discussion, which focuses on the awareness of such a bias, domestic violence must still be approached largely from this perspective. This emphasis on the role of the victim is very difficult to avoid, because a substantial portion of what we know about domestic violence comes from examination of the victim's choices as opposed to those of the perpetrator. This perspective is not an inherent flaw, because understanding the issues facing domestic violence victims is critical to providing assistance and increasing awareness. However, caution must be taken when examining abuse from this perspective if we are to avoid placing primary responsibility for the occurrence and continuation of domestic violence on the victim. This is critical, because it is through an examination of this social problem from multiple perspectives that we will be better equipped to address ending domestic violence as a responsibility of society as a whole.

See also **Addiction and Family; Child Abuse; Domestic Violence Interventions (vol. 2)**

Further Reading

Bosch, Kathy, and Walter R. Schumm, "Accessibility to Resources: Helping Rural Women in Abusive Partner Relationships Become Free from Abuse." *Journal of Sex and Marital Therapy* 30 (2004): 357–370.

Denmark, Florence, and Michelle Paludi, eds., *Psychology of Women: A Handbook of Issues and Theories,* 2d ed. Westport, CT: Praeger, 2008.

Family Shelter Service, "Learned Helplessness vs Survivor Hypothesis." http://www.familyshelterservice.org/pdf/survivor.pdf

Johnson, Michael P., "Patriarchal Terrorism and Common Couple Violence: Two Forms of Violence against Women." *Journal of Marriage and Family* 57 (1995): 283–294.

Johnson, Michael P., and K. J. Ferraro, "Research on Domestic Violence in the 1990s: Making Distinctions." *Journal of Marriage and Family* 62 (2000): 948–963.

National Center for Injury Prevention and Control, "Intimate Partner Violence: Definitions." October 21, 2008. http://www.cdc.gov/ViolencePrevention/intimatepartnerviolence/definitions.html

National Center for Victims of Crime, "Stalking Facts" (2009). http://www.ncvc.org/src/main.aspx?dbID=DB_statistics195

Neufeld, B. "SAFE Questions: Overcoming the Barriers to Detecting Domestic Violence." *American Family Physician* 53 (1996): 2575–2581.

Neufeld, J., J. R. McNamara, and M. Ertl, "Incidence and Prevalence of Dating Partner Abuse and Its Relationship to Dating Practices." *Journal of Interpersonal Violence* 14 (1999): 125–137.

Seligman, M.E.P., and S. F. Maier, "Failure to Escape Traumatic Shock." *Journal of Experimental Psychology* 74 (1967): 1–9.

Sokoloff, Natalie J., with Christina Pratt, *Domestic Violence at the Margins: Readings on Race, Class, Gender, and Culture.* New Brunswick, NJ: Rutgers University Press, 2005.

Strong, Bryan, Christine DeVault, and Theodore F. Cohen, *The Marriage and Family Experience,* 11th ed. Belmont, CA: Wadsworth, 2010.

Walker, Lenore E. A., *The Battered Woman Syndrome,* 2d ed. New York: Springer, 2000.

DROPOUTS

Jessica Ruglis

Colloquially, the term *school dropout* refers to a young person who has not completed high school. Linguistically, the choice of the word *dropout* places the responsibility and onus of leaving school solely on the individual. It obscures the pathways by which students ultimately "choose" to leave school, and the structures that lead to dropping out remain blameless. School dropout reflects not on the structures of the school the youth attended, on his or her schooling experiences, nor on the student's worlds and realities outside of school.

School dropout is a term that refers to a young person who does not graduate from school with a traditional diploma. These youth leave school by choice or by force or are pushed out due to "rationalized policies and practices of exclusion that organize" public high schools (Fine 1991, 6). In any event, the ultimate result is the same: a young person does not finish high school. Historic educational policies and practices mask the phenomenon of school dropout such that it rears itself as an outlier: a rare dysfunction of an individual failing within a system, and, like all social outcomes resulting from structural preclusion, it carries a detrimental blame-the-victim ideology. In the context of education, this ideology presents young people who drop out as failing to measure up to academic standards and their subsequent bleak social status and life outcomes as a natural consequence of education's ethos of equal opportunity for all.

Given that the graduation rate crisis disproportionately plagues students of color and low-income and special education students; recent immigrants; lesbian, gay, bisexual, transgender/transsexual, and queer/questioning youth; students with disabilities; homeless youth; youth caught in foster care; and youth caught in the criminal and juvenile justice systems, school dropout has a disparate impact, affecting youth who are already lacking in resources, opportunities, and voice.

A miseducation, however we name its end results, has substantial costs. For each youth and community disenfranchised by its school system, there are staggering economic and social impacts, heavy consequences for criminal justice, costs to civic and political participation, and grave implications for health. Dropouts are more likely to receive public assistance, be unemployed, live in poverty, end up in prison and on death row, die earlier, and suffer from a wide range of chronic and acute diseases and health problems. On average, dropouts earn $9,200 less per year than high school graduates and $1 million less over their lifetime than do college graduates. Beyond dropping out, children forced out of the school system are more likely to engage in conduct harmful to the safety of themselves, their families, and communities.

The Current Landscape of Graduation

Nationally, 68 percent of all students graduate from high school over the traditional four-year period; yet ethnic disparities in these graduation rates are striking. While 76.8 percent and 74.9 percent of Asian/Pacific Islanders and whites, respectively, graduate from high school, Native Americans, blacks, and Latinos all have graduation rates that hover around 50 percent. In some cases, Asian refugees—particularly Laotian, Cambodian, Vietnamese, and Hmong—and Pacific Islander students graduate at rates similarly as bleak. Immigration and socioeconomic status are important contextual variables in the success of immigrant students. On average, boys graduate at a rate 8 percent lower than girls, and graduation rates for youth attending high-poverty, racially segregated, urban schools fall between 15 and 18 percent behind their peers.

The data are similar for the special needs population, where only 32 percent of classified students with disabilities graduate from high school. Low-income children and children of color are overrepresented in special education (including being labeled as having emotional or behavior problems), school disciplinary actions, and in the juvenile and criminal justice systems—all of which correlate to school dropout. Compounding these statistics is the fact that children from low-income families are twice as likely to drop out of school as children from middle-income families and are six times more likely to drop out than children from high-income households. Ninth grade is thought to be the most critical year in influencing school dropout. A silenced history exemplifies this trend: between 1970 and 2000, the rate at which students disappeared from school between 9th and 10th grade *tripled*. And that does not include the leakage from 8th to 9th grade.

Data this staggering have inherent antecedents, leaving the current graduation rate crisis to illuminate a historical genesis of an institution that systematically fails entire groups of youth.

Historical Controversies of School Dropout

In closely examining the history of schooling, it becomes readily apparent that school dropout is a dialectic: it is both a deliberate *and* an unintended consequence of a system structured to maintain the status quo. This becomes evident through the ways by which schools ensure the development, success, and privilege of the white, dominant classes at the expense of those on the margins. The process of schooling is a means to assimilate and acculturate on one hand and to provide liberation, freedom, and educational, social, and economic equity on the other. Deeply contested and holding these two antithetical meanings, school dropout can no longer remain invisible. It has seeped through the cracks, appearing in the staggeringly low graduation rates and in real dollar costs to the criminal justice and health care systems at the expense of the educationally disenfran-chised. The facade of educational opportunity and the influence of differing ideologies seem to be the interface between these two conflicting forces.

The Muddled Roots of the School Dropout

Several educational practices throughout the history of schooling have been discussed in relation to school dropout. Academic tracking, a practice that has been around since the post–Civil War era, has always had the greatest percentage of low-income students and students of color occupying the lower academic tracks. These students are labeled and tracked into a marginal future, without the personal growth of one's own soul, aspi-rations, and spirit. With limited occupational and economic opportunity, being placed in a low academic track has always been a practice that serves as a precursor to school dropout.

One of the biggest misconceptions about young people who drop out is that they have no desire and motivation to learn, place little value on an education and learning, and are not interested in school. As it turns out, and as is detailed in the following sec-tion, schools often prevent young people from enacting their desire and motivation for learning and success. In fact, history is pervasive with examples of *social movements* for education, acts that can only be explained by both individual and a collective's desire and motivation for schooling.

Underfunding, chronic overcrowding, and poor schooling conditions are also his-toric educational practices that contribute to school dropout. Schools and districts that serve large immigrant populations, those of low income, and communities of color have been underfunded, overcrowded, and not well maintained. Subsequently, the quality of education achievable in these conditions pales in comparison to the educational opportunities and access to resources of their more privileged and white counterparts. Deliberate underdevelopment and a decrepit physical environment sig-nificantly shape educational limitations. For example, it has often been reported that overcrowding schools was a way to get young people to drop out. This was achieved through the practice of double-shift schooling, in which schools were filled beyond overcapacity to the extent that they needed to run several shifts of students through-out one single day. As a result, class time and total hours spent in school for each pupil decreased, and the time spent *out of school* increased. This practice, in essence, manufactured dropouts.

Contemporary Conflicts in School Dropout

School dropout is the end stage in a cumulative and dynamic process of educational disengagement and dispossession. The controversy and conflict surrounding who is to blame for dropout—the individual or the school system—are embedded into each cat-egory and represented by the range and scope of the data. The research reflects a diverse array of ideological and theoretical positions. Themes of alienation, lack of school engagement, and the nature of the school setting and culture that emerge from the literature are presented.

Causes of School Dropout Individual-Level Characteristics

Individual attributes associated with school dropout include feelings of alienation, disliking or feeling disconnected from school, decreased levels of school participation, and low educational or occupational self-expectations. Diminished academic aspirations may reflect the changing labor market and economic forces operating at higher levels of social organization. Additionally, when students feel that the locus of control for their success resides outside of themselves, they report feeling less academically inclined.

Compared to their counterparts who complete school, dropouts are less socially conforming; more likely to challenge openly their perceived injustice of the social system; less accepting of parental, school, social, and legal authority; more autonomous; more socially isolated; and less involved in their communities. For some young people, dropping out may be a form of resistance or critique of the educational system. And the effect of self-esteem on school dropout is contested, with some research showing an association and some not.

Behaviors associated with dropout include disruptive conduct; truancy; absenteeism; lateness; substance use; pregnancy and parenting; mental, emotional, psychological, or behavioral difficulties; and low participation in extracurricular activities. These behaviors may be influenced by differing school environments, again pointing to the role that inequitable schools play in shaping the production of school dropout.

The foremost cause of school dropout for adolescent women is teenage pregnancy, accounting for between 30 and 40 percent of the young women who leave school, although alternative evidence demonstrates that often young women stop attending school and *then* get pregnant. Adolescent men are also affected by teen pregnancy, as they may drop out to earn money to support a child. Compared to school completers, dropouts are more likely to be substance abusers, and to have started substance abuse early; more likely to be involved in the sale of drugs; and more likely to have friends engaging in behavior deemed to be socially deviant. Mental illness and emotional disturbance also account for a significant percentage of high school dropouts—reports state that between 48 and 55 percent of young people with mental and emotional troubles fail to graduate high school.

Individual school experiences greatly impact the likelihood of graduation. Students held back in school are more than *11* times as likely to leave school as their peers, and several studies identify grade retention (being held back a grade) as the most significant predictor of school dropout. Poor academic achievement, low self-expectations, low grades, lower test scores, and course failure all contribute to school dropout. Here, too, these individual factors must be viewed as manifestations of accumulating poor educational experiences. In fact, 45 percent of students report starting high school very underprepared by their earlier schooling.

Economic constraints also influence dropout. Surveys of dropouts show that having to get a job, conflicts between work and school, and having to support a family are important reasons for leaving school. However, the overwhelming majority of all dropouts report that education and graduating are important to success in life. Data indicate the high *value* that dropouts place on education and their strong *desire* for education, despite rhetoric on dropouts that argue the opposite.

Family Characteristics

Family characteristics associated with dropping out are low levels of family support, involvement, and expectations for education achievement; low parental education attainment; single-parent homes; parenting style; few study aids available at home; less opportunity for nonschool learning; financial problems; and low socioeconomic status. Low expectations for a child's academic success by adults have been shown to increase a child's likelihood of dropping out fivefold.

Residential or school mobility are also considerably linked to school dropout. Importantly, what often appears to be lack of parental involvement in education is actual life constraints of living in poverty, having to work more than one job, employment where parents cannot take time off of work, language barriers between the family and school personnel, or the symbolic representation of schools as unwelcoming institutions for parents who were not successful in schools themselves.

Many adolescents, especially young women, carry the burden of caring for their family, forcing them to leave high school due to social or health needs of their loved ones. Compared to school completers, dropouts are more likely to translate for family members, help to find health care for their family, and care for the elderly and children in their families. Young men are often forced to economically sustain their families. Family stress, parental substance abuse, physical or sexual abuse of children, lack of health insurance, family health problems, having to care for a family member, or the death of a loved one can contribute to the decision (or need) to drop out.

Neighborhood and Community Characteristics

Communities with high levels of crime, violence, drug-related crime, and arson have higher rates of school dropout than communities with fewer of these problems. Some studies indicate that communal social support promotes school engagement and improves chances for school graduation among racial and ethnic minority students. Similarly, cultural norms of schools and cultural and linguistic tensions between the home and community (and often country) from which students come contribute to educational disenfranchisement, leading to school dropout.

School Characteristics

Attributes of schools and school systems significantly influence dropout rates. Poverty again plays a central role, with a school's mean socioeconomic status being the most significant independent influence on graduation rates. In addition, higher levels of segregation, more students of color, more students enrolled in special education, and location in central cities or larger districts are also associated with lower graduation rates. It is neither an accidental correlation nor coincidence that race and ethnicity, socioeconomic class, and level of urbanization are implicated in higher rates of school dropout.

School climate is a central component of school engagement and, therefore, school completion. Punitive school policies (standardized testing, changing academic standards without supports, tracking, unfair and stringent discipline policies, frequent use of suspensions) all affect academic engagement and success. When social support and positive relationships with adults in the school are diminished, so is a young person's connectedness to school. And school engagement and connectedness are two widely supported causes of staying in school.

School Policies

High-stakes testing, a practice whereby student advancement is determined primarily by tests, also influences dropout rates. Comparing states that employ high-stakes testing to those that do not shows that states using such tests hold students back at much higher rates than states that do not.

More recent studies publish findings of "school pushout," in which school dropouts are forced out of school through a variety of policies and practices, like policing, discipline, and educational-tracking measures. School pushout is a concept that reframes the choice to leave school as a reflection of the larger educational systems, structures, and policies that have failed youth and that often ultimately force young people out of schools. Stemming from this phenomenon is the associated school-to-prison pipeline, a term that refers to policies and practices that ensure that when young people misbehave in school, they are turned over to the police and juvenile justice system.

School safety and discipline policies appear to have a strong effect on dropout rates. Student perceptions of unfair discipline, of low teacher interest in students, and of lack of attachment to an adult in the school all predict dropout. School disciplinary contact is among the strongest predictors of school dropout. Surveys of dropouts show that being suspended often and getting expelled contribute to the decision to drop out. Propensity for being a target of school discipline actions (number of office referrals, suspensions, and expulsions) is overwhelmingly racialized: low-income children, children of color, those in special education, and those labeled as emotionally disturbed are disproportionally impacted. Developmentally, school discipline has severe effects on a child's perception of justice, fairness, trust, capability, and self-worth and may contribute to feelings of social isolation and alienation and to engaging in high-risk behaviors.

Other school policies that have been associated with dropout include high student-to-teacher ratios, academic tracking, and a discrepancy between faculty and student demographic characteristics. Low levels of engagement to school also predict dropout. Related, a lack of sufficient programs for pregnant and parenting teens as well as comprehensive health and sex-education programs and availability of social services build barriers that make the success of particular groups of students nearly impossible. Schools that adopt such programs buffer school dropout with tremendous success.

The Controversy over Data Reporting

The issue of reporting data becomes controversial due to its absence and lack of any standardized, reliable, and valid data-collection formula. Until the No Child Left Behind Act (NCLB) of 2002, there was no federal mandate requiring graduation rate reporting. Before this, only some states kept graduation rate data. This law, while unearthing the chasm in public education, has also positioned itself in a way that can promulgate the crisis. This NCLB mandate provides little protection for low-performing students to not be pushed out of schools. Districts, in order to meet the incentives for improving their graduation rates and for meeting the annual yearly progress requirement, push lower-performing students into alternative school programs, where they are not counted as dropouts.

Also undermining any real attempt by NCLB to ensure equal educational attainment are two principles of the law. First, unlike the accountability mandates, which require test score and achievement data to be kept demographically—by income, race/ethnicity, special education status, and limited English proficiency—and for which adequate yearly progress must be made in at least one of these historically low-performing groups, when calculating the graduation rate, states must only count the overall rate; they do not have to record by demographics. This allows young people on the margins to be practically ignored and disparities in graduation rates to be silenced. Second, and also incongruent with the accountability mandates that stipulate that 100 percent of all students receive "proficient" test scores by 2014, states can establish their own formula for calculating graduation rates and their own graduation rate goals, which can range between 50 and100 percent. What NCLB has effectively done is to create a loophole that ensures, if not requires, students to be pushed out of schools in order to meet the more stringent accountability mandates—to which funding and school takeover sanctions are attached. By giving federal permission for states to aspire to a mere 50 percent graduation rate without having to record demographic data, the federal government has given the doorway for how to achieve 100 percent proficiency while maintaining the historic class and racial structure of society.

In recent years, several reports have published studies that examine and develop more accurate, comprehensive, and representative methods for calculating and capturing the landscape of educational attainment. Specifically, these measures are indicators of high school graduation rates rather than of the more traditional and common statistics that measure either dropout rates or high school completion rates. (Dropout rates can be calculated in one of three ways: event dropout rates, status dropout rates, and cohort dropout rates.) Each of these different measures will produce very different results. To date, most states calculate dropout rates, a figure that is not the equivalent of graduation rates (those reported here).

While these newer reports calculate nearly identical statistics on high school graduation rates, data used here are from a formula developed by Christopher Swanson of the Urban Institute. This formula is the best proxy for current graduation rates, and the subsequent research details the most "extensive set of systematic empirical findings on public school graduation rates available to date for the nation as a whole and for each of the states" (Swanson 2004b, 1). The method developed is called the Cumulative Promotion Index (CPI), and it is applied to data from the Common Core of Data (CCD), the U.S. Department of Education's database, as the measure to calculate high school graduation rates. The CCD database is the most complete source of information on all public schools and local education agencies in the United States. The CPI is a variation of cohort dropout rates in that it "approximates the probability that a student entering the 9th grade will complete high school on time [in four years] with a regular diploma. It does this by representing high school graduation as a stepwise process composed of three grade-to-grade promotion transitions (9 to 10, 10 to 11, and 11 to 12) in addition to the ultimate high school graduation event (grade 12 to diploma)" (Swanson 2004a, 7). It is important to emphasize that the CPI only counts students who receive high school diplomas as graduates and not those who earn a GED or other alternative credentials, thus overrepresenting the number of people "graduating" from high school. This is in keeping with the NCLB mandate for what constitutes a diploma. This index was created as a response to methods that are commonly used to determine educational attainment.

The more common statistical measures of dropout rates and high school completion rates have significant limitations. *Dropout rates*, meant to capture only the percentage of students that actually drop out of school, are based on underreported and underrepresented data, because there is no standard mechanism for reporting, coding, or accounting for students who drop out. Districts often title students who may have indeed dropped out or been pushed out as having transferred or moved or as missing. This false representation leads to an exaggerated picture of how well a school is doing. High school *completion rates* count General Educational Development (GED) graduates and students receiving alternative credentials as high school graduates. As such, data measuring high school completion differ greatly from those measuring graduation rates. Incorporating GEDs and other alternative credentials in graduation rates is problematic for two primary reasons. First, recipients of the GED or alternative certifications are not graduates of high school; therefore, their credentials cannot be attributed to the school system. Second, the economic and higher educational returns from students with a GED is not equivalent to those with a high school diploma.

The most common graduation and dropout statistics are cited from the National Center for Education Statistics (NCES), which calculates its data as high school completion rates but reports its data as a high school graduation rate of over 85 percent (2007). The NCES statistic has relatively low levels of national coverage and is computed using data from only 54 percent of U.S. school districts and 45 percent of the student population.

The NCES uses data from the Current Population Survey (CPS). The CPS, conducted by the U.S. Census Bureau, is a simple self-report survey conducted in noninstitutionalized settings and on people who are neither currently in school nor recently graduated. This measure surveys the general young adult population (ages 18–24), not school district information. Students may report GED attainment as high school completion, they may misrepresent their education level, and it may underrepresent low-income youth who are disproportionately dropouts. Youth in low-income communities are often harder to find and interview. The CPS also underrepresents black and Latino youth, who are incarcerated at high rates and are therefore excluded from participating in the survey because prisons are institutionalized settings. Collectively, this measure offers a much higher and nonreliable depiction of the state of high school graduation—one that masks the crisis.

Conclusion

The implications of how dropout is framed—either as an individual burden or as the fault of the institution—have drastically different consequences. For each young person disenfranchised by his or her school system, there is a fraying of the public belief in the common good, a threat to a collective sense of democratic belonging, substantial losses to communities, economic and social impacts, heavy consequences for criminal justice, costs to civic and political participation, and dire implications for health.

With increasing public and educational consciousness about the graduation rate crisis, many innovative and effective dropout-prevention programs are being created and implemented. With the move for schools to incorporate school-based health centers and other social service supports, young people are provided supports and resources that make their engagement and success in school possible. When schools and programs reflect the stance that schools need to support students, and not that students are deficient of success, this crisis has the ability to change.

See also **Government Role in Schooling; Juvenile Delinquency; Teen Pregnancy**

Further Reading

Fine, M., *Framing Dropouts: Notes on the Politics of an Urban Public High School.* Albany: State University of New York Press, 1991.

Franklin, C., et al., eds., *The School Practitioner's Concise Companion to Preventing Dropout and Attendance Problems*. New York: Oxford University Press, 2008.

Mishel, L., and J. Roy, *Rethinking High School Graduation Rates and Trends*. Washington DC: Economic Policy Institute, 2006.

Orfield, G., ed., *Dropouts in America: Confronting the Graduation Rate Crisis*. Cambridge, MA: Harvard Education Press, 2004.

Swanson, C., *The Real Truth about Low Graduation Rates: An Evidence-Based Commentary*. Washington, DC: Urban Institute, 2004a.

Swanson, C., *Who Graduates? Who Doesn't? A Statistical Portrait of Public High School Graduation, Class of 2001*. Washington, DC: Urban Institute, 2004b.

DRUGS

Nancy D. Campbell

Drugs enjoy a social significance different from other commodities, technologies, or artifacts. Celebrated by artists and visionaries from the 19th-century Romantics to the 20th-century Beats to 21st-century hip-hop musicians, drugs have been seen to shape minds and bodies in socially positive and problematic ways. Prescription drugs are credited with improving health, productivity, and well-being, whereas nonprescription drugs are blamed for destroying minds and bodies. How society views drugs depends on who produces them, how they are distributed and marketed, and who consumes them and how. Many controversies surround the workings of these fascinating, functional, and sometimes dangerous technologies.

Drugs as Pharmaceutical Wonders

History reveals a remarkable parade of "wonder drugs"—such as heroin, introduced in 1898 by the German pharmaceutical company Bayer as a nonaddicting painkiller useful for treating tuberculosis and other respiratory diseases. Bayer introduced aspirin a few years later as a treatment for rheumatoid arthritis but promoted it aggressively for relief of headache and everyday aches and pains. Today, aspirin is the world's most widely available drug, but there was a time when pharmacists smuggled it across the U.S.-Canadian border because it was so much more expensive in the United States than elsewhere. Cocaine, distributed to miners in the Southwest as an energizing tonic, was used much as amphetamines and caffeine are used in postindustrial society. Barbiturates; sedative-hypnotics such as thalidomide, Seconal, or Rohypnol; major and minor tranquilizers; benzodiazepines such as Valium; and painkillers or analgesics have all been promoted as wonder drugs before turning out to have significant potential for addiction or abuse and are also important for medical uses—for instance, cocaine is used as an oral anesthetic.

Wonder drugs are produced by pharmacological optimism—the myth that a drug will free human societies from pain and suffering, sadness, anxiety, boredom, fatigue, mental illness, or aging. Today, lifestyle drugs are used to cope with everything from impotence to obesity to shyness to short attention spans. Yet adverse prescription drug reactions are the fourth leading cause of preventable death among adults in the United States. Some drugs, we think, cause social problems; we think others will solve them. Drugs become social problems when important interest groups define them as such. Recreational use of illegal drugs by adolescents has been considered a public health problem since the early 1950s, when the U.S. public attributed a wave of juvenile delinquency to teenage heroin addiction. Since our grandparents' generation, adolescence has been understood as a time when many choose to experiment with drugs. Today, a pattern of mixed legal, illegal, and prescription drug use has emerged among the first generation to be prescribed legal amphetamines and antidepressants. Many legal pharmaceuticals have been inadequately tested in children, and the short-term effects and long-term consequences of these drugs are unknown.

Controversy and Social Context

Portrayed as double-edged swords, drugs do not lend themselves to simple pros and cons. Drug controversies can best be mapped by asking which interest groups benefit from current policies, whose interests are at stake in changing them, and how drugs are defined differently by each group of producers, distributors, and consumers.

The basic terms through which drug debates are framed are not natural and do not reflect pharmacological properties. The meaning of drug use is best thought of as socially constructed, because it is assigned meaning within social and historical contexts. Varied meanings were attributed to the major subcultural groups of opiate addicts in the early 20th-century United States. Opium smoking by 19th-century Chinese laborers in the United States was tolerated until the labor shortage that attracted them became a labor surplus. Although laborers have long used drugs to relieve pain, stress, and monotony, the larger population of 19th-century opiate addicts was white women, born in the United States, who did not work outside the home. Pharmacy records indicate that rates of morphine addiction were high among rural Southern women from the upper and middle classes—and almost nonexistent among African Americans. Morphine addiction among men was concentrated among physicians, dentists, and pharmacists—professions with access to the drug.

Why did so many native-born white people rely on opiates through the early 20th century? Prior to World War II, when antibiotics were found useful for fighting infection, doctors and patients had few effective treatments. Opiates were used to treat tuberculosis because they slow respiration and suppress cough, for diarrhea because they constipate, and for pain (their most common use today). Physicians and patients noticed that opiate drugs such as morphine and heroin were habit-forming, however. They used the term *addict* to refer to someone who was physiologically or psychologically dependent on these drugs. In the 20th century, physicians began to refrain from prescribing opiates except in cases of dire need. Improved public health and sanitation further reduced the need, and per-capita opium consumption fell. Despite this, the United States could still be termed a "drugged nation."

Since the criminalization of narcotics with the Harrison Act (1914), U.S. drug policy has been based on the idea of abstinence. There was a brief period in the early 1920s when over 40 U.S. cities started clinics to maintain addicts on opiates. This experiment in legal maintenance was short-lived. Physicians, once the progenitors of addiction, were prosecuted, and they began to refuse to prescribe opiates to their upper- and middle-class patients. By the 1920s, the opiate-addicted population was composed of persons from the lower or "sporting" classes. Drug users' median age did not fall, however, until after World War II. The epidemiology, or populationwide incidence, of opiate use in the United States reveals that groups with the greatest exposure to opiates have the highest rates of addiction.

Exposure mattered, especially in urban settings where illegal drug markets took root. Urban subcultures existed in the 19th century among Chinese and white opium smokers, but as users switched to heroin injection or aged out of smoking opium, the Chinese began to disappear from the ranks of addicts. Older dope-fiend subcultures gave way to injection heroin users, who developed rituals, argots or languages, and standards of moral and ethical behavior of their own. Jazz musicians, Hollywood celebrities, and those who frequented social scenes where they were likely to encounter drugs such as heroin, cocaine, and marijuana were no longer considered members of the respectable classes. The older pattern of rural drug use subsided, and the new urban subcultures trended away from whites after World War II. African Americans who had migrated to Northern cities began to enjoy increased access to illicit drugs that had once been unavailable to them. So did younger people.

Social conflict between the so-called respectable classes and those categorized as less respectable often takes place around drugs. Debates over how specific drugs should be handled and how users of these drugs should be treated by society mark conflicts between dominant social groups, who construct their drug use as normal, and subordinate social groups whose drug use is labeled as abnormal, deviant, or pathological. As historian David Courtwright (2001) points out, "What we think about addiction very much depends on who is addicted." How drugs are viewed depends on the social contexts in which they are used, the groups involved, and the symbolic meanings assigned to them.

Recent medical marijuana campaigns have sought to reframe marijuana's definition as a nonmedical drug by showing its legitimate medical uses and backing up that assertion with clinical testimonials from chronic pain patients, glaucoma sufferers, and the terminally ill. Who are the dominant interest groups involved in keeping marijuana defined as nonmedical? The voices most often heard defending marijuana's status as an illegal drug are those of drug law enforcement. On the other hand, the drug policy reform movement portrays hemp production as an industry and marijuana use as a minor pleasure that should be decriminalized, if not legalized altogether. Views on drug policy range from those who want to regulate drugs entirely as medicines to those who are proponents of criminalization. A credible third alternative has emerged called harm reduction, risk reduction, or reality-based drug policy. Asking whose voices are most often heard as authoritative in a drug debate and whose voices are less often heard or heard as less credible can be a method for mapping the social relations and economic interests involved in drug policy. Who was marginalized when the dominant policy perspective was adopted? Who lost out? Who profited? Although the frames active in the social construction of drugs change constantly, some remain perennial favorites.

Drug Panics and Regulation

Not all psychoactive substances used as recreational drugs are currently illegal. Alcohol and tobacco have been commonly available for centuries, despite attempts to prohibit them. Both typically remain legal, except where age-of-purchase or religious bans are enforced. Alcohol prohibition in the United States lasted from 1919 to 1933. Although Prohibition reduced per-capita consumption of alcohol, it encouraged organized crime and bootlegging, and repeal efforts led to increased drinking and smoking among the respectable classes. Prohibition opened more segments of the U.S. population to the recreational use of drugs such as the opiates (morphine and heroin), cannabis, and cocaine. Although cannabis, or marijuana, was not included in the 1914 legislation, Congress passed the Marijuana Tax Act (1937) during a period when the drug was associated with, for example, Mexican laborers in the southwestern United States and criminal elements throughout the country. Cocaine was relatively underused and was not considered addictive until the 1970s. Although cocaine was present in opiate-using subcultures, it was expensive and not preferred.

Social conflicts led legal suppliers to strongly differentiate themselves from illegal drug traffickers. The early 20th-century experience with opiates—morphine, heroin, and other painkillers—was the real basis for U.S. and global drug control policy. The Harrison Act was a tax law that criminalized the possession and sale of narcotic drugs. It effectively extended law enforcement powers to the Treasury Department, which was responsible for enforcing alcohol prohibition. After repeal of Prohibition, this unit became the Federal Bureau of Narcotics, the forerunner of today's Drug Enforcement Agency.

Pharmaceutical manufacturing firms began to use the term *ethical* to distance themselves from patent medicine makers. Pharmaceutical firms rejected the use of patents on the grounds that they created unethical monopolies. Unlike the patent medicine makers with their secret recipes, ethical firms avoided branding and identified ingredients by generic chemical names drawn from the U.S. Pharmacopeia (which standardized drug nomenclature). Ethical houses did not advertise directly to the public like pharmaceutical companies do today. They limited their business to pharmacists and physicians whom they reached through the professional press. Around the turn of the 20th century, however, even ethical firms began to act in questionable ways, sponsoring lavish banquets for physicians and publishing advertisements as if they were legitimate, scientifically proven theories. Manufacturing facilities were not always clean, so the drug industry was a prime target of Progressive campaigns that followed publication of Upton Sinclair's muckraking book *The Jungle*, which was about the meatpacking industry. The Pure Food and Drug Act (1905) created a Bureau of Chemistry to assess fraudulent claims by drugmakers. After more than 100 deaths were attributed to a drug marketed as "elixir of sulfanilamide," which contained antifreeze, in 1935, the U.S. Congress passed the Food, Drug, and Cosmetic Act (FDCA) in 1938. The FDCA created the Food and Drug Administration (FDA), the government agency responsible for determining the safety and efficacy of drugs and approving them for the market. Relying on clinical trials performed by pharmaceutical companies themselves, the FDA determines the level of control to which a drug should be subjected. In 1962, the FDCA was amended in the wake of the thalidomide disaster, and the FDA was charged not only with ensuring the safety and effectiveness of drugs on the market but also with approving drugs for specific conditions. Companies must determine in advance whether a drug has abuse potential or is in any way dangerous to consumers. Despite attempts to predict accurately which wonder drugs will go awry, newly released drugs are tested on only a small segment of potential users. For instance, OxyContin, developed by Purdue Pharma as a prolonged-release painkiller, was considered impossible to tamper with and hence not abusable. Soon known as "hillbilly heroin," the drug became central in the drug panic.

Drug panics are commonly recognized as amplifying extravagant claims: the substance at the center of the panic is portrayed in mainstream media as the most addictive or most dangerous drug ever known. Wonder drugs turn to "demon drugs" as their availability is widened and prices fall. This pattern applies to both legal and illegal drugs. Another major social frame through which drugs are constructed, however, is the assumption that medical and nonmedical use are mutually exclusive.

Medical use versus nonmedical use is a major social category through which drugs have been classified since the criminalization of narcotics. If you are prescribed a drug by a medical professional and you use it as prescribed, you are a medical user. The old divisions between medical and nonmedical use break down when we think about something like cough medicine—once available over the counter with little restriction despite containing small amounts of controlled substances. Today, retail policies and laws restrict the amount of cough medicine that can be bought at one time, and purchasing-age limits are enforced. Availability of cough suppressants in home medicine cabinets led to experimentation by high school students with "chugging" or "robo-tripping" with Robitussin and dextromethorphan-based cough suppressants.

Medication, Self-Medication, and Medicalization

Practices of self-medication blur the medical-versus-nonmedical category. In some places, illegal drug markets have made these substances more widely available than the tightly controlled legal market. Many people who use heroin, cocaine, or marijuana are medicating themselves for depression, anxiety, or disease conditions. They lack health insurance and turn to drugs close at hand. Legal pharmaceuticals are also diverted to illegal markets, leading to dangerous intermixing, as in the illegal use of legal benzodiazepines as "xaniboosters" to extend the high of an illegal drug. The social construction of legal drugs as a social good has been crucial to the expansion of pharmaceutical markets. The industry has distanced itself from the construction of illegal drugs as a serious social problem, but this has become difficult in the face of a culture that has literally adopted a pill for every ill.

Drug issues would look different if other interest groups had the cultural capital to define their shape. Some substances are considered to be essential medicines, whereas others are controlled or prohibited altogether. When drugs are not used in prescribed ways, they are considered unnecessary or recreational. Like the other frames discussed, this distinction has long been controversial.

The history of medicine reveals sectarian battles over which drugs to use or not use, when to prescribe for what conditions, and how to prescribe dosages. The main historical rivals were regular or allopathic physicians, who relied heavily on "heroic" doses of opiates and purgatives, and homeopathic physicians, who gave tiny doses and operated out of different philosophies regarding the mind–body relation. Christian scientists and chiropractors avoided drugs, and other practitioners relied primarily on herbal remedies. As organized medicine emerged as a profession, allopathic physicians became dominant. After World War II, physicians were granted prescribing power during a period of affluence and optimism about the capacity of technological progress to solve social problems. By the mid- to late 1950s, popular attitudes against using a pill for every ill turned around thanks to the first blockbuster drug, the minor tranquilizer Miltown, which was mass marketed to middle-class Americans for handling the stresses of everyday life. Miltown was displaced first by the benzodiazepine Valium and then by the antidepressants Prozac and Zoloft and the antianxiety drugs Xanax and Paxil. A very high proportion of U.S. adults are prescribed these drugs, which illustrates the social process of medicalization.

Medicalization is the process by which a social problem comes to be seen as a medical disorder to be treated by medical professionals and prescription drugs. Many of today's diseases were once defined as criminal or deviant acts, vices, or moral problems. Some disorders have been brought into existence only after a pharmacological fix has become available. During Depression Awareness Week, you will find self-tests aimed at young people, especially at young men. Typically, women medicalize their problems at higher rates, but the men's market is now being tapped. Health care is a large share of the U.S. gross national product, and pharmaceutical companies maintain the highest profit margins in the industry, so there are huge economic stakes involved in getting you to go to your doctor and ask for a particular drug. Judging from the high proportion of the U.S. population on antidepressant prescriptions at any given time, these tactics have convinced people to treat even mild depression. Antidepressants are now used as tools to enhance productivity and the capacity to balance many activities, bringing up another active frame in the social construction of drugs: the difference between drugs said to enhance work or sports performance and drugs said to detract from performance.

Performance enhancement drugs first arose as a public controversy in relation to steroid use in professional sports and bodybuilding. However, this frame is also present in the discussion of Ritalin, the use of which has expanded beyond children diagnosed with attention deficit and hyperactivity-related disorders. Amphetamines, as early as the late 1940s, were known to have the paradoxical effect of settling down hyperactive children and allowing them to focus, but today the numbers of children and adolescents diagnosed with attention deficit disorder and attention deficit hyperactivity disorder is extremely high in the United States. Stimulants such as cocaine, amphetamines, and caffeine are performance-enhancing drugs in those who are fatigued. Caffeine is associated with productivity in Western cultures but with leisure and relaxation in Southern and Eastern Europe, Turkey, and the Middle East, where it is consumed just before bedtime. Different cultural constructions lead people to interpret pharmacological effects differently. Today, caffeine and amphetamines are globally the most widely used legal and illegal drugs—the scope of global trading of caffeine exceeds even that of another substance on which Western societies depend: oil.

Performance detriments are typically associated with addictive drugs, a concept that draws on older concepts of disease, compulsion, and habituation. With opiates, delight became necessity as individuals built up tolerance to the drug and became physically and psychologically dependent on it. Addiction was studied scientifically in response to what reformers called the opium problem evident on the streets of New York City by the early 1920s. The U.S. Congress created a research laboratory through the Public Health Service in the mid-1930s where alcohol, barbiturates, and opiates were shown to cause a physiological withdrawal syndrome when individuals suddenly stopped using them. The Addiction Research Center of Lexington, Kentucky, supplied data on the addictiveness of many drugs in popular use from the 1930s to the mid-1960s. During that decade, the World Health Organization changed the name of what it studied to "drug dependence" in an attempt to destigmatize addiction. It promoted the view that, as a matter of public health, drug dependence should be treatable by medical professionals whose treatment practices were based on science. This view brought the World Health Organization into political conflict with the expanding drug law enforcement apparatus, which saw the problem as one to be solved by interrupting the international trafficking. Public health proponents lost out during the 1950s, when the first mandatory minimum sentences were put into place by the 1951 Boggs Act. These were strengthened in 1956. By the end of the decade, law enforcement authorities believed that punishment-oriented drug policies had gotten criminals under control. They were proven wrong in the next decade.

Drug Usage and Historical Trends

Patterns of popular drug use often follow the contours of social change. Several factors tipped the scale toward constructing drug addiction as a disease in the 1960s. The U.S. Supreme Court interpreted addiction as an illness, opining, "Even one day in prison would be a cruel and unusual punishment for the 'crime' of having a common cold" (*Robinson v. California*, 1962). Finding it "unlikely that any State at this moment in history would attempt to make it a criminal offense for a person to be mentally ill, or a leper, or to be afflicted with a venereal disease," the Court stated that prisons could not be considered "curative" unless jail sentences were made "medicinal" and prisons provided treatment. Four decades later, treatment in prison is still sparse, despite jails and prisons being filled with individuals on drug charges. In the late 1960s, civil commitment came about with passage of the Narcotic Addict Rehabilitation Act (1967), just as greater numbers of white middle-class youth entered the ranks of heroin addicts. Law enforcement was lax in suburban settings, where heroin drug buys and use took place behind closed doors, unlike urban settings. New drugs, including hallucinogens, became available, and marijuana was deeply integrated into college life. The counterculture adopted these drugs and created new rituals centered on mind expansion.

During this time, racial-minority heroin users and returning Vietnam veterans came to attention on the streets. In a classic paper titled "Taking Care of Business," Edward Preble and John J. Casey (1969) observed that urban heroin use did not reflect apathy, lack of motivation, or laziness, but a different way to pursue a meaningful life that conflicted with ideas of the dominant social group. Hustling activities provided income and full-time, if informal, jobs where there were often no legitimate jobs in the formal economy. The lived experiences of drug users suggested that many people who got into bad relationships with drugs were simply self-medicating in ways designated by mainstream society as illegal. Members of this generation of heroin users suffered from the decline of social rituals and cultural solidarity that had once held drug-using subcultures together and enabled members of them to hold down legitimate jobs while maintaining heroin habits in the 1950s and early 1960s.

By the 1970s, heroin-using subcultures were more engaged in street crime than they had once been. The decline of solidarity became pronounced when crack cocaine came onto the scene in the mid-1980s at far lower cost than powder cocaine had been in the 1970s. Reading Preble and Casey's ethnographic work, which was done 30 years before the reemergence of heroin use among middle-class adolescents and the emergence of crack cocaine, we see how drug-using social networks met members' needs for a sense of belonging by forming social systems for gaining status and respect. In the 1970s, the Nixon administration focused the "war on drugs" on building a national treatment infrastructure of methadone clinics distributed throughout U.S. cities. Methadone maintenance has enabled many former heroin addicts to lead stable and productive lives. For a time, it appeared the opium problem might be resolved through public health.

But there is always a next drug, and cocaine surfaced as the new problem in the 1980s. Powder cocaine had been more expensive than gold, so it was viewed as a jet-set drug and was used in combination with heroin. However, a cheaper form called crack cocaine became available in the poorest of neighborhoods during the 1980s. Mainstream media tend to amplify differences between drug users and nonusers, a phenomenon that was especially pronounced in the racialized representation of the crack cocaine crisis. Crack widened the racial inequalities of the war on drugs at a time when social policy was cutting access to health care and service delivery and when urban African American communities were hit hard by economic and social crisis. The pregnant, crack cocaine–using woman became an icon of this moment. Women had long made up about one-third of illegal drug users (down from the majority status of white women morphine users in the early 20th century), and little attention was paid to them. They were represented as a distinct public threat by the late 1980s and early 1990s, however. Despite so-called crack babies turning out not to have long-lasting neurobehavioral difficulties (especially in comparison with peers raised in similar socioeconomic circumstances), "crack baby" remains an epithet. Nor did crack babies grow up to become crack users—like all drug epidemics, the crack cocaine crisis waned early in the 1990s.

Like fashion, fads, or earthquakes, drug cycles wax and wane, and policies swing back and forth between treatment and punishment. Policy is not typically responsible for declining numbers of addicts. Other factors, including wars, demographic shifts such as aging out or baby booms that yield large pools of adolescents, new drugs, and new routes of administration (techniques by which people get drugs into their bodies), change the shape of drug use. Social and personal experience with the negative social and economic effects of a particular drug are far better deterrents to problematic drug use than antidrug education and prevention programs; punitive drug policy; incarceration, which often leads to increased drug exposure; and even drug treatment. Although flawed in many ways, drug policy is nevertheless important because it shapes the experiences of drug sellers and users as they interact with each other.

The War on Drugs and Its Critics

Just as drugs have shaped the course of global and U.S. history, so have periodic wars on drugs. The current U.S. drug policy regime is based on the Controlled Substances Act (1970), which classifies legal and illegal drugs onto five schedules that proceed from Schedule I (heavily restricted drugs classified as having "no medical use" such as heroin, LSD, psilocybin, mescaline, or peyote) to Schedule V (less restricted drugs that have a legitimate medical use and low potential for abuse despite containing small amounts of controlled substances). This U.S. law implements the United Nations' Single Convention on Narcotics Drugs (1961), which added cannabis to former international treaties covering opiates and coca. The Psychotropic Convention (1976) added LSD and legally manufactured amphetamines and barbiturates to the list. These treaties do not control alcohol, tobacco, or nicotine. They make evident the fact that drugs with industrial backing tend to be less restricted and more available than drugs without it, such as marijuana. Drugs that cannot be transported long distances such as West African kola nuts or East African qat also tend to remain regional drugs. Many governments rely heavily on tax revenue from alcohol and cigarettes and would be hard pressed to give them up. Courtwright (2001) argues that many of the world's governing elites were concerned with taxing the traffic, not suppressing it. Modernity brought with it factors that shifted elite priorities toward control and regulation as industrialization and mechanization made the social costs of intoxication harder to absorb.

Drug regulation takes many forms depending on its basis and goals. Hence, there is disagreement among drug policy reformers about process and goals. Some seek to legalize marijuana and regulate currently illegal drugs more like currently legal drugs. Some see criminalization as the problem and advocate decriminalizing drugs. Others believe that public health measures should be aimed at preventing adverse health consequences and social harms, a position called harm reduction that gathered ground with the discovery that injection drug users were a main vector for transmitting HIV/AIDS in the United States. This alternative public health approach aims to reduce the risks associated with drug use.

Conflicts between those who advocate the status quo and those who seek to change drug policy have unfolded. Mainstream groups adhere to the idea that abstinence from drugs is the only acceptable goal. Critics contend that abstinence is an impossible dream that refuses to recognize the reality that many individuals experiment with drugs, but only a few become problematically involved with them. They offer evidence of controlled use and programs such as reality-based drug education, which is designed to teach people how to use drugs safely rather than simply avoid them. Critics argue that the "just say no" and "drug-free" schools and workplaces have proven ineffective (see the entry on drug testing for a full account of how drug-free legislation was implemented). In arguing that the government should not prohibit consensual adult drug consumption, drug policy reformers have appealed to both liberal and conservative political ideals about drug use in democratic societies. Today's drug policy reform movement stretches across the political spectrum and has begun to gain ground among those who see evidence that the war on drugs War on Drugs has failed to curb drug use.

See also **Addiction and Family; Steroid Use by Athletes; Prescription Drug Costs (vol. 1); Drug Trafficking and Narco-Terrorism (vol. 2); DWI and Drug Testing (vol. 2); War on Drugs (vol. 2); Medical Marijuana (vol. 4); Off-Label Drug Use (vol. 4)**

Further Reading

Burnham, John, *Bad Habits: Drinking, Smoking, Taking Drugs, Gambling, Sexual Misbehavior, and Swearing in American History.* New York: New York University Press, 1994.

Campbell, Nancy D., *Discovering Addiction: The Science and Politics of Substance Abuse Research.* Ann Arbor: University of Michigan Press, 2007.

Courtwright, David, *Forces of Habit: Drugs and the Making of the Modern World.* Cambridge, MA: Harvard University Press, 2001.

DeGrandpre, Richard, *The Cult of Pharmacology: How America Became the World's Most Troubled Drug Culture.* Durham, NC: Duke University Press, 2006.

DeGrandpre, Richard, *Ritalin Nation: Rapid-Fire Culture and the Transformation of Human Consciousness.* New York: W. W. Norton, 1999.

Dingelstad, David, Richard Gosden, Brain Martin, and Nickolas Vakas, "The Social Construction of Drug Debates." *Social Science and Medicine* 43, no. 12 (1996): 1829–1838. http://www.uow.edu.au/arts/sts/bmartin/pubs/96ssm.html

Husak, Douglas, *Legalize This! The Case for Decriminalizing Drugs.* London: Verso, 2002.

Inciardi, James, and Karen McElrath, *The American Drug Scene,* 5th ed. New York: Oxford University Press, 2007.

McTavish, Jan, *Pain and Profits: The History of the Headache and Its Remedies.* New Brunswick, NJ: Rutgers University Press, 2004.

Musto, David, *The American Disease: Origins of Narcotics Control,* 3d ed. New York: Oxford University Press, 1999.

Preble, Edward, and John J. Casey, "Taking Care of Business: The Heroin Addict's Life on the Street." *International Journal of the Addictions* 4, no. 1 (1969): 1–24.

E

EARLY CHILDHOOD EDUCATION

CHRISTOPHER P. BROWN

Early childhood education (ECE) is a controversial and contested field. Since the Progressive Era, debate has existed over what role federal, state, and local government agencies should play in providing families and their young children with access to ECE programs. Within the field itself, there are disputes over issues such as what type of care should be provided to children and their families, what type of training early childhood educators should possess, and what type of instruction should take place and at what age.

Even with a majority of mothers within the United States in the workforce and numerous scientific studies demonstrating the importance of the early years of a child's life on later development and academic performance, society has yet to accept the idea that access to high-quality ECE programs should be a basic right for all children. A key reason for this is the patriarchal norms that dominate the American psyche. In general, society still defines the role of the mother as the primary caregiver of the child, and thus it is her responsibility to ensure that the child is cared for and ready to enter elementary school. Ideally, the mother is married and has husband who is able to support her and her child. While these images have been contested across numerous fronts, the nuclear family is still a key construct in federal policy and is used by many who oppose an expanding role of government into early childhood education.

A Definition of Early Childhood Education

The National Association for the Education of Young Children (NAEYC), the largest professional organization for early childhood educators, defines the early childhood years as those from birth through third grade, and thus this field of practice balances between systems of compulsory and noncompulsory schooling. This entry focuses on early childhood programs that serve children from birth through age five, including kindergarten.

The Status of Early Childhood Education within the United States

For children from birth through age five, early childhood services are offered through a patchwork system of care that includes public and private nonprofit agencies, religious organizations, corporations, for-profit enterprises, family child care providers, and public schools. Programs serve a range of ages, offer various types of services, and instill a range of curricula. For the most part, the early childhood community represents a fractured group of practitioners who are loosely coupled by licensure requirements that emphasize health, safety, and teacher and staff issues rather than academic expectations or curricula.

Government Support

While the debate over the role of government support for ECE continues, federal, state, and local governments do provide some funding for early childhood services and programs. Federal support for ECE exists through three main funding sources: (1) providing funding for child care services as an incentive to mothers who receive public assistance and are trying to enter the labor force; (2) providing funding for or access to services such as Head Start to children whom governmental agencies deem to be at risk due to factors such as poverty, language status, developmental delays, psychological issues, or a combination of these factors; and (3) providing financial support to families and corporations through tax credits.

The passage of the Personal Responsibility and Work Opportunity Reconciliation Act in 1996 altered previous federal social services by mandating recipients to achieve particular goals and reducing the length of time they could receive support, which increased the need for early childhood services for these families. For instance, the Temporary Assistance for Needy Families block grant replaced programs such as Aid to Families with Dependent Children, provides states with funds that they are to use to assist families in taking care of their children at home, and provides child care for parents so that they can participate in job training. The Child Care and Development block grant provides funds to states to subsidize the child care expenses of low-income working parents, parents who are receiving training for work, and parents in school.

The most well known federally funded early childhood program is Head Start, which operates through the Department of Health and Human Services (DHHS). The DHHS directly funds local grantees to provide Head Start programs to promote children's school readiness by enhancing their social and cognitive development. Head Start grantees are to offer children and their families' educational, health, nutritional, social, and other services.

Finally, the federal government offers two types of tax credits: (1) the dependent care tax credit for families who use out-of-home ECE services (which began as the child care tax deduction in 1954 and converted to a child care tax credit in 1972) and (2) tax credits for employers who establish or provide access for their employees to child care services (which began in 1962).

At the state and local level, funding is more eclectic. The availability of programs and services that extend beyond federal funding depends on the individual state or local community. Some (but not all) state governments supplement these federal funds, create their own programs for targeted populations, and encourage local participation in the process.

The most common form of state involvement in ECE is kindergarten, and the fastest growing program area among the states is prekindergarten (pre-K) for four- and sometimes three-year-olds. As of 2009, only 8 states require children to attend kindergarten, while the remaining 42 states require school districts to offer kindergarten. Forty states offer some form of pre-K funding to local school districts and community organizations, and three states—Oklahoma, Georgia, and Florida—offer all four-year-old children in their states access to prekindergarten, typically referred to as universal prekindergarten (UPK). Many states, such as New York, Illinois, Louisiana, and Iowa, are taking steps toward UPK. Other states, such as Maine, Oklahoma, Wisconsin, and West Virginia, offer pre-K for all through their school funding formulas.

Making the Case for Further Government Support of ECE

Those who support the expansion of federal, state, and local early childhood services typically make their case through two interconnected lines of reasoning. The first frames ECE as an investment. The second sees ECE as a necessary step to ready children for the increasing demands of elementary school.

The investment argument emerges from a collection of longitudinal studies that examine the effects of specific early childhood programs on a child's life. This research demonstrates that children who participate in high-quality early childhood programs are less likely as students to be retained or to require special education service and are more likely to graduate from high school. As adults, these children are more likely to be employed and not require social services and are less likely to be incarcerated (e.g., Reynolds, Ou, and Topitzes's 2004 analysis of the effects of the Chicago Child-Parent Centers). As a result, every dollar that is invested in high-quality ECE programs will save taxpayers from having to spend additional monies on supplemental education and social services for children through their lifetimes.

The readiness argument, which follows a similar line of reasoning as the investment argument, states that, in order to have students ready for the increasing demands of elementary school, government agencies need to provide families with access to high-quality early education services to ensure that their children are ready to learn.

Making the Case for Less Government Support of ECE

Those who oppose expanding the role of government also frame their argument through two lines of reasoning. The first, which takes a libertarian approach, contends that the government should limit its social responsibilities in taking care of children, except in the direst circumstances, and allow the market to deem the need and role of ECE (e.g., the Cato Institute). The second, which takes a more conservative approach, argues that the government should implement policies that encourage family members to stay home and care for their children, such as tax credits for stay-at-home family members or incentives for corporations to encourage part-time employment.

EARLY CHILDHOOD EDUCATION ORGANIZATIONS: PRO, CON, AND MORE

The following is a sample of organizations active in the debates surrounding early childhood education. Links to information about state early childhood education programs and family participation in such programs are provided.

Professional and Research Organizations That Support ECE

- National Association for the Education of Young Children: http://www.naeyc.org
- National Institute for Early Education Research: http://www.nieer.org
- Pre-K Now: http://www.preknow.org
- Foundation for Child Development: http://www.fcd-us.org
- Association for Childhood Education International: http://www.acei.org

Organizations That Oppose the Expansion of ECE

- Cato Institute: http://www.cato.org
- Reason Foundation: http://www.reason.org
- Concerned Women for America: http://www.cwfa.org

Statistics on Family Participation in ECE Programs

- National Center for Education Statistics: http://nces.ed.gov

Information about State Early Childhood Programs and Kindergarten

- Education Commission of the States: http://www.ecs.org

Early Childhood Education from the Progressive Era to Today

As the Progressive Era took shape, ECE emerged along two streams of care: the kindergarten movement and the day nursery movement. Within these two movements, issues of gender, class, and cultural affiliation not only affected the goals of each program but also which children and their families had access to these care and education services.

Kindergarten

The U.S. kindergarten movement began in 1854, when Margarethe Meyer Schurz founded the first kindergarten in Watertown, Wisconsin. These early kindergartens were supplemental programs that were designed to foster a child's growth and development and to provide mothers with a break from their children. (See Beatty 1995 for a detailed history of the development of kindergarten in the United States.)

Public kindergarten emerged in the 1870s through the work of individuals such as Susan Blow in St. Louis and spread across numerous cities. As these programs became part of education systems across the United States, stakeholders implemented them to achieve many goals—all of which framed kindergarten as a necessary and not supplemental service. For instance, some supporters saw these programs as a form of child rescue; others saw it as means to Americanize the influx of immigrants who were arriving in the United States; and many viewed these programs as form of preparation for elementary school. These programs steadily grew, because education and community stakeholders began to see more children as being unprepared for elementary school, and, thus, this construct of the deficient child infuses itself within the need for an expansion of early childhood services.

The idea of children following a normal developmental path emerged out of the work of child psychologists such as G. Stanley Hall, who began his child study experiments in Pauline Shaw's charity kindergartens in Boston. Hall's studies led him as well as many other psychologists to question what type of experiences should be taking place in kindergarten as well as in the home to prepare children for a successful life.

Day Nurseries

Prior to kindergarten or elementary school entry, the dominant understanding of children's early childhood experiences was that their mothers were to raise them in their homes. The day nursery movement emerged as an intervention for mothers who had to seek employment to take care of their families so that they would not have to institutionalize their children. These nurseries emerged as the philanthropic projects of wealthy women who wanted to assist working poor and immigrant mothers in getting back on their feet so that they could take their rightful place in the home. Day nurseries emphasized patriotism and hygiene as part of their instruction and only sought governmental assistance for regulatory purposes to improve nursery program conditions. Even though these programs had less-than-appealing reputations, the need for their services far outstripped their availability. In most instances—particularly in the South, rural areas, and for African American families—kith and kin provided the majority of care for these families. Ironically, many of these working mothers struggled to find care for their own children while working for wealthier families as the caretakers of their children. (See Michel 1999 for a detailed history of the day nursery movement and the positioning of mothers and women in general within this and other debates over the role of government in child rearing and education.)

Nursery Schools

Academically, the increased interest in understanding child development by the work of theorists and researchers such as Hall, Gesell, Freud, Piaget, and others led to the growing child study movement among universities. For instance, the Laura Spelman Rockefeller Memorial Foundation awarded significant sums of money to several colleges and universities to establish child study institutes. The institutes' lab schools began the nursery school movement, and middle-class families became attracted to the notion that science can enhance their child's development. Furthermore, this scientific emphasis on child development extended the view of ECE beyond the traditional academic notion of cognitive development that dominates elementary education. Early education included the child's social, emotional, physical, and cognitive development. This expanded view of learning caused conflict between early childhood educators and their elementary school colleagues as these programs became part of the elementary school environment.

The Federal Government Becomes Part of Early Childhood Education

The onset of the Great Depression resulted in a collapse of the day nursery movement for working mothers, and a majority of the ECE programs that remained were supplemental nursery programs used by middle-class families. In 1933, the Federal Emergency Relief Administration (FERA) changed this by starting a federally funded nursery school program as a means of employing schoolteachers and school staff. The custodial care of children was a secondary goal. The program was incorporated into the Works Progress Administration in 1934, when FERA was terminated.

As the Great Depression ended and World War II began, the funding for this program dwindled. However, the need for women's labor to support the war industry led to the Lanham Act, which funded over 3,000 child care centers to care for children whose mothers worked in defense-related industries.

When the Depression and the war ended, federal support for these custodial programs subsided, and mothers were to return home to care for their children. However, the kindergarten movement had come to be seen by education stakeholders as a much-needed vehicle for preparing children for school. Kindergarten survived these two national crises, and, by the 1940s, it became a permanent fixture of many school systems across the United States.

Project Head Start

For the next 20 years, the federal government abstained from funding ECE programs until the implementation of Project Head Start in 1965. This project emerged from the Economic Opportunity Act and the Elementary and Secondary Education Act as a part of the Johnson Administration's war on poverty.

This legislation shifted the role of the federal government in developing ECE and K–12 policy within the United States. Federal policymakers created legislation that defined the role of the federal government in ECE as a provider of intervention services that could alter the academic trajectory of particular populations of children. These policies identified the root cause of academic failure, which leads to economic failure, in the child's home environment. By identifying educational attainment as the means by which this cycle of poverty can be broken, policymakers defined the central role of ECE as readying students for school. ECE became a tool for intervention.

As soon as the federal government took on these roles in ECE and K–12 education, controversy arose. For instance, the Nixon administration responded to Johnson's Great Society education policies by creating the National Institute of Education, which investigated the return that society received for its investment in education. Furthermore, Nixon vetoed the Comprehensive Child Development Act of 1971, which was to expand the federal government's funding of child care and education while creating a framework for child services. Additionally, studies such as the Westinghouse Learning House's evaluation of Head Start in 1969 suggested that any gains in the IQs of students who participated in the program quickly faded, which raised concerns over the effectiveness of these government-funded programs.

Researchers responded to these critiques of Head Start by arguing that, while increases in IQ might not be sustainable, students who participated in such programs were more successful academically and socially as they continued through school than those students who did not receive these services. These longitudinal studies, which examined a number of early childhood programs other than Head Start, spawned the investment argument, which is outlined above.

This argument shifts the premise for funding ECE programs slightly. Rather than break the cycle of poverty for others, funding programs will save taxpayers money. Thus, this argument for ECE deemphasizes assisting families to be able to take care of their children at home, and, rather, it contends that experts in ECE can design and implement programs that prepare the child, and in some cases the family, for success in compulsory schooling and later life.

Standards for Early Childhood Education

The emphasis on student performance that emerged during the Reagan administration put pressure on early childhood educators to align their practices with K–12 education. While such pressure on ECE programs has been around since the 1920s, particularly for kindergarten programs (see Beatty 1995), organizations such as NAEYC began to produce position statements and documents that defined what empirical research identified to be appropriate teaching, learning, and assessment experiences for young children.

Although these empirically based responses deflected the pressures of accountability for children until later in their academic careers, recent federal and state standards-based accountability reforms have caused education stakeholders to again scrutinize what types of experiences students are having prior to their entry to elementary school. For instance, policymakers and early childhood stakeholders are debating the role of early learning standards, readiness assessments, and literacy and math instruction in early childhood programs.

Additional reforms that stakeholders are considering to improve children's preparation for elementary schooling include requiring student participation in full-day kindergarten programs, expanding prekindergarten services, improving the quality of early childhood programs, increasing training requirements for ECE teachers, and aligning early childhood programs across the field as well as with the K–12 education system. (See Cryer and Clifford 2003 for discussions surrounding ECE policy.)

Whatever policies emerge, the recent history of education reform demonstrates that these reforms will be linked to increased accountability expectations, making the expansion of the field dependent on the ability of ECE programs to improve student performance.

An added question that is somewhat unique to ECE is who should be providing these services. For-profit centers have a long history in ECE and provide care for a significant population of children and their families. These providers include national and international companies (e.g., the Australian-based publicly traded for-profit child care corporation ABC Learning, which is the world's largest provider of child care services and operates over 1,100 centers in the United States). Additionally, nonprofit and church-based centers provide a large portion of infant and toddler care for families. Thus, expanding or reforming early childhood services involves numerous stakeholders, and simply adding programs to the nation's public schools or implementing unfunded mandates has the ability to upset many who support as well as provide care for young children and their families.

Conclusion

ECE has a long and unique history in the United States. Those who support the field have framed its need in numerous ways. Current advocates argue that ECE is a necessity for families in which the primary caregiver works outside the home, is a smart investment of public resources, or is a basic right for all children. Those who oppose its expansion contend that the government agencies should not be involved in child rearing, should not pay for additional social services, or should implement policies that encourage families to stay at home and take care of their children. Either way, the battle over ECE boils down to how stakeholders perceive the role of government agencies in financing the care and education of young children, and thus the debate will continue as long as there are children and families who need or desire out-of-home care.

See also **Child Care; Government Role in Schooling**

Further Reading

Beatty, Barbara, *Preschool Education in America: The Culture of Young Children from the Colonial Era to the Present.* New Haven, CT: Yale University Press, 1995.

Cryer, Debby, and Richard M. Clifford, eds., *Early Education and Care in the USA.* Baltimore: Brookes Publishing, 2003.

Farquhar, Sandy, and Peter Fitzsimmons, eds., *Philosophy of Early Childhood Education: Transforming Narratives.* New York: Wiley-Blackwell, 2008.

Fuller, Bruce, et al., *Standardized Childhood: The Political and Cultural Struggle over Early Education.* Stanford. CA: Stanford University Press, 2007.

Goffin, Stacie G., and Valora Washington, *Ready or Not: Leadership Choices in Early Care and Education.* New York: Teachers College Press, 2007.

Michel, Sonya, *Children's Interests/Mothers' Rights: The Shaping of America's Child Care Policy.* New Haven, CT: Yale University Press, 1999.

Reynolds, A. J., S. Ou, and J. Topitzes, "Paths of Effects of Early Childhood Intervention on Educational Attainment and Delinquency: A Confirmatory Analysis of the Chicago Child-Parent Centers." *Child Development* 75 (2004): 1299–1328.

Siegel, Charles, *What's Wrong with Day Care? Freeing Parents To Raise Their Own Children.* New York: Teachers College Press, 2000.

EATING DISORDERS

Cynthia Childress

Diagnosis and treatment of eating disorders typically are relegated to psychiatry, although cultural critics and feminists have pointed out that culture, rather than merely individual psychology and home environment, may also play a role in causing eating disorders. The majority of people diagnosed with eating disorders are white women, although the number of eating disorder patients that are women of color and men is growing, which further complicates the debate on the cultural versus psychological causes.

Background

Eating disorders—most notably anorexia nervosa and bulimia nervosa—are common in Western cultures, although they occur with increasing frequency in poor and non-Western societies as well. Anorexia nervosa was first considered a disease, and one specific to women, during the mid-1800s; the first cases occurred in educated, middle-class white women. Social historicists such as Joan Brumberg, author of *Fasting Girls* (1988), see the rise in eating disorders among women at that time as a silent protest against expectations for the roles those women would play in society as passive, submissive women confined to the private sphere. Considering not only anorexia but also bulimia and other related eating disorders, explanations for their occurrences in women range from the pressure of having so many options that historically had not been available to women and the fear of making the wrong choices or failing to live up to expectations, to desperation to be as thin as possible in order to meet and exceed the social norms for female beauty, to more individual concerns such as hating one's body because of sexual abuse or punishing the body because of a lack of coping method for feelings of anxiety, anger, or even happiness and success.

These ideas about eating disorders inform and are informed by the clinical criteria for determining whether someone has an eating disorder and what kind is established in the *Diagnostic and Statistical Manual of Mental Disorders* (DSM), a book of diagnostic criteria for mental illnesses compiled by the American Psychiatric Association. Anorexia was the first eating disorder to be included in the DSM in the mid-1950s. The DSM added bulimia as a distinct category in 1980, and in 2000, a new category, eating disorder not otherwise specified, was added to assist doctors in diagnosing those who suffer from disordered eating but do not meet all the criteria for anorexia or bulimia. There are two other disorders that are not recognized in the DSM: binge eating disorder (BED) and compulsive overeating disorder (COE), both of which are thought by some professionals to deserve their own entries in the DSM's next edition, which will appear in 2013. Sufferers of both disorders are characterized by periodically going on large binges without purging and tend to be overweight, but the difference between BED and COE is that individuals with COE have an "addiction" to food. Both types of individuals, however, are said to use food and eating as a way to hide from emotions, to fill inner voids, and to cope with daily stresses and problems. Common for both disorders is a desire to hide behind the physical appearance of obesity, using it as a blockade against society.

Debates on the Causes of Eating Disorders

Psychological Explanations

There are many theories explaining how and why women develop eating disorders. Most explanations before the 1980s and 1990s constructed the problem and solution as being largely individual for each patient and her immediate family environment. In the classic psychoanalytic model, eating disorders are manifestations of a woman's psychosexual development. In that case, a woman or girl refuses to eat because she rejects her womanly body and what its health represents—sexual fertility. Along this line of thinking, then, a compulsive overeater may seek to cloak her sexuality in body fat.

These ideas subtly speak to cultural expectations for women's bodies and the judgment of what is beautiful or desirable in a woman, causing a second generation of critics to notice that the way in which social systems operate to reinforce negative messages to women about their bodies point toward patriarchy, defined as a system of interrelated social structures and practices in which men dominate, oppress, and exploit women. These social values are specific to our capitalistic society, in which the so-called cult of thinness supports food, diet, and health industries. "Weight concerns or even obsessions are so common among women and girls that they escape notice. Dieting is not considered abnormal behavior, even among women who are not overweight. But only a thin line separates 'normal' dieting from an eating disorder" (Hesse-Biber 1996). Twiggy, the waifish British fashion model of the 1960s, and the popular Mattel doll, Barbie, are often cited as icons of the impractical expectations society has for the size of women's bodies. It is commonly known that the average model during the 1950s wore a size 8 and the average woman a size 10; today the average model wears a size 2, and the average woman now wears a size 12. The rise in disparity between model size and real women's bodies parallels the rise of eating disorders, although experts are divided on the degree to which society is responsible. Joan Brumberg and most leaders of the eating disorder conversation agree that these images play a key role in the development of eating disorders, but psychiatrists say these coincidences might instigate disordered eating behaviors but are not enough to completely explain the development of the diseases anorexia and bulimia.

Biological Explanations

In the biological model, eating disorders are related to depression and bipolar disorder—both of which may be caused by chemical imbalances and thus corrected with medication. The only drug that has been approved by the U.S. Food and Drug Administration for the treatment of eating disorders is Prozac, to be used in bulimia patients. There are

HOW PREVALENT ARE EATING DISORDERS?

According to the National Association of Anorexia Nervosa and Associated Eating Disorders:

Over one-half of teenage girls and nearly one-third of teenage boys have tried to control their weight by skipping meals and fasting, vomiting, and taking laxatives.

For young women between 15 and 24 years old who suffer from anorexia nervosa, the mortality rate associated with the illness is 12 times higher than the death rate of all other causes of death.

One percent of adolescent girls have anorexia, 4 percent of college-aged women have bulimia, and 1 percent of all American women suffer from binge eating disorder.

Twenty percent of untreated eating disorder cases result in death, and 2 to 3 percent of patients treated for eating disorders do not survive.

many studies into medication for anorexic patients, and some trials have yielded individual successes, but because the anorexic's body chemistry is abnormal because it is in starvation mode, many drugs have little or no effect. Hesse-Biber criticizes the disease model of eating disorders, because it locates the problem as being within the individual rather than being outside oneself. She acknowledges that the disease model is good in that it frees patients from guilt, but she notes that this model benefits the health care industry—replacing a potential feminist view that society needs to be healed with a medical view that the victim needs professional treatment.

Family and Home Environment Explanations

Yet another model posits that eating disorders arise as symbolic representations of family dynamics. In this case, a power struggle between parent and child, especially the mother, may motivate a girl to find power over one thing she can control—what she eats. In this case, treatment and diagnosis involve the entire family. Feminist psychoanalyst Kim Chernin (1981) argues that eating disorders primarily develop as a response of overly controlling parents or environments that do not nurture a girl's journey from childhood to womanhood; psychiatrist Mary Pipher (1994) views eating disorders as responses to our culture's social dictate that a good woman is passive, quiet, and takes up very little space. Chernin and Pipher do agree, however, that eating disorders develop in situations that prevent the victim from saying or acknowledging to herself what she thinks, feels, or wants. In this way, then, eating disorders can be seen as survival strategies in response to emotional, physical, and sexual abuse; sexism; classism; homophobia; or racism—in other words, responses to trauma. Contemporary researchers and scholars mostly agree that eating disorder behaviors are coping mechanisms that give the sufferers a feeling of empowerment. By refusing to eat, bingeing, or bingeing and purging, a woman gains some influence over her environment. Control over the body becomes a substitute for control a woman may wish to have over her economic, political, or social circumstance. Thus, weight loss or gain may not be a primary motivation for disordered eating.

Increased Recognition of Eating Disorders among Racial Minorities

African American singer Dinah Washington died as result of an overdose of diet pills and alcohol; Puerto Rican poet Luz Maria Umpierre-Herrera writes about her struggle with anorexia; and African American writer Gloria Naylor writes about generations of eating disordered women in *Linden Hills* (Thompson 1996). According to Becky Thompson's research on minority women, many of them were taught to diet, binge, and purge by older relatives who had done so themselves, which suggests that, although statistics show that eating disorders are on the rise in U.S. minority cultures, this may simply be the result of more careful research rather than an actual sharp increase. Health professionals assume and are taught that eating disorders are a white women's disease, so in women of color eating disorder symptoms would be dismissed or treated as something else. Particularly because Hispanic and black women are culturally stereotyped as plump or obese, whereas Asian women are stereotyped as thin, doctors would ignore those visual cues as signs of eating problems. Exacerbating this situation is that most minority women also see eating disorders as a "white" problem, so they are more reluctant to recognize signs of disorder in themselves or seek help. This explains why most women of color who are treated for eating disorders are in more severe states than white women with the same disorders.

Women in African American and Hispanic communities have traditionally been larger than women in white communities, and minority communities have been more tolerant and even celebratory of the large female body as a symbol of health and wealth. One explanation for their larger size is food custom, but researchers have found that women in those communities also exhibit compulsive overeating behaviors, using bingeing as a way to cope with stress. Bingeing then is a way to find temporary relief from oppressive social and economic conditions such as sexual abuse, poverty, racism, and sexism. Since the 1980s, eating disorder diagnoses, particularly of anorexia, have risen among the African American population. Some experts note that this rise parallels the increasing affluence of middle-class black families, who find themselves embracing traditionally white values, including the obsession with thinness. This trend is also noted among upwardly mobile young Hispanic women and adolescents who see thinness as a key to success. A study conducted among a diverse selection of college-age women revealed that minority women who identified with their ethnic groups had fewer obsessions with thinness and realistic body goals compared to women who rejected their cultural identities and also subscribed to the thin ideal for themselves, resulting in a much larger percentage of eating-disordered behaviors (Abrams, Allen, and Gray 1993).

Increased Recognition of Eating Disorders among Men

The ratio of women to men with eating disorders is 9–1, although some researchers suspect that more men suffer from eating disorders and go untreated, particularly with bulimia, because it is easier to hide than anorexia (Crawford 1990). Like women of color, men with eating disorder symptoms may go unnoticed by physicians because they do not fit the classic diagnostic and treatment models, which tend to focus on women. Men who are more vulnerable to developing eating disorders participate in athletic activities that have regular weigh-ins, such as wrestling. Disordered eating and overexercising is sometimes ordered by a coach so that a team member will be a certain weight for a tournament, and this unnatural obsession with weight and weight control can lead to the wrestler using starvation as a means of weight control. Gay men may also be more susceptible to eating disorders because of the importance of appearance in gay culture. In a study comparing gay and straight men, homosexual men were found to be more preoccupied with their body sizes and appearances and more likely to suffer from body

FASHION WEEK IN MADRID

Madrid's 2006 Fashion Week was the first of its kind to place a ban on models with a body mass index below 18, a move that Australia's Fashion Week followed. A 5-foot 9-inch model weighing 125 pounds would have a body mass index of 18, which is the lowest healthy body mass range. This ban resulted in the turning away of 30 percent of the models scheduled to participate in the fashion week. Madrid's decision was a result of lobbying from groups such as Spain's Association in Defense of Attention for Anorexia and Bulimia, which argues that young women develop eating disorders as a result of trying to be as thin as the underweight fashion models. One turning point in the debate over model size for Madrid was the death of 22-year-old South American model Luisel Ramos, who suffered a heart attack after stepping off a runway in August of that year. She had been counseled that her career would jump start if she lost weight, so for three months she had been on a diet of green leaves and Diet Coke. Reactions to the ban from the fashion industry were mixed. Some designers refused to participate in Madrid's Fashion Week; others lauded the spirit of the ban. Most felt, though, that the fashion industry was being scapegoated for mental illnesses, when fashion merely reflects values society already holds. For eating disorder activists, this ban was seen as a major step toward having the fashion industry represent beauty at healthy weights and also having it assume a degree of responsibility for the health of its models, who so often starve themselves and are told by designers and agents to lose weight.

dysmorphia than their heterosexual counterparts (Crawford 1990). Experts forecast that eating disorders in all men will continue to rise as the marketing of men's health and beauty products becomes increasingly aggressive with "metrosexual" men, straight men who are overly concerned about their grooming, clothing, and overall appearance; and they, too, seek to make their bodies conform to the thin standard already set for women (Patterson 2004).

Conclusion

Debates will continue regarding whether eating disorders stem from biological, psychological, environmental, or structural factors. What researchers do know is that women of various socioeconomic backgrounds are disproportionately represented in the diagnosis and treatment of eating disorders, as defined by the DSM. Many eating disorder activists argue that the cult of thinness requires a more critical look at the culture at large, including gendered patterns of family life, girls' and boys' socialization, and the effects of various forms of oppression on individuals. Thus some activist-scholars argue that stopping the cycle of girls being socialized into the cult of thinness is a public, not a private, enterprise (Hesse-Biber 1996). Activism such as boycotting companies and products whose marketing includes the use of the thinness ideal is one approach that has been used by the Boston-based Boycott Anorexic Marketing group, which was effective during the mid-1990s in getting Coca-Cola and Kellogg to portray athletic instead of waifish women. More recently, this kind of activism has been taken on by marketers themselves, particularly with Dove's ad campaign that features women's bodies with "real curves." Groups such as the Eating Disorder Coalition have been lobbying the U.S. Congress to provide more money for eating disorder research and to force insurance companies to cover medical treatment. In addition, new research results continue to be released that points to other factors contributing to the prevalence of eating disorders among white, middle-class women as well as among men of various backgrounds and women of color—research that will surely shape future debates on their causes.

See also **Mental Health; Self-Injury and Body Image; Marketing to Women and Girls (vol. 1)**

Further Reading;

Abrams, S. K., L. Allen, and J. Gray, "Disordered Eating Attitudes and Ethnic Identity." *International Journal of Eating Disorders* 14 (1993): 49–57.

Bruch, Hilde, *The Golden Cage: The Enigma of Anorexia Nervosa.* Cambridge, MA: Harvard University Press, 1978.

Brumberg, Joan Jacobs, *Fasting Girls: The History of Anorexia Nervosa.* Cambridge, MA: Harvard University Press, 1988.

Chernin, Kim, *The Obsession: Reflections on the Tyranny of Slenderness.* New York: Harper Perennial, 1981.

Crawford, David, *Easing the Ache: Gay Men Recovering from Compulsive Disorders.* New York: Dutton, 1990.

Greenfield, Laura, *Thin.* HBO documentary. 2006.

Hesse-Biber, Sharlene, *Am I Thin Enough Yet? The Cult of Thinness and the Commercialization of Identity.* New York: Oxford University Press, 1996.

Maine, Margo, *Body Wars.* Carlsbad, CA: Gurze Books, 1991.

National Association of Anorexia Nervosa and Associated Disorders, 2010. http://www.anad.org

Patterson, Anna, *Fit to Die: Men and Eating Disorders.* Thousand Oaks, CA: Sage, 2004.

Pipher, Mary, *Reviving Ophelia: Saving the Selves of Adolescent Girls.* New York: Random House, 1994.

Rumney, Avis, *Dying to Please: Anorexia, Treatment and Recovery.* Jefferson, NC: McFarland, 2009.

Thompson, Becky W., *A Hunger So Wide and Deep: A Multiracial View of Women's Eating Problems.* Minneapolis: University of Minnesota Press, 1996.

ELDER ABUSE

Lasita Rudolph

Elder abuse is a serious issue that affects families and society. Elder abuse involves the acts of commission (abuse) and omission (neglect), as do other definitions of domestic violence. Unlike spouse and child abuse, which were defined as key social issues in the 1960s, elder abuse did not surface as a social problem until the late 1970s in congressional hearings examining the status of aging in the United States. The awareness generated through government and the media brought attention to the phenomenon. There are many questions about the prevalence of elder abuse and the vulnerability of certain categories of elders to abuse.

One thing that makes elder abuse difficult to discuss is that it is difficult to measure. Because domestic issues remain largely private, the true prevalence of elder abuse is not known. The best estimates, based on national samples and state data, indicate that about 5 percent of persons over age 65 will be abused in some way. It seems that spouse abuse is the most common abuse of those past retirement age, although abuse by adult children does contribute to the problem. Given the dependencies that most aged persons have, their reliance on others sets the stage for exploitation. Elders are potential victims whether they are being cared for in their own homes by family or at a nursing home by paid staff. There is evidence to suggest that, as today's elders are more likely to have retirement accounts and pension plans, their likelihood of being a victim of financial abuse is increasing.

What Is Elder Abuse?

Elder abuse is the sometimes intentional, but often times unintentional, mistreatment of a person over the age of 65. Elder abuse involves several aspects, including financial, physical, and emotional abuse. A special subcategory of physical abuse is sexual abuse. An inclusive definition of elder abuse would also consider neglect and self-neglect as additional aspects. Abuse of elders can lead to a worsening of the elder's health or even to death. Questions surround the causes of elder abuse as well as the ways that treatment and prevention should be approached. The different categories of abuse do not affect all elders in the same way.

Types of Elder Abuse

Physical Abuse

Physical abuse can be any of the following: pushing, kicking, slapping, choking, beating, punching, pinching, throwing, hitting, paddling, shoving, inappropriate restraints, assaulting, or harming with hand or objects. This force can lead to pain, injury, impairment, and disease of an elderly person. Given that humans get weaker and frailer as they age, abuse of elderly persons is particularly likely to result in injury. Additionally, these persons are less likely to be strong enough to defend themselves from attack and may even be confined to a wheel chair or bed due to their physical conditions. For the oldest old persons, age 85 and over, the consequences of physical beatings can be severe. The physical indicators of abuse are dehydration, malnourishment, sprains, dislocations, bite marks, internal injuries, unexplained bruises and burns, welts, skull fractures, lacerations, black eyes, and abrasions. Older persons, due to dementia or other memory-impairing conditions, may be unable to explain how their injuries occurred and may find it difficult to get assistance or intervention from law enforcement.

Sexual Abuse

Sexual abuse is any sexual activity performed on an elder without consent. Sexual abuse can be sexual intercourse, anal intercourse, or oral sex. Other sexual behaviors, however, can also be termed abuse if the elder is not a willing participant or is unable to provide consent. These activities include displaying one's genitals or making the elder display his or hers, watching while the elder does sexual things, or making the elder watch while the perpetrator does sexual things. It can even include watching pornography, taking pictures, and sex talk. The most likely perpetrator of sexual abuse is a family member. This is because the elder trusts the family member and allows closeness without knowing that the family member wants to do harm. It is also possible for an elder to be abused in a nursing home or for an outside caregiver to be the perpetrator of sexual abuse, but these cases are more limited. An elder with a severe disability is more likely to be abused because of dependency on the help of the nursing home staff or outside caregiver. Indicators of sexual abuse include genital or urinary irritation, frequent infections, vaginal or anal bleeding, bruising on the inner thighs, sexually transmitted diseases, depression, conversation regularly is of a sexual nature, severe agitation when being bathed or dressed, agitation during medical examination, and sudden confusion. Depending on the circumstances, sexual abuse can involve both physical and emotional elements.

Emotional Abuse

With emotional abuse, the elder is distressed, upset, depressed, experiencing withdrawal, and in emotional pain in this nonverbal or verbal situation. When elders are emotionally abused they become unresponsive, fearful, lack social interests, and evade others. Emotional abuse is equally likely to be perpetrated by a family member, nursing home staff, and outside caregivers. Elders may be particularly prone to emotional abuse, because they question their role in the family and society. Many persons perceive that, as they age, they are more of a burden on the family and have a harder time fitting in. They may feel that they deserve any treatment they receive because they cannot keep up mentally and physically with the younger generations. Some common types of emotional abuse include ignoring the elder, harassment and intimidation, insults and yelling, embarrassing or humiliating the elder, odd forms of punishment, and blaming. Also included are isolation from others or activities and not attending to the elder when necessary.

Financial Abuse

Financial abuse is the improper or illegal use of an elder's money and property. The financial abuser can be anyone but is most likely a family member because family members have more direct access to aged family members' resources. For various practical reasons, including fear of money management, tax savings, and inheritance, among others, elders may ask family members to tend to their financial concerns. Sometimes this takes the form of a power of attorney, where the family member is the legal guardian of the older person's estate and is authorized to act as his or her agent. Other times the arrangement is informal, and the older person just asks someone else to keep his or her bank accounts and take care of daily financial transactions. Government estimates indicate that approximately 5 million elders are victims of financial abuse each year, with most cases going unreported.

A dishonest person can take advantage of the elder, misinforming him about his assets or using the money for one's own needs. The person may even get the elder to consent to such things through threats or constantly harassing the elder about her financial status. Elders can be financially abused in many ways. They include exploitation and fraud by both primary and secondary contacts, signature forging, embezzling, and theft of property. Certain areas of fraud have targeted older persons and include home repair fraud, insurance fraud, medical fraud, telemarketing, and confidence games. Another egregious component is nursing home theft. Considering that most very old people are women, who often have fewer funds available at retirement than do men and often relied on their husbands to manage their funds prior to his death, the costs of financial abuse can be very high.

Neglect

Neglect can occur when the elder is in isolation, has been abandoned, or a caregiver refuses to provide the elder with essential needs, including physical and emotional needs. Just as neglect is the most frequent type of child abuse, neglect is considered the most common type of elder abuse. Self-neglect is also a problem with elders. This can occur when an elder neglects his own needs. There are two types of neglect: active and passive. Active neglect is defined as refusal or failure to fulfill the needs of the elder. This would be intentional neglect. Passive neglect is also failing to fulfill an elder's needs, but this type is unintentional. It has been known to occur in nursing homes that do not have the most qualified staff or the resources to meet the needs of the elder residents. Neglect is also done by family members and by outside caregivers. Examples of neglect include denial of needs such as food and water, lack of assistance with food and water (if required), improper supervision, inappropriate clothing for the type of weather, or inadequate help with bathing or other hygiene practices. Other examples are lack of access to the toilet, lack of diaper changing, strong smell of urine or feces, and physically restraining the elder without medical cause. Finally, refusing to seek required medical care for the elder is a type of neglect.

Brief History

Elder abuse first appeared on the public radar in the 1970s. However, many professionals did not care much about abuse of the elderly at the time and were more concerned with child abuse and abuse against women. Consequently, elder abuse was not taken very seriously. There was inadequate knowledge about the scope of the issue and what to do for such situations. There were few ways that family professionals could intervene in such cases. In the late 1970s, Congress began to hear of "granny battering" and became interested in this issue. As groups began to testify in Congress in defense of older Americans, the tide began to turn. In 1989, the Older Americans Act was proposed. While there was not a lot of money available to assist in stopping elder abuse, it was recognized as a problem, and, over time, more and more people became interested in this issue. The media helped to spread the word about elder abuse, getting the attention of medical professionals and the criminal justice system. Researchers began to attend to the issue as well. However, the extent of the problem remains hidden. The best estimates indicate that for every abuse case reported, there are about five more that are not reported.

Controversies in Elder Abuse

Although it is generally accepted that abuse is a problem in the culture that needs to be eradicated, the paths to decreased violence are often contradictory. Often experts suggest that one cannot end abuse without knowing the causes of abuse. Elder abuse shares some links with domestic violence causes in general, but because of the intergenerational nature of the abuse, there are some important differences. Another area of controversy involves whether gender plays a role in the status of both victim and perpetrator. Other questions remain as to the best course of action when dealing with older persons who have been abused and the role that the state plays in providing assistance to them.

Contributing Factors in Elder Abuse

There have been wide-ranging suggestions as to the factors that contribute to elder abuse. Not only have the ideas of "violence as a way of life" in U.S. society been blamed, but the cultural belief in the value of youth and devaluing of elderly, referred to as ageism, have been touted as a contributing factor. It seems likely that there are factors both within the culture as a whole and in the personal interactions of families that make abuse more likely to occur. Among the explanations in the literature are caregiver stress, victim disability, social isolation, perpetrator deviance, and victim-perpetrator dependency.

Situational factors can make caring for an elder particularly difficult. The caregiver may have emotional, psychological, financial, and mental problems of her own. These can become compounded when caring for an elderly person. A family member caring for an older relative may experience financial problems due to the material needs of the elder or missing work to care for the elder. The caregiving is particularly likely to compound any financial problems that were already there, leading to increasing stress for the caregiver. If the physical space is inadequate for the caring tasks, any poor housing conditions can become more concerning. Additionally, caregiving is stressful work, and many caregivers will feel overburdened after an extended time in the role. It is quite hard if persons are caring for more than one dependent at a time, such as caring for one's child and aging parent simultaneously. The more dependent on a caregiver the elder person is, the more the stress for the person caring for the elder.

Some of the dependencies that exist between an abusive caregiver and victimized elder relate to the tactics and responses developed in family life that can carry over into adulthood. For example, a history of psychological or mental health problems, physical abuse, or poor communication or relationships in a family may continue. There also may be personality problems and difficult behavior displayed by the elder that compound the problem.

Abuse in an institutional setting such as a nursing home might occur, because an elder is cared for in an institution that lacks proper resources. This might refer to the physical structure of the facility but also includes a lack of training for the staff, inadequate staffing relative to need, and stressful work conditions. It is important to remember that there is a component of today's society that argues the elderly are not important. They can no longer contribute to the economy and become costly. This approach suggests that elders feel unimportant as they age and become less critical in the operations of community life. The removal of older members from society and into nursing homes marginalizes elders, making them ripe for exploitation.

While each of these approaches may contribute to the abuse of any given elder, there is no definitive statement about which is the most powerful in explaining the phenomenon. Another variable in the abuse model is the gender of the victim and perpetrator.

Gender Issues in Elder Abuse

Are elders at differential risk of abuse by gender? Because the population of elderly is comprised of more women than men, due to women's greater life expectancy, women have a higher chance of becoming a victim. Not only are there more women, but in general women have less power in society. Research on violent crime shows that women are more likely the victims of assaults perpetrated by family members and acquaintances than those by strangers. Does this pattern hold for elders?

One of the critical elements in elder abuse seems to be dementia. Elders with dementia and related problems are more likely to be victimized. In three out of four cases where the wife abused her husband, he was suffering from severe dementia. In those cases where the son was the abuser, the man also suffered from mild dementia. Dementia featured less prominently in the cases of men being psychologically abused. Daughters, fathers, and sons all abused mothers with severe dementia. For most of the elderly women who are abused, it is generally by someone they live with. Regardless of sex, the worse the health of the elder is, the more likely that the elder will be abused. Overall, women are abused more than men. This is partly because women live longer but they suffer from different health issues. Elder women's health deteriorates more over the years, which makes them more prone to being abused.

Men and women are not equally likely to abuse elders. As the ones primarily responsible for caregiving, women have a greater likelihood of abusing elders. This is a point that has been quite controversial due to the assumption that men are more likely to use violence than women and that women are more nurturing than men. Although women relatives outnumber men relatives as abusers, it is wives who constitute the majority of abusers. In some studies, men have been found to be more likely to neglect an elder than are women. It is more likely that men financially abuse elders, and women physically abuse elders.

Help for the Elderly

The type of help proposed to counteract and decrease elder abuse depends on which of the explanations for abuse is applied. When the abuse is thought to be the result of caregiver stress, which is often associated with neglect, the abuse may be ameliorated

ELDER ABUSE IN OTHER SOCIETIES

Elder abuse is not limited to the United States, but has been defined as a problem in other societies, including South Africa, Australia, Greece, Hong Kong, Finland, Israel, India, Poland, Ireland, and Norway. Many countries do not have a consistent definition for elder abuse, nor do they research its prevalence and societal impacts. The least-common type of abuse reported in other countries is physical abuse. Some definitions ruled out self-neglect as a type of abuse. Physical abuse is very rare in some countries, because the culture espouses keeping harmony rather than using violence. Thus, abuse is culturally specific to the values and morals of the society. Some countries have few health care institutions available for the elderly. Failure to define behaviors as abuse may result from economic issues in different countries. They may not have adequate resources to take proper care of the elderly population that has increased as a result of longer life expectancy and lower mortality rates.

Three themes related to elder abuse that many countries have in common are dependency, economic conditions, and cultural change. Each of these can contribute to the likelihood of elder abuse. Dependency is a problem due to more responsibilities and demands placed on caregivers. Economic conditions are a problem because of unemployment, reductions in incomes, reductions of programs and services, and cutbacks of government assistance. Cultural change is a problem because of different traditions, industrialization, and new technologies. Differing values are also a problem, because the elder may still believe in doing things the way she was brought up, but her adult children may have a different way of doing things, creating conflict between elders and their families. In order to assist elders and prevent abuse, countries should first define and address the problem at hand. Second they have to understand the problem, know why it occurs, and want to end it. And last, they have to get assistance from the government, economy, and media so that it will be taken seriously.

by reducing how dependent the victim is on the caregiver. One way to assist is to bring services into the home so that the caregiver does not have to do everything. Meals on Wheels, respite care, skilled nursing care, housekeeping services, and so forth have all been proposed as strategies to reduce caregiver stress. Another component in reducing stress is the use of adult day care. Skill building and counseling for the caregiver have also been recommended.

If the abuse or mistreatment has more to do with the dependency, emotional or financial, between the perpetrator and the elder, which is often linked to physical abuse, the strategies change. Successful interventions might include mental health services, alcohol or drug treatment, job placement, housing assistance, or even vocational training. Sometimes emergency intervention is necessary, and courts may have to assign a guardian for the elderly person.

The National Center on Elder Abuse, part of the Administration on Aging of the U.S. Department of Health and Human Services, has been active in providing assistance to both caregivers and elders. It educates and advocates for better circumstances for senior citizens and is among the many groups focusing on elder abuse. It may be hard for an elderly person to come forward and ask for help after abuse, because he may not be able to do so, or may be afraid of getting hurt even worse. Elders can also have feelings of embarrassment, being ashamed of their victimization and expecting that no one will believe in them.

There is a lot that can be done to help. Abuse reporting hotlines are available to help caregivers and the elderly. Volunteers working at nursing homes can help identify problems or just be a friendly face who can listen to elders' concerns. One group called Beyond Existing was formed for victims of elder abuse. This group determines the exact abuse problem, talks over the problem with the elder, lets the elder meet others that were in a similar position, and helps the elder plan for the future. Finally, there is also help for elders through physicians, nurses, social workers, and case management workers.

As a public health issue, elder abuse is not expected to end but to increase. Elders are treated by health care professionals, social workers, and case management workers to make sure their needs are met. Health care professionals indicate that elder abuse adds to a health care system already experiencing problems. Nurses play an important role in the detection and resolution of elder abuse. They work as individuals or in a team setting to assess elder mistreatment. If any degree of abuse is present, the most important goal of the nurse is to maintain the safety of the elder and possibly remove her from that care setting. It is also the nurse's job to teach caregivers proper caring procedures for an elderly person, because they may lack the proper knowledge needed to care for an elder.

Physicians have an ethical and, in most states, a legal role in the recognition of and intervention in suspected cases of elder mistreatment. To be fully successful, physicians should be aware of legal issues, ethical issues, and communication needs and have a solid base in principals of geriatric care. Physicians must be able to detect mistreatment bruises from normal bruises. The presence of physical abuse marks and the stated causes of them must be documented. If a physician suspects mistreatment, he or she is expected to report it. It is also the responsibility of the physician to interview the elder to assess the elder's relationship with the caregiver. Social workers also have an important role in assessing elder abuse. Their main goal is to investigate any allegations of harm being done to an elder.

Conclusion

Elder abuse is a serious issue that society and families must examine and end. As U.S. society continues to age, the already large number of elders who are dependent upon others for daily care will only increase. To ensure that the aged are properly cared for, caregivers need support and training from a variety of sources and settings. Institutions should be monitored to ensure that they have all the proper resources to care for elderly patients, including a well-educated and not overburdened staff. The government plays a role through monitoring and legal regulation. Health care professionals should properly assess mistreatment of the elderly and get help right away.

See also **Elder Care**

Further Reading

Anetzberger, Georgia J., *The Clinical Management of Elder Abuse.* New York: Haworth Press, 2003.

Bonnie, Richard J., and Robert B. Wallace, *Elder Mistreatment: Abuse, Neglect, and Exploitation in an Aging America.* Washington, DC: National Academic Press, 2003.

Brownwell, Patricia J., and Stuart Bruchey, *Family Crimes against the Elderly: Elder Abuse and the Criminal Justice System.* New York: Garland, 1998.

Hoffman, Allan M., and Randal W. Summers, *Elder Abuse: A Public Health Perspective.* Washington, DC: American Public Health Association, 2006.

Nerenberg, Lisa, *Elder Abuse Prevention: Emerging Trends and Promising Strategies.* New York: Springer, 2008.

Payne, Brian K., *Crime and Elder Abuse: An Integrated Perspective.* Springfield, IL: Charles C. Thomas, 2005.

ELDER CARE

Kimberly P. Brackett

At both ends of the life course, infancy and old age, the question of care is paramount. Not only do discussions revolve around the quality of care available to assist with the needs of these groups, but costs and moral obligations compound the debate. Just as young parents must decide whether to place a child in day care or find an alternative so that the child may be cared for at home, adult children and their aging parents must decide how best to care for the aged. Is home care by a family member or skilled nursing care in an institutional setting most appropriate? Often families agonize over the decision of how to care for their loved one. Many times, financial limitations determine the options more than does personal preference.

Background

Even though the nuclear family has been the norm in U.S. society, caring for ill and elderly kin in one's home was common. Few options existed until the early 20th century, when nurses who were concerned about the health and care of elder citizens began to operate elder care facilities. Accelerated by the Great Depression, they opened their homes at a time when the elderly had few other choices but to accept their care. Nurses could use the meager income that elderly residents could provide from federal Old Age Assistance funds. Thus, nursing homes began as a for-profit enterprise. Nurses were the first professionals to begin research in the area of aging.

At the founding of the United States, few options to care for the elderly existed aside from their own wealth or the generosity of their children. Those who had neither were usually at the mercy of the poorhouses or almshouses that generally were responsible for all those who had no means of support, not just the frail elderly. By the early 1800s, many young folks were moving west to seek their fortunes, often leaving older relatives behind to fend for themselves. In the mid- to late 1800s, residential homes for the elderly began to appear. These were largely the result of benevolent societies such as the Masons and the Knights of Columbus. These voluntary and charitable residences were unlikely to provide medical care but were simply a place to live. Some may have had separate hospital areas where ill persons were housed. Some of the wealthier elderly began to live in so-called rest houses, which were often several rooms for rent in private homes. By the end of the 19th century, more options were emerging for elders. However, care in an institutional setting would not emerge en masse until the 1950s, largely as a result of changes to Social Security programs. In 1954, for example, a national survey found 9,000 nursing homes housing about 270,000 residents.

Elder care today has changed in response to the needs of patients and their desires. There are many different levels of care that are available, and families often find that they need to research them thoroughly to determine which is the most appropriate for their elder relative. Aside from care by a family member or care in the elder's own home, options include adult day care, assisted living, continuous care communities, independent living, and nursing homes. Adult day care provides respite care. This means the regular caregiver can use services to take a break from the rigors of caring. In independent living, residents live in a community setting where all of the maintenance is performed for them. Many amenities and the ability to furnish one's residence as desired make these attractive for healthy elders. There is generally no medical staff on site, however. Very similar to independent living is the continuous care community. These are sometimes touted as the most luxurious option for retirement living because of the desirable amenities. These communities provide, for a fee, the health care support and assistance that will change with the needs of the resident. Assisted living facilities provide significant support with the tasks of daily living, changing the services as needed by the resident. There is 24-hour security and support staff presence, food service, daily task assistance, and personal support like assistance in dressing, bathing, and so forth. In nursing home care, there is medical assistance available on site, more direct supervision of daily activities, personal support, and end-of-life care.

Caregiver Stress

Caring for a loved one is stressful. The literature suggests that the arrangement works best when there is at least some time for the caregiver and patient to be away from each other. This is where adult day care and other caregiver support tools can be particularly helpful. There are positive aspects to taking care of a loved one at home, usually because of the relationship between the caregiver and the elder. The satisfaction the caregiver feels, knowing that she is taking care of and helping the loved one, can help reduce the stress of the task and can improve her outlook on the role. People with higher rates of positive aspects of caregiving report less depression and more feelings of fulfillment. When the patient is mentally sharp and the relationship between caregiver and patient is close, the caregiving is viewed more positively. Likewise, the attitude one has going into the caregiving task is important in determining the attitude toward the task later. A difference between the races has been found for positive aspects of caregiving. African Americans report higher positive affect toward caregiving and lower anxiety. They also have comparatively lower socioeconomic status.

Older caregivers tend to view the caregiving more positively than do younger caregivers, who might see the task as a burden or interruption of their lives. Caregivers are particularly concerned with the quality of life that they can provide for their patients. When they feel that the loved one's quality of life is deteriorating, they may be more likely to seek alternatives to home care.

Nursing Home Issues

Often the decision to use a nursing home is seen as a last resort. Much of this comes from the stigma of being in an institutional setting. There are circumstances, however, in which a nursing home can be the most beneficial option. While most assume that care outside the home is chosen because the elder relative requires a level of care that can no longer be provided by family, there may be other factors that make nursing home care and similar supportive options attractive. Unlike with other housing options, true nursing homes admit residents only with a physician's order. *Nursing home* is used here to refer to both assisted living and nursing home–type care settings—what is more generally termed *institutional care.*

THE GENDER OF CAREGIVING

Women do more than their share of caregiving. Today men contribute to caregiving more than ever before, but women are still in the primary caregiver role. Estimates are that more than 70 percent of caregivers are women. This disproportionate burden on women might be the result of their socialization. Gender role attitudes are learned early in life and often indicate a gender-based division of labor in families. The most likely provider of care is a spouse. However, when that person becomes unable to provide care, an adult daughter is usually tapped to fulfill the tasks. The order of care providers reflects this gendered expectation: daughter, daughter-in-law, son, younger female relative, younger male relative, and then female nonrelative.

Not only do daughters perform more health care, they do it earlier in life and for longer periods of time than do men. Men usually provide financial and maintenance assistance, not direct personal care. Spouses are the most dependable caregivers, and, because women generally live longer than men, this usually means that wives are doing the bulk of the caring. Spouses generally provide care until the spouse dies or their own health deteriorates significantly. They report seeing the caring as part of the marriage contract. Spouses feel less role conflict and burden in taking care of the partner than do other family members.

Many elderly people do not want to impose on their families and want to remain independent as long as they can. When they can no longer live independently, the family is faced with the choice to care for the loved one at home or employ some type of residential facility, such as a nursing home. In some cases, particularly where there are few financial resources, a nursing home may be the most cost-effective option. Most residents have their care paid for by federal or state subsidies such as Medicare or Medicaid. While this may necessitate the surrender of all the elder's assets to the nursing facility, it may be the best long-term option.

Many of the benefits of nursing home care relate to the tasks of daily living that may become increasingly challenging as persons age. Included would be assistance with dressing, bathing, toileting, and other hygienic self-care. Additionally, for patients who are infirm, changing positions on a routine schedule and diapering can be hard for families but more easily managed with a trained staff. Other daily living tasks that nursing homes provide include food service and assistance with feeding, if needed. They also do laundry for residents and provide housekeeping services in their rooms or apartments.

Among the factors that are comforting to residents and family members are 24-hour security and trained staff caregivers. Additionally, social and recreational activities are available to provide leisure and enjoyment for residents. Given that the oldest and sickest elderly are likely to be in nursing care, the provision of medical supervision, including physician and other health care provider visits, is of benefit to the residents and families. Assistance is just a call button away, and someone can respond rapidly should an emergency occur.

Socially, many residents of institutional care are very satisfied with the situation. In a nursing home, there are staff and other residents with whom to interact, rather than just one caregiver. Communal living creates a bond with the other residents, who have, for the most part, had similar life experiences. This socially stimulating situation provides a daily activity schedule, and residents are encouraged to participate in it as they are able, thereby providing benefits to physical and psychological health. Even watching television is often done in a group context, thus encouraging interaction and shielding the elder from depression and loneliness.

There is a long-standing fear that nursing homes and other institutional settings are simply warehousing the elderly and that they do not take care of the elder as well as family members would. This stereotype leads to stress over the decision and fear of additional harm occurring as a consequence of the living situation. Most persons have a fear of institutionalization and prefer to stay in a familiar setting. Staying at home might also provide the elder with a sense of independence. Occasional reports of abuse of nursing home residents also make families and elders leery of such settings. While the abuse in these places draws media attention, elders are more likely to be abused by a family member at home than by a staff member at an institution.

Home Care Issues

Reciprocity, giving back to those who have given to you, plays a role whether consciously or unconsciously in the decision to care for an older relative at home. When one is a child, parents provide care; as parents age, children provide care. This creates a sense of being responsible for the care of one's elders. This can lead to guilt when factors limit the amount of care that a child can reasonably provide. This obligation is also mirrored in societal expectations that nursing care is a last resort.

Home care works best when there are multiple people in the family who can help provide it, including household maintenance, transportation, stimulation, and direct physical care. Loved ones who are in poor health necessitate more of a commitment on the part of caregivers. Caregiving involves much more than just providing medical assistance. Family roles and relationships may become altered in the process: economic difficulties, curtailed work and social activities, and exacerbation of family conflicts can all change the interaction dynamics in a family. It is, however, becoming increasingly possible for family caregivers to acquire the needed support to care for elders at home. When care is directed from home, the family can set up who the additional caregivers are, when they provide care, and under what circumstances. This sense of control can be positive for the family and the elderly relative.

It is sometimes less expensive to care for an elderly family member at home than in an institutional setting. Particularly if funds have been established for such purposes, family members can stretch the budget by performing tasks themselves rather than hiring them out. There may, however, need to be actual physical changes to the home to accommodate adequate care for the elder. The costs of remodeling may be prohibitive.

Having the elder at home makes it easier to interact with that person on a daily basis and monitor his health. This is much more convenient than having to arrange a time to travel to another location to visit and interact. Additionally, more family bonding can occur in the home than in an institutional setting. From the standpoint of the elder, it is a comfortable situation, because she can retain more of her personal belongings and may not have to consolidate items like persons in institutional care must do.

A benefit of home care that is sometimes overlooked is the ongoing contact that the elder has with the community. Rather than being forced to conform to a totally different routine, as occurs in some institutional settings, home care permits the elder to remain an enmeshed participant in the social life of the family and community. This occurs through continuing to see the same health care providers, attending the same church, visiting the same recreational facilities, and so forth.

Conclusion

Many issues will continue to influence the way that families make the decision about institutional care compared to home care. Among the most critical are the changing demographic patterns of the society. As the U.S. population continues to age, there will be more concern about having enough spaces for all those who wish to or need to reside in nursing homes. For persons who are older but still highly functional, having some decision-making ability over their own health is expected. One of the concepts that will likely be discussed more in the coming years is aging in place. Growing older without having to move to secure necessary support services as one's needs change can be beneficial. Advocates (such as the National Aging in Place Council) suggest that efforts should be made to support older persons remaining active participants in their communities and experiencing fulfilling interactions by living independently as long as their health permits them to do so. An intergenerational environment is the likely outcome. This approach is particularly supportive of those of low to moderate incomes, because they experience more financial constraints in the selection of care options.

More institutional facilities recognize this desire for independence and long-term participation in a residential community. Subsequently, they may offer a variety of services to provide long-term options for clients as they move from lower to higher levels of care need. For persons who are fortunate to be financially prepared for retirement and longevity expenses, the option of assisted living and other nursing home alternatives is attractive, suggesting that these types of facilities will be increasingly popular because residents are usually active participants in making the decision to live there.

As today's elders age, they are living longer than past generations due to increased nutrition, medical knowledge, and positive lifestyle choices. This means there are more oldest old (persons 85 years and older) who are likely to have several medical issues with which to contend and that require more complex chronic disease management. As family size has decreased, the persons who can share the burden of caregiving, both financially and directly, are fewer, requiring a greater commitment from those providing care. Likewise, the continuing high rates of women's employment suggest that there will be fewer traditional caregivers available to assume in-home care giving. Increased mobility for the population means that older people may not live in the same general locale as their potential family caregivers, giving more support to the idea that institutional care will increase as a percentage of all care for elders. Just because nursing and other institutional care is likely to increase, that does not mean that the decision about how to best care for elders will become any easier for families. Social pressures still suggest that the preferable pattern is for family to provide care as long as it is possible to do so.

See also **Elder Abuse; Health Care (vol. 1); Social Security (vol. 1)**

Further Reading

AARP, http://www.aarp.org

Berg-Weger, Marla, *Caring for Elderly Parents.* New York: Garland, 1996.

Digregorio, Charlotte, *Everything You Need to Know about Nursing Homes.* Portland, OR: Civetta Press, 2005.

Ebersole, Priscilla, and Theris A. Touhy, *Geriatric Nursing: Growth of a Specialty.* New York: Springer, 2006.

Henry, Stella Mora, with Ann Convery, *The Eldercare Handbook: Difficult Choices, Compassionate Solutions.* New York: HarperCollins, 2006.

Johnson & Johnson Caregiver Initiative,. http://www.strengthforcaring.com

National Aging in Place Council, http://www.naipc.org

EMPLOYED MOTHERS

SUSAN CODY-RYDZEWSKI

Maternal employment has been the subject of considerable debate for many years. Women's labor force participation rates have been steadily increasing since before the turn of the 20th century. In fact, over the past 100 years, the number of women who are employed for pay or seeking paid employment has increased from about 4 million in 1890 to almost 63 million in 2001. Furthermore, between 1980 and 2000, the paid labor force participation rate for mothers of school-aged children increased from 64 to 79 percent. For mothers of preschool children, the rate increased from 47 to about 65 percent. In 2009, nearly 60 percent of married mothers with children under the age of three were in the paid labor force. The percentage of mothers who return to work within one year after their child's birth has dropped slightly since the late 1990s, however. This has led some to suggest that there may be an increase of so-called neotraditional families—families in which women opt out of the labor force and in which spouses prefer traditional gender roles. Evidence seems to suggest that this opting out may be the result of a weak labor market more than a genuine change in gender role ideologies or a concern with family well-being. Labor force participation among women who must work—single parents and those with low levels of education—has continued to grow.

Looking Back

There is a popular misconception that women, especially wives, primarily worked inside the home until the second wave of the women's movement in the 1960s. This myth is largely based on U.S. nostalgia surrounding the period after World War II, in which women were encouraged to leave their jobs to make room for men and return to the home in fulfillment of their natural roles as wives and mothers. It should be made clear, however, that this return to homemaking and domesticity represented a reversal from previous, long-standing patterns.

In preindustrial America, almost everyone, including children, worked. Survival in agrarian economies depends on a stable and predictable supply of food; thus, all members of society must contribute in some way to food production. While some tasks were associated more with women than with men, there was considerable overlap in roles, and most work, including parenting, was performed by both women and men. Industrialization and urbanization led to an initial segregation of gender roles and of work. Men, single women, and women of color were expected to enter into the new paid jobs, while affluent, married women were expected to perform unpaid labor at home. This division of gender roles was supported by a belief system known as the ideology of separate spheres, which posits that work and family are separate domains and that each is better suited to the strengths and skills of either men or women. In summary, expectations for women and mothers vary according to current economic demands. Women's employment is dependent on various social-context variables, including available opportunities for women, economic constraints more generally (on men and women), as well as the perceived rewards and costs of the homemaking role.

Despite economic and social changes, this ideology has remained deeply embedded in U.S. culture and in the minds of most Americans. It appears that many continue to believe that women's natural place is at home. Even among dual-earner couples, it is more common for husbands to describe themselves as primary providers and for husbands and wives to describe wives as secondary providers or to describe their earnings as supplementary. Generally speaking, most couples consider housework and child care to be the province of women. As such, the domestic burden carried by wives results in a reinforcing cycle in which women's contributions to the paid labor force are severely compromised, and their commitment to it is perceived as weak. In other words, if women perform more housework, they are less able to contribute to their jobs or careers. This inability to contribute may be perceived as an unwillingness to contribute and thus a lack of professional commitment.

Work-Life Issues Today

Both the family and the workplace are so-called greedy institutions, demanding a great deal of time and energy from individuals. In fact, in the United States the full-time work week is quite a bit longer than in many Western European countries. Furthermore, individuals often find that these domains require the most from them during the same period of their lives. That is, the demands of work and family peak around the same time. Thus, many women and men feel that it is difficult to balance the demands of career, marriage, and family. This is particularly true of women, because they are expected to be the "kinkeepers"—maintaining a happy marriage, a stable and successful family, routines, rituals, and extended family ties. Not surprisingly, balance may be most difficult to achieve among dual-earner couples with preschoolers. To help achieve balance, one spouse, typically the wife, may choose to limit the time spent in the paid work force. Other strategies include seeking more flexible work schedules, although historically in the United States flexible options in the workplace have been scant. Some spouses may opt to work from home. However, studies have shown that women who work from home contribute more to housework than do men who work from home. Another consequence of the inability to balance work and family is a lack of leisure time, especially for wives. In one study, it was found that while husbands tend to relax in the evenings or enjoy a personal hobby, wives tend to be focused on housework and child care.

Because a belief in separate spheres remains firmly entrenched in American ideals, employed women, and especially mothers, often find that they not only confront conflicting role expectations but also social disapproval. Approval for working mothers seems to be on the increase, however. A 2001 survey of women found that over 90 percent of them agreed that a woman can be successful at both career and motherhood.

Today, a majority of mothers are employed. This trend has prompted a significant amount of negative attention, especially from social and religious conservatives. The primary concern seems to revolve around the potentially negative effects of maternal employment on child development and on family relationships more generally. The current ideal and expectation for so-called intensive mothering requires that women be available and receptive to their children's needs for most, if not all, hours of the day, every day of the week. There is no comparable expectation for fathers. Good fathering is normally defined as stable providing; thus, there is no contradiction between the roles of father and employee. For women, however, employment presents a challenge, at least ideologically, to the mothering role, because good mothering is not equated with providing. In fact, commitment to paid work is typically viewed as posing a threat to successful mothering. Women who wish to pursue both a career and motherhood may feel that they must choose between two opposing, mutually exclusive alternatives. The cultural contradiction of being a working mother has negative economic and professional ramifications for women. It has been found that not only does being married reduce the chances that a woman will be promoted, but being a mother does so as well. Women with preschool-aged children have lower rates of promotion than do other women, whereas the opposite is true for men. Motherhood has a definite negative impact on lifetime earnings—this is known as the motherhood penalty. This penalty has not declined significantly over the years.

Many of the concerns surrounding mothers' employment are unfounded; there is little, if any, empirical support for them. The primary concern surrounds the effects of maternal employment on the well-being of children. Furthermore, this seems to have been prompted by a larger concern with the rise of women's equality, threats to the masculine gender role, especially men's role as providers, and what some believe are the long-term, negative effects of the feminist movement. For the most part, Americans are accepting of mothers' employment if and when it is absolutely necessary to provide for basic necessities. Attitudes become more intolerant, however, of mothers who have careers and work for personal fulfillment. In fact, in recent years, there have been several instances of highly publicized cases in which children were harmed while under the supervision of a paid caregiver, such as a nanny. In such instances, it was the employed mother, not the hired caregiver or the employed father, who was held responsible for the child's well-being. Rarely, if ever, are fathers implicated in such cases.

A number of research studies have examined the question of what effect, if any, maternal employment has on child well-being. Among mothers who work outside the home during their child's first year of life, some negative outcomes have been found. However, many factors, such as the type and quality of child care, home environment, spousal attitudes toward women's employment, and gender role ideology need to be considered as well. After careful consideration of many of the studies examining the effects of women's employment on child outcomes, some have concluded that, in and of itself, maternal employment has little, if any, negative impact on child development or on child-parent relationships. In fact, some studies find that children benefit from maternal employment or from high-quality child care. Interestingly, a number of studies indicate that parents today spend as much or more time with children than in the past. For instance, it has been shown that, in 1975, married mothers spent about 47 hours per week with their children, whereas in 2000, they spent 51 hours per week with them. This increase seems to be the result of a decrease in time spent on personal care, housework, and marital intimacy.

Regardless of the child care arrangement, employed mothers may feel as if they are being asked to juggle and manage multiple roles—to do it all. The idea of the supermom is that of a woman who successfully manages a marriage, a family, and a career with time left over for herself. The reality is quite different from the image, however. Working mothers often report feeling overwhelmed with the kind and quantity of responsibilities they maintain. Not only are mothers expected to manage and execute tangible tasks such as meal preparation and transportation, but also psychological tasks such as planning and preparing for family routines. While husbands may serve as occasional pinch hitters, wives typically have an executive function, meaning that it is ultimately their responsibility to see that the household runs efficiently. Furthermore, the demands of the household are continuous and unrelenting; thus, household executives are never off duty.

Husbands and Housework

While women have made a substantial entry into the public sphere of paid work, men have not made a comparable entry into the private sphere of unpaid work. Even among dual-earner couples, wives perform the majority of unpaid labor in and around the home; this extra shift of work for employed wives has been referred to as the "second shift" or "double day." Ironically, just being married seems to increase the amount of housework that women perform, as single mothers spend less time in housework than do married mothers. Because of the uneven distribution of household labor and child care, there is a considerable leisure gap between mothers and fathers; that is, mothers have much less free and discretionary time than do fathers. Employed mothers often report feelings of physical and psychological exhaustion. Affluent couples may decide to hire outside help to assist with child care, household chores, or both. However, research indicates that it is still wives who initiate and coordinate such services. Other couples may rely on older children to assist with housework. This may be more common among single-parent households. Over 40 percent of children have been in some sort of nonrelative child care arrangement by the time they enter school. About 40 percent of children age 12 to 14 and 8 percent of those age 5 to 11 whose mothers were employed were in unsupervised self-care arrangements. Self-care is more common among white upper-middle-class and middle-class families. Lower-income, single-parent, and Latino families are much more likely to involve extended family members in the care of children.

Encouragingly, husbands' contributions to unpaid work have increased somewhat over the past 20 years or so. Husbands' involvement in household labor and parenting varies somewhat by race or ethnicity. African American couples, for example, are characterized by greater sharing and more egalitarianism. This may be due to higher rates of labor force participation among women of color as well as more cultural approval for a communal approach to parenting. Participation in housework is generally related to the relative earnings of spouses. That is, husbands of wives who earn a significant share of the total family income generally perform more housework than do husbands of wives who earn very little. Ironically, men may actually do less housework if and when they become unemployed. This may be an attempt to reclaim or hold onto an already threatened masculine identity.

See also **Child Care; Affirmative Action (vol. 1); Glass Ceiling (vol. 1)**

Further Reading

Blair-Loy, Mary, *Competing Devotions: Career and Family among Women Executives.* Cambridge, MA: Harvard University Press, 2005.

Crittenden, Ann, *The Price of Motherhood: Why the Most Important Job in the World Is Still the Least Valued.* New York: Henry Holt, 2002.

Galinsky, Ellen, *Ask the Children: The Breakthrough Study that Reveals How To Succeed at Work and Parenting.* New York: HarperCollins, 1999.

Hays, Sharon, *The Cultural Contradictions of Motherhood.* New Haven, CT: Yale University Press, 1998.

Hesse-Biber, Sharlene, and Gregg Lee Carter, *Working Women in America: Split Dreams.* New York: Oxford University Press, 2004.

Hochschild, Arlie Russell, *The Time Bind: When Work Becomes Home and Home Becomes Work.* New York: Henry Holt, 2001.

Landry, Bart, *Black Working Wives: Pioneers of the American Family Revolution.* Berkeley: University of California Press, 2002.

Padavic, Irene, and Barbara Reskin, *Women and Men at Work.* Thousand Oaks, CA: Pine Forge Press, 2002.

Williams, Joan, *Unbending Gender: Why Family and Work Conflict and What To Do About It.* New York: Oxford University Press, 2001.

EUTHANASIA AND PHYSICIAN-ASSISTED SUICIDE

Susan Cody-Rydzewski

In general, one can choose death by euthanasia and physician-assisted suicide. Broadly understood, euthanasia means "good death"; however, current usage depicts a specific kind of dying, which is usually accomplished by the act of someone other than the one who dies. Physician-assisted suicide is a particular form of suicide, or dying, where a physician who possesses relevant knowledge and skills assists the one who wishes to die. Various religious perspectives offer ways to deal with the challenges presented by death and dying, pain and suffering, freedom and responsibility in health care, and the value of human life. All of these are present at the intersection of euthanasia, physician-assisted suicide, and religion.

Typically, euthanasia and physician-assisted suicide occur in the context of health care when patients face death and dying. Death and dying are fundamental to (and inevitable in) the human condition. Historically, death and dying happened as a consequence of incurable disease, unforeseen accident, war, or murderous action. With euthanasia and physician-assisted suicide, however, one can take control over the circumstances, the mode, and the health state at the time of death. This represents a technological transformation of the dying process—a transformation that many argue brings about individual and social goods (philosopher Daniel Callahan refers to this kind of phenomenon as "technological brinkmanship"; see Callahan 2000, 40–41).

As the Hippocratic Oath indicates, the ethical, legal, and theological issues of euthanasia and physician-assisted suicide are not necessarily new. Dating back several centuries, the oath prohibits a Hippocratic physician from prescribing poisons and other materials for his patient (see Edelstein 1967; Rietjens et al. 2006; Ramsey 1974; Campbell 1994). Interestingly, this is not lost in a Christian version of the Hippocratic Oath: "Neither will I give poison to anybody though asked to do so, nor will I suggest such a plan" (Lammers and Verhey 1998, 108).

Nevertheless, the advances in medicine have brought new energy to this topic. Because many diseases remain incurable, the best that health care providers can do is manage one's painful symptoms as her illness marches on a path, often with intense suffering, before it ends in death. Many patients who have metastatic and terminal cancer experience this tragedy. For many commentators, this represents an intolerable reality. Instead, they wish to take matters into their own hands and seek voluntary euthanasia or physician assistance in their suicide.

From the perspective of various religions, these two practices—euthanasia and physician-assisted suicide—raise several ethical, legal, and theological issues. However, before discussing these issues, we will review the traditional distinctions of the term *euthanasia*. Then we will identify and describe the major ethical and legal issues in euthanasia and physician-assisted suicide. Finally, we will conclude with an overview of public policy considerations regarding both of these practices.

Traditional Distinctions of Euthanasia

Here, euthanasia is to be understood as the voluntary and intentional ending of a person's life. Many ethicists have made three critical distinctions in the debates over euthanasia. First, there is a distinction between voluntary and involuntary euthanasia. Voluntary euthanasia happens either by or at the request of the recipient of the act. Involuntary euthanasia occurs without the consent of the individual, either because the patient is incompetent, because the patient's wishes are not known, or because it is a policy to end the life of a person with certain traits (e.g., Nazi euthanasia policies). Most discussions of euthanasia reject any consideration of involuntary euthanasia, particularly in this last sense.

Second, there is a distinction between active and passive euthanasia. Active euthanasia occurs when someone performs an action that results in the death of the patient. Thus, one understands active euthanasia positively as the commission of a death-inducing action. Passive euthanasia occurs when someone does not perform an action, which results in the death of the patient. Thus, one understands passive euthanasia negatively as the omission of a life-preserving action. An example of active euthanasia is a doctor's injecting a lethal dose of drugs into a patient to bring about the patient's death. An example of passive euthanasia is a doctor's intent to kill a patient by refusing to administer antibiotics to a patient suffering from a treatable form of pneumonia. (There may be other morally justifiable reasons and circumstances why the physician would not provide antibiotics to a patient without intending the patient's death per se, but, for the sake of this example, we will consider the pneumonia to be the patient's only diagnosis.)

Third, there is a distinction between direct and indirect euthanasia. Here, one's intention plays a key role in establishing whether the action is direct or indirect. In addition, the Principle of Double Effect is applicable, which enables one to determine the nature of the agent's intent and whether the action is morally permissible. (In short, ethicists use the Principle of Double Effect to determine whether an act that produces both good and bad effects is morally permissible.) In direct euthanasia, an agent intends the death of the patient as the sole end. In indirect euthanasia, an agent does not intend the death of the patient either as the end sought or as a means to a further end. However, many prefer not to use the term *indirect euthanasia,* because this may confuse foregoing or withdrawing treatment with the intentional killing of a patient.

Historically, many confuse the last two distinctions: an active euthanasia act was direct; a passive euthanasia act was indirect. However, this is misleading because (1) there are two sets of criteria that distinguish these two terms (i.e., observation in the former, and the Principle of Double Effect in the latter), and (2) one distinction is descriptive of the action (i.e., commission versus omission), the other distinction is evaluative of the action (i.e., direct euthanasia is not morally permissible whereas an indirect euthanasia might be). Therefore, some ethicists suggest that these distinctions remain separate and avoided.

Additional reasons exist for avoiding these terms and they include the following: First, using the generic term *euthanasia* to speak of both direct killing and withdrawing therapy is confusing methodologically and psychologically. Second, many ethicists debate whether there is in fact a moral difference between active and passive euthanasia. Limiting the term *euthanasia* to the intentional killing of an individual at least circumvents that debate. Third, some ethicists think it is better to identify the moral legitimacy of foregoing or withdrawing a therapy as a separate issue. In this instance, one is focusing on benefit to the patient, which precludes considerations of killing the patient.

Many bioethicists frequently discuss the ethics of voluntary euthanasia in connection with the ethics of physician-assisted suicide. In fact, many see physician-assisted suicide as a form of voluntary euthanasia. However, there are key differences. First, suicide is a self-induced interruption of the life process and typically occurs in a nonmedical context; that is, many individuals who commit suicide in general are not suffering from a life-threatening disease. Second, while voluntary euthanasia and physician-assisted suicide may share motivations (e.g., mercy, compassion, and respect of autonomy), the ways in which one performs them differ significantly. In voluntary euthanasia, a physician or another person commits the act. In physician-assisted suicide, a physician cooperates but does not commit the act. Instead, the physician helps the patient commit the act. Third, many debate the distinction between voluntary euthanasia and palliative care. This does not occur in the context of physician-assisted suicide. Therefore, there are important issues to untangle in considering voluntary euthanasia in the continuum of care in modern hospitals. There is less of a need to disentangle issues between physician-assisted suicide and other forms of medical care.

Indeed, one study compared the clinical practices of terminal sedation (which is, according to the study, a palliative care protocol that induces a coma to relieve pain) and euthanasia in the Netherlands (Rietjens et al. 2006). These researchers found that both practices frequently involve patients who suffer from cancer. On the one hand, clinicians tended to use terminal sedation to address severe physical and psychological suffering in dying patients; on the other hand, clinicians tended to engage in euthanasia to protect patients' dignity during their last phase of life. In addition, clinicians employing terminal sedation tended to order benzodiazepines and morphine; clinicians participating in euthanasia tended to order barbiturates. Furthermore, the time interval between the administration of the drug and the patients' deaths ranged from one hour to seven days for terminally sedated patients and tended to be less than one hour for euthanized patients.

Ethical Issues

Several ethical issues involved in the debates over euthanasia and physician-assisted suicide remain controversial despite the lengthy debates over them. These issues relate to the various legal and theological issues, too. Here is a survey of some major ethical issues: human dignity, patient autonomy, prevention of harm, protection of the marginalized, and protection of professional integrity in health care.

First, among the most well known ethical issues in the debates over euthanasia and physician-assisted suicide is human dignity. Despite its pervasive use, the term suffers from ambiguity. At least two fundamental ways exist in which human dignity functions in ethical debates: as an expression of (1) intrinsic worthiness or (2) attributed worthiness. In the first sense, one may understand human dignity as an expression of intrinsic or inherent worthiness. This may directly relate to certain religious beliefs; in the Judeo-Christian traditions, the belief that God created humankind in his own image and likeness translates to an inviolable intrinsic worth. In contrast, one may understand human dignity as an attributed worth. On the one hand, one may suffer indignity as a result of the conditions or properties of one's life—for example, many would consider it undignified to live with a very poor quality of life as in complete dependence on machines to live and being bed-ridden. On the other hand, one may suffer indignity as the consequence of others' actions—for example, ignoring the incontinence of a bed-bound patient or neglecting senile elderly patients because of some repugnance to old age.

As a form of intrinsic worth, one may argue against euthanasia and physician-assisted suicide because such actions violate human dignity: intentionally killing a patient can never be an expression of respect for human dignity. As a form of attributed worth, one may argue for euthanasia and physician-assisted suicide because such actions may prevent such indignities. This is why some proponents suggest that euthanasia or physician-assisted suicide is a form of "death with dignity." However, in a now famous article, "The Indignity of 'Death with Dignity,'" the late theologian Paul Ramsey refuted this claim (Ramsey 1974).

Second, patient, or personal, autonomy relates to human dignity; here, autonomy is an exercise of self-rule whereby one controls the circumstances, the mode, and one's health status at the time of one's death. The fear of losing control over one's life is a powerful motivator for euthanasia or physician-assisted suicide. Individuals who seek physician-assisted suicide often do not want to live long enough to experience that loss of control and independence. For them, living in such circumstances could be a nightmare. When proponents of euthanasia and physician-assisted suicide seek a right to die, their concept of patient autonomy supports this right.

In these ways, one uses patient autonomy in support of voluntary euthanasia and physician-assisted suicide. However, this may confuse different notions of freedom. Indeed, the loss of control may seem like a loss of freedom, but, in general, this is only one kind of freedom lost: the freedom of choice. Alternatively, if one thinks of freedom as freedom of being—or freedom to be fully human—then a choice of death may be the ultimate imprisonment. That is, if humans are fundamentally relational (a belief prevalent among the world's major religions), then a choice to end all of one's relationships in choosing death would be an act that denies a basic aspect of what it means to be human.

Notwithstanding this alternative, if individuals experience suffering and indignity (i.e., the loss of control or the corresponding fear) as they approach death during a terminal illness, this may be more of a critique of society's inability to address the needs of the dying (Cahill 2005). In this sense, society may be effectively abandoning patients by not giving them the support and environment they need to flourish even in the last moments of physical life. Such circumstances make euthanasia and physician-assisted suicide logical choices.

Third, the prevention of harm is another ethical issue one finds in the debates over euthanasia and physician-assisted suicide. There are two aspects to this issue. On the one hand, proponents call for legalizing euthanasia or physician-assisted suicide (or both) as a way to regulate the practices. The intent behind this is to prevent harms to patients that are a direct consequence of the acts of euthanasia or physician-assisted suicide themselves. For example, without proper training or sufficient regulations, a patient may obtain and use an inadequate dose of lethal drugs. This may cause harm, because such a dose might not induce death and could leave the patient in an undesirable state (e.g., a coma). On the other hand, proponents argue for euthanasia and physician-assisted suicide as a means of preventing harms related to the illness the patient has or the treatments that the patient would need to endure (e.g., chemotherapy). In this sense, the patient prevents the harms by bypassing both the experience of the disease process and the risks or burdens of the treatments for the disease.

Of course, some opponents to euthanasia and physician-assisted suicide find this line of reasoning difficult to accept. For them, it seems illogical to prevent harm by causing the end of the patient's life. For some, the options of euthanasia and physician-assisted suicide are seen as failures of the health care system to deal adequately with the pain and symptoms of terminal illness and the dying process. Many claim that, with appropriate and accessible palliative care (pain and symptom management) and hospice care, the need or desire for euthanasia and physician-assisted suicide would diminish. However, this may not be as true as some hope: as discussed above, a principal concern is the loss of control, not the experience of pain per se.

Fourth, the protection of marginalized groups from a socially instituted policy of euthanasia constitutes another ethical issue. Here, the principal concern is to protect those who do not exercise autonomy in choosing euthanasia and who, in fact, may resist it. Therefore, this ethical issue results when involuntary euthanasia becomes a social practice supported by political power. This particular issue lives in the shadows of the Holocaust and Nazi euthanasia policies. Despite this tragic episode in human history, contemporary debates persist. For example, some proponents claim that involuntary euthanasia may be justifiable for the severely handicapped.

This issue also incorporates elements of a slippery slope argument. In this case, opponents claim that legalizing voluntary euthanasia and physician-assisted suicide jeopardizes the disabled and other marginalized groups, because such decisions reflect a belief that certain lives are not worth living. Opponents are concerned that the disabled community represents certain kinds of life that those who would support euthanasia would not want to live. Thus, even if legalized euthanasia was restricted to voluntary forms and physician-assisted suicide, such practices are only a short step away from involuntary euthanasia of the severely disabled and then (with one more short step) from the moderately or even slightly disabled. For these opponents, it would be quite possible to slip and tumble down the slope to widespread involuntary euthanasia.

To take this perspective further, if involuntary euthanasia of the severely handicapped never became a reality, there remains a concern that a culture that supports voluntary euthanasia would undermine programs and relationships that promote the livelihood and well-being of persons who are physically and mentally challenged. Thus, there may be decreasing support for social assistance programs and increasing pressure to participate in euthanasia or assisted suicide.

Finally, the practices of euthanasia and physician-assisted suicide may undermine the professional integrity of medicine (and other health care professions like nursing).

On the one hand, health care professionals do not want to abandon their patients at the end of life. On the other hand, health care professionals—as helping and healing professionals providing care—do not want to confuse their role or contribute in any way to an erosion of their professional ethos as healers. One concern is that this erosion may have a social consequence of confusing the role of healer and the role of executioner. In these circumstances, the trust in the physician-patient relationship is at risk; if physicians can no longer deal with death and dying appropriately and abandon their patients, patients will not trust doctors to be with them as they face their most difficult health crisis. Similarly, if a doctor supports euthanasia or physician-assisted suicide, a patient may be confronted with a doctor who may see euthanasia and physician-assisted suicide as the "easy way out" and may not trust her professional judgment about what is in her best interests.

Legal Issues in the United States

In 1991 and 1992, citizens in Washington and California, respectively, voted on two referenda; these referenda sought to sanction legally both euthanasia and physician-assisted suicide, or physician-assisted dying. In both cases, voters defeated these referenda by very narrow margins—about 54 percent to 46 percent in both cases. However, in 1994, the citizens of Oregon were asked to vote on Measure 16, which asked, "Shall law allow terminally ill adult Oregon patients voluntary informed choice to obtain physician's prescription for drugs to end life?" (quoted in Campbell 1994, 9). In this case, the measure passed, which ultimately led to the Oregon Death with Dignity Act (see "The Oregon Death with Dignity Act," in Beauchamp et al. 2008, 404–406). The critical difference between this Oregon statute and those proposed in Washington and California is its restriction to physician-assisted suicide.

When Oregonian voters approved this measure in November 1994 by a very narrow margin, Oregon became "the only place in the world where doctors may legally help patients end their lives" (Egan 1994, A1). However, that was not the end of the story. The day before the measure was to become law, its enactment was blocked by a court challenge. In August 1995, a federal judge ruled the measure unconstitutional because "with state-sanctioned and physician-assisted death at issue, some 'good results' cannot outweigh other lives lost due to unconstitutional errors and abuses" ("Judge Strikes Down Oregon's Suicide Law," A15).

In March 1996, the legal situation changed radically for the nine western states in the jurisdiction of the United States Court of Appeals for the Ninth Circuit, including Oregon. In an 8–3 ruling, this court struck down a Washington State statute that made assisting in a suicide a felony. While this ruling held only for the states in the Ninth Circuit, a very critical precedent was set. The grounds for the ruling were privacy and autonomy. Judge Stephen Reinhardt, writing for the majority, said: "Like the decision of whether or not to have an abortion, the decision how and when to die is one of 'the most intimate and personal choices a person may make in a lifetime,' a choice 'central to personal dignity and autonomy'" (Lewin 1996, A14). The ruling also argued that not only doctors should be protected from prosecution "but others like pharmacists and family members 'whose services are essential to help the terminally ill patient obtain and take' medication to hasten death" (Lewin 1996, A14). Thus, the window opened for a round of appeals and argumentation. Later, a unanimous ruling of the three-judge Second Circuit Court of Appeals in New York reinforced this ruling in April 1996. This court stated "that doctors in New York State could legally help terminally ill patients commit suicide in certain circumstances" (Bruni 1996, A1). As the ruling was appealed, a critical countrywide debate began.

Additionally, Michigan passed a law explicitly prohibiting physician-assisted suicide; this was in response to the activities of Jack Kevorkian, whose activities include physician-assisted suicide. However, this law has passed out of existence because of specific time limits. Furthermore, Kevorkian was brought to trial for acts committed while this law was in effect but was found not guilty based on the jury's decision that his intent was to relieve pain, not to cause death. Notwithstanding this, another murder charge was brought against Kevorkian in 1999. In this case, he was convicted and sentenced to prison.

Finally, three United States Supreme Court cases have become landmark cases in the legal and ethical debates over physician-assisted suicide. In 1997, the U.S. Supreme Court adjudicated on two related cases (Beauchamp et al. 2008). First, the main question before the Court in *Vacco v. Quill* was whether New York's prohibition on assisting suicide violated the Equal Protection Clause of the Fourteenth Amendment. The Court held that it did not. Second, the main question before the Court in *Washington v. Glucksberg* was whether the "liberty" (i.e., the right to refuse wanted life-saving medical treatment) specifically protected by the due process clause includes a right to commit suicide, which includes a right to assistance in suicide. The Court held that the right to assistance in suicide is not a fundamental liberty interest protected by the due process clause. In the 2006 case of *Gonzalez v. Oregon,* the main question before the Court was whether the Controlled Substances Act allows the U.S. attorney general to prohibit doctors from prescribing regulated drugs for use in physician-assisted suicide, notwithstanding a state law prohibiting it (Beauchamp et al. 2008, 413–418). The Court of Appeals held that the interpretive rule exercised by the attorney general to restrict use of certain drugs was invalid; the Supreme Court held that the Court of Appeals was correct: its decision was affirmed.

In summary, these cases have three implications. One, they demonstrate that it is not unconstitutional for states to ban assisted suicide while protecting patients' rights to refuse life-sustaining treatment. Two, one cannot claim that physician-assisted suicide is a fundamental liberty interest protected in the same way as the right to refuse treatment. Finally, the executive branch at the federal level cannot use the Controlled Substances

Act to restrict physician-assisted suicide at the state level (which basically protected the practice of physician-assisted suicide in Oregon).

Public Policy Considerations

In the end, there are many public policy considerations in the debates over euthanasia and physician-assisted suicide. However, there are four major considerations. The first consideration is, of course, the legalization and institutionalization of euthanasia and/or physician-assisted suicide. Here, institutionalization means the systematic integration of those interventions as organizational policy and professional practices. The legal issues in the United States mentioned above will continue to shape the possibility of legalization (or criminalization) of these practices. The second consideration is the fair availability and access to alternatives at the end of life; that is, public policy on euthanasia or physician-assisted suicide ought to consider adequate home health services, palliative care, and hospice as legitimate options to euthanasia and physician-assisted suicide. A third consideration includes adequate and necessary protections for marginalized individuals—especially the disabled, elderly, and sick—in society. If any public policy is to legitimize euthanasia and physician-assisted suicide, robust protections for these marginalized groups will be necessary. Finally, a fourth consideration is the protections for the health care professions, which ought to seek a separation between the roles of helping and healing and the roles of death-causing or -assisting. This will include sensitivity to the potential for conflicts of interest, reimbursement schedules, and the authenticity of both patient and provider judgments that choosing death is freely chosen. Many of the safeguards in Oregon's statute recognize these and other procedural issues involved in implementing a policy of physician-assisted suicide.

See also **Suicide and Suicide Prevention; Health Care (vol. 1); Social Justice (vol. 2); Biotechnology (vol. 4); Medical Ethics (vol. 4)**

Further Reading

Beauchamp, Tom L., et al., *Contemporary Issues in Bioethics*, 7th ed. Belmont, CA: Thomson Wadsworth, 2008.

Bruni, Frank, "Federal Ruling Allows Doctors to Prescribe Drugs to End Life." *New York Times* (April 3, 1996): A1.

Cahill, Lisa Sowle, *Theological Bioethics: Participation, Justice, and Change*. Washington, DC: Georgetown University Press, 2005.

Callahan, Daniel, *The Troubled Dream of Life: In Search of a Peaceful Death*. Washington, DC: Georgetown University Press, 2000.

Callahan, Daniel, *What Kind of Life? The Limits of Medical Progress*. Washington, DC: Georgetown University Press, 1995.

Campbell, Courtney S, "The Oregon Trail to Death: Measure 16." *Commonweal* 121, no. 14 (August 1994).

Edelstein, Ludwig, "The Hippocratic Oath: Text, Translation and Interpretation." In *Ancient Medicine,* ed. Oswei Temkin and C. Lillian Temkin. Baltimore: Johns Hopkins University Press, 1967.

Egan, Timothy, "Suicide Law Placing Oregon on Several Uncharted Paths." *New York Times* (November 25, 1994): A1.

Foley, Kathleen, and Herbert Hendin, eds., *The Case against Assisted Suicide: For the Right to End-of-Life Care.* Baltimore: Johns Hopkins University Press, 2002.

Gorsuch, Neil M., *The Future of Assisted Suicide and Euthanasia.* Princeton, NJ: Princeton University Press, 2006.

"Judge Strikes Down Oregon's Suicide Law," *New York Times* (August 4, 1995): A15.

Keown, John, ed., *Euthanasia Examined: Ethical, Clinical, and Legal Perspectives.* New York: Cambridge University Press, 1995.

Lammers, Stephen E., and Allen Verhey, eds., *On Moral Medicine: Theological Perspectives in Medical Ethics,* 2d ed. Grand Rapids, MI: William B. Eerdmans, 1998.

Lewin, Tamar, "Ruling Sharpens Debate on 'Right to Die,'" *New York Times* (March 8, 1996): A14.

McLean, Sheila, *The Case for Physician Assisted Suicide.* London: Pandora, 1997.

Mitchell, John B., *Understanding Assisted Suicide: Nine Issues to Consider.* Ann Arbor: University of Michigan Press, 2007.

Ramsey, Paul, "The Indignity of 'Death with Dignity.'" *Hastings Center Studies* 2, no. 2 (May 1974): 47–62.

Rietjens, Judith A.C., et al., "Terminal Sedation and Euthanasia: A Comparison of Clinical Practices." *Archives of Internal Medicine* 166 (2006): 749–753.

F

FOSTER CARE

Derrick Shapley

Defining foster care is a challenge. The most often stated definition for foster care is "care given outside a child's natural home for more than 24 hours when the child's home is not available to him or her excluding children at camps, in hospitals, or on weekend visits" (Stone 1970). This definition implies that the parents cannot provide adequate care for some serious reason. The essential element of foster care is child rearing responsibility shared with the child welfare agency, the original parents, the foster parents, the child care staff, and social workers. Foster care also has an expectation that it is of a limited duration; it is not a permanent method of child rearing but a temporary solution to a crisis in the home.

A simpler definition for foster care is "a generic term for children living in out-of-home care" (Curtis, Dale, and Kendall 1997). Historically, foster care was referred to as boarding out, implying that foster parents were almost always nonrelatives. These persons were reimbursed the expenses of caring for dependent children residing in their household on the assumption that the arrangement was a temporary one. The four basic types of foster care in the United States are family (nonrelative) foster care, kinship (relative) care, therapeutic foster care, and residential group care.

A thorough examination of the child welfare system, or foster care, in the United States finds that problems in foster care are similar to the issues that need to be addressed in the larger society as well. These issues include race, class, gender, government funding or lack thereof, and acceptance of people with mental and physical disabilities.

The foster care system is imperfect because it must deal with a myriad of complex social problems. When dealing with such complexities, it is impossible to create a perfect system. Our foster care system works with the worst aspects of social problems within U.S. society. As a result, a social worker's job is not easy. A child welfare worker, during the course of a typical work day, could have to remove a child from a family that has physically, emotionally, or sexually abused the child and then turn around and go to another house and attempt to find a solution for a child who has severe physical or emotional disabilities. Social workers are constrained by laws that limit what they can do. While they are thought to be the last line of defense in the care of a lost child, they rarely have adequate resources and community support to protect children who are in the direst situations.

Roughly 500,000 children are in foster care in the United States. African American children make up two-thirds of the foster care population and stay in foster care longer than the average child. About 30 percent of children in foster care have emotional, behavioral, or developmental problems, and the average age of a child in foster care is 10 years old.

The number of children in out-of-home care is enormous. According to the Child Welfare League of America (CWLA), in 2006, the national mean per state was 9,993, and the national median was 6,803. California had 92,344 children in foster care, the largest total in any state. Wyoming had the fewest children in foster care with 1,209.

Any attempt for a state to create a better foster care environment must first recognize the number of the children in foster care and then budget accordingly for an adequate caseload per social worker. The CWLA has set up recommended caseload standards for each state to follow. The CWLA recommends that one social worker should have at most 12 to 15 children that are in foster family care. The CWLA also recommends one supervisor for every five social workers. Additionally, there are guidelines suggesting that more than 12 initial assessments or investigations per month would be too much for one social worker.

Many states have strains on their budgets, which cause these recommendations to go unfulfilled. Instead states follow the guidelines that they have already established, which are likely to be less stringent than the CWLA recommendations. There is very little uniformity in foster care among the states. Our system of federalism as well as budgetary constraints in each state strain the uniformity in the child welfare process; therefore, varying standards of care among each state are bound to occur. In a way, each state is its own laboratory of experiments working to design a child welfare system that is responsive to each child within the state's budget limitations.

Background

English colonists arriving in the United States brought the Poor Law system with them. Long after the American Revolution, the well-established tradition continued to inform poverty practices. During the beginning of the 19th century, adults and children were cared for with very little or no distinction. Almshouses were gaining in popularity for the care of both the children and the elderly in large cities. Almshouses were privately funded (usually through churches) houses that cared primarily for the poor and destitute.

Agencies that cared for destitute children tended to spring up from two sources. The first of these was from public bodies that would act as representatives for the community as a whole. The second was from private donations and was exercised by benevolent individuals or associations. In 1853, Charles Loring Brace began the free foster home movement. Brace was concerned about the large numbers of homeless children and wanted to find families for them in the United States. He started advertising all across the country and would send children in groups of 20 to 40 in trains to their new destinations. Reverend Brace's work led to the creation of the Children's Aid Society and provided a framework for the establishment of a permanent foster care system in the United States.

In 1868, Massachusetts became the first state to pay for children to board in private family homes. In 1885, Pennsylvania became the first state in the United States to pass a licensing law. This law made it a misdemeanor for a couple to care for two or more unrelated children unless they were licensed to do so by the state. In 1910, Henry Chapin circulated statistics showing that orphanages sickened and killed large numbers of children. It was Chapin's belief that a poor home is better than a good institution. However, it was not until 1950 that the number of children in foster care outnumbered the number of children in institutions. In 1935, Aid to Dependent Children, which later became Aid to Families with Dependent Children (AFDC), was established through the Social Security Act of 1935. What AFDC and other antipoverty programs did was give financially struggling families an alternative to placing their children in institutions or losing them forever. The program was later expanded in the 1960s, and, with that expansion, federal funding for foster care was added.

While foster care has come a long way in the United States, there are still a host of problems within the current system. Many of these problems are vestiges of the old child welfare system. However, there are also new problems that social workers are just now beginning to see and that researchers are just now beginning to understand. With all these problems, there will still be a long history that will be written about foster care.

Foster Care Values

Foster care can be thought of as being based on three main values. First, maternal deprivation in the early years of life has an adverse effect on personality development, and later difficulties of the individual can be traced to a breakdown in this early relationship. This value shows the focus on child development at an early age and the need of social workers to become more engaged early with children from troubled homes.

The second value maintains that the parent-child relationship is of vital importance; all efforts must be made to restore it. No child should be deprived of his or her natural parents for economic reasons alone. If, for some extreme reason, a child's own parents cannot take care of him or her, another family is the best place for him or her. The child's own extended family is preferable to complete strangers.

The third value speak to the role of the foster parents in the foster care process. According to this value, the rights and interests of the child take priority over those of the parents in any plans affecting him or her. Natural parents and foster parents are to be understood as individuals with their own needs, but these needs cannot be permitted to affect the future of the child. If a child cannot be returned to his or her own family, whatever the reasons, the goal is to afford the child the needed security and feeling of belonging within the foster home by making arrangements permanent, preferably through legal adoption.

In addition to these three principal values, some scholars acknowledge three additional values for foster care. One value maintains that there should be a responsibility assumed by every community for seeing that a continuum of care and service is provided for children who must live outside their homes. No child should be lost because referrals are not made or adequate services are not available. Another value sets the goal for all children at minimal reasonable parenting, and this may not necessarily be tied to middle-class child rearing patterns. The final value is that criteria for evaluating foster parents should focus on their parenting abilities and their capacity to share these abilities with parents and agencies.

These values have helped to shape laws in the states and helped to define a foster care relationship. However, these values are not universally agreed upon. For example, how can one define what is in the best interests of the child? Is the best interest of the child going back to his or her natural parents? What if there is a history of abuse and domestic violence? These are all questions that have no easy answers. While one may be able to say that these values, in an ideal situation, may be good values, as was mentioned earlier, the foster care situation is not an ideal situation.

Another thing to consider about these values is that different decision makers may interpret these values differently. For example, what constitutes an extreme reason for taking a child away from his or her natural parents? What one person views as an extreme reason may be different than what another person views as an extreme reason. Another point of disagreement might be over what constitutes good parenting. Is spanking good parenting? Some may consider it to be so, while others may not. While the values may be perfectly reasonable, the interpretation of those values can turn into something that may be unreasonable.

The Foster Family

Research has indicated that "children who are placed in group homes are more likely to experience emotional disturbance and behavioral problems than those who are placed with families" (Perry 2006). According to Perry, this is because the foster family will provide a less disruptive environment for a youth than a group home, because a family environment is more structured to his or her normal life. Most social workers want to put children in the least disruptive environment possible in order for them to either keep or regain stability in their life.

So how can a foster family do this? A foster family must exhibit five things to be successful: communication, integration, flexibility, compassion, and patience. How a child reacts to a new environment will be based on the amount of success the parents, social workers, educational administrators, and other members of the community react to the child based on these five factors.

It is important that, before the child even reaches the foster family's home, there is an open line of communication between all the people involved in the child's life. This includes the foster parents, the child's case worker, the school administrators of where the child is moving, and the relatives of the child, if possible. The case worker is the person who needs to start the communication line, but it is the responsibility of everybody involved, and especially the foster parents, to maintain that communication line through the child's stay with the foster family.

Successful communication leads to the next step, which is successful integration. This integration process can take several forms based on the child's background and emotional experiences. Care must be taken in this process, because if there is a possibility—as there is in most cases—that the child will go back to a natural parent, then the integration must be flexible to make sure that the child can reestablish those ties to the natural parents. A successful foster family must treat the foster child as if he or she was a member of their immediate family. They must realize, however, that this child's needs may be different than those of their own children's (if they have children), so the structure the foster child lives under could possibly be different than the structure their natural children live under. This also needs to be explained to the natural children or other foster children in the household before the foster child comes to live with them.

Once the child arrives and is put in school, the communication line must hold firm to make sure that the teachers understand the child's problems and the best ways to address those problems. Parents and teachers need to make sure that they have adequate records from the child's past schools, and they need to speak regularly to see how the child is integrating into the classroom, such as with making friends, doing schoolwork, and getting involved in extracurricular activities. The administrators at the school also need to be made aware of any special medications or learning disabilities the child has in order to set acceptable guidelines for the child to follow and create the best learning environment possible.

A foster family has to be flexible. Children coming into their care will come with a wide range of social problems. These parents must be flexible enough to know that they cannot deal with a child who has been sexually abused in the same way they deal with a child who has lost both parents in a car accident. The school system also must be flexible enough to work with the parents and social workers to make the child's transition as smooth as possible.

The last two factors are interrelated: compassion and patience. If a foster family has compassion, they can begin to understand the problems the child is facing and work to find the help he or she needs. However, they must also be patient and realize that there are going to be bumps in the road. The process for a child whose social network has been severely disrupted is not short but a journey that the family will have to take with him or her throughout the child's entire stay.

Aging Out

Aging out refers to children who reach adulthood while in the foster care system. Each year, 20,000 children age out of the foster care program, and many of these children are still in need of support or services. Imagine a child who has just turned 18 and has been told to go out in the world with little to no social network. Imagining this leads a person to wonder not how a child learns to survive but how a child who is aged out is able to maintain his or her mental sanity. The unfortunate fact is that many of these children have a hard time coping with going out in the world without a social network. Only 2 percent of children who have aged out of foster care obtain a four-year college degree. Thirty percent of these children are without adequate health care, and 25 percent of these children have been homeless at some point in their life (Child Welfare League of America 2006).

These numbers for youths transitioning out of foster care are dramatic. They also cause one to pause and ask, what are the options? A system that can keep the children in foster homes a few more years in order to ease into the transition away from the foster care system is one avenue that probably needs to be examined. Also, scholarships for children in foster care for college or job training is another area that might be beneficial in assisting the transition from foster care to adulthood. Encouraging adoption may be another step in helping children to find a permanent family.

Although these ideas may ameliorate a crisis, they do not get to the root of the social problems that cause children to be placed in foster care. There needs to be an increased emphasis not only on what happens to children after they get out of foster care, but also preventing them from getting into foster care. Foster care is the intersection where all social problems meet, and, in order to stop children from entering the system, society must confront the social and structural problems within the country that created this intersection.

Conclusion

The future of foster care is complex, because it is not a uniform system. Each state has its own idea about how the system should work. All foster care agencies try to maintain certain values, but who interprets those values is a significant issue, and each state and even each judge can vary on those interpretations. Also, the state and federal funding that is devoted to foster care is unstable and prone to budget cuts. The future of foster care is going to be based on how well society handles other social problems. If society confronts the challenges of poverty, homelessness, health care, and so forth, then the future of foster care may be optimistic. However, if society does not confront these challenges, then the future may not be as bright.

So what can we predict about the future of foster care in the United States? We know already that there is a strong correlation between race, poverty, and entry into the foster care system. With the growing ranks of minorities in the United States, especially minorities from Central and South America, it is possible that minorities will come to dominate the ranks of children in foster care even more than they do presently.

Immigration also brings about a host of questions about the legal status of immigrants in the United States. How the states handle the children of immigrants may depend on citizenship status. This classification of children who may be undocumented will probably lead to many other issues within the foster care realm. Not least among the issues could be a language barrier between the child and available foster families.

No discussion about foster care can be complete without discussing the Personal Responsibility and Workforce Opportunity Reconciliation Act of 1996, also called welfare reform. The goals of welfare reform were to promote two-parent families and work among single mothers. However, an unintended consequence of this reform may have been an increase in the children who enter foster care. In 1984, 2.5 percent of children under the age of 18 lived in families where neither parent was present. There was an almost 60 percent increase from 1984 to 1998, when 4.2 percent of children lived in families where neither parent was present. While only a portion of this increase can be attributed to the federal welfare reform that was passed in 1996, many states experimented with various elements of welfare reform beforehand. The increase in children in foster care from various welfare reform initiatives could lead to a decline in child well-being in the United States, especially among poor families.

The challenges facing social workers all across the country are not going to get any easier. In order for foster care to improve, the system has to be more flexible but at the same time more structured, focused on prevention, address aging out, and less prone to budget instability at the federal and state levels. Policymakers must become aware of the dilemmas that social workers face on an everyday basis and create laws accordingly. Foster care is a complicated system and one that will have huge social implications for children well into the 21st century.

See also **Child Abuse; Juvenile Delinquency; Poverty and Public Assistance**

Further Reading

Bernstein, Nina, *The Lost Children of Wilder: The Epic Struggle to Change Foster Care.* New York: Vintage Books, 2001.

Children's Defense Fund, http://childrensdefense.org

Child Welfare League of America, *Special Tabulation of the Adoption and Foster Care Analysis Reporting System*. 2006. http://ndas.cwla.org/data_stats/access/predefined/Report.asp?PageMode=1&%20 ReportID=379&%20GUID={4859F5C2-DD74-4AF0-AD55-8360140347E3}#Table

Child Welfare League of America, *Quick Facts about Foster Care*. 2010. http://www.cwla.org/pro grams/fostercare/factsheet.htm

Curtis, Patrick A., G. Dale, and J. Kendall, *The Foster Care Crisis: Translating Research into Policy Practice*. Lincoln: University of Nebraska Press, 1997.

Krebs, Betsy, *Beyond the Foster Care System: The Future for Teens*. New Brunswick, NJ: Rutgers University Press, 2006.

Lindsey, D., *The Welfare of Children*. New York: Oxford University Press, 1994.

National Association of Former Foster Care Children of America, http://www.naffcca.org

National Foster Parent Association, *History of Foster Care in the United States*. 2007. http://www. nfpainc.org/content/index.asp?page=67&nmenu=3

Perry, Brea, "Understanding Social Network Disruption: The Case for Youth in Foster Care." *Social Problems* 53, no. 3. (2006): 371–391.

Pew Commission on Children in Foster Care, http://pewfostercare.org.

Stone, Helen D., *Foster Care in Question: A National Reassessment by Twenty-One Experts*. New York: Child Welfare League of America, 1970.

Wozniak, Danielle F., *They're All My Children: Foster Mothering in America*. New York: New York University Press, 2002.

G

GAMBLING

Daniel L. Smith-Christopher

The vast majority of Americans have gambled at least once. One can place bets on dog and horse races in 43 states, buy lottery tickets in 42 states, gamble for charity in 47 states, and play at commercial casinos in 11 states. As of 2010, all but two states (Hawaii and Utah) allowed some form of gambling. Gambling as a government-sponsored activity exploded in the late 20th century, and will clearly increase in the 21st century. Is gambling a moral and social problem? What are the social costs of problem gambling, and do they outweigh the social and economic benefits of increased state-sponsored gaming? Finally, how does the rise of Native American gambling in the late 20th century as a new income source for a traditionally deprived and impoverished minority population impact on the moral arguments for and against gambling? Although it may seem like a relatively recent social issue, the fact is that gambling has been a source of concern for many religious traditions for hundreds of years.

What Is Gambling?

Definitions of gambling are elusive, but a helpful suggestion has been made by M. D. Griffiths, a scholar and historian of gambling in Western culture, as "an exchange of wealth determined by a future event, the outcome of which is unknown at the time of the wager" (Dickerson and O'Conner 2006, 7). Gambling is therefore a type of a game in which financial loss or gain for the players is part of—or even the main point of— the results of the game. Games can be played exclusively for the financial aspects, or financial aspects can be introduced to games that otherwise do not have gambling as their primary intention (e.g., betting on races or professional sports).

The controversies surrounding gambling stem largely from the large sums of money that can become involved. Left to small sums, there are few objections to introducing financial loss or gain to otherwise innocent pastimes. When, however, significant gains or losses are made part of the activity, gambling can become a storm center of debate that has strong religious involvement. The significant moral and social issues surrounding the tremendous growth of the gaming industry in the United States (and worldwide—Australian gaming is, per capita, much greater than in the United States) include concerns about the social costs of so-called addicted or pathological gamblers, of organized crime, and even of the equitable distribution of gaming earnings.

Gambling in Western History

Games of chance, often accompanied with serious consequences in winning or losing, have been a part of human civilization for as long as we have written records. In Gerda Reith's (1999) important study, she notes that gambling of one kind or another has been an aspect of human play from the dawn of civilization. In ancient Greece, Plato believed that play, including games of chance, were among the more noble aspects of human activities; his fellow ancient Greek philosopher, Aristotle, on the other hand, believed gaming to be wasted effort and time. While there has always been a minority view in Western culture that has seen gaming, and gambling, as largely an innocent pastime, there is a dominant second tradition that stands closer to that ancient view of Aristotle by considering gambling a negative human undertaking.

Lotteries are perhaps the most widely attested form of large-scale gambling in Western history, and state-supported lotteries that are recorded in medieval Europe as early as the 15th century were intended to help raise funds to pay for military fortifications.

Gambling and Moral Judgment

It is hard to separate the history of gambling in human civilizations with the history of the very idea of chance. Through a good part of human history, there was no such belief in chance—it was believed that all events reflected the will of gods, spirits, or guiding deities. Various ancient religions routinely practiced a kind of casting of lots or dicelike devices in order to discover whether gods or spirits agreed with the course of actions determined by humans (e.g., whether a battle should be started on a certain day or month).

It would be difficult to find specific biblical injunctions against gambling, and within Judaism and Christianity, for example, there is a history of tense coexistence with gambling, particularly from the perspective of historical Judaism and the Roman Catholic Church. However, there is a tradition of a more intensively negative view in the Protestant Christian tradition, with similarities to Aristotle's notion of waste, and, later,

LOTTERIES

Every day, millions of Americans stop by a local store or visit a Web site, plunk down a few dollars, and hope for a miracle. Very few who play state lotteries will ever win any significant sums, and everyone except a handful of jackpot winners is guaranteed to lose more money buying tickets than they will gain in (mostly small) prizes over a lifetime. Yet these millions of Americans seem happy to continue playing—happy that some of the proceeds go to fund popular state programs such as schools and parks, and happy for the chance, however remote, of striking it rich.

The regeneration of a state lottery industry in the United States—the term *regeneration* is apt—has been one of the most striking developments in state government in the past 40 years. The trend began in 1964, when New Hampshire created the first modern state lottery. New York and New Jersey soon followed. By the mid-1970s, there were a dozen state lotteries, mostly in the northeast. After a 1975 federal law allowed more lottery advertising, other states began to enter the gambling business. As of 2010, 43 states and the District of Columbia featured some form of state-sponsored lottery game. Many of these states also participated in multistate games with jackpots in the hundreds of millions of dollars. Players bought over $60 billion in lottery tickets in 2008, with net proceeds of nearly $18 billion flowing into state coffers to fund a variety of governmental expenditures (North American Association of State and Provincial Lotteries n.d.). Still, it is important to keep these figures in proper perspective. Lotteries represent about one-fourth of the commercial gambling industry in the United States, as measured by gross revenue. They generate less than 3 percent of total state revenues, and in no state does a lottery contribute more than about 7 percent of revenue (Hansen 2004).

State lotteries may not dominate the gambling business or pay for a significant swath of state government, but they have nevertheless accounted for some of the most spirited and passionate public policy debates held in state capitals over the past quarter century. Proponents and opponents have made a series of arguments, touching on a range of concerns and issues: education, elder care, land preservation, fraudulent advertising, tax equity, the initiative and referendum process, organized crime, economic development, family values, and the proper role of morality in lawmaking. The nature and persuasiveness of the arguments made during state-by-state battles to create lotteries reveal much about how public policy is made and understood by public officials and average citizens alike.

The policy debates about state-run gambling in the United States have been energetic, complicated, and lengthy. While a large majority of states now have some kind of state lottery, these policy debates promise to continue. Not only will lottery proponents continue their push to create lotteries in the remaining states, but even within lottery states, there are frequent pressures to authorize new drawings and multistate options, change the mix of payouts and revenue earmarks, and expand state-sponsored gambling to encompass sports betting and other games. Competition from Internet-based gambling operations, some operating outside the bounds of current state and federal law, may also have a significant effect on the operations and politics of state lotteries in the early 21st century.

—John M. Hood

its associations with other activities seen as sinful (e.g., drinking and other forms of excess and, even more recently, organized crime). There are Islamic religious traditions that question gambling in much stronger terms than either Catholic Christianity or Judaism.

From Sin to Foolishness: Changing Western Attitudes

As strictly religious attitudes lost influence on European societies during the Enlightenment (18th century), religious condemnations began to be replaced with ideas that gambling was an irrational and wasteful pastime. Such an attitude toward the foolishness, rather than the immorality, of gambling can be heard in a 1732 poem by Henry Fielding:

> A Lottery is a Taxation,
> Upon all the Fools in Creation;
> And heaven be praised,
> It is easily raised,
> Credulity's always in Fashion:
> For, Folly's a Fund,
> Will never lose Ground,
> While Fools are so rife in the nation
>   (cited in Dickerson and O'Conner 2006, 2)

The Medicalization of Gambling: Problem and Pathological Gambling

It is in the 20th century that the notions of sinful gambling and irrational gambling began to be replaced with a medicalization of gambling as an illness that required intervention and therapy. Clearly, such attitudes were based on those cases where serious amounts of money were lost by those hardly able to handle such losses rather than on the minor or moderate amounts lost by casual gamers who fly to Las Vegas or Atlantic City in the United States for a few days of vacation.

A good part of the ancient and medieval opposition to gambling was based precisely on this notion that gambling was engaging in a kind of *secular* or *antireligious* consulting of higher powers. It is only when the very notion of *random chance* begins to be a widely held idea that gambling moves from being considered an irreligious activity to one that is considered irrational because of the randomness of such gaming, and, as an understanding of random actions and chance increased, so the awareness of risk in games of chance became a growing feature of the arguments of those who opposed this activity.

Finally, Reith points out that, as market economies developed in the West, attitudes toward gambling and risk-taking games changed from a religious view to views of its *risky character* or as a calculated opposition to high risk. One should engage in money-making activities that minimize risk, not only in business but also in leisure-time activities. As money making became quite literally a way of life for a growing class of merchants, the minimizing of risk also became a way of life—extending to leisure as well as work.

Some have argued that the gambling debate has been largely *overruled* by the very success of the industry and the dependence on that industry in many local economies around the United States. The debate continues to focus, however, on the issue of "problem gamblers."

Problem Gambling and Pathological Gamblers

The Australian Institute for Gambling Research has defined *problem gambling* as "the situation where a person's gambling activity gives rise to harm to the individual player, and/or his or her family, and may extend into the community" (Dickerson and O'Conner 2006, 11). Studies conducted by the National Opinion Research Center (NORC) at the University of Chicago examined social and economic changes attributed to *casino proximity*—a casino within 50 miles of a community—in 100 samples, and the federal government issued a major report by the National Gaming Impact Study Commission in 1999. The conclusions suggested that between 1 and 2 percent of gamblers (approximately 3 million people) can be classified as *pathological gamblers*, and another 3 to 4 percent are termed *problem gamblers* (about 3 to 8 million people), but it is clear that the vast majority of gamblers engage in gambling without measurably negative social or economic impact on themselves or their families. The NORC study concluded that the total societal costs of problem gambling were $4 billion each year but noted that this is a fraction of the social costs incurred by society in relation to drug and alcohol abuse, mental illness, heart disease, and smoking.

Pathological gambling, on the other hand, has a recently defined set of diagnostic criteria according to the American Psychiatry Association. Among the more common criteria with which to diagnose pathological gaming are assessing whether a person: (1) is preoccupied with gambling (constantly thinking about past games and getting money for future betting); (2) needs to gamble with increasing amounts of money to achieve desired level of excitement; (3) has repeated unsuccessful efforts to control, cut

GAMBLERS ANONYMOUS

Gamblers Anonymous is a popular 12-step program for problem gamblers modeled on Alcoholics Anonymous (AA). It is free and widely available, with over a thousand chapters in the United States. As in AA, participants in Gamblers Anonymous are encouraged to admit their powerlessness over their gambling problem and to invoke a higher power to help them conquer this problem. They are encouraged to seek support from their peers and from an assigned sponsor in overcoming their habit and to make amends to family members and others whom their gambling behavior has harmed.

back, or stop gambling; (4) is restless or irritable when attempting to cut down or stop gambling; (5) after losing money gambling, often returns another day to get even (chasing one's losses); (6) lies to family members, therapists, or others to conceal the extent of involvement with gambling; (7) has jeopardized or lost a significant relationship, job, or educational career opportunity because of gambling; and (8) relies on others to provide money to relieve a desperate financial situation caused by gambling.

Furthermore, the NORC study concluded that the presence of a casino in or near a community did not significantly increase crime; in some cases, small decreases in crime were noted.

On the other hand, opponents of gambling pointing out that, although the percentage of gamblers who are problem gamblers is low, it is precisely these problem gamblers who are among the most profitable clients of gambling establishments, and therefore they are the least likely institutions to argue for limitations on, or assistance for helping, problem gamblers who may wish to end their destructive behaviors.

Native American Gaming

One particularly interesting factor in the consideration of gambling as a social and moral issue is the rise of Native American gambling as a major industry on Indian land. Indian gambling is defined as gaming (including, but not limited to, casinos) conducted by a federally recognized tribal government and taking place on a federally established reservation or trust property. Although gaming brings in critically needed funds for often impoverished peoples, the total amount accounts for less than a quarter of the gambling industry revenues nationwide each year. A study written in 2005 found that 30 states are home to more than 350 tribal gaming establishments, operated by over 200 tribes that have decided to pursue gaming as a strategy for economic development (Light and Rand 2005).

About one-third of the approximately 560 tribes in the United States recognized by the federal government conduct casino-style gaming on their reservations. In some cases, tribes are located in states that do not allow any form of gambling (notably Utah), but, in other cases, the tribes have resisted gambling as a source of income—the most famous case being the Navajo, undoubtedly noteworthy because of their large population among Indian nations in the United States.

Nearly half of all tribal gaming enterprises earn less than $10 million in annual revenue, and one-quarter earn less than $3 million each year. On the other end of the spectrum, about 40 tribal casinos (or about 1 in 10) take in two-thirds of all Indian gaming revenues.

Before the rise of Indian gaming, the options available to many Indian tribes were quite limited. Often located on land considered useless to other Americans, Indians have traditionally suffered some of the highest unemployment in the United States, and have historically attracted the least economic investment.

NATIVE AMERICAN GAMBLING ENTERPRISES

Over the past two decades, gambling has grown exponentially in the United States owing in no small measure to Indian gaming, or the operation of gambling casinos on Native American reservations. By 2008, a peak year, revenues from such casinos had reached nearly $27 billion, according to the National Indian Gaming Commission. States and local communities throughout the nation continue to debate the merits of tribal casinos. Among the issues raised are the right of a marginalized population to self-governance and the pursuit of economic revival; the need of income-starved states for tax revenues and job opportunities; and the interest of the public in curtailing any potential harm from increased access to gaming, such as unregulated gambling, individual "addiction" (pathological gambling), and criminal activity.

In the 1970s and 1980s, a number of Indian tribes used their unique position as sovereign bodies within the United States to push for the development of games such as high-stakes bingo on tribal lands. As the number of proposals increased and as states and surrounding communities began to take a greater interest in these operations, the United States Congress was pressured to act. The resulting Indian Gaming Regulatory Act (IGRA) of 1988 established the terms for how Indian tribes could run bingo parlors and casinos, requiring public forums to discuss major issues (such as the building of new casinos) along with binding contracts setting out how gaming operations are to be conducted. Currently, the leading Indian gaming states are California and Oklahoma with, respectively, $7.3 billion and $2.9 billion in revenues generated in 2009.

While not distributed evenly among all Native Americans in the United States, it is impossible to deny that Indian gaming has initiated dramatic changes for the better for Native American tribal groups throughout the country. According to the 2007 Economic Census, while 13 percent of the total U.S. population fell below poverty level, nearly one-third of Native Americans lived in poverty, with unemployment rates reaching as high as 50 to 80 percent in some cases. But as a direct result of gaming, total Native American unemployment is down, educational opportunities have increased, and economic development in other areas of local investment is occurring. Furthermore, there appears to be relative consensus across available research that Indian gaming generates direct, indirect, and induced economic benefits for state and local communities.

From a Native perspective, tribes are independent nations by treaty rights, and therefore there is already a high level of compromise with state governments, which have significantly benefited from profit-sharing arrangements. In Native terms, reservation lands are to be seen in the same way as the federal government recognizes a foreign country, and there ought to be no more resentment, interference, or taxation imposed on them—any more than the United States would expect to impose taxes or rules, for example, on Canada or Mexico, if either country should build a casino near the U.S. border. From many federal and state governmental perspectives, however, there is a limit to tribal sovereignty, and, thus, modern arrangements worked out between tribal and state governments on revenue sharing already represent a significant compromise between the two historically different perspectives on the meaning of tribal sovereignty.

A number of issues have been raised, particularly by Native gaming, that have further complicated this special aspect of the overall issue of gambling. First, the success of many Indian gaming establishments has lent new urgency to those Indian groups seeking federal recognition. However, even though many of these groups have struggled for federal recognition for decades, there is a new pressure on the federal government to impose limits on such recognition because of the widely held belief that gambling opportunities are what is really behind groups seeking federal recognition. There are well over 250 Native groups seeking tribal recognition in the United States.

Second, tribal groups have sought to expand their land claims and work in partnership with outside gambling industry investors to increase their development. Why the Native developers are blamed for this, as opposed to the non-Native investors and industries that are investing in their projects, however, is often hard to determine—other than viewing it from the perspective of long-term prejudices and racism.

Third, Native economic development has resulted in new political clout. Once again, however, heavy investment in the political process by interested parties that include defense contractors, agricultural interests, and oil and automotive companies do not often raise the same concerns—and one can argue that Native Americans are simply exercising their economic power as others have done for a long time.

Conclusion

While there are no clear or direct religious teachings for or against gambling in religious traditions such as indigenous, Islam, Judaism, and Christianity, the increasing levels of personal risk, and the increasingly serious financial implications of professional gambling institutions, continue to make it a controversial activity from the perspective of many major religious traditions. In recent years, the medicalization of gambling has changed the terms of debate from an older religious-based argument about risk or about challenging the spirits or even testing God, to a debate about addictive and destructive behaviors that perhaps ought to be monitored in portions of the population in the same way that other medical or health risks are monitored as part of the responsibility of civil society.

See also **Addiction and Family; Consumer Credit and Household Debt (vol. 1); Internet (vol. 4)**

Further Reading

Barker, Thomas, and Marjie Britz, *Jokers Wild: Legalized Gambling in the Twenty-first Century.* Westport, CT: Praeger, 2000.

Castellani, Brian, *Pathological Gambling: The Making of a Medical Problem.* Albany: State University of New York Press, 2000.

Clotfelter, Charles T., and Philip J. Cook, *Selling Hope: State Lotteries in America.* Cambridge, MA: Harvard University Press, 1989.

Collins, Peter, *Gambling and the Public Interest.* Westport, CT: Praeger, 2003.

Dickerson, Mark, and John O'Conner, *Gambling as an Addictive Behaviour: Impaired Control, Harm Minimisation, Treatment and Prevention.* New York: Cambridge University Press, 2006.

Hansen, Alicia, *Lotteries and State Fiscal Policy.* Background Paper 46. Washington, DC: Tax Foundation, 2004.

Light, Steven Andrew, and Kathryn R. L. Rand, *Indian Gaming and Tribal Sovereignty.* Lawrence: University Press of Kansas, 2005.

McGowan, Richard A., *The Gambling Debate.* Westport, CT: Greenwood Press, 2008.

Morse, Edward A., and Ernest P. Goss, *Governing Fortune: Casino Gambling in America.* Ann Arbor: University of Michigan Press, 2007.

Mullis, Angela, and David Kamper, eds., *Indian Gaming: Who Wins?* Los Angeles: UCLA Indian Studies Center, 2000.

National Gambling Impact Study Commission, http://govinfo.library.unt.edu/ngisc

North American Association of State and Provincial Lotteries, "Resources," n.d. www.naspl.org

Pasquaretta, Paul, *Gambling and Survival in Native North America.* Tucson: University of Arizona Press, 2003.

Pierce, Patrick Ann, *Gambling Politics: State Government and the Business of Betting.* Boulder, CO: Lynne Rienner, 2004.

Reith, Gerda, *The Age of Chance: Gambling in Western Culture.* London and New York: Routledge, 1999.

GANGS

Karen L. Kinnear

Most young people join some type of social group. These groups help youths develop social skills, fulfill many of their emotional needs, offer an environment in which they are valued, provide them with goals, and give direction and structure to their lives. Some youths join groups that society considers prosocial, or are of benefit to society, such as Boy Scouts or Girl Scouts, Little League, or fraternities and sororities. Others will join groups that are considered antisocial, such as gangs.

What Is a Gang?

One of the first problems encountered by those who study gangs and gang behavior is how to define a gang. Is it just a group of people who hang around with each other? Can adults in a group be defined as a gang? Do the people in the group have to engage in some type of criminal behavior? From youths roaming the streets in Los Angeles following the riots in 1992 to youths rioting in Tonga in 2006 following demonstrations over a democratic government, news organizations refer to these groups as "gangs of youths" or "youth gangs." Defining gangs is often a highly political issue that reflects the interests and agendas of the various individuals and agencies involved, including law enforcement personnel, politicians, advocates, social workers, the media, and researchers.

Despite these conflicting views, several major elements can be found in most current definitions of gangs: a group of people, some type of organization, identifiable leadership, identifiable territory, use of symbols, a specific purpose, continual association and existence, and participation in some type of illegal activity. Most gangs today have other behaviors in common: they use graffiti to mark their territory and communicate with other gangs; they dress alike, often adopting a particular color as a gang color (for example, red for the Bloods, blue for the Crips); they often tattoo themselves with gang names or symbols; they abide by a specific code of conduct; they have their own specific language; and they have their own set of hand signs that help them recognize other members of their gang.

Gang Organization

Gangs are organized in a variety of ways, depending on their primary purpose, their level of structure, and the degree of control that the gang leaders have. Taylor (1990) categorized gangs as scavenger gangs, territorial or turf gangs, and instrumental or corporate gangs. Scavenger gangs are loosely organized and provide their members with a purpose for their lives. Many members are low achievers or school dropouts and are likely to exhibit violent behavior. Their crimes are usually not serious and are spontaneous. Territorial gangs may claim blocks, neighborhoods, specific buildings, or even schools as their home turf. These gangs are highly organized and have elaborate initiation rites as well as rules and regulations for controlling members' behavior. Members usually wear gang colors. Instrumental or corporate gangs usually have a clearly defined leader and a finely defined hierarchy of leadership, often a military-type structure. Crimes are committed for a specific purpose, usually profit of some sort, and not just for fun. Gangs may start off as scavenger gangs and, over time, become instrumental or corporate gangs.

Gangs are also made up of a variety of member types. "Wannabes" are usually younger people who want to become gang members or are seen as potential recruits by current members. Core members and leaders are more likely to be involved in the major activities of the gang. Veterans or "O.G." (for "old gangsters" or "original gangsters") are usually older youths or adults who are not actively involved in gang activity, have the respect and admiration of younger gang members, and work with gang leaders to help them achieve their goals.

Joining a Gang

Many theories attempt to explain why juveniles join gangs. Several of these theories are sociological in nature, focusing on structural and dynamic variables as causes of gang formation and behavior. Some of these variables include social environment, family, and economic conditions and opportunity. Most of the theories fall into one of six categories: bonding and control theory, opportunity and strain theory, labeling theory, subcultural or cultural conflict theory, social disorganization theory, and radical or sociopolitical theory.

Bonding and Control Theory

Family processes and interaction play a particularly important role in developing social bonds that may prevent young people from committing delinquent or criminal acts. Families of delinquents may spend little time together and provide less support and affection than families of well-behaved youths; parents may provide little or no supervision for their children. Bonding theory suggests that children who miss out on multiple opportunities to learn socially appropriate behavior may be more likely to join gangs.

Opportunity and Strain Theory

If young people do not believe that they have an equal opportunity to achieve the American dream of success, power, and money, they may grow up frustrated and may develop a sense of hopelessness, believing that they will not receive the same things from society as other people. The resulting depression or anger can lead to delinquent behavior. Prothrow-Stith (1991) believes that juveniles join gangs, including violent gangs, only when they believe that their future opportunities for success are limited.

Labeling Theory

According to sociologist George Herbert Mead (1934), an individual's self-concept is derived from how others define that individual. This concept provides the basis for labeling theory, which some have called self-fulfilling prophecy. Several theorists have applied this theory to juvenile delinquency. Goldstein (1991) believes the initial act of delinquent behavior (primary deviance) is not important in labeling theory; the subsequent delinquent acts perpetrated in reaction to society's response to the initial act (secondary deviance) are relevant.

Cultural Conflict or Subcultural Theory

Some researchers believe that delinquent behavior results from an individual conforming to the current norms of the subculture in which he or she grows up, even though these norms vary from those of the larger society (Thornton and Voight 1992). Youngsters who grow up in areas that have high crime and delinquency rates may come to believe that crime and delinquency are normal aspects of everyday life and therefore do not think that they are doing anything wrong when they misbehave or commit a crime.

Social Disorganization Theory

Thrasher (1927) was one of the first to propose social disorganization theory to explain why youths find gangs so compelling: youth join gangs because they do not feel connected to the existing social institutions. Thrasher believed these youth joined gangs because, to them, the gang was their own society, one that provided all of the gang member's needs. According to this theory, the formation of gangs is not abnormal, but rather a normal response to an abnormal situation (Spergel 1995). High rates of delinquency in an area indicate that social problems are present and may lead to gang formation (Delaney 2006).

Radical Theory

In the late 1970s, several researchers developed a sociopolitical perspective on crime and delinquency known as radical theory or the "new criminology." Believing that laws in the United States are developed by and for the ruling elite, radical theorists hold that these laws are used to hold down the poor, minorities, and the powerless (Bohm 2001).

Social Factors

As can be seen from the many theories concerning the existence and growth of gangs, many factors interact to lead youth to join gangs. Growing up in U.S. society today can be a challenge. When young people have little structure in their lives, when they have no purpose or can see no reason to excel in school, they may be more likely to join gangs. The gang gives their lives structure, makes them feel important and useful, protects them from a violent environment, and provides some sense of safety in numbers. Gang members are loyal to each other and to the gang, their group gets special attention in the community, and their association may provide financial rewards if the gang is selling drugs or involved in other criminal activities. Excitement is a part of gang life; members can get an adrenaline rush from some of their activities, and they may feel empowered by the backing and respect of other gang members.

Racial/Ethnic Gangs

Gangs frequently are composed of members from the same race or ethnic group, although a growing number of gangs are referred to as hybrid gangs. Whites usually join white gangs, Hispanics usually join Hispanic gangs, and African Americans usually join African American gangs. Researchers have found that these racial/ethnic gangs have several characteristics that are specific to their gangs.

Hispanic Gangs

Hispanic or Latino gangs generally have four levels of membership: peripheral, general, active, and hard core. Peripheral members identify with the gang but do not actively participate in the gang, especially in the criminal activities. General members readily identify themselves with the gang but are still working to gain respect. Finally, the hard-core members are active participants in the gang's criminal activity; in fact, these members are the ones who are in leadership positions. Hispanic gang members often set themselves apart from other gangs by using a slang language that is a combination of English and Spanish.

African American Gangs

According to several researchers, African American gang members stay in their gangs longer than gang members from other racial/ethnic groups. This can be explained in part by the lack of economic opportunities available to these youths. Spergel (1995) believes legitimate opportunities for African American youth to participate in viable economic activities are more limited than in any other community.

Asian Gangs

Asian youth may join gangs for many of the same reasons youth from other cultures join them. Asian youth whose parents are fairly new to the United States may feel alienated, overwhelmed, and out of place. The language barrier and other obstacles may encourage these youth to band together for protection and support. Asian gangs are usually organized for economic reasons, and members rarely commit crimes against other cultural or racial groups.

White Gangs

White gangs have the longest history among all racial/ethnic gangs; they were especially prominent in the late 1800s and early 1900s as many Europeans immigrated to the United States. In addition to the typical youth gang, white groups identified as gangs include stoners, heavy metal groups, satanic worshipers, bikers, and skinheads. White supremacist groups are popular gangs in many areas of the United States. They believe in the doctrines of Adolf Hitler and may be tied in with the Ku Klux Klan and the neo-Nazi movement. They dislike African Americans, Asians, Hispanics, Jews, gays, lesbians, Catholics, and any other group that they do not consider part of the white Aryan race.

Native American Gangs

Gang activity on Native American reservations is difficult to measure, in large part because reservations vary greatly in size and include both rural and urban areas. Research has indicated that gang activity on reservations primarily consists of unstructured and informal associations among youth (Major and Egley 2002). Native youth who have moved off the reservation and then return to the reservation may bring their gang associations with them and attempt to recruit new members. Some researchers believe that there is a direct causal relationship between the loss of cultural identity among the Native American children and their families and the problems of substance abuse and gangs on the reservation (Kilman 2006).

Hybrid Gangs

Hybrid gangs may have members from more than one ethnic group or race, members who participate in more than one gang or use symbols or colors from more than one gang, or rival gangs that cooperate in certain, often criminal, activities (Starbuck,

Howell, and Lindquist 2001). Communities throughout the United States are seeing an increase in the number of hybrid gangs, especially communities that had little or no gang activity prior to the 1980s or 1990s. Hybrid gangs may pose a serious problem to local law enforcement agencies because they do not mimic traditional gang characteristics or behavior; local law enforcement agencies may be lulled into a false sense of security, believing that their community does not have any gang activity.

Gang Alliances

Beginning in the 1960s, gangs began to adopt a variation of a common gang name, in essence, becoming a branch of another gang. For example, in Chicago, local gangs included the War Lords, California Lords, and Fifth Avenue Lords, all claiming to be related to and part of the Vice Lord Nation (Miller 2001).

The 1980s saw the expansion of gang alliances. Each alliance had its own set of symbols and other means of identifying and separating it from other gangs and gang alliances. Examples of these alliances include the People Nation (composed of Bloods [West Coast], Latin Kings, Vice Lords, El Rukn, Bishops, and Gaylords) and the Folk Nation (composed of Crips, Black Gangster Disciples, Black Disciples, Latin Disciples, and La Raza). Incentives for forming these alliances include the power associated with being part of a larger and more powerful organization and the coverage by the news media of these alliances, which creates publicity for these alliances.

Females and Gangs

Early studies of gangs usually did not consider females associated with gangs as gang members. They were seen, if at all, as girlfriends of gang members with only a superficial interest in gang activities. More recently, the role of the female has expanded to include a secondary role in gang activities. Females often are seen as providing help and support to male gang members by carrying weapons, offering alibis, and gathering information on rival gang members. Some female gangs are allied with a particular male gang, while others are totally autonomous. African American and Hispanic females are the most likely to participate in gang activities, although white and Asian females are forming and joining gangs in increasing numbers.

Gang Migration

Researchers are beginning to study gang migration—the movement of gang members from one area to another and the subsequent development of gangs in those new locations. In communities that are seeing the appearance of gangs in recent years, authorities believe that migratory gang members are moving into the area and recruiting local youth to establish a new branch of a gang. These migratory gang members may be seeking new sources of revenue through the development of drug distribution or other money-making criminal activities. Known as the importation model, this strategy involves attempts by gang members to encourage the growth of their gang in new cities and is often used to establish new money-making criminal enterprises (Decker and Van Winkle 1996). Knox and his colleagues (1996) refer to this as gang franchising, while Quinn and his colleagues refer to it as gang colonization (Quinn, Tobolowsky, and Downs 1994).

Gangs and Violence

Most experts agree that gang activity increased significantly during the 1980s and 1990s and continues to spread throughout the country today. Law enforcement, community organizations, and the news media offer many gang members the recognition that they crave. Stories about gang activities and gang violence are a concrete example to gang members that their gangs and their actions are important. In fact, some researchers believe that the news media influence the general public's view of gangs and creates the impression that gangs are more widespread and violent than they actually are. Prothrow-Stith (1991) explains that some inner-city youths believe the only way they can get any attention or recognition is to join a gang and participate in some type of criminal activity.

Researchers believe that a variety of factors have led to increasingly violent behavior on the part of gang members. The major factors are guns, territory, and drugs. Guns have become the weapon of choice for gang members, who are more likely to carry and to use guns than other juveniles. Gang members are able to obtain guns through both legal and illegal means. Gang members believe carrying a gun gives them increased power and masculinity, and they assume that their rivals are carrying a weapon, which justifies their possession of a weapon (Delaney 2006).

As the distribution and sale of drugs became more popular and profitable for gangs, the amount of territory that a gang controls became more important. Territory played a critical part in the life of many gangs as they built their power and influence. However, today that focus on territory may be changing. According to the National Youth Gang Center (2000), modern youth gangs are less focused on maintaining a certain territory than gangs in earlier years.

Even though a gang member sells drugs, it does not necessarily follow that he or she also uses drugs. In fact, some gangs involved in the distribution of drugs do not allow members to become users. For example, Ko-Lin Chin (1990) found that, while many of the early Chinese gangs in New York City distributed heroin, most of these gangs refused to use heroin themselves. Some researchers believe that gang structure is not conducive to organized drug dealing—gangs are too unorganized, unfocused, and unable to effectively operate a serious drug organization, and the gang-drug connection has been overstated (Klein, Maxson, and Cunningham 1988; Spergel 1995).

Why Youths Leave Gangs

Some individuals are able to walk away from gang activity on their own, without the help of outside intervention. As a youth gets older, he may lose interest in the gang, viewing the gang as a dead end (literally or figuratively). Or she may find other activities or interests that become more important than the gang. Others decide that they do not like or support violent activities. Some youth may discover that gang life does not meet their expectations. Finally, some gang members may discover that they are being used or exploited by the leadership and decide that they want to be needed, not used. In some cases, the home environment may improve, reducing the need for a youth to join a gang to feel part of a family. Some youths may realize that the benefits of being in a gang are not worth the increased likelihood of being incarcerated for gang activity.

Positive Function of Gangs

For the most part, young people are hurt by gang membership: they may get shot or killed, they may commit criminal acts, and they may end up in jail or prison. However, Klein (1995) found that there are positive aspects to gangs and gang life. For example, many young people who join gangs gain a measure of self-confidence and self-respect, and, in some cases, these young people will eventually see that gangs cannot give them what they want in life and will leave their gangs. In some cases, the skills that gang members learn, such as cooperation, organization, and teamwork, can be used to improve their neighborhoods and their futures, if applied in the right way. Finally, gangs may have a stabilizing effect on the communities in which they are found, by uniting communities against them and providing activities for the children and a focus on keeping the next generation out of gangs.

See also Juvenile Delinquency; Gang Injunction Laws (vol. 2); Juvenile Justice (vol. 2); Juveniles Treated as Adults (vol. 2)

Further Reading

Bohm, Robert M., *Primer on Crime and Delinquency Theory,* 2d ed. Belmont, CA: Wadsworth, 2001.

Chin, Ko-Lin, *Chinese Subculture and Criminality: Non-traditional Crime Groups in America.* New York: Greenwood Press, 1990.

Decker, S., and B. Van Winkle, *Life in the Gang.* New York: Cambridge University Press, 1996.

Delaney, Tim, *American Street Gangs.* Upper Saddle River, NJ: Prentice-Hall, 2006.

Goldstein, Arnold P., *Delinquent Gangs: A Psychological Perspective.* Champaign, IL: Research Press, 1991.

Kilman, Carrie, "Learning Lakota." *Teaching Tolerance* 2 (2006): 28–35.

Klein, Malcolm, *The American Street Gang: Its Nature, Prevalence, and Control.* New York: Oxford University Press, 1995.

Klein, Malcolm W., Cheryl L. Maxson, and Lea C. Cunningham, "Gang Involvement in Cocaine 'Rock' Trafficking." Project Summary/Final Report, Center for Research on Crime and Social Control, Social Science Research Institute, University of Southern California, Los Angeles, 1988.

Knox, G. W., et al., "Addressing and Testing the Gang Migration Issue." In *Gangs: A Criminal Justice Approach,* ed. J. M. Miller and J. P. Rush. Cincinnati: Anderson, 1996.

Major, Aline K., and Arlen Egley Jr., *2000 Survey of Youth Gangs in Indian Country. NYGC Fact Sheet #1.* Washington, DC: National Youth Gang Center, 2002.

Mead, George Herbert, *Mind, Self and Society.* Chicago: University of Chicago Press, 1934.

Miller, Walter B., *The Growth of Youth Gang Problems in the United States: 1970–1998.* Washington, DC: Office of Juvenile Justice and Delinquency Prevention, 2001.

National Youth Gang Center, *1998 National Youth Gang Survey.* Washington, DC: U.S. Department of Justice, Office of Justice Programs, Office of Juvenile Justice and Delinquency Prevention, 2000.

Prothrow-Stith, Deborah, *Deadly Consequences: How Violence Is Destroying Our Teenage Population and a Plan To Begin Solving the Problem.* New York: HarperCollins, 1991.

Quinn, J. F., P. M. Tobolowsky, and W. T. Downs, "The Gang Problem in Large and Small Cities: An Analysis of Police Perceptions in Nine States." *Gang Journal* 2 (1994): 13–22.

Spergel, Irving A., *The Youth Gang Problem: A Community Approach.* New York: Oxford University Press, 1995.

Starbuck, David, James C. Howell, and Donna J. Lindquist, "Hybrid and Other Modern Gangs." *Juvenile Justice Bulletin.* Washington, DC: Office of Juvenile Justice and Delinquency Prevention, 2001.

Taylor, Carl S., *Dangerous Society.* East Lansing: Michigan State University Press, 1990.

Thornton, William E., and Lydia Voight, *Delinquency and Justice,* 3d edition. New York: McGraw-Hill, 1992.

Thrasher, Frederic, *The Gang.* Chicago: University of Chicago Press, 1927.

GAY PARENT ADOPTION

JEFFREY JONES

Gay parent adoption or same-sex adoption refers to the adoption of children by individuals who prefer romantic partners of the same sex—gays and lesbians. Same-sex adoption is portrayed by the media as being a potentially good thing but with potentially detrimental side effects, most notably for the adopted children. This type of adoption is often made to look as if it might well be done but perhaps should not be for the sake of the children involved. With groups such as the religious right, fundamentalist Christian denominations, and private religiously affiliated adoption agencies backing the opposition to adoption by gays and lesbians and, on the other side, the American Civil Liberties Union, the Human Rights Campaign, and various LGBT (lesbian gay bisexual transgender)-friendly groups making up the proponents, the battle over same-sex adoption is well defined and entrenched in a deep and long-standing debate. That battle begins with the media and its portrayal of gay parent adoptions as against the agencies and advocacy groups and their perspectives on placing children in the homes and care of homosexual individuals.

Background

Adoption remained for a long time a rather homogeneous action, with the placement of children in the homes of middle-class, married couples. Over the course of the last three decades, adoption went through a metamorphosis, from being merely a source for married, middle-class couples to create families to being a pathway for a number of diverse and sometimes marginal populations to establish families of their own. According to estimates prepared by the Adoption and Foster Care Analysis and Reporting System, some 123,000 children in the public child welfare system were waiting to be adopted in late 2008. The average age of children awaiting placement in adoptive homes was between six and seven years of age. Many of these children who were awaiting adoption spent 38 consecutive months in foster care. That same year, only 55,000 children were adopted from public welfare agencies. Those who were adopted ranged in age from infants to teenagers and differed in race from Latino to white to African American. The adoptive parents were also diverse: 28 percent were single women, 3 percent were single men, and 2 percent were unmarried couples. Among these adoptive parents was a select group of gay and lesbian individuals and partners.

According to Ada White, director of adoption services for the Child Welfare League of America, many agencies do make placements with gay or lesbian parents, but they do not necessarily talk about these adopters. Agencies are not specifically tracking such adoptions and do not intend to track them. Consequently, the practice of adoption with many of these agencies is that they may place these children in homosexual homes but are not willing to make it public knowledge that they are doing so. The adoption of children by homosexual parents is often done so that others' knowledge of its occurrence remains minimal. The practices of adoption vary greatly from state to state and region to region and even from judge to judge. The Human Rights Campaign, the nation's largest gay and lesbian advocacy organization, has conducted research to determine that 21 states and the District of Columbia allow gay adoption. This would not be the case if the religious right had its way. It is suggested that the ability for gay and lesbian individuals to adopt would become much more limited, with a minimal number of states being welcoming of gay adoption.

Laws and Research

New Jersey was the first state to specify that sexual orientation and marital status could not be used against couples seeking to adopt. New Jersey also allows second-parent adoption, a legal procedure in which a coparent can adopt the biological or adopted child of his or her partner. New York soon followed, granting second-parent adoptions statewide and forbidding discrimination in adoption proceedings. California joined the party by enacting new domestic partnership legislation that legalized second-parent adoptions. On the opposite end of the spectrum, a number of states exclude gays and lesbians from adopting either as primary or as secondary adoptive parents. Florida stands out among the states in that gay adoption has been banned since 1977. Utah prohibits adoption by any unmarried couple or individual, regardless of sexual orientation. While Mississippi does not actually ban gay and lesbian individuals from adoption, same-sex couples are absolutely prohibited from adopting. The laws regarding same-sex adoption within most states are not actually on the books and are similar to accepted (or not accepted) practices within each state—based more on tradition than on legal precedent.

Since the turn of the millennium, there has been an increase in the number of children within the child welfare system in need of homes and a growing acceptance of nontraditional families looking to adopt them. Among those opposed to such adoptions, however, such as the religiously based organization Focus on the Family, there is a strong sentiment that placing children in the care of gay and lesbian individuals or partners is not in the best interest of the children. In April 2001, researchers Judith Stacey and Timothy Biblarz of the University of Southern California published findings regarding this issue in the *American Sociological Review*. The duo examined 21 studies concerning the effects of gay parenting. Their meta-analysis concluded: "There were subtle differences in gender behavior and preferences. Lesbian mothers reported that their children, specifically their daughters, were less likely to conform to gender norms in dress, play or behavior; more likely to aspire to nontraditional occupations, such as doctors or lawyers. They also discovered that children of gay and lesbian parents are no more likely to identify themselves as gay or lesbian than the children of heterosexual parents" (Stacey and Biblarz 2001). The latter part of their summary corresponds to what one might consider to be a fear among a majority of adoption agencies and judges—that children placed in homosexual-parented homes stand a greater chance than those in the general population of coming out as homosexuals. This suggests that the environment of a homosexual family is instrumental in the child's development as a gay person. This argument is regarded as a fallacy among members of the liberal left and by more and more of the general public, as the alternative, biological model of the origin of sexual orientation gains support. A similar aspect of the right's argument against the placement of children in homosexual-parented homes is that being raised in this fashion will have psychologically detrimental effects on the children. Stacey and Biblarz, in contrast, found that children of homosexual parents showed no difference in levels of self-esteem, anxiety, depression, behavior problems, or social performance but do show a higher level of affection, responsiveness, and concern for younger children, as well as seeming to exhibit impressive psychological strength.

Stacey and Biblarz also report that gay parents were found to be more likely to share child care and household duties. The children of gay partners reported closer relationships with the parent who was not their primary caregiver than did the children of heterosexual couples. The increase in affection and higher psychological strength that this study shows is, arguably, just part of the positive effects that gay adoption can have on children. In opposition to these and similar findings, however, are those who continue to believe that only heterosexual couples should adopt and that homosexuality is morally wrong. Some even claim that gays and lesbians are likely to abuse their children (see Stacey and Biblarz 2001).

The American Psychological Association (APA) has adopted the view that same-sex adoption is fine, as long as the best interests of the children are served in particular cases. In its Resolution on Sexual Orientation, Parents, and Children, from July 2004, the organization noted that, in the 2000 U.S. Census, 33 percent of female same-sex couple households and 22 percent of male same-sex couple households reported at least one child under the age of 18 living in the home. Opponents have expressed concerns over the idea of a minor living in a homosexual-parented household. Yet, according to research cited by the APA, there is no scientific basis for concluding that lesbian mothers or gay fathers are unfit parents based solely on their sexual orientation, and moreover households maintained by these individuals clearly can provide safe, nurturing, and loving environments in which to raise children.

The proponents of same-sex adoption argue in favor of the practice on the basis that both past and present research shows no difference in the health and success of the children of lesbian and gay parents as compared to the children of their heterosexual counterparts. There is no definitive indication of a disadvantage among children of gay and lesbian parents on the basis of their parents' sexual orientation. Home environments with gay or lesbian parents are just as likely to provide solid foundations of comfort and compassionate understanding as the homes of heterosexual couples. Data such as these supported the decision by the American Academy of Pediatrics to issue a policy statement endorsing adoption by same-sex couples.

In the view of opponents, homosexual parents do not act in the best interest of the child. A number of scholars, theorists, and researchers have posted the claim that gay parents subject children to unnecessary and increased risks. One notable suggestion is that children of gay parents are more likely to suffer confusion over their own gender and sexual identities, thus becoming more likely to claim a homosexual status later in their maturity. There are also claims that homosexual parents are more likely to molest their children; that these children are more likely to lose a parent to AIDS, substance abuse, or suicide; and that they are more likely to suffer from depression and other emotional disturbances. Arguments such as these abound, but there remains little or no scientific—or even consistent anecdotal evidence—in support of them.

Agencies

Regardless of one's position as to whether gay parents should be permitted to adopt, there are distinct differences in how each side is portrayed in the media and in various advocacy groups' Web sites. Agencies exist on both sides of the issue. The Evan B. Donaldson Adoption Institute has done extensive work in improving the knowledge of the public in this area. In 2003, the institute published a national survey titled "Adoption by Lesbians and Gays: A National Survey of Adoption Agency Policies, Practices, and Attitudes." Drawing on a number of surveys and studies, the report gives a plethora of statistics regarding the acceptance and placement of children into homosexual homes.

Among the findings are that: (1) lesbians and gays are adopting regularly, in notable and growing numbers, at both public and private agencies nationwide; (2) assuming that those responding are representative (and the results show that they are), 60 percent of U.S. adoption agencies accept applications from homosexuals; (3) about two in five of all agencies in the country have placed children with adoptive parents who they know to be gay or lesbian; (4) the most likely agencies to place children with homosexuals are public, secular private, Jewish- and Lutheran-affiliated agencies, and those focusing on special needs and international adoption. In addition to the specific findings, the study's results led to several major conclusions on the levels of policy and practice. These may be summarized as follows: (1) for lesbians and gay men, the opportunities for becoming adoptive mothers and fathers is significantly greater than is generally portrayed in the media or perceived by the public; (2) although a large and growing number of agencies work with or are willing to work with homosexual clients, they often are unsure about whether to or how to reach out to them; (3) because so many homosexuals are becoming adoptive parents, it is important for the sake of their children that agencies develop preplacement and postplacement services designed to support these parents.

In addition to the various types of programs that the adoption agencies utilize, ranging from special needs to international adoptions or a mixture of both, there is also a definite difference in the overall acceptance of adoption applications from homosexuals on the basis of the agency's religious affiliation. While Jewish-affiliated agencies were almost universally willing to work with LGBT clients, as were the majority of public agencies, private nonreligious, and Lutheran-affiliated agencies, only samples of Methodist and Catholic agencies were willing to consider applications from homosexuals. Twenty percent of all agencies responding to the study acknowledged that they had rejected an application from homosexual applicants on at least one occasion.

Not all of the agencies surveyed through the Donaldson Institute survey responded to the questions presented to them. Of those who willingly did respond, an estimated two-thirds of the agencies had policies in effect on adoption by gays and lesbians. Of those, an estimated 33.6 percent reported a nondenominational policy, 20 percent responded that placement decisions were guided by the children's country of origin, and another 20 percent said that religious beliefs were at the core of rejecting the homosexual applications. More than one-third of the responding agencies reported in follow-up phone calls that they did not work with homosexual prospective adoptive parents. On the other hand, an estimated two in five, or 39 percent, of all agencies had placed at least one child with a homosexual adoptive parent between 1999 and 2000. Owing to the fact that fewer than half of all agencies collect information on the sexual orientation of potential adoptive parents and do not actively track the statistics regarding the placement of children with adoptive parents who are homosexual, the Donaldson Institute was forced to estimate the number of such placements made. One adoption placement with a homosexual client per year was counted for statistical purposes. Based on these assumptions, there were an estimated 1,206 placements with homosexual parents (or roughly 1.3 percent of the total placements). This number is much higher in reality.

One aspect not yet discussed is the input of the birth parents in the proceedings of the adoption of their child. The Donaldson Institute delved into this issue and released the following findings: (1) About one-quarter of respondents said that prospective birth parents have objected to the placing of their child with gays or lesbians or have specifically requested that their child not be placed with homosexuals. At that time, nearly 15 percent of all agencies said birth parents had requested or chosen lesbian or gay prospective adoptive parents for their child on at least one occasion. (2) Although most agencies worked with lesbians and gays, only 19 percent sought them to be adoptive parents, and the vast majority of these (86.6 percent) relied on word-of-mouth for recruitment. Outreach efforts were made most often at agencies already willing to work with homosexuals (41.7 percent of Jewish-affiliated, 29.9 percent of private, nonreligiously affiliated, and 20 percent of public). (3) Similarly, adoption agencies focused on children with special needs were the most likely to make outreach efforts (32.1 percent) to gays and lesbians, followed by international-focused agencies (19.7 percent). (4) Nearly half of the agencies (48 percent) indicated an interest in receiving training to work with lesbian and gay prospective parents. Most likely to be interested were agencies already working with them; public, nonreligiously affiliated, and Jewish- and Lutheran-affiliated agencies. Additionally, special needs programs and those with mixed needs were more likely to be interested in training than were those focusing on international and domestic infant adoptions.

There seems to be a growing interest in and flexibility toward the idea that homosexual prospective parents may be a viable option for the placement of children into homes to ultimately give them a more stable and nurturing environment than one would find in child welfare systems. However, religious affiliation of the agency remains an important and prominent issue. Over half of the agencies held no religious affiliation (55.38 percent), while the rest represented a variety of faiths, the largest of which was Catholic-affiliated at 14.8 percent, with various other denominations reporting 5 percent or less. With as many placements as are being made, it is clear that, somewhere along the line, the individuals who work in these agencies do actually want to place these children in good, stable, nurturing homes. However, a number of the agencies to which this survey was sent declined to participate. Their reasons for declining ranged from: (1) agency does not make adoption placements (36.7 percent); (2) agency does not work with homosexual clients (34.1 percent); (3) interested but agency director too busy (13.3 percent); (4) no reason given or not interested in the study (12.5 percent); (5) incomplete data from returned survey (3.0 percent). While there is still 0.4 percent missing from this data set, it does give some startling ideas about the various agencies' reactions to this survey.

At the time of this survey, only Florida, Mississippi, and Utah had statutory bans on or prohibitive barriers to homosexual adoption. One of the more shocking discoveries of the Donaldson Institute research is that 17 adoption directors from other states incorrectly reported that lesbians and gays were barred from adopting children in their states; another 31 respondents were unsure of the states' law on adoption by homosexuals. This is slightly alarming, considering the work that has been done to include homosexuals in the adoption process, and yet it would seem that they are being excluded yet again but this time by ignorance. Despite being somewhat unaware of their states' legislation on homosexual adoption, there was a clear distribution of policy acceptance levels regarding homosexual adoption. According to the Donaldson Institute research, about 20 percent of all respondents said that their agencies, on one or more occasion, had rejected applications from gay or lesbian individuals or couples. The reasons for the rejections were as follows: (1) unrealistic expectations, (2) psychological problems, (3) questionable motives for adopting, (4) relationship problems, (5) placement with homosexuals violates agency policy, (6) applicant's lifestyle incompatible with adoption, (7) placement with homosexuals prohibited by country of origin, (8) sexual orientation of applicant incompatible with adoption, (9) lack of adequate social support, (10) financial problems, (11) placement with homosexuals violates community standards, and (12) medical problems with the applicant.

Conclusion

Generally, the presentation of gays and lesbians as adoptive parents has been biased by the group doing the presenting. Conservative media outlets and family-values groups such as the Family Research Council argue, largely on the basis of a preestablished moral line of thought, that the best home for a child is with two heterosexual married parents. These groups cite arguments against homosexuality in general, such as the so-called unnaturalness of same-sex partnerships or the potential for somehow damaging the children, as evidence for why homosexuals should be prevented from adopting. Increasingly, however, the opinions of the general public toward LGBT issues and individuals have become more accepting and positive. Moreover, because there are many more children awaiting adoption than there are homes into which they can readily be placed, gay and lesbian individuals and couples are increasingly seen as an untapped market. Anecdotal evidence suggests that, not only have gays and lesbians been more willing to adopt children with special needs, for example, but the outcomes are more positive than many critics predicted. As pressure mounts on states to solve some of their child welfare problems, particularly in the area of foster care, the prospect of opening adoptions to a field of underutilized but potential loving parents is a step in a beneficial direction.

See also **Adoption—International and Transracial; Domestic Partnerships; Foster Care**

Further Reading

American Psychological Association, "Sexual Orientation, Parents, and Children." 2004. http://www.apa.org/about/governance/council/policy/parenting.aspx

Black, James C., "Same-sex Parents and Their Children's Development." In *Same-Sex Marriage: The Legal and Psychological Evolution in America,* ed. Donald J. Cantor, Elizabeth Cantor, James C. Black, and Campbell D. Barrett. Middletown, CT: Wesleyan University Press, 2006.

Drescher, Jack, and Deborah Glazer, *Gay and Lesbian Parenting.* New York: Informa Healthcare, 2001.

Evan B. Donaldson Adoption Institute, "Adoption by Lesbians and Gays: A National Survey of Adoption Agency Policies, Practices, and Attitudes." 2003. http://www.adoptioninstitute.org

Family Research Council, http://www.frc.org

Hennon, Charles B., Bruno Hildenbrand, and Andrea Schedle, "Lesbian, Gay, Bisexual and Trans-gendered (LGBT) Families and Their Children." In *Family Influences on Childhood Behavior and Development,* ed. Thomas P. Gullota and Gary M. Blau. New York: Routledge, 2008.

Leung, Patrick, Stephen Erich, and Heather Kanenberg, "A Comparison of Family Functioning in Gay/Lesbian, Heterosexual, and Special Needs Adoption." *Children and Youth Services Review* 27 (2005): 1031–1044.

Mallon, Gerald P., *Lesbian and Gay Foster and Adoptive Parents: Recruiting, Assessing, and Supporting an Untapped Resource for Children and Youth.* Washington, DC: Child Welfare League of America, 2006.

Stacey, Judith, and Timothy J. Biblarz, "(How) Does the Sexual Orientation of Parents Matter?" *American Sociological Review* 66, no. 2 (2001): 159–183.

GAYS IN THE MILITARY

Carrie Anne Platt

From the time of the Revolutionary War to the era of "Don't Ask, Don't Tell," evidence of homosexuality has been grounds for exclusion or discharge from the U.S. military. The continued presence of lesbians and gays in the military has prompted heated debate over military necessity, personal rights, and the culture of the armed forces. The outcome of this controversy will likely affect other contemporary conflicts between lesbian and gay rights movements and traditional values.

Background

In June 2006, the Department of Defense found itself back in the middle of the controversy over gays and lesbians in the military. Researchers from the Center for the Study of Sexual Minorities in the Military had recently uncovered an official Pentagon document that classified homosexuality as a mental illness. Members of Congress and medical experts were quick to criticize the document, pointing out that the American Psychiatric Association had stopped classifying homosexuality as a mental disorder in 1973. This debate triggered a much larger dispute over how gay and lesbian service members should be classified by the military. Since the Department of Defense declared that "homosexuality is incompatible with military service" in 1982, gays and service members have become a topic of heated debate. Should sexual identity be a standard for inclusion or exclusion from the U.S. military? Does sexual identity have any impact on military performance? Should gay and lesbian individuals be allowed to enlist and serve as long as they do not reveal their sexual orientation? Should they be able to serve openly? What consequences do these military regulations have for the broader social debate over lesbian and gay rights in the United States? Politicians, military leaders, legislators, judges, activists, and service members have all struggled with these questions.

The introduction of "Don't Ask, Don't Tell, Don't Pursue, Don't Harass" in 1993 addressed some of these concerns, but not all. Don't Ask, Don't Tell, as the policy came to be known, officially prohibits the military from asking recruits or current service members about their sexual orientation. Supporters of this policy argue that allowing gays and lesbians to serve openly would be bad for troop morale and damaging to unit cohesion, which could significantly diminish military performance and put other soldiers at risk. They also point out that the military operates under its own rules and regulations, making it immune to state and federal antidiscrimination laws. Opponents of this policy argue that the military's current bias against lesbians and gays is equivalent to its previous opposition to racial integration. They contend that the stigmatization and harassment of gay and lesbian service members are violations of basic rights, and they view the numerous military investigations into the sexual lives of service members as governmental interference into private life. Finally, they argue that any benefits generated by Don't Ask, Don't Tell are outweighed by the high costs of investigations and discharge proceedings.

The Military's Regulation of Sexuality

U.S. military regulation of sexuality goes back as far as the Revolutionary War, when Lieutenant Gotthold Frederick Enslin became the first American soldier to be dismissed for homosexual conduct. In March 1778, Enslin was court-martialed and dishonorably discharged from the Continental Army for his actions. Contemporary conversations about gays and lesbians in the military often reference this incident, but it is important to note that Lieutenant Enslin's removal from the army was not based on his sexual orientation. He was removed for engaging in sexual acts that were prohibited by military law. Until World War II, the military had no specific laws or policies regarding homosexuals. The Articles of War of 1920 classified sodomy as a punishable offense, but were applicable to both straight and gay service members (Burrelli 1994).

The lack of specific regulations did not prevent the U.S. military from policing sexual conduct. The Newport Sex Scandal of 1919–1921 was one of the military's first systematic attempts to purge gay service members from the ranks. Afraid that sailors stationed at the Navy base in Newport, Rhode Island, were in danger of being morally corrupted by the local gay community, the Navy set out to investigate. It recruited several enlisted sailors to entrap and then testify against suspected "perverts" in court (Brenkert 2003). During the course of this investigation, a number of sailors were caught, court-martialed, and sent to prison. Prominent civilians, such as the Reverend Samuel Neal Kent, were also caught up in the dragnet, bringing the investigation—and Assistant Secretary of the Navy Franklin Delano Roosevelt—to national attention. Significantly, the scandal did not result from the Navy's findings but rather from the graphic accounts given by the young sailors who had volunteered for the investigation.

Lesbians and gays were not officially excluded from military service until World War II, when the introduction of standardized psychological screening shifted the military's focus from homosexual conduct to homosexual status. In 1942, the army revised its draft regulations to include criteria for differentiating between homosexual and "normal" draftees and added procedures for rejecting those who were not deemed normal by the screening protocol. Women who wished to enlist in the Women's Army Corps (WAC) were screened using the same criteria, although homosexuality did not become an official reason for disqualification until most of the WAC recruiting had been completed (Berube 1990). During this time, the high demand for service members meant that many of the regulations were loosened or ignored to allow gays and lesbians to enlist and serve. After the war was over, however, Congress enacted the Uniform Code of Military Justice, which standardized the military's restrictive approach to homosexuality across all branches of the armed services.

As the lesbian and gay rights movement emerged in the United States in the 1970s, military policy on homosexuality became the subject of both protest and legal challenge. Although this movement was unsuccessful in overturning the ban against gays and lesbians serving in the military, it did uncover enough inconsistencies in enforcement to prompt the military to review and revise its regulations in the early 1980s. The new policy sought to establish more uniform procedures for discharging lesbian and gay service members and to identify the extenuating circumstances under which those who had engaged in homosexual conduct might be retained. But the basic approach to lesbians and gays in the military remained—the first sentence of Department of Defense Directive 1332.14 reads: "Homosexuality is incompatible with military service."

Don't Ask, Don't Tell

The development and enactment of Don't Ask, Don't Tell in the early 1990s remains one of the most significant—and most contested—revisions of military policy on homosexuality. In 1993, shortly after taking office, President Bill Clinton announced that he planned to fulfill his campaign promise by lifting the ban on lesbians and gays in the military. He gave Secretary of Defense Les Aspin six months to draft a new policy that would end discrimination based on sexual orientation in the U.S. military. While waiting for this policy, President Clinton ordered the Department of Defense to stop asking military recruits about their sexual orientation and asked that those who were being discharged under the current policy be placed on standby.

KEY DATES

1778:	Lieutenant Gotthold Frederick Enslin becomes the first soldier dismissed from the U.S. military for homosexual conduct.
1919:	Navy orders first systematic investigation into allegations of homosexual conduct at Newport naval base. Numerous sailors are entrapped, court-martialed, and sent to prison.
1942:	United States Army begins to mandate screening of sexual orientation for all who enlist.
1950:	Uniform Code of Military Justice standardizes exclusion of lesbians and gays from all branches of the armed services.
1982:	Pentagon declares that "homosexuality is incompatible with military service."
1994:	Don't Ask, Don't Tell policy is enacted by the 1994 Defense Authorization Act.
2005 and 2007:	Representative Martin Meehan (D-MA) introduces and reintroduces the Military Readiness Enhancement Act, which seeks to overturn Don't Ask, Don't Tell (stalled).
2010:	President Barack Obama and congressional leaders announce that they will work to overturn Don't Ask, Don't Tell.

Clinton's proposals were strongly opposed by the joint chiefs of staff, high-ranking Pentagon officials, Senate Armed Services Committee (SASC) chair Sam Nunn (D-GA), and many conservative members of Congress. While Secretary of Defense Aspin commissioned studies on the current policy, both the SASC and the House Armed Services Committee held numerous hearings on the topic, during which Pentagon officials, military commanders, service members, and various experts testified on the potential impact of allowing lesbians and gays to serve openly in the U.S. military. The majority of the testimony offered was in opposition to lifting the ban (Herek 1996).

The final outcome of this controversy was "Don't Ask, Don't Tell, Don't Pursue, Don't Harass," a title that reflects the compromise reached in the new policy. Before Don't Ask, Don't Tell, military officials were permitted to ask potential recruits or current service members about their sexual orientation to prevent the enlistment or initiate the removal of gays and lesbians from the military. Don't Ask, Don't Tell prohibits military officials from asking direct questions about sexual orientation, but it also prevents gays and lesbians wishing to enlist and serve from saying or doing anything that would reveal their sexual orientation to others. They are also prohibited from engaging in any type of homosexual conduct, whether on duty or off duty. Also, if a commander believes that a service member has demonstrated a propensity for homosexual conduct, discharge proceedings can be initiated (Halley 1999). That lesbians and gays are now allowed to serve as long as they don't serve openly has done little to dampen the debate over gays and lesbians in the armed forces.

Arguments for Upholding the Ban

Individuals and organizations opposed to lesbians and gays serving openly in the U.S. military offer various arguments in support of their position. Moral values certainly play a role in this debate, but the most common arguments involve issues of military necessity and key distinctions between military and civilian law. During the congressional hearings held in 1993, for instance, Pentagon officials testified that gays and lesbians must be banned from military service to maintain necessary levels of troop morale, unit cohesion, and discipline.

These arguments have less to do with the actual performance in the military and more to do with the responses of heterosexual service members to lesbians and gays in their own units (Halley 1999). During basic training and deployment, military personnel live in close proximity to one another. Service members also have little to no privacy when they dress or shower. Proponents of banning lesbians and gays from military service argue that allowing homosexuals to train and reside with heterosexuals would be like giving men service members the opportunity to observe women service members in various states of undress. Service members would feel awkward or uncomfortable and troop morale would decrease significantly.

Openly gay or lesbian service members are also viewed as a threat to unit cohesion. Unit cohesion is generally defined as the fostering of mutual trust and commitment to one's fellow soldiers and is necessary for both overcoming hardship and achieving military objectives. Proponents of the ban contend that, even if military officers are instructed to exhibit tolerance, the homophobic culture of the military will lead to tension and additional violence between gay and straight service members (Herek 1996). They also argue that the inclusion of lesbians and gays in sex-segregated units will increase the possibility of sexual harassment and precipitate breakdowns in the chain of command.

Finally, those who support the military's right to exclude or discharge service members based on sexual orientation point out that the military acts under its own laws, rules, and regulations; that service members are faced with a number of restrictions on their personal behavior that would not be acceptable for civilians; and that the U.S. military is immune to both federal and state laws prohibiting discrimination (Ray 1993). Important distinctions between civilian and military law help to account for the failure of numerous legal challenges to Don't Ask, Don't Tell.

Arguments for Allowing Lesbians and Gays to Serve Openly

Because they are arguing against the status quo, gay-rights advocates and others who favor overturning the current ban have to both refute the arguments of their opponents and offer their own arguments for allowing lesbians and gays to serve openly in the military. They have uncovered studies commissioned by the Department of Defense and conducted independent research to dispute the claim that lesbian and gay service members are bad for troop morale or disruptive to unit cohesion. According to these advocates, recent surveys of enlisted military personnel show a marked increase in the number of service members who say they would be comfortable serving alongside lesbian and gay service members (Kuhr 2007).

From the perspective of advocates on this side of the debate, the military ban is symbolic of a more general refusal to grant full citizenship rights to lesbian, gay, and bisexual individuals. Like the right to vote or the right to enter into legal contracts, military service is a key marker of citizenship in the United States (Belkin and Bateman 2003). The controversy that surrounded the integration of African Americans into the U.S. armed forces in 1948 contained the same tension between military inclusion and social progress. Opponents of the ban point out that the military advanced similar arguments in this debate, stating that the integration of racial minorities would jeopardize military performance by dampening morale and damaging unit cohesion. Pursuing this analogy, they contend that the general success of racial integration in the U.S. military—and the number of foreign militaries who now allow lesbians and gay men to serve openly—suggests that overturning the ban would not adversely affect military performance.

Moving from principles to procedural issues, opponents of Don't Ask, Don't Tell argue that the policy costs too much and that the money and time it takes to investigate and discharge could be better spent elsewhere. According to a California blue ribbon commission report released in 2006, the policy cost U.S. taxpayers $364 million and resulted in the loss of almost 10,000 service members in its first decade (White 2006).

Conclusion

Nearly 30 years since the U.S. military said that "homosexuality is incompatible with military service," the country finds itself facing a combination of historical and cultural factors that are likely to have a significant impact on the debate over gays and lesbians in the military. In the face of an extended war in Afghanistan (and following an extended war in Iraq), the military has been forced to step up recruiting efforts and prolong tours of duty, but a troop shortage remains. It is clear that the discharge or exclusion of particular service members has come into conflict with military necessity.

At the same time, Don't Ask, Don't Tell has been denounced by dozens of former senior military officers and service members. John Shalikashvili, an army general who was head of the Joint Chiefs of Staff when the Pentagon adopted the policy, changed his mind and came out against it in early 2007. In 2005, Representative Martin Meehan (D-MA) introduced the Military Readiness Enhancement Act, which would allow lesbians and gays to serve openly in the military. The bill had 122 cosponsors but failed to pass the Republican-controlled House. It was reintroduced in 2007 and in

2009 (the latter time by Representative Patrick Murphy), gaining momentum this last time under backing from the White House under President Barack Obama. Senate leaders, too, announced that they would join the effort to overturn the ban, although an attempt to include a repeal measure in the 2011 defense appropriations bill failed owing to Republican opposition. Even in the event of passage in the near future, however, it would be up to top military leaders to implement any new policy according to military rules and regulations.

See also **Gay Parent Adoption; Social Justice (vol. 2)**

Further Reading

Belkin, Aaron, and Geoffrey Bateman, eds., *Don't Ask, Don't Tell: Debating the Gay Ban in the Military.* Boulder, CO: Lynne Rienner, 2003.

Berube, Allan, *Coming Out Under Fire: The History of Gay Men and Women in World War Two.* New York: Free Press, 1990.

Brenkert, Benjamin, "The Newport Sex Scandal, 1919–1921." *Gay and Lesbian Review Worldwide* 10, no. 2 (2003): 13–15.

Burrelli, David F., "An Overview of the Debate on Homosexuals in the U.S. Military." In *Gays and Lesbians in the Military: Issues, Concerns, and Contrasts,* ed. Wilbur J. Scott and Sandra Carson Stanley. New York: Walter de Gruyter, 1994.

Embser-Herbert, Melissa S., *The U.S. Military's "Don't Ask, Don't Tell" Policy: A Reference Handbook.* Westport, CT: Praeger Security International, 2007.

Estes, Steve, *Ask and Tell: Gay and Lesbian Veterans Speak Out.* Chapel Hill: University of North Carolina Press, 2007.

Frank, Nathaniel, *Unfriendly Fire: How the Gay Ban Undermines the Military and Weakens America.* New York: Thomas Dunne Books, 2009.

Halley, Janet E., *Don't: A Reader's Guide to the Military's Anti-Gay Policy.* Durham, NC: Duke University Press, 1999.

Herek, Gregory, "Why Tell If You're Not Asked? Self-Disclosure, Intergroup Contact, and Heterosexuals' Attitudes toward Lesbians and Gay Men." In *Out of Force: Sexual Orientation and the Military,* ed. Gregory Herek, Jared Jobe, and Ralph Carney. Chicago: University of Chicago Press, 1996.

Kuhr, Fred, "Gays in the Ranks: Who Cares?" *Advocate* (February 2007): 31–33.

Lord, James, *My Queer War.* New York: Farrar, Straus and Giroux, 2010.

Ray, Ronald D., *Gays: In or Out? The U.S. Military and Homosexuals: A Sourcebook.* Washington, DC: Brassey's, 1993.

Shilts, Randy, *Conduct Unbecoming: Lesbians and Gays in the U.S. Military, Vietnam to the Persian Gulf.* New York: St. Martin's Press, 1993.

Watson, Cynthia A., *U.S. Military Service: A Reference Handbook.* Santa Barbara, CA: ABC-CLIO, 2007.

White, Josh, "Don't Ask Costs More Than Expected: Military's Gay Ban Seen in Budget Terms." *Washington Post* (February 14, 2006): sec. A.

GENDER SOCIALIZATION

Amber Ault

When parents-to-be find out the sex of their child, family and friends begin to buy gifts according to gender. Girls receive pink clothing, and boys receive blue clothing. If parents choose not to know the sex of the child, generally clothing will be bought in gender-neutral colors like yellow and green. Buying babies' clothing in specific gendered colors begins the socialization process, which will continue when toys are purchased—dolls for girls, trucks for boys. The teaching of gender continues in society and carries over into schools.

Schools socialize students in multiple ways, starting in kindergarten. Schools teach young students about the society they live in and their expectations of behavior. Citizenship is stressed in early education through activities such as saying the pledge of allegiance and singing the national anthem. How to conduct oneself appropriately and listen to authority are also highly valued in early schooling. Much time is spent on sitting in your assigned seat, lining up properly, and learning to listen attentively to teachers (Thorne 1993).

Beyond these practical socializing factors, many researchers argue that schools also socialize according to gender. Teachers treat boys and girls differently based on different expectations of behaviors and intellect. Teachers tend to accept when boys act out more and justify boys' disruptions in the classroom as uniquely male features. Girls, however, are often reprimanded for similar behaviors, because teachers expect girls to be better behaved and less disruptive in class.

Teachers expect girls to be more studious and excel more in school, particularly in subjects like reading and writing; boys are favored in math and science. Girls receive better grades than boys, and they also receive more favorable evaluations from teachers. Teachers seem to appreciate girls' cooperativeness and ease at communication and consistently rank girls higher on in-classroom behaviors. Girls may be better adapted to schools or may have different expectations than boys.

Young students are affected by gender socialization. In elementary school, boys and girls choose who is popular based on typical constructions of gender. Boys are thought to be popular when they are athletic and described as tough or cool. Popular girls are chosen because of their physical appearance, social skills, and academic success (Adler, Kless, and Adler 1992).

The Feminization of Teaching

A subtler way that schools reinforce gender is through the feminization of teaching. The feminization of teaching refers to the fact that the majority of teachers in the United States are women. Throughout elementary and high school, teachers tend to be women.

The field of education tends to replicate traditional gender hierarchies seen in other work environments, such as business. Although women dominate the status of teachers, a much higher percentage of education administrators, from principals and superintendents to positions in government, are men. Also, in colleges, more men are faculty members than women, particularly in math, science, and engineering fields.

The feminization of teaching has a long history in the United States. As early as 1880, 80 percent of elementary school teachers were women (Urban and Wagoner 2004). Schools originally hired women to teach because they could pay them less than men and were thought to be more nurturing and caring. It is debatable whether women make better teachers, but the high number of women teachers and the low level of women administrators shape how education is developed and taught, as well as how it is perceived by boys and girls.

What teachers and society expect of, teach, and demonstrate to children directly affects their opinions of themselves, their abilities, and what they are to hope for in school and in the future. Girls may think they are supposed to be good writers but not good at math, or boys may think they should not be elementary school teachers because teaching is a women's job. It is hard to disentangle whether girls and boys learn differently or whether they are taught to think that boys and girls are different from an early age.

Where Are the Gender Gaps in Schools?

Debates over how and why children learn and perceive themselves in different ways continue, and evidence in schools shows that gaps exist between boys and girls in terms of achievement in the classroom, standardized tests, and completing schooling. These gaps vary. Some favor girls and others favor boys, beginning in elementary school and continuing throughout college and professional school.

Elementary School

Elementary school is the first formal schooling children receive, and it is primarily used to teach basic reading and math skills. In elementary schools, differences between boys and girls emerge. Since the 1950s, girls have consistently received higher grades in all elementary school subjects, even math and science, which are traditionally thought of as male subjects (Alexander and Eckland 1974). Girls receive better ratings by teachers, better grades on report cards, and are less likely to repeat grades. Boys are more likely to repeat grades or drop out of school (American Association of University Women 1998). Girls seem to excel in the early years of education; however, this is not the case when it comes to standardized testing.

On standardized tests, such as proficiency tests, gaps between boys and girls appear. Girls do significantly better on tests of reading and writing; boys do better on tests of science and math (American Association of University Women 1998). These gaps sometimes puzzle researchers who wonder why girls' abilities in the classroom do not translate to tests and why boys' high test achievement does not translate into the classroom.

High School

High school graduation rates suggest that girls are outpacing boys in schools and earning more degrees, but many obstacles stand in girls' ways for future success. Selection of classes becomes a cause of concern in high school. From early on, gaps in tests scores between boys and girls show that boys do better in math. The gap between math and science classes taken in high school is prevalent. Girls have increased their participation in math courses, but boys still take more advanced courses than girls. In science classes, boys are more likely to take all core classes, including biology, chemistry, and physics. Girls are less likely to take physics courses.

Conversely, girls take more English classes than boys, and boys are more likely to be enrolled in remedial English courses. Girls also take more foreign language, fine arts, and social science courses. Over time, girls have been increasingly taking more math and science courses, but they still lag behind boys.

Postsecondary

Historically, more men than women attended and completed college education, but this trend has recently changed. By 1980, men and women enrolled equally in college, and, currently, more than 56 percent of undergraduate students in the United States are women (Freeman 2004). Women enroll and complete bachelor's degree at higher rates than men; however, women's increased enrollment and attainment in college do not mean that equity has been reached. Many inequalities still exist for women in college.

Majors in college are highly sex segregated. Although women make up the majority of college students, certain fields seem regulated to men and women. Men earn a large majority of engineering, physical science, and computer science degrees. Women earn only 20 percent of engineering and 28 percent of computer science degrees. Women earn 41 percent of physical science degrees. The fields of business, mathematics, social sciences, and history have relativity equal numbers of men and women earning degrees. Women dominate the fields of education, completing 77 percent of degrees, and health professions, completing 84 percent of degrees.

Of interest, the fields that are clearly dominated by men, engineering and computer science, have the highest starting salaries of all college degrees; the fields dominated by women, education and health professions, have much lower starting salaries. The starting salaries of men and women after college cause concern for some scholars who believe that majors are a way to segregate men and women financially.

The types of degrees earned by men and women differ, as do the types of colleges and universities they attend. Even though women are more likely to be enrolled in college, the colleges that women enroll in are less likely to be prestigious, selective schools

(Jacobs 1999). This group largely includes prominent engineering schools. Women are more likely than men to enroll in two-year institutions such as community colleges.

Graduate and professional schools, like college majors, are sex segregated as well. Women are more likely to enroll in master's degree programs than men, but within these programs segregation similar to those seen in college occurs. The transition from master's to doctoral programs is less common for women, as they comprise only 45 percent of doctoral students. In professional fields, women's enrollment lags behind men. Roughly 39 percent of dentistry students and 43 percent of medical students are women. Law schools have almost reached parity in gender enrollment, with 47 percent of students being women.

SEXUAL HARASSMENT IN SCHOOLS

A pressing issue facing many students in U.S. schools is sexual harassment. Recognizing and preventing sexual harassment is difficult for educators and students, but the issue needs attention. Often, sexual harassment is considered a problem that afflicts workers only, yet sexual harassment is common at all levels of schooling. Sexual harassment in schools does not exclusively affect girls. A study conducted by the American Association of University Women found that 83 percent of girls and 79 percent of boys in grades 8 to 11 report being sexually harassed at school. Also, 62 percent of women and 61 percent of men in colleges report experiencing sexual harassment.

Peers overwhelmingly conduct sexual harassment in middle schools and high schools. Girls in schools are likely to be harassed for different reasons than boys. The most common types of sexual harassment that occur in schools include having rumors spread about a person, being forced into sexual acts, or enduring verbal attacks about looks or sexuality.

In college, peers mostly perpetrate sexual harassment. Concerns over sexual relationships between students and instructors or professors have prompted many schools to forbid such relationships. These relationships are troublesome because the professor is in a position of power over the student, often a young woman. Professors apparently can take on many roles in order to solicit relationships from young women, from threatening to decrease their grade to acting like a counselor or mentor to the student (Dziech and Weiner 1992).

Sexual harassment in schools is particularly harmful for women. The consequences of such experiences can cause girls emotional distress and is often associated with feelings of anger, fear, or embarrassment. Students who are sexually harassed may find it difficult to pay attention in class and their grades often suffer. In addition, they may skip class or drop out of school.

Although it is not likely to be a debate over whether sexual harassment is wrong, the issue is often overlooked or ignored in the education system. Affecting both boys and girls, sexual harassment should be discussed and addressed.

International Gender Gaps

Gender gaps in educational enrollment and completion of degrees exist in the United States, but what are the patterns of gender gaps in other countries? Similar gaps in standardized testing exist in other countries. In 2003, the Program for International Student Assessment tested 15-year-olds in math, science, and reading in 41 countries. Patterns similar to the United States are present in other countries. On average, boys performed better on tests of mathematics (Organisation for Economic Co-operation and Development [OECD] 2004). In 12 countries, however, the difference between boys' and girls' performance in math was not statistically significant. In all but one country, girls significantly outperformed boys on reading tests. In science tests, more variation occurs. In some countries, girls perform better than boys, but the opposite is true in other countries. On average, there is a minimal difference in science scores between boys and girls. Gender gaps seem to be consistent across countries, which is also true for educational enrollment.

In most industrialized countries, women have higher college enrollments than men. On average, they represent 53 percent of all students enrolled in tertiary education (OECD 2004). In some more conservative and traditional countries, such as Turkey and Germany, women still lag behind men in college enrollment, but in 13 industrialized nations, 55 percent of college students are women. In three countries, more than 60 percent of college students are women.

Gender gaps occur at all levels of schooling and across cultures, but the gaps do not always fall in one direction. Boys and girls have different advantages in schooling, creating a complex puzzle. Trends suggest that women have surpassed men, yet men still hold advantages in the work force. There is no clear answer explaining why girls excel in some areas and boys in others, and the controversies surrounding gender and education continue beyond how girls and boys learn and where they succeed.

Single-Sex Schools

The debates over how boys and girls learn, and why they succeed in different ways, lead some to argue for single-sex schooling in the United States. Those in favor of single-sex schools believe that, by schooling girls and boys separately, teachers can tailor their curricula according to gender. Opponents of single-sex schooling believe that there is no valid reason for segregating schools based on gender.

Single-sex schools have a complex history in the U.S. education system. Founders of public schools wanted to segregate all schools based on sex, but it was expensive and inconvenient to do so; so public schools were integrated. Although many colleges were, and remain, single-sex institutions, an increasing number of elementary and high schools are becoming single-sex, but not without controversy.

It is estimated that 237 schools have single-sex classrooms and 51 public schools are completely single-sex in the United States (National Association for Single Sex Public

WOMEN IN THE FIELD OF SCIENCE

In early 2005, Harvard University's then president, Lawrence Summers, suggested biological differences might be to blame for women's underrepresentation in the fields of science and engineering, pointing to statistical differences in standardized test scores. An immediate uproar over the remarks followed, launching a renewed interest in the controversy over women's performance in math and science. The debate has two contesting viewpoints. One view is that biological differences prevent women from being successful in science and engineering fields. The other view is that institutional forces and socialization prevent women from entering science and engineering fields.

The biological debate, discussed in this chapter, argues that men and women have different brains that have different specializations, which could benefit men in the participation in math, science, and engineering. The alternative argument, however, argues that the male-dominated fields such as math, science, and engineering discriminate against women, which limits their participation and success. In a report produced by the National Academies Press on the position of women in science and engineering (Committee on Maximizing the Potential of Women 2006), researchers found many obstacles that stand in women's way in these fields. First, they recognize that biological differences between the sexes may be present, but women are able to succeed in the sciences and have strong drives and motivations. Many women scientists have been extremely influential and successful in the sciences, such as Marie Curie, a physicist and chemist who was the first person to win two Nobel Prizes in different fields of science in 1903 and 1911. More recently, Linda Buck, a biologist, won the Nobel Prize in 2004 in the field of physiology.

Another obstacle for women in science is that at each educational transition, more and more women drop out of science fields. Women either opt out of or are weeded out of science programs as they progress through their education. Some suggest the presence of a science pipeline that disadvantages women. This pipeline refers to the trajectory that one must take to choose a science career. From elementary school to advanced degrees, women are not heavily placed on this pipeline. Also, within the fields of science and engineering, women face discrimination. Many science career and academic environments traditionally favor men, making women feel uncomfortable or unable to be successful. Finally, most people have implicit biases that suggest women are not good at math, science, or engineering. Often employers will hire a man over a woman for a scientific job, even if they have the same qualifications.

These barriers to women in the field of science support those who argue that society and the U.S. education system disadvantage women who would like to participate in the sciences. The debate over women in science continues as researchers continue to study both brain differences between the sexes and the socializing processes and discriminatory practices that impede women's participation in the sciences.

Education 2006). Many experts, parents, and students argue that students learn better when not distracted by the opposite sex, but others counter that claim by reasoning that the real world is not segregated by sex and therefore single-sex schools do not prepare students for the actual work environment (McCollum 2004).

Those in favor of single-sex schools believe that boys and girls learn differently. Boys enjoy competition and working alone, whereas girls learn through cooperation. Boys and girls interact in the classroom differently, with boys shouting out answers and testing boundaries; girls are more likely to follow rules and thoroughly analyze questions before answering. By placing girls and boys in separate schools, they learn in environments tailored to their sex.

Researchers and educators believe that single-sex schools benefit girls more than they benefit boys, causing girls to develop higher self-esteem than they would in a coeducational school. Girls in single-sex schools are also found to be more likely to be leaders in life and to pursue advanced degrees. In addition, girls in single-sex schools are twice as likely to pursue careers in science compared to girls in coed schools.

Although single-sex schools seem to benefit girls, they have many opponents. Some question the benefits of single-sex schools, for they tend to benefit girls from wealthier backgrounds that could skew their positive effects. Mainly, opponents of single-sex schools believe that coeducational institutions can spark different kinds of learning for every student. The diversity of having both boys and girls is beneficial to the understanding of ideas and viewpoints. They will better prepare students to interact with a more diverse population. Some question whether single-sex schools violate the Fourteenth Amendment to the Constitution, stating that schools must be integrated.

Some believe that single-sex schools are being used as a type of quick fix to problems in the U.S. education system. For example, in the 1990s, California attempted to operate single-sex schools, which seemed to succeed at first. However, over time, male-only schools became dumping grounds for boys with behavioral, educational, and emotional problems, which drove the schools to close. Although this case is extreme, the decision to implement single-sex schools is one that must be thoughtfully considered. In general, the majority of the U.S. public (68 percent) does not believe in single-sex schooling.

Conclusion

Women's position in the education system is likely to keep evolving as women continue to succeed in schools. These changes will be closely monitored by researchers and the public as questions are asked about testing gaps and college completion differences. The controversy over how males and females learn will continue as debate over brain differences and social differences continue. A free and equal education is expected in the United States, but how do we feel when one gender seems to be benefiting more than the other? Is there a middle ground between helping girls, who have traditionally been discriminated against in schools, succeed versus not wanting to diminish the success of boys?

See also **Nature versus Nurture (vol. 4)**

Further Reading

Adler, Patricia A., Steven J. Kless, and Peter Adler, "Socialization to Gender Roles: Popularity among Elementary School Boys and Girls." *Sociology of Education* 65 (1992): 169–187.

Alexander, Karl L., and Bruce E. Eckland, "Sex Differences in the Educational Attainment Process." *American Sociological Review* 39 (1974): 668–682.

American Association of University Women, "Gender Gaps: Where Schools Still Fail Our Children." 1998. http://www.aauw.org/research/girls_education/gg.cfm

Committee on Maximizing the Potential of Women in Academic Science and Engineering, *Beyond Bias and Barriers: Fulfilling the Potential of Women in Academic Science and Engineering.* Washington, DC: National Academies Press, 2006. http://www.nap.edu/catalog/11741.html#toc

Disch, Estelle, *Reconstructing Gender: A Multicultural Anthology.* Boston: McGraw-Hill Higher Education, 2009.

Dziech, B. W., and L. Weiner, *The Lecherous Professor: Sexual Harassment on Campus.* Urbana: University of Illinois Press, 1992.

Freeman, C. E., *Trends in the Educational Equity of Girls and Women: 2004.* Washington, DC: National Center for Education Statistics, 2004.

Gurian, Michael, *Boys and Girls Learn Differently! A Guide for Teachers and Parents.* Hoboken, NJ: Jossey-Bass, 2001.

Jacobs, Jerry A, "Gender and the Stratification of Colleges." *Journal of Higher Education* 70 (1999): 161–187.

McCollum, Sean, "Single-Sex Schools: Solution or Setback?" *Literary Cavalcade* 57, no. 2 (2004): 18–19.

Moir, Anne, and David Jessel, *Brain Sex: The Real Difference between Men and Women.* Quince Cottage, England: Delta Publishing, 1989.

National Association for Single Sex Public Education, http://www.singlesexschools.org

Organisation for Economic Co-operation and Development, "Learning for Tomorrow's World: First Results from PISA 2003." 2004. http://www.oecd.pisa.org

Thorne, Barrie, *Gender Play: Girls and Boys in School.* New Brunswick, NJ: Rutgers University Press, 1993);

Urban, Wayne, and L. Wagoner Jennings Jr., *American Education: A History* (New York: McGraw Hill, 2004).

U.S. Department of Education, "Title IX: 25 Years of Progress." June 1997. http://www.ed.gov/pubs/TitleIX/Index.html

GOVERNMENT ROLE IN SCHOOLING

Kevin R. Kosar

At the beginning of the 20th century, the role of government in schooling was to provide free public schools for children. So it was at the fin de siècle. What, then, changed? In

1900, schools were almost entirely the creatures of local governments. States played little role in their financing and operations, and the federal government was wholly absent. Come 2000, the role of local governments in schooling had ebbed while the role of state governments and the federal government had grown. Expressed as dollars, in 1900, local governments provided more than 80 percent of school funds; state governments contributed the rest. The federal government contributed none. By 2000, localities provided 43 percent of school funds, states 48 percent, and the federal government 9 percent.

These funding figures exhibit the growth of state influence over the schools. To cite just a few examples: State governments set high school graduation requirements, operate student learning testing and assessment programs, and dictate the certification requirements for teachers.

However, these numbers obscure arguably the most profound transformation in the government role in schooling, which is the dramatic rise in the power of the federal government to influence school operations. During the 20th century, the federal government went from having no role whatsoever to playing some part in virtually every aspect of schooling. Policies and actions of the federal government have affected schools' curricula and school policies toward minority (racial, language) and handicapped children, provided school lunches, funded cultural and arts programs and drug and alcohol abuse deterrence programs, and more. Furthermore, the growth of state education agencies and their development into highly professionalized entities was spurred, largely, by the federal government. Increasingly, the roles of state and local governments have been sculpted by actions of the federal government. As will be seen, the growth of the federal government's role in schooling has come through two means: federal court decisions and federal grants-in-aid policies.

The Colonial Era and After

Government's role as the provider of free education developed in fits and starts since the earliest settlement of North America. Though many children were educated by their parents or in private academies, some early localities and colonies did provide schools. In 1642, the Massachusetts Colonial Court decreed that, due to the "great neglect of many parents and masters, in training up their children in learning and labor, and other employments, which may be profitable to the commonwealth," we the court "do hereby order and decree, that in every town, the chosen men appointed to manage the prudential affairs…shall henceforth stand charged with the redress of this evil." The leaders of the towns could be fined and punished if they failed to remedy illiteracy among children, who were thought ignorant of "the principles of religion and the capital laws of this country."

The establishment of public schools was encouraged by the land management policies of the earliest federal governments of America. For example, the Northwest Ordinance of 1785 provided for the sale of Western lands by the federal government. As a condition of sale, it required that "[t]here shall be reserved the lot N. 16, of every township, for the maintenance of public schools within the said township." During the 19th century, the growth of government-sponsored schools accelerated. Many local governments, often nudged by states and zealous educators, established simple schools that would provide rudimentary educational skills training, such as reading and writing. Progress, though, was uneven, particularly in rural and low-income communities, where limited tax bases and the agrarian way of life inhibited the development of modern schools.

Government Provision but Not Compulsion

Private schools have existed since European settlers arrived in North America. While all levels of government have recognized a community interest in the education of children, this has not meant that government has an absolute power to compel student attendance to government-funded or "public" schools. This limited power was stated forcefully by the Supreme Court in *Pierce v. Society of Sisters of the Holy Names of Jesus and Mary* (268 U.S. 510 [1925]), when it struck down an Oregon law that required parents to send their children to a public school. The Court declared,

> We think it entirely plain that the Act of 1922 unreasonably interferes with the liberty of parents and guardians to direct the upbringing and education of children…under their control. As often heretofore pointed out, rights guaranteed by the Constitution may not be abridged by legislation which has no reasonable relation to some purpose within the competency of the state. The fundamental theory of liberty upon which all governments in this Union repose excludes any general power of the state to standardize its children by forcing them to accept instruction from public teachers only. The child is not the mere creature of the state; those who nurture him and direct his destiny have the right, coupled with the high duty, to recognize and prepare him for additional obligations.

Throughout the 20th century, this antagonism between the professed interests of communities in schooling children and the rights of parents over their children has recurred. Frequently, these disputes have been litigated and judges have had to rule on nettlesome issues, such as the right of parents to homeschool their children.

How the Federal Government Assumed a Role in Schooling

In its enumeration of the powers of the federal government, the U.S. Constitution makes no mention of schooling or education. Moreover, the Tenth Amendment of the Constitution declares: "The powers not delegated to the United States [government] by the Constitution, nor prohibited by it to the states, are reserved to the states respectively, or to the people," How, then, was the federal government able to assume a role in schooling? In great part, the vehicle has been grants-in-aid. Put succinctly, a grant-in-aid is an offer of funding by the federal government to states or localities. In exchange for the funds, the recipient of the grant must expend it on the purposes stipulated by the grant and obey the grant's mandates (i.e., "conditions of aid"). Thus, grants-in-aid, have provided the primary means through which the federal government has leapt over the federalism divide, which purported to separate governing responsibilities between the federal and state governments, and assumed a role in schooling.

The Growth of the Federal Role in Schooling, 1917–1958

In a pattern that was to be repeated during the 20th century, the establishment of the first major federal education policy was spurred by a crisis. As the federal government began to draft men to fight in World War I, it found that 25 percent of them were illiterate. President Woodrow Wilson, a PhD and former university president, found this troubling and favored education legislation to remedy this problem. He believed that the modern industrial economy and military needed workers and soldiers who were literate and skilled in industrial trades. Thus, one month before the United States formally entered World War I, President Wilson signed the Smith-Hughes Vocational Act (P.L. 64–347) on February 23, 1917.

The Smith-Hughes Act appropriated money "to be paid to the respective states for the purpose of co-operating with the states in paying the salaries of teachers, supervisors, and directors of agricultural subjects, and teachers of trade, home economics, and industrial subjects, and in the preparation of teachers of agricultural, trade, industrial, and home economics subjects." The act established the surprisingly powerful Federal Board for Vocational Education, which was empowered to set the requisite qualifications for an individual to be hired as a vocational education teacher. The board also could withhold federal funds from schools that violated federal education standards of what constituted appropriate agricultural, home economic, vocational, and industrial educational curricula. The statute mandated that states set up state vocational education boards that would work with the federal board.

Over this breakthrough, however, the federal government's role changed little over the next three decades. During the Great Depression, agencies such as the Public Works Administration (PWA), the Civilian Conservation Corps, and the National Youth Administration provided emergency funding to cash-strapped schools. In 1934, emergency aid reached approximately $2 million to $3 million per month. By 1940, PWA had helped local and state authorities build 12,704 schools with 59,615 classrooms. This brief expansion of the federal role in schooling, though, contracted once the Great Depression passed.

Between 1946 and 1958, the federal role suddenly spurted. On June 4, 1946, the School Lunch Act (P.L. 79–396, 60 Stat. 231) was signed into law by President Harry S. Truman. The law declared it "to be the policy of Congress…to safeguard the health and well-being of the Nation's children and to encourage the consumption of nutritious agricultural commodities and other foods, through grants-in-aid." The school lunch program required schools to provide low-cost or free lunches to children; in exchange, schools receive cash subsidies and food from the Department of Agriculture.

Impact aid (P.L. 81–815; 64 Stat. 967 and P.L. 81–874; 64 Stat. 1100) was enacted into law four years later (September 23, 1950, and September 30, 1950). This policy grew out of a 1940 program to fund infrastructure projects (sewers, recreational facilities, etc.) in areas where the federal government had a large presence (e.g., military installations, federal agencies, etc.). Mobilization for World War II created a huge growth in the size of the federal workforce. Military facilities occupied large swaths of land, which removed them from state and local tax rolls. (States and localities may not tax the federal government.) In time, the presence of these facilities and workers brought forth children who needed schooling. Impact aid was devised to reimburse these federally affected areas. Each year, communities provide the federal government with data on costs (e.g., educational costs) and receive reimbursement based upon a formula.

The launch of the *Sputnik* satellite by the Soviet Union on October 4, 1957, set off a media and political firestorm in the United States. While President Eisenhower downplayed the significance of the event, many inside and outside of Congress whipped up a frenzy. Senator Lyndon B. Johnson made especially fantastic claims. Control of space, he told the press, would make for control of the world, as the Soviets would have the power to control the weather and raise and lower the levels of the oceans. The schools were blamed for this situation. Prominent persons, such as former president Herbert Hoover and Senator Henry Jackson (D-WA), claimed that Soviet schools were producing far more brainpower than U.S. schools. In the name of national defense, many said, more federal education aid was needed. Less than a year later, the National Defense Education Act (NDEA, P.L. 85–864; 72 Stat. 1580) became law on September 2, 1958. Much of the NDEA benefited colleges, showering them with funds for research grants for technical training and advanced studies. Public high schools also benefited. Secondary schools were given funds to identify "able" students who should be encouraged to apply for federal scholarships for collegiate study in foreign languages, mathematics, and science.

Despite this growth in the federal role, many attempts to expand it further failed. Between 1935 and 1950, dozens of bills were introduced into Congress to provide general aid to public schools. Some of the bills would have raised teachers' salaries; others would have provided grants and low-interest loans to districts that needed to build bigger and more modern schools. In a hint of things to come, a number of bills were introduced that would have provided federal monies to create a floor in per-pupil spending. This latter proposal would have helped poor school districts, where property values were low, leaving schools grossly underfunded. All of the proposals to increase and equalize school funding stalled in Congress, blocked by members who saw little sense or propriety in an expansion of the federal role in schooling.

The Federal Government's Promotion of Equity in Schooling, 1954–1975

For much of its existence, the federal government did little to expand access to schooling for special needs and nonwhite children. On occasion, the U.S. Congress provided aid. For example, in 1864, the federal government helped found the Columbian Institution for the Deaf, Dumb, and Blind, which later became Gallaudet University. The federal government also aided in the development of schools for nonwhites. Subsequent to treaties signed with Native American tribes, the federal government funded and operated schools on Indian reservations. The federal government aided blacks by chartering Howard University in 1867 (Chap. CLXII; 39 Stat. 438). At the close of the Civil War, the federal government also forced confederate states to rewrite their constitutions to include provisions to require states to provide schooling for all children. (Previously, many black children and those in isolated rural areas lacked access to schooling.) Between 1954 and 1975, however, the federal government moved to the fore in expanding access to schooling.

The federal government's first major effort at ensuring equity in education came in the form of a Supreme Court decision. The case, *Oliver Brown et al. v. Board of Education of Topeka et al.* (347 U.S. 483), popularly known as *Brown v. Board of Education,* came on May 17, 1954. The Court noted that education was "perhaps the most important function of state and local governments." That said, it denied that states and localities could require children to attend racially segregated schools. Separate schooling was "inherently unequal," said the Court, and violated the Fourteenth Amendment's due process clause. States must, the Court declared, make schooling "available to all on equal terms." The upshot of the *Brown* case was the gradual demolition of states' racially segregated schooling. The *Brown* decision and those federal court decisions that followed it led to the federal policy of busing children to achieve racial desegregation. This policy was largely abandoned after 1980.

In the wake of America's "discovery of poverty" and rising violence in urban areas, the federal government greatly expanded its role in schooling and its funding of schooling through the enactment of the Elementary and Secondary Education Act of 1965 (ESEA, P.L. 89–10; 79 Stat. 27) on April 11, 1965. The act lifted the federal contribution to school funding to over 8 percent of total school funding. The ESEA provided funds for a number of school programs, the largest of which was Title I (also known as Chapter I). This program provided funds for schools to expend on compensatory education programs for nonwhite and poor children. The ESEA also provided funds to help state education agencies professionalize their operations. Over time, ESEA funds and mandates helped build state agencies into formidable educational administration agencies.

The federal government further expanded its role as promoter of equity in schooling with the enactment of the Bilingual Education Act of 1968 (P.L. 90–247; 81 Stat. 783, 816) on January 2, 1968, and the Education for All Handicapped Children Act of 1975 (P.L. 94–142; 89 Stat. 773) on November 29, 1975. Both of these acts established programs to help public schools to better teach underserved children. The former act provided funds for instruction in English and foreign languages. The latter act forbade school systems from excluding children with mental or physical handicaps from schools and provided funds for programs to help school these children.

Finally, the federal government expanded its role further still when it forbade states from denying schooling to the children of illegal immigrants. When the state of Texas enacted a statute to deny children of illegal immigrants the right to attend school, the Supreme Court struck it down. In *Plyler v. Doe* (457 U.S. 202 [1982]), the Court stated that, although these children did not have a fundamental right to schooling, the law did deny the children the equal protection under the law guaranteed by the Fourteenth Amendment to the Constitution because it erected "unreasonable obstacles to advancement on the basis of individual merit."

The Proliferation and Diversification of the Federal Government's Role in Schooling, 1976–1999

Over the next quarter of a century, the federal role in schooling became more diversified. The Office of Education was replaced by the Department of Education on October 17, 1979 (P.L. 96–88; 93 Stat. 668). This upgrading of federal administration solidified the federal government role in a number of areas, including compensatory education, bilingual education, vocational education, and educational research. New grants-in-aid programs proliferated; by the end of the century, the federal government funded school programs in arts education, physical fitness, school technology, antidrug and -alcohol dependency classes, character education courses, and more.

During this period, criticism arose over the efficacy of federal programs, such as Title I of the ESEA. In response, the federal government began creating policies to increase student learning as measured by tests. Congress enacted Goals 2000 (P.L. 103–227; 108 Stat. 125) on March 31, 1994, and amended the ESEA's Title I grants-in-aid program via the Improving America's Schools Act of 1994 (P.L. 103–382; 108 Stat 3518) on October 20, 1994, and the No Child Left Behind (NCLB) Act of 2002 (P.L. 107–110; 115 Stat. 1425) on January 2, 2002. Under the new Title I of NCLB, the conditions of aid required states and localities to experiment with school choice or voucher programs. Funds were provided for the development of privately operated but open-to-all-children charter schools. The new Title I also required local school districts to permit students attending underperforming schools to choose the public school they attended. As a further condition of aid, these policies required states to develop accountability systems consisting of academic standards and tests that would be used to hold schools accountable for student learning. By 2009, school districts and government officials, faced with a flood of "failing schools" under NCLB, were considering adjusting the accountability strictures and moving ahead with a program (Race to the Top) aimed at rewarding schools for demonstrating efforts designed to improve performance.

Conclusion

States and localities provide the vast majority of funds for public schools. It is these two levels of government that have the greatest power to prescribe schools' curricula, set the compensation and standards for the licensure of teachers and administrators, and oversee day-to-day school operations. Nevertheless, as the federal government has assumed a larger and larger role, more and more of what states do occurs within a context set by the federal government. Through court decisions and grants-in-aid programs, the federal government, despite its modest contribution to school funding, has taken a broad and significant role in the public schools.

See also **Charter Schools; Desegregation; Early Childhood Education; No Child Left Behind (NCLB); Nutrition in Schools; School Choice**

Further Reading

Angus, David L., and Jeffrey E. Mirel, *The Failed Promise of the American High School, 1895–1995.* New York: Teachers College Press, 1999.

Fusarelli, Bonnie C., and Bruce S. Cooper, *The Rising State: How State Power Is Transforming Our Nation's Schools.* Albany: State University of New York Press, 2009.

Howell, William G., ed., *Besieged: School Boards and the Future of Education Politics.* Washington, DC: Brookings Institution Press, 2005.

Kosar, Kevin R., *Failing Grades: The Federal Politics of Education Standards.* Boulder, CO: Lynne Rienner, 2005.

Manna, Paul, *School's In: Federalism and the National Education Agenda.* Washington, DC: Georgetown University Press, 2006.

McCluskey, Neal P., *Feds in the Classroom: How Big Government Corrupts, Cripples, and Compromises American Education.* Lanham, MD: Rowman & Littlefield, 2007.

Vinovskis, Maris A., *From a Nation at Risk to No Child Left Behind: National Education Goals and the Creation of Federal Education Policy.* New York: Teachers College Press, 2009.

H

HOMELESSNESS

Robert Hartmann McNamara

All of us are touched by homelessness in one way or another. One of the main reasons this particular social problem remains in the minds of many Americans is its visibility. While always a part of the U.S. social fabric, in the last 30 years Americans have been forced to confront the visibility of this group of people in a substantial way. This visibility has resulted in the public's attempt to conceal or minimize its significance, thereby exacerbating the problem.

Definitional Matters: Who Are the Homeless?

Part of the difficulty in dealing with homelessness has to do with how it is defined. In the 1970s, Mitch Snyder argued that a million Americans were homeless. In the 1980s, he and Mary Ellen Hombs (1982), in their report *Homelessness in America: A Forced March to Nowhere,* estimated the population at between 2 million and 3 million. Interestingly, in the absence of official statistics, advocates for the homeless, policymakers, and a host of others began using this figure. In response, in 1984 the Reagan administration directed the U.S. Department of Housing and Urban Development (HUD) to study the homeless population and to produce its own estimate.

To accomplish this, HUD contacted the most knowledgeable people it could find in each large U.S. city and asked them to estimate the number of homeless people in their metropolitan area. The department then selected a number near the middle of the range for each area. From this, HUD's best estimate of the homeless population was between 250,000 and 350,000 (Jencks 1995).

In response to the dramatic differences between Snyder and Hombs's and HUD's estimations, Snyder publicly admitted that he had no basis for their calculation, except that the number was large enough to warrant national attention on the problem. This playing of the "numbers game" has been, and continues to be, a pervasive problem in addressing the needs of the homeless. In his book, *Rude Awakenings*, White (1992) echoes this point and describes the tendency of service providers to inflate the size of the homeless population in an attempt to secure additional funding and to account for those individuals who are typically ignored in the definition of homelessness. He refers to this process as "lying for justice."

Part of the reason for the various estimates of the size of the population has to do with how the problem is defined and how it is measured. Defining the population is a difficult task at best. In one sense, however, it can be easily identified. For instance, according to the government definition, taken from the Stewart B. McKinney Act, a homeless person is "one who lacks a fixed permanent nighttime residence or whose nighttime residence is a temporary shelter, welfare hotel, or any public or private place not designed as sleeping accommodations for human beings" (PL 100–77). This definition, like others used by the government, excludes an important segment of the population. In the aforementioned HUD report, for example, a person is defined as homeless where, in addition to other living arrangements, "temporary vouchers are provided by public or private agencies" (p. 24). This definition excluded families in welfare hotels, presumably because their residence was long-term and no temporary vouchers were provided.

These different definitions are examples of the generally held usage of the term that correspond to three different political agendas. The first definition, used by Snyder and Hombs, is the most common one, but it does encounter some controversy when advocates employ it to contend that large numbers of homeless people remain on the street. The second definition, used in the HUD study, refers to the population served and is a favorite of public officials who would like to minimize the size of the population and demonstrate the adequacy of programs targeting the homeless. A third definition includes the population at risk—those who, though not currently on the street, are doubled up or might otherwise lose their housing. Typically found in estimates and projections of housing needs, it produces the largest number of homeless.

Essentially, there are only two options to choose from to obtain a census of the population. The first is what is sometimes known as a *point in time* study. This is a one-time survey of shelters, institutions, and the areas on the street where the homeless are likely to be found. This method is considered the most accurate of the two, but it is also the most expensive. It is also likely to identify the most visible portion of the population. The second method is to ask individuals whether they have ever spent any time in which they were homeless. This tends to depart from the government's definition as well as studies like HUD's, which ask about homelessness on any given night rather than at any other time.

While the HUD estimate and those made by advocates are extreme, more recently, the National Survey of Homeless Assistance Providers and Clients, conducted by the Urban Institute, found that between 446,000 and 842,000 people in the United States are homeless. This estimate is based on counts of homeless people from a sample of homeless service providers from across the country, To create an annual estimate of homelessness, Urban Institute researchers estimated that between 2.3 million and 3.5 million people per year experience homelessness (Cunningham and Henry 2008).

Profile of the Homeless

While the debate continues about the size of the homeless population as well as the most effective method of collecting data, there is much greater consensus on the characteristics of the homeless. And while no study has been accepted as the seminal work on the subject, especially since regional differences have been discovered, there are some fairly consistent themes that run through this population.

According to a 2010 report by the National Coalition for the Homeless, in general, the research suggests that the homeless population is younger than its historical counterparts and consists of about 50 percent minorities. According to the National Alliance to End Homelessness (2010), nearly 600,000 families and 1.3 million children experience homelessness in the United States. The research suggests that families make up anywhere between 30 percent and 55 percent of the homeless population, depending on whether it is in rural or urban areas (National Coalition for the Homeless 2009).

A report by the National Law Center on Homelessness and Poverty shows that children under the age of 18 represent about 39 percent of the homeless population, many of whom are under the age of 5. Additionally, about 25 percent of the homeless were between the ages of 25 and 34. The elderly, people aged 55 to 64, make up about 6 percent of the homeless population (Foscarinis 2008).

Most studies show that single homeless adults are more likely to be men than women, but only slightly. Single men make up slightly more than 51 percent of the total homeless population, while single women comprised about 17 percent. Part of the explanation for this trend has to do with changes in the economy. As the United States transitioned from an industrial to a service economy, many manufacturing jobs were moved to other countries. This meant that many members of the urban poor, who had few technical skills to begin with, were excluded from those job opportunities and eventually forced into shelters and onto the streets (Blau 1993).

About half (49 percent) of the homeless population are people of color. This makes sense if one recognizes that minorities have long represented a disproportionate percentage of people in poverty. Whites represent 35 percent, Hispanics about

13 percent, and Native Americans about 2 percent of the homeless population. The ethnic distribution of the homeless is affected by geography—homeless people in urban areas are much more likely to be African American, while the rural homeless consist primarily of whites, Native Americans, and Hispanics (National Coalition for the Homeless 2009).

Other variables, such as substance abuse and mental illness—two of the most common characteristics of the stereotypical homeless person—are also factors to consider in profiling this population. However, it must be noted that there are many problems with defining mental illness as well as which types of disorders are included in any given study. Additionally, the subjective nature of assessing mental illness must also be taken into account. A clinical diagnosis is not always the definitive way of identifying a disorder. Additionally, few studies have compared the incidence of mental illness among the general population. Thus, it is difficult to determine how extensive severe mental disorders are among the homeless compared to disorders for the rest of the population. According to the National Coalition for the Homeless (2009), approximately 16 percent of the single adult homeless population suffers from some form of severe and persistent mental illness.

Substance abuse is also a common feature of homelessness. In the 1980s, research on addictions found that the homeless had consistently high rates of addictive disorders. More recently, these rates have been called into question. According to recent accounts, the number is closer to 30–33 percent (National Coalition for the Homeless 2009).

Another common misperception of the homeless is that they are primarily veterans of military service (National Coalition for the Homeless 2009). Several studies indicate that veterans make up 33–40 percent of the homeless male population. This compares with about 34 percent of the general adult male population. However, Burton and James (2008) found that about 11 percent of the homeless population were veterans. The reasons for this disparity are still under scrutiny, but many questions remain about the impact of military service on homelessness.

Also in contrast to conventional wisdom, a significant portion of the homeless are employed. Most of the research shows that almost a quarter of the homeless population were engaged in some type of work, typically casual labor (National Coalition for the Homeless 2009).

The length of time one stays in a shelter can be misinterpreted to imply that homelessness is a short-term problem. For example, the data reveal that the range of time a person remains homeless is between 34 days and 11 months. The National Alliance to End Homelessness (2010) and the Urban Institute estimate that the average homeless experience lasted 7 months. While chronic homelessness represents a different set of challenges for policymakers and service providers than its temporary counterpart, the fact that so many people repeat their short-term episodes of homelessness warrants a long-term set of strategies.

Causes of Homelessness

In addition to identifying the characteristics of the homeless, much of the research has focused on the causes that resulted in the increase in the size and composition of the homeless population. Most of the research on homelessness identifies three main causal factors: a shift in the economy; the lack of affordable housing, such as the destruction of single-room occupancy (SRO) units through urban renewal efforts; and the deinstitutionalization of the mentally ill. There remains serious debate over which of these is most significant, but there is substantial evidence to suggest they all play a part in the problem.

First, Blau (1993) attempts to explain the causes of homelessness from an economic perspective in his book *The Visible Poor.* This analysis incorporates not only a relevant discussion of the shift to a service-oriented economy, which resulted in the decline of well-paying job opportunities for the poor, but also how this current trend has been occurring since the post–World War II era. Blau argues that, while moving production operations overseas helps the corporation's bottom line, it has a devastating impact on its workers. For many employees whose plants closed, it is a short step to living in a shelter or living on the streets. Exacerbating all of this was the social deregulation that took place in the 1980s during the Reagan administration, whereby many of the programs designed to help the poor—such as food stamps, Aid to Families with Dependent Children, the Comprehensive Employment and Training Act, and others—were eliminated, scaled back, or witnessed drastic changes in criteria. This affected the eligibility of hundreds of thousands of people.

Second, the lack of affordable housing influences homelessness. In his analysis of the problem in Chicago, Rossi (1989) concluded that the decline in SROs and other forms of inexpensive housing forced many poor Chicago residents to either spend a very large proportion of their income on housing, which perpetuates their impoverished status, or to resort to the shelters or the street. He goes on to argue that a major factor in explaining the decline of SRO housing units is the shrinkage of the casual labor market in many urban economies in the 1960s and 1970s.

Another significant event used to explain the rise of homelessness has been the deinstitutionalization of the mentally ill. Recall that about a third of today's homeless suffer from some type of diagnosed mental disorder. Deinstitutionalization of the mentally ill is a causal factor in the growth of the homeless population. Jencks argues that deinstitutionalization was not a single policy but a series of them, all of which tried to reduce the number of hospitalized patients and accomplished this by moving patients to different places. He argues that the policies implemented before 1975 worked; the ones after that did not (Jencks 1995).

Prior to 1975, a number of programs and events took place that led to the release of many formerly institutionalized patients. These changes imply a recognition on the part of the psychiatric community that hospitalization was a counterproductive measure.

This resulted in the release of any patient who could be cared for as an outpatient, and, if a patient was hospitalized, he or she was to be released as soon as possible. The second event was the development of drugs to treat schizophrenia, specifically thorazine. These drugs made it much easier to treat patients outside the institution (Jencks 1995).

The third event was the creation of several federally funded programs that gave patients the economic resources to survive as outpatients, specifically Medicaid and Supplemental Security Income (SSI). Medicaid paid for outpatient treatment but not hospitalization, and SSI was available for those who were incapable of holding a job because of a physical or mental disability. These programs led to the release of many people suffering from mental disorders but provided them with a means by which to continue their treatment and to maintain their economic viability without being hospitalized.

After 1975, many politicians pressured state hospitals to reduce their budgets due to an overall concern about rising taxes. As a result, most hospitals closed their psychiatric wards and discharged the remaining chronic patients. States compounded the problem by cutting their benefits to the mentally ill. The result of these decisions meant that more people suffering from serious emotional disorders were released into communities around the country (Jencks 1995).

In recent times, despite the considerable effort that has gone into eliminating homelessness as well as trying to address its chronic nature and intractable structural obstacles, the public's perception of the problem has changed. What was once sympathy for the plight of the homeless has, over time, transformed itself into a form of apathy. Evidence of this frustration comes in the form of city ordinances and efforts to make many of the behaviors of homeless people illegal. This general trend is often referred to as the *criminalization of homelessness*. Examples include aggressive enforcement of panhandling, loitering, and public intoxication statutes. Other legislation, as noted in Orlando, Florida, and Las Vegas, Nevada, in 2007, focused on prohibiting volunteers from feeding the homeless (Komp 2007). In all, the criminalization effort attempts to remove the homeless from the streets of U.S. cities by incarcerating or forcing the homeless to another community. However, such efforts are limited in their effectiveness and only serve as a stop-gap measure in dealing with the problem.

The Future of Homelessness in America

So what does the future hold for the homeless in America? In order to end homelessness, the severe lack of affordable housing to low-income people must be addressed and remedied. According to a 2007 poll, 90 percent of New York City residents believe that everyone has a basic right to shelter; 72 percent believe that, as long as homelessness persists, the United States is not living up to its values; 85 percent approve of their tax dollars being spent on housing for homeless people; and 62 percent believe the city should increase spending on programs for homeless people (Arumi, Yarrow, Ott, and Rochkind 2009). A 2007 poll found that 9 in 10 Americans believe that providing affordable housing in their communities is important, and fewer than half believe that current national housing policy is on the right track (National Association of Realtors 2007).

The past three decades have witnessed a striking shift in rhetoric and stated policy. While the Reagan administration publicly adopted the view that homelessness is a life-style choice and not a national policy concern, the Bush administration not only stated that homelessness *is* an important issue, it also made a commitment to ending chronic homelessness in the next decade (Cunningham, McDonald, and Suchar, 2008). Some policy shifts have accompanied the changed rhetoric, most notably during the 1990s, as funding for homelessness, housing, and other social programs increased. In addition, homelessness programs shifted away from crisis response toward longer-term aid. Currently, however, despite their stated commitment, recent economic changes have slowed efforts to address the housing and homelessness problem. While the problems experienced by the homeless remain or intensify, the ability of federal, state, and local governments to assist this segment of the population are hindered not only by the current economic recession but by changing public perception as well.

See also **Mental Health; Poverty and Public Assistance; Consumer Credit and Household Debt (vol. 1); Poverty and Race (vol. 1); Unemployment (vol. 1)**

Further Reading

Arumi, A. M., A. L. Yarrow, A. Ott, and J. Rochkind, *Compassion, Concern and Conflicted Feelings: New Yorkers on Homelessness and Housing.* Washington DC: Public Agenda, 2009. http://publicagenda.org/reports/compassion-concern-and-conflicted-feelings

Blau, J., *The Visible Poor.* New York: Oxford University Press, 1993.

Burton, C., and K. James,. "Homelessness and Veterans: Untangling the Connection." In *Homelessness in America,* Vol. 1, ed. R. H. McNamara. Westport, CT: Greenwood Press, 2008.

Cunningham, M. K., *A National Commitment to Ending Homelessness among Veterans.* Washington, DC: Urban Institute, 2009. http://www.urban.org/url.cfm/?ID=901263

Cunningham, M. K., and M. Henry, "Measuring Progress and Tracking Trends in Homelessness." In *Homelessness in America,* Vol. 1, ed. R. H. McNamara. Westport, CT: Greenwood Press, 2008.

Cunningham, M. K., S. McDonald, and N. Suchar, "Promising Strategies To End Homelessness." In *Homelessness in America,* Vol. 3, ed. R. H. McNamara. Westport, CT: Greenwood Press, 2008.

Foscarinis, M. "The Evolution of Homelessness: Trends and Future Directions." In *Homelessness in America,* Vol. 3, ed. R. H. McNamara. Westport, CT: Greenwood Press, 2008.

Hombs, Mary Ellen and Mitch Snyder, *Homelessness in America: A Forced March to Nowhere.* Washington, DC: Community for Creative Non-Violence, 1982.

Jencks, C., *The Homeless.* Cambridge, MA: Harvard University Press, 1995.

Komp, C., "Bans on Feeding Homeless Spread, Face Challenges." *New Standard* (2007). http://newstandardnews.net/content/index.cfm/items/3503

National Alliance to End Homelessness, *Fact Sheet: Family Homelessness.* 2010. http://www.endhomelessness.org/content/article/detail/1525

National Association of Realtors, *Field Guide to Affordable Housing.* 2007. http://www.realtor.org/library/library/fg327

National Coalition for the Homeless, "Factsheets." 2009. http://www.national homeless.org/fact sheets/index.html

Rossi, P., *Down and Out in America.* Chicago: University of Chicago Press, 1989.

Stewart B. McKinney Act (PL 100–77).

White, R. W., *Rude Awakenings: What the Homeless Crisis Tells Us.* San Francisco: Ice Press, 1992.

I

IMMIGRATION REFORM

Philip Martin

Public opinion polls find widespread dissatisfaction with the "broken" U.S. immigration system, which admits an average of 1 million immigrants a year and several hundred thousand unauthorized foreigners. Congress has debated comprehensive immigration reform for a decade but has been unable to enact the three-pronged package endorsed by President Barack Obama: tougher enforcement against unauthorized migration, legalization for most unauthorized foreigners, and new and expanded guest worker programs.

The Context for Immigration Reform

The United States had 38 million foreign-born residents in 2008, making up 12.5 percent of the 304 million U.S. residents (Pew Research Center 2010). Between 2000 and 2008, the number of foreign-born U.S. residents rose by 7 million, from 31 million to 38 million, while the number of U.S.-born residents rose by 16 million, from 250 million to 266 million. Immigration directly contributed one-third to U.S. population growth and, with the U.S.-born children and grandchildren of immigrants, over half of U.S. population growth.

The United States has the most foreign-born residents of any country, three times more than number-two Russia, and more unauthorized residents than any other country. About 10 percent of the residents of industrial countries were born outside the country.

The United States, with 13 percent foreign-born residents, has a higher share of immigrants among residents than most European countries but a lower share of foreign-born residents than Australia and Canada.

Immigration affects the size, distribution, and composition of the U.S. population. As U.S. fertility fell from a peak of 3.7 children per woman in the late 1950s to the replacement level of 2.1 today, the contribution of immigration to U.S. population growth increased. Between 1990 and 2010, the number of foreign-born U.S. residents almost doubled from 20 million to 40 million, while the U.S. population rose from almost 250 million to 310 million.

Mexico is the leading country of origin of foreign-born U.S. residents—30 percent, or 11.5 million, were born in Mexico, followed by 9 million born in Asia and 6 million born in Central America and the Caribbean. After Mexico, the leading countries of origins were the Philippines, 1.7 million; India, 1.6 million; China, 1.3 million; Vietnam, 1.2 million; El Salvador, 1.1 million; and Korea and Cuba, a million each. These eight countries, each accounting for over a million foreign-born U.S. residents, were 53 percent of the total.

In recent decades, immigrants have been mostly Asian and Hispanic; their arrival changed the composition of the U.S. population. In 1970, about 83 percent of U.S. residents were non-Hispanic whites and 6 percent were Hispanic or Asian. Today, two-thirds of U.S. residents are non-Hispanic white and 20 percent are Hispanic or Asian. If current trends continue, by 2050, the non-Hispanic white share of U.S. residents will decline to 52 percent, while the share of Hispanics and Asians will rise to a third.

The effects of immigration on the U.S. economy and society are hotly debated. Economic theory predicts that adding foreign workers to the labor force should increase economic output and lower wages, or lower the rate of increase in wages. This theory was supported by a National Research Council (NRC) study that estimated immigration raised U.S. gross domestic product (GDP, the value of all goods and services produced), one-tenth of 1 percent in 1996, increasing the then $8 trillion GDP by up to $8 billion (Smith and Edmonston 1997). Average U.S. wages, according to the NRC, were depressed 3 percent because of immigration.

However, comparisons of cities with more and fewer immigrants have not yielded evidence of wage depression linked to immigration. In 1980, over 125,000 Cubans left for the United States via the port of Mariel. Many settled in Miami, increasing Miami's labor force by 8 percent, but the unemployment rate of African Americans in Miami in 1981 was lower than in cities such as Atlanta that did not receive Cuban immigrants. One reason may be that U.S.-born workers who competed with Marielitos moved away from Miami or did not move to Miami.

Immigrants do more than work—they also pay taxes and consume tax-supported services. Almost half of the 12 million U.S. workers without a high school diploma are immigrants, and most have low earnings. Most taxes paid by low earners flow to the federal government as Social Security and Medicare taxes, but the tax-supported services most used by immigrants are education and other services provided by state and local governments. For this reason, some state and local governments call immigration an unfunded federal mandate and have sued the federal government for the cost of providing services to immigrants.

Many immigrants become naturalized U.S. citizens and vote; some hold political office, including California Governor Arnold Schwarzenegger. The U.S. government encourages legal immigrants who are at least 18, have been in the United States at least five years, and who pass a test of English and civics, to become naturalized citizens. There are often celebratory naturalization ceremonies on July 4 and other national holidays.

Naturalization rates vary by country of origin. Immigrants from countries to which they do not expect to return are far more likely to naturalize than immigrants from countries to which they expect to return. Thus, naturalization rates are far higher for Cubans and Vietnamese than for Canadians and Mexicans.

More Mexicans and Latin Americans are naturalizing, in part because their governments have changed their policies from discouraging to encouraging their citizens abroad to become dual nationals. However, rising numbers of naturalized immigrants have not yet translated into decisive political clout. There are more Latinos than African Americans in the United States, but, during the 2008 elections, African Americans cast almost twice as many votes as Latinos, reflecting the fact that many Latinos are not U.S. citizens and others did not register and vote. Latinos are sometimes called the sleeping giant in the U.S. electorate that could tilt the political balance toward Democrats as their share of the vote increases—two-thirds of the Latinos who voted in 2008 elections supported President Obama.

Immigration Reform: 1986–2008

The United States has had three major immigration policies throughout its history: no limits for the first 100 years, qualitative restrictions such as "no Chinese" between the 1880s and 1920s, and both qualitative and quantitative restrictions since the 1920s. During the half-century of low immigration, between the 1920s and the 1970s, U.S. immigration law changed only about once a generation.

Beginning in the 1980s, Congress changed immigration laws more frequently. The Immigration Reform and Control Act (IRCA) of 1986 embodied a compromise to reduce illegal migration. For the first time, the federal government received authority to fine U.S. employers who knowingly hired unauthorized workers while legalizing most of the estimated 3 to 5 million unauthorized foreigners in the United States. IRCA's sanctions failed to reduce illegal migration, largely because unauthorized workers used false documents to get jobs, and legalization was tarnished by widespread fraud that allowed over a million rural Mexican men to become U.S. immigrants because they asserted they had done qualifying U.S. farm work.

The September 11, 2001, terrorist attacks were committed by foreigners who had entered the U.S. legally; the attacks highlighted the failure of the U.S. government to track the activities of foreigners in the United States. In response to the attacks, the U.S. government established a tracking system for foreign students, gained the power to detain foreigners deemed to be threats to U.S. national security, and consolidated most immigration-related agencies in the new Department of Homeland Security.

Legal and illegal immigration continued after the September 11 attacks; U.S. leaders emphasized the distinction between desired immigrants and undesired terrorists. As the number of unauthorized foreigners rose from 8 million in 2000 to 12 million in 2007, Congress debated measures to deal with illegal migration, in part because employers complained of labor shortages as the unemployment rate dipped below 5 percent.

The congressional debate mirrored divisions among Americans. The House in 2005 approved an enforcement-only bill that would have added more fences and agents on the Mexico–U.S. border and made "illegal presence" in the United States a felony, which would likely complicate legalization. One result was demonstrations in cities throughout the nation that culminated in a "day without immigrants" on May 1, 2006.

The Senate took a different approach, approving the Comprehensive Immigration Reform Act (CIRA) in 2006 on a 62–36 vote in May 2006 to beef up border and interior enforcement and to provide an "earned path" to legalization—unauthorized foreigners would have to pay fees and pass an English test to become legal immigrants. CIRA 2006 would have created new guest worker programs to satisfy employers complaining of labor shortages.

There was strong resistance to an amnesty for unauthorized foreigners, prompting the Senate to consider a tougher bill in 2007. However, despite strong support from President George W. Bush and a bipartisan group of senators, the Comprehensive Immigration Reform Act of 2007 (S1348) stalled when proponents were unable to obtain the 60 votes needed to prevent a filibuster.

CIRA 2007's so-called grand bargain provided a path to legal status for the unauthorized in the United States, favored by most Democrats, and shifted future legal immigration toward foreigners with skills under a point system, favored by most Republicans ("Senate: Immigration Reform Stalls" 2007).

CIRA 2007 differed from CIRA 2006 in several important ways. First, CIRA 2007 included triggers, meaning that more border patrol agents would have to be hired, more border fencing built, and the mandatory new employee verification system working before legalization and new guest worker programs could begin. Second, CIRA 2007 required "touchbacks" for legalizing foreigners, meaning that unauthorized foreigners would have had to leave the United States, apply for immigrant visas abroad, and return to the United States legally. Third, CIRA 2007 would have changed the legal immigration system by admitting a third of U.S. immigrants on the basis of points earned for U.S. employment experience, English, education and other factors expected to increase the likelihood that a foreigner would be economically successful in the United States ("Senate: Immigration Reform Stalls" 2007).

CIRA 2007 failed because advocates toward the extremes of the no borders–no immigrants spectrum were more comfortable with the status quo than with a complex compromise whose impacts were unclear. The two key obstacles to CIRA 2007 were opposition to amnesty and fears that admitting guest workers would depress the wages of U.S. workers. Some analysts noted that the status quo persists, because it provides workers for many low-wage industries with relatively little risk of enforcement for employers or workers.

Both major presidential candidates in 2008 supported the comprehensive immigration reforms considered by the Senate in 2006 and 2007, but there was a difference in emphasis. John McCain called for border security before legalization, while Barack Obama stressed the need to enforce labor and immigration laws in the workplace to discourage employers from hiring unauthorized workers ("Senate: Immigration Reform Stalls" 2007).

The first priority of the Obama administration in 2009 was stimulating the economy, culminating in the $787 billion American Recovery and Reinvestment Act of 2009. Arizona Governor Janet Napolitano became Department of Homeland Security (DHS) secretary, and promised a different approach to enforcing U.S. immigration laws, including ending raids of factories and other workplaces to apprehend unauthorized foreigners. DHS also ended efforts begun by the Bush administration to have the Social Security Administration (SSA) include immigration-enforcement notices in the no-match letters the SSA sends to U.S. employers with 10 or more employees who pay Social Security taxes when employer-supplied information does not match SSA records.

Instead of surrounding factories and checking the IDs of workers, DHS's Immigration and Customs Enforcement (ICE) agency that enforces immigration laws inside the United States began to audit the I-9 forms completed by newly hired workers and their employers. ICE said that I-9 audits "illustrate ICE's increased focus on holding employers accountable for their hiring practices and efforts to ensure a legal workforce." ICE agents scrutinize the forms and inform employers of which workers appear to be unauthorized. Employers in turn inform these employees, asking them to clear up discrepancies in their records or face termination—most employees quit.

One of the employers whose I-9 forms were audited, American Apparel in Los Angeles, announced in 2009 that 1,800 workers, a quarter of its employees, would be fired because they could not prove they were legally authorized to work in the United States. American Apparel makes T-shirts and miniskirts in a pink seven-story sewing plant in the center of Los Angeles, and CEO Dov Charney has campaigned to "legalize L.A." by urging Congress to approve a comprehensive immigration reform.

Immigration Reform: 2010

Arizona in April 2010 enacted a law making it a state crime for unauthorized foreigners to be present, prompting Senate Democrats to announce a framework for a comprehensive immigration reform bill before demonstrations in support of legalization around the nation on May 1, 2010. The Democrats' framework was more enforcement oriented than the bill approved by the Senate in 2006, but Republicans predicted it would be difficult to enact immigration reform in 2010. President Obama seemed to agree when he said: "I want to begin work this year" on immigration reform.

Arizona, where almost half of the million foreign-born residents are believed to be unauthorized, enacted the Support Our Law Enforcement and Safe Neighborhoods Act (SB 1070) on April 23, 2010. Federal law requires foreigners to carry proof of their legal status, and SB 1070 requires foreigners to show IDs to state and local police officers who encounter them for other reasons but suspect they may be illegally in the United States—violators can be fined $2,500 or jailed up to six months. Arizona became the main point of passage to the United States for unauthorized migrants from Mexico about a decade ago, when unauthorized entry attempts shifted from California and Texas to the Arizona desert.

The Arizona law was criticized by President Obama, who said: "If we continue to fail to act at a federal level, we will continue to see misguided efforts opening up around the country." However, State Senator Russell Pearce (R-Mesa), author of SB 1070, expects the law to result in "attrition through enforcement"—that is, to reduce the number of unauthorized foreigners in Arizona. He said, "When you make life difficult [for the unauthorized], most will leave on their own." U.S. Senator John McCain (R-AZ), the Republican candidate for president in 2008, said: "I think [SB 1070] is a good tool" for Arizona because the federal government has not reduced illegal migration.

Critics, who predicted widespread racial profiling and mistaken arrests if the law goes into effect as scheduled on July 29, 2010, sued to block the implementation of SB 1070. The legal issue is likely to turn on whether Arizona police are engaged in lawful "concurrent enforcement" of immigration laws with federal authorities or in unlawful racial profiling. Since the 1940s, federal law has required immigrants to carry papers showing they are legally in the United States. A 2002 Department of Justice (DOJ) memo reversed a 1996 DOJ memo to conclude that state police officers have "inherent power" to arrest unauthorized foreigners for violating federal law.

The National Council of La Raza led a campaign of unions and church groups that urged governments, tourists, and businesses to boycott Arizona and urged major league baseball to move the 2011 All-Star Game scheduled for Phoenix if SB 1070 is not repealed. About 30 percent of major league baseball players are Hispanic, and half of the 30 major league teams train in Arizona.

Most Americans support the Arizona law. A Pew Research Center poll in May 2010 found 59 percent support for the Arizona law; only 25 percent of respondents supported President Obama's handling of immigration. Over 70 percent of Pew's respondents supported requiring people to present documents showing they are legally in the United States to police if asked, and two-thirds supported allowing police to detain anyone encountered who cannot produce such documents.

The Pew and similar polls suggest wide gaps between elites who favor more immigration and legalization and masses who oppose amnesty and immigration. Former president Bill Clinton on April 28, 2010, said: "I don't think there's any alternative but for us to increase immigration" to help the economy grow and to fix the long-term finances of Medicare and Social Security.

Senate Democrats released a 26-page outline of a comprehensive immigration reform bill on April 29, 2010, the Real Enforcement with Practical Answers for Immigration Reform (REPAIR). The Democrats' REPAIR proposal emphasized enforcement to discourage illegal migration in an effort to win Republican support, but the framework will not be put into legislative language until there are Republican supporters.

Under REPAIR, border enforcement benchmarks would have to be met before legalization can begin; a commission would be created to evaluate border security and make recommendations to Congress within 12 months. REAPIR calls for more border patrol agents and an entry-exit system to ensure that foreign visitors depart as required.

REPAIR would require all U.S. employers to check new hires within six years via an improved E-Verify system, the Biometric Enrollment, Locally-Stored Information, and Electronic Verification of Employment (BELIEVE). BELIEVE, to be funded by fees, would be phased in beginning with industries employing large numbers of unauthorized foreigners and require U.S. employers to use scanners to check the validity of new Social Security cards with biometric markers such as fingerprints presented by workers. Civil money penalties for knowingly hiring unauthorized workers would triple.

REPAIR offers a relatively simple path to legal status for an estimated 11 million illegal migrants. Unauthorized foreigners in the United States by the date of enactment would register and pay fees to obtain a new lawful prospective immigrant status that would allow them to live and work legally in the country. After eight years, they could become immigrants by passing English and civics tests and paying more fees. The proposal promises to clear the backlog in family-based immigration within eight years, in part by lifting caps on immediate relatives of legal immigrants (immediate relatives of U.S. citizens can immigrate without delay, but there are queues for immediate relatives of immigrants).

REPAIR would change the immigrant selection system. Foreigners who earn masters and PhD degrees from U.S. universities in science and engineering and have U.S. job offers could obtain immigrant visas immediately. New antifraud provisions would apply to employers seeking H-1B and L-1 visas for foreign workers with at least bachelor's degrees, including a requirement that all employers (not just H-1B dependent employers as currently) try to recruit U.S. workers before hiring H-1Bs and not lay off U.S. workers to make room for H-1B foreigners.

For low-skilled workers, REPAIR includes the Agricultural Jobs, Opportunity, Benefits and Security Act (AgJOBS) bill, which would legalize up to 1.35 million unauthorized farm workers (plus their family members) and make employer-friendly changes in the H-2A program. The H-2B program, which admits up to 66,000 foreigners a year to fill seasonal nonfarm jobs, would add protections for U.S. workers while exempting returning H-2B workers from the 66,000 cap if the U.S. unemployment rate is below 8 percent.

A new three-year H-2C provisional visa would admit guest workers to fill year-round jobs; H-2C visa holders could change employers after one year of U.S. work. H-2C visas could be renewed once, allowing six years of U.S. work, and H-2C visa holders could become immigrants by satisfying integration requirements. The number of H-2C visas is to be adjusted according to unemployment and other indicators, but employers could obtain an H-2C visa for a foreign worker even if the cap has been reached if they agreed to pay higher-than-usual wages and additional fees.

A new Commission on Employment-Based Immigration (CEBI) would study "America's employment-based immigration system to recommend policies that promote economic growth and competitiveness while minimizing job displacement, wage depression and unauthorized employment." The CEBI would issue an annual report with recommendations and could declare immigration emergencies when it concludes there are too many or too few foreign workers.

President Obama called the Senate Democrats' REPAIR proposal "an important step" to fix "our broken immigration system." Failure to enact immigration reform, Obama said, would "leave the door open to a patchwork of actions at the state and local level that are inconsistent and, as we have seen recently, often misguided."

Conclusion

The United States is a nation of immigrants that first welcomed virtually all newcomers, later excluded certain types of immigrants, and, since the 1920s, has limited the number of immigrants with annual quotas. Immigration averaged over 1 million per year in the first decade of the 21st century, plus an additional 500,000 unauthorized foreigners a year settled in the country.

Americans are ambivalent about immigration. On the one hand, most are proud that the United States welcomes foreigners seeking opportunity, including the ancestors of most Americans. On the other hand, Americans fear the economic, social, and cultural consequences of immigration. Congressional debates reflect these differences among Americans.

See also **Immigrant Workers (vol. 1); Immigration and Employment Law Enforcement (vol. 2); Racial, National Origin, and Religion Profiling (vol. 2)**

Further Reading

Archibold, Randal C., "U.S.'s Toughest Immigration Law Is Signed in Arizona." *New York Times* (April 23, 2010).

Borjas, George, *Heaven's Door: Immigration Policy and the American Economy*. Princeton, NJ: Princeton University Press, 1999.

Castles, Stephen, and Mark Miller, *The Age of Migration*. New York: Palgrave Macmillan, 2009.

Cornelius, Wayne A., Takeyuki Tsuda, Philip L. Martin, and James F. Hollifield, eds., *Controlling Immigration: A Global Perspective*. Stanford, CA: Stanford University Press, 2004.

Hsu, Spencer, "Senate Democrats' Plan Highlights Nation's Shift to the Right on Immigration." *Washington Post* (May 2, 2010).

International Organization for Migration, *World Migration Report*. 2010. www.iom.int/jahia/Jahia/policy-research/migration-research/world-migration-report-2010.

Martin, Philip L., and Elizabeth Midgley, *Immigration: Shaping and Reshaping America*. Washington, DC: Population Reference Bureau, 2006.

Martin, Philip, Manolo Abella, and Christiane Kuptsch, *Managing Labor Migration in the Twenty-First Century*. New Haven, CT: Yale University Press, 2006.

Migration News, http://migration.ucdavis.edu/

Pew Research Center, "Public Supports Arizona Immigration Law." May 12, 2010. http://pewresearch.org/pubs/1591/public-support-arizona-immigration-law-poll

"Senate: Immigration Reform Stalls," *Migration News* 14, no. 3 (July 2007). http://ruralwelfare.ucdavis.edu/mn/more.php?id=3294_0_2_0

Smith, James P., and Barry Edmonston, eds., *The New Americans: Economic, Demographic, and Fiscal Effects*. Washington, DC: National Academies Press, 1997.

United Nations Development Program, *Overcoming Barriers: Human Mobility and Development*. Human Development Report 2009. www.undp.org/hdr2009.shtml

INCLUSIVE SCHOOLING

J. Michael Peterson

Inclusive education is a movement that aims to have all students—including children with mild to severe disabilities, students considered gifted and talented, and students with other special needs—educated in general education classes with support and collaboration from specialists. Inclusive education had its beginning in the efforts of parents of children with disabilities, particularly severe disabilities, and professionals who were concerned about the segregated lives for which these children were being prepared in special education classes and schools. The movement has built on language in laws of countries throughout the world that has required, as in the United States, education in the least restrictive environment for students with disabilities. Over time, advocates of inclusive education for students with disabilities have broadened their focus to include goals of achieving broad-based diversity embracing also those from various cultural and ethnic backgrounds, students considered gifted and talented, second language learners, and others. Similarly, advocates of inclusive education have joined with other initiatives to reform and improve schools overall.

The movement toward inclusive education promoted first by advocates of students with disabilities naturally dovetails with other efforts to improve the capacity of schools and educators to meet the needs of children—particularly related to the education of children considered gifted and talented and the critique of tracking in schools. Educators and parents were concerned with limitations in traditional public schooling for children considered gifted and talented. While some have sought separate classes and programs for these students, others have helped to foster new perspectives on curriculum and instruction in public schools. The movement to create differentiated instruction has sought to provide strategies to allow children with different abilities to learn the same content together without separate and segregated classes while providing appropriate supports and challenges to high-functioning children. Having its roots in the needs of children, this approach has been supported by advocates of students with disabilities.

Inclusive Education and Ability Diversity

For many years, some educators have sought to detrack schools. Tracking is a practice in which separate series of classes are designed for children considered at different functioning levels but not labeled as having disabilities—typically low, average, and above average. While used in many schools, particularly in middle and high schools, many researchers have argued that the practice has only small positive effects on the academic and cognitive achievements of high-performing students while often impacting on them negatively socially. For students considered average or below average, the practice is actively harmful, contributing to a watered-down curriculum and drawing out high-functioning students who act as good models and guides for other students.

Inclusive education, along with differentiated instruction and detracking, is controversial. This controversy takes many forms and is embedded in many different educational communities. For example, despite a reasonable amount of research related to the value of heterogeneous, inclusive learning for students who are gifted and talented, many concerned with those students continue to believe and argue for separate, pull-out programs as the only viable option for students who are gifted. Similarly, some in the special education and disability community argue that only separate special education programs can serve students with disabilities well.

From another perspective, the debate about inclusive education deals with the roles of professionals in the educational process. For general education teachers, inclusive education requires that they learn how to effectively teach students at very diverse levels of abilities together who may also have other challenging characteristics. Some argue that this is what teachers must do regardless of whether students who are gifted or have disabilities are present in the classroom. These individuals believe that inclusive education helps improve teaching and learning for all children. Others argue, however, that this is an unreasonable and unlikely expectation for teachers.

Perhaps the professional debate is most intense in the professional groups of many specialists who provide support and services in public schools. These include social workers, speech therapists, occupational therapists, physical therapists, special education teachers, gifted education teachers, sign language interpreters, and many more. Inclusive education dramatically changes the roles of these professionals. Traditionally, such professionals work with children in separate clinical environments, most often a room with equipment and tools used by the specialist. In inclusive education, however, specialists work in collaboration with the general education teacher and provide their services in the content of the general education class. Each of these specialists has a professional organization in which the merits of clinical and integrated services have been highly debated. Within each of these professions, however, there is a strong and enduring movement toward inclusive education.

As the inclusive education movement has developed over the last 20 years, it has been interesting to watch the shift of the movement and the way that this is expressed in language. In the United States, early on some called the concept *supported education,* adapting the language of the field of supported employment, where individuals with disabilities would be trained and supported on a job rather than in a separate training environment. The term *integrated education* was used to describe situations in which students with severe disabilities attend some general education classes (most often nonacademic subjects like music, art, and physical education) while maintaining their base in a separate special education classroom. However, *inclusive education* quickly became the preferred term. During a three-month period in 1990, numerous people began to use this term based on a similar thinking process. They had an image of a group of people with their arms around each other who saw individuals outside the group. "Come join us!" the group would say. This was the concept of being included; thus, the term inclusive education. Over time, many have used the word *inclusive* as an adjective to other key terms, such as *inclusive teaching* and *inclusive schooling.* These latter terms are associated with educators, parents, and researchers who see inclusive education as an integral part of effective school reform.

What is clear about inclusive education is that it challenges deeply held assumptions about the educational process. The traditional model posits that students of different abilities must be placed in different groups—separate classes, separate schools, separate groups within classes. The assumption is that students cannot learn at their own level well if they are in a heterogeneous group—one, for example, in which a highly gifted student and a nonverbal student with a cognitive disabilities are learning U.S. history together. Interestingly, this oft-used example is based on an assumption rather than on any research. In fact, the available research tends to support the idea of an inclusive, heterogeneous approach to education. A recent review of literature failed to find any research support for this practice.

Public education is filled with statements about commitment to diversity. However, the elephant in the living room for schools is the natural distribution of a range of abilities across the human spectrum. We've heard the radio show from Minnesota, where "all kids are above average." That's the myth that all parents would like to believe—that their children are above average. Of course, when children are labeled with disabilities, part of what makes this hard for parents is that such a label is an official pronouncement that dashes the belief that their children are above average. In clear, cold, clinical terms, they are told that their children are below average.

With all the debates and discussion about education, it's hard to find a realistic discussion regarding how schools deal with ability diversity. Talk to any teacher, however, and ask the question: "What is the range of abilities of students in your class?" and he or she will likely tell you that those abilities range over three grade levels; some might even say four or five grade levels. Several research studies have validated these results in numerous school settings. Despite the reality, however, the usual discussion taking place in principles' and superintendents' offices and at school board meetings has to do more with what schools should be doing with special education students than with how to address the matter of the wide range in student abilities in general.

The concept of inclusive education, along with other related educational initiatives and movements, posits a different thesis regarding teaching students with ability differences. This thesis could be summarized as follows:

- Students learn and develop into full human beings when they learn together with students who are diverse in many characteristics, including gender, race, culture, language, and ability or disability.
- Educators have developed many strategies for instruction and teaching that will allow such inclusive teaching to be manageable for teachers and effective for all students, ranging from those with severe and multiple disabilities to students considered gifted and talented.

Research Findings and Applications

So what *does* the research say about the efficacy of inclusive education—that is, students with mild to severe disabilities, typical average students, students who are gifted and talented, racially and culturally diverse students learning together? As always, of course, research in any meaningful question is never finished. However, here are some conclusions that are clear from the present research base:

- Studies that have systematically compared outcomes from inclusive education and separate programs most often show that academic and social gains are higher in inclusive classes. In some studies, the results were mixed. It is notable that no studies showed segregated education to produce greater academic or social outcomes. It is also notable that research to date does not distinguish between the quality of practices in the general education classroom. The only comparison was between inclusive classrooms and separate classes. It would appear likely that *quality* inclusive teaching practices would increase the positive impact of inclusive education even more.
- For students with cognitive disabilities, the more they are included in general education classes, the higher their academic, cognitive, and social functioning.
- Students with mild disabilities make better gains in inclusive than in pull-out programs.
- The quality and outcomes of individualized education plans is improved for students with moderate to severe disabilities.
- There is no evidence that academic progress is impeded, but there is evidence that it is increased in inclusive classes for students without disabilities.
- Instruction may be improved for all students at all levels as teachers learn skills of multilevel and differentiated instruction.
- Friendships and social interactions for students with disabilities expand in school and carry over to after-school contexts.
- Students with mild disabilities are less often accepted and more likely rejected due to behavior than nondisabled students. However, teachers can used numerous strategies for addressing issues of ability diversity that change this impact and create better classroom conditions for all students.
- Students without disabilities view their involvement with peers with disabilities positively. They gain an increased appreciation and understanding of diversity and often improve self-esteem and behaviors.

While research makes it clear that inclusive education is a desirable, effective practice, some argue that educators are neither willing nor able to make inclusive education a reality. Numerous research studies have documented problems that include: (1) poor planning and preparation; (2) inadequate supports for students and teachers; and (3) negative and adversarial attitudes of educators.

Despite the fact that much segregated education exists, the movement toward inclusive education continues to grow—sometimes with major thrusts ahead, sometimes with retrenchment for awhile, and with a growth of quiet efforts on the part of individual schools and teachers. Several comprehensive studies have documented case studies of individual schools moving to implement inclusive education, including O'Hearn Elementary School in Boston, Souhegan High School in New Hampshire, and Purcell Marion High School in Cincinnati. The National Center on Educational Restructuring and Inclusion conducted a national study (1995) of hundreds of schools throughout the United States that were implementing inclusive education. Sixteen states have engaged in statewide initiatives for inclusive education. Other researchers and school change agents report that, when change efforts involve training, administrative leadership and support, in-class assistance, and other special services, the attitudes of teachers are positive. Some teachers view inclusive education as building on their existing positive teaching practices. Initially, teachers are often afraid of including students with severe disabilities. However, as teachers come to know such students and work with them, they come to value the experience and would volunteer to teach such students again. Finally, most teachers agree with the concept of inclusive education but are afraid they do not have the skills to make it work. As they have positive experiences with good administrative support, they become more comfortable and positive.

While some courts have ruled in favor of segregated placements, typically following failed attempts to include a child in a regular class, most have ruled in favor of inclusive education. Courts have upheld the principle of least restrictive environment and have stated that schools must, in good faith, consider inclusive placement of all students, no matter the severity of the disability, and students and teachers must be provided necessary supports and supplementary services. While the courts allow costs, amount of teacher time, and impact on other students to be considered, the standards are so high that denying an inclusive placement based on these issues is rarely supported.

These related concepts—inclusive education, differentiated instruction, and detracking—are being used in an increasing number of school reform models. In some cases, the focus is explicit and clear. In others, it is more implied by the stated values of the approach. The Coalition of Essential Schools, for example, has identified 10 principles of effective schooling. Schools move away from the 50-minute class period in high schools and develop larger blocks of instructional time, in which teachers work as interdisciplinary teams to engage students in substantive learning activities. Students demonstrate learning through substantive portfolios and yearly demonstrations to parents, other students, and the larger community. Accelerated schools stimulate the use of challenging and engaging teaching, typically reserved for gifted students, for all students, particularly those with learning challenges. The goal is to accelerate, not slow down, learning for *all* students through exciting, authentic teaching techniques or powerful learning. Accelerated schools engage teachers, administrators, parents, and the community to work together in teams to develop improved learning strategies for all students.

The Comer School Development Program brings another important perspective. According to James Comer, a psychiatrist, children need a sense of safety, security, and welcome if they are to learn. In his school development program, schools develop teams to facilitate partnerships with parents and communities and an interdisciplinary mental health team consisting of teachers, a psychologist, a social worker, and others to deal with holistic needs of both students and families. In each of these models, inclusive education is not specifically articulated as a component. However, the values and visions upon which each model is based often lead schools to incorporate inclusive education as a component of their school reform efforts when they use these models.

Whole schooling is a school reform framework that incorporates inclusive education as a central component of effective schooling for all children. The model posits that the purpose of public schools is to create citizens for democracy and the achievement of personal best learning for all students. The model is based on eight principles:

1. Create learning spaces for all.
2. Empower citizens for democracy.
3. Include all in learning together.
4. Build a caring community.
5. Support.
6. Partner with families and the community.
7. Teach all using authentic, multilevel instruction.
8. Assess students to promote learning.

Throughout the world in recent decades, and very recently in the United States, standards-based reform has been initiated with a goal to improve outcomes for students in public schools. The No Child Left Behind Act (NCLB), passed in 2002, initially aimed to have 100 percent of students pass standardized tests showing their proficiency in math and reading by the year 2014. (These goals later were reconsidered under the Obama administration.) In the United States, standards-based reform has been touted as a way of improving achievement and outcomes for all students, placing higher levels of accountability and expectations on public schools. In the United States, the NCLB law has come under increasing criticism as unrealistic and punitive, focusing on low levels of learning, limiting creativity and the education of the whole child.

Inclusive education can be viewed as both an extension of and, at the same time, in conflict with the concepts of standards-based reform and the laws designed for its implementation. On the one hand, many schools have decided that, if they are going to be evaluated on the performance of all students in the general education curriculum, students with disabilities need to be learning in general education classes, thus increasing their exposure and likelihood of doing well on standardized tests. On the other hand, standards-based reform identifies one set of expectations for all students. Thus, a fourth-grade student who is highly gifted, functioning on the eighth-grade level, will be expected to perform at the same level as a student with a cognitive disability, reading at the first-grade level. It is clear that, in this scenario, the gifted student is asked to perform far below her capacity, thus making the public school program irrelevant to her needs. The student with a cognitive disability is asked to function at a level far above his capacity. The result will be frustration and humiliation. For this student, no matter what effort he puts forth, he will be considered a failure. In this regard, NCLB and inclusive schooling could be seen as at odds with one another.

The movement toward inclusive education is truly international in thrust. In 1994, the country members of the United Nations adopted the Salamanca Statement, which articulated the rights of individuals with disabilities in society. This document particularly focused on schools and supported the concept and practice of inclusive education and called on member nations to use the document to reform their schools in this direction.

The idea of inclusive schooling can be expected to continue as a movement for reform in education. Clearly, the concept is connected at its essence with the concept of democracy. It is not surprising, consequently, to find that inclusive education is most practiced in countries that have a democratic political tradition and that segregated schooling is most firmly entrenched in authoritarian regimes.

One indicator of this trend has been the development of National Inclusive Schools Week in the United States, which has been growing in visibility since 2001 (see www.inclusiveschools.org). According to its Web site:

> National Inclusive Schools Week highlights and celebrates the progress of our nation's schools in providing a supportive and quality education to an increasingly diverse student population, including students with disabilities, those from low socio-economic backgrounds, and English language learners. The week also provides an important opportunity for educators, students, and parents to discuss what else needs to be done in order to ensure that their schools continue to improve their ability to successfully educate all children.

For those interested in the quality of schooling for students with wide ranges of abilities, monitoring the restructuring of schools to incorporate inclusive education as a central component may be one measure to watch in the coming years.

See also **Early Childhood Education; Government Role in Schooling; School Choice**

Further Reading

McGregor, Gail, and R. Timm Vogelsberg, *Inclusive Schooling Practices: Pedagogical and Research Foundations: A Synthesis of the Literature that Informs Best Practices.* Baltimore: Paul H. Brookes, 1999.

National Center on Educational Restructuring and Inclusion, *National Study of Inclusive Education.* New York: The Center, 1995.

Peterson, J. Michael, and Mishael M. Hittie, *Inclusive Teaching: The Journey towards Effective Schooling for All Learners,* 2d ed. Upper Saddle River, NJ: Prentice Hall, 2009.

Sapon-Shevin, Mara, *Widening the Circle: The Power of Inclusive Classrooms.* Boston: Beacon Press, 2007.

Tomlinson, Carol Ann, Kay Brimijoin, and Lane Narvaez, *The Differentiated School: Making Revolutionary Changes in Teaching and Learning.* Alexandria, VA: ASCD, 2008.

Vitello, Stanley J., and Dennis E. Mithaug, eds., *Inclusive Schooling: National and International Perspectives,* Mahwah, NJ: Lawrence Erlbaum.

J

JUVENILE DELINQUENCY

Tonya Lowery Jones

The role of the family as a social institution is essentially to prepare children for adulthood. To accomplish this task, the family is comprised of values and norms and different statuses and roles, all of which are devoted to achieving the goals of the family as well as that of society. However, this is no easy task. Families are often scrutinized when a child displays delinquent behavior. Of particular concern are the ways that families might promote or prevent juvenile delinquency. Among the areas of concern when examining the link between family and delinquency are traditional family values, child-rearing practices, the influence of the mass media, and parental responsibility.

Social scientists, too, have identified a variety of factors that they believe contribute to juvenile delinquency. These factors include the lack of parental supervision; a lack of discipline; a lack parental monitoring; the lack of attachment to prosocial institutions such as school, community, and church; low income; poor housing; a large family size; low educational attainment; associations with other delinquents; drug or alcohol abuse; and the criminal behavior of parents and siblings. Social scientists suggest that it is not just one single factor, but many factors working together, that increase the likelihood of juvenile delinquency.

Juvenile Delinquency in Perspective

In the United States, juvenile delinquency is a social problem affecting families, communities, and society as a whole. Federal Bureau of Investigation (FBI) statistics show that violent crime accounts for approximately 12 percent and that property crime accounts for approximately 88 percent of all serious crime in the United States. The FBI's Uniform Crime Reports estimate that about 1.4 million violent crimes and 9.8 million property crimes occurred nationwide in 2008, with 2.3 million people arrested for both types of offenses. Of those arrested in 2008 for violent and property crimes, about 415,000 (approximately 18 percent of the arrests) were persons under the age of 18, and of these arrests, about 118,000 (approximately 28 percent) were of persons under the age of 15 (U.S. Department of Justice, Federal Bureau of Investigation 2009). Given these statistics, it is understandable why there is concern over juvenile delinquency.

Juvenile delinquency refers to persons under a state-established age limit who violate the penal code. This means the law breaking was done by a child. In the eyes of the law, the only difference between a criminal and a delinquent is the person's age, and the state-established age limit varies from state to state. In the eyes of the law, a juvenile officially becomes an adult at 16 in 3 states, at 17 in 7 states, at 18 in 39 states, and at 19 in 1 state. Furthermore, delinquency is comprised of two parts. The first part includes property crimes like arson, burglary, larceny, and motor vehicle theft, while violent crimes include assault, robbery, rape, and murder, all of which would be considered crimes if committed by adults. The second part includes status offenses that are law violations that only apply to juveniles. This would include curfew violations, running away, and truancy. These status offenses are not violations of criminal law but are undesirable behaviors unlawful only for juveniles. It is believed that these offenses, if not dealt with, may lead to more serious delinquent behaviors in the future.

Therefore, the juvenile justice system takes steps to correct the behavior of juveniles and to try to change their behavior before they get involved in more serious property or violent crimes. It is the goal of juvenile courts, and has been since the first juvenile court was established in 1899, to prevent delinquent behavior and rehabilitate young offenders as apposed to just punishing them. This is why juveniles are not labeled *criminal* and their hearings are conducted in an informal atmosphere, where testimony and background data are introduced as opposed to a trial that determines guilt or innocence. In addition, the juvenile-court judge plays more of a parental role, reviewing the behavior of the juvenile offender in a less threatening environment than that of an adult criminal court. The juvenile court judge then determines an appropriate form of discipline, if any, and a course of action designed to prevent future delinquent behavior. Interestingly, many researchers believe that the majority of serious delinquent offenses are committed by a relatively small group of offenders and expect this delinquent population to maintain the antisocial behavior into adulthood.

Arenas for Debate

Family Values

The debate over the family's role in juvenile delinquency covers a variety of areas such as family values, child-rearing practices, the influence of the mass media, and parental responsibility. The central focus of this debate is on the lack of traditional family values in a so-called traditional family. Conservatives believe that alternative family forms like single-parent families, blended families, cohabiting families, and gay and lesbian families fail to instill traditional values in children. They believe that the traditional family is the foundation for strong values, norms, and an overall healthy society. Therefore, they push for a return to the traditional family, where mothers stay home and fathers are breadwinners, with a focus on traditional family values. In addition, they encourage parents to spend more time with their children and focus more on the family's needs as opposed to the individual's needs. For them, anything that threatens the family is considered a social problem. As a result, they believe that living together without marriage (i.e., cohabitation), premarital childbearing, divorce, and single parenting are social problems that weaken society and place children at risk. Conservatives point out that children are most affected by these social problems in that these factors not only increase their chances of ending up in a single-parent family, but they also increase their likelihood of living in poverty and put them at a higher risk for divorce as adults. The solution, according the conservatives, is to abolish no-fault divorce laws and discourage couples from living together in low-commitment relationships that favor so-called me-first values that support individualism over commitment.

Liberals, on the other hand, are more tolerant and supportive of the various alternative forms of families such as singlehood, cohabitation, single-parent families, blended families, and same-sex families. They believe people have the right to choose what type of family is right for them. They point out that family diversity is not new and that a variety of family forms have existed throughout history. In addition, liberals believe that this diversity is actually a solution to the historical problem of male-dominated households. They believe that the traditional family limits the opportunities of women and traps them in a male-dominated environment, which, in some cases, can be an abusive environment. According to liberals, alternative family forms are not the problem. The problem lies in the lack of tolerance for alternative family forms, in the push for the ideal traditional family (which discourages opportunities for women), and in poverty—all of which have a greater impact on women and children. Therefore, liberals feel the solution is to encourage more tolerance for alternative family forms, expand affordable child care programs so more women can work, and to enforce antidiscrimination laws so working women will be paid as much men.

Child Rearing

Much of the debate over child rearing in single-parent families is focused on the lack of parental supervision and the lack of guidance. Critics point out that, in many cases, single parents simply do not have enough time to meet the demands of adequate child rearing because of the demands placed on them to be the breadwinner and head of household as well as still maintain somewhat of a personal life. Unfortunately, the result is that children may not receive the parental supervision, guidance, and emotional support they need to develop into law-abiding adolescents. Consequently, more delinquent children come from single-parent families than two-parent families. Estimates are that children from single-parent families are about 10 to 15 percent more likely to become delinquent than are children with similar social characteristics from two-parent families (Coleman and Kerbo 2006). Children who are raised in an affectionate, supportive, and accepting home are less likely to become delinquents. Moreover, children whose parents model prosocial behavior in addition to adequately supervising and monitoring their children's behavior, friends, and whereabouts, as well as assist their children in problem solving and conflict resolution are less likely to engage in delinquent behavior. The bottom line is that parents have the ability to teach their children self-control, right from wrong, and respect for others, or they can teach their children antisocial, aggressive, or violent behavior. Therefore, children who grow up in a home with parents who are uninvolved or negatively involved are at greater risk for becoming juvenile delinquents.

Of course, critics of child rearing in single-parent families are not simply advocating more discipline. If parental discipline is too strict or too lenient, it can promote delinquency. There is strong evidence to show that children raised in single-parents families—specifically, mother-only homes—are at a greater disadvantage than those raised in two-parent families. Single-parent neighborhoods, particularly with high levels of mother-only households, have a higher rate of delinquency, because working single-mothers have less opportunity to adequately supervise their children, leaving them more vulnerable to the influences of deviant peers. Critics also point out that, in addition to higher rates of delinquency, children reared in single-parent families, specifically mother-only homes, are more likely to live in poverty, score lower on academic achievement tests, make lower grades, and drop out of high school.

The Mass Media

Another area for debate is the influence of the mass media on juvenile delinquency. The mass media refer to television, movies, music, video games, print media, sports, and the Internet. All of these have considerable influence over attitudes and behavior, especially among those under the age of 18. Not surprisingly, the mass media are a controversial agent of socialization because of how much they influence attitudes and behavior. Because we live in a society that seems to crave violence, it is no surprise that these different forms of mass media cater to the desires of the public by producing violent television shows, movies, music, video games, and overzealously cover violent incidents in the news. This excessive exposure to violence not only desensitizes us as a society, but for those in under the age of 18, these influences seem to have a number of serious effects. Some of the effects include: (1) *aggressive behavior:* media violence teaches children to be more aggressive so they tend to be less sensitive to pain and suffering; (2) *fearful attitudes:* media violence causes children to be more fearful of the world around them; and

(3) *desensitization:* media violence desensitizes children to real-life and fantasy violence, making it seem a normal part of everyday life. Exposure to media violence also increases a child's desire to see more violence in real-life and in entertainment, influencing them to view violence as an acceptable way to handle conflicts.

Other studies link excessive exposure to media violence to health problems, alcohol and tobacco usage, sexual activity, poor school performance, and more. These studies show that the effects of excessive exposure include: (1) decreased physical activity, which leads to obesity and other health problems; (2) photic seizures; (3) insomnia; (4) a decreased attention span; (5) impaired school performance; (6) decreased family communication; (7) increased sexual activity, which may lead to teen pregnancy and sexually transmitted diseases; and (8) an increased usage of alcohol and tobacco. Children ages 8 to 18 spend, on average, 44.5 hours per week (equivalent to 6.5 hours daily) in front a computer, watching television, or playing video games; by the time a child reaches age 18, he or she will have witnessed on television alone, with average viewing time, over 200,000 acts of violence, which include 40,000 acts of murder (Kirsh 2006). Children will view more than 100,000 acts of violence, including 8,000 acts of murder, by their first day in junior high school. Given the frequency of exposure to violence, children's violence and delinquency should not be surprising.

All media violence is not equal in its effects, however. The violence portrayed in cartoons is usually presented in a humorous fashion (67 percent of the time) and is less likely to depict long-term consequences (5 percent of the time) (BabyBag.com n.d.). Considering that the average preschooler watches mostly cartoons, this poses a greater risk for younger children because they have difficulty distinguishing between fantasy and reality. Therefore, they are more likely to imitate the violence they have seen. Researchers indicate that parents can be effective in reducing the negative effects of violent media viewing. Some of this can occur by parental understanding and utilization of television ratings. Other suggestions include watching television with one's child to permit discussion of difficult issues, turn the television off if the program is unacceptable, limit the time and type of programs watched, screen programs beforehand, and explain the differences between fantasy and reality.

Leonard Eron and Rowell Huesmann, psychologists at the University of Michigan who have studied the viewing habits of children for decades, found that the single factor most closely associated with aggressive behavior in children was watching violence on television. In testimony before Congress in 1992, they observed that television violence affects young people of all ages, of both genders, at all socio-economic levels. They noted that the effect is not limited to children who are already disposed to being aggressive(Bushman and Huesmann 2001). It is interesting that this has been a major issue for decades and that many key people, including former Surgeon General Dr. Jesse Steinfeld, have testified in numerous hearings on the topic, yet it is still a major issue.

Parental Responsibility

Parental responsibility is yet another area of concern regarding juvenile delinquency. Fundamentally, parental responsibility suggests that parents are to ensure that their children are protected, their needs are met, and their behavior is monitored. In addition, parents are responsible for socializing their children by instilling in them a sense of right, wrong, and the norms of society, helping them develop the skills they need to participate in society and shaping their overall development so that they are productive, law-abiding adolescents and adults.

However, when parents fail to ensure that their child or children develop into law-abiding adolescents, who is to blame? To what extent are parents responsible for their children's behavior? This has been an issue throughout U.S. history, and over time various types of legislation have addressed this specific question. Historically, the overall objective of these various laws was to require parents to provide the necessities for their children and to prohibit abuse or abandonment of minor children. However, due to the growing concern over juvenile delinquency, legislators have been prompted to expand laws regarding parental responsibility. More recently, parental responsibility goes beyond simply feeding, clothing, and loving one's children. Recent laws hold parents accountable for their child's actions by imposing various sanctions, including possible incarceration, fines, community service, and restitution. In addition, many states have enacted laws that require more parental involvement in juvenile court dispositions such as hearings, court-ordered treatment, counseling, training, rehabilitation and educational programs, and probation. Unfortunately, there is not enough comprehensive research on this subject to fully understand the effectiveness of parental responsibility laws. Whether the laws accomplish their intended purpose and have an effect on juvenile crime rates remains to be seen.

Conclusion

Solutions to the problem of juvenile delinquency are varied and have shown limited success at reducing crime among youth. Perhaps the slow pace of change is the result of the different schools of thought regarding the origins of delinquent behavior working in opposition to each other. Family, as the primary institution for rearing children, has been targeted as both the cause of and a preventive measure for juvenile delinquency. For some constituencies, the solution is encouraging traditional two-parent families with traditional values while discouraging other families forms such as single-parent families, cohabiting families, and same-sex families. For others, the solution is tolerance of alternative family forms and more focus on the overall well-being of children regardless of their parent's marital status or sexual orientation.

Social scientists have determined that it is not just one single factor that increases the likelihood of juvenile delinquency, but rather many factors in conjunction. Of the many factors, advocates have determined that a healthy home environment is the single most important factor and that adequate parental supervision is the second most important factor in decreasing the likelihood of delinquent behavior. Understandably, parents play a crucial role in a child's moral development, so it is their job to instill in their children a good sense of right and wrong and to promote healthy development in a healthy environment. Therefore, adolescents who live in a home environment with a lack of parental supervision and monitoring, poor or inconsistent discipline, a lack of positive support, a lack of parental control, neglect, and poverty are more likely to engage in delinquent behavior. On the other hand, for those adolescents in a positive home environment— which includes family support, nurturance, monitoring, and involvement—statistics show they are more likely to engage in prosocial behavior. In other words, children need parental affection, support, love, cohesion, acceptance, and parental involvement. When these elements are missing, the risk of delinquency increases.

See also **Addiction and Family; Foster Care; Juvenile Justice (vol. 2); Juveniles Treated as Adults (vol. 2)**

Further Reading

Agnew, Robert, *Juvenile Delinquency: Causes and Control,* 3d ed. New York: Oxford University Press, 2008.

BabyBag.com, "Facts about Media Violence and Effects on the American Family." http://www.babybag.com/articles/amaviol.htm

Brown, Kevin D., and Catherine Hamilton-Giachritsis, "The Influences of Violent Media on Children and Adolescents: A Public Health Approach." *Lancet* 365 (2005): 702–710.

Bushman, B. J. and L. R. Huesmann, "Effects of Televised Violence on Aggression." In *Handbook of Children and the Media*, eds. Dorothy G. Singer and Jerome L. Singer. Thousand Oaks, CA: Sage, 2001.

Caldwell, Roslyn M., Susan M. Sturges, and N. Clayton Silver, "Home Versus School Environments and Their Influences on the Affective and Behavioral States of African American, Hispanic, and Caucasian Juvenile Offenders." *Journal of Child and Family Studies* 16 (2007): 119–132.

Children and Television Violence, http://www.abelard.org/tv/tv.htm

Coleman, James William, and Harold Kerbo, *Social Problems,* 9th ed. Upper Saddle River, NJ: Pearson Prentice Hall, 2006.

Focus on the Family, http://www.family.org

Kirsh, Steven J., *Children, Adolescents, and Media Violence: A Critical Look at the Research.* Thousand Oaks, CA: Sage, 2006.

Media Awareness Network, http://www.media-awareness.ca/english/issues/violence/index.cfm

National Institute on Media and the Family, http://www.mediafamily.org/facts/facts_vlent.shtml

Office of Juvenile Justice and Delinquency Prevention: A Component of the Office of Justice Programs, U.S. Department of Justice. http://ojjdp.ncjrs.org/

Quinn, William H., *Family Solutions for Youth at Risk: Applications to Juvenile Delinquency, Truancy, and Behavior Problems.* New York: Brunner-Routledge, 2004.

Quinn, William H., and Richard Sutphen, "Juvenile Offenders: Characteristics of At-risk Families and Strategies for Intervention." *Journal of Addictions and Offender Counseling* 15 (1994): 2–23.

Siegel, Larry J., *Juvenile Delinquency: Theory, Practice, and Law,* 9th ed. Belmont, CA: Wadsworth, 2006.

Thompson, William E., and Jack E. Bynum, *Juvenile Delinquency: A Sociological Approach,* 8th ed. Boston: Allyn & Bacon, 2009.

U.S. Department of Justice, Federal Bureau of Investigation, *2008 Crime in the United States.* September 2009. http://www.fbi.gov/ucr/cius2008/index.html

M

MENTAL HEALTH

Donna R. Kemp

Mental health has been and still is a problematic policy area. People with mental illness have faced many problems from society throughout the ages. In the past, people with mental illness were often believed to be possessed by demons or the devil and were left in the care of their families or left to wander. They were sometimes mistreated. Eventually, society chose to hospitalize people with mental illness, but their status was reflected in Pennsylvania, where the first mental hospital was placed in the basement of the general hospital. Mental health has continued to be the poor stepchild of the wider health care arena.

History

Institutional care began in a few Arab countries; asylums were established as early as the eighth and ninth centuries to care for people with mental illness. Somewhat later in Europe, during the Middle Ages, the community began to seek confinement of people who were different. Some monasteries housed the mentally ill, usually treating them well. As societies became more urban and families became less able to care for persons with mental illness, eventually society chose to hospitalize people with mental illness.

In 1828, Horace Mann, an educational reformer, put forward a philosophy of public welfare that called for making the "insane" wards of the state. This philosophy was widely put into effect, and each state assumed responsibility for those with mental illness in that state. States often built their psychiatric hospitals in rural areas. Moral treatment and compassionate care were the main approach at this time, but with rapid urbanization and increased immigration, the state mental health systems began to be overwhelmed. Many elderly people who in rural areas would have been cared for at home could no longer be cared for when their families moved into the cities. Women, as well as men, frequently worked away from home, and there was no one to care for the elderly or see to their safety. Many people with brain-based dementias, probably caused by Alzheimer's or small strokes, became patients in mental institutions for the remainder of their lives. The institutions also had many cases of people in the last stages of syphilis. Many of those suffering from mental retardation, epilepsy, and alcohol abuse were also committed to the institutions; in hard economic times, the number of people admitted to the institutions increased.

By 1861, there were several state mental hospitals, and one federal hospital in Washington, DC. In the second half of the 19th century, attitudes changed and group and treatment practices deteriorated. Massive immigration to the United States led to a growing proportion of foreign-born and poor in the state hospitals. Most psychiatrists, community leaders, and public officials were native-born and generally well off and thus apt to be prejudiced against those who were neither (Rochefort 1993).

As more and more people were admitted to the institutions, the focus changed from treatment to custodial care. Commitment laws sent the dangerous and unmanageable to the state hospitals. More patients were alcoholic, chronically disabled, criminally insane, and senile. Treatment practices deteriorated. The institutions became overcrowded, and, by the late 19th century, the state hospitals were places of last resort, with mostly long-term chronic patients. Better treatment was found in small private psychiatric hospitals for those who could afford the care.

The 20th Century

As the 19th century drew to a close, a new idea, promoted by what is known as the eugenics movement, took hold. This movement held that insanity could be inherited. Professional conferences, humanitarian groups, and state legislatures increasingly identified insanity as a special problem of the poor. Insane persons were increasingly seen as possibly violent and incurable and as a threat to the community (Caplan 1969). These beliefs led to numerous state laws restricting the lives of people with mental disabilities, including involuntary sterilization laws and restrictive marriage laws. As a result, 18,552 mentally ill persons in state hospitals were surgically sterilized between 1907 and 1940. More than half of these sterilizations were performed in California (Grob 1983, 24).

Mental hospitals turned to the use of mechanical restraints, drugs, and surgery. Psychiatrists spent time diagnosing large numbers of patients rather than delivering individualized care. State legislatures did not increase budgets to meet the needs of the growing hospitals. Physical plants became overcrowded and deteriorated. Salaries were not adequate to attract good personnel. Superintendents no longer saw patients but spent their time on administrative tasks, and their influence declined as they became subordinate to new state boards of charity, which were focused on efficiency (McGovern 1985).

The first half of the 20th century saw some promising new treatment developments and attempts to establish community-based systems of services. In 1909, Clifford Beers founded the National Committee for Mental Hygiene to encourage citizen involvement, prevention of hospitalization, and aftercare for those who left the hospitals. The custodial institutions remained the main site of care, but some institutions developed cottage systems that placed more able patients in small, more homelike structures on the hospital grounds, and family care programs were created to board outpatients. All these approaches, however, served only a small part of the population.

Although the Division of Mental Hygiene was created in 1930 in the U.S. Public Health Service, it did not address institutional or community mental health care in general but only narcotics addiction. During the Great Depression of the 1930s and World War II, few resources were available to psychiatric institutions, but they continued to grow anyway. Some hospitals had as many as 10,000 to 15,000 patients. From 1930 to 1940, the number of people in state mental hospitals increased five times faster than the general population to a total of 445,000 (Rothman 1980, 374).

Four new therapies arose in the 1930s: insulin coma therapy, metrazol-shock treatment, electroshock therapy, and lobotomy. These treatments were given to thousands of patients, in many cases with devastating results; nevertheless, they were widely used until the appearance of antipsychotic medications in the 1950s.

The National Mental Health Act of 1946 brought the federal government into mental health policy in a significant way. The act created new federal grants in the areas of diagnosis and care, research into the etiology of mental illness, professional training, and development of community clinics as pilots and demonstrations. The act mandated the establishment of a new National Institute of Mental Heath (NIMH) within the Public Health Service to encourage research on mental health.

The states moved toward reform when, in 1949, the Governors' Conference released a report detailing the many problems in public psychiatric hospitals, including obsolete commitment procedures; shortages of staff and poorly trained staff; large elderly populations; inadequate equipment, space, and therapeutic programs; lack of effective state agency responsibility for supervision and coordination; irrational division of responsibility between state and local jurisdictions; fiscal arrangements damaging to residents; and lack of resources for research. In 1954, a special Governors' Conference on Mental Health adopted a program calling for expansion of community services, treatment, rehabilitation, and aftercare.

During the 1950s, the states pursued both institutional care and expansion of community services. In the mid-1950s, major deinstitutionalization of hospitals began. The introduction of psychotropic medicines to reduce and control psychiatric symptoms created optimism that some mental illnesses could be cured and others could be modified enough to allow persons with mental illness to function in the community. Because of the apparent success of the drugs, more emphasis was placed on a biochemical view of mental illness. The discovery and use of psychotropic drugs in the 1950s had a profound impact on the treatment of the mentally ill. Tranquilizing drugs were widely used in the state institutions and played a major role in deinstitutionalization. Early discharge programs became common, and the inpatient census of public psychiatric hospitals continued to steadily decline.

In 1955, the Mental Health Study Act was passed, leading to the establishment of the Joint Commission on Mental Illness and Health, which prepared a survey and made recommendations for a national program to improve methods and facilities for the diagnosis, treatment, and care of the mentally ill and to promote mental health. The commission recommended the establishment of community mental health centers and smaller mental hospitals. It laid the groundwork for the Community Mental Health Centers Act of 1963. During the 1960s, the civil rights movement and public interest law strengthened mental health policy and encouraged community mental health treatment and the decline of the role of psychiatric hospitals. The belief that the community would be involved in care for the mentally ill became more widely accepted, and the passage in 1965 of Medicaid and Medicare stimulated the growth of skilled nursing homes and intermediate-care facilities. In 1971, Title XIX of the Social Security Act (Medicaid) was amended to require institutional reform and the meeting of accreditation standards by facilities in order to receive federal funding. But the fiscal erosion of the 1970s and the 1980s took a heavy toll on state and local mental health programs.

In 1990, only one in five of those with mental illness received treatment (Castro 1993, 59). The National Institute of Mental Health estimated the cost of treating mental illness at $148 billion, which included $67 billion for direct treatment (10 percent of all U.S. health spending) and $81 billion for indirect costs such as social welfare and disability payments, costs of family caregivers, and morbidity and mortality connected to mental disorders (Castro 1993, 60).

In the U.S. Department of Health and Human Services, from which federal funding still largely comes, mental health programs were organized in 1992 into the Substance Abuse and Mental Health Services Administration, consisting of the Center for Mental Health Services, the Center for Substance Abuse Prevention, and the Center for Treatment Improvement. The institutes on mental health, drug abuse, and alcohol and alcohol abuse were shifted to the National Institutes of Health and began to focus only on promotion of research in mental health and substance abuse. The Department of Veterans Affairs and the Bureau of Indian Affairs in the Department of the Interior provided community mental health services directly in a number of locations.

Once states became responsible for the distribution of the federal grant funds for mental health, many funds were shifted from the community mental health centers to community mental health services more responsive to the needs of the seriously mentally ill (Hudson 1983). The complex intergovernmental array of organizations involved made coordination difficult.

Mental health care continued to be both inpatient and community based, but the site of inpatient care shifted from state institutions to general acute care hospitals in the community, with many people seen in psychiatric units in general acute care hospitals or in short-term public or private community inpatient facilities. Children began to be able to receive services in special community or residential treatment centers for children. The cost of inpatient care rose at all sites, but most sharply in general hospitals. Total costs were held in check because the length of stay decreased. Most of the decrease occurred in state mental hospitals and Veterans Administration facilities, even though those facilities had the longest stays (Kiesler and Sibulkin 1987). Community inpatient services were complemented by community outpatient services, such as the private practices of mental health professionals, family services agencies, community mental health centers, social clubs, day hospitals, halfway houses, group homes, assisted housing, and foster care.

Mental Health Policy and Services Today

In the 21st century, the history of modern mental health care continues to be complex and cyclical. There is a tug and pull between many of the viewpoints about mental illness. Should people with mental illness be free to manage their lives as they see fit, or should there be social control by the government? Is mental illness physical, environmental, or both? Is mental illness a part of physical illness, a brain disease or disorder?

As was the case in the 20th century, the United States continues to have no national mental health system. Each state has its own distinctive system. This approach allows for adjusting programs to the unique characteristics of different states and communities but has the disadvantage of creating disparities and differences in levels of community services. The private, nonprofit, and public sectors all play major roles in the delivery of services to people with mental illness. The system remains two-tiered, with lower-income people relying on the public sector and higher-income people on the private sector. People with insurance or sufficient income can access private mental health providers, from private psychotherapists, to general hospital psychiatric units in private and nonprofit hospitals, to private psychiatric facilities. The public mental health system remains the provider of last resort for people needing mental health services. However, there is a trend for more of these services being contracted out to the private sector rather than being provided by public agencies. The missions of most state mental health agencies focus resources on people with the most severe and persistent mental illnesses, such as bipolar disorder and schizophrenia.

The states remain the critical players in the development and maintenance of the public mental health system. "In fact, mental health more than any other public health or medical discipline, is singled out for exclusion and discrimination in many federal programs because it is considered to be the principal domain of the states" (Urff 2004, 84). In most states, the mental health system is administered by a state mental health agency. This agency may be an independent department but is most often an agency within a larger department, usually health or social services. As states downsize and close public psychiatric hospitals, services provided by private and nonprofit organizations take on increasing importance.

Who Are the Mentally Ill?

Mental disorders occur across the lifespan, affecting all people regardless of race, ethnicity, gender, education, or socioeconomic status. The World Health Organization has estimated that approximately 450 million people worldwide have mental and behavioral disorders, and mental disorders account for 25 percent of all disability in major industrialized countries (World Health Organization 2001, 7). The most severe forms of mental disorders have been estimated to affect between 2.6 and 2.8 percent of adults aged 18 years and older during any one year (Kessler, Berglund, Zhao, et al. 1996; National Advisory Mental Health Council 1993). About 15 percent of adults receive help from mental health specialists, while others receive help from general physicians. The majority of people with mental disorders do not receive treatment, and 40 percent of people with a severe mental illness do not look for treatment (Regier, Narrow, Rae, et al. 1993). Ronald C. Kessler, principal investigator of the National Comorbidity Survey Replication study, and colleagues (1996) determined that about half of Americans will meet the criteria for a *DSM-IV* (the American Psychiatric Association's *Diagnostic and Statistical Manual of Mental Disorders*) diagnosis of a mental disorder over the course of their lifetime, with first onset usually in childhood or adolescence. Based on their analysis, lifetime prevalence for the different classes of disorders were anxiety disorders, 28.8 percent; substance use disorders, 14.6 percent; and any disorder 46.4 percent. Median age of onset is much earlier for anxiety and impulse control disorders (11 years for both) than for substance abuse (20 years) and mood disorders (30 years) (Romano 2005).

The disease model of mental illness remains important. For the seriously mentally ill, it places a focus on finding and treating the causes of the emotional, behavioral, and/or organic dysfunction, with an approach based on diagnosis, treatment, and cure or recovery. The treatment focus is on short-term inpatient care, with the emphasis on medications and the ability to function in the community. Various services are provided to assist maintenance in the community, including housing, employment, and social services.

The mental health approach to people with less serious emotional disorders is focused on outpatient treatment, often through prescription of medication by a general practitioner. Primary care physicians provide at least 40 percent of mental health care. Employee assistance programs help employees in the workplace with assessment of mental health issues and referral to appropriate treatment sources. Those who are less seriously mentally ill are sometimes referred to in a derogatory way as the "worried well." When resources are short, conflict can arise as those who speak on behalf of the seriously and chronically mentally ill do not wish to see resources expended on the less seriously ill. However, many people at one time need assistance with a mental health problem in their lives, and failure to address their problems can lead to significant costs to society, including suicide.

Studies suggest that the prevalence of mental illness is about equal in urban and rural areas, but access to services is much more difficult in rural areas. Ninety-five percent of the nation's rural counties do not have access to a psychiatrist, 68 percent do not have access to a psychologist, and 78 percent lack access to social workers (California Healthline 2000).

Consumer Choice and Involuntary Treatment

What is now known as the consumer, or survivor, movement is generally recognized as having begun in the early 1970s, when several small groups of people who had been involved in the mental health system began to meet in several cities to talk about their experiences. They began to develop agendas for change.

Involuntary treatment is an issue that engages the attention of not only mental health consumers but family groups, providers, citizen advocacy groups, and law enforcement. On one side of the issue are those who would outlaw the use of force and coercion completely to protect individuals from dangerous interventions and abuse. They believe forced treatment violates basic civil and constitutional rights and erodes self-determination. They also believe forced treatment can lead to distrust and an avoidance of voluntary treatment. Those favoring involuntary treatment are found along a continuum, ranging from those who believe such treatment is justified only under extreme situations, when people are demonstrably dangerous to themselves or others, to those who believe involuntary treatment is acceptable based on a broad set of criteria.

Mental Illness and Criminal Justice

Along with homelessness and other negative outcomes of deinstitutionalization, the number of mentally ill in the correctional system has increased sharply. Crime, criminal justice costs, and property loss associated with mental illness cost $6 billion per year in the late 1990s, and people with mental illnesses are overrepresented in jail populations (U.S. Department of Health and Human Services 1999). Many of these inmates do not receive treatment for mental illness. A recent report by the Pacific Research Institute for Public Policy on criminal justice and the mentally ill noted that the total costs for state and local governments for arrest, processing in court, and jail maintenance of people with mental illnesses exceeds the total state and local government expenditures on mental health care (California Council of Community Mental Health Agencies n.d.). According to a 1999 Department of Justice report, more than 16 percent of adults in jails and prisons nationwide have a mental illness, and more than 20 percent of those in the juvenile justice system have serious mental health problems (Pyle 2002). There are more mentally ill people in U.S. prisons and jails (283,000 in 1998) than in mental hospitals (61,772 in 1996) (Parker 2001).

Recovery

Recovery is now a major element in health reform. William Anthony's (1993) "Recovery from Mental Illness: The Guiding Vision of the Mental Service System in the 1990s" used the phenomenon of recovery identified by Patricia Deegan and others to formulate a plan to become a guiding vision for the provision of mental health services. He used consumers' narratives of their recovery experiences to describe processes, attitudes, values, goals, skills, feelings, and roles that lead to a satisfying and contributing life even with limitations of illness. He stated that the process of recovery can occur without professional aid, but it can be helped by the support of trusted others, and it might be correlated with a reduction in the duration and frequency of intrusive symptoms. He held that individuals needed to recover from the consequences of illness, including disability, disadvantage, and dysfunction, as much as, or more than, from the illness itself. He argued that much of the disability, disadvantage, and dysfunction that people with mental illness experience are caused by the systematic and societal treatment of individuals who have psychiatric diagnoses. He believed that two models of service provision promote recovery: the psychiatric-rehabilitation model and the community-support-system model.

Conclusion

Mental health policy and services have traveled a long way from the days of the overcrowded state mental hospital. The civil rights movement brought many protections to people with mental illness. Yet the very deinstitutionalization of mental patients and the lack of funding for community care have led to new problems of homelessness and growing numbers of persons with mental illness in the criminal justice system. Although the stigma against people with mental illness is declining, many people with mental illness still have no access to treatment.

See also **Addiction and Family; Eating Disorders; Self-Injury and Body Image; Suicide and Suicide Prevention; Health Care (vol. 1); Insanity Defense (vol. 2); Social Justice (vol. 2)**

Further Reading

Anthony, W. A., "Recovery from Mental Illness: The Guiding Vision of the Mental Health Service System in the 1990s." *Psychosocial Rehabilitation Journal* 16 (1993): 11–23.

California Council of Community Mental Health Agencies, *The Development of California's Publicly Funded Mental Health System.* Prepared by S. Naylor Goodwin and R. Selix. http://www.cccmha.org

California Healthline, *Mental Health Neglected in Rural Areas. California Healthcare Foundation.* November 29, 2000. http://www.california healthline.org

Caplan, R. B., *Psychiatry and the Community in Nineteenth-Century America: The Recurring Concern with Environment in the Prevention and Treatment of Mental Disorder.* New York: Basic Books, 1969.

Castro, J., "What Price Mental Health?" *Time* (May 31, 1993): 59–60.

Frank, Richard G., and Sherry A. Glied, *Better but Not Well: Mental Health Policy in the United States since 1950.* Baltimore: Johns Hopkins University Press, 2006.

Grob, G. N., *Mental Illness and American Society, 1875–1940.* Princeton, NJ: Princeton University Press, 1983.

Grob, G. N., *The Mad among Us: A History of the Care of America's Mentally Ill.* New York: Free Press, 1994.

Hudson, C. G., "An Empirical Model of State Mental Health Spending." *Social Work Research and Abstracts* 23 (1983): 312–322.

Kelly, Timothy A., *Healing the Broken Mind: Transforming America's Failed Mental Health System.* New York: New York University Press, 2010.

Kemp, Donna R., *Mental Health in America: A Reference Handbook.* Santa Barbara, CA: ABC-CLIO, 2007.

Kessler, R. C., P. A. Berglund, S. Zhao, et al., "The 12-Month Prevalence and Correlates of Serious Mental Illness." In *Mental Health, United States, 1996,* ed. R. W. Manderscheid and M. A. Sonnenschein. DHHS Publication No. (SMA) 96–3098. Rockville, MD: Center for Mental Health Services, 1996.

Kiesler, C. A., and A. E. Sibulkin, *Mental Hospitalization: Myths and Facts about a National Crisis.* Newbury Park, CA: Sage, 1987.

McGovern, C. M., *Masters of Madness: Social Origins of the American Psychiatric Profession.* Hanover, NH: University Press of New England, 1985.

National Advisory Mental Health Council, "Health Care Reform for Americans with Severe Mental Illnesses: Report of the National Advisory Mental Health Council." *American Journal of Psychiatry* 150 (1993): 1437–1446.

Parker, Laura, "Families Lobby to Force Care." *USA Today* (February 12, 2001).

Pyle, E, "New Courts Aiming to Help Mentally Ill." *Columbus Dispatch* (December 26, 2002).

Regier, D. A., W. Narrow, D. S. Rae, et al., "The De Facto U.S. Mental and Addictive Disorders Service System: Epidemiologic Catchment Area Prospective 1-year Prevalence Rates of Disorders and Services." *Archives of General Psychiatry* 50 (1993): 85–94.

Rochefort, D. A., *From Poorhouses to Homelessness: Policy Analysis and Mental Health Care.* Westport, CT: Auburn House, 1993.

Romano, C. J., "Initial Findings from the National Comorbidity Survey Replication Study." *Neuropsychiatry Reviews* 6, no. 6 (2005). http://www.neuropsychiatryreviews.com

Rothman, D. J., *Conscience and Convenience: The Asylum and Its Alternatives in Progressive America.* Boston: Little, Brown, 1980.

Thompson, Marie L., *Mental Illness.* Westport, CT: Greenwood Press, 2006.

Urff, J., "Public Mental Health Systems: Structures, Goals, and Constraints." In *Mental Health Services: A Public Health Perspective,* 2d ed., ed. B. Lubotsky Levin, J. Petrila, and K. D. Hennessy. New York: Oxford University Press, 2004.

U.S. Department of Health and Human Services, *Mental Health: A Report of the Surgeon General—Executive Summary.* Rockville, MD: Department of Health and Human Services, 1999.

World Health Organization, *The World Health Report, 2001, Mental Health: New Understanding, New Hope.* Geneva: World Health Organization, 2001.

N

NEW RELIGIOUS MOVEMENTS

Tracy Sayuki Tiemeier and Michael Shally-Jensen

New religious movements have become big business, raising questions about their methods of recruitment, financial practices, and legitimacy. A new religious movement (NRM) is a spiritual or religious group that has emerged relatively recently and is unaffiliated with an established religious organization. Contemporary times find many NRMs growing at a fast rate. Such expansion could even be characterized as that of a growth industry, where an organization is in demand, expanding at a faster rate than the overall market. NRMs have become quite popular, no longer localized to a particular place or limited to a specific group of people. As people seek answers to their ultimate questions today, they have instant and equal access to NRMs (as much as to mainstream, established religions) through the Internet and mass media. As a result, the demand for information, materials, and contact with, by, and about NRMs has led to a flood of information, products, and services. From training seminars to collections of crystals, from red string Kabbalah bracelets to Scientology stress tests, memberships in and books and articles about new religious movements are on the rise.

What Is a New Religious Movement?

The term *new religious movement* arose as a designation for the many new religious organizations that formed in Japan after World War II. At that time, new religious freedoms and social upheaval provided fertile ground for such groups. The term was later used to describe other emergent religious groups around the globe.

The U.S. Immigration Act of 1965 lifted immigration restrictions from Asia, opening the doors to Asians, Asian religions, and their teachers. Groups such as the Unification Church (Family Federation for World Peace and Unification—popularly known as the Moonies) and the International Society for Krishna Consciousness (ISKCON—popularly known as the Hare Krishnas) attracted largely young, white, middle-class disciples. Asian religious groups provided responses to their problems that were different from mainstream U.S. traditions and became popular and controversial for this very reason.

The innovative and turbulent 1960s and 1970s also gave rise to other groups. While some employed more secular, psychological, and scientific methods and ideas, as in the case of the Church of Scientology, others drew on ancient or hidden traditions, as in the cases of the Covenant of the Goddess and the Order of the Solar Temple.

Other groups that had emerged in earlier times were also considered alongside these newer sects, and they, too, posed an alternative to mainstream U.S. religion. Some provided Christian alternatives, such as Christian Science, Jehovah's Witnesses, and The Church of Jesus Christ of Latter-Day Saints (Mormonism). Others emerged from African (La Regla de Ocha—Santería) or Native American (The Native American Church) beliefs and practices.

Scholars debate how "new" a movement has to be to constitute an NRM. While some would date a contemporary NRM to as early as the 19th century (such as the Baha'i Faith), others would argue that a new religious movement should have emerged no earlier than several decades before the present. Regardless, NRMs are not new in the sense that they pop up out of nowhere or within a spiritual vacuum. Some groups are centuries old or at least can trace their foundations or belief systems to ancient times. Indeed, NRMs often draw heavily on past revelations or traditions to authenticate their message. For example, Wicca claims an ancient past and lineage to distant pagan systems.

NRMs are often not religious in the traditional Western sense of maintaining belief in a named deity or deities, viewing core principles as stemming from a written text, or holding that faith is bound to ritual practices undertaken in an institutional setting. The Church of Scientology, for example, has specifically denied the label *religion* and instead emphasized its role in facilitating and maximizing personal development. The Self-Realization Fellowship, though it comes from a Hindu context, similarly does not require religious conversion or depend on any specific religious beliefs. Indeed, many groups have avoided the label *religion,* because it is understood as connoting the very thing that they originally found problematic and the very thing that their new adherents are seeking to abandon.

NRMs are widely categorized as *movements* because the term covers a wide range of organizational structures. Movements are generally fluid, but some new religious movements are highly organized and stratified.

KEY EVENTS IN THE HISTORY OF NEW RELIGIONS

1830—The Church of Christ (later called The Church of Jesus Christ of Latter-Day Saints) is founded by Joseph Smith.

1844—The beginnings of the Baha'i Faith, when the Báb (*gate*) starts teaching the local Persian Muslims about a coming prophet who would initiate a time of world peace.

1853—Mírzá Husayn'Alí receives a vision in prison that he is the prophet foreseen by the Báb and is the fulfillment of all the world religions.

1918—The Comanche chief Quanah Parker is credited with formalizing aspects of traditional peyotism to form the Native American Church.

1924—Paramahansa Yogananda establishes, in Los Angeles, the international headquarters of the Self-Realization Fellowship.

1930—Wallace Fard Muhammad teaches black power and Islam, marking the beginnings of The Nation of Islam.

1950—L. Ron Hubbard published *Dianetics: The Modern Science of Mental Health.* Four years later, he founds the Church of Scientology.

1955—Jim Jones founds the Wings of Deliverance, later to be called The People's Temple. The group sees Jones as a prophetic healer and incarnation of Christ.

1965—A. C. Bhaktivedanta Swami Prabhupada arrives in the United States and forms The International Society for Krishna Consciousness.

1960s—Wicca, a form of modern witchcraft first organized in the 1950s, receives increased notice as the name and other aspects take hold.

1968—Children of God, a blend of Jesus worshipers and hippie communitarians, is founded in California.

1971—The Movement of Spiritual Inner Awareness, based on meditation and mysticism, is founded by former Mormon Roger Delano Hinkins in California.

1974—Sun Myung Moon of the Unification Church holds a mass rally at Madison Square Garden in New York City, effectively launching the church as a movement in the United States.

1970s—The Rastafari movement gains hold in the United States, largely through the popularity of musician Bob Marley.

1975—Sōka Gakkai, a populist Buddhist new religion, founds an international umbrella organization.

1977—Maharishi Mahesh Yogi founds Transcendental Meditation as a modernization of classical yoga. The People's Temple is denied tax-exempt status and the group moves to Guyana, founding Jonestown.

1978—Mass murder-suicide in Jonestown; over 900 dead.

1980s—The New Age movement, drawing on occultism, esoteric beliefs, alternative medicine, and eco-spiritualism gains ground in the United States.

1984—Bhagwan Shree Rajneesh and his followers in Oregon undertake to poison members of the surrounding community in an effort to gain local political control.

1985—J. Z. Knight, emerging "channeler," makes her national television debut (on the *Merv Griffin Show*), sparking widespread interest in channeling.

1986—Shoko Asahara (b. Matsumoto Chizuo) founds Aum Shinrikyo in Tokyo, Japan. The movement blends Hinduism, Buddhism, and Christianity.

1992—Falun Gong, a "cultivation system" based on daily rituals of worship, is founded in China and spreads rapidly there and among Chinese communities elsewhere.

1993—The Bureau of Alcohol, Tobacco and Firearms raids the Branch Davidian compound in Waco, Texas. After a 51-day standoff, ATF agents moved in and stormed the complex. Over 80 died in a resulting fire.

1995—Aum Shinrikyo members release sarin gas in Tokyo subway, killing 12.

1997—Combining Christianity with UFO beliefs, members of Heaven's Gate kill themselves outside of San Diego when the comet Hale-Bopp appeared to them as the sign of the ship arriving to take their souls to heaven; 39 people dead.

2002—The Raëlians, who maintain that life on Earth was artificially created by extraterrestrial beings, announce that they have cloned a human being.

2008—Texas Child Protective Services seizes more than 400 children from the Yearning for Zion Ranch, a polygamist property in western Texas; charges of brainwashing and abuse are later found to be unsupported.

2010—Nine members of a Christian Identity group calling themselves the Hutaree are arrested in Michigan for plotting to kill police officers as a means of bringing about the End Time as described in the Book of Revelations.

New religious movements are sometimes called cults. While the word *cult* refers to a religious system of rituals, practices, and the people who adhere to it, the term today often carries a negative connotation of a controlling, distorted, even dangerous religious group. The term *new religious movement* is therefore a more neutral way to refer to a wider phenomenon of emergent religious/spiritual groups. Every religion is at some point new, and NRMs are composed of many different groups with widely divergent perspectives. While some new religious movements can indeed be dangerous to their adherents and to the general public, they are not all so. Nevertheless, until NRMs gain the acceptance of mainstream society, establishing the legitimacy of a new religious movement is often a sketchy proposition.

Who Joins and Why?

New religious movements vary widely in their beliefs and practices; however, such groups often represent alternative worldviews and practices vis-à-vis the mainstream, and they often offer distinct responses to the problems of their day. The answers they provide often seem more adequate to followers than those of the older, established traditions. Given widespread disillusionment with many established religious traditions, whether owing to scandals or to perceived backwardness, NRMs can offer attractive alternatives to the mainstream.

New religious movements in the United States are comprised largely of white middle-class young people—but not exclusively so. Groups recruit from the middle and upper classes. Adherents' families are generally well educated and financially stable. Many are in college or are college educated. They come, in other words, from mainstream society. Nevertheless, people attracted to NRMs are largely dissatisfied with mainstream religion and society, are interested in religious/spiritual matters, and are actively seeking individually and independently for fresh answers to their life questions. Seeking to "find themselves," people attracted to new religious movements want alternatives to the familiar, structured establishment of belief and practice.

It is often the case, too, that the downtrodden or less well-off find satisfaction in the pursuit of new religion. Certainly this is the case among many adherents of the Christian Identity movement, which overlaps in its tenets with radical antigovernmentism, racism, militarism, anti-intellectualism, and other such themes. Rejection of economic disparities similarly plays a part, too, whether formally stated or not, in the beliefs and activities of such groups as the Nation of Islam. And many Rastafarians and followers of Native American Religion are among the most economically challenged peoples in the country, even as they seek solace in rooting themselves in their cultural traditions. (Some observers, in fact, would count these last two faiths as no longer new religions but relatively well-established ones.)

Whatever their economic status, people in search of answers to their personal and social problems will often find complete solutions in new religious movements. The strong community identity these movements typically provide will give a sense of security and stability; the communal cooperation they offer will supply a sense of common goals for life-building; the discipline in practice they usually demand will cultivate a sense of self-mastery and knowledge; and the recruitment and financial activities they sometimes require can serve to build self-esteem.

NRMs and the Courts

While many countries grant their citizens religious freedom, conflicts between religion and the state are inevitable and can become more intense in the case of new religious movements—precisely because they engage in practices that many mainstream secular and religious people may find problematic.

New religious movements are often accused of harming or endangering adherents. Court cases have alleged that these movements inflict psychological and/or physical trauma or death. The practices enumerated include kidnapping, brainwashing, mind control, sexual abuse, alienation, harassment, and threats to families.

Charges of endangerment and violence have also been leveled at the criminal level. The mass murder–suicide in Jonestown is one example. Another well-known example occurred in 1984, when members of Rajneeshpurum near The Dalles, Oregon, sought to poison (via salmonella-laced food) people in the local populace who opposed the group's presence. In 2008, there were charges that children of members of the polygamist Yearning for Zion Ranch in Texas were being brainwashed and abused—charges that later proved unfounded. And in 2010, members of a Michigan Christian Identity group known as the Hutaree were charged with sedition and other crimes for seeking to overthrow the government.

Another major legal issue for NRMs has to do with their status as religious entities and their financial activities as related to that status. Tax exemption for religions and nonprofit organizations is granted in many countries, the United States included. Here, the question involves whether particular new religious movements qualify as protected religions and the legality of particular financial practices. An important issue raised in court cases is when an NRM becomes a legal religious entity. This is difficult to determine, because these movements are not typically organized according to traditional Western understandings of a religion, nor do they always behave like one. Courts have to discern whether a group is a smokescreen for illegal activities, such as a convenient means to qualify for tax exemption. Some new religious movements are indeed quite wealthy and run businesslike organizations, leading to questions about whether they are legitimate religions.

The Church of Scientology has been under constant scrutiny for this very reason. The church has had trouble with the Internal Revenue Service and was involved in a 10-year legal battle with the Food and Drug Administration over controversial medical practices. It took 48 years for New Zealand to formally recognize (in 2002) the Church of Scientology as a legal religious entity. Although Russia refused to re-register the church as a religion under the country's new laws on religion in 1997, the case was eventually taken to the European Court of Human Rights (*Church of Scientology Moscow v. Russia*), which sided with the church. In its decision of April 7, 2007, the Court found that the church was a religious entity entitled to the freedoms of association and of religion. The Italian Supreme Court ruled in 2000 that, while Scientology is indeed a religion—and therefore tax exempt—its drug-addiction program, Narconon, is not tax exempt. The Charity Commission of England and Wales rejected the church's application to register as a charity (giving it tax exemption like other religious entities registered as charities). Scientology was rejected as a religion, because British law requires a religion to include belief in a Supreme Being that is expressed in worship. Scientology is also involved in legal cases in other countries, such as Germany, where it is not accepted as a legitimate religion and instead is seen as a dangerous cult.

The U.S. Supreme Court ruled in 1989 that Church of Scientology members could not deduct auditing and training courses from their federal income taxes. Such courses, though integral to church membership, and costing thousands of dollars, are payment for services, and not free church contributions. Auditing is the main practice in Scientology for the practitioner to gain control of the mind and achieve the state of Clear. Although the church argued that auditing is a religious practice for achieving enlightenment and is comparable to the concept of tithing in other religious groups, the Court ruled that auditing is instead like church counseling, medical care, or other kinds of religiously sponsored services.

Other new religious movements have had similar troubles. Reverend Sun Myung Moon, founder of the Unification Church, was convicted by the United States on tax evasion charges prior to the group's recognition as a tax-exempt organization. Pagan and witchcraft groups have, not surprisingly, been challenged on their status as well. While U.S. courts generally recognize such groups as religious, the Supreme Court of Rhode Island revoked the Church of Pan's status, because the church's activities were entirely environmental in focus. In such cases, mainstream religions can also get involved; for legal issues involving new religious movements have implications for all religious groups and their practices.

Recruitment, Financial Practices, and the Business of NRMs

Recruitment and solicitation of funds have been particularly controversial for new religious movements, particularly their common method of public solicitation. Solicitation at airports and other public grounds has been banned in some places, because it is argued that these practices are a public nuisance, or even deceptive. For example, ISKCON members were arrested in 1987 in West Virginia for allegedly soliciting money for their community under the false pretense of feeding the poor.

Critics of NRM solicitation practices argue that groups use deceptive practices like misleading donors and recruits on how the money is spent, who the specific group is, or what membership entails. Nevertheless, new religious movements do not have the forum that established religions have for gathering members and funds. Thus, public solicitation is often the most efficient way of getting the message out. Other groups organize side projects and products, establishing quasi-businesses; selling paraphernalia, vitamins, or self-help books; offering cheap labor; designing Web sites; and so on. These practices are necessary for survival, but they also lead to questions of authenticity, legitimacy, and legality.

While some NRMs deny the material world and the accumulation of wealth (for themselves and their adherents), others either embrace it or at least teach that both are possible. Thus, some new religious movements have been extremely successful in gaining financial capital. One way to do this is by targeting mainstream businesses. Through workshops, special seminars, and self-help books, some NRMs have found success targeting business professionals.

Organizations that offer seminars to train businesspeople have proliferated since the 1970s. These training seminars teach businesspeople techniques of management, developed out of their own beliefs, methods, and practices. For example, the World Institute of Scientology Enterprises offers programs for businesses, teaching them management practices developed from Scientology founder, L. Ron Hubbard; the Osho movement, founded by Bhagwan Shree Rajneesh, offers Results Seminars; and Maharishi Mahesh Yogi's Transcendental Meditation offers master's degrees in business administration at its Maharishi University of Management.

New religious movements also recruit from among the general public. The Church of Scientology offers personality, stress, and IQ tests. Marketed products, Internet sites, and self-help books are all ways that individuals can take advantage of the offerings of NRMs. Through all of these, the exploration and experimentation in the self allows new religious movements to spread their message and grow.

Seeking prosperity for oneself and one's organization seems counter to the traditional notion of religions as not-for-profit and on individual disciples focusing on their own inner spiritual life. Yet many groups who support these kinds of business practices focus on the holism of life. If the divine is in all things, the material world is not in distinction from the spiritual world. Thus, self-empowerment leads to life empowerment, which leads to financial empowerment.

NRMs versus Sects

Overlapping with the concept of new religious movements is the concept of sects. The latter type of organization is generally seen as an offshoot of an established religion. In some cases, however, it is debatable whether a group is best viewed as a sect or as a distinctly new and different take on an old set of beliefs. For example, in the United States, among the fastest growing religious groups are churches belonging to a version of Pentecostalism that devote themselves to the so-called doctrine of prosperity. This doctrine claims that God provides material wealth to those he favors. Thus, by accruing money and worldly goods, the believer demonstrates the he or she is among the select. Beginning in the mid-20th century under a comparatively mild-mannered version promoted by Oral Roberts, and then extending into a range of popular televangelist programs in the latter part of the century, the prosperity gospel has since become a profitable industry for those who oversee it (primarily, the pastors of mega-churches and their media enterprises). The issue has become contentious enough that, at the end of 2007, Senator Charles Grassley opened a congressional investigation targeting a number of high-profile wealth gospel preachers. (As of mid-2010, the investigation remains open.)

Conclusion

As movements grow and organize themselves, they naturally seek to attract followers, sustain themselves, and increase their influence. This requires that new religious movements finance the spread of their message. Thus, charges of financial impropriety and exploitation of vulnerable people who are seeking alternatives in their lives are inevitable. To combat these charges, NRMs must prove that they are legitimate. To do so, they often point to experiential proof, revelation, and ancient wisdom in establishing their legitimacy. While new religious movements proliferate, they often rise and fall fairly quickly.

Only time will tell whether the new religions of today will become the mainstream religions of tomorrow.

See also Creationism, Intelligent Design, and Evolution; Religious Symbols on Government Property; Racial, National Origin, and Religion Profiling (vol. 2); Right-Wing Extremism (vol. 2); Deep Ecology and Radical Environmentalism (vol. 4)

Further Reading

Ashcraft, W. Michael, and Dereck Daschke, eds., *New Religious Movements: A Documentary Reader.* New York: New York University Press, 2005.

Clarke, Peter, *New Religions in Global Perspective.* New York: Routledge, 2006.

Cowan, Douglas E., *Cults and New Religions: A Brief History.* New York: Oxford University Press, 2008.

Dawson, Lorne L., *Comprehending Cults: The Sociology of New Religious Movements.* New York: Oxford University Press, 2006.

Gallagher, Eugene V., *The New Religious Movements Experience in America.* Westport, CT: Greenwood Press, 2004.

Gallagher, Eugene V., and W. Michael Ashcraft, eds., *Introduction to New and Alternative Religions in America.* Westport, CT: Greenwood Press, 2006.

Lewis, James R., *Legitimating New Religions.* New Brunswick, NJ: Rutgers University Press, 2003.

Partridge, Christopher, *New Religions: A Guide: New Religious Movements, Sects and Alternative Spiritualities.* New York: Oxford University Press, 2004.

Saliba, John, *Understanding New Religious Movements,* 2d ed. Walnut Creek, CA: AltaMira Press, 2003.

Wilson, Bryan, and Jamie Cresswell, eds., *New Religious Movements: Challenge and Response.* New York: Routledge, 1999.

NO CHILD LEFT BEHIND (NCLB)

LINDA MABRY

No Child Left Behind—these words convey an inspiring idea, an admirable goal for reform, and a shared value of universal access to high-quality education. As a national education policy adopted in 2002, No Child Left Behind (NCLB) aims at societal transformation by freeing historically underserved students from what supporters often call "the mediocrity of low expectations," demanding that public schools educate all students to meet standards. Accomplishment of this aim might finally resolve an argument that animated the Continental Congress that produced the Declaration of Independence—whether a government of the people, by the people, and for the people can be sustained in a population not fully literate, not fully educated—by educating everyone.

Yet NCLB has inspired more controversy than any previous educational policy in the United States. To grasp the arguments and to contextualize them historically, three questions will be explored:

1. Is 40 years of federal education policy, culminating in NCLB, more accurately described as *assisting and improving* public schooling in much-needed ways or as *hostile and harmful* incursions into the Constitution's reservation to the states of the provision of public education?
2. Are unintended *consequences* of NCLB-mandated testing outweighing planned or actual *benefits*?
3. Is test-driven accountability *rescuing* schools and students from intolerably low expectations or *abandoning* them and the enterprise of public education?

The explosion of test-related legislation and litigation and some invisible but inevitable problems of educational measurement will thread this discussion of assessment-related aspects of NCLB.

Federal Assistance or Constitutional Incursion?

Despite the Constitution's reservation of public education to the states, federal interest is nonetheless clear. In a democracy where it is the right and responsibility of all members to participate in decision making, education is fundamental to ensuring the electorate's capacity for comprehending complicated issues, seeking salient information and judging its accuracy, and comparing the campaign promises of elected representatives with their performance. Problems associated with state-level failure to make satisfactory education available to all were illustrated a half-century ago in the class action suit, *Brown v. Board of Education of Topeka, Kansas*, 1954. The persistence of efforts to include and exclude evolution from science curricula suggest continuing problems associated with the local level.

All three branches of the federal government have, in fact, played a role in public education. *Brown* and later cases demonstrate the role of the federal judiciary. The executive and legislative branches became active a decade after *Brown* with the Elementary and Secondary Education Act (ESEA) of 1965. Part of President Lyndon Johnson's "war on poverty," ESEA's centerpiece was Title I funding to assist disadvantaged students. In 1988, as the numbers and categories of these students grew, testing was introduced to monitor their progress and assure that federal funds were well spent. The 1994 reauthorization of ESEA, called the Improving America's Schools Act or Goals 2000, called for development of national standards and standards-aligned assessments for all students, tasks set for two bodies created by the same legislation—the National Council on Education Standards and Testing and the National Assessment Governing Board.

Eight years later, in 2002, as ESEA was again reauthorized, this time as NCLB, Goals 2000's six national goals remained unmet or unmeasurable—(1) all children ready to learn; (2) 90 percent high school graduation rate; (3) all children competent in core subjects (including arts and foreign languages); (4) United States ranked first in the world in math and science; (5) every adult literate and competitive in the work force; and (6) safe, disciplined, drug-free schools. Only 19 states had reached full compliance with the law; no national system of assessments had been created; the effort to calibrate state tests so that their scores could be compared had been abandoned; and neither national content standards nor opportunity-to-learn standards had been developed. Performance standards on the National Assessment of Educational Progress (NAEP) had been set, but the standard-setting process was found "fatally flawed" in multiple evaluations. Most states had adopted content standards, and, ultimately, to comply with NCLB, every state except Iowa had implemented standards-based assessments.

NCLB mandated reading and math proficiency by all students in grades three through eight within 12 years, to be measured by states' standards-based tests and confirmed by the state's NAEP scores; state participation in NAEP, previously voluntary, was required. State test scores were to be disaggregated for each of several subgroups of students identified by major racial and ethnic backgrounds, by disability, and by limited English proficiency, and each group was required to meet state proficiency standards. State improvement plans, including Adequate Yearly Progress (AYP) targets leading to 100 percent proficiency in 2014, were required to be submitted for U.S. Department of Education approval, the first time in January 2003.

The federal government could not compel states to attempt to meet NCLB requirements. Rather, the financial reward of choosing to participate in NCLB—the proverbial carrot—was continuation of the federal funding, an estimated 10 percent of most state education budgets, to which their struggling students had been declared "entitled" 40 years earlier by ESEA. The corresponding stick was a graduated series of penalties increasing in number and severity over time. Schools failing to meet student achievement goals have been identified as needing improvement and are required to do the following:

- In year two following NCLB implementation, develop an improvement plan, accept technical assistance, and make school choice available to any student in a school "in need of improvement" with the district paying transportation to the chosen school.
- In year three, all of the above plus provide approved supplemental services.
- In year four, all of the above plus take corrective action, such as hiring a new staff or adopting a new curriculum.
- In year five, restructure or face takeover by the state or a contractor.

Some saw these provisions as holding schools appropriately accountable for the educational outcomes of vulnerable students, giving the law teeth. Others saw them as threats to compel top-down change, which researchers had repeatedly found to be a hopeless reform trajectory.

A variety of reactions followed enactment of NCLB. Some reactions suggested NCLB was oppressive. Initially, Vermont declared that it would forego federal funding and accountability but later reversed this decision. In subsequent years, other states also considered and rejected opting out, but some did entertain legislation that allowed districts and schools to do so. The numbers of districts and schools that opted out grew.

A variety of reactions was also apparent in the first-round state improvement plans submitted in 2003 for federal approval. More differentiated than the federal government had expected, these plans prompted the first in a series of adjustments to requirements.

With such a multiplicity of responses, perhaps NCLB might be considered in terms of a multiple-choice item. For example, NCLB is best described as:

1. representing President George W. Bush's attempt to achieve ESEA's original hope of equal outcomes for all students.
2. furthering preexisting state trends toward testing and accountability and expanding on a national scale the Texas system instituted when Bush was governor, which produced (select one) the Texas miracle/the myth of the Texas miracle.
3. a violation of the U.S. Constitution.
4. imposing on states, districts, and schools a test-driven educational accountability system with severe penalties for compliance failures.
5. ensuring the failure of public education by setting unrealistic requirements for reading and math proficiency by all students in grades three through eight.

Or perhaps, since the right answer might depend on who was scoring this item, an essay question might be better. For example,

Is NCLB more about entitling students and improving their schools or threatening and punishing both?

Such a question can be taken as a frame for understanding the educational testing and accountability debates intensified by NCLB. The history of educational measurement has been dubbed a history of unintended consequences, to which some consider that Bush has contributed with NCLB. Bush himself described the policy as "real reform having real results" in a press conference December 20, 2004. Whether NCLB's results are positive or negative and, if the former, whether the gain is worth the pain are at issue.

Good Policy, Bad Effects?

Conflicting opinions exist not only among people but also within people. For example, in a small school district in January 2005, an assistant superintendent described NCLB to the author as "the moon shot in education. We might as well go for a big goal. We're

Federal Standards and Accountability Legislation Leading to the No Child Left Behind Act

	STANDARDS			ASSESSMENT			SANCTIONS		
	Standards Established	Deadline for Proficiency	Disaggregation of Performance	State Testing	High-Stakes National	Adequate Yearly Progress	Planned School Improvements	Restructuring of Schools	Public School Choice
Reagan administration/ George H. W. Bush administration (1981–1992)	Yes, voluntary standards	No	No	No	Proposed, NAEP as benchmark (not passed)	No	No	No	Proposed, tuition tax credits and Title I vouchers (not passed)
103rd Congress (1993–1994)	Yes, for Title I students	No	No	Yes, three tests between grades 3 and 12	No	Yes, but vague	Yes	No	No
106th Congress (1999–2000)	Proposed, for all students (only passed the House)	Proposed ten years (only passed the House)	Proposed (only passed the House)	Yes, three tests	Proposed, voluntary (implementation banned)	Proposed (only passed the House)	Proposed (only passed the House)	Proposed (only passed the House)	Proposed, (not passed)
George W. Bush presidential campaign (2000)	Yes	No	Partial	Yes, annual tests for grades 3–8	Yes, NAEP as benchmark	Yes	Yes	Yes	Yes
No Child Left Behind Act (2001)	Yes, mandatory for all students	Yes, 12 years	Yes, by race/ ethnicity, LEP, disability, and Title I students	Yes, annual tests for grades 3–8, one in 10–12	Partial, NAEP required but not linked to funding	Yes	Yes	Yes	Partial, plus supplemental services vouchers

Figure 1. Federal Standards and Accountability Legislation Leading to the No Child Left Behind Act (Adapted from Andrew Rudalevige, *The Politics of No Child Left Behind* [2003], http://educationnext.org/the-politics-of-no-child-left-behind)

going to be better for having tried." By the end of the school year, however, she was saying:

> I think [the law] has been both positive and vexing—positive in that it really has forced us to look carefully at what students are learning, especially those who are not yet learning to any standard this state considers appropriate. At the same time, it's been really vexing because, although we have put into place things that really help students and teachers, we don't know how we can keep on....I don't know if people are ultimately going to love me or curse me for this, but I've said I think it's time to take Title 1 dollars off the table. We did refuse it for two years, but we need the money, frankly.

Even the positive aspects can be vexing, as discussion of the following points will show: (1) Rising scores come with significant caveats, and evidence that they provide of school improvement does not always survive scrutiny. (2) While states develop their own improvement plans, the federal approval process limits their real options. (3) NCLB's wording protects districts and schools from new expenditures, but complaints and lawsuits charge that it is nonetheless an unfunded mandate.

Test Score Increases

There have been reports that scores on state reading and math achievement tests for students in grades three through eight are rising across the country. To NCLB proponents, this indicates that the bottom-line objectives are being attained, that reform is working. Although achievement gaps persist, test scores also offer evidence that some of the students who have been left behind in the past are beginning to catch up. NCLB promoted the credibility of the score increases by blocking some possibilities for gaming the system and thereby distorting test results, problems that had been reported with state tests:

- By requiring testing every student in grades three through eight every year, NCLB facilitated individual student progress monitoring. No longer was it necessary to compare fourth-graders in year one with fourth-graders in year two, a completely different student population.
- By requiring 95 percent student participation rates, NCLB diminished the possibility of skewing results by such manipulations as scheduling field trips for low-scoring students on test days, calling them to the school office, or suggesting their parents keep them home.
- By requiring comparison of each state's test scores to its scores on NAEP, NCLB checked any "dumbing down" of state tests that might raise scores by lowering expectations.

Even if tests remain imperfect, as test developers themselves acknowledge, few critics would argue that scores reveal nothing. Love tests or hate them, trust scores or harbor lingering doubts about their accuracy and meaning, not even the most acerbic critic can regret evidence from scores of improving educational outcomes for children and youth.

Cautions

Across time, student socioeconomic status has been so strongly and consistently correlated with test scores that it has been argued that zip codes, identifying the affluence of neighborhoods, tell as much about student performance as large-scale assessments do. It has even been joked that a high school senior's college performance can be better predicted by the number of cavities in his or her teeth than by the student's score on a college entrance examination, a whimsical allusion to the dental care available to the affluent. The correlation suggests that accountability based on test scores amounts, in effect, to holding students accountable for their parents' income and holding public schools, which must accept all the students in their catchment areas, accountable for factors beyond their control.

While state scores are rising, the NCLB requirement to compare each state's test scores to its NAEP scores is often failing to confirm reported state gains. For example, according to a 2006 *New York Times* investigation, NAEP math scores between 2002 and 2005 improved for poor, African American, and white fourth-graders, but NAEP reading scores declined slightly for African American and white eighth-graders and for eighth-graders eligible for free or reduced-price lunches. Mississippi declared 89 percent of its fourth-graders proficient readers, the highest percentage in the nation, but only 18 percent proved proficient in reading on NAEP.

The discrepancy signals invalidity. Because NAEP scores are less easily corrupted than scores on state tests, the discrepancy suggests that the invalidity is located in state testing—not for the first time. In the 1980s, the credibility of state test scores was called into question when a West Virginia physician, John J. Cannell, discovered that every state was claiming above-average scores, ushering into the measurement vernacular the "Lake Wobegon phenomenon," a reference to the fictitious community imagined by Garrison Keillor, where "all the children are above average." In the 1990s, Tom Haladyna and his colleagues found tests susceptible to a variety of types of "score pollution." In 2000, Center for Research on Educational Standards and Student Testing codirector Bob Linn showed that scores typically rise after a new test is implemented and typically return to original levels when the second test takes its place, suggesting that it is common for rising scores to exaggerate rising achievement. And in 2009, it was discovered through an investigation that school officials in Georgia were routinely correcting standardized tests submitted by students in order not to be penalized for poor performance and thus face the withdrawal of federal funds from their districts.

That the achievement gains suggested by rising scores may be an illusion is underscored by the fact that NAEP scores have remained fairly stable for 40 years. Flat NAEP scores also suggest that NCLB requirements are unrealistic. Many doubt that all third-through eighth-graders could achieve proficiency in literacy and numeracy. Assuming they could, Stanford University measurement expert Ed Haertel has calculated that the states with the best NAEP progress records would nevertheless need more than 100 years to reach 100 percent proficiency, not NCLB's 12 years.

Some of the cautions applicable to interpreting satisfactory progress toward NCLB requirements are technical. For example, while NCLB has stimulated high student participation in test-taking, it has also allowed each state to determine how many students in each subgroup (e.g., English language learners, special education students) must be enrolled for their scores to count in determining whether AYP targets have been met. States have set different minimum numbers of students in subgroups, which has proven problematic whether the minima are high or low. With a "low n," aggregated scores will be inconsistent (unreliable) from year to year, showing too much variability to tell whether progress is being made. With a "high n," the scores of students in the subgroup will not count toward AYP targets, making it impossible to tell whether these students are making progress or whether they are being left behind. There is no consensus about the right minimum number.

The *status models*, which have been federally approved for most states, base accountability on whether students reach a prescribed target or proficiency status, operationally defined as a cut-score on a test. Status models create uneven playing fields where students performing at lower levels than their age-mates—and the schools that serve them—have to make more progress to reach the required status. Alternatively, *growth models* have been developed, which compare a student's test performance in one year with his or her scores in succeeding years. Growth models permit measuring a student's improvement across time and the impact of the schooling the student has experienced. Yet, the U.S. Department of Education has approved only a few state requests to use growth models and only on a trial basis. As a result, in most states, poor students and their schools could be making greater progress than the more affluent, yet be judged as needing improvement in comparison with wealthier counterparts whom they have outperformed in terms of growth. President Barack Obama's Race to the Top program, in which states compete for federal monies based on a variety of criteria (including "turning around the lowest-achieving schools" and having "great teachers and leaders"), is meant to address some of NCLB's shortcomings.

School Improvements

In 2001, the Education Trust, a Washington, DC, policy group, listed 1,320 "high-flying schools" across the country in which half of the students were poor and half minority, yet scoring in their states' top thirds. Hope rose even faster than the reported score increases until researchers investigated the claims, which were based on single-subject gains, in single subjects, in single years. When Douglas at Harris Florida State University checked to see how many had made gains in two subjects, at two grade levels, over two years, all but 23 of the high-flying schools were grounded.

Researchers with the Civil Rights Project at Harvard University determined that the states reporting the biggest gains were those with the lowest expectations, that experienced teachers were transferring out of low-income minority schools, and that no significant headway had been made in closing the gap for minority and poor children since the 1970s–1980s with civil rights and antipoverty initiatives. Moreover, project researchers found that schools identified as needing improvement tended to enroll low-income students, to be racially segregated, and to fail to make the needed improvements. In a Hispanic P–5 school in Texas in 2005, Jennifer Booher-Jennings documented "educational triage," in which the overwhelming majority of instructional resources were concentrated on the "accountable kids," whose scores would figure in AYP determinations, and the "bubble kids," whose scores were near passing, at the expense of all others.

NCLB's assumption that educational accountability systems based on standards and standards-based tests will improve education has been tested independently. In 1996, the Pew Charitable Trusts awarded four-year grants to seven urban school districts to assist them in implementing standards-based reform. Five years later, as NCLB was nearing enactment, the Trusts reported that high-stakes accountability motivates educators to avoid penalties by raising test scores through less ambitious teaching, especially for low-performing students, and that emphasis on testing comes at the expense of curriculum, instruction, and professional development and prevents real improvement in student achievement. This comparison suggests that NCLB's logic was flawed from the start.

Saving or Abandoning Students and Public Education?

Options

States may refuse NCLB requirements and federal funding, although most, like Vermont, found they could not afford to do so. And NCLB came with a local price tag. Connecticut found itself facing $8 million in increased expenditures by 2008 related to NCLB and filed suit against NCLB's own prohibition against unfunded mandates, as did a Michigan school district and the National Education Association. Despite increased federal funding related to NCLB, such as grants to develop smaller learning communities in large high schools, NCLB has drained state and district coffers, whether through increased data collection, analysis, and reporting or through legal expenses.

Players

The special education impact has been problematic in two ways. One was exemplified by the lawsuit filed by two Illinois districts on the basis of conflicts between NCLB and the federal Individuals with Disabilities Education Act. The other has been the difficulty in raising the scores of students eligible for special services, a task so daunting that it became common knowledge in Washington that every district in the state not meeting the first AYP targets had failed on the basis of their special education subgroup. While some adjustments to the law have been made, this difficulty was predictable by educators, but they were left behind in the policy-making process.

Also left behind, according to an analysis of the policy-making process for one part of NCLB, the *Reading First* provisions, were professional education and educational measurement organizations, which have worked to provide policy analyses, conduct research on policy impact, and issue public statements. Commercial interests were not left behind, as witnessed by the recent furor over the U.S. Department of Education's narrowing of approved options regarding curricula and supplementary materials and also by this parody: No Psychometrician Left Unemployed.

As the 1990s' shift toward state legislation focused on tests rather than curriculum and professional development, NCLB has operated on an implicit theory of action that educators and students—the least powerful players in the system—would work harder if coerced. The results to date suggest that coercion may raise scores without raising achievement and may not close achievement gaps.

Reauthorization

Evidence suggests that schools categorized as needing improvement cannot bring all students to proficiency and are closed, that experienced teachers are leaving these schools behind, and promising students who want to transfer out of them outnumber the seats available in "high-flying schools." With the 2007 reauthorization of ESEA, consideration should have been given to the logical conclusion of these trends: NCLB might well leave public education behind. Nevertheless, the process of reforming it has already begun—in the guise of Race to the Top and other measures. To date, at least 27 states have adopted new national standards in English and math based, in part, on Race to the Top recommendations (Lewin 2010).

See also **Government Role in Schooling; Standardized Testing**

Further Reading

Abernathy, Scott Franklin, *No Child Left Behind and the Public Schools.* Ann Arbor: University of Michigan Press, 2007.

Bamberger, Michael J., Jim Rugh, and Linda Mabry, *RealWorld Evaluation: Working under Budget, Time, Data, and Political Constraints.* Thousand Oaks, CA: Sage, 2006.

Booher-Jennings, J., "Below the Bubble: 'Educational Triage' and the Texas Accountability System." *American Educational Research Journal* 42 (2005): 231–268.

Hayes, William, *No Child Left Behind: Past, Present, and Future.* Lanham, MD: Rowman & Littlefield, 2008.

Lewin, Tamar, "Many States Adopt National Standards for Their Schools. *New York Times* (July 21, 2010).

Linn, R. L., "Assessments and Accountability." *Educational Researcher* 29 (2000): 4–16.

Linn, R. L., E. L. Baker, and D. W. Betebenner, "Accountability Systems: Implications of Requirements of the No Child Left Behind Act of 2001." *Educational Researcher* 31 (2002): 3–16.

Ravitch, Diane, *The Death and Life of the Great American School System: How Testing and Choice Are Undermining Education.* New York: Basic Books, 2010.

Rebell, Michael A., and Jessica R. Wolff, eds., *NCLB at the Crossroads: Reexamining the Federal Effort To Close the Achievement Gap.* New York: Teachers College Press, 2009.

Reese, William J., *America's Public Schools: From the Common School to "No Child Left Behind."* Baltimore: Johns Hopkins University Press, 2005.

Sadovnik, Alan R., et al., eds., *No Child Left Behind and the Reduction of the Achievement Gap: Sociological Perspectives on Federal Educational Policy.* New York: Routledge, 2008.

Vinovskis, Maris, *From a Nation at Risk to No Child Left Behind: National Education Goals and the Creation of Federal Education Policy.* New York: Teachers College Press, 2009.

NUTRITION IN SCHOOLS

Ann Cooper and Lisa M. Holmes

The percentage of obese children in the United States today has more than doubled since 1970. More than 35 percent of the nation's children are overweight, 25 percent are obese, and 14 percent have type 2 diabetes, a condition previously seen primarily in adults. At the dawn of the 21st century, the Centers for Disease Control (CDC) reported that, of the children born in 2000, roughly one-third of all whites and half of all Hispanics and African Americans will develop diabetes in their lifetimes—most before they graduate from high school. At this rate, the CDC also reports, this group will be the first generation in U.S. history to die at a younger age than their parents. Processed foods favored by schools and busy moms for their convenience not only contribute to obesity; they also contain additives and preservatives and are tainted with herbicide and pesticide residues that are believed to cause a variety of illnesses, including cancer. In fact, current research shows that 40 percent of all cancers are attributable to diet. Many hundreds of thousands of Americans die of diet-related illness each year. People in the United States today simply do not know how to eat properly, and they do not seem to have time to figure out how, so fast food, home meal replacements, and processed foods take the place of good, healthy cooking.

Parents, pediatricians, and school administrators are increasingly concerned about children's health as it relates to diet. Most parents do not know what constitutes good childhood nutrition, and many feel they lack the time they would need to spend researching it. They rely, instead, on the United States Department of Agriculture (USDA)–approved National School Lunch program to provide their children with nutritionally balanced, healthful meals. The trouble is, the program alone cannot and is not doing so. While most schools continue to try to meet better nutritional guidelines, they are still not measuring up, and many are actually contributing to the crisis emerging over the last decade. Food is not respected; rather, it is something that must be made and consumed with increasing speed. In part, this is the result of the fact that there are more children than ever in schools with smaller cafeterias (often actually multipurpose rooms), forcing several short lunch shifts. Decreasing budgets, in many cases, have caused a decline in the quality of school meals.

For the most part, school lunch has deteriorated to institutional-style mayhem. Walk through the kitchen or lunchroom of almost any public or private school and "fast food nation" will ring with striking clarity. USDA-approved portions of processed foods are haphazardly dished out by harried cafeteria workers to frenzied students hurrying to finish their food in time for 10 minutes of recess. Nothing about the experience of being in a school cafeteria is calm—the din is deafening. Lunchrooms are vast open spaces filled with long tables flanked by dozens of chairs. There is no intimacy, no sense of calm, no respite from a morning of hard learning.

The noise and activity levels are not the only unpalatable aspects of lunchroom dining. A full 78 percent of the schools in the United States do not meet the USDA's nutritional guidelines, which is no surprise considering the fact that most schools keep the cost of the food for lunch under $1 per child. Also not surprisingly, children do not like the foods that are being served. A recent survey of local school children in northern Minnesota revealed the food is so abysmal that not even old standby favorites like cafeteria pizza and macaroni and cheese were given high marks. It is no wonder that kids are choosing fast foods, which are chemically engineered in many cases to be better tasting, over regular school lunch menu items. Children today are bombarded with food advertising that is reinforced by the careful placement of fast food chains in strip malls, nearby schools, and even on public school campuses. The big fast food chains have been aggressively and specifically targeting children for decades—they have even found ways to get inside schools and be part of the public school lunch menus. A mother from Aurora, Colorado, told the present authors that there is one Taco Bell and one Pizza Hut option available on every menu in her six-year-old son's lunchroom. She was told that the fast food program originally started as a "safety measure" to keep the high school and middle school students on school grounds, because, despite the fact that they had a closed campus, students were crossing busy streets to get to fast food restaurants near their schools. She thought "the fast food thing just trickled down to the elementary program." Of course the reality is that those schools were, and are, making money from million-dollar multiyear contracts with fast food companies.

School lunch menus have undergone some changes in recent years and are marginally improved, but nearly all schools continue to operate under the misguided notion that children prefer to eat frozen, processed, fried, sugary foods. Because most parents do not have time to spend in the kitchen the way the parents of generations past once did, the lunch lessons children are getting in school are the primary guideposts available to them. Poor in-school health and nutrition education is causing children and, by extension, their families to make bad food choices that are translating directly into big health problems—over $200 billion in health problems annually, in fact. Today, many parents, administrators, and concerned citizens are fighting to get fast food out of the nation's lunchrooms and improve the quality of school lunches from nutritional content all the way to the atmosphere in cafeterias. They believe that the tax money allocated to fund school lunches, which totals about $7 billion annually ($3 billion less than what was spent per month on the Iraq War), should be put to better use.

History of School Lunch

Most people assume that the school lunch program is a modern U.S. initiative. Not so. The very first school lunch program was started in Europe in the 1700s after teachers noticed that poor, malnourished children were having more difficulty concentrating than their well-fed classmates. Even more than three centuries ago, the ill effects of poor nutrition on health and education were so abundantly clear that they could not be ignored. The earliest programs were funded through the efforts of private charities with the humble goal of providing the most nutritious meals at the lowest possible cost—hallmarks that remain part of school lunch programs around the world today. When philanthropies could no longer support the needs of their communities, local and national governments stepped in to help. Parents were relieved to know that not only were their children being fed, but school attendance was soaring. At the same time, governments were able to almost guarantee themselves a larger number of healthier men to enlist in the armed services. From the beginning, the primary motivating factors behind school food programs were both charitable and political. The first U.S. school food programs, which started decades later, were no exception to this rule.

Major cities were among the first to put school food programs in place. Ellen H. Richards, home economics pioneer and the first woman admitted to the Massachusetts Institute of Technology (MIT), was a strong proponent not only for school meals but also for in-school nutrition education. During her tenure at as a professor at MIT, Richards spearheaded an effort to establish a Women's Laboratory and was successful in persuading the Women's Education Association of Boston to provide funding. Out of her work at the Women's Laboratory, Richards gathered research for several published works, two of which were *The Chemistry of Cooking and Cleaning* (1882; with Marion Talbot) and *Food Materials and Their Adulterations* (1885). In 1890, she helped open the New England Kitchen, whose purpose was to provide nutritious yet inexpensive food to working-class families in Boston while teaching them the principles of producing healthy, low-cost meals. Four years later, the Boston School Committee began receiving meals from the New England Kitchen, and Richards had almost single-handedly laid the foundation for a model of what was to eventually become the National School Lunch Program.

Philadelphia's first penny lunch program, organized and run by a private charity, also began in 1894, and its most significant contribution to today's school lunch program was the creation of the Lunch Committee of the Home and School League, the precursor to the modern-day Parent Teacher Association (PTA), which was instrumental in expanding the lunch program to nine other area schools.

About a decade later, in New York, Robert Hunter published *Poverty*, in which he made the assertion that between 60,000 and 70,000 children in New York City arrived at school with empty stomachs. It prompted a firestorm of investigative reports, including John Spargo's *The Bitter Cry of the Children*, published in 1906. In his book, Spargo supported Hunter's claims and urged society at large to take action on behalf of the children. Spargo's work in turn spurred further studies by physicians who began publishing reports about the malnutrition of New York City schoolchildren, which later led to a plea from the superintendent of New York City schools, William Maxwell, for a school lunch program where children could purchase healthy low-cost lunches every day. Maxwell's wishes were granted, and two schools were elected to participate in a trial run. Their success was undeniable, and two years later the New York City School Board approved the program and opened the door for a citywide school lunch program overseen by physicians with an eye toward honoring the ethnic and cultural traditions of the various school populations. Not surprisingly, the overall health of New York City's schoolchildren showed improvement very quickly. Ten years later, 17 public schools were participating in the program, and the first food safety measures, which included physical exams for food handlers as well as small pox vaccines, were established. As school lunch programs gained recognition and enjoyed greater successes, they began to pop up in towns and cities all over the country. Before the start of World War I, 13 states and Washington, DC, had some type of school food program in place.

As the war began, the school lunch program was expanded, due in no small part to the fact that approximately one-third of all young men attempting to enlist were turned away because of diseases attributable to malnutrition. At that time, the programs were still generally funded and operated by private charities, but when the Great Depression hit in the 1930s, private charities and individuals could no longer support school feeding programs, and hunger in the United States became more widespread. It was clear that the federal government would have to step in, both to combat hunger and to create much-needed jobs.

People were hungry, not because there was no food available but because they did not have the money to buy it, and, as a result, U.S. farmers were left with enormous agricultural surpluses and were in danger of losing their farms. In an effort to both assist farmers by purchasing their products and feed needy families and schoolchildren using agricultural surpluses, the Congress passed the Agricultural Act of 1935, Public Law 320, which required the cooperation of federal, state, and local governments to implement and establish a structure upon which future commodity distributions programs were built.

During this time, the Works Progress Administration (WPA) was organized to provide work on public projects to the unemployed, and school lunches were a perfect fit for the program. Not only did WPA workers cook and serve lunches, but they canned the fresh fruits and vegetables provided to them through the surplus program and through school gardens. Until that time, nothing had a greater impact on the National School Lunch Program than the WPA. By 1941, school lunches were being served by the WPA in every state to a total of about 2 million schoolchildren. The program was also responsible for employing more than 64,000 people in school lunch programs at that time. Just one year later, 6 million children were participating.

Unfortunately, with the onset of World War II, the school lunch program took a hit as surpluses were redirected to feed troops, but in 1943, Congress amended the Agricultural Act of 1935 to "provide school districts directly with funds for implementation of their school lunch programs."

At war's end General Lewis Blaine Hershey, director of Selective Services, declared that malnutrition was a national security risk and stated before Congress that the United States had 155,000 war casualties directly related to malnutrition. It became clear that strong federal legislation was necessary, and in the summer of 1946, the National School Lunch Act, Public Law 396, 79th Congress, was signed by President Harry S. Truman. The new law specified permanent funding through the Secretary of Agriculture "to assist with the health of the nation's children, and ensure a market for farmers" (USDA 1946). Section Two of the law states the purpose of the act:

> It is hereby declared to be the policy of Congress, as a measure of national security to safeguard the health and well-being of the Nation's children and to encourage the domestic consumption of nutritious agricultural commodities and other food, by assisting the States, through grants-in-aid and other means, in providing an adequate supply of foods and other facilities for the establishment, maintenance, operation, and expansion of nonprofit school lunch programs. (USDA 1946, 231)

With the passing of PL 396, the National School Lunch Program was given an unshakable foundation. The guidelines for administration of school lunch programs under PL 396 include:

1. Lunches must meet minimum nutritional requirements set by the Secretary of Agriculture.
2. Free or reduced-cost meals must be made available to children whom local authorities determine unable to pay.
3. Discrimination against children unable to pay is forbidden.
4. The program must be operated on a nonprofit basis.
5. Foods designated by the secretary as abundant must be utilized.

6. Donated commodity foods must be utilized.
7. Records, receipts, and expenditures must be kept and submitted in a report to the state agency when required.

Funds were also specifically set aside for the purchase of equipment so that money given to schools for food would be used only to purchase food. In 1954, the Special Milk Program was set in place, making surplus milk available to schools in much the same way as other surplus agricultural foods had previously been made part of the program.

Between 1955 and 1966, a decline in nutritional intake was reported by the Household Food Consumption Survey of 1965–1966 and resulted in the Child Nutrition Act of 1966, Public Law 89–642, allowing for increased funding to create programs whose sole purpose was to improve child nutrition. The Special Milk Program became part of the Child Nutrition Act, and through the Child Nutrition Act schools were provided nonfood assistance, which made funds available for the purchase of equipment as long as schools were able to cover 25 percent of their equipment costs. In 1966, a pilot breakfast program was given a two-year test run, and allowances were made for hiring more employees to run the school food programs. It was at this point that all school food programs, including those created for preschool children, were placed under the aegis of one federal agency, standardizing the management of school lunch programs across the country.

In the 1970s, nutritionists began taking a closer look at school meals and criticized the program for not taking into account students of different ages and body types. The same meals were being served to all students—athletes, obese children, undernourished kids, first-graders, and high school students alike. They also looked at sugar and fat content and questioned the general healthfulness of school lunches. It was at this time that nutritionists first began to look to the National School Lunch Program as a tool for educating children about good nutrition, and, in 1979, school districts were required to include children and parents in their school food programs, making them participants in the overall eating experience—from taste tests to menu planning and cafeteria design. After a decade of discussion on the subject of the healthfulness of school meals, new regulations were put in place that, among other things, included a provision that required different portion sizes for children of different age groups.

Also in the 1970s, vending machines made their appearance in public schools. There was some immediate concern on the part of parents and educators about the types of products being sold, and, as a result, the Secretary of Agriculture issued regulations in 1980 restricting the sale of sodas, gum, and certain types of candy. Unfortunately, the regulations were overturned in a 1984 lawsuit brought by the National Soft Drink Association. The judge presiding over the case stated that the Secretary of Agriculture had acted outside the bounds of his authority and was permitted only to regulate food sales within the cafeteria. So, although they were not allowed in cafeterias, vending machines once again found their way onto public school campuses around the country.

The 1980s were a time of great strain on the school lunch program. The Reagan administration forced budget cuts, causing meal prices to rise and some children to drop out of the program altogether. In an effort to save money and still appear to be meeting the federal guidelines for a healthy school lunch, the government made attempts to add certain foods to the "permissible" list. The one that made the most people sit up and take notice was the shocking allowance of ketchup as a vegetable. Also during the 1980s, many schools were forced to create noncooking kitchens, which, by default, increased the quantity of processed foods being served.

By the time President Bill Clinton took office, the USDA was still falling well short of meeting its own dietary guidelines in the public school system, which was not surprising in a program that for decades had been running on agricultural surpluses like milk, cheese, and high-fat meat products. As a matter of fact, the fat content of school lunches was well above recommended dietary guidelines, and meals were falling well short of students' needed nutrient values. Ellen Haas was appointed as Assistant Secretary of Agriculture in charge of Food and Consumer Affairs, and it became her job to oversee the National School Lunch Program. Haas and Secretary of Agriculture, Mike Espy, held a series of national hearings that were open to both experts and concerned citizens and put together their School Meals Initiative for Healthy Children in the summer of 1994. It required that schools meet USDA Federal Dietary Guidelines by 1998. The directive that an average of 30 percent or less of the week's calorie count come from fat (and only 10 percent from saturated fat) angered the major players in the meat and dairy industries who had been particularly reliant upon the school food program to take their surpluses. Nevertheless, Haas pushed forward, making her School Meals Initiative the first substantial revision to the National School Lunch Program in nearly 50 years. The hallmark of Haas's program was ease of implementation through the reduction of bureaucratic red tape.

Despite the fact that Haas's proposal became a federal mandate in 1994, more than a decade later, schools still struggled to meet its demands. Poultry, soy (incidentally, both tofu and soy milk are not considered part of a reimbursable meal), and a greater variety of fruits and vegetables were designated as permissible by the USDA, but fat content was down by only 4 percent and remained at about 34 percent on average. And while 70 percent of all elementary schools met government mandated nutrient guidelines, only 20 percent of secondary schools had been able to do so. To make matters worse, more snacks were being offered at school than ever before, and fast food chains were inching their way into the school system. Cash-poor schools looked to school snacks and fast food to help raise money for, among other things, extracurricular programs. Today, most schools still have no nutrition curriculum, and those that do use heavily biased educational materials donated by the meat and dairy industries. Students are being bombarded with an overwhelming amount of extremely persuasive advertising for high-fat, low-nutrient foods every day. In fact, food companies spend approximately $30 billion to underwrite about 40,000 commercials annually. It is nearly impossible for the National School Lunch Program to come out ahead, no matter how nutritious the meals become, if fast foods are among the choices in the lunchroom. When presented at school with a choice between a familiar Taco Bell selection and school cafeteria mystery meat, it is a no-brainer what most students will choose.

School meals reach nearly 27 million children each day; for some, what they eat at school is the most nutritious meal of their day, which is great news. Still, the childhood obesity crisis is at an all-time high. Children are getting fatter and fatter—in fact, nearly 20 percent of all U.S. children are considered obese by today's standards.

Some school districts, like Berkeley Unified School District in Berkeley, California, have found ways to work within the national guidelines while supporting an innovative interdisciplinary gardening and nutrition program that directly involves children in growing and cooking their own food, in conjunction with serving nutritious and delicious food in the cafeterias. Other schools have raised money for salad bars, and many school districts around the country have banned soda and vending machines. Private and charter schools like the Ross School on Long Island and Promise Academy in New York City are creating school food programs that are making their way, in bits and pieces, into the country's federally funded school lunch program. Progress is being made, but it is slow.

In 2006, through the Child Nutrition and WIC Reauthorization Act of 2004, the federal government mandated that each school district form a Wellness Committee and draft a Wellness Policy to establish standards for nutrition and good health in the public school system. The policies were required to address the quality of meals, regularity of exercise, and nutrition education. Unfortunately, there is no real national standard, nor is there any significant funding available to help school food administrators implement their plans. Parents and administrators continue to express their frustration, and educators on the front line continue to ask why the National School Lunch Program is overseen by the U.S. Department of Agriculture, whose primary purpose is to support the nation's farms through subsidy programs that require public schools to utilize high-fat, highly processed foods that are contraindicative to good nutrition. In 2007, at the behest of Congress, a committee made up of experts from the Centers for Disease Control and the Institute of Medicine compiled a comprehensive report on nutrition standards for foods in schools. As of mid-2010, however, most of its recommendations had yet to be acted upon in any systematic way, even while a growing number of individual school districts had instituted measures aimed at improvement.

See also **Government Role in Schooling; Marketing to Children (vol. 1); Genetically Modified Organisms (vol. 4); Obesity (vol. 4)**

Further Reading

Committee on Nutrition Standards for Foods in Schools, *Nutrition Standards for Foods in Schools: Leading the Way toward Healthier Youth.* New York: National Academies Press, 2007.

Cooper, Ann, and Lisa M. Holmes, *Bitter Harvest.* New York: Routledge, 2000.

Cooper, Ann, and Lisa M. Holmes, *Lunch Lessons: Changing the Way We Feed Our Children.* New York: HarperCollins, 2006.

Levine, Susan, *School Lunch Politics: The Surprising History of America's Favorite Welfare Program.* Princeton, NJ: Princeton University Press, 2010.

Pollan, Michael, *The Omnivore's Dilemma: A Natural History of Four Meals.* New York: Penguin Press, 2006.

Poppendieck, Janet, *Free for All: Fixing School Food in America.* Berkeley: University of California Press, 2010.

Schlosser, Eric, *Fast Food Nation.* New York: Harper Perennial, 2005.

USDA, National School Lunch Act, 79 P.L. 396, 60 Stat. 230. 1946.

O

OBSCENITY AND INDECENCY

Gwenyth Jackaway

Areas that have challenged the media's right to freedom of speech have long revolved around issues of human sexuality and expressions and language that violate standards of taste and decency. The history of censoring sexually explicit scenes considered to violate standards of decency goes back to the early days of film. As social mores and community standards have evolved over the years, so too have legal protections and the definition of what is acceptable and what is not on television, radio, and film. The changes in Federal Communications Commission (FCC) policy brought about by the "wardrobe malfunction" that exposed Janet Jackson's breast during her halftime performance with Justin Timberlake at the 2004 Super Bowl illustrate that these topics remain battleground issues for the media.

Obscenity

Given America's Puritan heritage, the long history of debate over the definition of obscenity, and the measures taken to stop it, should come as no surprise. Under British law in the time of the monarchies, sexually explicit writings and images were considered "obscene libel" and were outlawed. When the Puritans left Britain to pursue religious freedom, they brought their codes of sexual modesty and chastity with them. Hundreds of years later, despite the sexual revolution of the 1960s, the United States remains a country in which depictions of nudity and sexuality make many uncomfortable and are frequently met with calls for sanction or censorship. Despite the fact that the First Amendment provides for the separation of church and state, this is one area in which religious beliefs about sexuality and sin have consistently spilled over into the realm of law.

Throughout the 19th and 20th centuries, both the federal and state governments passed laws to stop the flow of material considered to be obscene or indecent. In 1842, Congress passed the first antiobscenity statutes, barring the "importation of all indecent and obscene prints, paintings, lithographs, engravings and transparencies." This statute was amended numerous times to include photographs, films, and phonograph records. The Comstock Act of 1873 made it illegal to use the U.S. postal system to distribute obscenity. At that time, obscenity was defined as material that has a "tendency to deprave and corrupt those whose minds are open to such immoral influences." This broad definition was used by both the U.S. Customs office and U.S. Postal Service to ban such works as Walt Whitman's *Leaves of Grass,* James Joyce's *Ulysses,* and Ernest Hemingway's *For Whom the Bell Tolls.*

With the arrival of cinema in the early 20th century, efforts to stop the flow of erotic imagery in the United States intensified. City and state censorship boards sprung up around the country to prohibit the exhibition of films containing sexually explicit scenes. In 1915, the Supreme Court upheld the practice of these censorship boards, arguing that film was not covered under the First Amendment. This gave the green light to film censorship all over the country. In response, the movie studios banded together in the 1930s to adopt the Hays Code, a set of self-imposed decency standards designed to "clean up" Hollywood and protect the studios from the loss of revenue caused by local censorship. These standards were later abandoned when the Supreme Court reversed its original position on cinema, granting the medium First Amendment protection in 1952.

By the middle of the 20th century, as sexual mores began to change, an increasing number of court cases began to challenge the various antiobscenity statutes around the country. Finally, in a series of rulings, the Supreme Court developed a legal definition for obscenity. Once they had defined this category of speech, they ruled that any form of communication meeting the criteria of obscenity is *not* protected by the First Amendment. This means that federal or state laws banning obscenity do not violate the First Amendment. Because of the great variety of sexual and moral standards throughout the country, the Supreme Court left it up to the states to determine whether, and to what extent, they would ban obscene communication.

Ironically, the issue of obscenity is one of those rare topics that has the power to unite political activists from both ends of the political spectrum. Conservative voters often express concern about obscenity on the basis of the threat that they feel it poses to the family. On the other hand, some liberals are also concerned about obscenity, arguing that pornography contributes to violence against women. Calls for censorship can come from both the right and the left, sometimes on the same issue, even if for very different reasons.

The development of new communication technologies has greatly complicated the issue of obscenity in the United States. In 1957, when first defining obscenity, the

Supreme Court included the "contemporary community standards" clause into the definition in an attempt to take into consideration the reality that sexual and moral standards vary widely by locale. Yet new means of transmitting sexual imagery have rendered this standard difficult to apply. When a small town decides that it does not want pornographic magazines in its local bookstore, residents seeking such material have the option of buying it in a larger city, where fewer restrictions exist. But whose values should determine the national standards regarding "taboo" material for electronic media? The Internet allows for the transmission of explicit imagery to anyone with a computer, regardless of where they live, making it very difficult to set or enforce obscenity or indecency laws governing computer communication. Each time a new communication technology is invented, providing new ways to disseminate controversial content, the national commitment to freedom of speech is tested once again. Given the political and religious diversity in the United States, the continuing development of communication technologies, and the ever-popular nature of sexually explicit media content, the issue of free speech and obscenity is sure to continue challenging future generations of Americans.

Indecency

In addition to concerns about sexually explicit media content, the United States also has a long history of identifying certain words and images as taboo, and therefore off-limits in "polite society." At one time in the nation's history, social convention served as an effective censor of "vulgar" language and gestures, and most people were willing to abide by the unwritten rules of convention. With the many social changes of the late 20th century, these rules, like so many others, were gradually tested. Because both radio and television are regulated by the U.S. government, these channels of communication have been the terrain on which the debate about the boundaries of propriety has taken place.

DEFINING OBSCENITY

The legal definition of obscenity was developed in a series of Supreme Court cases, most notably *Roth v. U.S.*, 1957, and *Miller v. California*, 1974. Currently, in order for a piece of mediated communication to be considered obscene—and therefore lacking First Amendment protection—the following conditions must be met:

1. An average person, applying contemporary local community standards, finds that the work, taken as a whole, appeals to prurient interest. (The legal definition of *prurient interest* is a morbid, degrading, and unhealthy interest in sex, as distinguished from a mere candid interest in sex.)
2. The work depicts in a patently offensive way sexual conduct specifically defined by applicable state law.
3. The work in question lacks serious literary, artistic, political, or scientific value.

The FCC, which sets the rules governing the broadcasting system, has defined indecency as "language or material that, in context, depicts or describes, in terms patently offensive as measured by contemporary community standards for the broadcast medium, sexual or excretory organs or activities." Indecent programming contains patently offensive sexual or excretory material that does not rise to the level of obscenity. Because obscenity lacks First Amendment protection, it cannot be broadcast on the public airwaves. Indecent speech, on the other hand, is covered by the First Amendment, and thus cannot be barred from the airwaves entirely. This poses a dilemma: how can a free society balance the rights of adults to consume adult-oriented material with the goal of shielding children from language or imagery that some feel is inappropriate for young audiences?

The solution, as devised by the FCC, in response to several key Supreme Court rulings, is known as the "safe harbor" provision, which prohibits the broadcasting of indecent material between the hours of 6:00 A.M. and 10:00 P.M. Broadcast companies, stations, and on-air personalities violating this rule are subject to fines. Like the laws prohibiting obscenity, rules restricting indecency are inconsistently enforced, with great fluctuations depending upon the political and religious climate predominating in the nation at any particular time. When the nation is in a more conservative period, greater concern is expressed about the transmission of such material.

The fines imposed on broadcasters by the FCC for indecency violations were, at one time, set at a relatively low rate of several thousand dollars per incident and were rarely enforced. This changed significantly following an incident involving singers Janet Jackson and Justin Timberlake, in which Jackson's breast was inadvertently exposed to a national audience watching the CBS television coverage of the halftime performance of the 2004 Super Bowl. In response to the tremendous public outcry about the event, particularly from conservative viewers, Congress and the FCC raised the indecency fines to over 20 times their original level. Viacom, then owners of the CBS network, were fined a record-breaking $550,000 for airing the incident, despite the fact that all parties involved claimed that it had been an accident.

During the same period, shock-jock radio personality Howard Stern, long famous for his off-color language and humor, became a target for public concerns about indecency on the airwaves. Clear Channel Communications, the national radio chain that had carried Stern's syndicated program, dropped him from its program lineup after being charged heavy fines for airing his material. In a move clearly designed to send a strong message, the FCC also issued fines of over half a million dollars to Stern himself for violating restrictions on broadcasting indecency. Some critics at the time argued that the real reason for the strong stand taken against Stern was that the radio personality had begun to use his airtime to criticize President George W. Bush.

Whether it was indecency or politics that turned Stern into a target, it was a new communication technology that provided the "solution." In a development that illustrates the power of new media to allow taboo messages to bypass existing restrictions on controversial speech, Howard Stern moved from broadcast to satellite radio, which, at the time of this writing, is not governed by content restrictions on indecency.

The Communications Decency Act

The Communications Decency Act attempted to introduce a wide range of broadcasting-type controls on the Internet. When the act passed into law on February 1, 1996, as part of the Telecommunications Reform Act, it met with protest from a broad range of groups promoting freedom of speech, from the American Civil Liberties Union to the Electronic Frontier Foundation (EFF). The EFF launched a blue ribbon campaign calling for Internet users to protest the legislation by displaying the anticensorship blue ribbon on their Web pages.

Critics charged that the Act was one of the most restrictive forms of censorship applied in the United States and that it turned the Internet from one of the most free forums for speech to one of the most tightly regulated. The act made it a crime to knowingly transmit any communication accessible to minors that could be considered "obscene, lewd, lascivious, filthy, or indecent." It also prevented any publicity of abortion services. Publishers of offending material could be prosecuted, and also those who distribute it—Internet service providers. In an attempt to avoid prosecution, they may have had to act as private censors. The penalty was a sentence of up to two years in prison and a $100,000 fine.

By June 1996, a three-judge panel in Philadelphia ruled that the act was unnecessarily broad in its scope, violating constitutional guarantees to freedom of speech. The act also infringed on privacy rights by empowering federal agencies to intervene in, for example, the sending of private e-mail between individuals.

On June 26, 1997, the U.S. Supreme Court agreed with the district court judges that the Communications Decency Act was unconstitutional. The judges pointed out that TV and radio were originally regulated because of the scarcity of frequencies in the broadcast spectrum, which is not true of the Internet. The judges stated that the concern to protect children "does not justify an unnecessarily broad suppression of speech addressed to adults. As we have explained, the Government may not 'reduc[e] the adult population…to…only what is fit for children.'"

After the Communications Decency Act was struck down, new legislation was passed: the Children's Internet Protection Act (CIPA). The federal statute requires Internet blocking of speech that is obscene, or "harmful to minors," in all schools and libraries receiving certain federal funding. CIPA, also known as the Internet Blocking Law, was also challenged. The EFF charged that the law damages the free speech rights of library patrons and Web publishers.

On June 23, 2003, the Supreme Court upheld CIPA. The court found that the use of Internet blocking, also known as filtering, is constitutional because the need for libraries to prevent minors from accessing obscene materials outweighs the free speech rights of library patrons and Web site publishers. However, many independent research studies show that Internet blocking software is incapable of blocking only the materials required by CIPA. The CIPA law is problematic because speech that is harmful to minors is still legal for adults, and not all library patrons are minors.

Conclusion

Debates regarding obscenity and indecency are so highly charged because they speak to core values and behavioral norms by which various groups and individuals expect or demand others to live. Thus, for instance, gay and lesbian literature, film, and television have often been coded as obscene or indecent when judged from a conservatively heteronormative value system, resulting in parental warnings being attached to programs that in any way mention, much less depict, gay or lesbian sexuality. Even medical terminology remains obscene and indecent to some, especially in media that are available to children. This poses the significant problem to regulators and producers of determining a standard definition of obscenity and indecency and predictably entails outrage and activism on behalf of those who disagree with the standard of the moment.

As the reactions to obscenity and indecency fluctuate, as rules and conventions ebb and flow, and as ever-developing media technologies introduce new battlegrounds, so too will our definitions of what should and should not be said or shown change in the future. Obscenity and indecency are likely to form the substance of many a debate long into the future, as we use media depictions and imagery as the fodder for vigorous discussion over what constitutes appropriate behavior both inside and outside of the media.

See also **Pornography; Shock Jocks, or Rogue Talk Radio; Violence and Media; Sex and Advertising (vol. 1)**

Further Reading

Bernstein, Matthew, *Controlling Hollywood: Censorship and Regulation in the Studio Era*. New Brunswick, NJ: Rutgers University Press, 1999.

Heins, Marjorie, *Not in Front of the Children: "Indecency," Censorship, and the Innocence of Youth*. New York: Hill and Wang, 2001.

Hilliard, Robert L., and Michael C. Keith, *Dirty Discourse: Sex and Indecency in Broadcasting*, 2d ed. Malden, MA: Blackwell, 2007.

Leff, Leonard J., *The Dame in the Kimono: Hollywood, Censorship, and the Production Code*. Lexington: University Press of Kentucky, 2001.

Lipshultz, Jeremy H., *Broadcast Indecency: FCC Regulation and the First Amendment*. Newton, MA: Focus Press, 1997.

Sandler, Kevin, *The Naked Truth: Why Hollywood Does Not Make NC-17 Films*. New Brunswick, NJ: Rutgers University Press, 2006.

Sova, Dawn B., *Forbidden Films: Censorship Histories of 125 Motion Pictures*. New York: Facts on File, 2001.

P

PORNOGRAPHY

Jane Caputi and Casey McCabe

Pornography is defined in the *New Oxford American Dictionary* as "printed or visual material containing the explicit description or display of sexual organs or activity, intended to stimulate erotic rather than aesthetic or emotional feelings." While pornography involving children is widely condemned, it remains a serious international problem. Pornography involving adults, although contentious, is a massive international media industry.

Pornography—from religious, commercial, social, cultural, artistic, feminist, and gay-friendly perspectives—is variously defined, criticized, and defended. While obscenity historically has not been protected under the First Amendment, very little material has been found by the courts to meet the standard for obscenity. The pornography industry is a multibillion-dollar one; novel technologies and media—beginning with the printing press and photography and continuing through film, home video, cable television, the Internet, and digital imaging—historically have worked to expand its reach. Researchers study the impact and effects of pornography on individuals as well as society: who uses pornography and why; how pornography influences attitudes and behaviors, including misogynist attitudes and violence against women; the history of pornography; textual analysis of stories and images; and pornography as a cinematic genre.

Feminists particularly have engaged in wide-ranging debate, with some viewing pornography as a cornerstone industry in promulgating sexist beliefs, actively oppressing women, and exploiting sexuality and others claiming pornography as a potentially liberatory genre, stressing the importance of maintaining the freedom of sexual imagination. In recent times, sexual and sexually objectifying and violent images, based in pornographic conventions, increasingly pervade mainstream culture, raising further debates as to their impact.

History

Sexually explicit and arousing stories and depictions have from earliest histories been part of human cultures—in erotic contexts as well as, and often simultaneously with, sacred, artistic, folkloric, and political. Modern pornography began to emerge in the 16th century, merging explicit sexual representation with a challenge to some, though not all, traditional moral conventions, for pornography was largely the terrain of male elites and represented their desires and points of view.

In the United States after World War II and spurred on by new sexological research, reproductive technologies, emerging movements for social justice, and the formation of the modern consumer economy, the state began to retreat from some of its efforts toward the regulation of sexuality. This allowed the emergence of the modern pornography industry. *Playboy* was launched in 1953, followed by a number of men's magazines, the large-scale production and dissemination of pornographic film and video, and the burgeoning of the industry through mainstreaming as well as enhancement by new technologies. Since 1957, the Supreme Court has held that obscenity is not protected by the First Amendment. In 1973, the Court gave a three-part means of identifying obscenity, including: Whether the average person, applying contemporary community standards, would find that the work appealing to the prurient interest; whether the work is patently offensive; and whether the work, taken as a whole, lacks serious literary, artistic, political, or scientific value. All three conditions must be met for it to be considered obscene.

"I ONLY READ IT FOR THE INTERVIEWS"

In the wake of hard-core pornography, many companies have been remarkably successful selling soft-core, "artistic," or "thinking man's" pornography. Such pornography usually eschews showing the actual act of intercourse in photographic form or close-ups in video form and lays claim to legitimacy by surrounding itself with the nonpornographic. Leading the pack here is *Playboy* magazine, whose interviews with major intellectuals, politicians, and other cultural elites have allowed the infamous excuse for those buying the magazine that "I only read it for the interviews." By avoiding the label of hard-core pornography, moreover, producers of many such images in this vein can also declare that they are merely continuing in the age-old tradition of art's fascination with the nude. As a result, soft-core pornography fills much late-night pay-cable programming, has worked its way down from the top shelf of the magazine rack, and often enjoys mainstream acceptance or at least tolerance.

In the contemporary period, Fortune 500 corporations like AT&T and General Motors now have affiliates that produce pornography, and, although it is difficult to obtain precise data, most researchers conclude that pornography in the United States annually results in profits from $5 billion to $10 billion, if not more, and globally $56 billion or more. Legal actions against pornography have virtually halted, highlighted by a 2005 obscenity case brought by the federal government against Extreme Associates, a production company featured in a 2002 PBS *Frontline* documentary, "American Porn." Extreme Associates has an Internet site for members and also makes films featuring scenes of men degrading, raping, sexually torturing, and murdering women. A U.S. District Court judge dismissed the case. There was no dispute that the materials were obscene. Rather, he found that obscenity laws interfered with the exercise of liberty, privacy, and speech and that the law could not rely upon a commonly accepted moral code or standard to prohibit obscene materials.

Definition and Debates

Pornography is generally associated with deliberately arousing and explicit sexual imagery, which renders it deviant for traditional patriarchal religious orientations that continue to associate sexuality with sin while equating chastity and strictly regulated sexual behavior in heterosexual marriage with goodness.

"Family values" functions as a byword for antipornography patriarchal positions that condemn not only all sexual representations but also women's sexual and reproductive autonomy as well as any nonheterosexual and nonmonogamous sexuality. Some pornography advocates critique this heterosexist morality, identifying themselves as "prosex." Others defend pornography by foregrounding it as a First Amendment issue. Both groups tend to defend sexual representations, as well as diverse adult consensual sexual practices, as a form of free speech and expression, as essential to the imagination, as an element of all of the arts, and as a potentially revolutionary force for social change.

Virtually all feminists argue that sexuality must be destigmatized, reconceptualized, and defined in ways that refuse sexist moralities. The association of sexuality with sin is a feature of specifically patriarchal (male-defined and dominating) societies. Such societies control and regulate female sexuality and reproduction, for example, by designating women as the sexual other while men stand in for the generic human; by mandating heterosexuality; and by basing that heterosexuality in supposedly innate gender roles of male dominance and female submission. These societies foster conditions that impose a sexual double standard, selecting some women (associated with men who have some social power) for socially acceptable if inferior status in the male-dominant family, and channel other women, girls, and boys and young men (those without social power or connections) into prostitution and pornography. Patriarchal societies give men, officially or not, far more latitude in sexual behavior, and pornography and prostitution—institutions historically geared to men's desires and needs—are the necessary dark side of patriarchal marriage and moralistic impositions of sexual modesty. In this way, pornography and conventional morality, though supposedly opposites, actually work hand in glove to assure men's access to women and male domination and female stigmatization and subordination.

Some feminists argue that as sexuality is destigmatized, sex work—including prostitution and pornography—can be modes whereby women can express agency and achieve sexual and fiscal autonomy. Those associated with what is defined affirmatively as queer culture—including gay, lesbian, transgendered, and heterosexual perspectives and practices that challenge conventional roles—often argue that open and free sexual representation is essential to communicate their history and culture and that social opposition to pornography is fundamentally based in opposition to sexual freedom and diversity.

Mainstream cultural critics of pornography point to the ways that contemporary pornography has become increasingly ubiquitous. They argue that pornography damages relationships between persons, producing unrealistic and often oppressive ideas of sex and beauty; that it limits rather than expands the sexual imagination; that it can foster addictive or obsessive responses; and that it increasingly serves as erroneous sex education for children and teenagers.

Antipornography feminists, while opposing censorship, point out that pornography is a historically misogynist institution—one whose very existence signifies that women are dominated. Pornography not only often openly humiliates and degrades women, but it brands women as sex objects in a world where sex itself is considered antithetical to mind or spirit. They contend that mainstream pornography defines sex in sexist ways, normalizing and naturalizing male dominance and female submission and, by virtue of its ocularcentric and voyeuristic base, promotes a fetishistic and objectifying view of the body and the sexual subject.

Andrea Dworkin and Catharine MacKinnon are well known for their radical feminist approach to pornography. In a model Civil-Rights Antipornography Ordinance, they propose an ordinance that would have nothing to do with police action or censorship but would allow complaints and civil suits brought by individual plaintiffs. The ordinance defines pornography in a way that distinguishes it from sexually explicit materials in general. Rather, pornography consists of materials that represent "the graphic, sexually explicit subordination of women" or "men, transsexuals or children used in the place of women." Their extended discussion delineates specific elements—for example, women being put into "postures or positions of sexual submission, servility or display"; "scenarios of degradation, injury, abasement, torture"; and individuals "shown as filthy or inferior, bleeding, bruised, or hurt in a context that makes these conditions sexual." Although several communities passed versions of this law, it was overturned in the courts as a violation of the First Amendment. At the same time, courts have recognized the use of pornography as a tool of sexual harassment that generates a hostile climate for women workers in offices, factories, and other job sites.

Numerous feminists link the practices and underlying themes of pornography to other forms of oppression. For example, Patricia Hill Collins links the style and themes of U.S. pornography to the beliefs and practices associated with white enslavement of Africans and their descendents—including bondage, whipping, and the association of black women and men with animals and hypersexuality.

Uses and Effects

Research has examined the role of mass-mediated pornography in causing harmful or unwanted social effects, including the furtherance of sexism as well as violence against women and/or willingness to tolerate such violence; profiles of those who work in pornography as well as those who enjoy it; and the potentially addictive aspects of pornography.

Research into the uses and effects of pornography has been conducted employing experimental studies, anecdotal evidence from interviews and personal stories, polling, and statistical data asserting connections between the existence or use of pornography and undesirable social phenomena. Two presidential commissions studied the effects of pornography, one beginning in the 1960s and the other in the 1980s. The first concluded that there were no harmful effects; the second concluded that sexually violent and degrading pornography normalized sexist attitudes (e.g., believing that women want to be raped by men) and therefore contributed to actual violence. These conclusions have been subjected to wide-ranging debate, for example, around the validity of information

DID YOU KNOW? CYBERPORNOGRAPHY AND HUMAN INTIMACY

From pornography's early expression in engravings to film and magazines, writing and research designed to understand pornography and its effects on human behavior and sexuality have occupied scholars from the social sciences to the humanities. With the rise of the Internet and the vast cyberporn industry, new questions about human sexuality have occupied researchers trying to explain the motivations and consequences of heavy use of—or even what some characterize as addiction to—online pornography. Pamela Paul and other health researchers have found disturbing consequences for male intimacy in those who are habituated to cyberporn. Many men accustomed to erotic responses from online pornography reported difficulty being aroused without it, even when having sex with their wives or girlfriends. One consequence of cyberporn, then, is a loss of erotic desire during sexual intimacy. Many men reported the need to recall or imitate the acts, behaviors, attitudes, and images of cyberporn in order to achieve sexual gratification, leaving them and their women partners at a loss for creative eroticism, individual expression, and interpersonal connection. Such sensibilities in the age of the Internet need not be unique to gender or sexual preference, and more research on the effects of mediated sexual experience are necessary to understand the complex nature of the relationship between human sexuality and media.

obtained from necessarily contrived laboratory experiments (usually with male students), the difficulty of defining common terms like *degradation,* the unwillingness of people to accurately report their own behavior, the political bias of the researchers, and so on.

Internationally, feminist researchers point out links between pornography and sex trafficking and slavery as well as the use of pornography in conquest, where prostitution is imposed and pornography is made of the subjugated women as well as men. For example, during the war between Serbia and Bosnia-Herzegovina and Croatia, Serbian forces systematically raped women as a tactic of genocide, and these rapes were photographed and videotaped. Sexual torture, photographed and displayed as kind of war pornography, also was practiced by U.S. troops against Iraqi prisoners in the U.S. prison at Abu Ghraib in Iraq in 2003. Subsequently, investigators released photographs of male Iraqis sexually humiliated and tortured by U.S. soldiers. There also were pornographic videos and photographs made of female prisoners, but these have not been released. Feminist activists argue that, in the case of war and forced occupation, pornography regularly is used to bolster the invading forces' morale and to destroy the self-regard of occupied peoples who are used for pornography as well as sex tourism.

Conclusion

Pornography is now openly diffused throughout U.S. society. Not only has it grown enormously as an industry, but, in mainstream imagery, other media outlets use typical pornographic images and themes in advertisements, music videos, and video games and to publicize celebrities and events. Pornography also has become a legitimate topic for academic study and the subject of college classes.

Research shows that more women now use pornography. As part of the feminist project of redefining sexuality, there has been a surge in erotic stories and images aimed at women audiences. Some feminists and those identified with queer communities have begun to produce what they consider to be subversive pornographies that challenge both traditional morality and the conventions of mainstream, sexist pornography—for example, by featuring models who are not conventionally beautiful and by valorizing nontraditional gender roles and nonheterosexist practices; by celebrating the body, sexuality, and pleasure; by acknowledging lesbian, gay, and transgender realities and desires; and by stressing women's sexual desire and agency.

Some applaud this expansion of pornography as reflecting greater sexual autonomy for women as well as a liberalization of social attitudes toward sexuality. Others argue that the mainstreaming of pornography does not produce or reflect freedom, but instead represents a backlash against the women's liberation movement and furthers the commoditization of sexuality—for example, in the ways that young girls are now routinely represented, often fashionably dressed, as sexually available. The system of patriarchal domination has always, one way or another, colonized the erotic. Modern pornography furthers the interests not only of sexism but also capitalism and other forms of domination. Sexuality, conflated with both domination and objectification, can more readily be channeled into, for example, the desire for consumer goods or the thrill of military conquest.

Visionary feminist thinkers aver that to be truly "pro-sex" we need to be critically "antipornography." Eroticism is humanity's birthright, a force of creativity, necessary to wholeness, and the energy source of art, connection, resistance, and transformation. Patricia Hill Collins urges both women and men to reject pornographic definitions of self and sexuality that are fragmenting, objectifying, or exploitative and instead articulate a goal of "honest bodies," those based in "sexual autonomy and soul, expressiveness, spirituality, sensuality, sexuality, and an expanded notion of the erotic as a life force."

See also **Obscenity and Indecency**

Further Reading

Brison, Susan J., "Torture, or 'Good Old American Pornography.'" *Chronicle Review/ Chronicle of Higher Education* (June 4, 2004): B10–B11.

Caputi, Jane, *The Pornography of Everyday Life* (documentary film). Berkeley Media. 2006. http://www.berkeleymedia.com

Collins, Patricia Hill, *Black Sexual Politics: African Americans, Gender, and the New Racism.* New York: Routledge, 2004.

Cornell, Drucilla, ed., *Feminism and Pornography.* New York: Oxford University Press, 2000.

Dines, Gail, Robert Jensen, and Ann Russo, *Pornography: The Production and Consumption of Inequality.* New York: Routledge, 1998.

Gutfield, G., "The Sex Drive: Men Who Are Hooked on Cyberpornography." *Men's Health* (October 1999): 116–121.

Hilden, Julie, "A Federal Judge Dismisses an Obscenity Prosecution on Privacy Grounds." 2005. http://writ.news.findlaw.com/hilden/20050131.html

Kammeyer, Kenneth C., *A Hypersexual Society: Sexual Discourse, Erotica, and Pornography in America Today.* New York: Palgrave Macmillan, 2008.

MacKinnon, Catharine, *Are Women Human? and Other International Dialogues.* Cambridge, MA: Harvard University Press, 2006.

McNair, Brian, *Mediated Sex: Pornography and Postmodern Culture.* New York: St. Martin's Press, 1996.

Paul, Pamela, *Pornified: How Pornography Is Transforming Our Lives, Our Relationships, and Our Families.* New York: Henry Holt, 2005.

PBS Frontline, *American Porn* (documentary), 2002.

Stark, Christine, and Rebecca Whisnant, eds., *Not for Sale: Feminists Resisting Prostitution and Pornography.* North Melbourne, Victoria: Spinifex Press, 2004.

POVERTY AND PUBLIC ASSISTANCE

Lane Destro

Public assistance programs are meant to relieve the hardships impoverished families experience as well as prevent families from remaining impoverished in the future or into the following generation. Over 12 percent of Americans—nearly 37 million people—are currently living below the poverty line. Even more Americans have income above the poverty line but still experience difficulties making ends meet. The poverty level for a family of four is just over $20,000 per year; this is roughly the equivalent of two parents each working a full-time, minimum-wage job five days a week for 52 weeks. Before discussing the policies that seek to help impoverished families, we should understand the characteristics of the Americans most likely to be impoverished today.

Families and persons most likely to be impoverished or affected by poverty are the elderly, minorities (especially African American and Latino), children, women, single mothers, young parents, people living in the South, the poorly educated, the unemployed, and those who live in very urban or very rural areas. Particular attention has been paid to the elderly poor in the United States, and programs such as Social Security and Medicare have alleviated a great deal of elderly poverty since their inception. Minorities face numerous challenges to employment and have less access to high-paying jobs, making them more likely to be impoverished than whites. It is important to note, however, that there is a greater absolute number of poor whites than there are poor minorities in the United States; it is a common misconception that most poor families are African American or Latino. Children make up a large percentage of impoverished Americans, because they have no source of personal income and are largely dependent on their parents for support. Women, similar to racial and ethnic minorities, face employment challenges and still make less money dollar-for-dollar than do men in comparable jobs. As the primary caregivers of their families, single mothers face even more difficulties in the workforce, because they have to manage work, child care, and parenting duties without the help of a partner. For these reasons, single mothers are also more likely than two-parent families to be impoverished.

Young parents, such as those who begin to have children while in their teens, face a greater likelihood of poverty than parents who postpone childbearing until later ages; this is due to their having little time to establish a career or finish higher education. Families living in the South or in urban or rural areas are at higher risk for poverty as well. Although poverty used to be a solely urban phenomenon, rural residents have become increasingly impoverished through the decline of small, family-owned farms and now face the same limited access to low-paying jobs as urban residents. Additionally, rural residents lack public transportation resources and often cannot retain a job because they have no reliable means of getting there. Urban residents and families living in the South lost good jobs that included benefits and a decent wage as industry moved out of these areas into lower-cost parts of the country (like the suburbs) and to other parts of the world. Individuals with low educational achievement and those who are unemployed are also more likely to be impoverished than individuals who have high levels of education and those who hold jobs.

Poverty can result in a number of complications for families, including low educational achievement due to living in neighborhoods with poorly funded schools and overfilled classrooms. Two of the most visible effects of poverty are poor health and subpar access to preventative health care. Families living in poverty often cannot afford health insurance without public assistance and therefore forgo preventative care such as yearly checkups, immunizations, prenatal visits, and cancer screenings, which results in allowing serious diseases to proceed or worsen undiagnosed. Families without health insurance often rely on hospital emergency care when necessary, which is a less-efficient and more-expensive option than visiting a family doctor or other primary care provider. Impoverished families also tend to neglect dental care; untreated dental problems have future implications for general health and access to employment. Fathers of impoverished families are the most likely family members to neglect health care, followed by mothers and then children.

Living in poverty can also cause poor nutrition, and several programs have tried to provide the resources for adequate nutrition, appropriate caloric intake, and access to nutritious foods. Homelessness and access to substandard housing also occur as a result of poverty, because families often cannot afford to pay market-priced rent, let alone purchase a home. Several assistance programs are in place exclusively to prevent families from being without a place to live, as well as to regulate the standards of housing available. Substandard housing has been held accountable for compromising children's health. Old lead paint on cracking banisters can cause lead poisoning, and mice, cockroaches, or other vermin have been cited as causing children's asthma.

Public Assistance Programs

Antipoverty programs remain among the most highly criticized of all government programs in the United States. Much of this can be explained by the misperceptions that average Americans have of persons who are in poverty and who receive public assistance. There is a long-standing stereotype that persons receiving public assistance are attempting to work the system or are cheating to qualify for additional benefits. However, all public assistance and antipoverty programs in the United States are means-tested programs, meaning a family's income has to fall below a specific guideline in order for that family to qualify for services. Public assistance programs are funded in part by the federal government and in part by state and local governments. The federal government sets guidelines for how families can qualify for programs as well as for how much funding each state must also contribute to the programs. Also referred to as the welfare system, public assistance is comprised of five major programs: Temporary Assistance to Needy Families (TANF); the food stamp program; the Special Supplemental Nutrition Program for Women, Infants, and Children (WIC); Medicaid; and Subsidized Housing Programs.

The United States did not have any comprehensive public assistance programs until President Franklin D. Roosevelt mandated that the government provide employment through public spending during the Great Depression. Public assistance continued to provide services to impoverished Americans until President Lyndon B. Johnson's War on Poverty attracted attention and, subsequently, scrutiny. Following the War on Poverty, the number of people accessing public assistance services grew rapidly. The enrollment for Aid to Families with Dependent Children (AFDC, a program that preceded TANF) increased by 270 percent, and enrollment for Medicaid (a program introduced in the 1960s) skyrocketed. The U.S. public continued to scrutinize the welfare system throughout the 1970s and 1980s, and all federally funded public assistance programs were eventually overhauled during the 1996 period of welfare reform under President Bill Clinton. The Personal Responsibility and Work Opportunity Reconciliation Act of 1996, commonly known as welfare reform, was hotly contested by advocates for the poor but did not end the debate over welfare. Although the number of people accessing social services has greatly declined since the 1996 reform (by as much as two-thirds), public assistance programs continue to undergo constant evaluations of their effectiveness.

Temporary Assistance for Needy Families

Temporary Assistance for Needy Families (TANF) is also referred to as cash assistance because it provides qualifying families with a monthly stipend of cash based on the number of persons present in a household and proportionate to the cost of living in their state. To qualify for TANF, recipients must generally have an income below the federal poverty level for their household size and must care for one or more dependent infants or children. Because mothers, rather than fathers, are more likely to have custody of their children, the vast majority of TANF recipients are women and their dependent children. Single persons not taking care of dependent children generally do not qualify for TANF.

Prior to the 1996 reform, TANF (then called AFDC) did not impose a time limit on recipient families, meaning that families could receive AFDC cash assistance indefinitely as long as they continued to meet the eligibility criteria. Opponents and critics of AFDC argued that the lack of time limits was not providing impoverished families with any incentive to get off assistance and go to work, and so post-1996 TANF instituted a federal standard of a 60-month lifetime limit per recipient. The second notable change of the reform called for stricter work requirements for its recipients, meaning a mother with children has to spend 10 to 40 hours per week participating in some kind of job training, job search, or educational program in order to remain eligible for TANF benefits.

Despite imposing time limits and work requirements, the 1996 reform also offered states some autonomy with respect to TANF. Individual states must follow the federal guidelines of the program but are allowed to amend the qualifying requirements if they so choose, meaning a family in one state might be permitted to have up to $2,000 in savings and still qualify for cash assistance, whereas another state might require families to have almost no assets in order to qualify. The lifetime limit for TANF can also be extended by individual states through the use of additional state funds, although some states have elected to make the 60-month limit noncontinuous (meaning a person can only be on TANF for 24 continuous months and then must leave welfare for at least a month before exhausting the rest of the time limit). States were also granted the ability to waive or change work requirements for recipients as part of various state-sponsored trial projects; this flexibility allowed states to experiment with TANF requirements in order to arrive at the best and most efficient way to move individuals from welfare receipt to employment.

The effectiveness of the change from AFDC to TANF is notable, as the number of individuals seeking cash assistance has declined by two-thirds. TANF is still not without controversy, however, as the program has been criticized for not significantly improving the lives of those who seek its assistance. Families that leave welfare often do not make a clean break from the program and get caught in an on-again–off-again cycle until they've exhausted their lifetime limit. Because families sometimes remain impoverished even after their TANF receipt, many argue that the program's role as a transition from poverty to nonpoverty and employment has not been fulfilled. The emphasis on work requirements for welfare recipients has been very well received, as critics of TANF and AFDC were opposed to the idea that one could qualify for cash assistance without making a concerted effort to find employment. The success of these work requirements is limited, however, because requirements restrict the time a mother has to spend with her children and can put a strain on child care arrangements. Often, work programs offer child care assistance and other benefits, such as help with resume writing or transportation assistance, but these are not universally granted to all of those enrolled. Work programs are also criticized by recipients as being useless or as not teaching them anything, and the employment they find is often that of the minimum-wage, service-sector variety and offers no health insurance. One major challenge TANF faces in the future is to assist families in eventually achieving permanent, gainful employment in order to make a successful permanent transition out of poverty.

Food Stamps

The food stamp program began in 1961 in response to physicians and army recruiters who noticed the pervasiveness of malnutrition within urban and rural populations. Created to provide a better opportunity for families to meet their basic nutritional needs, the food stamp program follows federal guidelines for qualification that are more lenient than those for TANF, meaning families who do not qualify for TANF may at least receive some food stamp assistance. If a family is already receiving TANF, they are automatically eligible for food stamps. If not receiving TANF, a family must have a gross income of less than 130 percent of the federal poverty level and less than $2,000 in assets (excluding the worth of their home and one car worth less than $4,500) to qualify. Food stamps may be used to purchase any type of food item except hot, prepared foods intended for immediate consumption. The amount of food stamps a family receives is based on the family size as well as the state's cost of living. An average family of three (one adult, two children) receives $200 per month in food stamps. Families must requalify for food stamps every six months to one year but are not required to report changes in income in between requalification periods.

The effectiveness of the food stamp program has been criticized because food stamp participants are still more likely to have poor nutrition than are non–food stamp participants. The 1996 National Food Stamp Survey found 50 percent of respondents still experience times without adequate food, and many households do not get enough folic acid or iron in their diets. Food stamps are not restricted only for the purchase of healthy foods, which leads some researchers to believe they have not improved impoverished families' nutrition and overall health. Food stamp participants are more likely to be obese, which could be due to families' choosing to purchase high-fat foods. However, families that receive food stamps tend to spend more on food than they would otherwise, and food stamp participants showed increased consumption of protein, vitamins A, B6, and C, and other important minerals.

Food stamp fraud presents another point of concern for the food stamp program because food stamp recipients sometimes sell food stamps for cash as opposed to using them to buy food. The going rate for food stamp resale is between 50 and 65 percent of face value, meaning $100 of food stamps is worth about $50 on the street. Studies have suggested, however, that the people selling food stamps also buy stamps. This indicates that families might be so strapped for cash that they prefer to sell stamps when they need cash, but then later buy their stamps back to purchase food. Scholars have proposed that the food stamp program can circumvent this issue by distributing stamps throughout the month rather than in a once-per-month lump sum.

WIC

Like the food stamp program, the Special Supplemental Nutrition Program for Women, Infants, and Children (WIC) was formed to provide nursing or pregnant mothers and children under five years old with better nutritional resources. WIC provides participants with certificates redeemable at participating markets for food items such as milk, cheese, cereal, beans, baby formula, and peanut butter in an amount equivalent to roughly $40 per month. These food items are sources of iron, vitamins A and C, calcium, and protein. WIC also provides participants with a nutritional education session each month when they come to get their WIC coupons and monitors the development of infants and children under five years old. Children are no longer eligible for WIC benefits after their fifth birthday, and mothers must be nursing or pregnant to qualify.

Participants must have incomes under 185 percent of the federal poverty level, although mothers and children under five years old automatically qualify if they are also receiving Medicaid. The more generous income guidelines have come under fire, because this allows more people to qualify for WIC and raises the cost of the program, although participation rates for WIC are much lower than they would be if every eligible individual participated. However, this underenrollment raises questions about whether WIC is truly serving the families who might need it the most. WIC, compared to the food stamp program, loses very little money to fraud, probably due to the food-item-specific nature of the program. The food coupons have very little resale value because they are restricted to certain food items and, furthermore, specific product sizes and brands.

Because WIC is the most-studied federal nutrition program, there is less controversy over whether WIC is effective compared to the food stamp program or the National School Lunch Program. WIC participation has reduced the incidence of low- and very low–birthweight babies, meaning public money spent on WIC saves on medical expenditures in the long run. Studies of WIC have also found positive health outcomes for toddlers, although not to the same extent as the outcomes for infants. Some have criticized the WIC program because it offers nursing mothers free formula and subsequently provides a disincentive to breast-feed. The health portion of the WIC program has begun to encourage mothers to breast-feed, but WIC mothers are still less likely to breast-feed than mothers not in the program. This program continues to cause controversy among health professionals and scholars who believe breast-feeding to be an important part of developing infants' immunity, the mothers' health, and the mother-child bond.

Medicaid

The Medicaid program seeks to provide federally and state-funded health insurance to qualifying low-income women and children. The Medicaid program also offers public health insurance to disabled (disability insurance) and elderly persons (Medicare). About half of all Medicaid recipients are low-income children and one-fifth are low-income women. Medicaid is the most expensive public service program, spending about $280 billion annually, with most of the costs going toward the health care and treatment of the elderly. The $47 billion that goes toward impoverished women's and children's health care is still very costly, especially when compared to the annual cost of TANF ($16 billion) and the food stamp program ($24 billion). Despite the program's vast spending, each year over the past decade, roughly 12 percent of all children in the United States have gone without health insurance. It is expected, however, that the Health Care and Education Reconciliation Act of 2010 will begin lessening that percentage.

Access to health insurance and preventative care is important for impoverished families' well-being, and Medicaid insurance provides very low-cost health care to families who qualify. As of the change implemented by the Deficit Reduction Act of 1984, any families who qualify for TANF are automatically eligible for Medicaid benefits as well. The Medicaid income cutoffs continued to become more generous, and more federal funding was set aside in order to guarantee more children's access to health care.

Medicaid benefits became available to pregnant women, two-parent families, and to teenage mothers living with their parents, as long as the incomes of these various types of households fell within the qualifying income guidelines. By the 1990s, families with incomes at 130 percent of the federal poverty line or below became eligible for Medicaid, with some states choosing to raise eligibility guidelines further, up to 185 percent of the poverty level. By October 1997, 41 of 50 states were using their own funds to raise the income guidelines for women and children.

Having Medicaid does not necessarily translate into having access to health services, because providers often restrict their practice to allowing only a certain percentage of Medicaid patients or refuse to see these patients at all. Additionally, the length of Medicaid doctor visits is, on average, shorter than the average non-Medicaid visit, which may indicate a lower quality of care for Medicaid patients. Medical institutions often cite Medicaid's slow reimbursement and excessive paperwork as a reason to prefer privately insured patients. Despite Medicaid's controversial position with practitioners, public health remains an important service that, at the very least, makes preventative and routine health care available and affordable to low-income women and their children.

Housing Programs

Although there are multiple kinds of housing programs, only two will be discussed here. Housing programs began in general with the passing of the Housing Act of 1949, which called for an end to unsafe, substandard housing. Some housing programs operate by offering incentives to contractors to construct low-income housing. In contrast, the programs discussed here provide low-cost housing to families at lower-than-market rent. Public housing developments are perhaps the most visible of these programs. These developments offer available units to families with income below the poverty level for rent proportionate to one-third of their monthly income.

Although public housing must meet a certain standard of cleanliness and construction, some housing developments have not uniformly met these guidelines. Public housing generally gets a bad reputation regardless of its quality or location. Families must often sign up for housing years in advance, due to the long waiting lists that exist for these units. In cities such as New York, over 100,000 families are on a housing waiting list. In contrast, the availability of public housing units in central Pennsylvania has motivated families to move to the area just to have access to housing.

The Section 8 program operates along the same income and benefit guidelines as public housing developments, except Section 8 allows families to select the housing of their choice. After a family gets past a waiting list longer than that for most public housing, Section 8 grants the family with a voucher and the family must find private-sector housing that meets the quality standards of public housing. If a family is able to do this, the voucher pays for a portion of the family's rent. This amount is typically proportionate to two-thirds of the market-rate rental price. As with public housing developments, the family ends up paying for one-third of the total rental amount.

Public housing is exceedingly helpful for the families who are able to get through the waiting lists, although a great deal of controversy remains over whether public housing developments are good and safe environments for children. The main issue public housing faces is providing all of those families in need with affordable housing options. As waiting lists indicate, this goal has not been met.

Ending Point

Poverty is clearly a problematic circumstance for families, and although antipoverty programs have had success in reducing the number of families in poverty, public assistance programs face various controversies of their own. Perhaps one of the most important issues with public assistance programs is their uniform neglect of fathers. Fathers cannot qualify for cash assistance unless they have full custody of their dependents, and fathers do not qualify for food stamps for the same reason. WIC is aimed only toward women and their children under five years old, and public housing does not typically provide housing services to men without families. In cases where the father is not married to the mother of his children, the father's presence in a public housing unit is actually illegal and may cause a mother and children to lose their housing subsidy.

In light of recent programs that promote marriage among low-income, unmarried parents (such as the Healthy Marriage Initiative), public assistance programs should consider expanding the eligibility requirements to men rather than restrict services to women and children only. Marriage programs do not cooperate with public assistance programs in a way that is productive for creating stable families; the fact that a mother can lose access to public housing if her partner lives with her is an indication of this. In order to successfully continue to provide impoverished families with much-needed resources, perhaps even a resident father's income, and encourage unity among families, public assistance will have to consider changing its policies in the future.

See also **Child Care; Foster Care; Homelessness; Health Care (vol. 1); Poverty and Race (vol. 1); Social Security (vol. 1); Unemployment (vol. 1)**

Further Reading

Allard, Scott W., *Out of Reach: Place, Poverty, and the New American Welfare State.* New Haven, CT: Yale University Press, 2009.

Almanac of Policy Issues, http://www.policyalmanac.org

Blank, Rebecca and Ron Hoskins, *The New World of Welfare.* Washington, DC: Brookings Institution Press, 2001.

Cancian, Maria, and Sheldon Danziger, eds., *Changing Poverty, Changing Policies.* New York: Russell Sage Foundation, 2009.

Chappell, Marisa, *The War on Welfare: Family, Poverty, and Politics in Modern America.* Philadelphia: University of Pennsylvania Press, 2010.

Currie, Janet M., *The Invisible Safety Net.* Princeton, NJ: Princeton University Press, 2006.

Grogger, Jeffrey, and Lynn A. Karoly, *Welfare Reform: Effects of a Decade of Change.* Cambridge, MA: Harvard University Press, 2005.

Pickering, Kathleen, et al., *Welfare Reform in Persistent Rural Poverty: Dreams, Disenchantment, and Diversity.* University Park: Pennsylvania State University Press, 2006.

Urban Institute, http://www.urban.org

PRAYER IN PUBLIC SCHOOLS

Ron Mock

The First Amendment to the United States Constitution includes two guarantees about religion:

> Congress shall make no law respecting an establishment of religion, or prohibiting the free exercise thereof.

The phrase *shall make no law respecting an establishment of religion* prohibits Congress from enacting any laws that have the effect of creating an official religion or committing the government's resources to supporting or promoting any particular faith. But the Constitution also says that Congress shall make no law. *prohibiting the free exercise* of religion. This provision protects the individual's right to follow his or her conscience, both in determining what to believe and in deciding what those beliefs require the individual to do.

Sometimes these two guarantees collide when people feel a need to practice their faiths in public settings. In the United States, the venue where the conflicts are greatest and most controversial is the public school.

History of the First Amendment as Applied to Public Schools

When the Constitution was first adopted, it had no explicit guarantee of religious freedom, other than a prohibition on using any "religious test" as a prerequisite for public office. The framers assumed that civil liberties would be protected by the states and that the Constitution did nothing to infringe them. But some Americans were concerned that, without clearer provisions in the new federal Constitution, the national government might act to undermine their rights. So, 12 amendments were proposed by the first Congress to address this worry. Of these, 10 were ratified by the states, including the First Amendment.

The First Amendment is directed at the federal government: "Congress shall make no law…" Public schools in the United States are run by the states or by the local governments created by the states, which are not mentioned in the First Amendment.

(At the time the First Amendment was adopted, some states had established churches, a practice that persisted into the early 19th century.) After the Civil War, Congress proposed, and the states ratified, the Fourteenth Amendment, which includes a provision forbidding any state to "deprive any person of life, liberty, or property, without due process of law; nor deny to any person within its jurisdiction the equal protection of the laws." The United States Supreme Court interpreted this provision to apply to religious freedom, declaring that the Fourteenth Amendment incorporates the First Amendment and religious freedom as part of the liberty that states must not infringe.

Since the middle of the 20th century, the Supreme Court has decided a steady stream of cases dealing with the First Amendment in public schools. Although there has been substantial confusion among the general public about what these cases mean, they can be summarized as follows:

- The constitutional ban on laws *respecting an establishment of religion* (the establishment clause) prohibits national, state, and local governments from offering any kind of support to any religious faith, whether it be in the form of money, facilities, or endorsement.

- The constitutional guarantee of religious liberty (the free exercise clause) allows citizens to practice their religious faith without interference from the government, unless there is a *compelling* issue of public safety or welfare. Even in the rare cases in which governments can restrict religious practice, the regulation has to be the least restrictive possible to achieve the compelling public purpose.

- In cases where a government agency has created a forum for public expression, it cannot restrict access to that forum based on the content of what is being expressed. In particular, it may not bar religious groups from using the forum because of the religious content of their speech or other activities.

Controversial Impact on Public Schools

Some of the uproar about religion in the public schools is based on misperceptions. It is not true, for example, that prayer is banned in public schools. Students and staff may pray privately at any time. Students can also pray publicly in settings where they initiate the prayer themselves, and employees of the school do not exercise control over what is said. Students can also express their religious views at any time they choose, subject to the normal rules schools can impose to keep order and protect the educational environment.

Students may not force *captive audiences* to participate or observe. Nor may they interfere with class discipline or disrupt the normal operations of the school. Otherwise, students are free to pray, study the scriptures, worship, and share their faith on school grounds to the same extent as any other kind of student activity and expression.

U.S. SUPREME COURT CASES INVOLVING THE FIRST AMENDMENT IN PUBLIC SCHOOLS

Everson v. Board of Education of Ewing Township, 330 U.S. 1 (1947): Court applies First Amendment ban on establishing religion to the states.

Engel v. Vitale, 370 U.S. 421 (1962): Public schools may not sponsor or mandate a short nondenominational prayer.

Abington School District v. Schempp, 374 U.S. 203 (1963): Public schools may not sponsor or mandate the reading of the Lord's Prayer or other Bible verses.

Tinker v. Des Moines Independent Community School District, 393 U.S. 503 (1969): Public schools may not ban specific kinds of nonobscene speech but may enforce content-neutral regulations for the purpose of maintaining order and a good learning environment.

Lemon v. Kurtzman, 403 U.S. 602 (1971): Public money may not be allocated directly to parochial schools, because doing so violates at least one part of a three-part test: (1) whether the government action has a secular purpose; (2) whether the primary effect of the government action advances or inhibits religion; or (3) whether the action brings government into excessive entanglement with religion, such as resolving doctrinal issues or the like.

Widmar v. Vincent, 454 U.S. 263 (1981): Public universities may not deny use of university facilities for worship if they are available for other student or community groups.

Wallace v. Jaffree, 472 U.S. 38 (1985): Public schools cannot set aside a minute of silence expressly for meditation or voluntary prayer.

Board of Education of the Westside Community Schools v. Mergens, 496 U.S. 226 (1990): The federal Equal Access Act of 1984 is constitutional, requiring public schools to allow students to organize religious groups if the school allows students to form similar groups for nonreligious purposes.

Lee v. Weisman, 505 U.S. 577 (1992): Public schools cannot sponsor prayers of invocation or benediction at graduation ceremonies.

Rosenberger v. The Rector and Visitors of the University of Virginia, 515 U.S. 819 (1995): If other student-initiated groups are given student activities funds, a public university may not deny those funds to student-initiated religious groups.

Santa Fe Independent School District v. Doe, 530 U.S. 790 (2000): Public schools cannot sponsor prayers of invocation or benediction at athletic events.

Good News Club v. Milford Central School, 533 U.S. 98 (2001): Public schools may not deny access to religious groups to use their facilities after school if they have allowed access to other community groups.

Employees, on the other hand, are restricted in some of the ways they might express their religious faith. Employees are free to practice their faith on their own time, or even with colleagues in settings that are entirely voluntary—after school hours in the faculty lounge, for example. But when students are involved, the Supreme Court has ruled that the employee's free exercise rights are limited by the students' right not to be subjected to a de facto *established* religion. So, while employees can be present to preserve safety and proper order even when students have organized themselves for prayer or scripture study, the employees cannot participate in the religious aspects of the activity or reward or punish students for their participation.

Setting aside the conflicts that arise from misunderstanding of the law—by parents as well as school staff and administrators—there is still controversy among religious leaders and lay people about the current interpretation of the Constitution as applied to public schools. Some religious groups have essentially accepted the current rules about prayer and other religious activities in public schools. The conservative Christian group Focus on the Family offers resources describing current law and suggestions for how to help students organize prayer meetings and share their faith on campus within the law. Moderate to conservative Christian attorneys pursue similar ends through organizations such as the American Center for Law and Justice and the Christian Legal Society's Center for Law and Religious Freedom.

But others feel that the Constitution should be interpreted to permit more freewheeling religious expression on public school campuses by students, community members, and employees alike. Most of the arguments fall into one of five categories:

- *The Christian nation argument:* The United States was founded as a Christian nation, and the Constitution should be interpreted in light of this. The ban on establishing a religion was not meant to exclude public expressions of Christianity by government officials, including teachers in schools.
- *The majoritarian argument:* In a democracy, when a community is in overwhelming agreement about what should happen in its schools, it should be able to implement that consensus.
- *The educational benefits argument:* There are positive educational benefits available to students from various religious activities.
- *The religious community argument:* All the major religions include a strong community emphasis, calling adherents to worship, study, or act jointly with others in public life, including school. True freedom of religion requires freedom to practice one's faith in this kind of community setting.
- *The religious accommodation argument:* Some of the private, individualized duties in many faiths have to be carried out in public or at times of the day that bring them into the school setting. Schools need to find ways to accommodate these practices or they will be prohibiting the free exercise of religion.

The first two lines of argument are most often made by Protestant Christians, naturally, since most of the framers of the Constitution were Protestants, and Protestants are by far the group most likely to constitute a dominant majority in school districts in the United States. They are both essentially arguments from the basis of political theory, saying public religious activity is appropriate because of the kind of nation the United States is, either by definition in its founding documents or by the political will of the current majority.

Other believers, however, including many Christians, object to the elevation of any specific faith to a privileged position in public institutions. For one thing, even in the most homogeneous communities in the United States, there are strong differences among citizens about matters of religious doctrine. Sometimes the differences are major, involving fundamental issues about the existence of God (or gods). Other times the disputes are about issues that seem minor to outsiders but are crucial to those who disagree, including issues ranging from the roles of men and women to matters of ethics or lifestyle. Those who framed the Constitution had similar disagreements among themselves.

Whatever the differences, to assemble a majority involves one of three choices, all of which are unacceptable: forcing some people to accept or participate in expressions of faith that violate their consciences; compromising on important issues in ways that will put everyone in uncomfortable positions; or finding a way to gloss over the differences. The result, according to these critics, is a bland *civil religion* that masks living faith and even distracts people from a true encounter with God.

Whatever the merits of the *Christian nation* or *majoritarian* arguments, they are clearly unpersuasive in the courts on *establishment of religion* grounds. There does not appear to be any realistic possibility that either approach will become the basis for U.S. law in the foreseeable future.

The *educational benefits* argument shifts focus to the educational purposes of schools. If we hope for our schools to educate the entire person, then we should encourage students to reflect on their moral and spiritual duties by exposing them to stories of faith and the basic teachings of religion. This line of reasoning is subtle and profound and has several layers of appeal.

On the surface, the argument for religious expression in school addresses prosaic concerns like discouraging disruptive behavior or encouraging scholarly virtues like discipline and hard work. If students are given a few moments at the beginning of the day to pray, to think about their duties to those around them, and to consider their deepest goals for their lives, there may be immediate and visible benefits in how well they do at their studies and how smoothly the school operates. This has been a persuasive line of reasoning in the courts, which have accepted such measures of moments of silence to start the day as long as school staff do not encourage (or discourage) students to use the time to pray or do other religious actions.

But the educational benefits of open religious practice or study in school might include more than just improving the educational atmosphere. If religion is an important factor in modern life, and if modern communications and transportation make it likely that students will encounter many faiths different than their own, then it might be valuable for students to learn about each other's faith in school. Study of religion and watching other faiths' practices would be good cross-cultural learning.

And there is an even deeper possible educational benefit. Because so much of students' time is spent in school, and because the public has a clear interest in developing virtuous citizens, then helping students to internalize solid values like honesty and caring for others is a public interest. Religion has traditionally promoted these kinds of values, a function that could be enhanced if religion and religious instruction were given freer rein in the public schools.

Focusing on the educational benefits of exposure to religion in this way does not ask schools to favor one faith over another. In fact, schools would be encouraged to make space for encounters with as many religions as possible—at least all those represented among the student population in the school. Courts have been open to this practice in schools, although they are still watchful, worried that activities that appear on the surface to be neutral toward various faiths might be mere covers for the advancement of one faith. For example, attempts by various states to provide for moments of silence before school have had mixed success in the courts. They have sometimes been rejected because people sponsoring the moments of silence went on record saying their goal was to encourage students to pray in school.

But the *educational benefits* argument is not always popular with parents, students, or even teachers. People worry that students may be converted to disfavored religions, either as a natural result of learning more about them or because they have been recruited to a new religious faith by people abusing the freedom to practice their faith at school.

The final two arguments (the *religious community* and *religious accommodation* arguments) have had more success in changing school practices. These focus on the believer's attempt to live faithfully to his or her religion. Here, the religious freedom side of the First Amendment comes into full focus, and the concerns about establishing a religion are least prominent. The claim here is that schools need to be flexible in their operation to allow students and employees to participate fully in the schools without forcing them into a position of having to violate the commandments of their faith.

Courts generally have been willing to accept, and in some cases even to require, attempts by public schools to make changes in their operations or programs to accommodate those who find the standard school experience to be contrary to their understanding of God's will. For example, schools have had to reschedule athletic events to permit students to participate without violating religious Sabbath-day requirements. Schools have altered menus to accommodate religious diets; created space in the school, and time in the day to allow Muslims to conduct required prayers; allowed students to opt out of dancing classes or other activities that violate their religious teachings; and many other forms of accommodation.

Conclusion

Courts in the United States developed their current interpretation of the First Amendment in a series of decisions since the mid-20th century. The boundary lines between what is and what is not permitted in the public schools are not yet settled firmly. But some areas of permissible activity have been clearly recognized, especially those involving voluntary nondisruptive activities organized by students. When students organize the events and do not seek special privileges not offered to other student groups, they can pray, study the scriptures, support each other, and even share their faith gently with other students who consent to hear their message.

See also **Creationism, Intelligent Design, and Evolution; Religious Symbols on Government Property; School Choice**

Further Reading

American Center for Law and Justice, http://www.aclj.org

American Civil Liberties Union, http://www.aclu.org/religion/index.html

Americans United for Separation of Church and State, http://www.au.org

Center for Law and Religious Freedom, http://www.clsnet.org

Dawson Institute for Church-State Studies (Baylor University), http://www.baylor.edu/church_state/splash.php

Dierenfield, Bruce J., *The Battle over School Prayer: How* Engle v. Vitale *Changed America.* Lawrence: University Press of Kansas, 2007.

First Freedom Center, http://www.firstfreedom.org

Fisher, Louis and David G. Adler, *American Constitutional Law.* Vol. 2, *Constitutional Rights: Civil Rights and Civil Liberties,* 7th ed. Durham, NC: Carolina Academic Press, 2007.

O'Brien, David M., *Constitutional Law and Politics.* Vol. 2, *Civil Rights and Civil Liberties.* New York: W. W. Norton, 2005 (especially chapter 6).

People for the American Way, http://www.pfaw.org/pfaw

The Rutherford Institute, http://www.rutherford.org

Solomon, Stephen, *Ellery's Protest: How One Young Man Defied Tradition and Sparked the Battle over School Prayer.* Ann Arbor: University of Michigan Press, 2007.

R

RELIGIOUS SYMBOLS ON GOVERNMENT PROPERTY

RON MOCK

Abraham Lincoln famously described America's democratic dream as "government of the people, by the people, and for the people," a vision that is shared by billions of people around the world. The first commitment of democratic government, then, is to enact laws, carry out policies, and behave in ways that embody the aspirations and values of the people.

Many people draw their most important values and sense of identity from their religion. Since their faith is central to their lives, they long to live with others of similar convictions so they can help each other build lives that draw upon and reflect their faiths. People have migrated, at risk to their lives, across oceans and continents and settled in wildernesses, deserts, jungles, and other harsh environments to have a chance to build communities of faith. The United States was built in large part on the contributions of several different religious communities, from Puritans in Massachusetts, Quakers in Pennsylvania, Catholics in Maryland and the desert Southwest, Lutherans in the upper Midwest, Mennonites in several northern states stretching from Kansas to Pennsylvania, Baptists in the South, Mormons in Utah, and many others. A snapshot of the United States today would include the descendants of all these religious communities, and hundreds of others, stretching outside Christianity to include Jews, Muslims, Hindus, Buddhists, Baha'i, and others.

But as soon as a political system is erected that incorporates more than one faith, a conflict arises: whose religious convictions get to be embodied in the policies and activities of the government? Should the work week include a Sunday Sabbath day of rest to accommodate Christian beliefs? Or Saturday, as most Jews and some Christians would prefer? Or Friday, in accord with Muslim beliefs? What should be taught in schools about the origins of the universe, or values of right and wrong, or the relative roles of women and men in life, and many other topics?

Conflict over religious dimensions of community life can become intense because people believe the stakes are so high. If someone is teaching my children falsehoods about God and the universe and how they should live, they are threatening both the quality of life in this world and, possibly, dooming my children to eternal death rather than eternal life in heaven. Unfortunately, human history is scarred with battles over control of government policy between different religious groups, including some of the bloodiest wars ever. As this is written, struggles over how to reflect people's religious faiths in their government are especially bloody in places like Iraq, Afghanistan, Pakistan, India, Lebanon, and Israel, and Palestine.

America's founders were aware of this danger. So the First Amendment to the United States Constitution begins with the statement:

> Congress shall make no law respecting an establishment of religion, or prohibiting the free exercise thereof.

With these words, the framers of the Constitution hoped to build a hedge of law around the deep passions evoked by our religious faiths. The principle of government *by the people* was given a limitation: even if most of the people wanted to, they would not be able to use the machinery of the federal government to establish their faith as the official faith of the entire nation. The free exercise clause ("Congress shall make no law…prohibiting the free exercise [of religion]") guarantees that the government will not be used to suppress faith. And the establishment clause ("Congress shall make no law respecting an establishment of religion") prevents the government from favoring one faith, even when directed by a clear majority of the people.

This article will focus on how the establishment clause has been interpreted by the courts in the United States to determine whether it is constitutional for a government agency to display religious symbols or engage in other religious activities or expression, such as prayers or slogans.

Interpretation of the Establishment Clause

At the time the First Amendment was ratified, some state governments had established churches, which included appropriations of tax money to the coffers of specific Christian denominations. These churches were disestablished over the next few decades, so that by the time the Fourteenth Amendment was ratified after the Civil War, there were no churches with official *established* status anywhere in the United States.

The Fourteenth Amendment says, in part:

No state shall make or enforce any law which shall abridge the privileges or immunities of citizens of the United States; nor shall any state deprive any person of life, liberty, or property, without due process of law; nor deny to any person within its jurisdiction the equal protection of the laws.

The Fourteenth Amendment has been interpreted by the United States Supreme Court to incorporate various parts of the Bill of Rights, thereby extending civil rights protections to citizens against possible actions by the states. In the case of *Cantwell v. Connecticut* (1940), the Supreme Court ruled that the prohibition against establishing a religion was one of the rights incorporated in the Fourteenth Amendment, thus making official what had been observed in practice for a century: no state could *establish* a particular faith by specially favoring it over another faith.

But this leaves a wide range of issues, where democratic dynamics push government to reflect citizens' religious commitments, but the Constitution prohibits the government from endorsing any religion. The Supreme Court has upheld some practices that bring religious faith into contact with the activities of governments, such as opening legislative sessions with prayer at the state level (*Marsh v. Chambers* 1983); passing laws barring some commercial activity on Sunday (*McGowan v. Maryland* 1961); displaying a Christian nativity scene on public property along with non-Christian symbols such as Santa Claus, reindeer, a Christmas tree, and Christmas presents (*Lynch v. Donnelly* 1983); and granting property tax exemptions to religious worship organizations (*Walz v. Tax Commission of the City of New York* 1970).

Other practices have been ruled unconstitutional, including laws requiring the posting of the Ten Commandments in public school classrooms (*Stone v. Graham* 1980); school-organized prayers in classrooms (*Abington School District v. Schempp* 1963), at football games (*Santa Fe Independent School District v. Doe* 2000) and at graduations (*Lee v. Weisman* 1992).

These cases left laypeople (and lawyers) confused about what is, and what is not, permissible. Part of the problem is that the Supreme Court has not stuck to one single test for deciding matters. In some of the cases, the Court applied a three-part test first outlined in *Lemon v. Kurtzman* (1971):

1. Is the purpose of the government's action primarily secular?
2. Does it have the primary effect of encouraging or discouraging religious faith?
3. Does it threaten to entangle the government in the internal affairs of a religious group, especially in making judgments about questions of faith or doctrine?

School prayers, for example, do not meet the *Lemon* test, because courts have trouble believing the purpose of a prayer is not primarily religious. Multifaith Christmas displays do better, because it is easier to defend them as having either no religious purpose, since so many contrasting faiths are on display, including completely secular symbols such as Santa Claus. But these simple generalizations do not cover every case. If school prayers led by district employees, or involving captive audiences at sporting events or graduations, are not constitutional, why is it constitutional to have Congress or a state legislature pay a chaplain to offer a prayer to open its daily sessions?

Sometimes the Court has taken pains to point out that religion has played a major role in U.S. history, and still does in the lives of most Americans. This point is used in two ways. Some justices (especially William Rehnquist, Antonin Scalia, and Clarence Thomas) have employed it to argue that the framers of the First Amendment could not have meant to bar some interdenominational expressions of religious conviction by the government. They point to many examples of official congressional actions or presidential addresses that invoke faith in God, including prayers, resolutions, proclamations, and other communications, which were made while the First Amendment was being ratified, and which continued unabated right after ratification. This is a classic *originalist* argument, insisting that the Constitution needs to be applied today consistently with how the original authors of the Constitution would have understood it when they adopted it. Thus, evidence that so many governmental leaders thought opening Congress with a prayer was not a form of establishing a religion, means the establishment clause was not seen at the time as covering interfaith prayers at government functions.

Most Supreme Court justices have not been originalists. They believe the Constitution should be applied in light of things we have learned since it was originally adopted. Thus, the original idea that *separate but equal* was an acceptable way to provide *equal protection of the laws* under the Fourteenth Amendment does not bind us today, according to the nonoriginalist view, since we learned long ago that *separate but equal* does not work as advertised. But even many nonoriginalists invoke the role of religion in American life to suggest that government acknowledgement of religion is acceptable if it is more descriptive than prescriptive—that is, if it objectively acknowledges or reports what people believe without endorsing or promoting (or criticizing) those beliefs. So a Christmas scene with secular symbols mixed in with religious symbols from a variety of faiths passes muster because it depicts (without endorsement) the range of views one could find in the community.

But other justices see most forms of government recognition of religion as violating the Constitution, essentially on the grounds that anything that throws positive (or negative) light on a faith has the effect of helping (or hindering) it, and thus functions as an endorsement (or critique) even when it is not intended to be.

None of these three broad approaches has garnered enough support to command a stable majority of the Court.

The 2005 Ten Commandments Cases

On June 27, 2005, the Supreme Court decided two cases involving displays of the Ten Commandments on government property. All of the dynamics that made this area of the

U.S. SUPREME COURT CASES INVOLVING RELIGIOUS SYMBOLS ON GOVERNMENT PROPERTY

Cantwell v. Connecticut, 310 U.S. 296 (1940): the First Amendment applies to the states and prevents them from regulating public speech based on its religious content.

Everson v. Board of Education of Ewing Township, 330 U.S. 1 (1947): Court applies First Amendment ban on establishing religion to the states.

McGowan v. Maryland, 366 U.S. 420 (1961): States or localities may restrict commercial activity on Sunday.

Engel v. Vitale, 370 U.S. 421 (1962): Public schools may not sponsor or mandate a short nondenominational prayer.

Abington School District v. Schempp, 374 U.S. 203 (1963): Public schools may not sponsor or mandate the reading of the Lord's Prayer or other Bible verses.

Tinker v. Des Moines Independent Community School District, 393 U.S. 503 (1969): Public schools may not ban specific kinds of nonobscene speech but may enforce content-neutral regulations for the purpose of maintaining order and a good learning environment.

Walz v. Tax Commission of the City of New York, 397 U.S. 664 (1970): States may grant tax exemptions to houses of worship.

Lemon v. Kurtzman, 403 U.S. 602 (1971): Public money may not be allocated directly to parochial schools because doing so violates at least one part of a three-part test: (1) whether the government action has a secular purpose; (2) whether the primary effect of the government action advances or inhibits religion; or (3) whether the action brings government into excessive *entanglement* with religion, such as resolving doctrinal issues or the like.

Stone v. Graham, 449 U.S. 39 (1980): States may not require the Ten Commandments to be posted in public school classrooms.

Marsh v. Chambers, 463 U.S. 783 (1983): State legislatures may open their sessions with prayers from a chaplain employed by the state.

Lynch v. Donnelly, 465 U.S. 668 (1983): A local government may display a Christian nativity scene on public property along with non-Christian symbols such as Santa Claus, reindeer, a Christmas tree, and Christmas presents.

Lee v. Weisman, 505 U.S. 577 (1992): Public schools may not sponsor prayers at graduation ceremonies.

Santa Fe Independent School District v. Doe, 530 U.S. 290 (2000): Public schools may not sponsor public prayers before school sporting events.

Van Orden v. Perry, 545 U.S. 677 (2005): A state may maintain a monument displaying the text of the Ten Commandments when there is no evidence the state had a religious motive for doing so and the display is in a context that does not communicate an essential intent to advance or endorse religious faith.

McCreary County v. American Civil Liberties Union, 545 U.S. 844 (2005): Counties may not post the Ten Commandments publicly when it is clear the intent for doing so was to endorse or advance religion.

law so murky were at work in these cases: competing visions of constitutional interpretation; contrasting views about the propriety of acknowledging religion on government property; even disagreement over how central religion has been in the development of the country. At first glance, the results were even more confusing than normal, since in one case the display of the Ten Commandments was upheld as constitutional, while in the other it was ruled to be impermissible. Each vote was five to four, with Justice Stephen Breyer voting in the majority each time.

In *Van Orden v. Perry* (2005), the state of Texas maintained a plaque on a six-foot tall monument on the grounds of the state capitol, on which was inscribed the Ten Commandments. The monument was donated in 1961 to Texas by the Fraternal Order of Eagles, a national service club, as part of a campaign against juvenile delinquency. The Eagles were hopeful that, if young people were more aware of the rules of behavior in the Ten Commandments, juvenile crime would diminish. The donation to Texas was part of a campaign in which similar monuments were donated to state governments around the nation. There were 16 other monuments of similar scale on the 21-acre grounds around the capitol, none of the rest of which involved religious texts.

The inscription on the monument quotes from the Old Testament book of Exodus, although in somewhat condensed form. It starts in bold, centered text with Exodus 20:2, "I AM the LORD thy GOD" and then lists each of the Commandments. The text was framed by symbols—two stone tablets like the ones on which God wrote the original Ten Commandments, two stars of David (a Jewish symbol), and the Greek letters chi and rho (a Christian symbol).

In *McCreary County v. American Civil Liberties Union* (2005), two Kentucky counties tried three times to get the Ten Commandments posted on their courthouse walls. In the first attempt, the Ten Commandments were displayed by themselves prominently in the courthouse. The text of the display was similar to the one in Texas, except that the preamble "I AM the LORD thy GOD" was omitted. In Pulaski County, there was a ceremony when the display was hung in which a county official made comments about the existence of God. When the American Civil Liberties Union sued in court seeking an injunction ordering the displays to be removed, the counties each adopted a resolution explaining that the Ten Commandments were "the precedent legal code upon which the civil and criminal codes" of Kentucky were founded, and stating that county leaders shared with America's Founding Fathers an "explicit understanding of the duty of elected officials to publicly acknowledge God as the source of America's strength and direction." These resolutions directed that the displays be expanded to include eight excerpts from other historical documents in which there was some reference to God (such as Pilgrim's Mayflower Compact and the passage from the Declaration of Independence in which the Continental Congress had said that all "men are endowed by their Creator with certain inalienable rights").

When the federal district court ordered the displays removed because they lacked any secular purpose and were distinctly religious, the counties created a third display. This one included nine documents of identical size, one of which was the Ten Commandments (in a more complete text). The others were the Magna Carta, Declaration of Independence, Bill of Rights, the Preamble to the Kentucky Constitution, Mayflower Compact, *Star Spangled Banner,* the National Motto (*In God We Trust*), and a picture of Lady Justice. Each document was accompanied by a statement of its historical and legal significance. The one for the Ten Commandments explained that they had "profoundly influenced the formation of Western legal thought and the formation of our country" and provided "the moral background of the Declaration of Independence and the foundation of our legal tradition."

These two cases reached the United States Supreme Court at about the same time and were argued in the fall of 2004. The opinions in both cases were announced on the same day the following June.

In *Van Orden,* five justices voted to uphold the display of the Ten Commandments on the grounds of the Texas capitol, while four voted to rule it was unconstitutional. In *McCreary,* five justices voted to rule the displays were unconstitutional, while four voted to uphold them.

The four justices who would have upheld both displays used two principal lines of argument. First, Justices Scalia, Rehnquist, and Thomas argued that government was not barred from favoring religious practice, because the original framers of the constitution would not have intended such a thing—an originalist argument. Justice Anthony Kennedy did not join in that view but did agree with the other three justices that, in each of these two cases, the intent of the displays was secular: to reduce juvenile delinquency in the Texas case and to inform citizens of some of the main historical sources of the modern legal system in the Kentucky case. Since there was a legitimate secular purpose, strong enough by itself to justify the creation of the displays, they would be acceptable under the *Lemon* test, or any other test, according to these justices.

The four justices who would have ruled all the displays unconstitutional (Sandra Day O'Connor, John Paul Stevens, Ruth Bader Ginsburg, and David Souter) used, either explicitly (in *McCreary*) or implicitly (in *Van Orden*), the *Lemon* test. They found that the displays had a primary religious intent, to go along with at least some religious effect on those who saw them. In *McCreary,* the religious intent was easy to discern in the second phase of the project, including the resolution that pointed to God as the source of America's strength, and in the focus on religious texts in the display. Whereas the four justices in the minority in *McCreary* generally ignored the first two attempts to get the display done, the majority opinion (by Souter) assumed that the motive behind the first two attempts was the genuine one, and the third version of the display with its assertion of broader educational goals was an attempt to cover up the religious motive with "secular crumble."

The same kind of evidence was not available in *Van Orden*, so the four disapproving justices focused instead on the design of the monument and the lack of any attempt by Texas to integrate the 17 displays on the capitol grounds into any kind of coherent treatment of Texas's legal, political, or social history. Since the context provided no clues about why the monument was there, other than the monument's own content, and since the monument featured the phrase "I AM the LORD thy God" and religious symbols, according to these justices, people looking at the monument would be likely to see it as an endorsement of Judaism and/or Christianity.

Neither of these two views carried the day. Justice Breyer wrote a separate opinion in *Van Orden* in which he rejected the *Lemon* test for borderline cases where government connects itself to a message or symbol with religious content. He saw *Van Orden* as just such a borderline case, requiring him (and his fellow justices) to exercise *legal judgment*, by looking at the entire situation to determine whether there was anything about it that violated the purposes for the First Amendment, which were:

1. To assure the fullest possible scope of religious liberty and tolerance for all;
2. To avoid the public and political divisiveness that often grows out of religious differences; and
3. To maintain "separation of church and state" so that each authority (religious and political) can do the work for which it is best suited.

In *Van Orden*, Breyer thought there was no danger of observers being coerced or unduly influenced toward Judaism or Christianity by the old monument, which had caused so little controversy for so long and which was in a setting that did nothing to reinforce a religious message. But in *McCreary*, Breyer joined the majority opinion declaring the Kentucky displays unconstitutional, presumably persuaded that the history of the projects, with the clear evidence of religious purposes, moved that case out of the borderline region, so no special exercise of judicial judgment was required.

The Current State of the Law on Public Display of Religious Texts or Symbols

The results of the *Van Orden* and *McCreary* cases are instructive from a practical point of view, although not so much from a legal point of view. If a display of objects with religious content is to be attempted, it needs to be justified entirely by secular purposes fitting to the level of government and needs to be carried out consistently with those purposes. A display about a secular topic—such as the history of the development of law or about motives for settling a frontier—can include religious material pertinent to that purpose. So the Ten Commandments could go into a display on the history of the law. Or a diary from a settler expressing thanks for God's protection and commitment to a vision of serving God could be part of a display about frontier life. But these items would have to be justified based on their secular importance, tied to objective evidence that law draws important inspiration from the Old Testament (a difficult proposition for any individual state's laws, although perhaps not so difficult for the history of human law in general), or that large numbers of pioneers were motivated by religion (in some areas, a very easy case to make). These justifications cannot be added on as afterthoughts as ways to cover up what is really a religious motivation.

The unresolved differences on the Court trouble legal theorists, but they do tend to point remarkably clearly toward a fairly stable range of outcomes. If a government is considering a public display that is worth putting up without the religious symbol or text, and if the religious material is in the display only to make it more accurate (and thus does not overrepresent the role of religious faith in the subject of the display), then it probably would pass constitutional tests.

Nevertheless, it is important to note that the legal theory upon which future courts will judge these cases is still unsettled and even a little messy. Although the twin precedents of *Van Orden* and *McCreary* do go some way toward narrowing the scope of practical uncertainty, they did not clarify the legal definition of unacceptable government behavior in representing or displaying religious faith.

See also **Creationism, Intelligent Design, and Evolution; Prayer in Public Schools**

Further Reading

American Center for Law and Justice, http://www.aclj.org

American Civil Liberties Union, http://www.aclu.org/religion/index.html

Americans United for Separation of Church and State, http://www.au.org

Center for Law and Religious Freedom, http://www.clsnet.org

Dawson Institute for Church-State Studies (Baylor University), http://www.baylor.edu/church_state/splash.php

Dunn, Charles W., ed., *The Future of Religion in American Politics.* Lexington: University Press of Kentucky, 2009.

First Freedom Center, http://www.firstfreedom.org

Fisher, Louis, and David G. Adler, *American Constitutional Law.* Vol. 2, *Constitutional Rights: Civil Rights and Civil Liberties,* 7th ed. Durham: Carolina Academic Press, 2007.

Lane, Frederick S., *The Court and the Cross: The Religious Right's Crusade to Reshape the Supreme Court.* Boston: Beacon Press, 2008.

Nussbaum, Martha Craven, *Liberty of Conscience: In Defense of America's Tradition of Religious Equality.* New York: Basic Books, 2008.

O'Brien, David M., *Constitutional Law and Politics.* Vol. 2, *Civil Rights and Civil Liberties.* New York: W. W. Norton, 2005 (especially chapter 6).

People for the American Way, http://www.pfaw.org/pfaw

The Rutherford Institute, http://www.rutherford.org

Stark, Rodney, *What Americans Really Believe: New Findings from the Baylor Surveys of Religion.* Waco, TX: Baylor University Press, 2008.

S

SCHOOL CHOICE

Ronald G. Corwin

The term *school choice* refers to programs or initiatives under which parents may select the school to which their child goes. The school choice movement endeavors to expand parents' options. Currently, a number of alternatives are available to most parents both within and outside school districts. Districts provide open enrollment plans, specialized magnet and vocational schools, small schools-within-schools, and locally managed public schools. Of these alternatives, open enrollment, arguably, has been the most controversial.

Open Enrollment Programs

Open enrollment programs allow students to attend any public school in their district or often throughout a state. First enacted in Minnesota in 1988, these programs currently are available in 29 states. However, only 14 percent of children in grades 1 through 12 participate. The low participation can be attributed to the fact that transfer programs threaten the ability of neighborhoods to control who attends their schools. Districts take advantage of loopholes allowing them to refuse students or to set quotas based on space availability and other reasons, and most states do not provide funds for transportation.

Although open enrollment programs may benefit individual students, the schools themselves are left unchanged or in worse condition. In particular, if a small school loses some students, it may need to cut staff and programs and increase class size.

These cuts can prompt still more students to transfer, introducing still another round of cuts.

Independent, Publicly Financed Schools

Notwithstanding a wide range of options available within public school districts, during the past two decades the school choice movement has dramatically evolved into a restless push for publicly financed schools that operate *outside* districts. The quest by parents to be free of district control explains the popularity of education vouchers and various charter schools. In both cases, parents use public tax monies to send their children to self-governing, independent schools that operate without close oversight from local school boards. Most local taxpayers have no say in what happens in such schools. Both charter schools and voucher schools have been promoted on the basis of free market ideologies rooted in claims about market-driven organizations outperforming traditional public school monopolies. In truth, such claims may be premature.

Voucher Schools Compared to Charter Schools

Education vouchers set aside a specified amount of public money that parents may use to pay their child's tuition to a receptive private (or, in a few cases, public) school. Receiving schools are known as *voucher schools*. The private sector is diverse. The Catholic Church enrolls almost half of all private school students. But one in three is in a school affiliated with a wide array of religious organizations and sects, and others are in nonsectarian schools. Most private schools are for elementary students, but some of them are high schools, and many more are combined K–12. Also, private schools are widely dispersed throughout central cities, the urban fringe, and large towns, but one in five is located in a rural area. Few Catholic schools are small (fewer than 50 students), and over one-third are large (300 or more students); this pattern is reversed for nonsectarian schools. One in four private schools serve wealthy, elite families, and the percentage of private schools with poor students is less than half that of public schools. Three-fourths of all private school students are white, but, in one out of five Catholic schools, over half the students come from minority backgrounds. Most Catholic schools have some students who qualify for subsidized meals, but other private schools are much less likely to have such students. Private schools are far less likely than public schools to enroll students with limited English proficiency.

Charter schools are publicly funded, tuition-free, nonsectarian public schools that have been released from many of the laws and rules that govern school districts, including, for example, rules pertaining to teacher qualifications, curriculum, and calendar. Funds allocated to the school district follow the student to the charter school. Like private schools, they are also very diverse. About three-quarters of charter schools nationwide are new start ups; most of the others are existing public schools that have converted to charter status. In practice, many charter schools are indistinguishable from other public schools. However, they are expected to take innovative approaches likely to improve student achievement. And some do. In fact, some charters are runaway mavericks, while others feature distinctive and sometimes controversial Waldorf, Montessori, or "back-to-basics" approaches. Still others are not schools in the usual sense. Nearly one-third of them are not classroom based. Eight percent operate as home schools, others are classified as independent-study schools, and several dozen online cyber-charters have no visible physical boundaries or school buildings. There are even some charter *districts* that have converted all of their schools to charters.

Control of Charter Schools

Depending on the state, charters can be launched by parents, educators, community members, state universities, private firms, or any entity designated by the state. Charter schools are managed by their own governing boards, and most are legally independent. Eleven states grant them independence outright, and eight others permit them to be independent. The 20 states that require their charters to operate as part of a school district account for about one-fifth of the nation's 3,600 charter schools. Their legal status notwithstanding, as conceived, charter schools are supposed to operate autonomously, although their actual freedom varies widely in practice.

Authorized by state statutes, charter schools operate under a contract with an overseeing chartering agency. Over three-fourths of all charters are sponsored by local school boards. In addition, intermediate, county and state boards of education, as well as state education agencies, universities, and colleges sometimes act as sponsors. Sponsors approve long-term contracts. Theoretically, they can also revoke or refuse to renew contracts, but in practice a sponsor's actual control over schools varies enormously. Adding to the ambiguity, several states require each school to negotiate with the sponsor over which decisions it is permitted to control, and the outcomes of these negotiations are not always clear. It does seem clear, though, that many charter schools are precariously straddling a bewildering paradox as autonomous, often legally independent schools, physically located within school districts that are responsible for them but not permitted or inclined to interfere with them.

Selectivity in Charter Schools

Unlike private schools, which select students, charter schools are legally required to accept students who apply, provided there is space and provided the child meets criteria that may be mandated by the states or set by the school. However, in practice, charter schools are not available to most students because of mandates and because of official and informal policies. Often charter schools give priority to local neighborhood children, either by mandate or by policy. Some states limit enrollment to low-income or low-achieving students. Most charter schools say they are oversubscribed, in which case they are allowed to select students randomly or from first-served waiting lists.

Some charters target recruiting practices to preferred types of families, some have formal or informal admission criteria (including recommendations, academic records, tests, or aptitudes), others counsel out the less preferred individuals, and many expel difficult students. Just how frequently charters use these informal practices is difficult to document. Most schools deny having any special admission requirements, but one in four charters admit to them. Many others require applications and interviews. Moreover, a large percentage of charters require or expect parents to work on behalf of the school as a condition for admission. While that may seem like a good idea, parent contracts exclude families that are unable to participate or choose not to participate. Given this arsenal of available exclusionary techniques, the admission practices of charters and voucher schools are not as divergent as they appear on the surface.

Historical Roots of the School Choice Movement

The school choice movement has been explained and justified in at least three ways:

1. White-flight parents, seeking to escape desegregation programs mandated under the 1954 *Brown v. Board of Education* decision, enrolled their children in private schools, which in turn created a demand for publicly financed vouchers.

2. Reformers advocated government-financed schools that would provide options for low-income minority parents dissatisfied with their children's assigned public school. Some voucher programs and charter schools have been reserved for minorities, while some others are required to maintain some form of racial and/or income balance. However, the aggregate national data showing that charters enroll a high percentage of minorities are misleading. State-by-state data show that a few charters have an abundance of minorities, but most enroll only a handful of minority students.

3. Some reformers have succeeded in convincing politicians to support vouchers and charter schools under the implausible promise that competition from independent publicly financed schools will force public schools to reform in order to retain students.

Just one year after the *Brown* decision, the Nobel Prize–winning economist Milton Friedman introduced a plan to give parents public money they could use to enroll their children in any receptive private or public school of their choice. But it was not until 1990 that Milwaukee, Wisconsin, used vouchers and tax credits to create the nation's first publicly financed urban school choice program. The school choice ideology got a substantial boost in the early 1990s as frustrated parents realized that school districts were incapable of meeting their needs. Critics were quick to cite low test scores, high dropout rates, overcrowding, and other negative statistics as evidence that traditional schools were failing to prepare the literate, skilled workers needed in a specialized, technological world marketplace. Frustrated parents, the critics argued, started looking for options, and independent choice schools emerged to do the job.

Criticisms of Bureaucracy

The problems often have been blamed on intractable bureaucracy and uncaring officials. But bureaucracy is not primarily responsible for the shortcomings of school districts. There were awesome societal forces beyond their control, including immigration, higher retention rates, and urbanization, all of which produced mammoth schools unable to meet personal circumstances. This society did not—or maybe could not—provide the resources and leadership that districts needed to cope with the drastic social changes that swept over them. In any case, frustration with bureaucracy does not account for why choice advocates pushed to make choice schools independent from public school districts. They said public educators were incapable of changing and too often were uninterested in doing so. Yet, in the early 1990s, even as vouchers and charters were being vigorously promoted, social conditions were already forcing school districts to adapt. They were ripe for sweeping internal reforms and were in fact experimenting with a host of reforms.

It was not necessary to force parents to leave school districts to give them viable choices. Choice advocates could have chosen to use their clout to push for choices within school districts. Instead, they chose to press for independent schools operating outside districts. Why? The short answer is that a nationwide ideological movement, which took hold starting in the 1950s, had gained momentum. This so-called laissez-faire movement called for the privatization of almost every commodity and service in the public sector. School choice advocates hitched their ideological wagon to a questionable free-market dream.

The Impetus for Charter Schools

Charter schools entered the picture in the early 1990s as a derivative of the voucher concept and, just as importantly, as a competitive alternative to school vouchers. For example, in 1993, California voucher activists placed a public initiative on the ballot to assess the voters' interest in school vouchers. Their opponents felt compelled to give the public another way to regain control over the way their children were taught. The compromise was legislation authorizing charter schools to form. There seems little doubt that the promise of charter schools helped defeat the 1994 California voucher initiative. However, the charter school concept itself had become tainted by close association with private school vouchers, which in turn caused the school establishment to turn its back on charter schools. To meet the objections of educators, the California legislature imposed compromises, including caps on the number of charter schools that could be created.

Are Choice Schools Better Than Regular Schools?

In exchange for being released from most rules, charter schools are supposed to be more accountable than other schools, a provision that supposedly includes closing schools that fail to perform adequately. There are two types of accountability criteria: market and contractual. *Market accountability* means that a choice school must sustain adequate levels of enrollment. Voucher schools are subject to this type of accountability. *Contractual accountability* means that the school must fulfill a contract with sponsors under terms set by state legislation, which can include stipulations about meeting student achievement goals. Charter schools are subject to both forms of accountability.

In practice, both are problematic. Market accountability provides no assurance that a school is providing a sound education and operating legally. Contractual obligations, especially those pertaining to student achievement, are difficult for understaffed agencies to monitor or measure. Consequently, few charter schools have been closed for failure to produce good results. At the same time, more than 400 have been closed for fraud and mismanagement, and there are probably many others that have not been caught or sanctioned. Corruption and negligence are the unspoken downside of independence.

Charter schools, and even private schools that accept vouchers, were presented to the public as a way to improve student achievement. The bargain was *better outcomes in exchange for deregulation and independence.* In particular, it was understood that if charter schools could not demonstrate improved student achievement, they would be shut down. In addition, some advocates convinced legislatures that competition from charter schools would force public schools to improve. The preponderance of evidence has not supported either claim. Yet both programs remain strongly entrenched in state and federal budgets, sometimes because they are promoted by passionate advocates making claims based on trivial differences and wildly inconsistent data.

The Vast Gap between the Claims and the Evidence

Advocates say that:

- Choice schools lead to higher levels of learning.
- No study points to substantially poorer performance of choice schools.
- There is a surprising consensus among studies showing students enrolled in choice programs benefit academically.
- Data showing charter school students do worse on national tests than other students are baseless.
- Fourth-grade school students across the nation are more proficient in reading and math than students in nearby public schools.
- Competition from a few independent schools produces improved test scores among students in regular schools.

- Competition from charter schools is the best way to motivate the ossified bu-reaucracies governing education.
- Charters are reinventing public education.

In contrast, however, various researchers have concluded that:

- Student achievement in general has not been positively enhanced by charter schools.
- Some studies comparing charter schools and regular schools suggest a positive impact and others a neutral or negative impact.
- The majority of charter schools have failed to raise, and sometimes have lowered, student achievement compared to regular public schools in the same area.
- With some notable exceptions, charter schools are remarkably similar to regular schools.
- Charter schools are not doing anything regular schools wish to emulate.
- There is little going on in charter schools that merits the attention of anyone seeking powerful ways to engage children and youth in learning.
- Innovation in curriculum and instruction is virtually nonexistent in charter schools.
- Charter schools have produced no convincing data to illustrate that, on the whole, they are prudent or productive investments.

Further confounding the picture, some researchers overstate the implications from the data and, in some cases, distort the data themselves. For example, comparing a sample of charters with nearby regular schools, one researcher claims to have found a 3 percent difference in math proficiency and a 5 percent difference in reading, which she believes is significant (Hoxby 2004). Not only are the differences relatively small, but they were inflated because the author excluded the lowest-performing charter school students be-cause they attended schools serving at-risk students, who the author supposes are not comparable to students in nearby public schools—even though a large portion of most public schools enroll the same type of student. Moreover, the study was represented as a national study when, in fact, the schools included represented only one-third of existing charter schools, and the students included account for fewer than 12 percent of charter school students.

Diversity of Outcomes

So, are choice schools superior? It is obvious that advocates on both sides of the question are arguing over inconsistent and often trivial differences. The rancorous ongoing debate only confirms that studies have not substantiated the overblown claim that choice schools are out-performing regular schools in meaningful ways. At best, the picture is mixed. It could not be otherwise given the diversity of choice schools. They take too many different forms to be treated as a meaningful unit that can be sensibly compared to conventional public schools—which of course also differ widely among themselves. Choice schools are not comparable either in programs or in students' qualifications and therefore cannot be held accountable to common measures. The only thing charter schools have in common is their legal form—which is to say, the charter that authorizes someone to start a school. And the only salient feature the more than 7,000 private schools share is their nonpublic standing.

Is Competition Reforming Regular Public Schools?

What about the claim that competition from choice schools is causing school districts to improve? The short answer is that it probably is not happening. Reason suggests that schools will sometimes take notice when they start losing enough students and money. However, the research has not identified where that might happen, how big the loss must be, how much competition it takes, or what actions schools will take to improve student outcomes. This research has been plagued by defective analyses, including: inflating the significance of small differences, incorrectly aggregating individual scores to meaningless levels of abstraction, preoccupation with averages that obscure variation, and failure to identify where competition does and does not have an effect.

A few schools in a district are probably not going to provide real competition, and they certainly are not going to assure that regular schools will miraculously improve. Improvement takes leadership, skills, and resources—none of which is guaranteed by competition. On the contrary, competition can have a corrosive effect by draining off resources. Ultimately, competition might only cause schools to flail blindly without direction.

Problems with the Research on School Achievement

Using classroom tests to compare samples of schools is inappropriate for the following reasons.

Hazards of Aggregating Test Scores of Individuals to Schools

The idea that the success of a national program can be assessed with standardized tests comes from an obsolete industrial model that treats schools as factories processing students as raw materials—with average test scores reflecting the quality of the product. However, in the first place, a school does not control most of the so-called production process. The way students perform on tests depends on many extraneous forces, such as language proficiency, family structure, parental guidance, peer group influences, job and travel experiences, and the like. More importantly, standardized tests are constructed to maximize differences among *individuals* and so are inappropriate measures of higher-level *organizational units* like schools, school districts, and programs. The greater the variance among individuals at the classroom level, the smaller the differences become when their scores are used to represent schools, districts, or states.

Fallacies of Statistical Averages

Reporting averages that compare schools, programs, or states can mislead parents who are trying to find a suitable school for their children. Studies typically pool all included charter schools, across all classrooms, districts, and states represented, and then report the mean for that pool, without breaking out important differences among various types of schools and without taking into account the range of scores. *Within a school,* many students could be doing poorly even if the mean score reflects well on the school. For example, a school can increase its average score even when the students who improve are the ones in the upper part of the distribution. And *among diverse schools, districts, and programs,* mean scores only obscure the critical differences among them. Statistical means do not, for example, reveal the facts that many public schools are as good as private schools and that students who attend the best public schools outperform most private school students.

Given the enormous differences among both choice schools and regular schools, averages and other measures of central tendency are not only meaningless but also deceptive. Suppose that charter schools within a state or within a school district have higher average scores than regular public schools. That signifies only that some are better; but some may be worse. The question is how many are better? It is always possible that a few schools are pulling up the average, masking the poor performance of most other schools. What is most critical is the percentage of schools in the top, middle, and bottom of the distribution of charter schools and how those percentages compare with the distribution of public schools. Those distributions are seldom reported, and, consequently, parents have no way to assess the risk they are taking in sending their child to a charter school, even when average scores in the area are relatively favorable.

Implications of the Research

Putting aside inflated claims on both sides of the question, the only reasonable conclusion that can be justified by the evidence so far is this: even if some students are marginally better off in choice schools, the differences appear small and inconsistent enough that it does not make much difference, causing some to question why massive federal and state programs in favor of choice schools are in place. The fact that *some* choice schools may be good, even exceptional, is little comfort for parents who must make decisions about whether to risk sending their children to a *particular* school. Given the wide differences among schools, the risk is high. For parents, average scores are not helpful. They need better information. However, rather than sorting it out, researchers report only averages and then incorrectly aggregate data collected from individuals in classrooms to the levels of districts, states, and programs. Standardized test scores were not constructed for the purpose of comparing diverse types of schools or other macro units like school districts and states.

Conclusion

While independence from school districts has been vaunted as a solution to the problems confronting public schools, as things stand, independence appears to be a counterproductive dead-end. Autonomous schools are products of random market forces. There is no guarantee that they will locate where the need is greatest, or be well designed and able to meet the most challenging problems. Further, there appears to be no perceptible difference between many charters and regular public schools. And many charter schools seem to abuse their freedom, while many others are struggling to survive. In the name of independence, some students are being shortchanged with watered-down versions of comprehensive school programs, sitting in substandard buildings and facilities, being taught by inexperienced and sometimes poorly trained teachers.

This does not mean that there are no excellent choice schools. On the contrary, there are many exceptionally good ones. But there is no compelling evidence for the proposition that schools that operate independently are better than regular schools. And even if it could be shown that independent schools are marginally better, the difference could be explained by the small size of most choice schools or by good teachers, strong parental support, and a host of other reasons unrelated to independence.

The promise that it would be possible to demonstrate across-the-board achievement gains in favor of independent choice schools was impossible from the start, not necessarily because choice schools are inadequate, but because proponents promised too much and certainly more than can be demonstrated with test scores. However, charter schools, and even voucher schools, can be useful, provided they are linked more closely with school districts. For it *is* known that, while some choice schools are floundering, others are performing at least as well as regular schools or in some cases even as well as blue-ribbon public schools. These charter schools could be helpful to school districts if only they were made part of districts rather than being independent of them. The school choice debate artificially sets schools against one another when competition is not the solution. School districts need help.

In many conventional schools, unions may control teacher assignments, and, as a consequence, the best teachers are able to avoid the most challenging schools. However, if a district operated its own charters, it could use them strategically to entice good teachers into hard-to-staff schools and to address other districtwide problems, including those associated with at-risk students, English learners, special education students, and others.

See also **Charter Schools; Government Role in Schooling; No Child Left Behind (NCLB)**

Further Reading

Betts, Julian R., and Tom Loveless, eds., *Getting Choice Right: Ensuring Equity and Efficiency in Education Policy*. Washington, DC: Brookings Institution Press, 2005.

Bracey, Gerald W., *The War against America's Schools: Privatizing Schools, Commercializing Education*. Boston: Allyn & Bacon, 2001.

Cookson, Peter W., and Kristina Berger, *Expect Miracles: Charter Schools and the Politics of Hope and Despair*. Boulder, CO: Westview Press, 2003.

Corwin, Ronald G., and E. Joseph Schneider, *The School Choice Hoax: Fixing America's Schools*. Lanham, MD: Rowman & Littlefield, 2007.

Feinberg, Walter, and Christopher Lubienski, *School Choice Policies and Outcomes: Empirical and Philosophical Perspectives*. Albany: State University of New York Press, 2008.

Hoxby, Caroline M., *Achievement in Charter Schools and Regular Public Schools in the United States: Understanding the Differences,* Cambridge, MA: Harvard University and National Bureau of Economic Research, 2004.

Lockwood, A. T., *The Charter School Decade*. Lanham, MD: Scarecrow Press, 2004.

Ravitch, Diane, *Death and Life of Great American School Reform: How Testing and Choice Are Undermining Education*. New York: Basic Books, 2010.

Walberg, Herbert A., *School Choice: The Findings*. Washington, DC: Cato Institute, 2007.

SELF-INJURY AND BODY IMAGE

Margaret Leaf

Self-injury tends to be associated with young women and girls, whereas injuring others is associated with young men and boys. Both behaviors may be understood as forms of gendered violence, directed outward for men and boys and inward for women and girls. While boys learn to act *through* their bodies with physical violence, girls learn to act *on* their bodies with self-inflicted violence.

Background

Adolescence and young adulthood are rife with both physiological transformations (for example, puberty) and social transitions (for example, changing schools, shifting orientation from family to peers) that young people often experience as distressful. However, there is evidence suggesting that the ways people respond to this distress are gendered. Specifically, girls and women are more likely to direct their distress inward, taking it out on themselves, while boys and men are more likely to direct their distress outward, taking it out on others. This can be seen in the higher rates of other-directed violence among boys and young men and higher rates of eating disorders and self-injury among young women.

Of these responses to distress, self-injury has only recently received attention from the media and scientific communities, increasing public attention and debate about the

SELF-INJURY AWARENESS, PREVENTION, AND TREATMENT

Awareness of self-injury is increasing, as evidenced by the movement for a Self Injury Awareness Day, set for March 1 of every year, on which people may promote awareness by wearing an orange ribbon.

As awareness increases, prevention becomes easier. First and foremost, self-injurers may be best served by being listened to and encouraged rather than stigmatized or ignored. Building allies in communities and schools, raising awareness, and promoting a sense of power among young people—particularly young women—are all essential steps toward prevention.

Treatment for self-injury is available in many places, in many forms. The S.A.F.E. (Self-Abuse Finally Ends) program supports a national hotline: 1-800-DONTCUT. There are also many therapists, counselors, and other mental health professionals who specialize in treating self-injury. Visit http://www.selfinjury.com for more information.

topic. First and foremost, these debates center on the definition of self-injury. Currently, most researchers view self-injury as some type of deliberate harm to one's own body without conscious suicidal intent. However, definitions of the behavior vary greatly in terms of social acceptability, severity, and frequency. For example, some researchers include such behaviors as interfering with wound healing (that is, picking at scabs) and nail biting in their definition, while others specify much more severe and stigmatized behaviors such as self-castration and bone breaking. Additionally, some researchers focus on repetitive self-injurious behaviors, such as head banging or self-hitting, particularly among people who are differently abled. Finally, researchers even disagree about what to call the behavior. While *self-injury* is probably the most common term used, other terms include *cutting, deliberate self-harm, self-abuse, self-injurious behavior, self-mutilation,* and *suicidal* or *parasuicidal behavior.*

In addition to disagreement about how to define self-injury, there is also disagreement about who engages in self-injury and how common it is. Estimates of the prevalence of self-injury vary from less than 1 percent to 4 percent in the general population and from 15 percent to 35 percent among adolescent and college-aged samples (Briere and Gil 1998; Favazza 1996; Gratz 2003; Laye-Gindhu and Schonert-Reichl 2005; Whitlock, Powers, and Eckenrode 2006). These differences are mostly due to the fact that there are no nationally representative data on self-injury, so most samples are small or highly specific (for example, students sampled in a university class). Also, while most research has focused on self-injury among white women in the United States, there is a growing body of research on self-injury among other racial groups and in other countries, particularly among Asian women (see Bhardwaj 2001 and

TALKING ABOUT IT: SELF-INJURY ONLINE

A 2006 study by Whitlock, Powers, and Eckenrode identified over 400 online message boards dedicated to the topic of self-injury, with girls and women between the ages of 12 and 20 visiting the boards more than men. The study found that these message boards provide a relatively anonymous forum for self-injurers to share personal stories and problems, voice opinions and ideas, and give and receive support—all of which may be particularly helpful for adolescents and young adults who may have no one else to confide in. However, the study also found that some message boards may encourage self-injury, when, for example, they provide instructions for new self-injury techniques or promote self-injury as a pleasurable, painless behavior.

Marshall and Yazdani 1991 on self-harm among Asian women; Kinyanda, Hjelmeland, and Musisi 2005 on self-harm in Uganda). Additionally, there is some research suggesting that self-injury is more prevalent among gay, lesbian, and bisexual people (Adler and Adler 2005; Alexander and Clare 2004, Whitlock, Powers, and Eckenrode 2006) as well as among prison populations. One of the few consistencies across most studies is that self-injury typically begins during adolescence or young adulthood and tends to persist for an average of 10 to 15 years, though it may continue for decades (Favazza 1996; Muehlenkamp 2005). Some research indicates that self-injury may be likely in some elderly populations, due in part to higher rates of depression and isolation (Dennis et al. 2005).

For the most part, media depictions of self-injury paint it as a uniquely adolescent and female problem, as evidenced by movies such as *Thirteen* and *Girl, Interrupted,* as well as talk shows such as *Oprah* featuring only female guests who self-injure (Brickman 2004). Yet, because there are no nationally representative data on the prevalence of self-injury, it is unclear to what extent women really are likely to self-injure or whether it is a media myth. While a few clinical and community studies have shown that self-injury is as common among men as it is among women (Briere and Gil 1998; Gratz 2003), other studies show that self-injury is less common among men and may be carried out differently among men as well. For example, a study of 2,875 students at Cornell University and Princeton University found that 17 percent had self-injured at some point in their lives, and women were about one and a half times as likely as men to be repeat self-injurers (Whitlock, Powers, and Eckenrode 2006). Additionally, women were more than twice as likely as men to scratch or cut themselves, while men were almost three times as likely as women to punch an object. This difference in the method of injuring reflects a bigger pattern: women and girls may be more likely to act on their bodies—for example, by cutting or scratching themselves with an object—while men and boys may be more likely to act through their bodies by punching someone or something else.

Self-Injury as Gendered Violence

Whether inflicted through punching an object or punching, cutting, scratching, or burning oneself, self-injury can be seen as a form of violence toward oneself and one's body. For instance, James Gilligan (2004, 6) defines violence as

> the infliction of physical injury on a human being by a human being, whether oneself or another, especially when the injury is lethal, but also when it is life-threatening, mutilating, or disabling; and whether it is caused by deliberate, conscious intention or by careless disregard and unconcern for the safety of oneself or others.

This somewhat broad definition of violence differs from more traditional definitions because, although it is limited to physical injury, it includes the act of injuring oneself. Self-injury, according to this definition, is a form of violence, regardless of whether the self-injurer interprets it as such. Self-injury meets all of Gilligan's qualifications: it involves the infliction of physical injury on a human being by a human being (oneself), it is mutilating and sometimes life threatening, and it is done by deliberate, conscious intention. Viewing self-injury as a form of violence allows us to compare it to the other-directed or outward forms of violence more common among men.

James Messerschmidt's study of adolescent boys' violence toward others in *Nine Lives* (2000) is a particularly useful reference. In this book, Messerschmidt considers the social settings—such as family, school, neighborhood, and even one's own body—that influence and are influenced by violence. He also takes an explicitly gendered approach to violence, arguing that social settings also influence and are influenced by gender. In other words, one's family, one's school, and even the larger society (for example, the media) influence how we define masculinity and femininity and how we behave according to these definitions. From this perspective, gender is not just about one's biological male" or female status, but instead it is something that we *do* in everyday social interactions, including how we walk and talk, dress, sit, and eat, and even how we do violence.

In *Nine Lives*, Messerschmidt argues that boys are not violent by nature, but they are more likely to become violent if they have been in social settings that define sexually and/or physically fighting back as the appropriate expression of masculinity or the best way to "be a man." For instance, John, a young man who experienced severe sexual abuse at the hands of his father, learned that "dominating someone sexually" was "what a male just did" (37). On the other side of the coin, Sam came from a nonviolent home but was abused by peers at school because of his body size and shape (short and overweight). Lacking the physical resources to fight back, he instead made up for the masculinity threats at school by sexually assaulting the young girls he babysat. As these cases illustrate, the masculinity "lessons" do not come from just one source but can grow out of any one or more of a variety of settings—family, school, neighborhood, or even one's own body.

Within this framework, self-injury can be seen a form of violence that stems from a variety of social sources. Furthermore, self-injury may be as gendered as other forms of violence. While lessons in masculinity taught the boys in Messerschmidt's study to inflict violence on others, lessons in femininity lead some women (and fewer men) to inflict violence on themselves. Girls and women learn from various social settings—the media, family, school, peers—that they are inferior, and some women and girls take this out on themselves and their bodies (Brown 2003). This self-inflicted violence is manifested in the various body projects women and girls engage in, from restrictive dieting to starving oneself, and from piercing to cutting (Brumberg 1997). Whereas boys learn to act *through* their bodies with physical violence, girls learn to act *on* their bodies with self-inflicted violence.

Control, Body Image, and Societal Messages

Why are girls and women more likely to act *on* their bodies? Some argue that control is at the center of the picture. Like many self-injurers, some of the boys in Messerschmidt's study had been physically, sexually, and/or emotionally abused at home or at school, resulting in a sense of helplessness and lack of control. In turn, they sought and gained a sense of control by physically and sexually assaulting others, often people whom they viewed as weaker (for example, girls and younger boys). But girls and women sometimes view themselves as weaker or inferior as well, and so instead of trying to control those who are more powerful (that is, men), they try to gain control of girls, including themselves. Lyn Mikel Brown (2003), for example, argues that fighting between girls exists in part because of girls' struggle for power, voice, and legitimacy. The limited power to which girls have access often stems from "qualities they either have little control over, don't earn, or openly disdain," such as their bodies and appearance, and so they take their frustration out on each other and themselves (32).

Furthermore, when this search for control is combined with poor body image and self-esteem, it often results in self-harming practices such as extreme dieting and exercise, disordered eating, and self-injury. From a young age, women and girls are bombarded with images of unrealistically thin and beautiful women in the media. Often these images are so airbrushed and digitally altered that even the models themselves do not measure up. These images, along with other social influences, set a standard of femininity that is thin and beautiful, sexy but sweet, yet relatively passive and powerless. One of the few "appropriate" sources of power regularly advertised to girls and women is sexiness through their bodies and appearance. As a result, girls and women sometimes go to great lengths to fit the sexy media image. Because this image is virtually unattainable, their efforts become self-destructive rather than self-enhancing. Adolescent women and girls may be particularly susceptible to this, given the powerlessness they often feel amid the myriad physical, hormonal, and social changes they have to contend with. While it is difficult, if not impossible, to argue that media images and societal messages directly cause girls and women to engage in self-harming behaviors, they certainly do not help girls and women gain the sense of control and independence they may be seeking.

Conclusion

Although self-injury has only recently received mass media attention, it is not a new problem. People have been self-injuring in cultural and religious rituals, and likely in private as well, for centuries (see Favazza 1996). While the definitions and explanations of self-injury and the responses to it have varied greatly, the practice itself has not changed dramatically: people inflicting violence on themselves without necessarily intending to die. Like violence toward others, violence toward the self results, at least in part, from social surroundings. If boys' and men's violence toward others stems from settings that define fighting back and controlling others as appropriate and valued expressions of masculinity, then perhaps girls' and women's violence toward themselves results from social settings that define fighting back and controlling others as inappropriate. Instead, girls and women are encouraged to control themselves, to be pretty, nice, and quiet, and this results in either turning aggression down—like young girls who learn to lower their voices when fighting—or turning it toward themselves (Brown 2003). Until these messages change, girls and women will continue to find ways to take it out on themselves, with boys and men sometimes taking it out on them too.

See also **Eating Disorders; Mental Health; Marketing to Women and Girls (vol. 1); Sex and Advertising (vol. 1)**

Further Reading

Adler, Patricia A., and Peter Adler, "Self-Injurers as Loners: The Social Organization of Solitary Deviance." *Deviant Behavior* 26 (2005): 345–378.

Alexander, Natasha, and Linda Clare, "You Still Feel Different: The Experience and Meaning of Women's Self-injury in the Context of a Lesbian or Bisexual Identity." *Journal of Community and Applied Social Psychology* 14 (2004): 70–84.

Berman, Jeffrey, and Patricia Hatch Wallace, *Cutting and the Pedagogy of Self-Disclosure.* Amherst: University of Massachusetts Press, 2007.

Bhardwaj, A., "Growing up Young, Asian and Female in Britain: A Report on Self-harm and Suicide." *Feminist Review* 68 (2001): 52–67.

Bordo, Susan, *Unbearable Weight: Feminism, Western Culture, and the Body.* Berkeley: University of California Press, 2004.

Brickman, Barbara J., "'Delicate' Cutters: Gendered Self-Mutilation and Attractive Flesh in Medical Discourse." *Body and Society* 10, no. 4 (2004): 87–111.

Briere, John, and Eliana Gil, "Self-mutilation in Clinical and General Population Samples: Prevalence, Correlates, and Functions." *American Journal of Orthopsychiatry* 68 (1998): 609–620.

Brown, Lyn Mikel, *Girlfighting: Betrayal and Rejection among Girls.* New York: New York University Press, 2003.

Brumberg, Joan Jacobs, *The Body Project: An Intimate History of American Girls.* New York: Random House, 1997.

Dennis, Michael, Penny Wakefield, Caroline Molloy, Harry Andrews, and Trevor Friedman, "Self-harm in Older People with Depression: Comparison of Social Factors, Life Events and Symptoms." *British Journal of Psychiatry* 186 (2005): 538–539.

Favazza, Armando R., *Bodies under Siege: Self-Mutilation and Body Modification in Culture and Psychiatry.* Baltimore: Johns Hopkins University Press, 1996.

Gilligan, James, "How to Think about Violence." In *Violence and Gender: An Interdisciplinary Reader,* ed. P. R. Gilbert and K. K. Eby. Upper Saddle River, NJ: Prentice Hall, 2004.

Gratz, Kim L., "Risk Factors for and Functions of Deliberate Self-Harm: An Empirical and Conceptual Review." *Clinical Psychology: Science and Practice* 10, no. 2 (2003): 192–205.

Groves, Abigail, "Blood on the Walls: Self-Mutilation in Prisons." *Australian and New Zealand Journal of Criminology* 37 (2004): 49–65.

Hodgson, Sarah, "Cutting through the Silence: A Sociological Construction of Self-Injury." *Sociological Inquiry* 74, no. 2 (2004): 162–179.

Kinyanda, Eugene, Heidi Hjelmeland, and Seggane Musisi, "Psychological Factors in Deliberate Self-harm as Seen in an Urban African Population in Uganda: A Case-control Study." *Suicide and Life-Threatening Behavior* 35 (2005): 468–477.

Laye-Gindhu, Aviva, and Kimberly A. Schonert-Reichl, "Nonsuicidal Self-harm among Community Adolescents: Understanding the 'Whats' and 'Whys' of Self-harm." *Journal of Youth and Adolescence* 34 (2005): 447–457.

LifeSIGNS Self-Injury Guidance and Network Support, *Self-Injury Awareness Booklet,* 2d ed., 2005. http://www.selfharm.org/publications/sia/index.html

Marshall, Harriette, and Anjum Yazdani, "Locating Culture in Accounting for Self-harm amongst Asian Young Women." *Journal of Community and Applied Social Psychology* 9 (1999): 413–433.

Messerschmidt, James W., *Nine Lives: Adolescent Masculinities, the Body, and Violence.* Boulder, CO: Westview Press, 2000.

Milia, Diana, *Self-Mutilation and Art Therapy: Violent Creation.* London: Jessica Kingsley, 2000.

Miller, Dusty, *Women Who Hurt Themselves.* New York: Basic Books/HarperCollins, 1994.

Muehlenkamp, Jennifer J., "Self-Injurious Behavior as a Separate Clinical Syndrome." *American Journal of Orthopsychiatry* 75, no. 2 (2005): 324–333.

Nixon, Mary K., and Nancy L. Heath, eds., *Self-Injury in Youth: The Essential Guide to Assessment and Intervention.* New York: Routledge, 2009.

S.A.F.E. Alternatives, "Self Abuse Finally Ends." 2010. http://www.selfinjury.com

Strong, Marilee, *A Bright Red Scream: Self-Mutilation and the Language of Pain.* New York: Penguin, 1998.

Whitlock, J. L., J. E. Eckenrode, and D. Silverman, "The Epidemiology of Self-Injurious Behavior in a College Population." *Pediatrics* 117 (2006): 1939–1949.

Whitlock, Janis L., Jane L. Powers, and John Eckenrode, "The Virtual Cutting Edge: The Internet and Adolescent Self-Injury." *Developmental Psychology* 42 (2006): 407–417.

SHOCK JOCKS, OR ROGUE TALK RADIO

David Sanjek

The emotional persuasiveness of person-to-person communication over the radio has been evident since the birth of the medium. Something about a voice emanating out of the very air commands an audience's attention. Many radio personalities have employed that power without any thought to pushing the envelope of acceptable speech, while others have engaged in questioning their limits almost without license. When does public speech possibly pollute the airwaves, and has the very medium itself been shocking audiences, in one way or another, throughout its history?

The term *shock jock* has come into vogue as a shorthand designation for a radio personality who uses the power of his or her microphone to either rile up or titillate the audience. One can distinguish between two types of shock jocks. First are those with an ideological axe to grind who ridicule if not ravage the views of their opponents. The currently most popular of those figures (Rush Limbaugh, Michael Savage) tend to be conservative in their politics, although those in opposition to their positions attempted to establish a beachhead, the Air America network (2004–2010), to counter their preeminence on the dial. The second type of shock jock appeals to listeners through either disregarding or intentionally deflating the rules of publicly permissible speech as propounded by the Federal Communications Commission (FCC). The currently most popular of those figures (Howard Stern, Opie and Anthony) litter their broadcasts with sexual innuendo and, on occasion, outright obscenity. The ultimate aim of both camps, admittedly, comes down to ratings and the maximization of their share of the audience; yet, in some cases, shock jocks act in a deliberate manner in order to convince the public to adopt their positions and act upon them in such a way as to influence public life.

Radio as a Shocking Medium

While contemporary shock jocks engage in a form of extreme public speech not heard by past generations over the airwaves, the very medium of radio has possessed a capacity to shock since its very beginning. Admittedly, audiences accepted and accommodated radio as a form of public communication in relatively short order after the first national broadcast by the RCA network in 1921. However, we should recall that each consumer invites the participation of others into their lives by choice. In its essence, radio can be thought of as a kind of desired or designated intrusion, a fact that was authoritatively demonstrated in recent times by the excessive amplification of boom boxes. Once radios became reasonably affordable, around 1927, the technology came to be thought of as a kind of acoustic hearth, though audiences expected those who entertained them to wipe their shoes, so to speak, before they crossed the threshold of their homes.

This desire not to be disturbed or dismayed by what was broadcast over the air particularly applied to announcers and later disc jockeys—the predecessors to and, in some cases, influences upon present-day shock jocks. On-air personalities received considerable leeway to display the full range of their idiosyncrasies, but announcers were expected to be virtually invisible and extinguish any quirks from their personalities. Some compared the phenomenon of their voices to God, as they came invisibly out of the very air, and they were expected, like the deity, to promote and not abuse community standards.

Rockin' Is Our Business

This trend began to change with the emergence of the disc jockey, a position that, while not inaugurated by Martin Block and his show *Make Believe Ballroom* in 1934, is by many associated with him as its originator. He gave a name and defined personality to a figure that heretofore remained anonymous, even if the music he played was the audience-friendly pop tunes of the day. Disc jockeys adopted an even more colorful role with the emergence of rhythm and blues and subsequently rock and roll in the 1940s and 1950s. They broke the moderate mold not only by the type of music they played but also, and more importantly, through the manner with which they presented it. Individuals like Hunter Hancock of Los Angeles, the black announcers on Memphis's WDIA (Nat Williams and Rufus Thomas), and most famously Alan Freed of Cleveland and later New York injected a more raucous tone to their position. They concocted idiosyncratic vocabularies, solicited the opinions of their teenage listeners, and enthusiastically advocated the music they played. Even now, tapes of their broadcasts retain a vibrancy and audacity that time has not erased.

Many parents and some politicians feared the power these men held over their children and worried that the repertoire they featured threatened the very fabric of society. Some less open-minded citizens even called attention to and chastised the disc jockeys for playing music that they felt encouraged racial integration. When government investigations called attention to the fact that many of these men accepted payments for records they played, known at the time as payola, hearings were held in Washington and some careers ended, Freed's most notably. The furor that followed toned down the audacity of the disc jockeys, as less threatening figures, like *American Bandstand*'s Dick Clark, adopted a posture that parents found acceptable. Nonetheless, the transformation of the on-air announcer from a virtual nonentity to an audacious individual with a definite personality was complete.

Voices in the Night

Some individuals saw in radio the opportunity to speak, person to person, through a microphone and conceived of their broadcasts as a sphere of self-expression. None, perhaps, succeeded more in shocking portions of the public with his adoption of the airwaves as a kind of personal podium than Jean Shepherd. It was not that he had a polemical axe to grind, but, instead, Shepherd thought of the medium as a means for transforming the minds of his listeners toward a more imaginative, even anarchic way of thinking. Some think that Shepherd single-handedly invented talk radio, even though his antics had their predecessors, like Los Angeles's Jim Hawthorne, who from the 1940s to the 1960s played records backward and invited listeners to call in, only to hold his receiver up to the microphone and allow them to address the audience at large. Shepherd started his pioneering broadcasts on New York's WOR in 1955. Much of the time, he engaged in a kind of storytelling about his youth that one hears today in the monologues of Garrison Keillor about Lake Wobegon. (The popular film *A Christmas Story* [1983] adapts Shepherd's work and employs him as its narrator.) He also would sometimes solicit his listeners to engage in group actions that bear a surprising resemblance to the contemporary phenomenon of flash mobs; he would announce a time and place for them to meet and engage in some spirited action, a practice he called "the Milling." Other times, he urged them to throw open their windows and shout slogans to the open air, something like the broadcaster Howard Beale in the film *Network* (1976). Station owners and some listeners found Shepherd disturbing as he not only broke conventions but also refused to bend to preconceived formats. His ultimate aim, he stated, was to combat "creeping meatballism," a poetic phrase for objectionable forms of conformity.

Exploding the Playlist

If Shepherd shocked some by treating his broadcasts as a kind of public conversation, then the advocates of free-form radio in the 1960s triggered equally aggressive responses by expanding, if not exploding, the barriers that existed as to what kind of material, either music or speech, might be broadcast. Most disc jockeys were cobbled by playlists dictated by management and exercised little to no influence over their choices. Even if they did, their shows were routinely defined by particular genres of expression. It was considered unfashionable to mix disparate styles; rock was kept apart from country, or rhythm and blues from concert music. The airwaves were, in effect, ghettoized, with little intermingling of material. Correspondingly, audiences tended to associate themselves with distinct bodies of sound and self-censored what they did not want to hear.

This straightjacket upon the repertoire presented on radio was removed in large part by the practices advocated by the San Francisco–based disc jockey Tom Donahue. A veteran of a number of markets, Donahue quit KYA in 1965 when controls over his material reached the breaking point. He turned instead to the newly emerging technology of FM and the opportunity presented by the troubled station KMPX to initiate a new approach. Starting in 1967, Donahue exhorted his fellow disc jockeys to play the kind of music they would for their friends and disregard any form of niche thinking. The result was a kind of sonic smorgasbord that paralleled the mashing together of forms of expression that could be heard in the city's premier music venues at the time: the Fillmore West and the Avalon Ballroom. Donahue encouraged his news staff to adopt a similarly unorthodox stance, and it resulted in what the news director, Scoop Nisker, characterized as "the only news you can dance to." Other stations, particularly on the FM bandwidth, followed Donahue's lead. Much as audiences appreciated the transformation, the radicalization of radio staff dismayed the owners of KMPX. They objected to the spillover of anarchy from the airwaves to the office spaces. This led to a strike, and, eventually, Donahue's migration to KSAN. Free-form radio itself eventually fell prey to the segmentation that affected U.S. society as a whole, when the antiwar movement and the counterculture of the 1960s collided with the self-involvement of the following decade. Many, if not most, radio stations returned to a predetermined and circumscribed playlist, yet for many the shock of hearing such a wide array of sounds remains one of the high points of the radio medium.

Seven Dirty Words

Donahue's expansion of the forms of expression included on radio drew upon certain programming practices of the noncommercial network known as the Pacifica Foundation. A group of stations in New York, Los Angeles, Washington, DC, Berkeley, and Houston, the foundation was founded by Lewis Hill in 1949. The inaugural signal, KPFA in Berkeley, initiated the organization's commitment to spurning advertising as well as government or corporate support, and to permitting free speech over its airwaves. Over the years, the organization has assimilated any number of points of view and styles of presentation, some of which resemble the first-person mode of Jean Shepherd (Bob Fass's "Radio Unnameable," heard on New York's WBAI) while others promote specific segments of the political or social spectrum, though customarily from a left-of-center perspective. Many listeners, should they chance upon a Pacifica station by accident, would be shocked and find the range of voices a virtual cacophony, the adoption of off-center ideologies strident in the extreme. Faithful consumers, however, regard Pacifica as the lone exception to the medium's virtual expulsion of radical perspectives and acceptance if not promotion of the almighty dollar.

The most shocking element of Pacifica's history and a groundbreaking influence upon what kind of speech could be aired occurred when WBAI broadcast an infamous track, "Seven Words You Can Never Say on Television," from comedian George Carlin's 1972 *Class Clown*. (A routine featured on Carlin's subsequent album, *Occupation: Foole* [1973], covered much of the same material.) This list of commonly used expletives was perhaps not officially prohibited from radio, yet a complaint to the FCC was made by a father who heard the track with his son. The FCC did not reprimand WBAI but put the station on notice that, "in the event subsequent complaints were received, the Commission will then decide whether it should utilize any of the available sanctions it has been granted by Congress." Pacifica appealed the notice, which was overturned by the Court of Appeals. The FCC brought the matter to the Supreme Court, which came down in favor of the FCC in 1978. This decision codified indecency regulation in U.S. broadcasting. Even though subsequent rulings amended its dictates, such as the

SHOCK-JOCK POLITICS

Depending upon one's perspective, whether any individual amounts to a shock jock depends upon where one stands in the political spectrum. For those on the right, Rush Limbaugh speaks truth to power; for those on the left, Rachel Maddow (now a television host as well) holds those who wield power inappropriately to the fire of necessary criticism. Nonetheless, sometimes individuals are hired and promoted to the public as fair and polite when even a cursory investigation of their public activities reveals that they are partisan in the extreme.

Take the hiring by CNN Headline News in January 2006 of Glenn Beck to host a one-hour prime-time talk show. The president of the network, Ken Jautz, describes Beck as follows: "Glenn's style is self-deprecating, cordial; he says he'd like to be able to disagree with guests and part as friends. It's conversational, not confrontational." However, when one consults Beck's comments on the air prior to his hiring, they do not come across as either civil or conversational. They seem little more than one-sided invective. For example, he apparently so loathes the antiwar politician Dennis Kucinich that he stated in 2003, "Every night I get down on my knees and pray that Dennis Kucinich will burst into flames." The next year, he crossed the line even more emphatically when he characterized Michael Berg, the father whose son was beheaded in Iraq, as "despicable" and a "scumbag" because he deigned to criticize President George W. Bush.

Perhaps the most indefensible, if not alarmingly over-the-top, comment from Beck came in his attack on the filmmaker Michael Moore. In 2005, he mused on the air about killing him: "I'm thinking about killing Michael Moore, and I'm wondering if I could kill him myself, or if I would need to hire someone to do it. No, I think I could. I think he could be looking me in the eye, you know, and I could just be choking the life out—is this wrong?"

It remains a quandary what is more disturbing: that CNN would hire and defend a man who makes these kinds of statements or whether he was being anything other than disingenuous when he inquired of his audience if his sentiments were over the top?

provision that some questionable speech is permissible if children are not part of the audience, the decision holds to this day. There remains a window of opportunity for shocking language between the hours of 10:00 P.M. and 6:00 A.M., but, otherwise, none of the seven dirty words should pass the lips of anyone heard over the air during the course of the rest of the day.

Can They Say That?

The jumping-off point for the present-day profusion of shock jocks is hard to isolate. Nonetheless, it remains clear that, while the announcer on WBAI took the words out of George Carlin's mouth, these current performers do not achieve any of their audacity secondhand. It is also important to stress how virtually all of them emerged from more mainstream broadcasting as disc jockeys as well as how much they acknowledge their debt to and the influence of on-air personalities from the past, like Jean Shepherd. Some may as well have watched, or even been fans of, two short-lived television figures who virtually broke through the third wall of the screen, so vehement were their opinions: Joe Pyne and Alan Burke. Pyne broadcast a syndicated show from Los Angeles from 1965 until his untimely death from cancer in 1970; Burke appeared in New York City from 1966 to 1968 and turned to Miami-based radio during the 1970s and 1980s. It may seem more than a bit of a leap from the "Shut up, creep!" of Pyne and Burke to the outright obscenity of the current shock jocks, but a lineage between the two certifiably exists.

Other legal and institutional factors contributed to the emergence of the shock jocks. During the course of the Reagan administration, the FCC began to lean less heavily on the regulatory throttle, in particular so far as station ownership was concerned. More and more entities were brought up by broadcasting conglomerates, such as Clear Channel, and owners sought formats that could appeal across broad geographical and ideological segments of the population. Sexual innuendo, frat-boy shenanigans, and spirited diatribes against one's opponents fit the bill. Also, the regulations regarding the need for all sides of an issue to be publicly aired became trimmed, so that the aggressive defense of polemical positions did not require any counterpointed alternative. The adoption of the airwaves as a personal soapbox therefore acquired the sanction of both the law and the corporate bottom line.

Don Imus unleashed his loose cannon on WNBC in New York City in 1971; Howard Stern joined him there in 1982; Rush Limbaugh began his career in 1984 in Sacramento, California; Michael Savage unleashed his vitriol over San Francisco's KGO in 1994. While all four of them commonly stretch the boundaries of taste and legally protected speech, each operates under his own agenda. Stern, the "King of All Media," aims to goose the adolescent mentality of listeners any way he can; Imus oscillates between the outrageous and the ideological, maintaining a need both to crack a crude joke and tweak the sensibilities of those he considers unwise or effete; Limbaugh engages his loyal listeners as a virtual cheerleader for their common conservative social and political philosophy; and Savage savages that which he dislikes with an acid tongue and the utter conviction of a true believer. All four men have also successfully engaged in media other than radio, publishing books and appearing in films or on recordings. Each maintains a loyal and considerable following as well as receives some of the highest salaries in broadcasting.

None of them continue, however, without opposition or outcry. The phenomenon of the shock jock certainly has been a mainstay of columnists and op-ed writers for some time, and many individuals need only the slightest provocation to bang the drum about these men's latest foolhardiness or faux pas. Most notably, the comedian Al Franken published a best-seller, *Rush Limbaugh Is a Big Fat Idiot,* in 1996 and subsequently achieved his own on-air slot with Air America as a proponent of the liberal opposition. At the same time, sanctions of a more serious nature have been threatened against shock jocks. Stern in particular tussled repeatedly with the FCC, and some feel that part of the reason he signed up with the satellite system Sirius radio in 2006 was to circumvent the restrictions applied to terrestrial broadcasting. For the most part, broadcasters continue in their established modes of calculated offense, engaging their fans as broadcasting's bad boys and shocking their detractors as near-criminal abusers of the public airwaves.

Crash and Burn

The phenomenon of shock jocks in general, and Don Imus in particular, occupied a brief but heated news cycle in April 2007. For years, Imus committed and subsequently apologized for a number of definitely offensive and debatably funny comments that amounted to little more than sophomoric exercises in sexism and racism. From referring to the African American journalist Gwen Ifill as a "cleaning lady" to characterizing Arabs as "ragheads" to denigrating the African American sports columnist Bill Rhoden as a "*New York Times* quota hire," Imus has engaged for years in a free-for-all of invective. While one might argue that these comments amount to protected speech in the service of comedy, albeit a fairly sophomoric category of comedy, they nonetheless come across as hurtful, possibly hateful, and certainly mean-spirited.

One of the paradoxes of Imus as a personality, however, remains that this schoolyard potty mouth coexists in a kind of Jekyll-Hyde or symbiotic relationship, depending upon one's perspective, with a thoughtful, well-prepared, and consistently intelligent interviewer. Many individuals who frequent Imus's microphones praise him as one of the most astute and committed commentators on the public airwaves; *New York Times* columnist Frank Rich repeated these remarks at the climax of Imus's latest, and most incendiary, collision with the limits of free speech. For years, the program oscillated back and forth between the cerebral and the coarse, and many listeners, and some participants, chose to ignore the elements of that dialogue that offended or bored them.

This process came to a head on April 4, 2007, when Imus and his cohort, Bernard McGuirk, dismissed the Rutgers University women's basketball team as "nappy-headed hos." This was Imus's retort to McGuirk's characterization of the predominantly African American squad as "some hard-core hos." Almost immediately, a torrent of anger ensued, and two days later Imus apologized for the dialogue: "It was completely inappropriate and we can understand why people were offended. Our characterization was thoughtless and stupid, and we are sorry." Imus, however, ratcheted up the anger when he appeared on the Reverend Al Sharpton's radio program on April 9 and referred in passing to some of his critics as "you people." Plans were set in place for him to meet with the team and its coach. However, due to the public anger, loss of sponsors, and complaints from other African American employees at NBC, the network fired Imus and ended *Imus in the Morning* immediately. The meeting with the Rutgers squad proceeded, and their coach reported that the team members did not themselves call for Imus's firing.

Aside from the heat and fury of the moment, the question remains whether Imus's firing will trigger more focused attention upon shock jocks and whether the possibility of censorship will extend to those of a more right-wing persuasion who engage in invective and rancor on as regular a basis as did Imus.

See also **Obscenity and Indecency; Violence and Media; Conglomeration and Media Monopolies (vol. 1)**

Further Reading

Awkward, Michael, *Burying Don Imus: Anatomy of a Scapegoat.* Minneapolis: University of Minnesota Press, 2009.

Colford, Paul, *Howard Stern: King of All Media.* New York: St. Martin's Press, 1996.

Douglas, Susan, *Listening In: Radio and the American Imagination.* Minneapolis: University of Minnesota Press, 2004.

Fisher, Marc, *Something in the Air: Radio, Rock, and the Revolution that Shaped a Generation.* New York: Random House, 2007.

Imus, Don, *God's Other Son.* New York: Simon & Schuster, 1999 [1981].

Jamieson, Kathleen Hall, and Joseph N. Cappella, *Echo Chamber: Rush Limbaugh and the Conservative Media Establishment.* New York: Oxford University Press, 2008.

Laser, Matthew, *Uneasy Listening: Pacifica Radio's Civil War.* London: Germinal Productions and Black Apollo Books, 2006;

Laser, Matthew, *Pacifica Radio: The Rise of an Alternative Network,* rev. ed. Philadelphia: Temple University Press, 2000.

Limbaugh, Rush, *The Way Things Ought To Be.* New York: Pocket Books, 1992.

Milbank, Dana, *Tears of a Clown: Glenn Beck and the Tea Bagging of America.* New York: Doubleday, 2010.

O'Connor, Rory, *Shock Jocks: Hate Speech and Talk Radio: America's Ten Worst Hate Talkers and the Progressive Alternatives.* San Francisco: AlterNet Books, 2008.

Savage, Michael, *The Political Zoo.* Nashville: Nelson Current, 2006.

Shepard, Jean, *In God We Trust: All Others Pay Cash.* New York: Doubleday, 1966.

Shepard, Jean, *Wanda Hickey's Night of Golden Memories and Other Disasters.* New York: Doubleday, 1976.

Stern, Howard, *Private Parts.* New York: Simon & Schuster, 1993.

Walker, Jesse, *Rebels on the Air: An Alternative History of Radio in America.* New York: New York University Press, 2001.

STANDARDIZED TESTING

Sandra Mathison

Standardized tests are administered under standard conditions, scored in a standard way, and result in quantifiable results; they can include multiple choice or performance-based questions (like essays); and, while usually administered to groups, they may also be individually administered. Standardized tests are used in schools for a variety of reasons (to determine the achievement or aptitude of individual students; to evaluate programs and curricula for improvement; to hold schools accountable), and they may be either low stakes (that is, having no or low-level rewards and consequences) or high stakes (that is, having serious consequences attached to the scores).

Standardized testing in schools has always been controversial. The controversy centers on the uses and misuses of the tests; cultural, class, and gender biases in the tests; whether they are benign or have a negative effect on those who take them; and whether they are a good indicator of the quality of learning or schools. Standardized tests have both the promise to reward merit and the reality of advantaging the already advantaged; the means

TIMELINE OF STANDARDIZED TESTING EVENTS

- 1845: Administration of the Boston Survey, the first known written examination of student achievement.
- 1895: Joseph Rice developed common written tests to assess spelling achievement in Boston schools.
- 1900–1920: Major test publishers are created: The College Board, Houghton-Mifflin, Psychological Corporation, California Testing Bureau (now CTBS), and World Book open for business.
- 1901: The first common college entrance examinations are administered.
- 1905: Alfred Binet and Theodore Simon develop the Binet-Simon Scale, an individually administered test of intelligence.
- 1914: Frederick Kelly invents the multiple choice question.
- 1916: Louis Terman develops a U.S. version of the Binet-Simon Scale, which becomes a widely used individual intelligence test, and he develops the common concept of the intelligence quotient (or IQ).
- 1917: Army Alpha and Beta tests are developed by Robert Yerkes, then president of the American Psychological Association, to efficiently separate potential officers from soldiers as the United States entered World War I.
- 1926: The Scholastic Aptitude Test (SAT), adapted directly from the Army Alpha Test, is first administered.
- 1955: The high-speed optical scanner is invented.
- 1970: The National Assessment of Educational Progress is created.
- 1980s: Computer-based testing is developed.
- 2001: No Child Left Behind is signed into law, reauthorizing the Elementary and Secondary Education Act, and using student achievement test scores to hold schools accountable.
- 2009: Race to the Top, a federal program designed, in part, to emend No Child Left Behind, is launched; by mid-2010, 27 states have implemented new math and English standards based on the program's recommendations.

to overcome racism and a source or racism; and the means of establishing accountability in schools and a constraint on what a good education is.

Beginning in kindergarten, standardized test results are used to sort, track, and monitor the abilities, achievements, and potentials of students. A concern is that standardized test results may be weighed more heavily than they ought to be, that decisions once made cannot or will not be reversed, and that other compelling information may be ignored. The uses of standardized testing are far-ranging. While there is considerable variation from one school district to the next, children will be administered at least one, but typically many more, standardized tests each year. Except for Iowa and Nebraska, every other state administers English and mathematics state-mandated tests from grades 3 to 8, and, of those 48 states, 31 administer state-mandated tests in at least two of grades 9 through 12.

Mental Measurement Goes to School

The use of standardized student achievement testing in U.S. schools dates back to 1845 with the administration of the Boston Survey. Horace Mann, then secretary of the Massachusetts State Board of Education, oversaw the development of a written examination covering topics such as arithmetic, geography, history, grammar, and science. The test battery, 154 questions in all, was given to 530 students sampled from the more than 7,000 children attending Boston schools. Mann was moved to create these tests because of what he perceived to be a lack of consistency and quality in the Boston schools.

This was followed not long after by Joseph Rice's work, also in Boston. In the decade beginning in 1895, Rice organized assessment programs in spelling and mathematics in a number of large school systems. Much as Horace Mann wanted to see more consistency in what was taught in schools, Rice was motivated by a perceived need to standardize curriculum.

About this same time, in 1904, E. L. Thorndike, known as the father of educational testing, published the first book on educational measurement, *An Introduction to the Theory of Mental and Social Measurement.* He and his students developed many of the first achievement tests emphasizing controlled and uniform test administration and scoring.

But the real impetus for the growth of testing in schools grew out of the then developing emphasis on intelligence tests, particularly those that could be administered to groups rather than individuals, work that built on the basics of Thorndike's achievement tests. In 1917, the Army Alpha (for literate test takers) and the Army Beta (for illiterates) intelligence tests were developed. Robert Yerkes, Louis Terman, and others took up the challenge during World War I of helping the military to distinguish between those recruits who were officer material and those who were better suited to the trenches. Within a year and a half, Terman and his student Arthur S. Otis had tested more than 1.5 million recruits.

Terman also created the Stanford Achievement Test, which he used in his longitudinal study of gifted children and from whence came the term *intelligence quotient,* or IQ. So taken with Terman's work, the Rockefeller Foundation supported his recommendation that every child be administered a "mental test" and in 1919 gave Terman a grant to develop a national intelligence test. Within the year, tests were made available to public elementary schools.

Test publishers quickly recognized the potential of testing in schools and began developing and selling intelligence tests. Houghton-Mifflin published the Stanford-Binet Intelligence test in 1916. The commercial publication of tests is critical since many of the efficiencies of the testing industry, such as machine scanning, resulted from efforts to gain market share. In turn, the ability to process large quantities of data permitted ever more sophisticated statistical analyses of test scores, certainly with the intention of making the data more useful to schools, teachers, and counselors.

Until the onset of the current high-stakes testing movement, achievement and ability tests served a number of purposes, but in his 1966 book *The Search for Ability: Standardized Testing in Social Perspective,* David Goslin summarized what were at the time the typical uses of standardized tests in schools:

- to promote better adjustment, motivation, and progress of the individual student through a better understanding of his abilities and weaknesses, both on his own part and on the part of his teachers and parents
- to aid in decisions about the readiness of the pupil for exposure to new subject matter
- to measure the progress of pupils
- to aid in the grade placement of individuals and the special grouping of children for instructional purposes within classes or grades
- to aid in the identification of children with special problem or abilities
- to provide objective measures of the relative effectiveness of alternative teaching techniques, curriculum content, and the like
- to aid in the identification of special needs from the standpoint of the efficiency of the school relative to other schools

While Goslin's list represents the emphasis on local uses of testing, at this same time, during the administration of John F. Kennedy, there was a growing interest in national assessment. During this period, Ralph Tyler was called upon to oversee the development of a national testing system, which would become the National Assessment of Educational Progress (NAEP), first administered in 1969 by the Education Commission of the States. The creation of NAEP allowed for state-by-state comparisons and a common metric for all U.S. students, and all states are now required to participate in NAEP testing.

The Technical and Sociopolitical Nature of Measurement

The development of standardized means for measuring intelligence, ability, and achievement coincided with a remarkable explosion of scientific knowledge and technological advance across a wide range of domains. The industrial growth during most of the 20th century and the information technology growth of the late 20th century are the context for the use and development of assessments that differentiate individuals for the allocation of scarce resources such as jobs, postsecondary education, and scholarships.

Without the power of more and more advanced and complex technology, both in terms of data management and statistical analysis, it is doubtful that student assessment would be the driving force of the accountability demanded in the current standards-based reform movement. The development of testing technology is a series of changes, each responding to a contemporary constraint on testing, and each of which enhanced the efficiency of testing—that is, the ability to test more people at less cost and in less time. Charles Pearson's invention of factor analysis in 1904, Lindquist's invention of the optical scanner in 1955, the development of item response theory in the early 1950s by Fred Lord and Darrell Bock, as well as the variant developed by Georg Rasch in 1960, and the development of matrix sampling by Darrell Bock and Robert Mislevy in the 1960s and 1970s are examples of these technological enhancements. A number of areas in student assessment remain astonishingly unsophisticated, such as, for example, strategies for standard setting. In many ways, the educational measurement community has operated on the assumption that appropriate uses of assessment in schools is a matter of making good tests and being able to manipulate the scores in sophisticated ways. However, testing is also a sociopolitical activity, and even technically sound measures and procedures are transformed when they are thrown into the educational policy and practice arena.

There is and has been great optimism about what testing and measurement in schools can accomplish. Robert Linn, contemporary father of educational measurement, suggests in his 2000 *Educational Researcher* article that we are overly optimistic about the promises of what can be delivered:

> I am led to conclude that in most cases the instruments and technology have not been up to the demands that have been placed on them by high-stakes accountability. Assessment systems that are useful monitors lose much of their dependability and credibility for that purpose when high stakes are attached to them. The unintended negative effects of high-stakes accountability uses often outweigh the intended positive effects. (19)

Eugenics and Testing

Early U.S. work on mental measurement was deeply informed by a presumed genetic basis for intelligence and differences. In 1905, the French psychologist Alfred Binet developed a scale for measuring intelligence that was translated into English by the American psychologist Henry H. Goddard, who was keenly interested in the inheritability of intelligence. Although Binet did not hold the view that intelligence was inherited and thought tests were a means for identifying ways to help children having difficulty, Goddard and other U.S. hereditarians disregarded his principles. Goddard believed that "feeble-mindedness" was the result of a single recessive gene. He would become a pioneer in the American eugenicist movement.

"Morons" were Goddard's primary interest, and he defined morons as "high grade defectives" who possess low intelligence but appear normal to casual observers. In addition to their learning difficulties, Goddard characterized morons as lacking self-control, susceptible to sexual immorality, and vulnerable to other individuals who might exploit them for use in criminal activity.

Lewis Terman was also a eugenicist and popularized Binet's work (that is, Goddard's translation of it) with the creation of the Stanford-Binet Test. A critical development, and one that still sets the parameters for standardized testing, was Terman's standardizing the scale of test scores—100 was the average score and the standard deviation was set at 15. Terman (along with others, including E. L. Thorndike and R. M. Yerkes) promoted group testing for the purpose of classifying children in grades three through eight, tests that were published by the World Book Company (the current-day Harcourt Brace). The intent of these tests was clear: to identify the feeble-minded and curtail their opportunity to reproduce, thus saving America from "crime, pauperism, and industrial inefficiency." Although lively discussion (most especially with Walter Lippman) about the value of and justifiability of Terman's claims was waged in the popular press, this eugenicist perspective persisted.

In addition, Terman's classifying of student ability coincided with ideas emerging among progressive educators in the 1910s. Progressives believed curriculum and instructional methods should be scientifically determined, and Terman's tests and interpretations fit the bill. Few seriously questioned his assumptions about the hereditary nature of intelligence or that IQ was indeed a valid measurement of intelligence. By "scientifically" proving that recent immigrants and blacks scored lower than whites due to an inferior mental endowment, he catered strongly to the nativism and prejudice of many Americans.

Although most contemporary experts in mental measurement eschew these eugenicist beginnings, the debate lives on, manifest more recently in the work of Herrnstein and Murray in the much-debated book *The Bell Curve*. The authors of this treatise have used intelligence testing to claim African Americans are genetically intellectually inferior. But their arguments are connected to class as well, and herein may lie the most obvious connections to the advocacy of testing by powerful politicians and corporate CEOs. Questions and answers they pose are:

How much good would it do to encourage education for the people earning low wages? If somehow government can cajole or entice youths to stay in school for a few extra years, will their economic disadvantage in the new labor market go away? We doubt it. Their disadvantage might be diminished, but only modestly. There is reason to think that the job market has been rewarding not just education but intelligence. (96)

Race and class, which are inextricably linked in contemporary society, remain important considerations in measurement and assessment. There is ample evidence that suggests achievement tests are better predictors of parental income than anything else.

Biases in Standardized Tests

Standardized tests used in schools have always been criticized for their potential biases, especially since the test developers may be different from many students taking the tests, and these authors may take for granted their cultural, class, racial upbringing, and education. Although test developers strive to develop fair tests, it is difficult to make a single test that accurately and fairly captures the achievement of a student, rather than their life experiences. For example, a test item that asks about the motion of two trains moving on parallel tracks may be obvious to adults but quite confusing to a child who has never had occasion to ride on a train. Or the obvious class bias in the oft-cited analogy question on the SAT—runner is to marathon as oarsman is to regatta. The bias in standardized test questions may be based on cultural, class, ethnic, gender, or linguistic differences.

The increased use of standardized tests called high-stakes tests—those where the results are used to make important decisions resulting in rewards or punishments—has, however, reinforced the disadvantages standardized tests present for students of color and those living in poverty. High-stakes testing is disproportionately found in states with higher percentages of people of color and living in poverty. A recent analysis of the National Educational Longitudinal Survey shows that 35 percent of African American and 27 percent of Hispanic eighth-graders will take a high-stakes test, compared to 16 percent of whites. Looked along class lines, 25 percent of low socioeconomic–status (SES) eighth-graders will take a high stakes test compared to 14 percent of high-SES eighth graders. Students of color are more likely to take high-stakes tests, and they also score lower than white students. With the advent of high-stakes testing, dropout rates for students of color have increased, either because they do not do well on the tests required for graduation or because they are pushed out by school districts that are judged by their overall test scores.

Effects of Standardized Tests on Test Takers

Although standardized tests are meant to facilitate educational decision making at many levels, it is important to consider the experience of the test taker. Generally, policymakers, test developers, and educational bureaucrats assume the taking of standardized tests will be benign, with relatively modest positive or negative effects on children. Research, however, suggests standardized testing contributes to unhealthy levels of student stress, resulting sometimes in serious mental health problems and even suicide.

Although less dramatic, there is also concern that emphasizing performance on standardized tests (and even grades) diminishes students' motivation to learn. Rather than focusing on the value of learning, educational contexts that emphasize outcomes focus students on getting the grade or test score—emphasizing what is required to do well on the test rather than focusing on genuine learning. Lifelong learning and critical thinking are not key educational outcomes when the focus is on tests scores.

Standardized Tests and Accountability

Despite cautions about the value of standardized testing, test scores are now the common language used by education bureaucrats, politicians, and the media to summarize the quality, or lack of quality, of schools. This is a recent use of standardized tests though, and the last decade has seen a turn to high-stakes testing. While test scores have been used within the education bureaucracy for many decades, it was not until the late 1970s, when the College Board reported declines in SAT scores, that these scores become the means for describing the quality of schools. And the debate about the meaning and value of those scores for such purposes began immediately.

Culturally, Americans are drawn to statistical and numerical indicators, which are perceived to be factual and objective. Perhaps this is a result of public policy debate in a complex democracy where there is a tendency to gravitate to simple means for resolving differences in deeply held value positions. Perhaps it is a romance with technology and science. In a few decades, standardized test scores have infiltrated the popular culture as the obvious, inevitable indicator of the quality of education and schooling. In such a short time, we have forgotten there are many other sorts of evidence that have been and can be used to describe the quality of schools and schooling.

TABLE 1. An Illustration of Standardized Testing across the Life of a Student

Grade	Test
*for remedial students only; **Johns Hopkins Talent Search test for gifted program.	
Kindergarten	Boehm Test of Basic Concepts
1st	Gates-MacGinitie Reading Test*
2nd	Gates-MacGinitie Reading Test*
	Stanford Diagnostic Math Test*
	Terra Nova (reading and math)

(continued)

TABLE 1. *(continued)*

Grade	Test
3rd	Gates-MacGinitie Reading Testing* Stanford Diagnostic Math Test* Terra Nova (reading & math) School and College Ability Test (SCAT)** Cognitive Abilities Test (CogAT)
4th	Gates-MacGinitie Reading Test* Stanford Diagnostic Math Test* School and College Ability Test (SCAT)** State English Language Arts Test State Math Test State Science Test
5th	Gates-MacGinitie Reading Test* Stanford Diagnostic Math Test* Terra Nova (reading and math) School and College Ability Test (SCAT)** State Social Studies Test
6th	Terra Nova (reading and math) School and College Ability Test (SCAT)**
7th	Terra Nova (reading and math) Cognitive Abilities Test (CogAT)
8th	State English Language Arts Test State Math Test State Science Test State Social Studies Test State Foreign Language Test State Technology Test
9th–12th	State Graduation Exams: English Language Arts Mathematics Global History and Geography U.S. History and Government Science Language other than English PSAT SAT

The reporting of test scores in the media, primarily in newspapers, is now expected and often uncritically examined. Typically, the test scores on state-mandated standardized tests are published annually in local newspapers. Little, if any, information is provided about the meaning of the scores. Topics like measurement error (which, for example, would tell one that on the SAT, a difference of at least 125 points between two scores is necessary to be confident there is any real difference between the two test takers) and test validity (whether the standardized test being used is one that was developed for that particular use) are usually not included, either because they are not understood by education reporters or are perceived as too complex for the average reader. Similarly, schools and districts are often ranked—an absolute folly given the error in the scores and the conceptual problem of truly being able to justifiably rank order hundreds of things.

While test developers have always cautioned that tests should be used for the purposes for which they were developed, this desire for a simple common metric to judge a student's learning, the quality of a school, a teacher's performance, or a state or country's educational attainment has led to more misuses of tests. More and more standardized tests are required, and too often tests are being used in ways they were not intended to be used. The most common example of this is when general achievement tests developed specifically to create a spread of scores from very low to very high with most scores in the middle (like the Iowa Test of Basic Skills) are used to determine what students have actually learned. James Popham, notable measurement expert, likens this misuse to taking "the temperature with a tablespoon."

Conclusion

Standardized tests have been a part of education and schools for many decades and will continue to be a part of the educational landscape. Controversy will surely continue to surround their uses and the psychological, social, and political aspects of their use.

See also **Government Role in Schooling; No Child Left Behind (NCLB)**

Further Reading

Baker, Joan M., *Achievement Testing in U.S. Elementary and Secondary Schools.* New York: Peter Lang, 2005.

Hursh, David W., *High-Stakes Testing and the Decline of Teaching and Learning.* Lanham, MD: Rowman & Littlefield, 2008.

Mathison, Sandra, and E. Wayne Ross, *Defending Public Schools: The Meaning and Limits of Standards-Based Reform and High-Stakes Testing.* Westport, CT: Praeger, 2004.

Nichols, Sharon Lynn, and David C. Berliner, *Collateral Damage: How High-Stakes Testing Corrupts American Schools.* Cambridge MA: Harvard Education Press, 2007.

Phelps, Richard P., ed., *Defending Standardized Testing.* Mahwah, NJ: Lawrence Erlbaum, 2005.

STEROID USE BY ATHLETES

Rob Beamish

The World Anti-Doping Agency's (WADA) "2008 Prohibited List" states clearly: "Anabolic agents are prohibited." The list prohibits 47 *exogenous* anabolic androgenic steroids (AAS), 21 *endogenous* AAS, and five *other anabolic agents.* Steroid use in any sport governed by WADA's code is subject to a two-year suspension the first time and lifetime suspension the second time. According to WADA, the code preserves "what is intrinsically valuable about sport...The intrinsic value is often referred to as 'the spirit of sport': it is the essence of Olympism: it is how we play true....Doping is fundamentally contrary to the spirit of sport."

Following the Canadian government's inquiry into the use of drugs in sports, Chief Justice Charles Dubin articulated similar reasons for banning AAS. The use of banned drugs is cheating, Dubin maintained. Drugs threaten "the essential integrity of sport" and destroy "its very objectives." Drugs "erode the ethical and moral values of the athletes who use them, endangering their mental and physical welfare while demoralizing the entire sport community."

Although the primary objection to AAS in sports is ethical, concerns over their physiological impact have also influenced the ban. First synthesized in 1935, it was then noted that, despite the initial, positive response by some scientists, the conservative medical establishment was wary of a synthetic hormone that might "turn sexual weaklings into wolves and octogenarians into sexual athletes." The concern today is the negative side effects from AAS, even though almost all are reversible in postpuberty males (and knowingly accepted by females). Nevertheless, sports leaders have used the potential negative side effects as a deterrent to AAS use and grounds for their ban.

Two further sentiments underlie the AAS ban in sports, although they are rarely noted. The first concerns the symbolic power and significance of sports and the association of steroids with certain reprehensible events in sports or social history. The second is a fear of the unrestricted, scientifically assisted pursuit of the outer limits of athletic performance. Increased musculature and steroids' performance-enhancing attributes cause concern about where the use of unrestricted science, technology, and pharmacology might ultimately lead.

Background

The moral arguments against AAS and sports' symbolic importance stem from Baron Pierre de Coubertin's efforts to create the modern Olympic Games as a unique moral and educational program. Feeling that late 19th-century Europe was falling into spiritual decline, Coubertin wanted to reestablish its traditional values through a far-reaching, innovative, educational project. His plan grew out of the philosophy of the "muscular Christian" and the spirituality of the ancient games. Character, Coubertin maintained, "is not formed by the mind, it is formed above all by the body." Sports, as it was practiced in the British public schools, could revitalize the moral and spiritual fiber of Europe's youth.

Coubertin's image was inspiring. "The athlete enjoys his effort," Coubertin wrote (2000 552). "He likes the constraint that he imposes on his muscles and nerves, through which he comes close to victory even if he does not manage to achieve it. This enjoyment remains internal…, Imagine if it were to expand outward, becoming intertwined with the joy of nature and the flights of art. Picture it radiant with sunlight, exalted by music, framed in the architecture of porticoes." This was "the glittering dream of ancient Olympism" that "dominated ancient Greece for centuries."

Coubertin's project would create "an aristocracy, an elite"—"a knighthood" of "brothers-in-arms." Chivalry would characterize the Games—"the idea of competition, of effort opposing effort for the love of effort itself, of courteous yet violent struggle, is superimposed on the notion of mutual assistance" (Coubertin 2000, 581). Chivalrous brothers-in-arms, bonding in the cauldron of competition, would forge Europe's new moral elite.

Winning was irrelevant to Coubertin; character development in the struggle to win a fair, man-to-man contest (the gender is intentional) against a respected opponent, within a chivalric code of conduct was everything. Performance enhancement of any type—even physical training—was completely foreign to the ethos of Olympism. The true "essence of sport" was far loftier than crass, competitive sports; it centered on the character development upper-class youths gained on the playing fields of Rugby, Eton, and elsewhere in civilized Europe.

One cannot emphasize enough how this idealized image serves as the key reference point for AAS policies at the present time.

Symbolism was central to the modern Olympic Games from their inception. To achieve the appropriate solemnity, Coubertin launched his project "under the venerable roof of the Sorbonne [where] the words 'Olympic Games' would resound more impressively and persuasively" (cited in Beamish and Ritchie 2006, 32). It was, however, the 1936 Games in Nazi Germany and the long shadow of World War II that demonstrated the Games' symbolic power.

Nazi Propaganda Minister Joseph Goebbels was a master at manipulating information and emotions for political gain. The Nazis frequently used imposing, emotive, Wagnerian-styled *gesamtkunstwerke*—total works of art—in enormous venues such as sports stadiums, to blend music, choreography, costume, and neoclassical architecture into captivating, exhilarating, and emotionally draining experiences. Knowing the power that well-crafted propaganda had on the hearts and minds of the masses, the 1936 Games let Goebbels use the Promethean symbolic power of the Olympics to project the commanding presence of Nazi Germany across Europe.

The Games' marquee icon—the chiseled, muscular, racially pure Aryan, crowned with a victor's olive wreath, rising above the goddess of victory atop the Brandenburg Gate—embodied the Nazi's quest for world domination. The image soon included the cold-blooded brutality of German troops as they conquered Europe and marched on to Moscow.

In the post–World War II period, amid the ashes of destruction and defeat, rumors that Hitler's Secret Service had taken steroids while perpetrating the Holocaust and destroying Eastern Europe were added to the image of Nazi barbarism. The 1936 Games linked steroids, ruthless aggression, moral depravity, and totalitarianism into one stark, chilling entity.

Admiring the Nazis' use of the Games to project their power, the Soviet Union joined the Olympic movement for similar ends. At the 1952 Games—the first post–World War II confrontation between the superpowers—Soviet success quickly dispelled any notion of U.S. superiority.

Confirming at the 1954 world weightlifting championships that the Soviets had used testosterone to enhance performance in world competitions, U.S. physician John Ziegler developed methandieone, or Dianabol, to level the playing field. Dianabol quickly spread from weightlifters to the throwers in track and field and on to other strength-based sports. By the early 1960s, steroids were commonplace in world-class sports, and the unfettered use of science to win Olympic gold would increasingly dominate nations' and athletes' approach to sports after 1954.

Key Events

From the outset—and enshrined in the Olympic Charter in 1962—the Modern Games were restricted to amateur athletes. The type of competitor that Coubertin and the International Olympic Committee (IOC) wanted was the turn-of-the-20th-century British amateur. Only the well-educated, cultured, physically active, male aristocrat had the appropriate appreciation of sports to realize Coubertin's goals. Well before 1952, however, the IOC had little control over the athletes who competed, and it failed miserably in achieving Coubertin's educational objectives. Nevertheless, the IOC—especially Avery Brundage (president from 1952 to 1972)—struggled to maintain the Games' integrity. The Olympics, Brundage claimed, "coming to us from antiquity, contributed to and strengthened by the noblest aspirations of great men of each generation, embrace the highest moral laws....No philosophy, no religion," he maintained, "preaches loftier sentiments." But the social pressures outside the movement quickly overwhelmed those lofty claims.

Throughout the 1950s and 1960s, Cold War politics, expanding consumerism, and the growth of television with its vast commercial resources and thirst for targeted audiences increasingly pressured the IOC to open the Games to the world's best athletes. Furthermore, developments in sports science encouraged athletes to devote longer periods of their lives to the pursuit of Olympic gold and financial reward—Olympic athletes became increasingly professional. By 1970, pressure grew to replace the amateur rule with a new eligibility code. The 1971 code remained restrictive, but a 1974 revision opened the Games to the best athletes money could buy and governments and sports scientists could produce.

Danish cyclist Knud Jensen's death at the 1960 Olympics, allegedly from amphetamine use, symbolized the value athletes placed on victory. The IOC established a medical committee in 1961 to recommend how to prevent or control drug use by athletes. The 1964 recommendations included athlete testing, signed athlete statements confirming they were drug-free, and heavy sanctions. Rule 28, added to the charter in 1967, prohibited any "alien or unnatural substances" that created an unfair advantage; although banned in 1967, the IOC did not test for AAS until 1976.

The Nazis and Soviets had used the Games to occupy center stage internationally and symbolically project their importance to the world. The German Democratic Republic (GDR) developed similar aspirations—especially after Munich was awarded the 1972 Games. The decision to hold the Olympics on the soil of the GDR's most bitter rival—the Federal Republic of Germany—was pivotal in the history of AAS use by world-class athletes. The GDR initiated "State-Plan 14.25"—an extensive, high-level, classified, laboratory research program involving substantial state resources—to develop a scientifically based program of steroid use. By the 1976 Olympics, AAS were fully integrated into the GDR's high-performance sports system as a matter of state policy.

Throughout the 1970s and 1980s, the Games increasingly centered on the all-out pursuit of victory. For nations, Olympic gold signified strength, power, and international supremacy; for athletes, it meant wealth and celebrity.

Ben Johnson crushed Carl Lewis and shattered the 100-meter world record in the 1988 Games' premier event, but his positive test for stanozolol created a major crisis. In short order, *Sports Illustrated* ran articles on steroids in sports, and the Canadian government and the U.S. House of Representatives began investigations into AAS use in sports. The entire credibility of the Olympic movement was at stake—was the IOC serious about steroids and the purity of the Games? Steroid use, it was clearly evident, was widespread.

In March 1998, French customs officials found erythropoietin (EPO) in the TVM cycling team's van, and criminal charges followed. Then in July, mere days before the Tour de France began, the Festina team was implicated in the EPO scandal. But it was IOC President Juan Antonio Samaranch's comments that shocked the world. Drugs could damage an athlete's health as well as artificially improve performance, Samaranch observed. If it only improves performance, he continued, it did not matter: "Anything that doesn't adversely affect the health of the athlete, isn't doping." Potentially implicating the IOC in whitewashing AAS use, Samaranch's comments forced the IOC to establish an independent body to oversee drug testing from then on.

Created in 1999, WADA hosted a world conference on drug use that led to its June 2002 draft of the World Anti-Doping Code. A subsequent draft in October led to unanimous adoption of version 3.0 in March 2003 at the second world conference. Despite WADA's efforts, steroid use did not stop; AAS users simply found ways to avoid detection. In July 2003, track coach Trevor Graham gave the American Anti-Doping Agency a syringe containing the designer anabolic steroid tetrahydrogestrinone (THG). Graham alleged that Victor Conte, through the Bay Area Laboratory Co-Operative (BALCO), was giving THG to world-class U.S. athletes at their request. BALCO was just beginning. President George W. Bush's 2004 State of the Union Address focused on education reform, Medicare, the Patriot Act, the war on terrorism, and military engagements in Afghanistan and Iraq. The president turned next to family values and the war on drugs. "One of the worst decisions our children can make is to gamble their lives and futures on drugs," Bush warned (Associated Press, 2004). To make the right choices, children need good role models, but, Bush maintained, "some athletes are not setting much of an example….The use of performance-enhancing drugs like steroids in baseball, football and other sports is dangerous, and it sends the wrong message—that there are short cuts to accomplishment, and that performance is more important than character." Bush challenged professional sports 'to get rid of steroids now.'"

Within days, the *San Francisco Chronicle* published allegations that Greg Anderson, homerun king Barry Bonds's personal trainer, had ties to BALCO and gave Bonds THG. The *Chronicle* alleged that Anderson supplied Jason Giambi, Gary Sheffield, and others with AAS. Steroids and BALCO were now linked within America's national pastime.

In May 2004, U.S. sprinter Kelli White admitted to taking THG supplied through BALCO. In December 2005, the Lausanne-based Court of Arbitration for Sport suspended 100-meter world record holder Tim Montgomery for THG use, stripping him of his 2002 record. In November 2006, a federal grand jury indicted Graham for three counts of making false statements to the Internal Revenue Service Criminal Investigation Division officials around the BALCO investigations. And in October 2007, sprinter Marion Jones was stripped of her medals and records for taking BALCO-supplied THG.

From a trailerlike office operation (BALCO), run by a self-aggrandizing schemer-entrepreneur (Conte) assisted by his "steroid guru" (Patrick Arnold), BALCO now symbolized the sleaziest aspects of athletes' greed and lust for record performances and celebrity.

On March 17, 2005, Denise Garabaldi and Don Hooton told the House of Representatives' Oversight and Government Reform Committee that steroids had killed their sons. Subpoenaed to testify, Mark McGuire evaded questions, Rafael Palmeiro denied he had used AAS, and Jose Conseco said his book *Juiced* told the full story. The event forced Bud Selig to appoint former Senate Majority Leader George Mitchell to conduct an independent investigation into steroid use in baseball. Mitchell's report identified 86 players as users and led to Chuck Knoblauch, Andy Pettitte, Roger Clemens, and personal trainer Brian McNamee testifying before the committee in February 2008. The reality of AAS use by athletes had never been so clear, although its full extent is still shrouded in secrecy. Some athletes, such as Mark McGuire, have begun admitting on their own (albeit belatedly in his case) that they were indeed involved with using AAS.

Conclusion

The future of steroid use by athletes depends upon how four fundamental issues and sets of questions are answered: It is clear that the Olympic Games do not embody Coubertin's principles and goals; they are a commercial extravaganza that nations exploit for international status, while athletes use them for fame and money. One must ask whether the principles that really underlie contemporary, world-class, high-performance sports justify the exclusion of performance-enhancing substances such as AAS. On what grounds should officials try to restrict scientific performance enhancement in commercial, entertainment spectacles where the ultimate attraction is athletic performance at the outer limits of human potential? What principles apply?

What are the long-term health implications of AAS use by athletes (and by people in the general population)? How safe or dangerous are steroids—unmonitored or monitored by physicians? What are the emotional and cognitive effects that lead to, and may result from, AAS use? Do existing laws on AAS possession and use protect or endanger users?

AAS are not confined to enhancing athletic performance. Athletes are just one source of ideal body images that saturate commercial and entertainment media. "Megarexia"—muscular dysmorphia—has become a serious issue among a growing percentage of young men (and some women). Does the sports ban on AAS help limit the spread of muscular dysmorphia among contemporary youth, or are there more significant factors? Does the WADA ban on steroids limit AAS use among young athletes and nonathletes? If not, what would?

Finally, one must consider the widespread use of drugs in people's lives today. What are the fundamental concerns and issues related to the increasing use of over-the-counter, prescription, and illegal drugs? Where do steroids fit into those concerns? To reduce steroid use, what changes have to occur in the broader culture?

See also **Drugs**

Further Reading

Assael, Shaun, *Steroid Nation: Juiced Home Run Totals, Anti-Aging Miracles, and a Hercules in Every High School.* New York: ESPN Books, 2007.

Beamish, R., and I. Ritchie, *Fastest, Highest, Strongest: A Critique of High-Performance Sport.* London: Routledge, 2006.

Coubertin, B. P., *Olympism: Selected Writings*. Lausanne, Switzerland: International Olympic Committee, 2000.

Fourcroy, Jean L., ed., *Pharmacology, Doping, and Sports: A Scientific Guide for Athletes, Coaches, Physicians, Scientists, and Administrators*. New York: Routledge, 2009.

Hoberman, John, *Testosterone Dreams: Rejuvenation, Aphrodisia, Doping*. Berkeley: University of California Press, 2005.

Rosen, Daniel M., *Dope: The History of Performance Enhancement in Sports from the Nineteenth Century to Today*. Westport, CT: Praeger, 2008.

Todd, J., and T. Todd, "Significant Events in the History of Drug Testing and the Olympic Movement: 1960–1999." In *Doping in Elite Sport: The Politics of Drugs in the Olympic Movement*, ed. W. Wilson and E. Derse. Champaign, IL: Human Kinetics Press, 2001.

Yesalis, C., and Bahrke, M., "History of Doping in Sport." *International Sports Studies* 24 (2002): 42–76.

SUICIDE AND SUICIDE PREVENTION

Michael A. Church and Charles I. Brooks

One of the most baffling experiences for many of us to accept is the purposeful taking of one's own life. For those who have never been suicidal, it is difficult to comprehend such an act. In reality, analyses show that there are many different reasons for suicide. Ernest Hemmingway took his life after becoming increasingly depressed about overwhelming medical problems. The noted psychiatrist Bruno Bettelheim did not want his family to be encumbered by his chronic and debilitating illness. Still others grow weary of their feelings of depression, hopelessness, drug/alcohol abuse, and/or other practical or psychological problems leading to suicidal behavior. Clearly, this is a very personal act decided upon for varied reasons.

It is estimated that well over 30,000 people commit suicide yearly (Centers for Disease Control and Prevention 2007). However, experts believe that this is a gross underestimate of the actual number, because so many ambiguous deaths are ruled accidental. Moreover, it is estimated that at least 10 persons attempt suicide for every 1 who completes the act.

Some have argued that an individual would have to be psychotic or insane to perform such an act. However, psychological autopsies that involve case study analyses of the histories of those who commit suicide do not support such a contention. Although it is clear that most suicidal individuals usually have one or more psychological disorders, this is not always the case. Moreover, most individuals who commit suicide do not appear to be out of touch with reality (i.e., psychotic). Along these lines, it should be noted that suicide is not classified as a psychological disorder in the most recent diagnostic manual (the American Psychiatry Association's *Diagnostic and Statistical Manual of Mental Disorders*, 4th ed., or *DSM-IV*) used by mental health professionals.

Correlates

Obviously, we cannot perform experiments to delineate factors that cause suicide. Therefore, we are left with correlational analyses of these acts. Interestingly, studies have shown that those who attempt suicide are different than those who "succeed." Attempters are likely to be white housewives between 20 and 40 years of age who are experiencing marital or relationship problems and who overdose with pills. Those who actually end their lives tend to be white men over 40 years of age who are suffering from ill health and/or depression, and they shoot or hang themselves (Diekstra, Kienhorts, and de Wilde 1995: Lester 1994; Fremouw, Perczel, and Ellis 1990).

Suicide Statistics

- Suicide is the eighth leading cause of death in U.S. men.
- Married people are less likely to kill themselves than those who are divorced.
- Suicide rates are highest during the spring and summer months.
- The suicide rate among college students is twice as high as those who are not in college, and one in five students admits to suicidal thoughts sometime during college.
- Men commit suicide about three times more often than women, although women attempt it about three times more frequently.
- Physicians, lawyers, law enforcement personnel, and dentists have the highest rates of suicide.
- Socioeconomic status is unrelated to suicide, although a marked drop in socioeconomic status is associated with greater potential for suicide.
- Suicide rates are lower in countries where Catholicism and Islam are a strong influence.
- Native Americans have very high rates of suicide compared with Japanese Americans and Chinese Americans.
- Suicide rates tend to be low during times of war and natural disasters, which tend to create cohesiveness and purpose in a greater percentage of people.
- The majority of people who commit suicide communicated their intent prior to the act.
- Men over 65 years of age are the most likely group to commit suicide.
- Men are more likely to use violent means to kill themselves than women (e.g., firearms versus pills, respectively), although women are increasing their use of methods more likely to be successful.
- About 60 percent of suicide attempters are under the influence of alcohol, and about 25 percent are legally intoxicated.
- The majority of suicide victims show a primary mood disorder.
- Childhood and adolescent rates of suicide are increasing rapidly, and suicide is the third leading cause of death among teens.

- Although depression is correlated with suicide, hopelessness is more predictive of the act. (For information on this and the other items in the above list, see Berman 2006; Centers for Disease Control 2007; Leach 2006; and Shneidman 1993.)

Common Characteristics of Suicide

Suicide victims almost always show ambivalence caused by the built-in desire to survive and avoid death. Still, the goal is to end psychological pain that they see as permanent. They have reached a point of seeing the future as hopeless. Tunnel vision is a common state for the suicidal, wherein they are unable to see the "big picture." Death is viewed as the only way out. Other options and the impact of suicide on significant others are minimally considered, if at all. Thus, the act undertaken is one of escape—an act, moreover, that is often typical of their lifelong coping styles.

Theoretical Orientations

Theories of suicide generally focus on sociological, psychodynamic, and biological causes. Sociocultural explanations were originally advanced by the French sociologist Emile Durkheim (1951). He postulated three types of suicide: egoistic, altruistic, and anomic. Egoistic suicide results from an individual's inability to integrate one's self with society. Lack of close ties to the community leaves the individual without support systems during times of stress and strain. Durkheim argues that highly industrialized and technological societies tend to deemphasize connection with community and family life, thereby increasing vulnerability to suicide. Altruistic suicide involves the taking of one's life in order to advance group goals or achieve some higher value or cause. Examples include some terrorist and religious acts. Anomic suicide occurs when dramatic societal events cause an individual's relationship with society to become imbalanced in significant fashion. Higher suicide rates during the Great Depression and among those who were freed from concentration camps after World War II serve as examples.

Psychodynamic explanations were derived from Freudian theory, which says that suicide is anger turned inward. Presumably, the hostility directed toward self is, in actuality, against the love object with whom the person has identified (e.g., the mother, the father, or some other significant relation). Interestingly, research analysis of 165 suicide notes over a 25-year period showed that about one-quarter expressed self-anger. However, the majority either expressed positive self-attitudes or neither. Thus, although some suicides may involve anger turned toward oneself, it appears other emotions and factors are also relevant (Tuckman, Kleiner, and Lavell 1959).

Biological explanations have focused on the fact that suicide, like many other psychological phenomena, can run in families. That is, there is evidence that suicide and suicide attempts are higher among parents and close relatives than with nonsuicidal people. Additionally, patients with low levels of the metabolite 5-HIAA (which is involved in the production of serotonin, a brain neurotransmitter) are more likely to commit suicide (Asberg, Traskman, and Thoren 1976; Van Praag 1983). Such persons are more likely to possess histories of impulsive and violent behavior patterns (Edman, Adberg, Levander, and Schalling 1986; Roy 1992). Of course, this evidence is correlational in nature and does not indicate whether low levels of 5-HIAA are the cause or the effect of certain moods and emotions or whether they are directly related.

Children, Adolescents, and College Students

Although suicide almost always leaves one with a deep sense of loss, it is particularly tragic when it occurs with a young person. In many ways, those belonging to the youth population are the most vulnerable to making irreversible decisions (their last) without receiving much, if any, support or help and without fully understanding the ramifications of the suicidal act, including how it will affect others.

There is evidence that family instability and stress is correlated with suicide attempts (Cosand, Bouraqe, and Kraus 1982). Many suicidal children have experienced traumatic events and the loss of a parental figure before age 12. Their parents have frequently been abusers of drugs and/or alcohol. Their families have been found to be under greater economic stress than matched (control group) families. The families of suicide attempters also showed a higher number of medical problems, psychiatric illnesses, and suicides than the control group families.

Carson and Johnson (1985) say that 20 percent of college students have experienced suicidal ideation during their college years. Research has shown that students who commit suicide tend to be men, older than the average student by about four years, more likely to be a graduate as opposed to undergraduate student, more often a foreign or language/literature student, and to have performed better academically as an undergraduate than as a graduate student (Seiden 1966, 1984). Further analyses have shown that, despite excellent academic records, most college undergraduates who commit suicide are dissatisfied with their performances and pessimistic about their abilities to succeed. Along these lines, they tend to show unrealistically high expectations for themselves and perfectionist standards and often feel shame over their perceived failings. Additionally, a frequent stressor is the failure to reach expectations or loss of a close interpersonal relationship. A precipitating factor is often the breakup of a romantic relationship. Also, suicide attempts and suicides are more likely to occur with students who have experienced the separation or divorce of their parents or the death of a parent.

Assessment

Clinical psychologists use various tests, such as the Beck Depression Inventory, Beck Hopelessness Scale (BHS), and Beck Scale for Suicide Ideation, to help assess suicide probability. These and other types of psychological tests can be used to supplement clinical interviews, patient histories, and other information as data that can help determine suicidal risk. These measures depend on the honesty of the respondent because they do not have validity scales that can determine people who are deliberately denying their true feelings and intentions. Interestingly, Exner's Rorschach system can be used to predict suicide risk. The test includes a suicide constellation score that allows for prediction of those who possess heightened potential for such. Because the Rorschach is comprised of ambiguous stimuli, it is very difficult to fake. Although all of these measures can be used to complement other inputs, the BHS has been found to be particularly helpful in predicting eventual suicide (Beck, Steer, Kovacs, and Garrison 1985).

Suicide Prevention

Most suicidal victims display signs of their intent. Families, coworkers, primary care doctors, mental health professionals, and others need to be aware of these signs and then act appropriately in terms of the specific context. Of course, laypeople are not expected to be able to predict the likelihood of a suicide attempt with the accuracy of a trained professional. However, friends, coworkers, and family members are certainly in a better position to see day-to-day changes in potential suicide victims' moods and earlier behaviors in ways a professional cannot. As a result, family members and acquaintances may be able to intervene effectively or get the sufferer needed professional help. For example, knowing that men, particularly the depressed elderly, are more likely to commit suicide than other demographic groups can alert us to warning signs in that group. Suppose we know such a man who lives alone and recently lost his wife after a sustained illness. Add to this information the fact that he seldom sees his family or friends and possesses a gun. Certainly, risk factors are present in that case. Obviously, such factors do not mean that the man *will* attempt to take his life. However, we should be alert to the higher risk of such an act taking place in this situation.

Both laypeople and professionals should be aware that people who have thought out a plan for their suicide are more likely than those without a plan to try it. Generally, the more detail they can provide about their plan, the more serious they are about carrying it out. Also, they often communicate their intent to others and provide indirect behavioral clues. For example, they may make out a will or change insurance policies, give away prized possessions, or go on a lengthy trip. At any rate, their presuicidal behavior in retrospect is often seen as somewhat unusual or peculiar. Of course, previous suicide attempts are often a precursor to a "successful" one and are a major risk factor. Still, we need to keep in mind that some suicide victims have neither tried suicide before nor communicated their intent to anyone.

With respect to suicide prevention, the phenomenon of subtle suicide (Church and Brooks 2009) is relevant. Subtle suicide typically involves a long-term pattern of self-destructive behaviors, thoughts, and feelings that ultimately drag a person down in a self-defeating fashion. As with overt suicide, subtle suicide involves deep ambivalence about living. Sufferers have a desire to live, while, at the same time, there is an equal or greater wish that their life will end. Although not actively suicidal, the subtly suicidal engage in neglectful, self-defeating, risky and self-destructive behaviors that inevitably lower the quality and sometimes length of their lives. A downward spiraling effect occurs that can eventually lead the subtly suicidal to become overtly suicidal. In other words, some people pass through an extended period of being uncommitted to living before ending their lives. Professional and family interventions may be effective in getting these individuals committed to living more fully and out of a "subtle suicide zone," where they compromise their own physical, psychological, and social well-being.

The main point to emphasize here is that many people take a long, slow slide downhill that may or may not be apparent to those close to them. We need to keep in mind that over half of those who commit suicide have made no previous attempt (Zhal and Hawton 2004b; Stolberg, Clark, and Bongar 2002). Over time, some people who have been subtly suicidal become overtly so, particularly as their lives deteriorate and they become more hopeless in their outlook. Interventions as early in the process as possible stand to save lives and enhance the quality of life for the potential victim and significant others. Thus, early detection of people who are becoming or have become suicidal—regardless of whether they suffer from serious psychological disorders—is a first line of defense in the effort to prevent suicide. Many people can avoid the process of dealing with active suicidal ideation and behavior altogether if they get the prerequisite support and help.

A second form of prevention involves crisis intervention. The objective here is to intervene appropriately when an individual calls for help with suicidal ideation, gesture, or attempt. The focus is on maintaining contact with the potential victim. The contact could be on the telephone or in person in a hospital, mental health clinic, or other location. In all instances, the objective is to give helpful support and feedback. Constructive feedback can help in a number of ways, including (but not limited to):

- Bringing calm to the situation.
- Minimizing loneliness and alienation.
- Reducing the tunnel vision that many suicidal people have in this state.
- Combating hopelessness.
- Giving empathy.
- Offering practical options and choices.
- Making referrals to other professionals.
- Initiating an involuntary or voluntary psychiatric hospitalization.

Follow-up treatments can be crucial in preventing future attempts. Even with treatments, there is an increased risk, as those who have a previous attempt are at a five times greater risk to die by suicide (Stolberg, Clark, and Bongar 2002).

Some successful prevention studies have been done with particular high-risk groups. One program placed older men in roles where they are involved with social and interpersonal activities that help others. These activities have been found to help them cope with feelings of isolation and meaninglessness (Maris, Berman, and Silverman 2000). A similar program involved adolescents with suicidal ideation and behavior and/or mood or substance abuse history (Zhal and Hawton 2004a). Finally, working with adults who had made previous attempts, Brown and colleagues (2005) found that 10 cognitive therapy sessions targeted at suicide prevention reduced subsequent suicide attempts by 50 percent over an 18-month period. The same subjects' feelings of depression and hopelessness, moreover, were lower than the comparison group (Brown et al. 2005). These are just a few of the studies that have shown clear evidence of how suicide prevention can be used effectively.

See also **Euthanasia and Physician-Assisted Suicide; School Violence (vol. 2)**

Further Reading

Asberg, M., L. Traskman, and P. Thoren, "5HIAA in the Cerebrospinal Fluid: A Biochemical Suicide Predictor?" *Archives of General Psychiatry* 33 (1976): 1193–1197.

Beck, A. T., and R. A., Steer, *Manual for Revised Beck Depression Inventory.* San Antonio: Psychological Corporation, 1987.

Beck, A. T., and R. A. Steer, *Manual for Beck Hopelessness Scale.* San Antonio: Psychological Corporation, 1988.

Beck, A. T., R. A. Steer, M. Kovacs, and B. Garrison, "Hopeless and Eventual Suicide: A 10-Year Prospective Study of Patients Hospitalized with Suicide Ideation." *American Journal of Psychiatry* 142 (1985): 559–563.

Beck, A. T., R. A. Steer, and W. F. Ranieri, "Scale for Suicide Ideation: Psychometric Properties of a Self-Report Version." *Journal of Clinical Psychology* 44 (1988): 499–505.

Berman, A. L., "Risk Management with Suicidal Patients." *Journal of Clinical Psychology: In Session* 62 (2006): 1971–1984.

Brown, G. K., T. Have, G. R. Henriques, S. X. Xie, J. E. Hollander, and A. T. Beck, "Cognitive Therapy for the Prevention of Suicide Attempts. A Randomized Control Trial." Journal of the American Medical Association 294, no. 5 (2005); 563–570.

Carson, N. D., and R. E. Johnson, "Suicidal Thoughts and Problem Solving Preparation among College Students." *Journal of College Student Personnel* 26 (1985): 484–487.

Centers for Disease Control and Prevention, *Suicide Facts at a Glance.* 2007. http://www.cdc.gov/nipe/dvp/suicide/

Church, M. A., and C. I. Brooks, *Subtle Suicide: Our Silent Epidemic over Ambivalence about Living.* Westport, CT: Praeger, 2009.

Cosand, B. J., L. B. Bouraqe, and J. F. Kraus, "Suicide among Adolescents in Sacramento County, California, 1950–1979." *Adolescence* 17 (1982): 917–930.

Diekstra, R. F., C.W.M. Kienhorts, and E. J. de Wilde, "Suicide and Suicidal Behavior among Adolescents." In *Psychological Disorders in Young People,* eds. M. Rutter and D. J. Smith, Chichester, England: John Wiley.

Durkheim, E., *Suicide*. New York: Free Press, 1951.

Edman, G., M. Adberg, S. Levander, and D. Schalling, "Skin Conductance Habituation and Cerebrospinal Fluid 5-Hydroxyindeactic Acid in Suicidal Patients." *Archives of General Psychiatry* 43 (1986): 586–592.

Exner, J. E. Jr., *The Rorschach: A Comprehensive System*. Vol. 1, *Basic Foundations*, 3d ed. New York: John Wiley, 1993.

Fremouw, W. J., W. J. Perczel, and T. E. Ellis, *Suicide Risk: Assessment and Response Guidelines*. Elmsford, NY: Pergamon, 1990.

Leach, M. M., *Cultural diversity and Suicide: Ethnic, Religious, Gender and Sexual Orientation Perspectives*. Binghamton, NY: Haworth Press, 2006.

Lester, D., "Are There Unique Features of Suicide in Adults of Different Ages and Developmental Stages?" *Omega Journal of Death and Dying* 29 (1994): 337–348.

Maris, R. W., A. C. Berman, and M. M. Silverman, *Comprehensive Textbook of Suicidology*. New York: Guilford Press, 2000.

Roy, A., "Suicide in Schizophrenia." *International Review of Psychiatry* 4 (1992): 205–209.

Seiden, R. H., "Campus Tragedy: A Study of Student Suicide." *Journal of Abnormal and Social Psychology*, 71 (1966): 389–399.

Seiden, R. H., "The Youthful Suicide Epidemic." *Public Affairs Report* 25 (1984): 1.

Shneidman, E. S., *Suicide as Psychache: A Clinical Approach to Self-Destructive Behavior*. Northvale, NJ: Jason Aronson, 1993.

Stolberg, R. A., D. C. Clark, and B. Bongar, "Epidemiology, Assessment and Management of Suicide in Depressed Patients." In *Handbook of Depression*, ed. I. H. Gotlib and C. L. Hammen. New York: Guilford Press, 2002.

Tuckman, J., R. Kleiner, and M. Lavell, "Emotional Content of Suicide Notes." *American Journal of Psychiatry* 16 (1959): 59–63.

Van Praag, H. M., "CSF 5-H1AA and Suicide in Nondepressed Schizophrenics." *Lancet* 2 (1983): 977–978.

Zahl, D. L., and K. Hawton, "Media Influence on Suicidal Behavior: An Interview Study of Young People." *Behavior and Cognitive Psychotherapy* 32, no. 2 (2004a): 189–198.

Zahl, D. L., and K. Hawton, "Repetition of Deliberate Self-Harm and Subsequent Suicide Risk: Long-term Follow-up Study of 11,583 Patients." *British Journal of Psychiatry* 185 (2004b): 70–75.

SURROGACY

Sarah Fish

Surrogacy is a form of reproductive assistance in which one woman bears a child for another woman to rear. While it sounds like a simple proposition—something a woman might do for another out of the goodness of her heart—it is far more complex than it initially sounds. Likewise, the ethical, moral, and legal controversies surrounding surrogacy continue to be revealed.

Surrogacy: A Brief U.S. History

Surrogacy, as scientific assistance for pregnancy and birth, became a part of public discourse around the mid-1970s, despite its having been mentioned in the Bible in Genesis. The first documented instance in the United States comes from an anonymous advertisement in the mid-1970s requesting the help of a surrogate mother. According to the advertisement, the surrogate would receive from $7,000 to $10,000 for her services and $3,000 for medical expenses. The amount established in the 1970s has been the accepted minimum form of assistance for all commercial surrogacy cases. It is important to note that the fees given to surrogate mothers today are not necessarily payments for a child. Most states have made it illegal to pay a woman for a child, so the payments given to a surrogate are couched in phrases like "medical assistance, food, and shelter." This is done to eliminate the stigma of baby selling.

The first time a surrogacy case went to court was in 1981. Unlike the more widely known cases like Baby M and *Johnson v. Calvert,* this particular case was about payment. The case was a challenge to Michigan laws that would not allow a payment in exchange for relinquishing parental rights. Leading this case was the so-called father of surrogate motherhood, Noel Keane. He challenged Michigan laws regarding payment to surrogate mothers, but the trial did not go in his favor, and the state upheld its law against fees being paid for a child. In fact, Michigan was so staunchly opposed to surrogacy that it tried to ban surrogacy contracts outright in 1988 and was the first state in the nation to take a stand on surrogacy.

During the 1980s, surrogacy became a more prevalent form of assisted reproductive technology, but it also became more entrenched in legal battles. The law was unable to keep up with the emerging technologies, and before anyone could reconfigure concepts of parenthood, cases like Baby M and *Johnson v. Calvert* took the national stage. When the Baby M case hit the New Jersey courts in 1986, both the United Kingdom and the United States had had their first successful in vitro fertilizations, and surrogacy had taken on new dimensions. The jargon surrounding surrogacy shifted, creating four categories of cases:

1. Traditional surrogacy: a case in which a couple decides to have a child through a surrogate mother, and the husband provides the sperm and the surrogate provides the ovum. In this case, the surrogate mother is the genetic and gestational mother.

2. Gestational surrogacy: a case in which a couple decides to have a child through a surrogate, and the husband and wife provide the necessary gametes. In this case, the surrogate is not genetically linked to the child. Also, gestational surrogacy can occur with the use of anonymously donated sperm and ova, thus creating some potentially difficult legal issues (see *Jaycee B. v.*

the Superior Court of Orange County 1996 and *In re Marriage of John A.B. and Luanne H.B.* 1998).

3. Commercial surrogacy: a case in which a couple pursues surrogacy usually through an agency, paying for the agency services as well as providing financial assistance to the surrogate mother.

4. Noncommercial surrogacy: a case in which a couple pursues surrogacy, usually through a private agreement, in which no fees are exchanged between the couple and the surrogate mother.

The four types of surrogacy are not mutually exclusive. A surrogacy cannot be traditional and gestational at the same time nor commercial and noncommercial concurrently. However, it can be a traditional, commercial surrogacy or even a traditional, noncommercial surrogacy. Depending on the combination of labels, the moral, ethical, and legal ramifications of each surrogacy case increases. Several legal cases have involved surrogacy, but three have received the most media attention: *In re the Matter of Baby M, Johnson v. Calvert,* and *In re Marriage of John H.B. and Luanne A.B.* The three cases have set the precedents for all surrogacy cases and have brought various issues into the national discourse.

The Case of Baby M

When the New Jersey Supreme Court ruled on *In re the Matter of Baby M* in 1988, the case had received an enormous amount of national attention. The case was the first of its kind, with the surrogate mother demanding that the court acknowledge her parental rights. The case of Baby M was a traditional, commercial surrogacy.

William and Elizabeth Stern, the intended parents, had contracted an agreement with Mary Beth Whitehead as the surrogate mother. According to the contract, Whitehead would undergo artificial insemination with Mr. Stern's sperm, carry the child to term, and, upon the child's birth, would relinquish her parental rights to the Sterns. In exchange for fulfilling the contract, Whitehead would receive $10,000.

As the pregnancy advanced, Whitehead had reservations about giving up the child and decided that she wanted to keep it. Upon the birth of Baby M, Whitehead fled to Florida against court orders. When the case went before the Superior Court, the judge upheld the legality of the surrogacy contract and demanded that Whitehead return the child to the Sterns.

Upon appeal, the case went before the New Jersey Supreme Court, where it garnered national media attention. The court, without precedents for surrogacy cases, treated the arrangement between the Sterns and Whitehead as they would a custody battle between divorced parents. Because Elizabeth Stern had no apparent claim to the child, the court did not consider her intent in having a child. The court reversed the Superior Court's decision on the basis that the contract between the Sterns and Whitehead was illegal. Because the contract outlined payment for a child and the relinquishment of parental rights rather than payment for medical expenses, the contract violated New Jersey public policy and was null and void.

The court, having dismissed the surrogacy contract, then dealt with the issue of custody and the child's best interests. In the hearing, it was decided that the Sterns could provide the best possible environment for Baby M, so they were awarded custody. Unlike the Sterns, Whitehead had recently divorced and was struggling financially—two things the court considered while deciding the best interests of Baby M. However, because she was deemed the biological mother, the court granted her visitation rights.

Baby M was the first case that addressed the lack of a legal framework for dealing with surrogacy issues. Without laws specifically governing surrogacy, the court had to treat traditional surrogacy as it would a custody battle between separated parties. As a result of the media attention, however, nearly every state considered laws to allow, ban, or regulate surrogacy. The Baby M case marks the beginning of public legal and ethical discussions of surrogacy issues. In the middle of the trial, a 1987 poll from the *New York Times* found that a majority of people believed that surrogacy contracts should be upheld—even if the courts seemed to rule otherwise.

The Case of Johnson v. Calvert

Six years after the New Jersey Supreme Court handed down its decision regarding traditional surrogacy in the Baby M case, the California Supreme Court handed down a decision that would inform the general consensus toward gestational surrogacy: *Johnson v. Calvert*. In this case, Mark and Crispina Calvert sought to have a child through a surrogate mother, Anna Johnson.

Anna Johnson offered to be the surrogate mother for the Calverts. Unlike the case of Baby M, where the surrogate also supplied the ovum, Johnson provided the necessary gestation for the child, and Mrs. Calvert provided the ovum. By using in vitro fertilization, Johnson carried the Calverts' genetic child. Under the contractual agreement between the two parties, Johnson would receive $10,000 in installments to help finance medical expenses and basic needs. The Calverts would also insure her life with a $200,000 life insurance policy. In return, Johnson would carry the child to term and recognize the sole parental rights of the Calverts. However, the Calverts and Johnson had a falling out, and both parties filed custody suits.

According to California law (under the Uniform Parentage Act), both Crispina Calvert and Anna Johnson had equal claims to the child, because the law acknowledged the role of genetic and gestational mothers as legal mothers. However, the court decided in favor of Mrs. Calvert based on a consent-intent definition—a definition that has subsequently affected all gestational surrogacy cases. By a consent-intent argument, the legal parents are the people who consented to the procedure with the intention of taking on parental responsibility. The court argued that any woman could have gestated the resulting child, but only Mrs. Calvert could have provided the ovum. As a result, Mrs. Calvert was the legal mother.

The Case of Jaycee B.

Like the two previous cases, the trials involving Jaycee B. took the national stage, as once again the law struggled to deal with issues that arise from surrogacy. However, unlike Baby M and *Johnson v. Calvert*, Jaycee B. was not a surrogacy case; in fact, the trials surrounding this child were more about child support and deciding the legal parents. The trials were labeled as a surrogacy case gone awry, because Jaycee B. was the result of a rather unusual surrogacy. This case involved a gestational surrogacy in which the genetic material (the sperm and ovum) used to create the child belonged to neither of the intended parents. The intended parents had used anonymous donor sperm and ova, and, under California law, donors are not acknowledged as legal parents.

When the intended parents of Jaycee B., John and Luanne, divorced one month prior to the birth of the child, questions of parentage arose. When John filed for divorce, he listed no children from the marriage and refused to pay child support for Jaycee B. In the media, reports labeled the child as legally parentless because the genetic parents were anonymous donors and the surrogate mother had filed for custody, only to take her petition back when Luanne assured her that Jaycee would be fine. As the divorce trial continued, John refused to acknowledge the child as his own because he was not the biological father. He argued that, because he was not genetically linked to the child, he should not have to pay child support.

The first trial in the matter of Jaycee B. concluded in 1996, *Jaycee B. v. Superior Court of Orange County*. The first trial was meant to decide whether John should pay child support. The Appellate Court declared that, because he had signed the surrogacy contract as an intended parent, he owed child support until such time as a court officially labeled him as other than the father of the child. In 1997, the case became more complicated when a higher court decided that John had no support obligations, that the surrogacy contract was unenforceable, and that Luanne would have to officially adopt the child.

The second trial in the matter of Jaycee B. concluded in 1998, *In re Marriage of John A.B. and Luanne H.B.* This specific trial dealt with the issue of parentage. The court decided that the intended parents of a child of donor gestation are the legal parents. John had argued that, because he had only signed the surrogacy contract and no other legal paperwork, he could not be considered the legal father and thus was not responsible for child support. The 1998 court decision upheld the consent-intent definition of parenthood established by *Johnson v. Calvert*, even in the absence of complete legal written documentation, but with John's full awareness of the situation. Regardless of the lack of a genetic link between John and Jaycee, he was, by intent, her father. The trials involving Jaycee B. were not necessarily surrogacy cases—no surrogate mother was protesting her parental rights—but the trials illustrate what can happen when U.S. laws do not account for the special needs of surrogacy cases.

Does Surrogacy Aid Infertile Couples or Exploit Women?

The biggest praise that surrogacy receives is that it enables infertile couples to have children that are genetically linked to at least one parent, if not both. In 1999, a study found that 2 million to 3 million couples were infertile. Infertility data, combined with the fewer numbers of children readily available for adoptions, suggest that fewer couples would ever experience their desired parenthood. Surrogacy, when compared with the costs of legal adoption, may be an economically competitive form of having children.

The process can be expensive, with a surrogacy costing a couple anywhere from $10,000 to $60,000 depending on whether the surrogacy is commercial or noncommercial, traditional or gestational. Average domestic adoption costs are $9,000, and the expense increases with a foreign adoption. Both adoption and surrogacy carry a weighty cost for agency and legal fees. In an adoption, the birth mother is not paid anything to compensate her for her pregnancy and childbirth. However, because the intended parents may pay money to the surrogate mother, many critics view surrogacy as exploitation.

The case of Baby M caused an explosion of moral and ethical debates regarding surrogacy. Because the contract between the Sterns and Whitehead outlined that she would be paid upon the birth of the child and her filing to relinquish her parental rights, the courts viewed this as baby selling. Under contract, Whitehead would receive money for additional medical needs, but the $10,000 from the contract was to be given to her upon the birth of Baby M and not before and not in the case of an abortion. Radical feminist critics lashed out about surrogacy, claiming that the act exploited women and children and that it undermined the basic mother-child bond. The stigma of baby selling continues in the dialogue about surrogacy. Even today, when it is widely recognized that surrogacy contracts cannot outline payment for children or the relinquishing of parental rights, critics argue that labeling the payments as being for medical expenses, food, or clothing is a façade. Women are being paid to have children and give them to the purchaser.

The issue of women being paid for pregnancy and childbirth brings up more controversial topics like exploitation of women and children and the commoditization of human capital. Because surrogacy is such an expensive procedure, the process favors the privileged classes while harming lower-class women; rich couples can exploit lower-class women with the promise of money that they might not otherwise be able to earn. Because lower-class women may need the money, they would be more willing than other women to act as surrogates, and, because the current system under which surrogacy operates has little follow-up for surrogates, critics argue that these women are seen as persons of use rather than persons worthy of respect.

Because a monetary figure is attached to a woman's body and the resulting child, critics contend that we have created a market for human capital; we are buying and selling people. Studies question the possible negative effects on a surrogate mother, such as the labels that society places on her and the consequences of separating a mother and child. Others wonder at the outcome for a child who learns that she or he is the result of a surrogacy arrangement. Very few studies follow up on these questions.

However, when we discuss surrogacy and exploitation, we must consider the varying definitions of exploitation. Because harm is a subjective feeling, different surrogate mothers may relate different experiences. A first possible definition of exploitive surrogacy is that the intended parents gain while the surrogate mother is harmed. In this case, the intended parents gain from hurting someone else. Because the intended parents have the economic power, they can demand whatever they wish from the surrogate, and, in return, she is left to acquiesce. A second possible definition of exploitative surrogacy is that both the intended parents and the surrogate gain from the experience, but the intended parents gain more. In this case, the intended parents gain a child and the surrogate gains some kind of monetary compensation. However, because society places a high value on a child's life, but not one that is necessarily monetary, the exchange for a child and $10,000 for expenses is not a fair arrangement. A third possible definition of exploitive surrogacy is that the intended parents gain from an immoral practice. Because surrogacy violates an inherent social norm or religious viewpoint, it has to be exploitative.

The difficulty in assessing accurate data on the exploitative nature of surrogacy is the fact that harm is subjective. Undoubtedly, Whitehead and Johnson might recount similar feelings from their surrogacy experiences, but the unnamed surrogate from the Jaycee B. case might relate a different experience. While they might make the news headlines, in fact less than 1 percent of surrogate mothers change their minds and want to keep the children. Most espouse a more altruistic motive to becoming surrogate mothers. Able to have children, they decided to give a gift to another couple. The *Johnson v. Calvert* case judges cited that a majority of surrogate mothers made between $15,000 and $30,000 per year in income separate from any possible assistance from the surrogacy. Less than 13 percent made below $15,000 per year.

It has been suggested that the primary motive for women to serve as surrogates is the money that they can earn doing so. Money may not be the driving factor for surrogate mothers that some critics of the practice suggest. Early studies of the practice also found women's enjoyment of pregnancy, guilt over a past abortion, or giving a child up for adoption as potential motives in addition to financial compensation. Defenders of surrogacy argue that a woman who chooses to be a surrogate mother solely for some kind of payment would actually make less for the time she invested than if she worked at a low-paying job. Because these women choose to be surrogates—a 24-hour, nine-month job for a minimum of $10,000 of assistance—there must be some other motivation. If these women choose to be surrogates, the issue of exploitation seems irrelevant. It does not make sense that a woman would commoditize her body, as critics claim, for $1.54 per hour. This figure is derived from the following information: an average pregnancy lasts 270 days for 24 hours each day, totaling 6,480 hours. If a surrogate mother receives the minimum $10,000 of assistance, she makes $1.54 per hour. If she receives $20,000 in assistance, it comes out to $3.09 per hour.

Of course, to consider raising the minimum accepted assistance given for medical and basic needs might also lead to more women choosing to be surrogate mothers because of the money rather than for more charitable motives. Ultimately, surrogacy cannot exist without surrogate mothers. We have yet to find a means of fertilizing an ovum and sperm and gestating the embryo without a gestational mother. The question is: does surrogacy help more than it hurts?

Genetics or Gestation: Who Becomes the Legal Mother?

Despite the scientific developments with artificial reproductive technologies, the law has not moved fast enough to consider surrogacy cases. The federal government has been unable to provide a general law for surrogacy like the equivalent in the United Kingdom, the Surrogacy Act of 1985. The only time federal legislation for surrogacy was introduced was in 1989 when Representative Thomas A. Luken (D-Ohio) and Representative Robert K. Dornan (R-California) introduced two different bills.

Representative Luken presented the Surrogacy Arrangement Bill, which criminalized commercial surrogacy. Anyone who willingly made commercial arrangements—intended parents, surrogate mothers, and agencies—would be subject to legal action. Representative Dornan introduced the Anti-Surrogate Mother Bill, which criminalized all activities relating to surrogacy. The bill would have also made all current surrogacy contracts—commercial and noncommercial—null and void. No one has been able to create a federal surrogacy law, and, as a result, the laws vary from state to state.

GIVING BIRTH TO ONE'S GRANDCHILDREN

In 1991, in one of the most pleasant and well-publicized surrogacy arrangements, a South Dakota woman gave birth to her granddaughter and grandson. Arlette Schweitzer, 43 at the time of the birth, underwent in vitro fertilization by using the eggs from her daughter, Christa, and sperm from her son-in-law, Kevin—the first documented arrangement of this type in the United States. Christa (22 at the time of the birth) had been born with functioning ovaries but without a uterus. Upon learning of this, Mrs. Schweitzer volunteered to gestate her own grandchildren. This gestational surrogacy gained publicity through a TV movie in 1993, *Labor of Love: The Arlette Schweitzer Story*. In 2004 Arlette Schweitzer recounted her surrogacy experience in the book *Whatever It Takes*.

The Baby M case began the legal discussions of surrogacy and prompted debate in law reviews regarding the legal definitions of surrogacy between 1988 and 1990. The New Jersey Supreme Court's decision to treat Whitehead as the legal mother of Baby M was the first case of its kind to decide that legal motherhood is defined by genetics. Because Mrs. Stern had no role in the creation of Baby M, apart from her intent to be a mother, the court did not consider her in the case until it tried to decide the best interests of the child. With a legal vacuum for dealing with surrogacy, the court had to treat the case as a custody battle and treated the surrogacy contract as an adoption contract. However, within a few years, most states had considered some laws dealing with the issues that originated with Baby M.

By the time *Johnson v. Calvert* received national attention, California had already begun a legal dialogue for deciding parentage: the Uniform Parentage Act. According to this act, legal mothers could be determined by either genetics or gestation. This posed a problem with *Johnson V. Calvert* because, according to this definition, both Johnson and Mrs. Calvert had legal claims to the resulting child. The court decided the case based on a consent-intent definition, which claimed that, without the intentions of the Calverts, there would have been no child. The case also solidified the role of genetics in determining legal motherhood. In fact, many people at the time argued that a genetic definition of motherhood would be the best for surrogacy cases. The genetic argument eliminates any potential inconsistencies in surrogacy law, and it is the one contribution to a child that no one else could supply. In the instance that genetics and gestation were bound in the same woman, legal motherhood would be indisputable.

But, again, because surrogacy laws change from state to state, there are no consistent laws for the process. California is the one state that has stayed the most up to date by considering various laws and standards for determining legal motherhood. Currently, there are three different tests for legal motherhood that courts use when deciding cases: intent-based, genetic contribution, and gestation. As previously mentioned, the intent-based definition of legal motherhood originated with *Johnson v. Calvert*. Because there would be no child without the intent of the intended parents, the intended mother is the legal mother. The genetic contribution test is the most foolproof method for determining legal motherhood, because it is the contribution that only the biological donor parent provides. The gestation test is a common law assumption that the birth mother is the legal mother because she devoted time to gestating the child.

The fact that there are three tests for determining legal motherhood, and that each of these tests contradicts the other in some places, suggests a need for more uniform law regarding surrogacy. However, in considering federal laws that would regulate surrogacy at the state level, legislators would have to decide exactly what defines a parent. With only one law to govern surrogacy, there may not be room to consider the special circumstances that can arise from surrogacy cases that do not begin as surrogacy cases, like the trials involving Jaycee B.

Surrogacy as Deviant to Notions of Motherhood

Today, it is impossible to discuss surrogacy apart from issues that range from artificial insemination and donor egg transplantation, the controversy over same-sex couples, and U.S. concepts of motherhood. When discussing the moral, ethical, and legal questions surrounding surrogacy, most people get more than agitated. For some, surrogacy is immoral based on religious convictions. For others, surrogacy exploits women and children, making people commodities much in the way that the 18th- and 19th-century slave trade made people commodities. And yet for others, surrogacy is one of the only chances that they will ever have to have a child.

Surrogacy has enabled couples who may not have been able to have biological children to finally have children. This includes infertile couples as well as same-sex couples. With the rise of same-sex marriage controversies in the early part of the 21st century, surrogacy can become enmeshed as well. Religious zealots against homosexuality may lump surrogacy, despite its ability to give children to heterosexual couples, into a category of immoral behavior. Because surrogacy can provide children for same-sex partners, and because same-sex relationships are labeled morally wrong by these groups, surrogacy must also be morally wrong.

But if we strip down surrogacy to its basic components—that a woman might decide prior to conception to choose to gestate a child for someone else to raise—then we may find that the notions of U.S. motherhood are compromised. If U.S. culture heralds a natural mother-child bond and maternal instinct, then what does surrogacy challenge about our notions of motherhood? If a woman willingly decides to gestate a baby for another couple, what does that say about the notions that mother knows best?

On the one hand, surrogacy does perpetuate the idea that women should become mothers. By allowing infertile couples to have children in ways other than adoption or fostering, more women can become the mothers that society expects them to become. For most people, the act of gestation alone might make a woman a mother. But what kind of mother is she if she does not keep the child? Is a surrogate mother worse than a woman who gives up a child for adoption if the surrogate mother decides before she is pregnant that she will not keep the child?

Some of the same stigmas and stereotypes of adoption are repeated in surrogacy. Over the last 30 years, there has been considerable research into both adoption and surrogacy but very little into the women who give up the children. Arguably, it is because surrogate mothers are deviant mothers. They do not conform to U.S. concepts of motherhood and so have been left out of mainstream research. Surrogate mothers do not reinforce ideas like the naturalness of mothering and the maternal instinct. Despite the fact that the surrogacy cases that have received the most media attention—Baby M and *Johnson v. Calvert*—seemed to argue that women do have an instinctual desire to be mothers, fewer than 1 percent of surrogate mothers have ever contested for any parental rights.

Surrogacy, despite increased popularity as a form of assisted reproductive technology, is still on the outskirts of the U.S. legal framework. Apart from California, most state governments do not have laws guaranteeing the security of either the intended parents or the surrogate mother. The U.S. legal system does not make it possible for a child to have two moms and one dad, or even just two dads (excepting California in a decision from 2005 that changed the Uniform Parentage Act). Because of these limitations, the jargon associated with surrogacy cases is divided, allowing for separations between normal motherhood and deviant motherhood. Surrogacy is either traditional or gestational. It can either be commercial or noncommercial. The language of surrogacy reinforces inherent U.S. notions of good mothers, and a surrogate mother does not fit that role.

See also **Reproductive Technology (vol. 4)**

Further Reading

Crockin, Susan L., and Howard W. Jones Jr., *Legal Conceptions: The Evolving Law and Policy of Assisted Reproductive Technologies.* Baltimore: Johns Hopkins University Press, 2010.

Markens, Susan, *Surrogate Motherhood and the Politics of Reproduction.* Berkeley: University of California Press, 2007.

Schweitzer, Arlette, *Whatever It Takes.* Mandan, ND: Crain Grosinger, 2004.

Shalev, Carmel, *Birth Power: The Case for Surrogacy.* New Haven, CT: Yale University Press, 1989.

Shanley, Mary London, *Making Babies, Making Families: What Matters Most in an Age of Reproductive Technologies.* Boston: Beacon Press, 2001.

T

TEEN PREGNANCY

Santarica Buford

The United States has the highest rates of pregnancy, abortion, and childbirth among teenagers in industrialized nations, a fact that results in considerable social anxiety and controversy. Teen pregnancy is defined as pregnancy among girls and young women age 19 years and younger. A phrase that is used to draw attention to the problems of this behavior is *children having children*. Teen pregnancy leads to adolescents raising children before they are emotionally or financially ready to do so. The rate of teen pregnancy has steadily decreased since reaching an all-time high in the 1990s. The rates have fallen because teenagers today have shown an increased use of long-acting birth control and slight decreases in sexual activity.

Today fewer American young people get married as teens, compared with young people 50 years ago. They do not, however, avoid sexual relationships until marriage. Because they are involved in premarital sexual relations, often with little planning for pregnancy and for the prevention of sexually transmitted diseases (STDs), teens become parents early. This has been a factor in the increase in single-mother families. There are different reasons why teenage girls become pregnant. Teenage girls are likely to become pregnant if they were sexually abused at a young age, in need of someone to love them, or planned for motherhood. Other pregnancies were unintended, because most teens tend to be poorly prepared with contraception and tend to underestimate their chances of conceiving.

Background

Twenty-nine million adolescents are sexually active in the nation, and the number is increasing each year. More than 850,000 teenage girls will become pregnant each year, and close to 500,000 of them will give birth. Estimates are that three-fourths of these pregnancies are unintended. About 90 to 95 percent of teens who carry the pregnancy to term will keep their babies. Surprisingly, the nation's highest teen birth rate occurred in 1957, with 96.3 births per 1,000 teenage girls, compared to 41.9 births per 1,000 teenage girls in 2006. These numbers seem to suggest that teen parenting was more of a problem in the past. That is misleading, however. Most of the births from the 1950s and 1960s were to older teens who were married to their partners. These teens, who married young and had high fertility rates, were the parents of the baby boom generation. Economic instability, a hallmark of teen parenting today, was ameliorated in the 1950s by a strong economy and the likelihood of finding a family-wage job with only a high school education. Because so-called good jobs were available to those with only a high school education, young marriage and childbearing was encouraged by the social circumstances. Also, there was a strong propaganda machine extolling the virtues of stay-at-home mothers. There was a stigma on girls who were out-of-wedlock mothers, so much so that many pregnant teens were sent to live with relatives until the birth, when the infant was then placed for adoption. The alternative was a so-called shotgun wedding in which the couple was persuaded to marry before the pregnancy began to show. In the 1950s and 1960s, more than half of the women who conceived while they were single married before the child was born.

Today, the story is a very different one. The overwhelming majority of teen pregnancies are among unmarried teens. Eighty percent of teenage births occur outside of a marital relationship, and most of the girls have no intention of marrying the father of the child. As the social stigma of teen pregnancy has decreased dramatically over the last 30 years, so has the pressure to marry in order to legitimize a birth. Pregnant teens attend school alongside nonpregnant teens. This is quite a contrast from the days when pregnant girls were forced to drop out or were sent to the reform school for students with behavior problems so that they would not corrupt the nonpregnant girls. The financial circumstances of today's teen mothers are often quite desperate, and many end up seeking public assistance funds. Education beyond high school has become essential for constructing a middle-class life, but many teen mothers experience a truncated educational history, quite unlike what those teen mothers of 50 to 60 years ago experienced when their husbands had high-paying jobs.

A brief discussion of the trends in teen birth in the last 20 years can help us to understand why teen pregnancy has been described as such a problem. In 1986, the birth rate among 15- to 19-year-old women was 50 births per 1,000, but by 1991 that rate had climbed 24 percent to 62 per 1,000. However, over the next five years, the rate fell to 54 births per 1,000 women ages 15 to 19 (Darroch and Singh 1999). In 2005, the teen birth rate in the United States was 40 births per 1,000 teenage girls. Most data are concerned with the 15- to 19-year-old group because they have higher rates and constitute a much larger proportion of the births to teen mothers. Today research shows that pregnancies among young girls ages 10 to 14 have fallen to their lowest level in the past decade. Thus, in the late 1980s and early 1990s, politicians, families, religious leaders, and educators began to worry about the increases in teenage births and asked what solutions would help turn the trends around.

Race and Ethnicity

Racial and ethnic groups in the United States do not all have the same teen pregnancy and birth rates. Fertility rates among American women are different because of religion, age, and socioeconomic status. During the 1970s and 1980s, African American women had the highest fertility rate, Hispanics had the second highest, and white women had the lowest. Today, however, it is Hispanic women with the highest rate, followed by African Americans and whites. The rate of teen births among blacks has dropped more dramatically than the rates of any other ethnic group. According to the Centers for Disease Control and Prevention, in 2005, the birth rate for Hispanic teens was 82 births per 1,000 girls ages 15 to 19. Comparable data for black and non-Hispanic whites were 61 per 1,000 and 26 per 1,000, respectively. The group with the lowest teen birth rate was Asian and Pacific Islander teens, at 17 per 1,000.

The reasons that birth rates among races differ are because of socioeconomic factors, family structure, and perceived future options. Risk factors for teen pregnancy include living in rural areas and inner cities, where many minority groups are clustered. White adolescent girls are less likely than black or Hispanic girls to carry their pregnancies to term. Because of their economic status and parental pressure, many will end their pregnancies through abortion. Often minority women, particularly those on public assistance, cannot afford abortion, and legislation has changed so that government funds will not cover elective abortion.

Likewise, education and religion can play a role in teen births. Girls who perceive few educational or employment opportunities (usually minority girls) may be more interested in becoming mothers. Pregnancy and mothering may be a way to avoid going to work in low-paying, dead-end jobs. At least they can have control in one aspect of their lives. This is more likely to be the case for black girls. One study in Alabama found more than 20 percent of black teens between the ages of 14 and 18 wished that they were pregnant. For Hispanics, socioeconomic status is also important. However, Roman Catholicism, which disapproves of both birth control and abortion, also plays a role. Hispanic culture places a high value on children, particularly in their ability to contribute to the family group.

Intervention

With the changing patterns of teen pregnancy described above and concerns over the long-term consequences for society from children being reared by teen parents or single parents, calls for intervention have increased. Specifically, prior to the welfare reform of 1996, there was increasing concern over public funds supporting these families and frequent unsubstantiated charges that teens, and other poor single mothers, were having more babies just to increase their welfare benefits. In 1992, the U.S. government realized the importance of considering the experiences of teenage mothers and began pregnancy prevention programs in earnest. These programs, which largely target girls under the age of 16, were designed not only to discourage sexual activity but to educate young people about safer sexual practices. They generally worked off the assumption that all teen pregnancies were unwanted or unintended. While that does seem to be the majority experience, it does not fully describe teen childbearing.

Optimists predicted that these types of programs would reduce the numbers of teen pregnancies by half and increase the provision of sex education and contraceptive services for young people. It did, however, become an issue with parents as well as religiously conservative groups. While there are no definitive data, there is a concern that sex education will encourage teenagers to have sex by making them think more sexual thoughts or providing the sense that adults condone teenage sexual experimentation. Some school districts were concerned about parental reaction should they institute the federal program. Education proponents argued that if teenagers are not educated about sex, they will not know how to protect themselves, and the result will be pregnancy or an STD. Teenagers are curious and they are going to experiment regardless of whether they have had sex education. Proponents argued that another reason why teenagers have sex is peer pressure, and comprehensive sexuality education could help counter that.

Beginning with the George H. W. Bush administration, these education programs focused heavily on teaching young people about abstaining from sexual behavior until marriage. While this drew praise from conservative religious and political groups, it was not well received by those who work directly with teens, suggesting that it was too naive of an approach given the saturation of U.S. media with sexual images. Critical of the emphasis on abstinence of most government programs, sexuality researcher Ira Reiss (1991) has said on many occasions that vows of abstinence break far more easily than do condoms.

The government has not been the only organization working on the issue of teen pregnancy. In 1996, the National Campaign to Prevent Teen and Unplanned Pregnancy, a nonprofit private nonpartisan organization, was founded with the sole goal of reducing teen pregnancy rates by 30 percent in 10 years. Through grassroots work and media influence, it has been largely successful. Despite the decreases in teen pregnancy in recent years, the problems that teen mothers and their children face are daunting.

Problems with Teen Pregnancy

Politicians, educators, clergy, and the general public debate whether teen pregnancy is a serious problem in the United States. The negative consequences of teen pregnancy and parenting have been well documented by public and private agencies, including the well-regarded Annie E. Casey Foundation. The areas of concern include the children, the mothers, and society as a whole. Advocates stress that teen pregnancy is a serious problem, because teen pregnancy is linked to many negative circumstances for both teen parents and their children.

Health

Early childbearing puts teen girls at risk for health problems, both mentally and physically. Teens are at higher risk of death than older women during delivery; two to four times higher by some estimates. Young girls are faced with medical problems such as anemia, hemorrhage, and high blood pressure. These complications are particularly likely in the 10- to 14-year-old age group. Sexually active teens also have high rates of STD transmission, some of which can be passed on to their infants at birth. Infection during pregnancy can cause health problems with the fetus and miscarriage.

Primarily due to inadequate nutrition, adolescents are three times more likely to have a baby with low birth weight or to be delivered prematurely. Infants born to teenage mothers, then, are at greater risk for developmental and physical problems that require special medical care. The younger the teen is, the higher the chance that her baby will die in the first year of life.

Most teenage girls do not admit to being sexually active. When a young girl becomes pregnant, she may not tell anyone because she is in denial or is scared. When a teen does not reveal that she is pregnant, she puts herself and the fetus in serious danger. Teens are less likely to receive prenatal care when they hide their pregnancies from their family. Early and adequate prenatal care, preferably through a program that specializes in teenage pregnancies, ensures a healthier baby. The mother's and baby's health can depend on how mature the young woman is about keeping her doctor appointments and eating healthy. Sometimes, due to insurance limits or government policies, unmarried teens can be denied funding from the government or insurers, making safe pregnancies and deliveries difficult.

Adolescent mothers are more prone to smoke, use drugs, or consume alcohol during pregnancies than are older mothers. Their children are at increased risk of growth delay and dependence on chemical substances from the drug use. Adolescents' children are often in need of speech therapy, because they are behind in development. Teen mothers are less prepared for the tasks of child rearing, know less about child development, and are more likely to be depressed than other mothers.

Adolescent mothers and their children are faced with the same effects as most single-mother families. Single-mother families are one parent raising the children and taking on the role of mother and father. Coupled with teen mothers' greater chances of living in poverty and having a special-needs child, the tasks of parenting can seem overwhelming. This leads to high levels of stress. Additionally, studies indicate that these young women can have difficulty forming stable intimate relationships later. These concerns are compounded when the teen has inadequate social support.

Economy

One of the largest concerns regarding teen pregnancy is the poverty status of the teens and babies. Pregnancy reduces the likelihood of completing one's education, which—because the less educated a person is, the harder it is to have a good job with benefits—leads to poverty. Around 40 percent of teen mothers receive their high school diplomas. Low academic achievement is both a cause and consequence of teen pregnancy. Estimates suggest that about one-half of all teen moms will receive welfare payments within five years of the birth of their first child. This percentage increases to three-quarters when only unmarried teen mothers are considered.

Teenage childbearing places both the teen mother and her child at risk for low educational attainment. Her children will look at her as a role model; if she got pregnant early and dropped out of school, they may feel they should, too. Women who grow up in poor families are more likely to have been the offspring of a teen pregnancy. The children of teen mothers are more likely to be living in poor neighborhoods where schools may be underfunded, are unsafe, or are of low quality, thus not preparing them for the future. The children of teen mothers, perhaps due to diminished opportunities, can suffer from depression and low self-esteem.

Social Support

The support of family and friends is very helpful and much needed in the circumstance of teen pregnancy. Family and friends might make it possible for the teen to stay in school and continue her education. They can encourage adequate nutrition and prenatal health care. It is clear that there are substantial societal costs from teen pregnancies in the form of lost human capital and public welfare outlays, but support for the teen can assist her in positive parenting and active economic participation.

Teenagers may become sexually active for a number of reasons. Depending on how mature their bodies are, whether they are spending time around sexually active people, or how much television viewing and magazine reading they do, they may develop attitudes consistent with the group. This is why it is not uncommon for friends to become teen mothers and for sisters to have similar early pregnancy experiences. The social network is important in the outcomes. Teens are more at risk of becoming pregnant if they grow up in poverty, use alcohol or drugs, have no support from their family, have fewer friends, and have little interest or involvement in school activities.

There are differences in how families respond to the pregnancy of a teen daughter. More white girls live independently with their child after the birth, suggesting that their parents may be less accepting of such an outcome. Unfortunately, the children of

CROSS-CULTURAL COMPARISONS OF TEENAGE PREGNANCY

Data are consistently clear: teenagers in the United States are significantly more likely than comparable women in other developed countries to become pregnant. The Netherlands, Norway, Sweden, Iceland, France, Australia, New Zealand, Great Britain, and Canada are among the countries that have much lower rates of teen pregnancy than the United States. This leads those who work with teens to hypothesize about what is different for U.S. teens. Several factors are proposed. One is access to contraceptives and other family planning services. Many other nations have national health care systems that significantly reduce the costs of such services, making them easily accessible to all persons. Additional suggestions include American teen's ambivalence toward sexuality. Even though the media are saturated with sexual themes, they rarely communicate responsible attitudes toward sexuality. Risk-taking behaviors and an alienation of some groups from what are considered middle-class values have also been considered.

teens are disproportionately represented among the ranks of children who are abused and neglected, particularly when compared with the children of single mothers in their twenties. The children of teen mothers have a greater chance of themselves becoming teen parents, participating in delinquent acts, and being incarcerated.

Positives of Teen Pregnancy

While it seems that all of the news is bad regarding teen parenting and that more problems are created than solved, some positives can be found in the experiences of teens. Some teens might actually benefit from early childbearing. A small number of teens planned to have their children. These teens are not likely to abuse or neglect their children. They usually finish school and go on to successfully support themselves and their families. These are the teens who are most likely to be married, either before or after the birth, to the father of the child.

General stereotypes of teen mothers describe them as single, poor heads of families, but most teen mothers age 15 to 19 are not living independently with their children. The vast majority lives with relatives, including parents and, sometimes, husbands. By ethnicity, it is whites who are most likely to be living independently and with husbands. African American and Mexican American teens are most likely to be living with family members. This coresidence can provide significant support, both emotionally and financially. Through child care and other family-provided services, young mothers may be able to finish school and gain solid employment. In this way, pregnancy and mothering may only delay, not deny, their pursuit of successful adult lives. Some economists have indicated that black teens gain less of an economic advantage by waiting to have children than do white teens. The common stereotype of irresponsible teens who behave irrationally by becoming pregnant may need to be reconsidered when it is a response to deficient and discriminatory opportunities.

In some cases, teen pregnancy can be a way out of a troubled home life. Teens suggest that the true benefits of childbearing are having someone to love and someone who loves them. Sometimes the birth of a child can help them to heal scars from their own childhood. Some teens have suggested that they have used pregnancy as a way to leave an abusive home.

Controversies of Teen Pregnancy

Is Teen Pregnancy a Problem?

Although the number of teen pregnancies reached a historic low in 2004, this does not take the focus away from the situation, because teenage girls are still getting pregnant. Politicians, columnists, educators, researchers, and communities continue to argue that it is a serious problem. Almost every bad situation in society is blamed on teen pregnancies. Single parenting, poverty, delinquent children, school failure, drug abuse, child abuse, and crime have all pointed to teen pregnancy and birth as contributing factors. It seems that politicians use these data to raise the alarm in society and draw the public to their campaigns, often with the suggestion that ending poverty will be possible if teen pregnancies stop. Teen pregnancy can contribute to a given young person's chances of being poor, but it does not cause poverty. Many of these girls were living in poverty before getting pregnant. Consequently, teen pregnancy may just be the scapegoat for other social problems.

Sociologist Kristin Luker (1996) argues that adolescent girls are placed in the middle of a conflict between political factions that debate the issue of abstinence-only sex education compared with more comprehensive approaches. She argues that the phenomenon of teen pregnancy has been misidentified. Specifically, she indicates that teen pregnancies do not occur only in the United States. Although our rates might be higher, the problem is not uniquely ours. However, the racial and social class distribution of teen births causes many in the United States to see them as a problem. Significantly, the rates have been declining and are not out of control largely due to improved contraceptive use, particularly of long-acting contraception that does not require daily administration. Given that rates of sexual activity have increased over the same period that teen birth rates have declined, the pregnancy rates could be significantly higher than they are. Young people are physically mature at early ages today—the consequence of better nutrition and overall health—and development of their sexuality accompanies that. Luker also reminds us that the teen birth rate is not new; the mothers of the baby boom often began their child rearing in their late teens.

One of the interesting co-issues of teen pregnancy is why teen mothers are treated so much worse than are teen fathers. Young women face many more negative attributions than do young men. The message to young women seems to be, "we are okay with you exploring your sexuality; just don't get pregnant while doing so." Given that it takes both partners for conception, one wonders when the fathers will receive comparable scrutiny.

Should Pregnant Teens Marry the Fathers of Their Babies?

A popular suggestion for decreasing the negative effects of adolescent childbearing is for teens to marry the fathers of their children. They already receive pressure to declare the father's identity in order to receive state child support payments through public assistance. In the past, teens were more likely to marry before the birth. Today, however, only about 20 percent of teens marry the child's father before the birth.

When teens are encouraged to and actually get married, their children have a better prospect for success later in life simply because they will have a two-parent family. The two-parent family has many documented advantages over single-parent families. Greater financial stability and more complete socialization of children are cited as reasons why teens should marry. Teens might even hear the suggestion that they have already made one mistake by becoming pregnant; they don't want to make another by failing to provide legitimacy for the child. Teen marriages are actually more stable when children are present, but, on the whole, teen marriages are particularly prone to end in divorce.

Marrying, then, might be the bigger mistake. Most teenage girls do not get pregnant by a teenage boy but by an older man. Data indicate that more than 50 percent of the fathers of teen mothers' babies are between the ages of 20 and 24, around 30 percent of the fathers are adolescents themselves, and 15 percent are 25 or older. When teen mothers do marry, they tend to become pregnant again very quickly.

The suggestion that teens should marry the fathers of their babies fails to consider the long-term issues. The higher rates of dissolution were mentioned above. In both the United States and abroad, premarital pregnancy is correlated with a higher rate of divorce. When men are at least five years older or younger than their wives, they are more likely to divorce. There are also maturity and readiness factors to consider. Lack of coping skills, inadequate preparation for marriage, and fewer life experiences contribute to marital dissatisfaction. There also might be less support from the couple's friends and family for the marriage, which decreases the social pressure for the couple to stay together.

Is Adoption the Answer?

In the current climate of decreased negativity toward nonmarital childbearing, it seems unlikely that large numbers of teens will surrender their babies for adoption. With the stigma of teen parenting has significantly decreased, they may face more negativity for giving the child up for someone else to rear. It has always been the case that more white girls than black girls placed their children for adoption, and that pattern holds today.

However, the rapid decline in numbers of healthy white infants available via adoption has changed the adoption industry and pushed more families to adopt internationally.

Adoption may be the answer in that it permits the teen to get on with her life and allows her child the opportunity to have a two-parent family. Those teens who place their infants for adoption tend to be older, white, have higher educational goals, and are more likely to complete additional job training. They are more likely than teens who rear their children themselves to delay marriage and to live in higher-income households. Certainly there is initial sorrow and regret over the decision to relinquish a child, but these tend to be short-term experiences.

Conclusion

Teenage mothers and their children are at risk of difficulty in the areas of social environment, education, and economics. The major focus on teen parents is on the socio-economic outcomes of the mother. Literature on teenage mothers continues to show negative long-term consequences for early childbearing, including consistently low levels of education and a greater dependency on welfare. In some cases, people tend to see teen parents as uneducated, intolerant, impatient, insensitive, irritable, and prone to use both verbal and physical punishment. There is evidence that they are more likely than other parents to abuse their children. Economic success greatly depends on continuing school and not having more children. Older literature describes teen mothers as neglectful and unintelligent, but as research is updated, there are more positive effects of teenage parenting for the women and children involved.

See also **Abortion; Birth Control; Poverty and Public Assistance**

Further Reading

Annie E. Casey Foundation, http://www.aecf.org

Centers for Disease Control, "Preventing Teen Pregnancy: An Update in 2009." http://www.cdc.gov/reproductivehealth/AdolescentReproHealth/AboutTP.htm

Darrock, J. E., and S. Singh, "Why Is Teenage Pregnancy Declining? The Roles of Abstinence, Sexual Activity, and Contraceptive Use." In *Occasional Report*, no. 1. New York: Alan Guttmacher Institute, 1999.

Davis, Deborah, *You Look Too Young to Be a Mom: Teen Mothers on Love, Learning, and Success.* New York: Perigee, 2004.

Furstenberg, Frank F., *Destinies of the Disadvantaged: The Politics of Teenage Childbearing.* New York: Russell Sage Foundation, 2007.

Gottfried, Ted, *Teen Fathers Today.* Brookfield, CT: Twenty-First Century Books, 2001.

Hoffman, Saul D., and Rebecca A. Maynard, *Kids Having Kids: Economic Costs and Social Consequences of Teen Pregnancy.* Washington, DC: Urban Institute Press, 2008.

Luker, Kristin, *Dubious Conceptions: The Politics of Teenage Pregnancy.* Cambridge, MA: Harvard University Press, 1996.

National Campaign to Prevent Teen and Unplanned Pregnancy, http://www.thenationalcam
    paign.org

Planned Parenthood Federation of America, http://www.plannedparenthood.org

Reiss, Ira L., "Sexual Pluralism: Ending America's Sexual Crisis," *SEICUS Report* 19 (1991): 5–9.

Williams-Wheeler, Dorrie, *The Unplanned Pregnancy Book for Teens and College Students.* Virginia
    Beach, VA: Sparkledoll Productions, 2004.

V

VIDEO GAMES

Garry Crawford

Video games are an important entertainment industry and common leisure pursuit, played by people the world over. However, video games continue to be deeply controversial. Playing video games is often viewed as mainly the activity of adolescent boys, and games are seen as isolating and antisocial, creating a generation of socially dysfunctional and unfit children. Worse still, it is alleged that the often high levels of violence in many video games encourage heightened aggression in the vulnerable young minds of those who play them.

The origins of digital gaming can be traced back to the 1950s, but it was not until the late 1970s and 1980s that digital gaming began to develop as a common leisure activity. Today, video games are a major global industry. Global game sales exceed $48 billion, with the largest game market still undoubtedly in the United States, where game sales in 2008 reached nearly $12 billion. A recent poll by the Entertainment Software Association (ESA) suggested that 42 percent of all Americans planned on purchasing at least one game in the following year. Game sales are now comparable to cinema box office takings, and today more video games than books are sold in the United States and United Kingdom.

Gender

Contrary to popular belief, video game playing is not restricted solely to male adolescents. The ESA suggests that 82 percent of video game players are over the age of 17.

NAME OF THE GAME

The term *video games* is sometimes used to refer to all forms of electronic/digital games played on games consoles, computers, arcade machines, cell phones, and other gaming hardware, and sometimes it is used specifically to refer only to console games. To avoid confusion, some authors and organizations have adopted other terms such as *digital games* or *entertainment software* to refer to all forms of electronic gaming.

Though digital gaming is by no means a level playing field when it comes to gender, the ESA suggests that 47 percent of gamers are female, and in Johannes Fromme's study of over 1,000 German schoolchildren, almost a third of girls (and 55.7 percent of boys) claimed to "regularly" play digital games; it has been suggested that in Korea women make up to close to 70 percent of gamers (Krotoski 2004).

However, statistics on game-playing patterns, particularly in relation to gender, can hide continuing discrepancies and imbalances between the gaming patterns of men and women. Studies suggest that, on average, women continue to be less likely to play video games than men, and those who do play tend to play a lot less frequently than their male counterparts. In particular, these discrepancies are much greater for adult men and women. This is most likely because women's leisure time continues to be more restricted and fractured than men's and because video games continue to be created and marketed primarily toward men and feature stereotypically masculine themes, such as violence and male participation sports, with female characters often absent or sexualized within games (Crawford and Gosling 2005). Technology also continues to be primarily controlled by men (such as the placing of game machines in "male" spaces, such as the bedrooms of brothers), which means that game machines and gaming are infrequently seen as belonging to women within households.

Gaming as Violent

It is evident that violence or violent themes and action are present in a large proportion of video games, with some of the most successful and popular games such as the *Grand Theft Auto* series or *God of War* involving high levels of violent content. Games are now being used for military training and recruitment, such as *America's Army*. Because of this, some express concern that violence in video games can lead to heightened aggression. In particular, due to the interactive nature of gaming, some authors suggest that violence in video games could be more damaging than that seen in television and film. While television viewers are (largely) passive, video games often require players to actively direct the (in-game) aggression, and hence the aggression and violence is more "participatory" (Emes 1997). However, the relationship between violent games and gamers (as with violence on television and viewers) is far from conclusive. In particular, such research has been heavily criticized for its inconsistent methodologies and small and unrepresentative sample groups. It has also been criticized for overestimating the ability of games to influence the specific attitudes and behavior of individuals or groups and for seeing gamers as passive and vulnerable to representations of violence within games (Bryce and Rutter 2003).

Gamers as "Mouse Potatoes"

A further criticism often leveled at video gaming is that it is an antisocial and isolating activity, producing a generation of passive "mouse potatoes." However, this wholly negative attitude toward video gaming continues to be questioned in ongoing research. One study of over 200 London schoolchildren found no evidence to suggest that those who regularly played video games had fewer friends (Colwell and Payne 2000). Gamers are not "absent," but rather constitute active participants within the games they play. Digital gaming is an expression of human performance and can be a very sociable activity—with gamers playing each other online, meeting at conventions, and, more commonly, playing with friends or family members. In particular, research undertaken for the Interactive Software Federation of Europe suggests that 55 percent of gamers play with others.

Likewise, the argument that playing video games can negatively affect levels of sport participation has been challenged by several authors. For instance, Fromme's study of German schoolchildren found no evidence to support the assertion that playing video games reduces a child's participation in sport. On the contrary, his survey produced some evidence to suggest that daily use of digital games was positively associated with increased levels of sport participation. Similarly, a study of U.K. undergraduate students

MASSIVELY MULTIPLAYER ONLINE ROLE PLAYING GAMES (MMORPGS)

One of the biggest gaming phenomena of recent years has been the rapid growth of MMORPGs, such as *World of Warcraft*, *EverQuest*, and *Lineage*. These games allow the player to create characters (avatars) that they control and to play out adventures in an online world inhabited by other players from all over the (real) world. Games often allow characters to develop careers not just as warriors or wizards but also dancers, miners, or doctors; some games also allow players to own vehicles, pets, and property (such as houses and shops) and even get married. These games have proved hugely popular with many players, with *EverQuest* frequently referred to by gamers as EverCrack due to its "addictive" qualities. Nick Yee, who until 2009 ran a research Web site (the Daedalus Project) on MMORPGs, suggests that, on average, gamers who play MMORPGs spend 22 hours per week at them. By 2009, the number of players of *World of Warcraft* was about 12 million—greater than the population of Greece.

found no evidence to suggest that playing video games could have a negative affect on patterns of sport participation, but rather that sport-related video games could actually inform and increase both the interest in and knowledge of sport of some game players (Crawford 2005).

Gaming Theory

Video games have also grabbed the attention of researchers eager to understand the interaction between gamers and the games they play. However, different researchers and authors have adopted different approaches to studying video games. In particular, it is possible to identify a divide between theorists (such as Murray 2001), who have sought to understand video games by drawing on and developing a film and media studies approach, and those (such as Frasca 2003), who adopt a more psychologically influenced focus upon patterns of play (a perspective called ludology).

Adopting a media/film studies approach to video games does not simply mean that video games are viewed as interactive films, but it provides certain tools to help gain a more in-depth understanding of video games. For instance, some argue that games can be understood as a text, just as any other media form, such as a book, television show, or film. This text can then be studied to look for meanings, both obvious and hidden. From this perspective, it is also possible to study the narratives (stories and themes) within games in the same way we can with film or to study the rules and conventions of gaming using similar tools to those employed in understanding poetry.

However, some question whether video games can be understood as a text in the same way as older media forms (such as television, radio, and cinema), because, unlike these, video games are not set and rigid but can vary depending on how the player interacts with them (Kerr, Brereton, and Kücklich 2005). This is a similar argument offered by a ludology approach, which suggests that, while traditional media (such as films) are representational (i.e., they offer a simple representation of reality), video games are based on simulation, creating a world that gamers can manipulate and interact with.

Nevertheless, the degree of flexibility within a game should not be overemphasized. In particular, the degree of interactivity a gamer has with, or over, video games has been questioned by numerous authors. For instance, new technologies (such as DVDs) are frequently introduced and sold to the market using the selling point of their increased interactive qualities. The user's level of control or interaction with the medium, though, is still restricted by not only the limitations of technology but also the aims of the designers and manufacturers.

A limitation with early studies that draw on both film/media and ludology approaches is that, in many cases, gamers were frequently seen as isolated individuals rather than understood within a wider social setting. However, there is an increasing awareness of the need to include an understanding of the role and importance of gaming within its social setting, such as how people talk about games with friends and family, how they fit into leisure patterns and everyday lives, and how they can inform some people's identity and sense of who they are (Crawford and Rutter 2007).

Conclusion

Video gaming today is a major leisure and cultural activity, engaged in by many people all around the world, often taking up a sizable proportion of their leisure time. As with any cultural activity, it is impossible to categorize this as either wholly good or bad. Video games are often violent and can be sexist, homophobic, and racist—as can any media form, such as film, music, and literature. However, video games are also an important industry; they allow people to relax and can be a source of conversation and identity for many. It is therefore important that we understand gaming within a wider social and cultural setting—sometimes as shocking, sometimes awe-inspiring, but more often a relatively normal and mundane pastime engaged in, and discussed, by many.

See also **Violence and Media; Internet (vol. 4)**

Further Reading

Bissell, Tom, *Extra Lives: Why Video Games Matter.* New York: Pantheon, 2010.

Brown, Harry J., *Video Games and Education.* Armonk, NY: M. E. Sharpe, 2008.

Bryce, Jo, and Jason Rutter, "Gender Dynamics and the Social and Spatial Organization of Computer Gaming." *Leisure Studies* 22 (2003): 1–15.

Colwell, John, and J. Payne, "Negative Correlates of Computer Game Play in Adolescents." *British Journal of Psychology* 91 (2000): 295–310.

Crawford, Garry, "Digital Gaming, Sport and Gender." *Leisure Studies* 24, no. 3 (2005): 259–270.

Crawford, Garry, and Victoria K. Gosling, "Toys for Boys? Women's Marginalization and Participation as Digital Gamers." *Sociological Research Online* 10, no. 1 (2005). http://www.socreson line.org.uk/10/1/crawford.html

Crawford, Garry, and Jason Rutter, "Playing the Game: Performance in Digital Game Audiences." In *Fandom: Identities and Communities in a Mediated World,* ed. Jonathan Gray, Cornel Sandvoss, and C. Lee Harrington. New York: New York University Press, 2007.

Egenfeldt-Nielsen, Simon, et al., *Understanding Video Games: The Essential Introduction.* New York: Routledge, 2008.

Emes, Craig E., "Is Pac Man Eating Our Children? A Review of the Effects of Video Games on Children." *Canadian Journal of Psychiatry* 42 (1997): 409–414.

Entertainment Software Association, http://www.theesa.com

Frasca, Gonzalo, "Simulation versus Narrative: Introduction to Ludology." In *The Video Game Theory Reader,* ed. Mark J. P Wolf and Bernard Perron. New York: Routledge, 2003.

Fromme, Johannes, "Computer Games as a Part of Children's Culture." *Game Studies* 3, no. 1 (2003). http://www.gamestudies.org/0301/fromme

Gee, James Paul, *What Video Games Have to Tell Us about Learning and Literacy,* 2d ed. New York: Palgrave Macmillan, 2007.

Kelly, R. V., *Massively Multiplayer Online Role-Playing Games.* Jefferson, NC: McFarland, 2004.

Kerr, Aphra, Pat Brereton, and Julian Kücklich, "New Media—New Pleasures?" *International Journal of Cultural Studies* 8, no. 3 (2005): 375–394.

Krotoski, Aleks, *Chicks and Joysticks: An Exploration of Women and Gaming.* London: Entertainment and Leisure Software Publisher's Association, 2004.

Murray, Janet H., *Hamlet on the Holodeck: The Future of Narrative in Cyberspace.* Cambridge, MA: MIT Press, 2001.

Newman, James, *Videogames.* New York: Routledge, 2004.

Perron, Bernard, and Mark J. P. Wolf, eds., *The Video Game Theory Reader 2.* New York: Routledge, 2008.

Rutter, Jason, and Jo Bryce, eds., *Understanding Digital Games.* Thousand Oaks, CA: Sage, 2006.

Vorderer, Peter, and Jennings Bryant, eds., *Playing Video Games: Motives, Responses, and Consequences,* Mahwah, NJ: Lawrence Erlbaum, 2006.

Yee, Nick, *The Daedalus Project.* http://www.nickyee.com/daedalus

VIOLENCE AND MEDIA

Talmadge Wright

Concerns about media and violence have historical roots going back to the Victorian era, when the newly emerging middle classes expressed anxiety over the working class reading "penny dreadfuls" instead of more wholesome fare such as "morally uplifting" literature. The modern era, on the other hand, led to numerous studies that have become known as the "media effects" literature, which has sought to demonstrate a causal connection between media representations and acts of real violence. While some claim to have demonstrated behavioral effects of media violence, critics charge that the research is flawed in various ways. Many also claim that debates over media and violence are often a cover for other anxieties that remain too threatening for many people to talk about. What are the real issues being concealed by the debates over media and violence?

For the past 40 years, researchers have been investigating what effects exposure to violent images have on children and adults, especially with regard to stimulating aggression or aggressive thoughts. The results of this mountain of studies remain inconclusive, with causal links between images of violence and actual violent or aggressive behavior hard to track with any degree of accuracy. Early studies attempted to document the impact that violent movie images had on children, followed by television images and now video game interactions. Critics say these research models are flawed and suffer in differing degrees from inadequately defined objects of study, inconsistent definitions, misapplied research methodologies, experimental limitations, and grossly simplified models of human behavior. Nevertheless, these studies have shaped public debate on the relationship of media technology, play, and child development. A brief word is in order about what concepts these studies have been based upon and the definitions of violence and aggression that underlie them.

The obvious question to ask is what is meant by violence and aggression with regard to media and its effect on people. The problem resides in both the conflation of real violence with its representation in TV, film, or video games and in what activity is presumed to be violent or aggressive. In some studies, the Three Stooges, Roadrunner, and Bugs Bunny are placed in the same category as horror slasher films and real news violence, simply based on the actions of the characters involved—who hit whom, how often, and so on. There is no meaningful distinction drawn between real and fictional violent representations or between types of fictional violent representations and their contexts. The second point is the meaning of effects. It is presumed that media have effects on people, but what those effects are is presumed to revolve around aggressive or passive activity, as if these are the only ways to understand how media influences individual behavior. For example, we rarely ask what kind of effect book reading, bicycling, or playing football has on subjects unless we have a predetermined answer in mind. Thus, some people would object to others reading certain kinds of books because of the violent or sexual imagery conveyed through words. However, this speaks less to the position of the reader and more to the concerns of the one objecting to the material. In other words, what is measured, if anything, is more the subjective concern of the researcher or the offense to those who would act as moral arbiter and less the actual effect on the subject in question. Those skeptical of media effects studies charge that researchers consistently draw spurious causal connections between data that remain mere correlations and point to the following conceptual confusion and logical flaws: (1) the simplistic theories of self used by some psychologists and child development specialists; (2) the moral agendas of political figures and those with a religious or cultural objection to media representations; and (3) legitimate concerns by parents who perceive their children as "out of control."

Models and Traditions of Research

Social learning theory, developed by psychologist Alberto Bandura in the 1970s, is a modification of B. F. Skinner's behaviorist theories applied to adolescents and aggression. His research attempted to understand the interactions between the self and environment (reciprocal determinism) and set the initial standard for conducting studies of media and violence. Based on principles of observational learning or modeling therapy and self-regulation, Bandura illustrated his points with the famous Bobo doll studies. In these experiments, he had a fellow experimenter strike a Bobo doll, designed for that very purpose, while children observed on a TV monitor. When given the Bobo doll, the same children proceeded to strike the doll as they had witnessed. This was considered evidence that children model the behavior of others. What was not considered was the meaning the Bobo doll had for the children. The doll was designed to be struck, so this tells us little about aggression connected to modeling behavior, other than the children figured out this is what you are supposed to do with this type of toy. What was demonstrated was the authority of the experimenter more than any inherent aggression as a by-product of modeling behavior.

Bandura claimed that effective modeling depended on various degrees of attention, retention, motor reproduction, and motivation. He argued that children model the behavior of adults and other children, including media representations; hence, the concern over the consumption of violent media images. While this can explain the fact that people do model the behavior of others—even virtual others—it cannot explain what that modeling means to the individual. The issue of motivation is central but cannot be answered by this type of behaviorist framework, because it does not offer an explanation for how interpretation can modify behavior. How do children, in fact, understand violent media representations, and do they make distinctions between real and fictional violence?

Anderson and Bushman's General Aggression Model (GAM), based on the earlier work of Bandura and others, attempted to go beyond the limitations of social learning theory, assigning priority to feelings, thoughts, and physical responses to violent media in specific situations leading to a presumed interpretation on the part of the subject. The problem, however, resides in how the GAM understands violence and aggression. The GAM perspective is often guilty of conflating the violence of horror films and shooter video games with the supposed earlier violence of Pac-Man, argued as desensitizing the public to real-life violence. Again, the issue is one of understanding the differences between real-life aggression and violence and fantasy aggression or violence. This conflation is made consistently by critics of violent media representations.

The catharsis model, meanwhile, assumed that consuming violent media works to *lower* aggression, to "let off steam." A favorite position of defenders of violent films, TV shows, and video games, the catharsis model was based on the work of Seymour Feshbach and Robert D. Sanger, in *Television and Aggression: An Experimental Field Study*, conducted in 1971. This model attempted to offer evidence that people can benefit from consuming violent fantasies since they can provide a safe way of coping with anxieties and general fears. Unfortunately, their studies have not been adequately replicated and remain more of a hypothesis than a testable reality.

The cultivation theory of George Gerbner, former dean of the Annenberg School for Communication at the University of Pennsylvania, proposed a broader cultural or ideological critique of violent media. Often referred to as the "mean world syndrome," cultivation theory used content analysis and surveys, avoiding the problems of the experimental laboratory setup. Cultivation theory argued that heavy consumption of media led to the cultural effects of political passivity and a greater tolerance for real-world violence. The problem here is that fearful people may be drawn to watching more television for a variety of reasons, which points out the additional problem of not addressing individual variations in how people consume and understand media.

Critics of Effects Research

Jonathan Freedman, in *Media Violence and Its Effect on Aggression: Assessing the Scientific Evidence,* examined most of the experimental studies conducted on violence in media and found them lacking in consistent definitions of what constitutes aggression or violence and containing flawed methods of research and a continuing confusion of correlation with causation. The work of Barker and Petley in their volume, *Ill Effects: The Media/Violence Debate,* along with the work of David Gauntlett in that same book, deepens the critique voiced by Freedman. One of the major flaws of these studies is their set of assumptions about human subjects. These assumptions give no room for people, children, or adults to interpret or make sense of their own actions. Meaning, though, is important. How we understand fantasy and reality, imagination and reason, aggressive play and real assault, is critical in our ability to assess risk to ourselves and to others. The media effects perspective, unfortunately, does not take meaning seriously, assuming that people are either overtly or covertly manipulated into believing and acting the way that they do simply by exposure to media images. The larger social context within which we understand images, our everyday lives, families, social groups, and so forth is almost never integrated into this type of research on media and violence.

For example, Jeffrey Goldstein argues that the absence of volition in media effects research combined with not taking seriously the social context of media consumption distorts the understanding of the role media play in the lives of children and adults. Some researchers take this lack of choice even further, arguing that the meanings we make of media violence are not significant, because our making sense of the world is only accomplished through predetermined social lenses that condition us to look at the world in a very specific way—what is often called interpolation. This position is refuted by the research of James Tobin, who in *Good Guys Don't Wear Hats: Children's Talk about the Media* looked at how children actually understood the film medium, violent or otherwise, and pointed out the wide variety of interpretations children make of their experiences with media. Violent images may frighten one child and simply bore another. One cannot find a given interpretation as the correct one way to understand fictional violence over any other.

The real social lives of humans, our families, friends, and authority figures—that is, the larger social context—do indeed shape our responses to violent media images. The degree to which each of these variables influences behavior, and the combination of these multiple influences on behavior, has proven to be the most difficult measure for media researchers. Further complicating research models remains the distinction between fantasy violence and real violence, a differentiation especially important for children. Children must make these distinctions in order to understand how to survive

MORAL PANICS AND MEDIA FEARS

Moral panic was a term originally developed by Stanley Cohen in his 1972 book *Folk Devils and Moral Panics: The Creation of Mods and Rockers*. He described the organized public campaign of harassment against the emerging youth subculture of mods and rockers by the media and agents of public control, law enforcement, politicians and legislators, action groups, and the public at large. This panic over an emerging youth subculture was stimulated by converting mods and rockers into folk devils, as repositories of public anxieties over widespread social change. Erich Goode and Nachman Ben-Yehuda in *Moral Panics: The Social Construction of Deviance* as well as Barry Glassner's *The Culture of Fear: Why Americans Are Afraid of the Wrong Things* and Karen Sternheimer's *It's Not the Media: The Truth about Pop Culture's Influence on Children* extend this analysis to all types of media representations. Earlier examples of media moral panics can be seen during the 1950s with the moral campaign, organized by Dr. Fredric Wertham, a New York psychiatrist, that attacked horror comic books as contributing to juvenile delinquency. As John Springhall points out in his book, *Youth, Popular Culture and Moral Panics: Penny Gaffs to Gangsta-Rap, 1820–1996*, these patterns of social dread reflected the anxiety and fears of an emerging middle class over a corruptible working class who ignored socially "uplifting" reading in favor of "dime novels" or "penny dreadfuls." Harold Schechter, in *Savage Pastime: A Cultural History of Violent Entertainment*, describes the extreme forms of entertainment that both the middle and working classes of pre-Victorian Europe enjoyed, making modern-day panics over television, film, and video game violence seem silly by comparison.

in the real world. Adults can more easily blur these distinctions if they have already established what is real and what is fantasy to begin with. Tobin's studies demonstrate that children make this distinction between fantasy and reality at a very early age.

Hence, it is not surprising that advertisers and filmmakers work hard to break these barriers down in order to cement audience identification with the product or film work at an early age. However, the fact that customers, whether children or adults, play with these boundaries through their own critiques, jokes, parodies, imitations, and other forms of meaning-making, indicates that humans are active producers often at odds with commercial producers.

Moral Panics and Moral Entrepreneurs

The persistence of controversy around media effects research may be understood as a deeper crisis in how we think of children, technology, and threats in the modern world. These periodic concerns expressed as anxiety over media violence are given the term *moral panics*.

Moral panics are public campaigns that often call for censorship or express outrage at behavior or fantasies of particular lower-status social groups when those same groups are perceived as escaping the control of the dominant status group. They occur often during periods of social and technological change and may crystallize around a particular emotional issue. The early Salem witch burnings were facilitated by the panic induced by male clergy members who felt threatened by the increasing power of women in the church. Closer to our time period, concerns over comic books, pool hall attendance, heavy metal and rap music, television violence and sex, films, and a host of media activities have come under public scrutiny for their supposed corruption of morals and youth. In the 1980s, the Parents Music Resource Center went after heavy metal bands for their supposed effect on youth and the belief that such music caused teenage suicides. Today, it is conservative groups like Focus on the Family attacking Barbie dolls and Shrek or the Parents Television Council decrying acts of television violence and gore, while liberal groups attack the computer games *Manhunt* and *Grand Theft Auto* for their racial and gender stereotypes and simulated sex in hidden codes. While racists and sexist attitudes persist in U.S. society, the degree to which media cause those attitudes has yet to be demonstrated by effects research, and media and First Amendment scholars argue that the values of an open society and that the attendant civil liberties enjoyed therein outweigh unproven media effects assertions.

What is interesting is that, in most of the qualitative studies of children and media violence, when asked whether they were affected by violent images, most children responded with the assertion that they were not affected, but their younger peers were affected. Middle-class parents often voiced the same concerns—they are not affected but those lower-class folks down the block might be harmed. In other words, the panic over media and violence can be clearly viewed as a panic over status and power, with the

MORAL ENTREPRENEURS AND MEDIA CONSUMPTION

Originally coined by the sociologist Howard Becker in his 1963 work, *Outsiders: Studies in the Sociology of Deviance*, moral entrepreneurs work as crusading reformers attempting to clean up what they perceive as the failure of lower-status groups. With humanitarian intents, such groups and individuals often work in a paternalist fashion to shape the behavior of those in social classes below them, usually taking on and being offended by the representations of working- or lower-class culture. Moral entrepreneurs work to mobilize social groups and the public at large against what they perceive as threats to the dominant social order, helping to define what is considered deviant behavior. The use of labeling and stereotyping often operates in constructing definitions of what is deviant. These labels are, in turn, used by moral entrepreneurs to support their actions against the offending representations. For example, by invoking moral outrage against rock music, the Parents Music Resource Center signaled to concerned parents that it shared their values and concerns. This solidarity is, in turn, cemented by creating an out group, while reinforcing the prejudices of the in group.

higher-status groups—parents over children, middle class over working or lower class, whites over blacks, and so on—asserting their so-called moral authority in order to protect some supposed moral boundary of society.

The fact that these concerns over media and violence are most often promoted by advocacy groups who claim that they have children's welfare at stake, as well as media pundits, politicians looking for votes, and professional experts and organizations, indicates that the issue of media violence is one that lends itself to the work of moral entrepreneurs. Occupying a privileged position in society, such moral entrepreneurs are able to exploit their social position to assert their authority in reinforcing conventional "common-sense" folkways that appeal to many parents anxious over the behavior of their children.

"Out of Control": Fears of Youth and Technology

The third point, that parents feel their children are out of their control, is understandable given the rapid rates of technological change, the decrease in public play areas, the rise of the Internet, and the expansion of widespread social and political inequality leading to less opportunities in life for members of both the working and middle classes. According to Henry Jenkins of the University of Southern California's Annenberg School for Communication, the moral panic that surrounds the issues of violence and media can be traced to fear and anxieties over adolescent behavior, a fear of new technology, and the expansion of youth culture throughout the media landscape into all areas of everyday life. In addition, the deep fear of the intermingling of the private and public spheres of everyday life is expressed not only in terms of parental fear of children being exposed to media violence but also in images of sexuality and online predatory behavior. Given the widespread adult ignorance of technology and science, it should not be surprising that when their son or daughter knows more about the technology than they do, parents feel at a distinct disadvantage. Such competency on the part of one's children raises a host of questions about parental authority as well as ideas of childhood innocence, which is challenged as children gain more knowledge through the Internet, television, and film.

Conclusion

The old Victorian myth of innocent children without greed, desire, or competency is under attack. The response by parents is often to either demonize children, ignore them, or idealize them as little angels, all revealing a lack of understanding of the complex reality of childhood in the modern world. But seeing technology and media violence as destroying the innocence of childhood is just as misleading as assuming that children are powerful liberators of modern technology and can easily withstand onslaughts of media violence. What is required, as Gerard Jones points out in *Killing Monsters: Why Children Need Fantasy, Super Heroes, and Make-Believe Violence,* is for children to feel safe in playing with their fantasy monsters, whether it is in a book, on television, in film, or in a video game. Playing with and killing monsters in a fantasy world may be just another way to keep these monsters from becoming our everyday harsh realities.

See also **Video Games; Marketing to Children (vol. 1); Internet (vol. 4)**

Further Reading

Anderson, Craig A., and B. J. Bushman, "Human Aggression." *Annual Review of Psychology* 53 (2002): 27–51.

Anderson, Craig A., Douglas A. Gentile, and Katherine E. Buckley, *Violent Video Game Effects on Children and Adolescents: Theory, Research, and Public Policy.* New York: Oxford University Press, 2007.

Bandura, Albert, *Aggression: A Social Learning Analysis.* Englewood Cliffs, NJ: Prentice Hall, 1973.

Bandura, Albert, *Social Learning Theory.* New York: General Learning Press, 1977.

Barker, Martin, and Julian Petley, eds., *Ill Effects: The Media/Violence Debate.* New York: Routledge, 2001.

Becker, Howard, *Outsiders: Studies in the Sociology of Deviance.* New York: Free Press, 1997.

Buckingham, David, *After the Death of Childhood: Growing up in the Age of Electronic Media.* Malden, MA: Polity, 2005.

Cohen, Stanley, *Folk Devils and Moral Panics,* 3d ed. London and New York: Routledge, 2002.

Feshbach, Seymour, and Robert D. Singer, *Television and Aggression: An Experimental Field Study.* San Francisco: Jossey-Bass, 1971.

Freedman, Jonathan L., *Media Violence and Its Effect on Aggression: Assessing the Scientific Evidence.* Toronto: University of Toronto Press, 2002.

Gauntlett, David, "The Worrying Influence of 'Media Effects' Studies." In *Ill Effects: The Media/ Violence Debate,* eds. Martin Barker and Julian Petley. New York: Routledge, 2001.

Gerbner, George, Larry Gross, Michael Morgan, and Nancy Signorielli, "Growing Up with Television: The Cultivation Perspective." In *Media Effects: Advances in Theory and Research,* ed. Jennings Bryant and Dolf Zillman. Hillsdale, NJ: Lawrence Erlbaum, 1994.

Glassner, Barry, *The Culture of Fear: Why Americans Are Afraid of the Wrong Things.* New York: Basic Books, 1999.

Goldstein, Jeffrey H., "Does Playing Violent Video Games Cause Aggressive Behavior?" *Playing by the Rules: The Cultural Policy Challenges of Video Games Conference,* Cultural Policy Center, University of Chicago. October 27, 2001. http://culturalpolicy.uchicago.edu/conf2001/papers/ goldstein.html

Goldstein, Jeffrey H., *Why We Watch: The Attractions of Violent Entertainment.* New York: Oxford University Press, 1998.

Goode, Erich, and Nachman Ben-Yehuda, *Moral Panics: The Social Construction of Deviance,* 2d ed. Hoboken, NJ: Wiley-Blackwell, 2009.

Jenkins, Henry, *Fans, Bloggers, and Gamers: Exploring Participatory Culture.* New York: New York University Press, 2006.

Jones, Gerard, *Killing Monsters: Why Children Need Fantasy, Super Heroes, and Make-Believe Violence.* New York: Basic Books, 2002.

Schechter, Harold, *Savage Pastime: A Cultural History of Violent Entertainment.* New York: St. Martin's Press, 2005.

Springhall, John, *Youth, Popular Culture and Moral Panics: Penny Gaffs to Gangsta-Rap, 1820–1996.* New York: St. Martin's Press, 1998.

Sternheimer, Karen, *It's Not the Media: The Truth about Pop Culture's Influence on Children.* Boulder, CO: Westview Press, 2003.

Tobin, Joseph, *Good Guys Don't Wear Hats: Children's Talk about the Media.* New York: Teachers College Press, 2000.

Trend, David, *The Myth of Media Violence: A Critical Introduction.* Hoboken, NJ: Wiley-Blackwell, 2007.

Bibliography

Family, Marriage, and Divorce

AARP, http://www.aarp.org

Adoption Media, http://www.adoption.com

Ahrons, Constant, *We're Still Family: What Grown Children Have to Say about Their Parents' Divorce*. New York: Harper Paperbacks, 2005.

Almanac of Policy Issues, http://www.policyalmanac.org

American Civil Liberties Union, http://www.aclu.org/religion/index.html

Berg-Weger, Marla, *Caring for Elderly Parents*. New York: Garland Publishing, 1996.

Cantor, Donald J., et al., *Same-Sex Marriage: The Legal and Psychological Evolution in America*. Middletown, CT: Wesleyan University Press, 2006.

Celello, Kristin, *Making Marriage Work: A History of Marriage and Divorce in the United States*. Chapel Hill: University of North Carolina Press, 2009.

Child Welfare League of America, http://www.cwla.org

Clayton, Obie, et al., eds., *Black Fathers in Contemporary American Society: Strengths, Weaknesses, and Strategies for Change*. New York: Russell Sage Foundation, 2005.

Coles, Roberta L., and Charles Green, eds., *The Myth of the Missing Black Father*. New York: Columbia University Press, 2010.

Coontz, Stephanie, *The Way We Never Were: American Families and the Nostalgia Trap*. New York: HarperCollins, 1992.

Crittenden, Ann, *The Price of Motherhood: Why the Most Important Job in the World Is Still the Least Valued*. New York: Henry Holt, 2002.

Demo, David, and Mark A. Fine, *Beyond the Average Divorce*. Thousand Oaks, CA: Sage, 2009.

Dorow, Sara K., *Transnational Adoption: A Cultural Economy of Race, Gender, and Kinship*. New York: New York University Press, 2006.

Douglas, Susan, and Meredith Michaels, *The Mommy Myth: The Idealization of Motherhood and How It Has Undermined All Women.* New York: Free Press, 2004.

Drescher, Jack, and Deborah Glazer, *Gay and Lesbian Parenting.* New York: Informa Healthcare, 2001.

Duerr, Jill, and Bruce Fuller, eds., *Good Parents or Good Workers? How Policy Shapes Families' Daily Lives.* New York: Palgrave Macmillan, 2005.

Emery, Robert E., *Marriage, Divorce and Children's Adjustment,* 2d ed. Thousand Oaks, CA: Sage, 1999.

Family Research Council, http://www.frc.org

Focus on the Family, http://www.family.org

Gailey, Christine Ward, *Blue-Ribbon Babies and Labors of Love: Race, Class, and Gender in U.S. Adoption Practice.* Austin: University of Texas Press, 2010.

Hamer, Jennifer, *What It Means to Be Daddy: Fatherhood for Black Men Living Away from Their Children.* New York: Columbia University Press, 2001.

Hays, Sharon, *The Cultural Contradictions of Motherhood.* New Haven, CT: Yale University Press, 1998.

Heins, Marjorie, *Not in Front of the Children: "Indecency," Censorship, and the Innocence of Youth.* New York: Hill and Wang, 2001.

Henry, Stella Mora, with Ann Convery, *The Eldercare Handbook: Difficult Choices, Compassionate Solutions.* New York: HarperCollins, 2006.

Hetherington, E. Mavis, and John Kelly, *For Better or For Worse: Divorce Reconsidered.* New York: W. W. Norton, 2002.

hooks, bell, *Ain't I a Woman: Black Women and Feminism.* Boston: South End Press, 1981.

Johnson and Johnson, Caregiver Initiative. http://www.strengthforcaring.com

Mandel, Deena, *Deadbeat Dads: Subjectivity and Social Construction.* Toronto: University of Toronto Press, 2002.

Metz, Tamara, *Untying the Knot: Marriage, the State, and the Case for Divorce.* Princeton, NJ: Princeton University Press, 2010.

National Aging in Place Council, http://www.naipc.org

National Council for Adoption, http://www.adoptioncouncil.org

Patton, Sandra, *BirthMarks: Transracial Adoption in Contemporary America.* New York: New York University Press, 2000.

Pinello, D. R., *America's Struggle for Same-Sex Marriage.* New York: Cambridge University Press, 2006.

Quiroz, Pamela Ann, *Adoption in a Color-Blind Society.* Lanham, MD: Rowman & Littlefield, 2007.

Rimmerman, Craig A., and Clyde Wilcox, *The Politics of Same-Sex Marriage.* Chicago: University of Chicago Press, 2007.

Rose, E., *A Mother's Job: A History of Day Care 1890–1960.* New York: Oxford University Press, 1999.

Strong, Bryan, Christine DeVault, and Theodore. F. Cohen, *The Marriage and Family Experience,* 11th ed. Belmont, CA: Wadsworth, 2010.

United States Department of Health and Human Services, http://www.hhs.gov

Yancy, George A., and Richard Lewis Jr., *Interracial Families: Current Concepts and Controversies.* New York: Routledge, 2009.

Children and Young People

Agnew, Robert, *Juvenile Delinquency: Causes and Control,* 3d ed. New York: Oxford University Press, 2008.

Bernstein, Nina, *The Lost Children of Wilder: The Epic Struggle to Change Foster Care.* New York: Vintage Books, 2001.

Bitensky, Susan H., *Corporal Punishment of Children: A Human Rights Violation.* Ardsley, NY: Transnational, 2006.

Brown, Lyn Mikel, *Girlfighting: Betrayal and Rejection among Girls.* New York: New York University Press, 2003.

Brumberg, Joan Jacobs, *The Body Project: An Intimate History of American Girls.* New York: Random House, 1997.

Child Welfare Information Gateway, http://www.childwelfare.gov

Child Welfare League of America, *Quick Facts about Foster Care.* Washington, DC, 2010. http://www.cwla.org/programs/fostercare/factsheet.htm

Childhelp USA Foundation, http://www.childhelpusa.org

Children's Defense Fund, http://childrensdefense.org

Clark, Alison, and Virginia Allhusen, *What about Childcare.* Cambridge, MA: Harvard University Press, 2005.

Crowley, Jocelyn, *The Politics of Child Support in America.* New York: Cambridge University Press, 2003.

Disch, Estelle, *Reconstructing Gender: A Multicultural Anthology.* Boston: McGraw Hill Higher Education, 2009.

Donnelly, Michael, and Murray A. Stras, eds., *Corporal Punishment of Children in Theoretical Perspective.* New Haven, CT: Yale University Press, 2005.

Krebs, Betsy, *Beyond the Foster Care System: The Future for Teens.* New Brunswick, NJ: Rutgers University Press, 2006.

Lindsey, D., *The Welfare of Children.* New York: Oxford University Press, 1994.

National Association of Former Foster Care Children of America, http://www.naffcca.org

National Foster Parent Association, *History of Foster Care in the United States.* Washington, DC, 2007. http://www.nfpainc.org/content/index.asp?page=67&nmenu=3

Pew Commission on Children in Foster Care, http://pewfostercare.org

Pickering, Kathleen, et al., *Welfare Reform in Persistent Rural Poverty: Dreams, Disenchantment, and Diversity.* University Park: Pennsylvania State University Press, 2006.

Prothrow-Stith, Deborah, *Deadly Consequences: How Violence Is Destroying Our Teenage Population and a Plan to Begin Solving the Problem.* New York: HarperCollins, 1991.

Quinn, William H., *Family Solutions for Youth at Risk: Applications to Juvenile Delinquency, Truancy, and Behavior Problems.* New York: Brunner-Routledge, 2004.

Ramsey, Sarah H., and Douglas E. Abrams, *Children and the Law in a Nutshell,* 2d ed. St. Paul, MN: Thomson/West, 2003.

Urban Institute, http://www.urban.org

Waldfogel, Jane, *What Children Need*. Cambridge, MA: Harvard University Press, 2008.

Wozniak, Danielle F., *They're All My Children: Foster Mothering in America*. New York: New York University Press, 2002.

Zigler, Edward, Katherine Marsland, and Heather Lord, *The Tragedy of Child Care in America*. New Haven, CT: Yale University Press, 2009.

Family and Economic Issues

Blair-Loy, Mary, *Competing Devotions: Career and Family among Women Executives*. Cambridge, MA: Harvard University Press, 2005.

Blank, Rebecca, and Ron Hoskins, *The New World of Welfare*. Washington, DC: Brookings Institution Press, 2001.

Blau, J., *The Visible Poor*. New York: Oxford University Press, 1993.

Cancian, Maria, and Sheldon Danziger, eds., *Changing Poverty, Changing Policies*. New York: Russell Sage Foundation, 2009.

Chappell, Marisa, *The War on Welfare: Family, Poverty, and Politics in Modern America*. Philadelphia: University of Pennsylvania Press, 2010.

Currie, Janet M., *The Invisible Safety Net*. Princeton, NJ: Princeton University Press, 2006.

Grogger, Jeffrey, and Lynn A. Karoly, *Welfare Reform: Effects of a Decade of Change*. Cambridge, MA: Harvard University Press, 2005.

Hesse-Biber, Sharlene, and Gregg Lee Carter, *Working Women in America: Split Dreams*. New York: Oxford University Press, 2004.

Hochschild, Arlie Russell, *The Time Bind: When Work Becomes Home and Home Becomes Work*. New York: Henry Holt, 2001.

Jencks, C., *The Homeless*. Cambridge, MA: Harvard University Press, 1995.

Landry, Bart, *Black Working Wives: Pioneers of the American Family Revolution*. Berkeley: University of California Press, 2002.

McNamara, Robert Hartmann, *Homelessness in America*. Westport, CT: Greenwood Press, 2008.

Padavic, Irene, and Reskin, Barbara, *Women and Men at Work*. Thousand Oaks, CA: Pine Forge Press, 2002.

Williams, Joan, *Unbending Gender: Why Family and Work Conflict and What to Do about It*. New York: Oxford University Press, 2001.

Family Medical, Behavioral, and Ethical Issues

Ali, Syed F., and Michael J. Kuhar, eds., *Drug Addiction: Research Frontiers and Treatment Advances*. Boston: Blackwell, 2008.

Annie E. Casey Foundation, http://www.aecf.org

Assael, Shaun, *Steroid Nation: Juiced Home Run Totals, Anti-Aging Miracles, and a Hercules in Every High School*. New York: ESPN Books, 2007.

Beamish, R., and Ritchie, I., *Fastest, Highest, Strongest: A Critique of High-Performance Sport*. London: Routledge, 2006.

Bonnie, Richard J., and Robert B. Wallace, *Elder Mistreatment: Abuse, Neglect, and Exploitation in an Aging America.* Washington, DC: National Academies Press, 2003.

Bruch, Hilde, *The Golden Cage: The Enigma of Anorexia Nervosa.* Cambridge, MA: Harvard University Press, 1978.

Brumberg, Joan Jacobs, *Fasting Girls: The History of Anorexia Nervosa.* Cambridge, MA: Harvard University Press, 1988.

Burnham, John, *Bad Habits: Drinking, Smoking, Taking Drugs, Gambling, Sexual Misbehavior, and Swearing in American History.* New York: New York University Press, 1994.

Campbell, Nancy D., *Discovering Addiction: The Science and Politics of Substance Abuse Research.* Ann Arbor: University of Michigan Press, 2007.

Caron, Simone M., *Who Chooses? American Reproductive History since 1830.* Gainesville: University Press of Florida, 2008.

Castellani, Brian, *Pathological Gambling: The Making of a Medical Problem.* Albany: State University of New York Press, 2000.

Centers for Disease Control, "Preventing Teen Pregnancy: An Update in 2009." http://www.cdc.gov/reproductivehealth/AdolescentReproHealth/AboutTP.htm

Cheever, Susan, *Desire: Where Sex Meets Addiction.* New York: Simon & Schuster, 2008.

Chichetti, Dante, and Vicki Carlson, *Child Maltreatment: Theory and Research on the Causes and Consequences of Child Abuse and Neglect.* New York: Cambridge University Press, 1997.

Church, M. A., and Brooks, C. I., *Subtle Suicide: Our Silent Epidemic over Ambivalence about Living.* Westport, CT: Praeger, 2009.

Clark, Neils, *Game Addiction: The Experience and the Effects.* Jefferson, NC: McFarland, 2009.

Connell, Elizabeth B., *The Contraception Sourcebook.* New York: McGraw-Hill, 2002.

Conrad, Peter, and Joseph W. Schneider, *Deviance and Medicalization: From Badness to Sickness.* Philadelphia: Temple University Press, 1992.

Courtwright, David, *Forces of Habit: Drugs and the Making of the Modern World.* Cambridge, MA: Harvard University Press, 2001.

Crosson-Tower, Cynthia, *Understanding Child Abuse and Neglect.* Boston: Allyn & Bacon, 2007.

Crouse, Janice Shaw, *Children at Risk: The Precarious State of Children's Well-Being in the United States.* New Brunswick, NJ: Transaction, 2010.

Davis, Deborah, *You Look Too Young to Be a Mom: Teen Mothers on Love, Learning, and Success.* New York: Perigee, 2004.

DeGrandpre, Richard, *The Cult of Pharmacology: How America Became the World's Most Troubled Drug Culture.* Durham, NC: Duke University Press, 2006.

Dickerson, Mark, and John O'Conner, *Gambling as an Addictive Behaviour: Impaired Control, Harm Minimisation, Treatment and Prevention.* New York: Cambridge University Press, 2006.

Dodge, Kenneth A., and Doriane Lambelet Coleman, *Preventing Child Maltreatment: Community Approaches.* New York: Guilford Press, 2009.

Ehrenreich, Nancy, ed., *The Reproductive Rights Reader: Law, Medicine, and the Construction of Motherhood.* New York: Routledge, 2008.

Finklehor, David, *Childhood Victimization: Violence, Crime, and Abuse in the Lives of Young People.* New York: Oxford University Press, 2008.

Flowers, R. Barri, *Domestic Crimes, Family Violence and Child Abuse: A Study of Contemporary American Society.* Jefferson, NC: McFarland, 2000.

Foley, Kathleen, and Herbert Hendin, eds., *The Case Against Assisted Suicide: For the Right to End-of-Life Care.* Baltimore: Johns Hopkins University Press, 2002.

Fourcroy, Jean L., ed., *Pharmacology, Doping, and Sports: A Scientific Guide for Athletes, Coaches, Physicians, Scientists, and Administrators.* New York: Routledge, 2009.

Frank, Richard G., and Sherry A. Glied, *Better but Not Well: Mental Health Policy in the United States since 1950.* Baltimore: Johns Hopkins University Press, 2006.

Furstenberg, Frank F., *Destinies of the Disadvantaged: The Politics of Teenage Childbearing.* New York: Russell Sage Foundation, 2007.

Gebbie, Alisa E., and Katharine O'Connell White, *Fast Facts: Contraception.* Albuquerque: Health Press, 2009.

Gelles, Richard J., *Intimate Violence in Families.* Thousand Oaks, CA: Sage, 1997.

Ginsberg, Faye, D., *Contested Lives: The Abortion Debate in an American Community,* rev. ed. Berkeley: University of California Press, 1998.

Glasier, Anna, and Alisa Gebbie, eds., *Handbook of Family Planning and Reproductive Healthcare.* New York: Churchill Livingstone/Elsevier, 2008.

Gorsuch, Neil M., *The Future of Assisted Suicide and Euthanasia.* Princeton, NJ: Princeton University Press, 2006.

Grob, G. N., *The Mad among Us: A History of the Care of America's Mentally Ill.* New York: Free Press, 1994.

Herring, Mark Youngblood, *The Pro-Life/Choice Debate.* Westport, CT: Greenwood Press, 2003.

Hesse-Biber, Sharlene, *Am I Thin Enough Yet? The Cult of Thinness and the Commercialization of Identity.* New York: Oxford University Press, 1996.

Heyman, Gene M., *Addiction: A Disorder of Choice.* Cambridge, MA: Harvard University Press, 2009.

Hoberman, John, *Testosterone Dreams: Rejuvenation, Aphrodisia, Doping.* Berkeley: University of California Press, 2005.

Hoffman, Allan M., and Randal W. Summers, *Elder Abuse: A Public Health Perspective.* Washington, DC: American Public Health Association, 2006.

Husak, Douglas, *Legalize This! The Case for Decriminalizing Drugs.* London: Verso, 2002.

Inciardi, James, and Karen McElrath, *The American Drug Scene,* 5th ed. New York: Oxford University Press, 2007.

Kelly, Timothy A., *Healing the Broken Mind: Transforming America's Failed Mental Health System.* New York: New York University Press, 2010.

Kemp, Donna R., *Mental Health in America: A Reference Handbook.* Santa Barbara, CA: ABC-CLIO, 2007.

Kurst-Swanger, Karel, and Jacqueline L. Petcosky, *Violence in the Home: Multidisciplinary Perspectives.* New York: Oxford University Press, 2003.

Leach, M. M., *Cultural Diversity and Suicide: Ethnic, Religious, Gender and Sexual Orientation Perspectives.* Binghamton, NY: Haworth Press, 2006.

Lord, Alexandra M., *Condom Nation: The U.S. Government's Sex Education Campaign from World War I to the Internet.* Baltimore: Johns Hopkins University Press, 2010.

Lowinson, Joyce H., et al., eds., *Substance Abuse: A Comprehensive Textbook*. Philadelphia: Lippincott Williams & Wilkins, 2005.

Luker, Kristin, *Abortion and the Politics of Motherhood*. Berkeley: University of California Press, 1984.

Luker, Kristin, *Dubious Conceptions: The Politics of Teenage Pregnancy*. Cambridge, MA: Harvard University Press, 1996.

Maris, R. W., A. C. Berman, and M. M. Silverman, *Comprehensive Textbook of Suicidology*. New York: Guilford Press, 2000.

Markens, Susan, *Surrogate Motherhood and the Politics of Reproduction*. Berkeley: University of California Press, 2007.

Maxwell, Carol J. C., *Pro-Life Activists in America: Meaning, Motivation, and Direct Action*. Cambridge, England: Cambridge University Press, 2002.

May, Elaine Tyler, *America and the Pill: A History of Promise, Peril, and Liberation*. New York: Basic Books, 2010.

McBride, Dorothy E., *Abortion in the United States: A Reference Handbook*. Santa Barbara, CA: ABC-CLIO, 2008.

McBurnett, Keith, and Linda Pfifner, eds., *Attention Deficit Hyperactivity Disorder: Concepts, Controversies, New Directions*. New York: Informa Healthcare, 2008.

McTavish, Jan, *Pain and Profits: The History of the Headache and Its Remedies*. New Brunswick, NJ: Rutgers University Press, 2004.

Miller, Dusty, *Women Who Hurt Themselves*. New York: Basic Books/HarperCollins, 1994.

Miller, William R., and Kathleen M. Carroll, *Rethinking Substance Abuse: What the Science Shows, and What We Should Do about It*. New York: Guilford Press, 2006.

Mitchell, John B., *Understanding Assisted Suicide: Nine Issues to Consider*. Ann Arbor: University of Michigan Press, 2007.

Monteleone, James A., *A Parent's and Teacher's Handbook on Identifying and Preventing Child Abuse*. St. Louis: G. W. Medical Publishing, 1998.

Musto, David, *The American Disease: Origins of Narcotics Control*, 3d edition. New York: Oxford University Press, 1999.

National Association of Anorexia Nervosa and Associated Disorders, http://www.anad.org

National Association to Protect Children, http://www.protect.org

National Campaign to Prevent Teen and Unplanned Pregnancy, http://www.thenationalcampaign.org

National Children's Advocacy Center. http://www.nationalcac.org

Nerenberg, Lisa, *Elder Abuse Prevention: Emerging Trends and Promising Strategies*. New York: Springer, 2008.

Nixon, Mary K., and Nancy L. Heath, eds., *Self-Injury in Youth: The Essential Guide to Assessment and Intervention*. New York: Routledge, 2009.

Nutt, David, et al., eds., *Drugs and the Future: Brain Science, Addiction, and Society*. Burlington, MA: Academic Press, 2006.

Page, Cristina, *How the Pro-Choice Movement Saved America: Freedom, Politics, and the War on Sex*. New York: Basic Books, 2006.

Patterson, Anna, *Fit to Die: Men and Eating Disorders*. Thousand Oaks, CA: Sage, 2004.

Planned Parenthood Federation of America, http://www.plannedparenthood.org

Prevent Child Abuse America, http://www.preventchildabuse.org

Riddle, John M., *Eve's Herbs: A History of Contraception and Abortion in the West.* Cambridge, MA: Harvard University Press, 1997.

Rose, Melody, *Safe, Legal, and Available? Abortion Politics in the United States.* Washington, DC: CQ Press, 2007.

Rosen, Daniel M., *Dope: The History of Performance Enhancement in Sports from the Nineteenth Century to Today.* Westport, CT: Praeger, 2008.

Rumney, Avis, *Dying to Please: Anorexia, Treatment and Recovery.* Jefferson, NC: McFarland, 2009.

S.A.F.E. Alternatives, "Self Abuse Finally Ends." 2010. http://www.selfinjury.com

Shalev, Carmel, *Birth Power: The Case for Surrogacy.* New Haven, CT: Yale University Press, 1989.

Shrage, Laurie, *Abortion and Social Responsibility: Depolarizing the Debate.* New York: Oxford University Press, 2003.

Sokoloff, Natalie J., with Christina Pratt, *Domestic Violence at the Margins: Readings on Race, Class, Gender, and Culture.* New Brunswick, NJ: Rutgers University Press, 2005.

Solinger, Ricki, *Pregnancy and Power: A Short History of Reproductive Politics in America.* New York: New York University Press, 2005.

Strong, Marilee, *A Bright Red Scream: Self-Mutilation and the Language of Pain.* New York: Penguin, 1998.

Thompson, Marie L., *Mental Illness.* Westport, CT: Greenwood Press, 2006.

Timimi, Sami, *Naughty Boys: Anti-Social Behavior, ADHD and the Role of Culture.* New York: Palgrave Macmillan, 2005.

Weschler, Toni, *Taking Charge of Your Fertility.* New York: HarperCollins, 2006.

Williams-Wheeler, Dorrie, *The Unplanned Pregnancy Book for Teens and College Students.* Virginia Beach, VA: Sparkledoll Productions, 2004.

Family and Media

BabyBag.com, "Facts about Media Violence and Effects on the American Family." http://www.babybag.com/articles/amaviol.htm

Barker, Martin, and Julian Petley, eds., *Ill Effects: The Media/Violence Debate.* New York: Routledge, 2001.

Bissell, Tom., *Extra Lives: Why Video Games Matter.* New York: Pantheon, 2010.

Buckingham, David, *After the Death of Childhood: Growing up in the Age of Electronic Media.* Malden, MA: Polity, 2005.

Children and Television Violence, http://www.abelard.org/tv/tv.htm

Egenfeldt-Nielsen, Simon, et al., *Understanding Video Games: The Essential Introduction.* New York: Routledge, 2008.

Entertainment Software Association, http://www.theesa.com

Freedman, Jonathan L., *Media Violence and Its Effect on Aggression: Assessing the Scientific Evidence.* Toronto: University of Toronto Press, 2002.

Gee, James Paul, *What Video Games Have to Tell Us about Learning and Literacy,* 2d ed. New York: Palgrave Macmillan, 2007.

Glassner, Barry, *The Culture of Fear: Why Americans Are Afraid of the Wrong Things.* New York: Basic Books, 1999.

Goldstein, Jeffrey H., *Why We Watch: The Attractions of Violent Entertainment*. New York: Oxford University Press, 1998.

Hilliard, Robert L., and Michael C. Keith, *Dirty Discourse: Sex and Indecency in Broadcasting*, 2d ed. Malden, MA: Blackwell, 2007.

Jamieson, Kathleen Hall, and Joseph N. Cappella, *Echo Chamber: Rush Limbaugh and the Conservative Media Establishment*. New York: Oxford University Press, 2008.

Jenkins, Henry, *Fans, Bloggers, and Gamers: Exploring Participatory Culture*. New York: New York University Press, 2006.

Jones, Gerard, *Killing Monsters: Why Children Need Fantasy, Super Heroes, and Make-Believe Violence*. New York: Basic Books, 2002.

Kammeyer, Kenneth C., *A Hypersexual Society: Sexual Discourse, Erotica, and Pornography in America Today*. New York: Palgrave Macmillan, 2008.

Kirsh, Steven J., *Children, Adolescents, and Media Violence: A Critical Look at the Research*. Thousand Oaks, CA: Sage, 2006.

Lipshultz, Jeremy H., *Broadcast Indecency: FCC Regulation and the First Amendment*. Newton, MA: Focus Press, 1997.

McNair, Brian, *Mediated Sex: Pornography and Postmodern Culture*. New York: St. Martin's Press, 1996.

Media Awareness Network, http://www.media-awareness.ca/english/issues/violence/index.cfm

National Institute on Media and the Family, http://www.mediafamily.org/facts/facts_vlent.shtml

O'Connor, Rory, *Shock Jocks: Hate Speech and Talk Radio: America's Ten Worst Hate Talkers and the Progressive Alternatives*. San Francisco: AlterNet Books, 2008.

Paul, Pamela, *Pornified: How Pornography Is Transforming Our Lives, Our Relationships, and Our Families*. New York: Henry Holt, 2005.

PBS Frontline, *American Porn* (documentary). 2002.

Sandler, Kevin, *The Naked Truth: Why Hollywood Does Not Make NC-17 Films*. New Brunswick, NJ: Rutgers University Press, 2006.

Schechter, Harold, *Savage Pastime: A Cultural History of Violent Entertainment*. New York: St. Martin's Press, 2005.

Springhall, John, *Youth, Popular Culture and Moral Panics: Penny Gaffs to Gangsta-Rap, 1820–1996*. New York: St. Martin's Press, 1998.

Sternheimer, Karen, *It's Not the Media: The Truth about Pop Culture's Influence on Children*. Boulder, CO: Westview Press, 2003.

Tobin, Joseph, *Good Guys Don't Wear Hats: Children's Talk about the Media*. New York: Teachers College Press, 2000.

Trend, David, *The Myth of Media Violence: A Critical Introduction*. Hoboken, NJ: Wiley-Blackwell, 2007.

Vorderer, Peter, and Jennings Bryant, eds., *Playing Video Games: Motives, Responses, and Consequences*, Mahwah, NJ: Lawrence Erlbaum, 2006.

Religion and Society

Alters, B. J., and S. M. Alters, *Defending Evolution: A Guide to the Evolution/Creation Controversy*. Sudbury, MA: Jones and Bartlett, 2001.

Americans United for Separation of Church and State, http://www.au.org

Bowler, Peter J., *Monkey Trials and Gorilla Sermons: Evolution and Christianity from Darwin to Intelligent Design.* Cambridge, MA: Harvard University Press, 2007.

Center for Law and Religious Freedom, http://www.clsnet.org

Cowan, Douglas E., *Cults and New Religions: A Brief History.* New York: Oxford University Press, 2008.

Dawson, Lorne L., *Comprehending Cults: The Sociology of New Religious Movements.* New York: Oxford University Press, 2006.

Dierenfield, Bruce J., *The Battle over School Prayer: How* Engle v. Vitale *Changed America.* Lawrence: University Press of Kansas, 2007.

Dunn, Charles W., ed., *The Future of Religion in American Politics.* Lexington: University Press of Kentucky, 2009.

Frawley-O'Dea, Mary Gail, *Perversion of Power: Sexual Abuse in the Catholic Church.* Nashville: Vanderbilt University Press, 2007.

Gallagher, Eugene V., *The New Religious Movements Experience in America.* Westport, CT: Greenwood Press, 2004.

Gallagher, Eugene V., and W. Michael Ashcraft, eds., *Introduction to New and Alternative Religions in America.* Westport, CT: Greenwood Press, 2006.

Giberson, Karl, *Saving Darwin: How to Be a Christian and Believe in Evolution.* New York: HarperOne, 2008.

Larson, Edward J., *Trial and Error: The American Controversy over Creation and Evolution,* 3d ed. New York: Oxford University Press, 2003.

Lewis, James R., *Legitimating New Religions.* New Brunswick, NJ: Rutgers University Press, 2003.

McMackin, Robert A., et al., eds., *Understanding the Impact of Clergy Sexual Abuse: Betrayal and Recovery.* New York: Routledge, 2009.

Miller, Kenneth R., *Only a Theory: Evolution and the Battle for America's Soul.* New York: Viking Press, 2008.

Numbers, Ronald J., *The Creationists: From Scientific Creationism to Intelligent Design,* rev. ed. Cambridge, MA: Harvard University Press, 2006.

Nussbaum, Martha Craven, *Liberty of Conscience: In Defense of America's Tradition of Religious Equality.* New York: Basic Books, 2008.

Partridge, Christopher, *New Religions: A Guide: New Religious Movements, Sects and Alternative Spiritualities.* New York: Oxford University Press, 2004.

People for the American Way, http://www.pfaw.org/pfaw

Petto, Andrew J., and Laurie R. Godfrey, *Scientists Confront Intelligent Design and Creationism.* New York: W. W. Norton, 2007.

Plante, Thomas G., ed., *Sin against the Innocent: Sexual Abuse by Priests and the Role of the Catholic Church.* Westport, CT: Praeger, 2004.

Rutherford Institute, http://www.rutherford.org

Saliba, John, *Understanding New Religious Movements,* 2d ed. Walnut Creek, CA: AltaMira Press, 2003.

Scott, Eugenie C., *Evolution vs. Creationism: An Introduction,* 2d ed. Berkeley: University of California Press, 2009.

Solomon, Stephen, *Ellery's Protest: How One Young Man Defied Tradition and Sparked the Battle over School Prayer*. Ann Arbor: University of Michigan Press, 2007.

Stark, Rodney, *What Americans Really Believe: New Findings from the Baylor Surveys of Religion*. Waco, TX: Baylor University Press, 2008.

Wilson, Bryan, and Jamie Cresswell, eds., *New Religious Movements: Challenge and Response*. New York: Routledge, 1999.

Schools

Abernathy, Scott Franklin, *No Child Left Behind and the Public Schools*. Ann Arbor: University of Michigan Press, 2007.

Angus, David L., and Jeffrey E. Mirel, *The Failed Promise of the American High School, 1895–1995*. New York: Teachers College Press, 1999.

Baker, Joan M., *Achievement Testing in U.S. Elementary and Secondary Schools*. New York: Peter Lang, 2005.

Beatty, Barbara, *Preschool Education in America: The Culture of Young Children from the Colonial Era to the Present*. New Haven, CT: Yale University Press, 1995.

Betts, Julian R., and Tom Loveless, eds., *Getting Choice Right: Ensuring Equity and Efficiency in Education Policy*. Washington, DC: Brookings Institution Press, 2005.

Boger, John Charles, and Gary Orfield, eds., *School Resegregation: Must the South Turn Back?* Chapel Hill: University of North Carolina Press, 2004.

Bracey, Gerald W., *The War against America's Schools: Privatizing Schools, Commercializing Education*. Boston: Allyn & Bacon, 2001.

Buckley, Jack, and Mark Schneider, *Charter Schools: Hope or Hype?* Princeton, NJ: Princeton University Press, 2007.

Bulkley, K., and P. Wohlstetter, eds., *Taking Account of Charter Schools: What's Happened and What's Next*. New York: Teachers College Press, 2004.

Carnoy, Martin, et al., *The Charter School Dust-Up: Examining the Evidence on Enrollment and Achievement*. Washington, DC: Economic Policy Institute; New York: Teachers College Press, 2005.

Clotfelter, Charles T., *After Brown: The Rise and Retreat of School Desegregation*. Princeton, NJ: Princeton University Press, 2006.

Committee on Nutrition Standards for Foods in Schools, *Nutrition Standards for Foods in Schools: Leading the Way toward Healthier Youth*. New York: National Academies Press, 2007.

Cookson, Peter W., and Kristina Berger, *Expect Miracles: Charter Schools and the Politics of Hope and Despair*. Boulder, CO: Westview Press, 2003.

Cooper, Ann, and Lisa M. Holmes, *Bitter Harvest*. New York: Routledge, 2000.

Cooper, Ann, and Lisa M. Holmes, *Lunch Lessons: Changing the Way We Feed Our Children*. New York: HarperCollins, 2006.

Corwin, Ronald G., and E. Joseph Schneider, *The School Choice Hoax: Fixing America's Schools*. Lanham, MD: Rowman & Littlefield, 2007.

Cryer, Debby, and Richard M. Clifford, eds., *Early Education and Care in the USA*. Baltimore: Brookes Publishing, 2002.

Cummins, Jim, and Merill Swain, *Bilingualism in Education: Aspects of Theory, Research, and Practice*. New York: Longman, 1986.

Dunn, Joshua M., and Martin R. West, eds., *From Schoolhouse to Courthouse: The Judiciary's Role in American Education*. Washington, DC: Brookings Institution Press, 2009.

Farquhar, Sandy, and Peter Fitzsimmons, eds., *Philosophy of Early Childhood Education: Transforming Narratives*. New York: Wiley-Blackwell, 2008.

Feinberg, Walter, and Christopher Lubienski, *School Choice Policies and Outcomes: Empirical and Philosophical Perspectives*. Albany: State University of New York Press, 2008.

Frankenberg, Erica, and Gary Orfield, eds., *Lessons in Integration: Realizing the Promise of Racial Diversity in America's Schools*. Charlottesville: University of Virginia Press, 2007.

Franklin, C., et al., eds., *The School Practitioner's Concise Companion to Preventing Dropout and Attendance Problems*. New York: Oxford University Press, 2008.

Freeman, C. E., *Trends in the Educational Equity of Girls and Women: 2004*. Washington, DC: National Center for Education Statistics, 2004.

Fuller, Bruce, ed., *Inside Charter Schools: The Paradox of Radical Decentralization*. Cambridge, MA: Harvard University Press, 2000.

Fuller, Bruce, et al., *Standardized Childhood: The Political and Cultural Struggle over Early Education*. Stanford, CA: Stanford University Press, 2007.

Gandara, Patricia, and Megan Hopkins, *Forbidden Language: English Learners and Restrictive Language Policies*. New York: Teachers College Press, 2010.

Garcia, Eugene E., *Teaching and Learning in Two Languages: Bilingualism and Schooling in the United States*. New York: Teachers College Press, 2005.

Goffin, Stacie G., and Valora Washington, *Ready or Not: Leadership Choices in Early Care and Education*. New York: Teachers College Press, 2007.

Gunderson, Lee, *English-Only Instruction and Immigrant Students in Secondary Schools: A Critical Examination*. Mahwah, NJ: Lawrence Erlbaum, 2007.

Gurian, Micael, *Boys and Girls Learn Differently! A Guide for Teachers and Parents*. Hoboken, NJ: Jossey-Bass, 2001.

Hayes, William, *No Child Left Behind: Past, Present, and Future*. Lanham, MD: Rowman & Littlefield, 2008.

Hursh, David W., *High-Stakes Testing and the Decline of Teaching and Learning*. Lanham, MD: Rowman & Littlefield, 2008.

Hyman, Irwin A., *Reading, Writing, and the Hickory Stick. The Appalling Story of Physical and Psychological Abuse in American Schools*. Lexington, MA: Lexington Books, 1990.

Kluger, Richard, *Simple Justice: The History of* Brown v. Board of Education *and Black America's Struggle for Equality,* rev. ed. New York: Knopf, 2004.

Kosar, Kevin R., *Failing Grades: The Federal Politics of Education Standards*. Boulder, CO: Lynne Rienner, 2005.

Levine, Susan, *School Lunch Politics: The Surprising History of America's Favorite Welfare Program*. Princeton, NJ: Princeton University Press, 2010.

Lockwood, A. T., *The Charter School Decade*. Lanham, MD: Scarecrow Press, 2004.

Manna, Paul, *School's In: Federalism and the National Education Agenda*. Washington, DC: Georgetown University Press, 2006.

Mathison, Sandra, and E. Wayne Ross, *Defending Public Schools: The Meaning and Limits of Standards-Based Reform and High-Stakes Testing.* Westport, CT: Praeger, 2004.

McCluskey, Neal P., *Feds in the Classroom: How Big Government Corrupts, Cripples, and Compromises American Education.* Lanham, MD: Rowman & Littlefield, 2007.

McGregor, Gail, and R. Timm Vogelsberg, *Inclusive Schooling Practices: Pedagogical and Research Foundations: A Synthesis of the Literature that Informs Best Practices.* Baltimore: Paul H. Brookes, 1999.

Merseth, Katherine K., with Kristy Cooper, *Inside Urban Charter Schools: Promising Practices and Strategies in Five High-Performing Schools.* Cambridge, MA: Harvard Education Press, 2009.

Miron, G., and C. Nelson, *What's Public about Charter Schools? Lessons Learned about Choice and Accountability.* Thousand Oaks, CA: Corwin Press, 2002.

Mishel, L., and J. Roy, *Rethinking High School Graduation Rates and Trends.* Washington, DC: Economic Policy Institute, 2006.

Nichols, Sharon Lynn, and David C. Berliner, *Collateral Damage: How High-Stakes Testing Corrupts American Schools.* Cambridge MA: Harvard Education Press, 2007.

Orfield, Gary, ed., *Dropouts in America: Confronting the Graduation Rate Crisis.* Cambridge, MA: Harvard Education Press, 2004.

Orfield, Gary, and Chungmei Lee, *Racial Transformation and the Changing Nature of Segregation.* Cambridge, MA: Civil Rights Project at Harvard University, 2006.

Peterson, J. Michael, and Mishael M. Hittie, *Inclusive Teaching: The Journey towards Effective Schooling for All Learners,* 2d ed. Upper Saddle River, NJ: Prentice Hall, 2009.

Phelps, Richard P., ed., *Defending Standardized Testing.* Mahwah, NJ: Lawrence Erlbaum, 2005.

Poppendieck, Janet, *Free for All: Fixing School Food in America.* Berkeley: University of California Press, 2010.

Powers, Jeanne M., *Charter Schools: From Reform Imagery to Reform Reality.* New York: Palgrave Macmillan, 2009.

Ravitch, Diane, *Death and Life of Great American School Reform: How Testing and Choice Are Undermining Education.* New York: Basic Books, 2010.

Rebell, Michael A., and Jessica R. Wolff, eds., *NCLB at the Crossroads: Reexamining the Federal Effort to Close the Achievement Gap.* New York: Teachers College Press, 2009.

Reese, William J., *America's Public Schools: From the Common School to "No Child Left Behind."* Baltimore: Johns Hopkins University Press, 2005.

Sadovnik, Alan R., et al., eds., *No Child Left Behind and the Reduction of the Achievement Gap: Sociological Perspectives on Federal Educational Policy.* New York: Routledge, 2008.

Salomone, Rosemary C., *True Americans: Language, Identity, and the Education of Immigrant Children.* Cambridge, MA: Harvard University Press, 2010.

Sapon-Shevin, Mara, *Widening the Circle: The Power of Inclusive Classrooms.* Boston: Beacon Press, 2007.

Smrekar, Claire E., and Ellen B. Goldring, eds., *From the Courtroom to the Classroom: The Shifting Landscape of School Desegregation.* Cambridge, MA: Harvard Education Press, 2009.

Swanson, C., *The Real Truth about Low Graduation Rates: An Evidence-Based Commentary.* Washington, DC: Urban Institute, 2004.

Swanson, C., *Who Graduates? Who Doesn't? A Statistical Portrait of Public High School Graduation, Class of 2001.* Washington, DC: Urban Institute, 2004.

Thorne, Barrie, *Gender Play: Girls and Boys in School.* New Brunswick, NJ: Rutgers University Press, 1993.

Urban, Wayne, and L. Wagoner Jennings Jr., *American Education: A History.* New York: McGraw-Hill, 2004.

Vinovskis, Maris A., *From a Nation at Risk to No Child Left Behind: National Education Goals and the Creation of Federal Education Policy.* New York: Teachers College Press, 2009.

Walberg, Herbert A., *School Choice: The Findings.* Washington, DC: Cato Institute, 2007.

Wells, Amy Stuart, et al., *Both Sides Now: The Story of School Desegregation's Graduates.* Berkeley: University of California Press, 2009.

About the Editor and Contributors

Editor

Michael Shally-Jensen is former editor-in-chief of the *Encyclopedia Americana*, executive editor of the *Encyclopedia of American Studies*, and editor of numerous other books and reference publications. He received his PhD in cultural anthropology from Princeton University, having specialized in aspects of American culture and society. He lives in Amherst, Massachusetts.

Contributors

Amber Ault is a sociologist with training in anthropology and social work; a background in teaching, advising, and academic coaching; and interests in health, wellness, exercise, and creating healthy, inclusive, diverse institutional environments.

Rob Beamish is associate professor of sociology at Queen's University, Kingston, Ontario. His research interests include the use of performance-enhancing substances in sport. He is coauthor, with Ian Ritchie, of *Highest, Fastest, Strongest: A Critique of High-Performance Sport* (2006). He has also published a two-volume textbook of sociology.

Rachel Birmingham is currently a doctoral student in human development and family studies at Auburn University. She completed her master's degree in family, youth, and community services at the University of Florida, with a specialization in family violence studies. She has been certified by the Florida Coalition against Domestic Violence.

Paul Boudreau is a Catholic priest of the Diocese of Norwich, Connecticut, and a freelance writer. He coauthored, with Alice Camille, *The Forgiveness Book* (2008). He serves the Blessed Kateri Tekakwitha Parish in Banning, California.

Kimberly P. Brackett is distinguished teaching associate professor of sociology and head of the Sociology Department at Auburn University, Montgomery, Alabama. She received MA and PhD degrees from the University of Florida. Her specialties include family, gender, and social psychology, and it is in these areas that she teaches.

Glenn Branch is deputy director of the National Center for Science Education, a nonprofit organization affiliated with the American Association for the Advancement of Science, which defends the teaching of evolution in the public schools. His articles on creationism and evolution have appeared in such publications as *Academe, The American Biology Teacher, BioScience, Free Inquiry, Geotimes,* and *USA Today.* With Eugenie C. Scott, he is the editor of *Not in Our Classrooms: Why Intelligent Design Is Wrong for Our Schools* (2006).

Charles I. Brooks is professor and chair of the Department of Psychology, King's College, Wilkes-Barre, Pennsylvania. He received a master's degree in psychology from Wake Forest University, and a doctorate in experimental psychology from Syracuse University. He has taught at King's College since 1975 and was designated a distinguished service professor in 1993. He has authored or coauthored more than 40 scholarly publications in psychology.

Christopher P. Brown is an assistant professor in the Department of Curriculum and Instruction at the University of Texas at Austin. His research interests include the intersection of education policy, curriculum, and instruction; standards-based accountability reform; and early childhood/early elementary education.

Santarica Buford is pursuing an advanced degree in social work at Auburn University, having completed her undergraduate studies in sociology and marriage and family. Her future goals involve counseling and work with pregnant teens and domestic violence victims.

Nancy D. Campbell is an associate professor of science and technology studies at Rensselaer Polytechnic Institute in Troy, New York. She is the author of *Using Women: Gender, Drug Policy, and Social Reproduction* (2000), *Discovering Addiction: The Science and Politics of Substance Abuse Research* (2007), and, with J. P. Olsen and Luke Walden, *The Narcotic Farm: The Rise and Fall of America's First Prison for Drug Addicts* (2008). She has also written on the history of harm reduction drug policy, sweat-patch drug testing, and feminist science studies.

Jane Caputi is professor of women's studies at Florida Atlantic University, Boca Raton. Among her publications is *Goddesses and Monsters: Women, Myth, and Power in Popular Culture* (2004).

Cynthia Childress is a PhD candidate in the Department of English at the University of Louisiana at Lafayette, specializing in women's literature and feminist theory.

Michael A. Church is associate professor of psychology at King's College in Wilkes-Barre, Pennsylvania. He received his master's and doctoral degrees in psychology from the University of Miami. He has taught at King's College since 1976, and has been a licensed clinical psychologist with a private practice since 1980. He is a member of the Council of National Register of Health Service Providers in Psychology.

Susan Cody-Rydzewski is associate professor of social sciences at Georgia Perimeter College, Dunwoody. She received her doctorate from the University of Florida and currently teaches courses in marriage and family, gender and society, social problems, and sociology of religion. She has published articles on work and family conflict and women's experiences working within male-dominated occupations, such as ministry.

Hayley Cofer completed a bachelor of arts degree in sociology with a concentration in marriage and family at Auburn University at Montgomery, Alabama.

Ann Cooper is a noted author, chef, educator, and enduring advocate for better food for all children. A graduate of the Culinary Institute of America, Hyde Park, New York, she has been a chef for more than 30 years, including positions with Holland America Cruises, Radisson Hotels, and Telluride Ski Resort as well as serving as executive chef at the renowned Putney Inn in Vermont. She has published four books, including *Lunch Lessons: Changing the Way We Feed Our Children* (2006) and *In Mother's Kitchen: Celebrated Women Chefs Share Beloved Family Recipes* (2005), both coauthored with Lisa Holmes.

Ronald G. Corwin is a professor emeritus of sociology at Ohio State University, has also taught at Teachers College, Columbia University, and has served as director of basic research in the U.S. Department of Education. He has been a vice president of the American Educational Research Association and has held elected positions in the American Sociological Research Association. Author or coauthor of a dozen books and two dozen contributed chapters, he also edited a series of books on educational research.

Garry Crawford is a senior lecturer in sociology at the University of Salford (United Kingdom). His research interests focus primarily on media audiences and fan cultures. In particular, he has published on sport fan culture, including the book *Consuming Sport: Sports, Fans and Culture* (2004). He also coauthored, with T. Blackshaw, *The Sage Dictionary of Leisure Studies* (2009) and has written on digital gaming patterns.

Lane Destro is a Sulzberger/Levitan fellow in sociology at Duke University's Center for Child and Family Policy. Her research interests include demography, methodology, and racial disparities in wealth acquisition.

Sarah Fish is an adjunct instructor in the Department of English and Philosophy at Auburn University, Montgomery, Alabama. She holds a master's degree from Auburn and is currently a PhD candidate there.

Erica Frankenberg is director of research and policy for the Initiative on School Integration, part of the University California, Los Angeles's Civil Rights Project. She received her doctorate in educational policy from the Harvard University Graduate School of Education. She is coeditor, with Gary Orfield, of *Lessons in Integration: Realizing the Promise of Racial Diversity in America's Schools* (2007).

Aaron D. Franks is proprietor and chief executive officer of A1 Health and Fitness. His interests include furthering his academic pursuits as well as improving the lives of others.

Nicole D. Garrett is a graduate research assistant in the marriage and family therapy program at the University of Kentucky. Her research interests include couple dynamics, methods of improving relationship quality, and adolescent behavior and emotional health.

Lee Gunderson is a professor and former head of the Department of Language and Literacy Education at the University of British Columbia, where he teaches undergraduate and graduate courses in second language reading, language acquisition, literacy acquisition, and teacher education. He has served as a preschool teacher, a primary-level elementary teacher, a reading specialist, a principal and vice principal in a bilingual school, and a teacher of the learning disabled. He has conducted long-term research that explores the achievement of approximately 25,000 immigrant students.

Lisa M. Holmes graduated from Wellesley College with a degree in English and began her career as a writer with a six-year stint as a travel journalist for Frommer's. She later shifted her focus, adding chef and chocolatier to her resume after receiving her professional culinary training at the Culinary Institute of America in Hyde Park, New York. Her publications, coauthored with Ann Cooper, include *Lunch Lessons: Changing the Way We Feed Our Children* (2006) and *In Mother's Kitchen: Celebrated Women Chefs Share Beloved Family Recipes* (2005).

John M. Hood is president and chairman of the John Locke Foundation, a public policy think tank in North Carolina. A graduate of the University of North Carolina–Chapel Hill's School of Journalism, Hood is a syndicated columnist whose articles have appeared in such publications as *Reader's Digest,* the *Wall Street Journal,* and the *National Review.* He has also authored three books.

Jonelle Husain is a doctoral student in sociology and research associate at the Social Science Research Center at Mississippi State University. Her research focuses on social constructions of trauma in the context of postabortion healing groups.

Gwenyth Jackaway is associate professor of communication and media studies at Fordham University. Her research and teaching interests include freedom of speech, children and media, and media effects. She has authored a number of articles and book chapters as well as the book *Media at War: Radio's Challenge to the Newspaper, 1924–1937* (Praeger, 1995).

Jeffrey Jones is a freelance writer living in Montgomery, Alabama. His interests include representations of homosexuality in contemporary art, pagan symbolism in Renaissance art, queer theory, and gay rights advocacy.

Tonya Lowery Jones holds a master's degree in sociology and a bachelor's degree in criminology, both from Auburn University in Auburn, Alabama. She is currently an adjunct sociology instructor at Auburn University (Auburn and Montgomery campuses), Southern Union State Community College, and Chattahoochee Valley Community College.

Donna R. Kemp is professor of public administration and graduate coordinator of the Department of Political Science at California State University, Chico, California. Her published works include *Mental Health in America: A Reference Guide* (ABC-CLIO, 2007) and *Mental Health in the Workplace: An Employer's and Manager's Guide* (Praeger, 1994).

Karen L. Kinnear is a paralegal and a professional researcher, editor, and writer with more than 25 years of experience in sociological, economic, statistical, and financial analysis. Her published works include *Gangs* (2d ed., 2008) and *Childhood Sexual Abuse* (2d ed., 2007), both published by ABC-CLIO.

Kevin R. Kosar is the author of *Failing Grades: The Federal Politics of Education Standards* (2005). His writings have appeared in many professional journals, and he has lectured at the New York University's Robert F. Wagner Graduate School of Public Service and at Metropolitan College of New York's School for Public Affairs and Administration. He has worked for a New York City not-for-profit corporation that helps children in some of New York City's lowest-performing schools and has served as a peer reviewer for the U.S. Department of Education's Teaching American

History Grant Program and Presidential Academies for American History and Civics programs. He earned his doctorate in politics at New York University.

Chinh Q. Le served as assistant counsel at the National Association for the Advancement of Colored People Legal Defense and Educational Fund, Inc. in New York for five years. During that time, he represented plaintiffs in school desegregation and educational equity cases, including several class action cases, and counseled defendants in voluntary school integration litigation. He has also been involved in matters related to voting rights and higher education affirmative action. Le received his JD degree from the University of Virginia School of Law, where he served as notes editor of the *Virginia Law Review.* He is presently an associate in the New York office of Jenner & Block LLP.

Margaret Leaf is a PhD candidate in sociology at Florida State University. Her research interests include self-injury, rape, and sexual behavior, all of which she has published papers about in professional journals.

Linda Mabry is professor of education at Washington State University. Her research interests include state and national assessment systems and teacher-developed assessments. Current projects include a follow-along study of No Child Left Behind (NCLB) in two states and development of a public statement on educational accountability for the American Evaluation Association. Her publications include *Real-World Evaluation: Working Under Budget, Time, Data, and Political Constraints* (2006), coauthored with Michael J. Bamberger and Jim Rugh.

Philip Martin is professor of agricultural and resource economics and chair of the Comparative Immigration and Integration Program at the University of California, Davis. He is the editor of *Migration News* and the *Quarterly Rural Migration News.* His research interests include farm labor, labor migration, and immigration issues. He has testified before Congress and state and local agencies on immigration. His recent publications include the book *Importing Poverty? Immigration and the Changing Face of Rural America* (2009).

Sandra Mathison is professor of education at the University of British Columbia. Her research interest is in educational evaluation, and her work has focused especially on the potential and limits of evaluation to support democratic ideals and promote justice. Her most recent research is on the effects of state-mandated testing on teaching and learning. She is editor of the *Encyclopedia of Evaluation* (2004), coeditor (with E. Wayne Ross) of *Defending Public Schools: The Nature and Limits of Standards Based Reform and Assessment* (2008), and coauthor (with Melissa Freeman) of *Researching Children's Experience* (2008). She is editor-in-chief of the journal *New Directions for Evaluation.*

Casey McCabe received a master's degree in women's studies from Florida Atlantic University. She received a bachelor of arts degree from the University of Connecticut.

Robert Hartmann McNamara is associate professor of political science and criminal justice at the Citadel. He is the author or editor of several books, including (as editor), *Homelessness in America* (Praeger, 2008). McNamara has served as a senior research fellow for the National Strategy Information Center, the Policy Lab, the Police Executive Research Forum in Washington, DC, and the Pacific Institute for Research and Evaluation in Baltimore.

Lori McNeil is an assistant professor of sociology in the Department of Sociology and Anthropology at Long Island University, C. W. Post Campus. She received her MA and PhD degrees from Western Michigan University.

Gary Miron is chief of staff at the Evaluation Center and professor of education at Western Michigan University. He has extensive experience evaluating education policies and school reforms. In recent years, he has evaluated charter school reforms in six states and conducted a federally sponsored study of the correlates of success in charter schools. He also conducted an evaluation of student achievement in schools operated by Edison Schools Inc. He has authored or edited eight books and has published more than 20 articles and book chapters.

Ron Mock is associate professor of political science and peace studies at George Fox University, in Newberg, Oregon. He holds an master's degree in public administration from Drake University and a JD from the University of Michigan. His research and teaching interests include conflict resolution, community mediation, state and local government, and issues in law and society.

J. Michael Peterson is professor in the College of Education at Wayne State University, where he teaches courses related to inclusive teaching and transition from school to adult life. He obtained his doctoral degree in vocational education, special needs from the University of North Texas. He has previously been a faculty member at Mississippi State University and director of the Developmental Disabilities Institute at Wayne State University. He is director of the Whole Schooling Consortium, an international network of educators, university faculty, parents, and schools. He has published some 80 articles and monographs, including (with Mishael M. Hittie) *Inclusive Teaching: Creating Effective Schools for All Learners* (2d ed., 2009).

Carrie Anne Platt is assistant professor of communication at North Dakota State University. She received her MA and PhD degrees from the Annenberg School for Communication at the University of Southern California, where she was a Walter

R. Fisher Fellow. Her research and teaching focuses on cultural politics, public rhetoric, and electronic communication.

Lasita Rudolph is pursuing an advanced degree in marriage and family therapy after having received a bachelor of arts degree in psychology from Auburn University at Montgomery, Alabama.

Jessica Ruglis is a Kellogg Health Scholar at Johns Hopkins University. She received her PhD in urban education from the Graduate Center of The City University of New York. A former teacher, she also holds a master's degree in urban public health/community health education from Hunter College, a master of art in teaching in secondary science education from Union College, and a BS degree in human biology from University at Albany.

David Sanjek is on the Faculty of Arts, Music, and Social Sciences at the University of Salford (United Kingdom). He has taught classes in popular music and media studies at New York University, Hunter College, Fordham University, and the New School for Social Research. From 1991 to 2007, he was the director of the Broadcast Music Incorporated Archives in New York City. A member of the editorial boards of the *Journal of Popular Music Studies, Popular Music and Society, American Studies,* and the *New Grove Encyclopedia of American Music,* he has published widely on popular music, film, media studies, copyright law, and popular culture.

Derrick Shapley is currently working toward his PhD in sociology at Mississippi State University. He earned a bachelor of arts degree in political science and history from Auburn University and a bachelor of science degree in sociology from Athens State University. His research interests include rural sociology, poverty, political sociology, sociology of religion, and social theories.

Amanda Singletary works with the Alabama Department of Human Resources as a foster care social worker. She is pursuing a master's degree in community counseling at Troy State University Montgomery.

Daniel L. Smith-Christopher is a professor of theological studies and director of peace studies at Loyola Marymount University. He appears regularly on television as a consultant and scholarly commentator on documentaries broadcast by A&E, Discovery, the History Channel, the National Geographic Network, and PBS (Public Broadcasting Service) and is the author of numerous works of scholarship.

Angela Sparrow is currently a Periclean Scholar in Ghana with Elon University, where she is studying human services.

Tracy Sayuki Tiemeier is an assistant professor of theological studies at Loyola Marymount University. Her research and teaching interests include comparative theology, Hindu-Christian dialogue, contemporary theological anthropologies and identity politics, Asian and Asian American theologies, feminist theologies, and postcolonial theory.

Taralyn Watson received her bachelor of liberal arts degree from Auburn University at Montgomery, Alabama.

Marion C. Willetts is an associate professor of sociology at Illinois State University. Her areas of specialization include families—particularly cohabitation and coupling policies—and stratification—most notably poverty. She has published numerous articles in journals such as *Journal of Marriage and Family, Journal of Family Issues,* and *Journal of Divorce and Remarriage.* Her most recent research is a policy analysis of licensed domestic partnership ordinances.

Donald Woolley completed his doctoral work in sociology at North Carolina State University. He has since worked at Duke University as a researcher in the Fast Track study within the Center for Child and Family Policy and in the Healthy Childhood Brain Development and Developmental Traumatology Research Program within the Department of Psychiatry and Behavioral Sciences, Division of Child and Adolescent Psychiatry. Woolley also teaches as an adjunct assistant professor in the Department of Sociology and Anthropology, Elon University.

Talmadge Wright is an associate professor of sociology at Loyola University of Chicago. His recent research has focused on digital gaming, though he has also published work on homelessness, social inequality, usage of social space, mass media, popular culture, and other subjects.

Annice Yarber is an assistant professor of sociology at Auburn University at Montgomery, Alabama. She teaches courses on the sociology of health and illness, human sexuality, divorce and remarriage, and human behavior and the social environment. Current research interests include adolescent sexual health, African American male sexual behavior, as well as the influence of neighborhood context on the health of various groups.

Index

minimum wage and, 233
Sarbanes-Oxley effects on, 55
technological boosts to, 34, 175
Proffitt v. Florida (1976), 435
Profiling, racial. *See* Racial/national origin/
religion profiling
Profiling of criminals. *See* Serial murder and
mass murder
Progressive taxes, 75
Prohibition, 206, 728, 920
Project Head Start, 934
Proportionality (criminal justice), 414–419,
436, 721–722, 724
Proposition 21 (California), 553
Proposition 27 (California), 801
Proposition 69 (California), 446
Proposition 103 (Arizona), 801–802
Prosecutorial Remedies and Tools against the
Exploitation of Children Today (PRO-
TECT) Act (2003), 426
Prostitution, 515, 522
Protecting the Rights of Individuals Act
(2003), 582–583
Protection of Lawful Commerce in Arms Act
(PLCAA, 2005), 511
Protectionism
effects of, 119–120, 249–250
free trade vs., 114
import dumping, 78, 81
subsidies and, 140
Proteomics, 1309
Protestant families and corporal punishment,
853–854
Protocol to Prevent, Suppress, and Punish
Trafficking in Persons (Palermo Protocol),
520, 523
Prozac, 922, 938–939
Psychological addiction, 766–767
Psychostimulant medications. *See* Adderall;
Ritalin
Psychotropic Convention (1976), 926
Public assistance programs, 1107–1108
Public Citizen (consumer advocate), 274
Public Company Accounting Oversight
Board, 407
Public Company Accounting Reform and
Investor Protection Act (2002). *See* Sar-
banes-Oxley Act
Public defender system, **625–629**
historical background, 626–627
indigent defense services, 627–629
legal developments, 627
stresses to the system, 629

Public election financing, 84, 88–89
Public Health Service (U.S.), 1337
Public Law 480 (1954), 140
Public nuisance laws, 498, 500
Public option (health care), 157
Public services usage, 162
Public Works Administration (PWA), 1019
Pulley v. Harris (1984), 436
Pure Food and Drug Act (1905), 921
Pure Food and Drug Act (1906), 728
Puritans, 1121
Pyne, Joe, 1152

Quakers, 1121
Quality of life, 1435–1437
Quid pro quo sexual harassment, 706
Quota Law (1921), 163

Race and racism, 1385–1389, 1405
as cultural construct, 633
in immigration law, 536–537, 541
in juvenile justice, 550, 551, 552, 554, 555
racial profiling, 631–649
in sentencing/death penalty, 357–359, 430,
437, 555
See also Affirmative action; Glass ceiling;
Minorities, racial and ethnic
Race to the Top program, 1022, 1081
Racial harassment, 125–126
Racial/national origin/religion profiling,
631–649
Arizona law regarding, 646–648
case vs. class probability, 644–645
definition of, 631
DNA profiling and, 446–447
drug interdiction and, 635
federal judge's experience of, 636
federal/local policing agreements, 645–646
Henry Louis Gates Jr. incident, 648
historical background, 632–633
key events, 632
legal cases/legislation, 633–634, 636–637
ongoing debate, 648–649
police corruption and, 598
reasons for/against, 642–644
research on, 634–636
social justice and, 712, 713–714
terrorist profiling, 642–644
unauthorized immigrants and, 637–639
by U.S. Customs, 642
Racketeer Influence and Corrupt Organizations (RICO) Act (1970), 373
Radical theory (of gangs), 990

DATE DUE

MAY 0 7 2013		
MAY 0 2 2014		